BEYOND SWAT

BENJAMIN D. HOPKINS and MAGNUS MARSDEN
(*Editors*)

Beyond Swat

*History, Society and Economy along
the Afghanistan-Pakistan Frontier*

HURST & COMPANY, LONDON

First published in the United Kingdom in 2013 by
C. Hurst & Co. (Publishers) Ltd.,
41 Great Russell Street, London, WC1B 3PL
© Benjamin D. Hopkins, Magnus Marsden and the Contributors, 2013
All rights reserved.
Printed in India

The right of Benjamin D. Hopkins, Magnus Marsden and the Contributors to be identified as the authors of this publication is asserted by them in accordance with the Copyright, Designs and Patents Act, 1988.

A Cataloguing-in-Publication data record for this book
is available from the British Library.

ISBN: 978-1-84904-206-2

www.hurstpublishers.com

This book is printed on paper from registered sustainable
and managed sources.

CONTENTS

Acknowledgements vii
About the Contributors ix

Introduction: Rethinking Swat: Militancy and Modernity along the Afghanistan–Pakistan Frontier   *Benjamin D. Hopkins* and *Magnus Marsden*   1

1. Swat in Retrospect: Continuities, Transformations and Possibilities
   Charles Lindholm   17

SECTION 1
CONTINUITY AND CHANGE

2. The Abdali Afghans between Multan, Qandahar and Herat in the Sixteenth and Seventeenth Centuries   *Christine Noelle-Karimi*   31
3. A History of the "Hindustani Fanatics" on the Frontier
   Benjamin D. Hopkins   39
4. *Kashars* against *Mashars: Jihad* and Social Change in the FATA
   Mariam Abou Zahab   51

SECTION 2
LOCATING FRONTIER WORLDS

5. A History of Linguistic Boundary Crossing Within and Around Pashto   *Shah Mahmoud Hanifi*   63
6. The Road to Kabul: Automobiles and Afghan Internationalism, 1900–40   *Nile Green*   77
7. Being a Diplomat on the Frontier of South and Central Asia: Trade and Traders in Afghanistan   *Magnus Marsden*   93

SECTION 3
CLASS, PATRONAGE AND THE STATE: BEYOND THE EXCEPTIONAL PASHTUN?

8. Class, Patronage and Coercion in the Pakistani Punjab and in Swat
   Nicolas Emilio Martin   107

CONTENTS

9. Exceptional Pashtuns?: Class Politics, Imperialism and Historiography
   Nancy Lindisfarne   119
10. Class, State and Power in Swat Conflict   *Robert Nichols*   135

SECTION 4
THE TALIBAN, PASHTUNS AND SWAT

11. The Swat Crisis   *Sultan-i-Rome*   149
12. Producing Civil Society, Ignoring *Rivaj*: International Donors, the State and Development Interventions in Swat   *Urs Geiser*   163
13. Crisis and Reconciliation in Swat through the Eyes of Women
    Anita M. Weiss   179
14. Public Visibility of Women and the Rise of the Neo-Taliban Movement in Khyber Pakhtunkhwa, 2007–9   *Sana Haroon*   193

SECTION 5
TRIBES, CONFLICT, AND STATE-BUILDING IN AFGHANISTAN AND PAKISTAN

15. Custom and Conflict in Waziristan: Some British Views
    Hugh Beattie   209
16. Studying Pashtuns in Barth's Shadow   *Richard Tapper*   221
17. If only there were Leaders: the Problem of "Fixing" the Pashtun Tribes   *Antonio Giustozzi*   239
18. Lessons on Governance from the Wali of Swat: State-building in Afghanistan, 1995–2010   *David B. Edwards*   249

Notes   265
Bibliography   331
Index   359

ACKNOWLEDGEMENTS

The origins of this volume lay in a conference that we organized in the summer of 2010, entitled "Rethinking the Swat Pathan". We felt it was time to rigorously contest the staid platitudes that have become accepted knowledge about this region. It falls to us here to acknowledge and thank the many people and organizations who made the "Rethinking the Swat Pathan" conference, and subsequently this volume, a reality.

The British Academy, the Malaysian Commonwealth Studies Centre (Cambridge), the Leverhulme Trust (UK), the School of Oriental and African Studies (SOAS), and Hurst & Co. made the conference possible through their generous assistance. In particular, Michael Dwyer, Graham Furniss, Anil Seal and Jonathan Spencer all helped to ensure that the conference came to fruition. SOAS kindly provided facilities and support for the conference; Jane Savory and Rahima Begum worked very hard over several months to ensure that the two days ran smoothly, as did Paul Rollier. All of these people deserve our special thanks. Tahir Sharaan, Khadija Abbasi, Zia Shahriyar, and Haseeb Amar were very helpful in ensuring that the conference's findings were presented to as wide an audience as possible, including press in the region. While their papers are not published here, we wish to thank Ashraf Ghani, Conrad Schetter, Anatol Lieven, Vazira Zamindar, Zuzanna Olszewska and Mukulika Banerjee for presenting their work at SOAS, as well as for their very significant contributions to this book's topic of study more generally. Unni Wikan was also a vital presence at the conference, and her attendance was greatly appreciated.

With regard to the present volume, special thanks are due to Charles Lindholm and Christine Noelle-Karimi who offered insightful and constructive comments on the Introduction. All of the book's chapters also benefited from the Hurst reviewer's report. As ever, Michael Dwyer has been instrumental in guiding the book to publication and supporting our wider scholarly efforts. Most importantly, we would like to thank Fredrik Barth for making the trip to London and actively participating in the conference. Professor Barth shared his memories of Swat and presented with great eloquence and wit his vision of anthropology, ethnography and theory which remain, as we hope to show in this book, as relevant today as when he started his career. It is to Fredrik Barth, as well as the people of the region he studied, that we dedicate this book. It goes without saying that all mistakes, substantive or otherwise, are our own.

Benjamin D. Hopkins and Magnus Marsden

ABOUT THE CONTRIBUTORS

Mariam Abou Zahab, a specialist on Pakistan and Afghanistan, was awarded a PhD in political science by the Institut d'Etudes Politiques de Paris (Sc.Po). She is a researcher affiliated with the Centre d'Etudes et de Recherches Internationales (CERI) and a lecturer at the Institute of Oriental Languages (INALCO), both in Paris. Her research focuses on Shiism, sectarianism and jihadi groups in Pakistan, the social and political dynamics of Pakistan's tribal areas, and Pashtun society in Pakistan and Afghanistan more generally. Her recent publications include: "'I shall be waiting for you at the door of Paradise': The Pakistani Martyrs of the Lashkar-e Taiba (Army of the Pure)" in A. Rao, M. Böck and M. Bollig (eds), *The Practice of War: The Production, Reproduction and Communication of Armed Violence* (Oxford: Berghahn 2007); "Between Pakistan and Qom: Shi'i Women's Madrasas and New Transnational Networks" in M. Van Bruinessen, F. Noor and Y. Sikand (eds), *The Madrasa in Asia: Political Activism and Transnational Linkages* (Amsterdam University Press, 2008); "Salafism in Pakistan: The Ahl-e Hadith Movement" in R. Meijer (ed.), Global Salafism: Islam's New Religious Movement" (London: Hurst, 2009); "The SSP: Herald of Militant Sunni Islam in Pakistan" in L. Gayer and C. Jaffrelot (eds), *Armed Militias in South Asia: Fundamentalists, Maoists and Separatists* (London: Hurst, 2009); "Sectarianism in Pakistan's Kurram Tribal Agency" in H. Abbas (ed.), *Pakistan's Troubled Frontier* (Washington: The Jamestown Foundation, 2009); "Deobandi Groups and Ahl-e Hadith" in *Islamic Affairs Analyst* (Jane's, 2009); "Unholy Nexus: Talibanism and Sectarianism in Pakistan's Tribal Areas" in L. Gayer (ed.), *Guerres et sociétés en AfPak* (Paris: CERI, 2009); "La Frontière dans la tourmente: La talibanisation des zones tribales", *Outre-terre* (Paris, 2010/1, no. 24); "Des Talibans aux néo-talibans: chronique d'un movement social" in *Les crises en Afghanistan depuis le XIXe siècle, Etudes de l'Irsem* (April 2010, no. 1, Paris). She is co-author with Olivier Roy of *Islamist Networks: The Afghan-Pakistan Connection* (London/New York: Hurst/Columbia University Press, 2004) and co-author with Shuja Nawaz et al. of *FATA: A Most Dangerous Place* (Washington: CSIS, 2009).

Hugh Beattie read history at Cambridge, then moved into social anthropology at the School of Oriental and African Studies, and undertook field research in Afghanistan in the late 1970s. Subsequently he has undertaken extensive research in the British Library's Oriental and India Office archive. He is lecturer in Religious Studies at The Open University. His interests include Islam, anti-colonial

ABOUT THE CONTRIBUTORS

resistance and the state, the history of Sikhism, and militant Christianity in the USA. His book *Imperial Frontier Tribe and State in Waziristan* (Richmond: Curzon Press, 2002) uses insights drawn from social anthropological research into Pashtun socio-political organization and culture to explore the British relationship with the Pashtun tribes of Waziristan in the later nineteenth century. He is currently working on a follow-up volume covering the first half of the twentieth century.

David B. Edwards is W. Van Alan Clark '41 Third Century Professor of the Social Sciences, Williams College, Williamstown, MA. He has been conducting research on and writing about Afghanistan for more than twenty-five years. A graduate of Princeton University (BA, 1975) and the University of Michigan (PhD, 1986), he is the author of two books on Afghanistan (*Before Taliban: Genealogies of the Afghan Jihad*, University of California Press, 2002 and *Heroes of the Age: Moral Fault Lines on the Afghan Frontier*, University of California Press, 1996), along with numerous articles on Afghan history, religion and culture. Edwards is also the co-director and producer of the film *Kabul Transit* (Bullfrog Films, 2006), which has been an official selection at the Los Angeles Film Festival; the International Documentary Festival in Amsterdam; and the Independents Night series at the Lincoln Center in New York City. Edwards has received two research fellowships from the National Endowment for the Humanities, as well as grants from the Andrew Mellon Foundation, the Fulbright Commission, and the National Science Foundation. In 2002 he was named a Carnegie Scholar by the Carnegie Corporation of New York. At present he is working on a book dealing with the changing relationship between violence, governance and legitimacy in Afghanistan and Pakistan.

Antonio Giustozzi is an independent researcher associated with the Crisis States Research Centre of the London School of Economics and Political Science (LSE). He is the author of several articles and papers on Afghanistan, as well as three books, *War, Politics and Society in Afghanistan, 1978–1992* (Washington: Georgetown University Press, 2002), *Koran, Kalashnikov and Laptop: the Neo-Taliban Insurgency, 2002–7* (London/New York: Hurst/Columbia University Press, 2207) and *Empires of Mud: War and Warlords in Afghanistan* (London/New York: Hurst/Columbia University Press, 2009). He also edited a volume on the Taliban, *Decoding the New Taliban* (London/New York: Hurst/Columbia University Press, 2009), featuring contributions by specialists from different backgrounds. He is currently researching issues of governance in Afghanistan, from a wide-ranging perspective which includes understanding the role of the army, the police, subnational governance and intelligence gathering.

Nile Green is a Professor of South Asian and Islamic History at the University of California, Los Angeles (UCLA). He was previously Lecturer in South Asian Studies at the University of Manchester and Milburn Research Fellow at Lady Margaret Hall, Oxford University. His research focuses on the history of Islam and the Muslim communities of South Asia (India, Pakistan, Afghanistan), Iran and the Indian Ocean. His books include *Indian Sufism since the Seventeenth Century: Saints, Books and Empires in the Muslim Deccan* (London: Routledge, 2006); *Religion, Lan-*

ABOUT THE CONTRIBUTORS

guage and Power (edited with Mary Searle-Chatterjee, London: Routledge, 2008); *Islam and the Army in Colonial India: Sepoy Religion in the Service of Empire* (Cambridge University Press, 2009); *Bombay Islam: The Religious Economy of the West Indian Ocean* (Cambridge University Press, 2011); *Sufism: A Global History* (Blackwell, 2011); and *Saints, Migrants and Settlers: Sufis and Societies in Early Modern India* (Oxford University Press, forthcoming).

Urs Geiser, PhD, is Senior Researcher with the Development Study Group, Department of Geography, University of Zurich, Switzerland. His research focuses on the social and political dimensions of rural development, with special attention to the contestation and negotiation of institutions that define access to, and control over, means of livelihood. He conducts empirical research in Pakistan, South India and Switzerland. Recent publications include U. Geiser and S. Rist (eds), *Decentralisation Meets Local Complexity: Local Struggles, State Decentralisation and Access to Natural Resources in South Asia and Latin America*. Vol. 4, (University of Berne Press, Berne, 2009). And on Swat proper: U. Geiser "Contested Forests in North-West Pakistan: The Bureaucracy between the 'Ecological', the 'National', and the Realities of a Nation's Frontier" in G. Cederloef and K. Sivaramakrishnan (eds), *Ecological Nationalisms—Nature, Livelihoods and Identities in South Asia* (Seattle: University of Washington Press, 2006, pp. 90–111).

Shah Mahmoud Hanifi is an Associate Professor of History focusing on the Middle East and South Asia at James Madison University in Virginia, USA, where he is the Coordinator of the Middle Eastern Communities and Migrations Program. He is the author of *Connecting Histories in Afghanistan* (Stanford University Press, 2011); "Henry George Raverty and the Colonial Marketing of Pashto," in Cythnia Talbot (ed.), *Knowing India: Colonial and Modern Constructions of the Past* (Yoda Press, 2011); "Quandaries of the Afghan Nation," in Shahzad Bashir and Robert D. Crews (eds), *Under the Drones: Modern Lives in the Afghanistan-Pakistan Borderlands* (Harvard University Press, 2012); "Shah Shuja's 'Hidden History' and its Implications for the Historiography of Afghanistan," *SAMAJ: South Asia Multidisciplinary Journal*, 2012, http://samaj.revues.org/3384. Hanifi has received grants from the Social Science Research Council, the Council of American Overseas Research Centers, the American Historical Association, the Asian Development Bank, and James Madison University for research conducted in Australia, Europe, North America, and South Asia.

Sana Haroon received her PhD at the School of Oriental and African Studies, Department of South Asian History in 2004. She held the Isobel Thornley Doctoral Fellowship in 2003–04, and the Past and Present Foundation Postdoctoral Fellowship at the Institute of Historical Research in 2004–05. She has held the post of Assistant Professor at Zayed University in Dubai and at IBA Karachi, and is currently the Malathy Singh Visiting Lecturer at the South Asian Studies Council at Yale University. Haroon published a study of the history of religious mobilisation in the Pakhtun "Tribal Areas", *Frontier of Faith* (London/New York: Hurst/Columbia University Press, 2007). She has worked on the rise of Deobandi Islam in the North-West Frontier Province of colonial India, and is currently working on a project studying the rise of Islamic revivalism across Muslim north India.

ABOUT THE CONTRIBUTORS

Benjamin D. Hopkins is an Assistant Professor of History and International Affairs at the George Washington University in Washington DC. He completed his doctorate at the University of Cambridge, where he was a Junior Research Fellow at Corpus Christi College. His works include *The Making of Modern Afghanistan* (Basingstoke: Palgrave Macmillan, 2008) which explores the construction of the Afghan state in the early nineteenth century, as well as *Fragments of the Afghan Frontier* (London/New York: Hurst/Columbia University Press, 2012), co-authored with Magnus Marsden, which examines the historical antecedents and everyday lived experience of governance along the Afghanistan/Pakistan frontier. His research interests include the colonial legacies shaping the Afghan political topography and the effect of such legacies on processes of globalisation. He is currently working on a monograph entitled *The Imperial Frontier*.

Charles Lindholm is University Professor of Anthropology at Boston University. His fieldwork in Swat led to an ethnography (*Generosity and Jealousy: The Swat Pukhtun of Northern Pakistan*, New York: Columbia University Press, 1982) and a collection of essays (*Frontier Perspectives: Essays in Comparative Anthropology*, Karachi: Oxford University Press, 1996). His work on Swat gave him the courage to write a comparative historical anthropology of the Middle East (*The Islamic Middle East: Tradition and Change*, Oxford: Basil Blackwell, 2002). Most of his other work has focused on the intersection between psychological and political anthropology, with a special interest in identity, charisma, emotion, and the ambiguities of egalitarianism. His most recent books are *Culture and Authenticity* (Oxford: Basil Blackwell, 2007) and *The Struggle for the World: Liberation Movements for the 21st Century* (Stanford University Press, 2010—co-authored with José Pedro Zúquete).

Nancy Lindisfarne taught Social Anthropology at the School of Oriental and African Studies (SOAS), University of London for many years. She has done fieldwork in Iran, Afghanistan, Turkey and Syria and published numerous articles on gender, marriage and Islam in the Middle East. As Nancy Tapper she is the author of *Bartered Brides: Politics, Gender and Marriage in an Afghan Tribal Society* (Cambridge University Press, 1991). As Nancy Lindisfarne, her volume of short stories, *Dancing in Damascus*, about elite families in Syria appeared first in Arabic (Beirut: Al Mada, 1998) and then in English (State University of New York, 2000). *Thank God, We're Secular*, about nationalism, secularism and practised Islam, was published by İletişim (Istanbul) in 2001. A direct antecedent to her paper in this volume was "Starting from Below", her 2002 Richards Lecture, sponsored by the Centre for Cross-Culture Research on Women and Gender, University of Oxford. The lecture has been reproduced a number of times, most recently in H. Armbruster and A. Laerke (eds), *Taking Sides: Ethnics, Politics and Fieldwork in Anthropology* (Oxford: Berghahn, 2008). Nancy retired from teaching in 2001 to study art at Central St Martins School of Art and Design in London. "Street Aesthetics", an exhibition of her photographs of Iran, travelled to London and Manchester. More recently, "Reconsidering Iran", an exhibition of her prints, paintings and photographs, was held at Wolfson College, University of Oxford.

Magnus Marsden is Senior Lecturer in Social Anthropology with reference to the study of South and Central Asia at the School of Oriental and African Stud-

ABOUT THE CONTRIBUTORS

ies, University of London. He completed his PhD at Cambridge University and was also a Junior Research Fellow at Trinity College, as well as the Graduate Officer at the Centre of South Asian Studies, University of Cambridge. He has conducted fieldwork in northern Pakistan, and, more recently, Afghanistan and Tajikistan. His publications include *Living Islam: Muslim Religious Experiences in Pakistan's North-West Frontier* (Cambridge University Press, 2005) and, with Benjamin D. Hopkins, *Fragments of the Afghan Frontier* (London/New York: Hurst/ Columbia University Press, 2012). He is also the editor with Kostas Retsikas of *Articulating Islam: Anthropological Approaches to Muslim Worlds* (Dordrecht: Springer, 2012). He is currently working on a monograph entitled *Trading Worlds: Afghan Merchants across Modern Frontiers*.

Nicolas Emilio Martin specialises in the anthropology of South Asia, particularly Pakistan, where he has conducted research in rural Punjab since 2003. His research focuses on the effects of patronage and kinship networks upon rural state institutions and explores how the appropriation of the state and its resources by landowning elites not only results in poor service delivery by state institutions, but also in endemic political violence and criminality. Nicolas' work examines how broad economic and social changes erode traditional ties of patronage and how this process is related to the rise of Islamic militancy in Pakistan. In addition to his academic research in Pakistan, Nicolas has also worked there since 2001 in various fields including micro-credit, human rights and earthquake relief (following the October 2005 earthquake in Kashmir). Nicolas has been a visiting scholar at Quaid-I Azam University in Islamabad. He is currently a Teaching Fellow in the Department of Social Anthropology at the London School of Economics.

Robert Nichols is Professor of History at Richard Stockton College, New Jersey. His history PhD is from the University of Pennsylvania. His research and teaching explore interregional, colonial, and modern history in South Asia and the Indian Ocean. He has studied state and society relations in Peshawar, Pakistan, including analysis of the discourses and practices of state-builders dating to the Mughal Empire. He has researched the dynamics of circulation and mobility, especially by Pashtuns across the Indian Ocean, including migration to the oil economies of the Gulf. His publications include the books *Settling the Frontier: Land, Law and Society in the Peshawar Valley, 1500–1900* (Oxford University Press, 2001) and *A History of Pashtun Migration, 1775–2006* (Oxford University Press, 2008). He edited *Colonial Reports on Pakistan's Frontier Tribal Areas* (Oxford University Press, 2006). Articles and book chapters by him include "Afghan Historiography: Classical Study, Conventional Narrative, National Polemic" in *History Compass* (3, 2005, AS 141, pp. 1–16, Oxford: Blackwell).

Christine Noelle-Karimi is a senior scientist at the Institute of Iranian Studies of the Austrian Academy of Sciences. Her research concerns relationships of power and their manifestations in local, regional and state settings. Her dissertation ("State and Tribe in Nineteenth-Century Afghanistan") deals with the genesis of the modern Afghan state and its impact on the relationship between the state-supporting elite and local powerbrokers. Her second dissertation ("Herat and the Mapping of Khurasan from the Fifteenth to the Nineteenth Centuries," forth-

ABOUT THE CONTRIBUTORS

coming) explores the changes in concepts of statehood and territoriality since early modern times and traces the transition from fluid models of political cohesion to modern notions of the nation state. Her current research is devoted to travelogues within the Persophone world from the late eighteenth to the early twentieth century, and inquires into the relationship between individual perceptions of the landscape and constructions of political space.

Sultan-i-Rome is Assistant Professor of History, Government Jahanzeb College, Saidu Sharif, Swat, Khyber Pakhtunkhwa, Pakistan. His major publications are *Swat State (1915–1969): From Genesis to Merger; An Analysis of Political, Administrative, Socio-Political and Economic Developments* (Oxford University Press, 2008) and *The North-West Frontier (Khyber Pukhtunkhwa): Essays on History* (Oxford University Press, 2012). His forthcoming book, *Land and Forest Governance: Transition from Tribal System to Swat State to Pakistan* is in the process of being published by Oxford University Press. His other publications include numerous articles/books chapters. Sultan-i-Rome is a Life Member of the Pakistan Historical Society and a sitting member of its Executive Committee, the Council of Social Sciences Pakistan (COSS), as well as the Pukhtu Adabi Board. His fields of interest includes the history, culture and natural resources of the region.

Richard Tapper is Emeritus Professor of Anthropology in the University of London, BA (Cambridge, 1964), PhD (London, 1972). He taught anthropology with special reference to the Middle East at the School of Oriental and African Studies, University of London, between 1967 and 2004. His main research interests include the study of Iran, Afghanistan and Turkey, pastoral nomadism, ethnicity, tribe/state relations, anthropology of Islam, anthropology of the state, media in the Middle East, documentary film and Iranian cinema. His recent books include *Frontier Nomads of Iran: a Political and Social History of the Shahsevan* (Cambridge University Press, 1997); (with Ziba Mir-Hosseini) *Islam and Democracy in Iran: Eshkevari and the Quest for Reform* (London: I.B. Tauris, 2006); (ed. with Sami Zubaida) *A Taste of Thyme: Culinary Cultures of the Middle East* (London: I.B. Tauris, 2000); (ed.) *Ayatollah Khomeini and the Modernization of Islamic Thought* (SOAS, 2000); (ed.) *The New Iranian Cinema: Politics, Representation and Identity* (London: I.B. Tauris, 2002); (ed. with Jon Thompson) *The Nomadic Peoples of Iran* (London: Azimuth, 2002); (ed. with Keith McLachlan), *Technology, Tradition and Survival: Aspects of Material Culture in the Middle East and Central Asia* (London: Frank Cass, 2004).

Anita M. Weiss received her doctorate in sociology from UC Berkeley and is now professor and head of the department of International Studies at the University of Oregon. She has published extensively on social development, gender issues, and political Islam in Pakistan. Her books include *Power and Civil Society in Pakistan* (co-editor with Zulfiqar Gilani and contributor, Oxford University Press, 2001); *Walls Within Walls: Life Histories of Working Women in the Old City of Lahore* (Westview Press, 1992, republished by Oxford University Press, 2002 with a new preface), and *Culture, Class, and Development in Pakistan: The Emergence of an Industrial Bourgeoisie in Punjab* (Westview Press, 1991). Recent publications include "A

ABOUT THE CONTRIBUTORS

Provincial Islamist Victory in NWFP, Pakistan: The Social Reform Agenda of the Muttahida Majlis-i-Amal," in *Asian Islam in the Twenty-First Century*, ed. John L. Esposito and John Voll, 145–73 (Oxford University Press, 2008), and "Population Growth, Urbanization and Female Literacy" in *The Future of Pakistan*, Stephen P. Cohen and others, 236–48 (Brookings, 2011). Her current research project is analyzing how distinct constituencies in Pakistan, including the state, are grappling with articulating their views on women's rights. Professor Weiss is a member of the editorial boards of *Citizenship Studies* and *Globalizations*, is on the editorial advisory board of Kumarian Press, is a member of the Research Advisory Board of the Pakistan National Commission on the Status of Women, and is the vice president of the American Institute of Pakistan Studies (AIPS).

Map of Afghanistan and surrounding countries, Benjamin D. Hopkins and Magnus Marsden (2012).

INTRODUCTION

RETHINKING SWAT
MILITANCY AND MODERNITY ALONG THE AFGHANISTAN-PAKISTAN FRONTIER

Benjamin D. Hopkins and *Magnus Marsden*

In 1959, one of the most important works in modern anthropology was published. Fredrik Barth's *Political leadership among Swat Pathans* detailed the societal workings of the Swat valley, a remote corner of north-western Pakistan. For generations of students, Barth's book has set the terms of approach to a region—the borderlands of North-West Pakistan and Afghanistan—continually invested with global significance, especially over the past thirty years.[1] Almost immediately after its publication, the work sparked a critical debate amongst anthropologists that laid the ground for *the* key thematic concerns of the discipline's approach to politics.[2] The main concerns of the debate include the relationship between religion and politics, as well as individual strategising and class conflict; the nature of processes of state-formation; and the role played by cultural values, especially those of honour, in shaping patterns of violence in the Muslim-majority societies of the modern Middle East.

Yet Barth's work had broader implications outside anthropology. It built upon a tradition of ethnographic inquiry first authored by British scholar-administrators in the nineteenth century and familiar to many historians.[3] This familiarity has enabled historians to employ the approaches he advanced as the standard starting point for many attempts to reflect on past forms of social, political and cultural organisation in this region and places further afield. *Political Leadership among Swat Pathans* remains a seminal work, required reading for anyone interested in the North-West Frontier and the dynamics of tribal social structures and state formation there and beyond.[4]

While in 1959 Swat stood as a largely forgotten, if romanticised, periphery of a faded empire, more recently it has been thrust to the center of international attention. In 2008 it was transformed into a South Asian theatre of the so-called "Global War on Terror" by an uprising of the "Taliban" and subsequent military intervention by the Pakistani army. The conflict led some anthropologists to refocus awareness on the insights the discipline had brought to understanding Swat decades before.[5] These contributions, however, lacked the theoretical and empirical rigour required to bring the anthropological story of Swat up to date. Equally important, they proved unable to impress the globally powerful political discourses with scholarly understanding. Such discourses often locate the region's problems in its inherent primitivism and the fanaticism of its populace. These images caricature the Pushtun as being above all committed to a static, violent culture defined by custom, tradition and religious bigotry.[6] Pashtun culture is posited as one founded upon cultural values fundamentally different from, and often incomprehensible to, those of the so-called "West." With the prevalence of such images, which have achieved the status of respectable knowledge largely because of the absence of a sizeable or vocal scholarly community to challenge them, the nuances of the region and its inhabitants have been elided into simplistic tropes. One example, representative of much written about Swat and the Frontier more generally, baldly states that "[t]o be a Taliban today means little more than to be a Pashtun tribesman who believes that his fundamental beliefs and customary way of life, including the right to bear arms to defend the tribal homeland and protect its women, are threatened by foreign invaders."[7]

This book takes up the challenge posed by the power of such images. Returning to Barth's work and the reactions it sparked, the volume explores the relevance of such scholarly debates to understanding the key dynamics affecting the region and its people today. The contributions are written by anthropologists and historians with long-standing research experience in Afghanistan and Pakistan, as well as expertise in one or more of the region's languages. Each chapter explores varying yet interconnected dimensions of the region's culture, society and politics over a broad span of history. They relate these themes to key issues in the Swat debate started by Barth over fifty years ago. While the authors locate their discussions in the context of the specific socio-historic settings with which they are concerned, they do not limit their conclusions to those contexts. Rather, like Barth, the contributors assert the relevance of their findings to wider debates about the dynamics shaping this and other comparable frontiers.[8]

The book's chapters make carefully considered parallels between Swat and other societies, both within the Frontier and beyond. This is not to say that Swat is a template for understanding Frontier society in its full complexity. But the thematic concerns that arise from in-depth studies of Swat maintain purchase in geographical locations beyond it, both in Pashtun contexts along the Frontier and in non-Pashtun ones further afield. The parallels the authors make cross temporal as well as spatial boundaries. In doing so, they open up theoretically innovative lines of scholarly inquiry about the Afghanistan-Pakistan Frontier, the nature of Islamic militancy and its connections to ethnicity, and the relationship between anthropology and history. Given the extent to which writings about this region over the past ten years have been largely utilitarian, researched with politics and policy in mind rather than scholarship, such innovation is urgently needed.[9]

Each of the chapters is based on long-term fieldwork and/or archival research. Such research methods enable scholars to ask questions of a type rarely asked in the expanding body of literature on the region's politics. While important, too

INTRODUCTION

often this literature is constrained by contemporary concerns, and repeats caricatures of the Frontier. As a result, less is known about the interactions between older and newer social dynamics there, the shifting nature of local understandings of "the state" and political leadership, Islam's role in shaping people's everyday lives and relations, and people's conceptions of being human in a context of political flux, violence, and uncertainty. This trend undermines attempts to understand the region on its own terms and gauge its relevance to broader global processes.

This volume, providing serious scholarly anthropological and historical insight into the dynamics of the diverse communities of the Afghanistan-Pakistan frontier, will not be welcomed by all. Over the past decade, foreign and local governments active along this frontier have constantly consulted anthropologists and historians. But policy-makers often have a narrow, utilitarian understanding of the value of these disciplines. The practical purpose of such consultations is to offer insights into the nature of local "tradition"—the rules, norms and values that govern "community life"—in order to shape political and military action.[10] For scholars sanguine about past experiences in the region, these interactions can often be frustrating.[11] As they are rarely in a position to frame such encounters—the ways in which they take shape and proceed, or indeed the content and understandings communicated—some question the ultimate value of such public or policy engagement.[12] But it is important for scholars to remain involved, even if their voices are emasculated or ignored. The abdication of the public responsibilities of regional scholars—to challenge and dispute caricatures of this region and help shape informed understandings of it—is harmful not only to the scholarly community itself, but to the larger publics involved.

As an historian and an anthropologist who have worked on Afghanistan as well as the Afghan-Pakistan borderland over this tumultuous decade, we have witnessed important changes in the attitudes of policy-makers towards our disciplines, as well as those with whom we work and study.[13] Intellectuals from the region have accused both anthropology and history of presenting a simplified picture of society in this complex arena, which has worked to the detriment of the region's people.[14] The picture of "the Frontier" that such critics rightly challenge is one that defines the region's make-up above all in terms of immutable ethnic groups and unchanging, primitive tribes—socio-political "blocs" inhabited by unthinking folk imprisoned by tradition. Such representations of "the Frontier" are, as many scholars have previously noted, themselves "colonially-derived", as well as being invented and reinforced by regional elites.[15] These critiques are not of history and anthropology themselves, but rather of the outcomes they have produced with regard to the region. Nevertheless, as the chapters of this book show, such a reading of scholarly work on this region, while understandable given the current and past context, is simplistic. It overlooks the contribution these disciplines have made to understanding this region, and many others like it, in terms both of their significance to the unfolding forms of global modernity and of the importance of "tradition" to the lifeworlds of its inhabitants.

By bringing Barth's work, and that of his colleagues, into conversation with debates about the region today, our aim is to show its importance in understanding contemporary dynamics. The essays in this book examine that continuing relevance, exploring the region according to varying social perspectives, analytical lenses, geographic locales, and temporal moments. Yet this work's purpose is not simply to demonstrate that Barth's work continues to be germane. Rather, it is to remind us of the deeper significance and contribution that scholarship can make. The value of anthropology and history lies not in scholars writing policy-friendly accounts or assisting in programmes such as the US Human Terrain System. Such forms of knowledge production are best left to the growing band of "Afghan" and North-West Frontier "experts".[16] Instead, the "utility" of scholarly work is located in its capacity to theorise and develop a conceptual language to address issues important to the places and people it studies, to ask and frame questions of broader historical and societal significance.

As its title suggests, this volume is not only about Swat or Pashtuns. Neither, indeed, was Barth's work which has inspired it. Rather, the following essays engage in a theoretically rich discussion sparked by Barth, but one firmly grounded in historical and ethnographic detail. Swat and its Pukhtun and non-Pukhtun inhabitants, as Barth so clearly showed in 1959, are representative of places and people similarly situated in geographically and temporally distinct locales. This introduction highlights the key themes tying the book's chapters together and places them in the wider historical and anthropological context. It demonstrates the continuing validity of his original suppositions by focusing on four of the most important themes which have arisen out of Barth's work and the ensuing debates around it: continuity and change in frontier worlds; geographical imaginaries of the frontier; tribe and ethnicity; and status and class. By looking at each in turn, this essay and the volume as a whole seek to underline again the continuing importance of Swat and its people to the wider world of which they are a part.

Continuity and change in frontier worlds

What is the nature of social and political change in a region that is so often defined by its supposed timelessness and primitivism? The following contributions consider change in both the short and the long term along the Frontier, from the immediacy of the post-9/11 violence of the "Taliban" in Swat to the contested political norms of Abdali Afghans in the sixteenth century. The region's society and past are not considered merely within the frame of local history and culture, but more broadly in terms of how global geopolitics have long been embedded in and are a part of "the local" here.[17] From the regional competitions between the Mughals and Safavids to the paramountcy of the British Raj, to the ideologically laden conflict of the Cold War, to the unfolding and seemingly unending "Global War on Terror", this region has been a central participant in a broader global history.

Historians of the Frontier have long used anthropological approaches to better understand the complexity of this region's worlds. This book offers a renewed effort to understand the transformations and continuities of life in the region, as well as the relationship between history and anthropology. The role of history in cognizing the Frontier has often been Janus-faced: either this region is depicted as one acted upon by transforming processes unleashed from the outside, whether British colonialism, Soviet imperialism or the recent US intervention; or, con-

INTRODUCTION

versely, the Frontier is portrayed as mired in an unchanging savage past, a temporal as well as a geographical periphery.[18] The chapters in this volume reject both these impressions, and instead present a far more nuanced picture which balances the complex interaction between continuity and change here.

Important continuities between the Frontier's past and present are evident in all the volume's contributions. Christine Noelle-Karimi's chapter evinces one such continuity: the capacity of elites to simultaneously forge ties with and relate to multiple imperial formations. She explores the highly cosmopolitan political world inhabited by the Abdali Pashtun nobility, nurtured by networks of trade between Multan, Qandahar and Herat. Likewise, the durability of the relationship between Frontier forms of reformist Islam and modern material culture, especially technology, is another continuity between past and present. Islamic militancy and modern technology are often held to be opposed to one another—an attitude visible in the surprise that NATO commanders showed at the Afghan Taliban's skill in their media war.[19] Yet religious reformers have long been adept at participating in the material culture of modernity. Nile Green's chapter on Urdu travelogues in the early twentieth century underlines how important vernacular print has been in spreading diverse ideas about religion. Recognising such continuities is imperative. It shows how processes bear the imprint of local actors, agencies and dynamics, rather than simply resulting from "Western" policies and actions.

Those local actors, inhabitants of the Frontier, are not simply the pawns of global trends and "outside" influences. Robert Nichols' chapter reminds the reader how much the Swat uprising of 2008, far from being another front of global jihadism with scant local pedigree, was deeply rooted in the area's history. He reveals a "complex historical pattern of resistance to colonial and postcolonial state institutions perceived to be oppressive, illegitimate, and lacking moral authority". Similarly, Mariam Abou Zahab's chapter focuses on the relationship between militant Islam and social conflict in the Waziristan tribal region of Pakistan's North-West. Abou Zahab argues that the tendency to see this relationship in terms of external factors alone, notably foreign support for militant Islam, fails to grapple with a deeper, underlying question: Why do such forms of militant Islam gain traction along the Frontier? Both authors analyse the profound social and cultural changes in Frontier society over the past thirty years—for example in the practice of hospitality, a Pashtun custom widely held to be static and unchanging by analysts—and show how these are driven as much by internal as by external factors. Yet they also tie those changes to the continuities marking Frontier society, for example in the complex causes that inform the outbreak of particular local conflicts. Their analysis reminds us of the profound importance of the local, as well as the past, in understanding the nature of apparently global phenomena.

Detailing both the "local" and the "past" is Sultan-i-Rome's contribution. His chapter offers a deeply grounded analysis of the rise of the Taliban and their assumption of power in Swat. Rome points us towards both continuities and ruptures with the past, marking that rise and enabling the continued appeal of these social forces. Rome's contribution is complemented by Hugh Beattie's examination of British imperial efforts at gaining control of the region. Beattie's chapter, which details British operations in Waziristan during the late nineteenth and early twentieth centuries, reminds us that when looking at both continuities and change here, it is not only local actors we need to bear in mind. The similarities between the tactics of Beattie's British Indian troopers in the 1900s and today's British squaddies and American marines operating in the same area are striking. Likewise, Benjamin D. Hopkins' chapter on "Hindustani Fanatics" brings to the fore the continuities of religious dissent marking the Frontier's past and present. By examining a colony of Muslims from the Indian plains who took up resistance along the Frontier, and whom the British termed "Fanatics", Hopkins traces their continued physical and spiritual presence right up to the end of the British Raj in 1947. While there is no direct link between these "talibs", as the British sometimes termed them, and today's Taliban, the lineages and languages of resistance are strikingly consonant between the two.

Recognising continuities is important, not only as an academic exercise but also for their implications for modern policies in the region. Such recognition enables a more nuanced understanding of ways in which rupture and change are important. How processes of change have affected and been affected by the Frontier's inhabitants is an important consideration for how this region is actively shaped today.[20] As Barth previously recognised, and a number of contributors to this volume emphasise, issues including the ongoing monetisation of local economies, the expansion of unequal global labour markets into the Frontier, and the continual re-working of patron-client networks are all discernable in the region's past and will continue into its future. Charles Lindholm's contribution to the volume, reflecting on his fieldwork in Swat in the late 1970s, offers a personal and humane account of how these changes swept across the region and affected the everyday lives of its peoples. His reflections on Swat, past and present, give a unique insight into how seemingly the timeless values of honor and hospitality, as well as issues of status, have assumed new idioms of expression. The "real Pakhtun" of Barth's and Lindholm's days have transformed into the "real Muslim" of today.

Between Central Asia and the Indian Ocean: locating the Frontier

Where does the Frontier belong—South Asia, the Middle East, or Central Asia? Is it best referred to as a non-space or a "space in-between," as the title of Rory Stewart's book suggests?[21] And is geographical mapping the only, or indeed the most appropriate way to conceive of this region? What about its cultural affinities—its participation in a Persianate world, a South Asian cultural sphere, and a Turkic social world? And what of its peoples' participation in circuits of movement extending into Inner Asia, the Indian Ocean, the Persian Gulf and beyond?[22] Why should such attempts to map the region matter at all?[23] Regardless of whether they should matter, the practical reality is that they do, both academically and politically.

Academically, the complexity of the Frontier's location is best captured by Barth himself. One would assume that fieldwork in Pakistan's north would lead to a career in the anthropology of South Asia. But Barth, and many of the participants in the debate around his work, including Charles Lindholm and Akbar Ahmed, chose instead to conduct further ethnographic fieldwork elsewhere. Barth's subsequent work was conducted in the Arabian peninsula and the Indonesian archipelago, amongst other settings; Lindholm went on to explore theoretical issues that located Frontier experiences in Middle Eastern culture; Ahmed focused more generally on the study of Islam.[24] As the trajectories of these scholars suggest, the Frontier, and more generally Afghanistan, has no natural home in area studies, but instead is located between the study of various cultural areas.[25] While there is excellent scholarship on the Frontier, it is often portrayed as a periphery or liminal region, appended as a special case to wider comparative courses on the Middle East, South or Central Asia. Its academic treatment is significant as different disciplines and area studies make competing claims about having "superior" knowledge of the region. Such claims play a central role in denoting the acceptable forms of knowledge about both the Frontier and Afghanistan. For scholars, as we explore, they frame the way the Pakistan-Afghanistan frontier may be understood and discussed. More insidiously, for policy-makers and the military they offer the opportunity to render this knowledge usable in concrete ways.

A number of scholarly interventions have centred on the way the Frontier's location is conceptualised. Some have sought to locate the region according to its social organisation. Do Swat's social structures and its stratification better resemble the Indian caste system, or the occupational groups and guilds of the Middle East?[26] Others have sought to locate the Frontier through comparative considerations of its cultural composition, arguing that the region's political dynamics have been informed by the standards and practices of a Turko-Persian Islamic ecumene.[27] According to such arguments, the contemporary cultural boundaries between South and Central Asia are the legacy of colonial state-building, Cold War politics, and the post-World War II reorganisation of the academy along the lines of area studies. Yet another way of locating the Frontier has been to treat it as a particular type of political space, one defined by the border that traverses it—a borderland.[28] Others have ethnicised the Frontier, calling it "tribal" or more specifically "Pushtun". More nuanced analyses treat it as peripheral yet intimately tied to the wider Persianate cultural world.[29]

Each of these types of categorisation carries within it both promise and problems. For example, the ethnicisation of the Frontier as exclusively "Pashtun" is both simplistic and factually inaccurate, ignoring not only the co-existence of but also rich interaction between heterogeneous cultural worlds there. Shah Mahmoud Hanifi's contribution emphasises that the urban centres of the "Pashto-world"— Quetta, Peshawar, Kabul and Qandahar—are contexts where Pashto exists in relationship to other "major" as well as "minor" languages of the Frontier, including Baloch, Dari, Hindko, not to mention Urdu and English more recently. Likewise, the term "borderland" defines a space by the presence of a border placed within it. Yet the significance of that border to people's lives is contested on a daily basis and varies according to the location, class, and ethnicity of those who interact with it.

Rather than defining the Frontier according to one or another criterion, we conceive of it as a region historically characterised by its internal heterogeneity.[30] This region, like other comparable ones—the Sahara, the Caucasus, the Indian Ocean, Zomia or upland South East Asia—is defined by patterns of circulation and movement. Its peoples and places are connected to one another, yet also different. Addressing the historic dynamics of patterns of "dependence and interdependence", which have tied the region together while at the same time fragmenting it, inevitably raises questions about the Frontier's future political shape.[31] Policy circles often talk of the need for a "joint solution" to Afghanistan and Pakistan's problems—the so-called "Af-Pak" strategy of Richard Holbrooke. Conversely, there are renewed and continuing rumours that regional separatisms seek new independent states, such as Baluchistan or Pashtunistan. Neither approach—treating it as a homogeneous whole or conversely as divided territories—does justice to the complexity of the Frontier's simultaneously centrifugal and centripetal character.

Imaginaries of the Frontier are not limited to those associated with the modern-day nation-state. Islamist movements active within and beyond the region think of the Frontier as an ethical-moral "space" where Muslims can forge an ideal type of Islamic polity.[32] Other local movements and actors reach back in history, conceptualising it as part of a pre-national Khorasan, for example.[33] The Frontier, both historically and today, has fed people's imaginations in fertile and influential ways. While often discounted as unrealistic, these imaginaries give the lie to the rich conceptual ordering that the region's inhabitants confer on a complex and interrelated social world. They do not limit their gaze to the simplistic national and ethnic categories external powers feel comfortable with.

Images of the Frontier are central to understanding its past and present, as well as constructing its future. They are the product of considerable investment, intellectual and otherwise, by their authors, who have their own agendas. One example of these images is the renewed focus on this region as part of the Silk Road, historically as well as today. Major international organisations, such as the Aga Khan Foundation, depict the Frontier and the wider contexts to which it is connected as a melting pot of peoples ideally located to profit from old trading routes carrying new products, most importantly those from China. Yet these organisations have commercial, religious and political interests in the region. This is part of a conscious construction of a new type of connective capitalist space that transcends old national and ethnic divisions.[34] Images of the Frontier such as this are embedded in and arise out of political economies, constructed by both local and global actors. Scholars need to critically examine them and the abstract conceptions of "space" on which they are based as historical and anthropological phenomena, rather than simply reproduce them.

The view of the region as a great inland highway is not simply the construction of modern multinational organisations like the Aga Khan Foundation. It is also visible in the great Muslim poet and philosopher Allama Iqbal's portrayal of Afghanistan in the 1930s, documented here by Nile Green. Iqbal described Afghanistan a "highway" that connected the Muslim-majority regions of Central and South Asia to one another, the development of which would lead to the liberation and release of Islamic creativity by Muslim communities in both regions. He considered these "dry roads" and skies as connective of the Muslim *umma*, distinct from the contemporary ubiquitous sea transport, which Iqbal thought of as "imperial" and central to the development of European colonialism. While Green's Muslim dignitaries travelling through Afghanistan reflected on its importance to the *umma*, today Magnus Marsden spends many hours conversing with young men who have "returned" to their "homeland" from Pakistan, where many were born. These young men remember their return through the icon of

Afghanistan's roads. Indeed, they make decisions about whether to stay or go according to their experiences of these roads, claiming to have learned to take pleasure in the "uniqueness" of long Afghan car journeys along bad roads that Land Cruisers share with nomads' camels.[35] There is a deep pool of spatial imaginings of the region which local actors draw upon today, very different from yet not simply prior to those of colonial map-makers.

The Frontier is no simple "space in-between" or "borderland" lying on the periphery of the regions and forces which shape it. Rather, it is a region with a long history of both interaction with and definition of the more familiar areas surrounding it. Historically, its peoples have long acted as middlemen between the Indian Ocean world and the steppes and great Islamic cities of Central Asia, such as Bukhara and Samarqand.[36] They are now involved in the same processes, but on a larger, global canvas, as is documented here in Marsden's chapter. He demonstrates how complex forms of economic and commodity-mediated life have emerged in the region now and in the past, driven in the main by local actors. Sophisticated trading institutions and relations developed over time and form an important dimension of the region's dynamics. The agents of these institutions, the Frontier's traders and merchants (*tojirha*), as well as self-defined *busnismine* (businessmen), have mediated its interaction with a range of wider worlds, and profoundly affected the region itself.

The Frontier's significance is not limited to itself. It tells us about other comparable regions that are divided by national borders yet also connect world regions to one another. The traders Marsden documents in his contribution literally embody these connections. They clearly show that neither the Frontier or Afghanistan is now, nor was not in the past, some homogeneously rural region, free of market influences and social relations mediated by capitalist-like logics.[37] Rather, it is both tied to and an active participant in global networks of exchange, migration and movement, and is, as such, an author of these logics. Ultimately, the placing of the Frontier is an important intellectual, economic and political exercise, the process of which is as revealing as the result.

The Taliban: beyond ethnic chauvinism, tribal primitivism and Muslim fundamentalism

The war in Afghanistan and Pakistan's North-West has, from 2001, sparked a flurry of interest in the social and cultural organisation of the region. Within days of the attacks on America in September 2001, publics in Europe and America were inundated with colourful maps of Afghanistan, showing the geographic distribution of the country's "ethnic groups". Such maps, and the analysis, implicit or explicit, of the region which accompanied them, were met by many scholars of the region with dismay. On the one hand, these maps were often incorrect, omitting the presence of major communities throughout the country. More problematically, they territorialised Afghanistan's ethnic groups in ways directly reminiscent of the cartographic practices of the British colonial-scholar administrators of the nineteenth century.[38] The maps depicted Afghanistan's ethnic groups as distinct communities defined by rigid differences in social organisation, cultural values and beliefs. These timeless, objective differences were all dimensions of their "identities" that directly shaped their political affiliations. Scholars of the social sciences and humanities rejected such understandings of ethnicity long before 11 September and have questioned the nexus between ethnic identity and political affiliation in this region.[39] Barth himself explored the mutability of ethnicity in his work *Ethnic Groups and Boundaries*, published in 1969. More recently, scholars have demonstrated the ways in which ethnic identity markers are contextually enacted and performed, rather than defining every feature of a person's being.[40]

Popular understandings of ethnicity and its relationship to collective identity and political affiliation crystallise most detrimentally in depictions of the Pukhtuns. Pukhtuns are frequently said to inhabit the "unruled", indeed unruleable regions of the Afghanistan-Pakistan border.[41] They are often portrayed as the main font of support for the Taliban and militant Islam, with Pervez Musharraf once famously remarking that "all Taliban are Pushtun, but not all Pushtun are Taliban". The Pashtuns are depicted not only as religious fanatics, but also as tradition-bound tribesmen whose moral universe is limited by the cultural values of honour and hospitality. Indeed, the so-called Pashtun "code of honour", the Pushtunwali, is widely treated as "the secret to understanding" not only Pashto-speakers, but all Afghans.[42] Yet it is unhelpful to simply challenge a stereotype or depiction of a people with a counter-narrative. Replacing the image of Pukhtuns as religious fanatics with one where they are tradition-bound tribesmen advances our understanding of the region little, but instead reinforces simplistic stereotypes about its diverse peoples.[43]

Rather than contesting stereotypes head-on, a strategy that tends to re-create simplistic ways of looking at the world, several of the chapters in this book take a more multi-dimensional approach to the identities of the region's peoples, especially the Pukhtun. Richard Tapper's contribution explores how far "Durrani Islam" and "Taliban Islam" overlap. He considers the extent to which the forms of Islam embraced by the Taliban resemble those he observed in the everyday life of Durrani Pashtuns prior to the Soviet invasion. Urs Geiser's chapter examines how state-sponsored development projects of the 1980s and 90s, despite their claim of participatory approaches, proceeded to usurp and undermine "traditional" social structures and institutions. The way the Pashtun were constructed intellectually by the state and development agencies has had, and continues to have, important implications for their role in, and relationship with, the Pakistani state-building agenda.

One of the key issues for both the Pakistani state and more broadly the international development community has been the Pashtun's, and the Taliban's, treatment of women. Anita Weiss' contribution shows how the Taliban's reign in Swat, and the Pakistani army's offensive to expel them, were fear-inspiring for many of its female inhabitants. This chapter moves away from understandings of the experiences of women based on Pukhtun cultural values or religious zealotry, and instead brings the focus squarely onto violence. Likewise, Sana Haroon's chapter illustrates the extent to which fear was central to women's experience of the Taliban. She explores the important overlaps between local ideas about gender and public space and the Taliban's actions towards women. Such overlaps were based on an inchoate "perception of malignant and dangerous" dimensions of the region's moral life. Yet

INTRODUCTION

this was no simple elision between Pashtun custom and Islamic stricture. The Taliban actually inverted "norms which favour familial control over women's sexuality and punishment" by entering the domain of the private and taking decisions for families concerning the education of their daughters. Haroon's chapter is a reminder that the Taliban's relationship with Pukhtunwali is not simply one of either adopting or resisting it on the basis of its perceived relation to Islam.

The almost singular focus on the Pukhtun as a problem obscures how the region's heterogeneity—ethnic, religious, and linguistic—has historically frustrated attempts at building exclusive nation-states.[44] By privileging the Pashtun, especially as negative actors, Western policy circles ignore the importance of the Frontier's and Afghanistan's non-Pashtun communities in its past, present and future. Indeed, dealing with Afghanistan's heterogeneity has grown ever more difficult as political claims grounded in ethnicity and the re-reading of past injustices become increasingly important within and beyond this region. These issues are as important in Pakistan as in Afghanistan; the 2009 decision to change the name of Pakistan's North-West Frontier Province to Khyber Pakhtunkhwah has generated debate amongst non-Pashto speakers in the Province about the effect of the name change on their identities and political position within it. How history plays into the present in such circumstances is a complicated question.

David Edwards' chapter explores that question by asking if the strategies of state-building pursued by the Wali of Swat, documented by Barth, are relevant to understanding strategies of state-building pursued by President Hamid Karzai today. According to Edwards, like the Wali, Karzai makes and breaks alliances with figures of authority across Afghanistan's diverse political field—alliances that, importantly, cross ethnic, linguistic and religious boundaries. Yet there are significant differences between the context in which the Wali of Swat pursued his strategies of political consolidation, and that in which Karzai works today. Edwards' discussion raises the question of whether the old and regionally important models of state-building Karzai employs suit today's circumstances. If not, could this partly explain his apparent failure to fashion an Afghan state?

Ethnicity is not the only problematic category of identity widely used to define the Frontier's social make-up; one as powerfully omnipresent along the Frontier is "tribe", a term used in diverse and multifarious ways. Some, especially politicians, employ it as a proxy for the term "ethnic group". The future stability of Afghanistan, they argue, requires a settlement that will "bring in all of the tribes".[45] This language not only carries connotations of unchanging primitivism; it also de-politicises conflicts in the country by ignoring the role of class, status and political conviction. As anthropologists and historians have long known, however, not all along the Frontier think of themselves as belonging to "tribes". Indeed, characterising Afghanistan as a homogeneous "tribal society" is a source of extreme resentment for many in the country and beyond, especially its intellectuals and elites. The current American-led military operations in the region have added to local sensitivities concerning the use of the term "tribe".

Western capitals, in both their political and public discourses, have too often used concepts of tribe to refer to a state of primitivism and primordial identities that inevitably lead to fratricidal violence. On the ground, Western forces have invested heavily in an effort to "know the tribes", most especially through the US Human Terrain System programme, in order to better control them.[46] But as with ethnicity, little is gained by rejecting the concept of "tribe" out of hand. Rather, such terms need to be deployed in a sensitive and nuanced manner.

Scholarly uses of the term tribe are indeed much more sophisticated than merely indicating a form of polity defined by its primitiveness. Historically, "tribe" is identified with forms of social structure and connected cultural ideologies that lie beyond and often seek to challenge the realm, institutions and values of "the state". Historians, however, have demonstrated how "tribes" and "states" in many contexts were wrought out of shared rather than divergent political and social processes. Anthropologists have also challenged the notion that tribes and states inhabit different political and cultural orders.[47]

Antonio Giustozzi's chapter engages these debates. Focusing on the Shinwari, who live in Ningahar, Kunar and Pakistan's tribal areas, he traces the convoluted relationship between tribal leaders and state officials in Afghanistan. The Afghan state, he argues, has sought to exert its authority over such spaces by cultivating connections with tribal leaders, who themselves affiliate with the state in order to benefit from the resources it may provide them. Afghanistan's political situation, according to Giustozzi, continues to reflect these political dynamics. As with Edwards' analysis, the balance between violence and alliance is central to Giustozzi's account of state-building and consolidation. Tribe, then, though problematic as a cultural category, allows us to focus on forms of political life—the making and breaking of alliances, and the politically-informed decision-making processes that go into these—that are, if anything, highly rational and calculating rather than signs of atavistic and primitive forms of politics.

Class and status

Class and status are important social realities along the Frontier which have received scant attention over the past decade. All the book's contributions emphasise, to a greater or lesser extent, that ignoring these realities, and more broadly the global political economies they are tied to, obscures some of the central driving forces of this region. It is important to recognise that just as geopolitics has historically been embedded in the "local", so too have global economic practices and transformations, making these supposed economic peripheries centres of global economic change.[48] Further, rather than a simplistic dialectic of class formation and conflict, the volume's contributions collectively argue for a complex model of political economy. The conscious deployment of the political language of class proved an important dimension of the Swat Taliban's discourse and practice. In contrast, many in Afghanistan chose to join or leave the Taliban and other political organisations on the basis of their projected understandings of the future, rather than for any overt sense of "class consciousness".[49] Individual strategising and its collective outcomes require further exploration to disentangle the relative importance of class, religion and imperialism in understandings of the "Taliban".

It is well known, for example, how families in Afghanistan spread their loyalties across a wide range of political positions to safeguard their assets and influence in an unstable political environment. This strategy of sons, documented in other politically unstable areas such as Northern Ireland, has been widely practiced by many Afghan elites. Indeed, over the past thirty years the children of rural elites became "educated peasants", democrats and socialists, only now to identify themselves as urban and educated opponents of the Taliban while being at the same time allies of the Mujahidin leaders for whom they work. In this context, what conceptual purchase do the dichotomous categories "urban bourgeoisie" and "rural poor" really have?

Other chapters complicate simplistic understandings of the supposed "special relationship" between Pukhtuns and the Taliban, turning their focus towards the political economy which has enabled the movement's emergence. Nancy Lindisfarne's contribution argues that scholars have focused on dimensions of the Taliban movement's ideology that appear most alien to them. As a result, she suggests, they have failed to explore its anti-imperial and class dimensions. Robert Nichols also challenges the tendency to locate the Swat Taliban in relation to cultural explanations that depict it as the current stage in an ongoing process of Islamisation. Such modes of analysis, he argues, need to focus more on the region's political economy, recognising its relation to local, national and global contexts. For Nichols, the Taliban leadership in Swat were successful in winning support for their movement by raising issues connected to everyday Swati experiences of class inequality.

These are issues addressed ethnographically by Nicolas Martin in his chapter on the state and class as experienced by the rural poor in Pakistan's Punjab Province. Martin's contribution leaves the Frontier for Pakistan's breadbasket, but his Punjab is comparable to Barth's Swat in a number of ways. Competition for land between aspirant and established landlords marks political life; the state and its services are a revenue source for the landlords; patron–client relationships have morphed from ones built on social obligations and proximity to ones that are outwardly political and economic. Recent developments in the religious landscape of the Punjab, moreover, render it comparable to Swat in other ways. The Punjab has seen growing levels of Taliban-like militant activity. Martin's chapter shows the extent to which debates about Swat describe similar processes affecting the social dynamics of contexts beyond the frontier world. It is an important contribution to the volume as it clearly de-exceptionalises the Pushtuns, drawing parallels between developments in the Punjab and Swat.

For all the focus on issues of class, status and political economy, both in Barth's *Political Leadership* and in the ensuing debate, there is relatively little attention paid to merchants and trade, or their effect on political economy and state-building. This is in stark contrast to the extensive body of work on South Asia that places merchants and traders at the heart of processes of state-building.[50] In the context of the Frontier, merchants and traders are widely depicted as little more than one-dimensionally immoral "profiteers" who have enriched themselves from the region's war economy. Such a position is difficult to dispute if one views the region through the distanced spectacles of a Western political economist. Yet merchants and traders are also of historic significance to society and politics in Afghanistan and the wider region.[51]

Trading builds on logics that bring people together as equivalent sources of profit rather than distinguishing them on the basis of ethnicity. But trade is not simply an economic activity.[52] It is informed by forms of social and cultural activity revolving around the exchange of things and ideas whose importance is human in scale. Over the past thirty years of political upheaval many people from diverse backgrounds have turned to trade to survive, yet in the process have also crafted new moral and cultural worlds. In this context as in others, being a trader refers not only to people's flexibility in relationship to flows of capital, but also to their ability to continually remake themselves, act independently, and emerge from cataclysmic conflict unscathed. As Ashraf Ghani argued in his presentation at the conference where the chapters of this volume were first presented, a more rounded understanding of the region requires consideration of the importance of traders and merchants both today and in the past to multiple domains of life within it.[53]

Structure of the book

While the contributions to this volume all engage the cross-cutting themes discussed thus far, we have nevertheless organised their presentation into discrete sections for those wishing to focus on particular episodes. These sections are: Continuity and Change; Locating the Frontier; Class, Patronage and the State; Taliban, Pashtun and Swat; and finally, Tribe and State. Before the volume delves into the individual sections, it begins with Charles Lindholm's reflective essay on his experiences in Swat over thirty years ago. Continuity and Change includes the contributions by Christine Noelle-Karimi, Mariam Abou Zahab and Benjamin D. Hopkins. While all raise issues which speak across the volume as a whole, these contributions sit well together because of their focus on change, or the lack of it, over time in this space. The second section, Locating the Frontier, includes the contributions of Shah Mahmoud Hanifi, Nile Green and Magnus Marsden. While they too engage the volume's themes broadly, these contributions complement one another in how they conceptualise the Frontier as a particular type of imagined and enacted space.

Class, Patronage and the State, which includes chapters by Nicolas Martin, Nancy Lindisfarne and Robert Nichols, looks to the centrality of class as an idiom through which to understand the upheavals of the recent past. This is followed by the contributions of Sultan-i-Rome, Urs Geiser, Anita Weiss and Sana Haroon, which collectively compose the section Taliban, Pashtun and Swat. These contributors detail the specific experiences of the Swat Valley and its inhabitants, while tying those experiences back to the volume's broader conceptual discussions. Finally, the section Tribe and State includes chapters by Antonio Giustozzi, Richard Tapper, David Edwards and Hugh Beattie. These contributions offer a detailed examination of the mutually constitutive relationship between "tribes" and the state, and critically question both the validity and utility of such categories. All the contributions, either implicitly or explicitly, engage the themes we have outlined in this introduction, while at the same time raising a host of other considerations which are often in conversation with one another. It is that conversation we hope to foster and enrich through this volume.

INTRODUCTION

Conclusion

Although this volume brings insight to a wide variety of issues of critical importance along the Frontier, we still lack important perspectives on this world. Our call has been for greater attempts to think through the Frontier on its own terms. The globally important nature of the Afghanistan-Pakistan region is clear. While the attempts of competing forces to legitimise different visions of it focus on the present American-led efforts, the Frontier has long been shaped by its own ever-changing dynamics. Moreover, it is important as both an imagined and material dimension of the lives of people in many of the world's countries. The costs of the now decade-long war in Afghanistan have been enormous for all involved. The US alone has spent nearly $500 billion directly on the conflict in Afghanistan.[54] Thousands of young men and women from the US, UK and their NATO allies have served and been injured in what has become the longest war of the twenty-first century.

Often minimised or ignored in discussions of the current conflict is the cost to the region's inhabitants. Their views of the contemporary role played by outside powers are regularly overlooked or even dismissed. Yet they are shaped by past experiences of violence at the hands of these same powers. For example, it is widely asserted in Afghanistan that British support of the Taliban in Helmand and elsewhere is central to the latter's ongoing success. Likewise, it is common to hear the argument across the country that the current intervention is in fact driven by the desire to plunder Afghanistan's treasures; treasures that the British and others have in the past been forced to leave behind. Specifically, people in Badakhshan talk about German forces entering the region's many shrines by night to steal the treasures inside.

To many commentators from outside the region, such talk sounds like conspiracy theories, to be dismissed as irrational if not "grotesque".[55] Such dismissals, however, fail to account for the local experiences and expectations of external actors, past and present.[56] Public reports of the Pentagon's assessment of Afghanistan's mineral wealth understandably lead to suspicions about foreign motives in the country.[57] At the same time, Afghans' assertions that the British have returned to Helmand and the South in order to re-establish old relationships with powerful actors they once knew have a long pedigree. Such assertions could be interpreted as deriving not from a lack of rationality but rather from the workings of political processes. As several of the chapters of this book show, out of conflicts emerge alliances. Moreover, these rumours also point to the economic practices that Afghans have developed in the context of constant political flux and economic uncertainty.[58] Rather than conspiracy, this is a mode of thinking about the past and its relationship to the present that reveals how people in Afghanistan and connected contexts see the ties that bind their world to that beyond, as well as embarking upon practices that seek to bring consistency to the fluid world they inhabit.

The Frontier reveals globally important forces and trends. Academically, it has furnished social science scholarship with key concepts, thanks in large part to the pioneering work of Fredrik Barth. The chapters in this volume plainly show the continuing relevance and ongoing significance of that work. With great clarity, he recognised the centrality of political processes, as opposed to culture, in the forging of individuality. As he wrote in 1959,

In Swat persons find their place in the political order through a series of choices, many of which are temporary or revocable. This freedom of choice radically alters the way in which political institutions function. In systems where no choice is offered, self-interest and group advantage tend to coincide, since it is only thorough his own group that any individual can protect or improve his own position. Where, on the other hand, group commitments may be assumed and shed at will, self-interest may dictate action which does not bring advantage to the group; and individuals are able to plan and make choices in terms of private advantage and in a personal political career. In this respect the political life of Swat resembles that of Western societies.[59]

Barth's analysis remains a salutary reminder that the problems faced by current international engagements along the Frontier derive from their tendency to exaggerate cultural differences rather than speak to the common human modes of behaving that are equally, if not more, visible. By reminding us both of the mutability of culture and of the importance of politics, Barth's analysis presents a radical, yet familiar understanding of the Frontier which has too long been ignored.

1

SWAT IN RETROSPECT

CONTINUITIES, TRANSFORMATIONS AND POSSIBILITIES

Charles Lindholm

Swat in 1977

When I left Pakistan in at the end of 1977, I completed over a year and a half of fieldwork in a Swati village I have called "Shin Bagh" (Green Garden).[1] Surrounded by lush fields and hidden behind thick stone walls, it seemed to exist in a world of its own. Although a government police force existed, and although military jeeps occasionally raised dust on the main road, neither the police nor the military dared or cared to intervene in local matters. Whatever authority there was rested with the local khans.

At that time, the Pukhtun code of honor (Pukhtunwali), which enjoined hospitality, revenge and refuge, as well as the custom of paying bride price and a prohibition of divorce, was assumed to be as Islamic as fasting in Ramadan or praying five times a day. To be a pious Muslim meant being a good Pukhtun. The function of the village mullahs was to teach the basics of religious practice to children, to lead the prayers in the village's mosques and to preside over necessary ceremonies of birth, circumcision, and death. Their opinions were not sought on political matters, and their moral influence was confined mainly to inveighing against the evils of women. Other religious figures were even more peripheral. A couple of Sufi shaikhs from the region were said to have loyal disciples in the village, but most people considered these Sufis to be charlatans at best, dangerous magicians at worst. Sometimes long-haired wandering *malangs*, feared for their ability to curse and derided for their dirty clothes and bad habits, begged for *paisa* (a Pakistani coin, a hundredth of a rupee) and bread in the village lanes, beating away dogs and children with their walking sticks. Families reckoned to be somehow descended from the Prophet or his companions (*Sayyidan* and *Miagan*) cultivated strips of land (*tseri*) between villages that had been granted to them by the

17

khans a few generations ago in payment for their occasional roles as mediators in disputes. Ideally speaking, they were expected to behave in a manner diametrically opposed to that of the warrior khans—that is, they were not to carry weapons and were supposed to be studious, self-abnegating, and pious. In practice, these expectations were rarely met, since most members of the holy lineages tended to emulate the Pukhtun mode of life instead of symbolically reversing it.

In those days, there were no intrusive loudspeakers in the village mosques. Electricity was new and unreliable; cooking was mostly done over smoky fires. Tea had been introduced within the lifetime of the older men, who had also experienced the periodic circulation of fields and villages (*wesh*). Now that *wesh* had ceased, apple trees were growing in the fertile soil, tobacco had been introduced, and people were becoming accustomed to cash instead of barter. Yet I met men who had never seen a five-rupee note. The rhythm of the seasons was slow. I spent my days collecting notes and my nights playing cards with my Pukhtun friends and philosophizing by the flicker of lamplight. Sometimes, we listened to the mesmerizing drone of Nahshanas on Radio Kabul. It seemed as if things would never change.

This sense of timelessness was an illusion. Transformations were already well underway as new roads allowed outsiders to lift the veil of Swat, revealing its long famed beauty. As Khushal Khan Khattak declared two hundred years ago: "In climate Swat is glorious, lovelier far than Kabul. Its air and verdure are like Kashmir. Everyplace is by nature a garden of flowers."[2] Capitalizing on the valley's natural resources, efforts were underway to turn it into the "Switzerland of Pakistan." A ski resort was being built and there were plans for a golf course. Down the road, a few miles from Shin Bagh, on a picturesque rapids, an American woman opened an inn catering to foreign tourists, Punjabis, and other lowlanders escaping Pakistan's summer heat.

But, despite appearances, Swat was hardly a paradise when I was there, any more than it had been when Khushal wrote his verse, which goes on to say: "Yet (Swat) has no garden, no fragrance, no freshness, because the Yusufzai have made it a desert." And elsewhere, he laments: "Friendship and kinship are lies. Everyone pursues his personal interest... God has taken back humanity from man. Wild animals are far better than such creatures." As I soon discovered, the potential for inhumanity was never far beneath the bucolic surface. When my host's brother-in-law, a well-respected, jovial and handsome young man, suddenly and horribly died, the official explanation was cholera, but the gossip was that he had been poisoned by arsenic. The prime suspect was his first wife, who had been dishonored when he took a second. Nothing could be proven, and life went on.

Feuds between men also led to killings. One evening my host, riding back to the village on his motorbike, came across a newly slain body lying in a ditch, oozing blood. His first thought was how much the dead man's bullet-pierced embroidered vest resembled one of his own. His second was that he should continue quickly on his way, since the killer might be lurking nearby. By the time he arrived back in the village, he had forgotten the incident, and only remembered it much later in the evening. The violent death of someone he didn't know was not really newsworthy to him.

But in fact "normal" violence, though always a danger, was limited by a number of factors. A story I have told before is worth repeating. One of my friends brought a Hindu to visit him as a guest in the village. There were some rumblings among the villagers about a Muslim's duty to slay infidels, and the visitor feared that he might be killed. He was told: "Do not worry. Your death will be avenged." Though this assurance sounds like cold comfort, what it meant was that in Pukhtunwali violence towards a guest was the same as violence towards the host, and would lead to the same result: retribution. However, hotheaded, impetuous vengeance was not the norm. On the contrary, the real Pukhtun bided his time, waiting for the right moment to set things right. In one case I knew of, a man burst into a hospital room to kill the already dying elderly brother of someone who had shot his father some thirty years ago. As a local proverb says: "The Pukhtun took revenge after a hundred years and said: 'I took it quickly.'" In a context where insults are never forgotten, guns are ubiquitous, and revenge is slow but certain, people generally control their tempers and act with discretion. When another friend of mine found that someone had cut his fruit trees down in the night, he said, "Thank God, I have many enemies" and did nothing, since he didn't know (or could plausibly claim not to know) whom to blame, and could interpret the attack as an affirmation of his high status.

In fact, the more elite the clan, the more its members actively avoided blood feuds. This was for several reasons. For one, they held land in various places, and could not cultivate it if a feud was going on; so it was in their interest to avoid violence. For another, their widespread marital ties militated against feuds with their in-laws who were also their allies. Disputes between affines were therefore likely to be negotiated. And finally, their party (*dullah*) alliances, which cross-cut lineage ties and were the main sites for political rivalry, were superseded by the requirements of loyalty to close patrilateral kin. As one of my friends told his brother: "I will take revenge if you are killed, but otherwise we are enemies." In other words, while men often opposed their brothers, patrilateral uncles and cousins and even fathers in factional *dullah* disputes, they could not remain allies with members of their faction who actually did physical harm to their patrilineal kin. This meant that *dullah* politics did not tend to lead to serious violence or insult, since that would break up the alliance. These factors generally kept fights between powerful khans from spreading too far or going on too long. And, if disputes did burst into violence, elite families had the wherewithal to convene, house and feed a *jirga* (council) of respected elders and religious figures until a settlement was reached. In general, only lesser men died in disputes, and their deaths were either avenged among themselves or settled by negotiations instituted and enforced by their patrons.

The erosion of stability

However, despite the appearance of balance, danger signs were visible everywhere during my stay in Swat. For one thing, despite substantial out-migration, the population of the valley was becoming increasingly dense—about equal to that of Bangladesh per acre of arable land. The hills, denuded of trees that had been sold for a few paisa, were eroding rapidly. Land washed away in the rainy season and dried out in hot weather. Even the stately chinar trees, which grew in the local graveyard and supplied the only shade in the village, had been cut down and sold by the village elders for almost nothing. Since firewood was rare, dry dung had to do as fuel for cooking. Food was usually scarce and hunger was commonplace. Even though I was the guest of a khan, he had no cows or buffalo, so we had to trade for dairy products, and often lived mainly on bread and rice. Clearly, an ecological disaster was brewing, fostered by the "tragedy of the commons." Even though most of the villagers knew that cutting the trees on the hills was causing erosion and destroying the land, they chopped them down and sold them anyway, since otherwise someone else was sure to do so.

At the same time, the old feudal system of mutual interdependence between patron landlords and client workers was slowly being eroded by the encroachment of a cash economy and an influx of migrant labor. Traditionally, the khans made sure their dependents had food on the table and were not harassed; they contributed to bride price and mediated disputes; when the crops were divided, the shares for the farm workers and other village servants (barbers, carpenters, mullahs, etc.) were apportioned first. In return, clients and their families worked for and, if need be, fought alongside their patrons; they lived near them, knew them well, depended on them, and respected them. And they had a degree of autonomy and power, since the client's labor and loyalty could be offered to a rival patron, whose prestige and position would be improved. Although it was asymmetrical, this relationship of mutual dependency combined with a degree of voluntary association provided a degree of stability and continuity.[3]

However, during my stay in Swat a number of khans were already being drawn to the costly pleasures of life in Peshawar and were becoming absentee landlords, uninterested in maintaining lifelong ties to local clients. Instead they hired migrant workers and tenant farmers whose relationships with their employers were purely monetary and who could easily be fired. This brought into the valley a large group of impoverished Pukhtun from different regions who had neither loyalty to the local elite nor any connection with the indigenous tribal framework. It also turned former feudal clients into mere landless laborers, dependent on the vicissitudes of the market for survival and owing allegiance to no one. In the service of what they saw as their rational self-interest, the khans destroyed the main sources of their own legitimacy, paving the way for the arrival of new and revolutionary modes of authority that would eventually extinguish their world.

As they had done for generations, but now with even more frequency as they lost their protective ties to their patrons, Swati workers sought employment in Karachi, Dubai and the other Gulf States, or even in Malaysia or Germany. Their families relied on their remittances for survival. When the migrants returned, they often had great ambitions, but their savings were eaten up by showy capital expenditures: big houses, new cars, and fancy wedding celebrations. Prospects for productive investment were limited: only so many taxi businesses could make a profit. Landownership remained the basis for respect, and was still controlled by local khans, who, on pain of ostracism, could only sell to one of their own. On their side, many young khan men were tired of farming, which yielded little income, while pride kept them from migrating abroad as laborers or working as employees. Frustrated in their ambitions, they complained bitterly that the valley was "*tang*"—narrow.

Pervasive poverty, unemployment, and lack of opportunity heightened discontent and inspired insurrection. For example, a Gujar from the mountainous region of Biha led his fellows in a rebellion against his Shamakhel patrons, eventually defeating them and stripping them of some of their land. As a result, he became a khan in his own right. In the region of Lalkoo, local Miagan, hoping to appropriate high quality rice land to augment their own unproductive *tseri*, secretly manufactured a cannon and attacked the town of Bodigram before they were finally defeated. North of Swat, in the Kingdom of Dir, sharecroppers forcibly appropriated the land they worked. The same scenario took place in the Malakand Pass as tenant farmers from Bajaur, Mahmand, and elsewhere claimed fields as their own. Closer to my own home, one of my friend's uncles was killed by mountain Gujars when he tried to collect rent from them.

In this era of discontent and anxiety, democratic elections seemed to offer ordinary people some hope of change. The populist and nationally dominant Pakistan People's Party (PPP) had as its slogan a demand for "*roti, kapra, makam*" (food, clothing, shelter). However, in Upper Swat the PPP was primarily a reconstituted version of the old *dullah* of Khan Bahadur, who had dominated the region during the reign of Wali (the former King).[4] What mattered to these traditional leaders was not the socialistic ideology of the national PPP, but who one's allies were, and how much they could be trusted. This pragmatic attitude was expressed in a PPP rally I witnessed at a local man's house: the PPP flag was raised, armed bodyguards looked fierce, and the attending khans were given tea and shook hands with the candidate. No speeches were made; there were no promises of redistribution or reform among this group of insiders. The purpose was plain: a demonstration of power and loyalty.

Yet, there were indications that a more profound ideological shift was in the making. The PPP candidate was not one of Khan Bahadur's sons or close cousins, as might be expected, but rather a young and handsome minor khan who employed all the rhetoric of class warfare to appeal to the local sharecroppers and servants and to the Gujars who inhabited the more remote upland valleys. His opponent, supported by a coalition between the secular PNA (People's National Alliance) and the religious JUI (Jamiat-i-Ulema-i-Islam), was a conservative village mullah (Maulana Abdul Rahman), presaging a pattern that would soon become the norm. But at that time, he was seen primarily as a stalking horse for the *dullah* of Khan Bahadur's old enemies, the Mahmatkhel.

However, some Pukhtun did publicly embrace the religious ideology espoused by the JUI and reviled the PPP as "socialist" and "unIslamic." As one told me: "If the rich fulfilled their Islamic duties, there would be no need for reform. But Islamic duties are not fulfilled, the society is not just, and when people do call for reform, they are labeled *kafir* (infidels)." To back up his words, he, like many others, began growing his beard, symbolizing his new adherence to activist Islam. There was a degree of self-interest involved. The JUI/PNA platform opposed any form of land redistribution; help for the poor would come from Islamic charity, not from structural change. The status quo would remain, legitimized by Muslim precepts.

On the other side of the political fence, although PPP rhetoric meant nothing to the powerful leaders of Khan Bahadur's *dullah*, it did appeal to some younger Khans who believed they could win the loyalty of the destitute and dependent. These idealistic and ambitious men told me that "the people" would support them because, unlike their venal elders, they treated the poor well, interceded for them, protected them, and mediated their disputes fairly. In their conversations, they cited the examples set by the great *malik*s (leaders) of previous generations, who were revered by all (at least in memory). According to legend, *malik*s in the past were honorable, honest magistrates and benefactors of the people, who generously funneled the revenues from fines and taxes to their poor dependents and to their loyal allies. The young PPP khans hoped that they too could fill that role. However, even for those Pukhtuns who were sincerely moved by PPP rhetoric, the cry for justice ended when there was a threat to their own property. For example, an educated and liberal young khan who was considered a model of the "new generation" shot one of his sharecroppers dead when the man instigated other workers to strike.

Meanwhile, violence against the rich and powerful was on the rise: a spate of robberies and murders were committed along the main road, reported to be the work of Gujars. They left behind the beheaded bodies of well-dressed victims as a sign of contempt. The bandits who perpetrated these brutal crimes were feared, but also celebrated in popular songs and stories. Even in peaceful Shin Bagh landless laborers and servants voiced strong complaints about their khans. Some told me outright that their Pukhtun landlords cruelly oppressed their helpless tenants. Others, less damning, said that the village landlords were simply aloof and did not care about the plight of the poor. Sharecroppers told me that above all they would like to own their own land, though the prospect seemed hopeless. As one said, "I would migrate anywhere if I was given land for myself and my family. But the khans would move with us, and take any land for themselves."

So, even though the elections in Swat were generally and accurately seen as a battle between *dullah*s and traditional elites, new elements had come into play. The old guard of khans could no longer dominate simply because they were strong, wealthy men upholding the traditional masculine values of a "real Pukhtun." Instead, in public their mouthpieces spouted either the language of populism or that of Islam, while both were alike in crying out for justice and reform. This rhetoric inflamed a populace suffering from the collapse of the protections and continuity offered by the old feudalistic system and increasingly experiencing hunger and other effects of overpopulation. The elections, it was generally hoped, might offer real change, and voters came out en masse, most of them casting ballots for the PPP. Their hope was crushed in 1977 when General Zia declared martial law after the national PPP landslide. Nevertheless, as a result of these elections, politics in Upper Swat clearly began to extend beyond the interminable *dullah* struggles for prestige and power. At the same time, disappointment with the results led to popular alienation from the democratic political process and a susceptibility to more radical solutions.[5]

Sources of insurgency

The seeds of present discontent were already sown when I left Swat in 1977. Since then, most of the elite khans, further weakened by the erosion of their ties to the countryside and the delegitimization of their old roles as mediators and moral exemplars, have retreated to suburban homes in Peshawar or London, where they lament the loss of their traditional authority.[6] At the same time, many local opponents of the status quo, once divided by adherence to either religious or socialist paths to change, found common ground in the ideology of neo-fundamentalist Islam, as enunciated in local terms by the TNSM (Tehrik-i-Nifaz-i-Shariat-i-Muhammadi) movement and its descendants, the MMA (Majlis-e-Amal) and the TTP (Tehrik-i-Taliban Pakistan). The proclaimed goal of bringing justice to the deprived and impoverished through strict and impersonal implementation of Islamic law (sharia) united the social justice rhetoric of the PPP with the religious claims made by the JUI/PNA alliance. As the old system of mutual obligation broke down, so did constraints on violence. Class rage was focused on the remaining big khans and on the wealthy and successful. As a result, what had been popular discontent turned into a revolution: decapitation—that old Gujar sign of contempt—became a general method of political execution.

Although the pieces were in already in place in 1977, a number of intertwined factors precipitated the recent eruption. One was the American conquest of Afghanistan in 2001 and subsequent interference in the NWFP. As a result, the people of Swat became all too aware that their local struggles could be framed as part of a global battle for the survival of Islam. After 2001, what had once been a mere battle for local power was interpreted as a cosmic war between the forces of good and evil, with all the intensification and zealotry that implies. The Afghan war also brought about a massive demographic shift, as multitudes of refugees poured across the border, placing further pressure on the scarce resources in the region and destabilizing an already fragile social structure. In contrast, in 1977 America was conceived by Swatis to be a far-distant place where the sun rose in the West, people were buried standing up, and frogs were eaten: in other words, a myth. There was no fear that Islam was threatened by Americans, no sense that international enemies were conspiring against the believers, no massive influx of de-territorialized immigrants.

Magnifying these factors was the arrival in Swat of foreign and domestic preachers and teachers who advocated the neo-fundamentalist textual originalism of the Deobandi and Wahhabi schools of Islam, which asserted that only the words of the Koran were binding. Trained in an austere and simplistic faith that devalued culture and interpretation, they attacked traditional forms of Islamic authority such as the sacralized authority of the family of the Wali, asserted that their own version of Islam was universal, changeless, transparent, and absolute, and drew attention to the disjunctures between Pukhtunwali and the faith. Domination by the khans, in their eyes, was an abomination.[7] This attitude increasingly resonated with the experiences of Swatis, especially those who had brought back neo-fundamentalist ideas about Islam from their stints as migrant laborers in the Gulf States, Saudi Arabia, and elsewhere.

A final exacerbating factor was the huge increase in the power of the Pakistani state in Swat. As I mentioned above, during my stay no officials lived in the village, and few taxes, if any, were paid. Police kept their distance. Visits by authorities were by invitation only, to celebrate weddings, engagements, or funerals, or to preside over expressions of *dullah* solidarity disguised as political rallies. Disputes were mostly settled by personal negotiation and, if that failed, by the mediation of a local khan or, perhaps, of respected Sayyidan or Miagan living on the nearby *tseri* land. Cases were taken to the official courts only as a last resort, with full knowledge of the time and money that would be eaten up in dealing with corrupt judges and paying off witnesses. Yet, it was recognized that the judgment of the Wali was legitimate, since his authority was both sacred and backed up by force.

As noted, the khans' loss of authority as mediators and judges coincided with their withdrawal from the feudal system of reciprocal obligations. When they left the dirt and travail of the villages in pursuit of the much cleaner and easier life of the city, their absence opened a space for the insertion of the state. Moreover, the official displacement of the Wali as ruler and final arbiter of justice left a vacuum that was quickly filled by the installation of civil courts. Most people did not see this as a shift from arbitrary "*qadi*" justice to a more impersonal and equitable system. Rather, the state courts were widely considered to be dishonest, unpredictable, and inefficient. Even worse, Swatis believed that Pakistani magistrates and officials only pretended to rule impartially and honestly when in actual fact they were self-interested, corrupt, and in thrall to infidel Americans. So, the Pakistani state was undermined and delegitimized by its perceived hypocrisy as well as its lack of integrity and manifest inefficiency.

Without the religiously mandated and historically legitimized judgments of the Wali, without the mediations formerly provided by the khans, and without any legitimacy attached to the government court system, what remained was recourse to the sharia, promoted by the Deobandi missionaries as the straightforward, incorruptible, and universal source of justice. The rebels of the TNSM, MMA, and TTP argued that the sharia should be implemented immediately, and the government courts disbanded. As for the traditional justice meted out by the khans, it was obsolete; the khans had proved unfit to rule, it was time for a new day to dawn. And so it has, but without much light being shed.

The populist uprisings in Swat that exploded in the last few years have been traumatic events in which civil government was overthrown, police, the military, and the paramilitary attacked, local elites beheaded, government and "unIslamic" buildings and property destroyed. In Upper Swat, where I once worked, special targets of the rebels were the agents of the old political system. Afzal Khan was the leader of the Mahmatkhel *dullah* that had once supported the JUI, a national religious party. Sultanat Khan, his major opponent, was the head of Khan Bahadur's *dullah*, which had ruled the region for a generation with the support of the Wali. According to my informants, Afzal Khan was almost killed by the insurgents, despite his history of alliance with the party of the pious. This was because he had long been in power as an elected official in the National Assembly but had done nothing to alleviate the sufferings of the people. In particular, he was accused of mistreating and displacing the Gujars who were his tenants. Attacks on Sultanat Khan and his *dullah* allies were more predictable. Their power and wealth, combined with their history as oppressors of the poor, made them obvious targets. For the MMA and Taliban, both families represented the worst of the old order.

The doctor and the suicide bomber

However, in Shin Bagh, where I did my research, the villagers held the rebels at bay outside the walls. Many of them interpreted the proclamation of a *jihad* (holy war) as a ploy that would allow foreign immigrants and local bandits to take over the village's lands and pillage its resources. Their basic philosophy was "better the devils we know than the ones we don't." Barred from Shin Bagh itself, the insurgents attacked those buildings erected along the main road during the long years of peace. Among these were a school and a free clinic/guesthouse that had been built and supported by one of my friends, an elite local khan who had become a cosmopolitan and secular medical doctor with an international reputation. His personal mission in Swat was to alleviate some of the suffering, backwardness, and misery of his homeland.

When the Taliban rebellion occurred, the doctor and his family felt they could no longer safely stay in Swat, and they retreated, like so many Pukhtun, to their modern primary home in Peshawar. His clinic and the school, defenseless on the main road, were raided and defaced; the furniture and medicines were stolen. However, neither building was destroyed, unlike the government sponsored girls' school nearby, which was razed to the ground. A week later the doctor received a phone call at his Peshawar compound. The caller proudly identified himself as a suicide bomber and claimed responsibility for the attack on Shin Bagh. At the same time, he apologized for the actions of his men against the clinic and school. Fazlullah, the leader of the MMA, had decreed that the doctor's things should be kept safe and returned to him when possible; all the stolen items had been put aside in a safe place except for the foam mattresses, which the Mujahidin needed, as they were sleeping on the hard ground. The caller then asked: "Do you know me? I studied in your school until the eighth class. You gave us books and paid our tuition. But I had to stop my schooling because of poverty." A few days later, when the rebels were under ferocious attack by the Pakistani army, he called again to tell the doctor where he could find his goods, which indeed were later recovered intact.

The root causes and contradictions of the insurgency are encapsulated in this story. The self-described suicide bomber was motivated to join the rebels by a combination of poverty, ignorance, and a sense of injustice. For him the old PPP call for "*roti, kapra, makam,*" once uttered by Pakistan's leaders, later by the radical young khans and their erstwhile followers, was now linked to a religious demand for sharia law and installation of "true Islam." The MMA and TTP rebels, in their innocence, saw this as a simple prescription that could be immediately realized. All that was necessary was to install "real Muslims" (who had supplanted "real Pukhtuns" in popular estimation) in positions of leadership, and justice would inevitably reign. At the same time, the caller respected the secular doctor's goodwill and integrity, and felt honor bound to right the wrongs he and his men had done to him. This story hints at the complexities of the Swati situation, where modern class hatred and neo-fundamentalist notions of Islam combine in unpredictable ways with old habits of respect and honor. The ultimate outcome of this volatile mixture is yet to be determined.

In my previous writings on Swat, and in this article as well, I have focused mostly on the masculine world of politics and power, on genealogical linkages and *dullah* alliances, on the relation of old disputes to new ones. I have related tales of betrayal and chicanery, of heroism and revenge, of the narrowness and factionalism of village life, of the consequences of breaking custom and of being shamed, of the ways and means of gaining respect in a constant battle between co-equals. This orientation makes sense. Violence, war, honor, betrayal, and political manipulation were what the men I talked to talked about.[8] For them, the words of Khushal were self-evidently true: "To gamble life and limb, honest and fearless—that is the work of a real man." And they accepted as well the truth of the proverb: "The Pukhtun is never at peace unless he is at war." Today, with the surge of violence in the region and the involvement of the superpowers, warfare and strategy remain at the forefront of our scholarly and journalistic writings on this troubled region.

But focusing on this harsh aspect ignores a softer side of Pukhtun character, as expressed best in the poetry of an equally great Pukhtun poet, the mystic Rahman Baba, who praises the heartfelt hospitality, friendship, kindness, generosity, and selflessness that many of us have experienced in Swat, even from people in the poorest circumstances.[9] I sometimes was ashamed to realize that a family had slaughtered their only chicken in order to feed me, an honored guest. Like other visitors before me, I had to learn not to express admiration for anything, since it would then immediately be given to me, with no refusal possible. This characteristic generosity is revealed as well by the charity of successful Pukhtun, like my doctor friend, who have not forgotten the sufferings of the impoverished and oppressed. Emphasis on warlike characteristics also obscures the sacrifices made by Pukhtun men and women who hope for a better future for themselves and their children. I include many of the present day insurgents in this category. Although they are categorized as "the bad guys" in the polarized worldview of the West, I believe that most of them are sincerely searching for a way to achieve some degree of justice and humanity in the bleakest of circumstances. The doctor and the suicide bomber may not be so far apart after all.

As for prescriptions for the future, my ambitions as a pundit are minimal. I have no confidence in my own ability to predict the future or to steer policy. I do want to remind my readers that people from Swat, like other Pukhtun, have long been adventurous and resilient entrepreneurs, traveling far and wide in pursuit of adventure and profit, quickly and successfully adapting to circumstances wherever they may be. The Pukhtun worldview, which first of all assumes that the Pukhtun are the equals (if not the superiors) of anyone else, and secondly assumes that hard work, austerity, and dedication are manly virtues, makes them the modern equivalents of Weber's Calvinist entrepreneurial capitalists. Unhappily, this formidable capacity for work and innovation can only flower outside the repressive confines of the Swat Valley. A valuable contribution to peace and prosperity in Swat and the region would therefore be to invest in schools that teach practical skills as well as religious training. This could coincide with providing start-up support for innovative local entrepreneurs. Given the weakness and fractioning of the Pakistani state, such programs are unlikely to be implemented, but something might be possible, especially with the aid of successful expatriates who would contribute to projects if they could be assured their money would not be wasted or stolen.

Although the situation in Swat may seem hopeless, it is worth recalling that the Red Shirts, who were the most devoted and militant devotees of Gandhi in Pakistan, who endured the most violent retaliation from the British, who were humiliated and martyred for their acts of passive resistance, were Pukhtuns.[10] When Abdul Ghaffar Khan amalgamated the precepts of Islam with those of Pukhtunwali and convinced his followers that victory and respect could be gained by stoic acceptance of pain and suffering, the tribesmen's supposedly innate tendency to violence and revenge was transmuted. Self-sacrifice was placed within the framework of resistance to foreign oppression and the achievement of a better and more humane society in the future. Devotion to this ideal inspired the Red Shirts to submit to discipline, to hold back from vengeance, to passively accept torture and—eventually—to succeed.

That this example has been more or less forgotten in Pakistan and in general is due to the historical fact that the Red Shirts' devotion to the Gandhian ideal stood against the separatist wave that finally prevailed. But simply because the movement was on the wrong side of history does not mean that its message of social transformation through self-transformation was mistaken. Honor and respect are always emergent properties capable of being negotiated and altered according to circumstances, interests, and ideals. This means that the mysticism of Rahman Baba can, in principle, be reconciled with the heroic masculinity of Khushal. That was the reason I ended my ethnography of Swat, and this reconsideration of it, with the word "love."

SECTION I

CONTINUITY AND CHANGE

2

THE ABDALI AFGHANS BETWEEN MULTAN, QANDAHAR AND HERAT IN THE SIXTEENTH AND SEVENTEENTH CENTURIES

Christine Noelle-Karimi

The existing historical narrative places the Abdali/Durrani Afghans in two contexts. First, they figure as the tribal elite that participated in Ahmad Khan Sadozai's attempted state-building in the wake of Nadir Shah's assassination in 1747. The upward and spatial mobility of the Abdali leaders is generally regarded as the outcome of their advancement within the ranks of Nadir Shah's army. In keeping with this interpretation, the nascent Afghan state is understood to represent Nadir Shah's military and administrative legacy. Furthermore, the Abdalis literally followed in Nadir Shah's footsteps and retraced some of his military campaigns. By focusing their military activities on India, Ahmad Shah Sadozai and his fellow tribesmen may be said to have operated within the territorial framework opened up by Nadir Shah's eastern conquests. The second context assigned to the Abdali confederacy is that of a strictly circumscribed space. The area around Qandahar is cast as the ancestral homeland of the Abdalis, and Ahmad Shah's choice of this city as the capital of his realm is seen as a natural consequence of the fact that his kinsmen were already based there.

While both representations are correct in their broad outlines, they tend to reduce the role of the Abdalis at once in terms of historical and territorial scope. On the one hand, the emphasis on the emergence of this confederacy in the middle of the eighteenth century creates an artificial turning point. It seems to imply that the Abdalis did not exist as a viable entity in pre-Nadirid times and that their rise in power and subsequent territorial conquests occurred *ex nihilo*. On the other hand, the projection of Qandahar as their timeless fatherland blurs the understanding of the fluidity of spatial relations in early modern times. Although Qandahar was indeed central to Abdali concerns, the often-quoted territorial ownership of that region is a relatively recent phenomenon. It is best understood as the result of land grants made by Nadir Shah to the future Ahmad Shah and his fellow tribesmen in return for military services.[1]

In the following, I will argue that the Abdali elite were by no means merely a local phenomenon but rather positioned themselves within a network extending from Multan in the east to Herat in the west well before the time of Nadir Shah. Their rise in power did not develop from a political void; it was the outcome of strategic linkages, with the Mughals/Safavids in particular, in the contest over the control of Qandahar. The emergence of the Abdali elite presents a test case for the scope of tribal mobility in early modern times.[2] Before proceeding to the narrative of events in the sixteenth and seventeenth centuries, I will briefly discuss the strategic importance of the three urban centers in question and present the available sources, namely European travelogues, Safavid and Durrani court chronicles, and Persian histories with a regional focus.

Multan, Qandahar and Herat formed nodal points in the overland trade between India, Central Asia and Iran. In early modern times, European travelers noted Multan's large-scale export of cotton and indigo[3] and Qandahar's role as an entrepôt for Central Asian horses.[4] The trade route connecting the three cities was coveted by Mughals and Safavids alike. While Multan in the east and Herat in the west were firmly incorporated into one or the other polity, Qandahar changed hands a dozen times after 1522 until it finally fell to Iranian control in 1649. These conflicts must have affected the population around Qandahar, yet the Safavid sources tell us very little about the local circumstances. If Afghans are mentioned at all, they figure as rebellious elements in the Mughal realm. In 1550 the Herati author Amir Mahmud b. Khvand Amir describes them as the unruly subjects of Babur (1483–1530) in the early part of his reign in Kabul.[5] Iskandar Beg, who immortalized the achievements of Shah 'Abbas I (r. 1588–1629), portrays the Afghans as the rebellious troops who expelled the Mughal ruler Humayun to Persia in 951/1543–44 and as "unfortunate" elements in the struggle for power following Emperor Akbar's death in 1605.[6] Towards the end of the seventeenth century, the author of *Dastur-i shahriyaran* refers to the Mughal army as a combination of "Baluch, Afghan, Rajput, and Patan."[7]

One of the few Safavid sources that dwells on the circumstances in and around Qandahar is the *'Abbasnama*. The author, Muhammad Tahir Vahid Qazvini, devotes an ornate text to the events that took place during the reign of 'Abbas II from 1642 to 1663. In particular, he magnifies the campaign the teenage King undertook to Qandahar in 1648–49. In keeping with the Safavid projection of Iran as a Shiite realm, Qazvini pictures the conflict with the Mughals and their allies in religious terms. He reports that the leadership of the Afghans protecting the citadel of Qandahar was driven by "absurd Sunni fanaticism" (*ta'assub-i madhhab-i batil-i tasannun*). It is in this light that the decision of the local Abdali leader Shah Husain Sultan to flee to India after the Safavid conquest of Qandahar is cast. Shah Sultan Husain turned to Shah Jahan (r. 1628–58) and instigated him to undertake the first of a rapid succession of military campaigns against the Safavids in Qandahar.[8]

While Safavid sources hardly acknowledge the Afghans as political and military actors, French missionaries and travelers of the time attest to their powerful position vis-à-vis their Mughal and Safavid overlords. In 1690, Sanson perceived the Afghans as a distinct and influential group courted by the Safavid rulers:

THE ABDALI AFGHANS

The [Safavid] King maintains a large garrison in the Province of Kandahar for fear of an attack by the Baluch and the Afghans inhabiting the mountains. These people live in tents in the manner of the first human beings. They are bellicose and skilled in the use of bow and arrow, but they [also] are bad thieves and have no mercy on caravans. They inhabit Scythia and are subjects of the Mughal Emperor. He is not really their master, and they only serve whoever offers most. Persia treats them with caution and grants them such great privileges and advantages that even if she cannot attach them fully to her cause, she at least reduces their inclination for doing harm.[9]

The French traveler Thevenot, who visited India in 1666, briefly mentions the population around Qandahar in his travel memoirs. Although he does not identify the local inhabitants as Afghans, he captures the wide field of opportunities opened by overlapping Mughal and Safavid interests: "There are some small Rajas in the Mountains, who are suffered to live in liberty, paying some easie Tributes; And these Gentlemen have always stuck to the strongest side, when the Country came to change its Master."[10]

These cursory impressions are complemented by a later Persian history of the eighteenth century which does not pertain to any specific imperial context. The *Majma' al-tavarikh dar tarikh-i inqiraz-i safaviya va vaqayi'-i ba'd* ("The juncture of history concerning the decline of the Safavids and subsequent events") offers a regional perspective on the developments in the eastern Iranian lands up to 1792. A native of Mashhad, its author, Muhammad Khalil Mar'ashi, belonged to one of the families vying for power in Khurasan after the death of Nadir Shah. His account of local affairs until the year 1750 reflects an interesting moment in time when the Safavids had vanished but had not yet been supplanted by a new imperial power and its narrative. Muhammad Khalil produced the *Majma'* after migrating to Murshidabad in Bengal in 1778. Writing in Indian exile and basing his account on the notes of his father, who had left Khurasan as early as 1751–52, the author was far removed from his homeland both in a geographical and chronological sense.[11]

Meanwhile, the rise of the Durrani empire based in Qandahar gave rise to a new body of historiography focusing on the ruling Sadozai lineage and its entitlement to power. A case in point is the *Tarikh-i husainshahi*. The author, Imam al-Din Husaini, joined the Durrani court in Lahore in 1796–97 and composed different portions of the work in Peshawar and Lucknow. It is perhaps no coincidence that his narrative engages in genealogical reasoning which bears resemblance to notions of Afghan ethnogenesis developed under Mughal auspices in the seventeenth century. Like Ni'matullah's *Tarikh-i Khan Jahani*, it identifies Qais 'Abd al-Rashid, a descendant of Jacob and a contemporary of the Prophet, as primogenitor of the Afghan tribes.[12] The Abdalis/Durranis are traced to 'Arif b. Tirin, a descendant of Qais, on whom the Chishti saint Abu Ahmad of Herat (d. 355/966) allegedly conferred his own title of "Abdal".[13] Reflecting Abu Ahmad's rank within the hierarchy of saints and being closely associated with the Chishti shrine of Herat, this title is understood to have enhanced the standing of Abdal's lineage among the greater group of Pashtuns. The projection of royal legitimacy on the basis of genealogical reasoning combined with saintly sanction is by no means special to the Sadozai period. Employing these ingredients, the authors of the time followed a well established formula for the construction of authority.

Afghan histories produced in the nineteenth century likewise correlate the establishment of the Afghan state with the progression of genealogy and seek to identify early historical precedents heralding the eventual ascent of the royal Sadozai lineage. For our purposes, the accounts of two authors of Abdali descent are of particular importance. Based in Multan, 'Ali Muhammad Khan Khudakka Sadozai produced a detailed description of the Abdalis in Safavid/Mughal times, tracing the fortunes of various Sadozai lineages in Khurasan and India. Entitled *Tadhkirat al-muluk-i 'alishan* ("Memoir of Excellent Kings"), this source provides a narrative grid for the local events that took place between the late sixteenth and late seventeenth centuries. It also gives some insights into the career of the Sadozai Abdalis as a military elite under both Mughal and Safavid auspices. 'Ali Muhammad Khan Khudakka completed his book in 1835. Against the backdrop of the decline of Sadozai power and the conquest of Multan by Ranjit Singh in 1818, the work reads as an attempt by a member of the "old" Multani elite to capture the former grandeur of his lineage.[14]

Of equal value is Sultan Muhammad b. Musa Barakzai Durrani's *Tarikh-i sultani* ("royal history"), which was composed in 1865 and covers the history of the Afghans from their genealogical origin to the incorporation of Herat into the Muhammadzai state in 1279/1863. Sultan Muhammad is the first Afghan historian to make use of the concept of "Afghanistan" as a political entity and to project it back into earlier historical periods. In the first section of the book, which was apparently added immediately prior to its printing in Bombay in 1298/1881, the author describes the confines of Afghanistan, its climate, agricultural products, and urban centers. A member of the urbanized Durrani elite, Sultan Muhammad based his narrative on oral information and written sources of Iranian, Indian and British provenance. Spanning the entire expanse from the mythical Israelite background of the Pashtuns to the Lodi dynasty (1451–1526), his account of early Pashtun history follows seventeenth-century Mughal sources, such as the *Tarikh-i Firishta* and the *Tarikh-i Khan Jahani*.[15]

Given their focus on genealogy, the last sources mentioned may be understood as an enunciation of Pashtun identity. Yet, used in combination with the available Iranian accounts, they also furnish data which allow us to map relationships of power and exchange. On the basis of this evidence, I will attempt to reconstruct the reach of Abdali networks and their evolution during the Safavid/Mughal era.

In the late eighteenth century Mar'ashi described the Afghan realm as follows:

> The Afghans [*firqa-yi afaghina*] are a people inhabiting the lands between Khurasan and Hindustan. Their land extends from the Rud-i Nilab [upper Indus] … in the east to the dependencies of Herat in the west. In the north it comprises the surroundings of Bajaur and the Hindu Kush adjoining the border of Ghurband and Kahmard, which belong to the dependencies of Badakhshan and Balkh; in the south it includes the towns of Sivi [Sibi] and Dahadar [?], which belong to the dependencies of Bhakkar and Sivistan. In recent times, the majority [of the Afghans] have been obedient to Kabul and Multan, which are a part of Hindustan. A minority are obedient to Qandahar and Herat, which are a part of Iran. Among the two foremost Afghan tribes the Abdalis dwelling around Herat are the greatest. The second strongest group are the Ghilzais residing in the environs of Qandahar. Throughout the time one of the leaders of these two tribes has served the government of the King of Iran and has been addressed as *Sultan*. This was also the case during the time of [the last Safavid ruler] Shah Sultan Husain [r. 1694–1722].[16]

THE ABDALI AFGHANS

This statement is interesting in several respects. For one thing, it conflates information from different historical periods. The division of the Afghans between Kabul and Multan, on the one hand, and Qandahar and Herat on the other reflects the state of affairs in the seventeenth century, when the Safavid empire reached its greatest extent. The statement identifying Herat as the stronghold of the Abdalis, by contrast, seems to refer to the situation in the early eighteenth century, prior to Nadir Shah Afshar's rise to power. The second interesting aspect is that Mar'ashi portrays the Afghans as an integral component of the Mughal and Safavid states and emphasizes their long-standing relationship of service with both parties. Mar'ashi also gives some information on the arrival of the Abdalis in the region of Herat. According to his version of events, they began to make their presence felt there in the late sixteenth century, precisely in the year 1000/1591–92, when "a number of incidents" caused them to leave the "Kuhistan" of Kabul.[17]

The Multan connection of the Abdali Afghans is highlighted both by 'Ali Muhammad Khan Khudakka and by Sultan Muhammad Durrani. Both authors produce a coherent narrative based on the coordinates of Sadozai genealogy. They focus on Sado (Asadullah, 1558–1627), the forefather of this illustrious lineage, and delineate a logical progression beginning with Sado's political career, continuing with the fortunes of his descendants in Qandahar, Multan and Herat, and culminating in the successful Sadozai bid for royal power in 1747. In their version of events, the Sadozai Afghans assume a central role in local politics and insert themselves into imperial strategies. While Khudakka and Sultan Muhammad concur on the broad outlines of this story, they present us with numerous actors and, moreover, differ on matters of genealogy as well as the lifespan and sphere of influence of individual Sadozai leaders. As this article is primarily concerned with highlighting the major contours of Abdali history rather than working out chronological minutiae, the following account will be exclusively based on Khudakka's version of events.

Sado's career coincided with Akbar's occupation of Qandahar in 1595 and the Safavid reconquest of the city and province under Shah 'Abbas I in 1622. According to the *Tadhkirat al-muluk-i 'alishan*, he served the Mughals as tax collector in the area around Qandahar until the region changed hands again in 1622. At the same time he maintained lively contacts with the Safavid court. It is said that he paid his respects to 'Abbas I (r. 1588–1629) in Herat and impressed him with his accomplishments in archery, among other things.[18] Subsequently he sided with the Safavids in the conquest of Qandahar. In exchange for his services, he received the title of *sultan* and control over the citadel at Shahr-i Safa, an important coordinate along the trade route between Qandahar and Kabul, as well as the revenues of the surrounding country. Sado's close interaction with the imperial powers affected local power relations. The Abdali confederacy became stronger with respect to the neighboring Ghilzais and Hazaras. In addition, the fact that Sado was a Mughal/Safavid representative granted his own family a leading position within the Abdali confederacy.

Over the next generation Qandahar reverted to Mughal rule, while the local leadership stayed in place. Sado's second son Maudud Khan (1584–1644) entertained a close relationship with the long-standing Safavid Governor of Qandahar, 'Ali Mardan Khan. 'Ali Mardan Khan was appointed by Shah 'Abbas and held his post until, in 1636, charges of embezzlement put an end to his relations with Isfahan. Encouraged by the Governor of Multan, he entered negotiations for the submission of Qandahar to Shah Jahan (r. 1628–58) and eventually handed over the citadel to the Mughals in 1638. The stability of the local configurations of power is reflected by the fact that Maudud Khan Sadozai subsequently supported the Mughal forces in a military confrontation with the Safavid army.[19]

Over time, however, the continued conflict between the Safavids and the Mughals for the possession of Qandahar translated into, and was enhanced by, the rivalry between different Sadozai subdivisions. This internal competition opened the door for successive waves of migration to Multan. The first such internal confrontation arose among two of Sado's grandsons, the paternal cousins Shah Husain b. Maudud and Khudadad b. Khizr. The local dispute among these two men over the control of Shahr-i Safa expanded into an imperial conflict, as each of them sought to bolster his cause by tapping alternative sources of power. When Shah Husain Khan managed to evict Khudadad Khan from Shahr-i Safa with the assistance of the Mughal Governor of Qandahar, the latter sided with the Safavids. Perhaps overstating the impact of Sadozai activities, the *Tadhkirat al-muluk-i alishan* informs us that Khudadad Khan convinced Shah 'Abbas II (r. 1642–66) to embark on a military campaign against Qandahar, which resulted in the capitulation of the Mughal Governor in February 1649.[20] During the two following Mughal sieges of Qandahar in 1652 and 1653, Khudadad successfully defended the citadel of Qandahar in the name of the Safavids. In return for his services, he gained the title of *sultan*, and the Safavid Governor of Qandahar placed him in charge of the entire territory outside the city gates.[21]

Meanwhile, Khudadad's rival Shah Husain Khan entered Mughal service and accompanied the Princes Aurangzeb and Dara Shukuh on their unsuccessful campaigns to Qandahar. Shah Jahan acknowledged his services by bestowing the title of "Vafadar Khan" on him and granting him an estate in Rangpur (in the modern district of Muzaffargarh).[22] When Aurangzeb became Emperor (r. 1658–1707), he conferred further *jagirs* in Multan, Sialkot and Lahore on the Sadozai nobleman.[23]

One generation later, we hear of activities by Khudadad's son Hayat along the highway between Qandahar and Herat. This expansion of activities by a member of the Sadozai lineage into the region of Herat may be attributed to the fact that Hayat Khan's maternal relatives belonged to a section of the Nurzai Abdalis which had moved to the region west of Herat at some point in the past.[24] Hayat Khan's activities in the surroundings of Herat apparently met with the opposition of the Safavid overlords. In 1680–81 he was forced to withdraw after suffering defeat at the hands of the Safavid troops.[25] According to Mar'ashi, this move was primarily occasioned by a conflict over the payment of revenues:

I have heard that in the time of Shah Sulaiman [r. 1666–1694] and Shah Sultan Husain they [the Abdalis] amounted to approximately 60,000 families. The Safavid Kings have always addressed their leaders as *sultans*... Towards the end of Shah Sulaiman's era, the leadership of the Abdalis rested with Hayat Sultan Sadozai... He happened to have an argument with one of the revenue collectors of the Governor of Herat. This dispute turned into a fight, the revenue collector was killed, and the affair dragged on with the Governor of Herat. Hayat Sultan and his brother Lashkar Khan feared punishment for the murder, and [they feared] the stern justice of the Qizilbash governors, who tended to beat and dishonor the grand army leaders on account of the slightest offence. They fled to Multan along with 5,000–6,000 related families.[26]

Upon his arrival in Multan, Hayat Khan was immediately confirmed as a member of the local elite. Aurangzeb granted him a large *jagir* in addition to a monthly cash stipend of 10,000 rupees.[27] Thus two rival Sadozai clans, the descendants of Shah Husain and the descendants of Khudadad Khan, came to play a preponderant role in the economic and political life of Multan. Shah Husain Khan's family retained a highly influential position in Multan throughout the Mughal period and eventually served as the governors (*nayib nizam*) of the province from 1738 on. Both branches of the family built their own palaces and cultivated famous mango groves in the vicinity of the city.[28] Some of the Multani Abdalis gained a reputation as camel traders.[29]

When Hayat Khan left for Multan in 1682, he was accompanied by his relative Zaman Khan (b. Daulat b. Sarmast b. Sher b. Khizr). This information is noteworthy in light of the fact that Zaman Khan's son Ahmad, who was born in Multan in the palace of Shah Husain Khan, later went on to found the Durrani empire.[30] The Sadozai Abdalis thus furnish a prime example of the formation of a military and economic elite under the auspices of Mughal overlordship. This was by no means a unique phenomenon.[31] Yet it was their convenient location at the outposts of the Mughal and Safavid polities that eventually allowed the Sadozai Abdalis to make the leap from a local aristocracy to an imperial elite. Spanning the region between Multan, Qandahar and Herat, they were in the best possible position to develop into an independent regional force parallel to the crumbling of the overarching state structures in the eighteenth century.

There is no evidence concerning the scope of Sadozai commercial activities. Nor do we know whether they formed trade networks similar to those of the *poyanda* traders, the Pashtun nomads who provided the commercial linkage between the markets in northern and central India and those in Central Asia.[32] Yet it is certain that the Sadozai elite of Multan maintained regular contact and exchange with their kinsmen in their homelands. The leadership moved back and forth between Multan and Qandahar at frequent intervals and were equally at home in the eastern and western strongholds. In this context it comes as no surprise that Ahmad Shah eventually carved out his kingdom around the commercial centers of Herat, Qandahar, and Multan. These places had come to form fixed coordinates within the political horizon of the Sadozai Abdalis in the previous generations and offered the greatest scope for advancement within the shifting configurations of power in the early eighteenth century.

The above narrative highlights the limitations and potential of the early modern Persian historiography. The sources discussed provide a specific instance of mapping. The political terrain is cast in terms of genealogical relationships, and the narrative focuses on great personages. The conflation of genealogical and political space in these sources obscures certain strata of information which would be of interest to the present-day historian. Hayat Khan's migration to Multan at the head of several thousand families allows for the conclusion that the social and spatial mobility of the elite implied far-ranging movement for the followership. Otherwise, the genealogical grid imposed seems to prescribe static affiliations and to disregard the possibility of fluctuations over time and interchanges with other local or imperial identities. At the same time, the material provides a unique glimpse of the urban centers and the way they were embedded in regional relationships of power. We learn about the scope of movement and the strategies open to the Abdali tribal elite in a setting of overlapping imperial claims. The sources give us a sense of early modern notions of space and the forces of cohesion at work. The patterns of Abdali circulation between towns and the tribal hinterland reveal a political realm created and maintained by movement. Agency is linked to a spatial dynamic, and power is actualized in the course of a constant bargaining process.

3

A HISTORY OF THE "HINDUSTANI FANATICS" ON THE FRONTIER

Benjamin D. Hopkins

The Pakistani army's recent operations in Swat propelled, for a fleeting moment, this remote and picturesque landscape, often referred to as the "Switzerland of Pakistan", to the centre of world attention. The army's violent occupation of Swat pitted government forces against a tribal *lashkar* (army) of "Taliban" militants estimated to number 3,000.[1] This *lashkar*, under the command of Maulana Fazlullah, had previously driven the army out of the valley after a "reign of terror" including targeted assassinations and executions of local police, supposed informants, and other officials deemed enemies of their cause.[2] Foreign observers have characterised these events as heralding a new front in the "Global War on Terror" as the Taliban and their creed of "Islamo-fascism" supplant the power of civilised authorities in the valley. Pakistan's offensive to retake the valley followed heavy pressure from its Western allies, especially the US, which has viewed the deteriorating security situation in the country with dismay.

Much of the analysis of current events in Swat, and indeed along the Frontier as a whole, is divorced from any substantive understanding of the historical context shaping the region. General assertions about the "wild", "violent" and "tribal" past of the Frontier ruled by "custom" and "tradition" abound, with little effort to critically engage such characterisations. The current bout of Islamic militancy is thus seen as unsurprising on this "savage frontier" which has long been marked by religious fanaticism.[3] Indeed, Swat is no stranger to religious militancy or violence. The current Taliban under Maulana Fazlullah trace their genealogy to Tehrik-i-Nifaz-i-Shariat-i-Muhammadi (TNSM) of the 1990s, which similarly challenged central state authority through violence clothed in religious rhetoric.[4] But to link current violence simplistically to past "fanaticism" is to fundamentally misconstrue and fail to understand both. The region has a deeper history of violent resistance speaking a religious idiom, but it is one with a sophisticated pedigree and is of lasting consequence.

BEYOND SWAT

One of the most interesting episodes of that deeper history is the long-standing presence of a colony of "Hindustani Fanatics" who traced their origins to the *jihad* of Sayyid Ahmad of Rai Bareilly in the early nineteenth century. From the inception of their rule along the Frontier in 1849 until their withdrawal from the subcontinent in 1947, the British watched this colony. The rather curious tale of the Hindustani Fanatics holds a greater significance than simply as an enduring episode of religious resistance on a peripheral frontier. Rather, these Fanatics and the Frontier they inhabited were central to defining the attitudes and actions of the British Indian colonial state towards its Muslim subjects. Further, their legacy, or rather the legacy of those attitudes which they helped shape, continues to possess an insidious power over contemporary understandings of violence and religion on the Frontier today. Echoes of British administrators' fears of "seditious Wahabis" may be heard in today's denunciations of "Islamo-fascists" with roots in an unbridled embrace of Saudi-backed Wahabism.[5]

This essay offers a brief history of the colony of Hindustani Fanatics located in Swat and the surrounding area. It focuses on the colonial period between 1849 and 1947 in order to examine the effect this colony had both on the locality in which it was situated, and also more broadly on the colonial state and colonial public sphere. Through an examination of the century-long tenure of the Hindustani Fanatic colony on the Swat frontier, the colony's legacy both for the colonial state as well as the frontier society in which it was embedded becomes clear. The colony's experience is both representative and constitutive of the nature of religious resistance along the Frontier and its continuing relevance today.

The "Frontier Fanatics"

Swat, like neighbouring Chitral, Dir, and Bajaur, is a rugged and mountainous realm, especially in its more remote reaches. Its central valley lies roughly 100 miles northwest of Islamabad and approximately 50 miles northeast of Peshawar. Swat's population consists mainly of Yusufzai Pashtun who migrated to the valley during the sixteenth century.[6] Colonial and post-colonial ethnographers, most famously Fredrik Barth, have often depicted the Yusufzai's tribal structure as the central organising principle of Swati society.[7] But tribes are not the only entities that have provided social structure. Charismatic religious leadership has also been an important part of Swat's past, particularly by the Akhund of Swat, Abdul Ghuffar (1794–1877). Difficulty of access has historically made Swat and its surrounding areas largely autonomous, if not independent, though they normally maintained a nominal tributary relationship with the imperial powers ruling South Asia. During the epoch of British rule over the subcontinent, Swat remained outside the formal orbit of political control until early years of the twentieth century. In 1915, Swat was established as a princely state, a status it maintained until it was fully integrated into Pakistan in 1969, along with Chitral and Dir.[8]

Swat's physical remoteness and its political autonomy often made it a centre of resistance to centralising political authorities of the north Indian plains. This resistance was not only undertaken by local tribesmen, but also by foreigners who found refuge along the periphery of Swat's remote mountain vastness.[9] In the nineteenth

A HISTORY OF THE "HINDUSTANI FANATICS" ON THE FRONTIER

century, initially Sikh and subsequently British dominion over parts of South Asia was violently contested by a core of foreign religious resisters, mainly from Bengal and the United Provinces (modern Uttar Pradesh), and later from the Punjab, who at times made common cause with neighbouring tribesmen. These rebels, whom the British termed Hindustani Fanatics, became a fixture of the Frontier for over one hundred years, preceding and apparently outlasting British rule.

The Hindustani Fanatics, or *mujahidin* as they called themselves, arrived on the Frontier in the late 1820s, led by Sayyid Ahmed of Rai Bareilly who famously waged a *jihad* against Sikh suzerainty along the Frontier.[10] Following his death in 1831 at the battle of Balakot, Sayyid Ahmed's surviving followers retreated into the mountains of Swat and established a colony near a village called Sitana on the Indus River, in Buner country.[11] Over the subsequent years, they cultivated connections with like-minded supporters in north India, centred in the main around Patna.[12] These supporters apparently collected subscriptions for the colonists, as well as recruits from amongst poor Muslim villagers of rural Bengal.[13] The Fanatics made peace with the local tribesmen through a combination of political manoeuvring and the maintenance of low profiles. Their contestation of Sikh rule consisted of periodic raiding and kidnapping, mainly of Hindu *bania* merchants.[14] This remained the case as the British assumed authority from the Sikhs along the Frontier following the second Anglo-Sikh War in 1849.

The British were well aware of the presence of the Hindustanis and their previous activities against the Sikhs. The British first "discovered" what they believed to be the Fanatics' machinations against the colonial state when a channel of secret and seditious communication was uncovered between the colony and its supporters in Patna in 1852, implicating a *munshi* (native secretary) of the Fourth Native Infantry regiment in Rawalpindi.[15] In January 1853, the Company decided it was time to chastise the Fanatics and dispatched an expedition. But despite the Fanatics' avowed hostility to the infidel *sarkar*, the 200–300 assembled Hindustanis dispersed upon the appearance of British forces.[16]

Like most of the Frontier, the Fanatics remained quiet during the events of 1857. This silence led to a split amongst the colonists, with a breakaway faction party forming a new colony, which became an "asylum for bad characters".[17] The British, deciding they could no longer countenance the Hindustanis' rebellious activities, mounted a serious expedition to destroy the colonists. Unlike four years earlier, the Sepoys met fierce resistance from the Hindustanis, but nonetheless destroyed the Fanatics' colonies.[18] But the colonists themselves survived, retreating even further into the mountain vastness of Swat. By the summer of 1863, they had resettled their former colonies at both Sitana and Mangal Thana. Such a direct challenge to British authority, if left unchallenged, was a dangerous threat to their prestige. So by the autumn of the same year, a major expedition was assembled to finish the Fanatics once and for all.[19]

In October, the British launched what became known as the Ambela campaign. Despite plans for a quick and surgical strike, the Raj found itself bogged down in a brutal frontier war with the tribesmen through whose territory they attempted to pass.[20] After two months, the commitment of over 9,000 troops, and nearly 900 British casualties, the forces of the Raj were able to overcome the fractious tribal alliance they faced. A negotiated settlement led to the destruction of the Fanatics' redoubts by local tribesmen under the supervision of Lieutenant Colonel Reynell Taylor, achieving the expedition's ostensible objective.[21] Success, however, came at a high price as the Ambela campaign proved one of the costliest and bloodiest little frontier wars the Raj mounted in the nineteenth century.[22]

The Ambela campaign marked an important, and ultimately short-lived, rupture in British attitudes towards the Hindustani Fanatics on the Frontier. However, its effects on attitudes towards their Muslim subjects in the subcontinent were of greater consequence. In practical terms, it led to the break-up of the colony, which struggled to re-establish itself in tribal territory for the next twenty years. Indeed, the Raj would not violently engage the Fanatics on such a scale ever again, and the Fanatics abstained from embroiling themselves with British arms until 1888.[23] Yet Ambela became a catalyst for a colonial crackdown on the Fanatics' "Wahabi" supporters in British territories. This crackdown led to the famous trials of 1865–71, in which a number of men were accused, tried and convicted of waging war against the Queen (IPC §121) by facilitating material support to the colony at Sitana. More important than the judicial offensive the colonial state undertook was the rhetorical one mounted most vociferously by W.W. Hunter, who authored his polemic *Our Indian Musalmens* at this time. Hunter explicitly linked the Wahabi conspirators with the Ambela campaign against the Fanatics. He also insinuated a connection between these and a larger Muslim conspiracy which sat at the heart of the Mutiny.

Interestingly, Hunter's linkages and insinuations, which together painted an insidious and disturbing picture of Muslim conspiracy, were neither endorsed by nor echoed in official circles. Furthermore, those circles had discounted the idea that some sort of apocryphal Muslim conspiracy had lain at the heart of the 1857 revolt, with L. Bowring's report in 1859.[24] While the British were busy prosecuting a number of their supporters, they treated the now homeless Fanatics with marked leniency.[25] The British thought little of the danger posed directly by the Fanatics. Indeed, the biggest stated fear was not of their ability to orchestrate violence, but rather that their suppression by the British Indian state would turn them into martyrs.[26]

Even at the height of the Wahabi scare, British officials evinced marked indifference to surviving Fanatics who remained in tribal territory. By 1883, those survivors had regrouped and built a "mud fort on the banks of the Indus". This new colony included nearly 600 fighting men, the majority of whom came from Bengal, though others came from the Punjab, Delhi and the UP. They were well armed and were reported to have arms for 2,000 men, as well as two Bengali gunsmiths.[27] Despite the Wahabi trials, the colonists apparently continued to receive cash remittances from India unhindered,[28] and it was even rumoured that they had obtained percussion caps for their muskets from Jullundur in the Punjab.[29] But the Fanatics' unity of purpose was shattered by disagreement over their relative silence and inactivity vis-à-vis the British, leading once again to the more militant amongst them to abandon the colony in protest.[30]

Despite their apparent preparations for war, the Fanatics in the main refrained from confronting the British. Even during disturbances in 1885 involving the Bunerwals, their old hosts in Sitana, the Fanatics remained on the sidelines. It was reported that the tribesmen's willingness to compromise with the British made

A HISTORY OF THE "HINDUSTANI FANATICS" ON THE FRONTIER

the Hindustanis wary of directly joining in tribal uprisings, even if these potentially forwarded their ultimate aim of expelling British authority from the area.[31] The Fanatics' reputation as religious warriors suffered from their notable lack of anti-British activities.[32] The British believed the consequent loss of importance in the eyes of their tribal hosts made their life along the Frontier rather uncomfortable.[33]

For the remainder of the nineteenth century, and into the early years of the twentieth, the Fanatics refrained from openly antagonizing the British, even though these years proved some of the most tumultuous for the Raj along the Frontier. Their participation in the 1897 Frontier revolt proved to be nothing noteworthy,[34] and during the 1908 disturbances they made only a "half-hearted attempt to stir up trouble."[35] Their relative silence did not mean, however, that the colony was not active. New recruits regularly arrived, with 120 from Bengal, the North-West Province and the Punjab appearing between April and July 1895 alone. The British described these men as "all men of no position, being of the faqir and 'talib-ilm' class" who arrived in twos and threes, passing themselves off as religious wanderers in British territories. They joined a colony estimated at 580 inhabitants, 300 of whom were fighting men organised into one company of one hundred and four companies of fifty men each. These included twenty-four *sowars*, fourteen gunners and twenty drivers. However, the arrival of new recruits was offset by the attrition of those who dispersed to their homes in British India, thought to be somewhere in the range of twenty to thirty per year.[36] One estimate put their strength at the turn of the century at 900 fighting men with nearly 800 Martini-Henry rifles.[37]

Despite their numbers, officials continued with the line adopted in the wake of the Ambela campaign, which was to treat the Fanatics as people of no consequence. The Commissioner of Peshawar wrote in 1899:

> The least notice taken of these people the better. Even if they ask for permission to come to India, I would treat them openly as of no account, and simply say that they might come or go as they please provided they behave themselves, and live out of the Punjab. I would, however, watch them as a precaution, and if they were found intriguing mischievously deport them again.[38]

In 1903, their long-serving leader Maulvi Abdulla died. It was thought the "Fanatic" colony might break up and its inhabitants disperse back to their homes. Instead, fifty more recruits arrived from Bengal in that year alone.[39] They eventually relocated to a place called "Smast" on the Barandu River, twelve miles from their old redoubt at Sitana; this proved their final settlement which they occupied continuously until the end days of the Raj in 1947.[40]

The activities of the *mujahidin* attracted British attention during World War I, when they appeared to be at the heart of trouble brewing on the Frontier. They allied themselves with a local religious notable, the Haji Sahib of Turangzai, who proved a source of anti-colonial intrigues along the Frontier after he fled Peshawar in 1915.[41] Further, colonial authorities believed the *mujahidin* to be in contact with the Afghan government, as well as Indian nationalists. Despite these connections, the British continued to consider the Fanatics benign. This assessment appears to have been shared by their supporters in British India, who dispatched "several persons of substance... from Bengal, the Punjab, and other places in India, and have accused them [the Fanatics] of deriving an income for many years from the enemies of the British Government, without making any return in the way of hostile action".[42]

George Roos-Keppel, the Chief Commissioner of the North-West Frontier Province, offered a concise picture of both the Fanatics and British attitudes towards them in a letter he wrote to the Foreign Secretary of the Government of India in October 1915:

I have been keeping an eye on the Hindustani fanatics and so far have found nothing to show that they are particularly active or dangerous. There are about four or five hundred of them in Chamla, living under a communistic system but ruled by their Amir, as the chief fanatic is called, the majority of them are the descendents of the Mujai-ud-din of mutiny days but from time to time since individuals mostly from the neighbourhoods of Lucknow and Moradabad have joined them and have also settled down and married there. In the course of the last fifteen years a good many of them have been to see me and I have had long talks with them and have come to the conclusion that their fanaticism is the trade by which they live and that they are not at all anxious to be committed to any warlike acts. At the same time in order to get their "shukarana" they are bound to show some hostility towards us. A deputation goes every year to the Amir and receives presents from him but the deputation has several times been warned that Mujai-ud-din will get no more money from Cabul [sic] unless they do something to deserve it. They also get contributions from various parts of India. I am told that quite recently a Hindustani visited the fanatics and asked to see their Amir who, however, distrusted the visitor and declined to see him. The man went away without giving his name; he was escorted to the Indus by one of the fanatics and on leaving gave him a sealed parcel for the Amir, which, when opened, was found to contain Rs. 2,000/-.[43]

In the same letter, however, the Fanatics were implicated in the disappearance of fifteen students from the Lahore Medical College who apparently fled to Asmas in the hope of joining an anti-British *jihad*.[44]

Despite Roos-Keppel's reference to "our old friends of Mutiny times", and his assessment that they were "professional fanatics...[who] have loudly beaten the drum of Islam but simultaneously sent messengers to assure me that they had no intention of doing anything more serious,"[45] the Fanatics participated in disturbances along the Frontier during the war and actively agitated against the British war effort. At one point, posters appeared in the villages of Mardan "with a manifesto from the Amir of Hindustani Fanatics that the day of liberty has dawned, Russians and English having been defeated by the Turks and Germans."[46] The colony was later implicated in what became known as the "Silk Letter case" which centred around clandestine and seditious communications between Indian nationalists and the Afghan government.[47] The Fanatics' renewed activity, after years of relative silence, aroused the attention of the British and led them to step up efforts both at surveillance as well as suppression of the colony.

Yet the colonists' relationship with the colonial state was not marked by hostility exclusively. In 1916 Amir Niamatullah, the leader of the Fanatics, addressed the Chief Commissioner of the North-West Frontier Province seeking to establish peace with the *sarkar* which would ensure the colony would no longer be the object of government harassment. His letters were prompted by the arrest of couriers who were bringing collections for the colony from British India worth over Rs. 8,000.[48] Niamatullah's letters vacillated uncomfortably between threat and petition. He insisted that the colony had been at peace with the Government for years, but that if the Government continued to hassle it by stopping the free movement of its peaceful members, the *mujahidin* would be forced to raid British territories and assault those of Britain's ally the Nawab of Amb.[49] After some negotiation, conducted on behalf of the *mujahidin* by a former Extra Assistant Commissioner and Sub-judge in the Lyallpur District, a settlement was reached.[50] In return for taking responsibility for all members of the colony and ensuring they did not behave in a hostile fashion towards the colonial state, the British would allow the *mujahidin*, as they were now referred to, free intercourse with the Indian plains and would release those who had been arrested, restoring their property to them.[51]

Niamatullah's successful overtures to Roos-Keppel were part of a longer history of accommodation which both the Fanatics and the Raj had authored. Since their bloody encounter during the Ambela campaign in 1863, a half-century had passed with relatively little violence between the two parties. The British had refrained from launching punitive military expeditions against the Fanatics, though they did occasionally engage members of the colony in the course of operations against the independent tribes. Likewise, the Fanatics in the main did not take any concerted action to antagonise British authorities. This inaction led to splits within the *mujahidin* community, but these generally did more harm to the Fanatics than to the British. Further, it appears to have undermined their position amongst the independent tribes, no longer secure following the Ambela campaign in any case. It is in this context that Niamatullah's overtures must be seen. This was, after all, the third distinct episode of communication between the leadership of the Fanatic colony and British authorities (the others being in 1885 and 1898). What is striking about all of this is that despite the rhetoric of religious rebellion and violence, the Fanatics seem to have settled into a relationship with the Raj full of the former while in the main bereft of the latter.

The seeming *entente cordiale* arrived at between Niamatullah and Roos-Keppel had its sceptics in both British and *mujahidin* ranks. C.R. Cleveland of the Criminal Intelligence Office wrote to A.H. Grant, the Foreign Secretary, expressing his department's reservations about Roos-Keppel's secret peace. He noted,

Sir George appears to contemplate a future in which the fanatics will be at secret peace with us, while their supporters in India will imagine that they are hostile and will continue to vent their jehad [sic] feelings by sending subscriptions, emissaries and disciples secretly to the fanatics. We are satisfied that on the part of the Indian jehadis their relations with the fanatics have been tinged all through with a feeling of guilt and sedition, and we are extremely reluctant that similar conditions should prevail in the future. It is very unhealthy and probably dangerous for a number of persons in India to continue to feel that they are secretly aiding and abetting the enemies of Government and we are most anxious to remove the outward appearance and inner consciousness of guilty practices from the whole community of Ahl-i-Hadis and Muhammadis. Concealed and secret peace with the Amir of the fanatics will fail apparently to change the practice of the Indian jehadis[sic] from political guilt to harmless religion.[52]

Within the *mujahidin* camp the agreement led to a rift, with many of those dissatisfied at the new footing on which relations stood, fleeing to Chamarkand in order to remain implacably hostile towards the British.[53] The Chamarkand colonists lived around the tomb of Mulla Hadda, an important local religious figure, which made it impossible to attack them without agitating the tribesmen.[54] Originally an offshoot colony of Asmas, Chamarkand now became the centre of anti-British activities, in clear contravention of the wishes of Niamatullah,[55] who was murdered in 1921 for his rapprochement with Roos-Keppel.

It was at this time that the *mujahidin* entered their final phase of hostile activism against the British. The colonies, in particular the more militant one at Chamarkand, were connected with both Indian nationalists and Bolshevik agents. It was believed that they provided a conduit for weapons to the Bengali "terrorists" and the Akali Sikhs.[56] Chamarkand was thought to receive Rs. 1000 per month from the Central Khilafat Committee and played a crucial role as a conduit between Indian "revolutionaries", Kabul and the Soviets.[57] By 1925, the British had evidence of senior colonists meeting with the Soviet minister in Kabul[58] and receiving a substantial subsidy from the Bolsheviks.[59]

In addition to the Bolsheviks and Indian nationalists, the Fanatics also received support from the Afghan government. As early as the 1880s the *mujahidin* attempted to solicit support in the form of annual allowances. The Afghans proved consistently fickle, linking their support to explicit activities by the *mujahidin*, such as advocacy of Kabul's line amongst the tribes in independent territory or fomenting disquiet aimed at destabilising British paramountcy, which benefited the Afghan government. The *mujahidin* found themselves increasingly dependent on the Afghan subsidies as subscriptions from British India fell.[60] Kabul seems to have offered its largesse in the late 1920s, but it suspended its annual subsidies from December 1934.[61] In return for their investment, Afghan authorities appear to have exercised a considerable amount of control over the *mujahidin*, going so far as to warn the contingent in Waziristan not to act in support of anti-British tribal activities without orders from the Afghan Foreign Office.[62] However, incessant infighting meant the *mujahidin* were considered a poor investment by Kabul.[63]

Although the British recognised that the Chamarkand *mujahidin* on their own presented little danger,[64] their potential as a key link between dissatisfied Indian nationalists, intriguing Russian agents, and an untrustworthy Afghan government was unsettling. An intelligence assessment from 1925 noted:

> The Chamarkand colony is extremely dangerous in some ways, but it has not itself the influence to further the general scheme which the Bolsheviks have at heart, and for the purpose of spreading Bolshevism among the masses in British India the colony can achieve very little of itself. The danger lies in its use as a link, or agency, between the Russians and the Extremist leaders of British India, and it is certain that it is chiefly of this purpose that it is being financed by the Russians.[65]

Consequently, the British sought to sow dissension between the Asmas and the Chamarkand colony, using the former to curb the excesses of the latter.[66] Although they considered Chamarkand a potential "wasps nest", an undisclosed "series of long, patient, and thoughtful steps" had rendered the colony "quiet and harmless."[67] Indeed, the British saw it as a potential "emergency safety-valve" for the "diehards" of the parent colony.[68] Chamarkand remained small, numbering only "49 Hindustanis and 14 Punjabis under Maulvi Siraj-ud-din, Bengali, a representative of the Asmas Amir, Rahmatullah [and] 4 Punjabis with Maulvi Fazal Ilahi" in 1927.[69]

During roughly a decade of activism from 1922 to 1934, the *mujahidin* undertook activities aimed at undermining British rule. They attempted to establish "anti-British" schools along the Frontier, successfully setting up two with Russian money channelled through Chamarkand.[70] Recruits and subscriptions continued to trickle to the *mujahidin* from British India, but the colonies became increasingly reliant on Afghan subsidies. They published a newspaper, *Al-Mujahid*, originally in Persian but later in Pashto as well,[71] in which they wrote articles decrying British atrocities,[72] supporting the actions of the Afghan government,[73] and informing the readership of events in the wider world.[74] The British thought the paper did a "good deal of harm"[75] and banned it from their territories, declaring Chamarkand to be a "revolutionary organisation."[76] Some of the *mujahidin* were implicated in a terrorism case in the Punjab, which led to the colony at Chamarkand and its inhabitants being declared parties to a conspiracy to wage war against the King-Emperor.[77] Yet despite British fears of the Bolshevik menace employing a motley collection of religious fanatics to spread its seed in South Asia, as well as concerns regarding Afghan intrigues along the Frontier, little came of the *mujahidin*'s efforts.

Handicapped by perpetual infighting over leadership, the *mujahidin* participated minimally in uprisings against the British along the Frontier, such as the revolt led by the Faqir of Ipi in 1936. Nonetheless, the British continued to watch the Fanatics' colonies until their withdrawal from the subcontinent in 1947. During World War II the *mujahidin* remained largely quiet, although in 1942 they were mentioned on "Azad Hind" radio from Berlin as a contact point for all anti-British activities who wanted to communicate with the Axis powers.[78] In terms of their relationship with the rapidly developing politics of Indian nationalism, they seemed largely indifferent. At one point, however, the *mujahidin* assumed an anti-Congress stance, warning through *Al-Mujahid* that a purely Hindu Congress sought to establish Hindu dominance in India.[79] They also spread pro-Muslim League propaganda in Bajaur in the run up to Partition in 1947.[80] The last entry regarding the *mujahidin* in the British records appears in the weekly intelligence summary from Peshawar for the week ending 21 June 1947. It simply reads "Jemadar Muhammad Ayub Mujahiddin [leader of Chamarkand] has been touring Bajaur collecting harvest money (*zakat*)."[81] As for their post-independence fortunes, these have yet to be explored. However, local tribesmen of Bajaur are said to remember Chamarkand as "*Da Mujahidino kali* (village of the Mujahidin)."[82]

Legacies

The Frontier Fanatics appear to have outlasted British power in the subcontinent, making their uninterrupted presence in the area over a century in length. This in itself is a rather amazing feat. Although they were outsiders to the tribal societies which they found themselves embedded in, and often at odds with, the Fanatics carried on a precarious existence and established a home on the Frontier lasting multiple generations. They were in regular contact with sympathetic supporters in north India whose spiritual and material support proved key to their survival. They successfully recruited local tribesmen into rebellion against the Raj, most spectacularly during the Ambela campaign of 1863. The Fanatics' survival on the Frontier is itself a unique story. However, before it is simply dismissed as an interesting but ultimately idiosyncratic episode, it is necessary to consider both the reasons for the Fanatics' longevity, as well as the effects it had both on the Frontier and on the wider colonial sphere of South Asia.

In large part the Hindustanis survived and indeed thrived as a community in the independent tribal areas because of their ability to embed themselves within local social systems through a common idiom of belonging, as well as their apparent utility and value to local tribes as sources of capital—economic, social and political. Additionally, the regular arrival and departure of recruits from British territories seem to have continuously renewed the colonies' population. At least some of these recruits brought their families, and many of the reports regarding the health of the Fanatic colonies refer to the presence of women and children. The changing ethnic composition of the community also affected its ability to survive, with Pashtun tribesmen increasingly playing a role after the First World War. Yet there is little evidence to indicate the colonies formed anything more than a symbiotic relationship with their local hosts. There is no indication that *mujahidin* intermarried with local tribes, and Pashtun social mores militated against such a possibility. The colonists thus formed an integral, but unincorporated part of local society on the Frontier.

What, if anything, does the *mujahidin*'s century of activism on the Frontier tell us about the nature of revolt and religiously inspired violence in the region? In a way, they represent a kind of ideal type from which one can derive a pattern. We see a charismatic religious leader with a call to reform, misunderstood by external powers, but one with deep linkages and resonances in local religious rhetoric, understandings and sensibilities—namely Sufism. The leader's reliance on a religious brotherhood renders his relations comprehensible within local social systems. This may be furthered by possible claims of belonging and relation which go deeper than simply religious affinity, as in the case of Sayyid Ahmed of Rai Bareilly. These connections enable the leader—who has a core following of foreign adherents who are themselves totally alien to the tribal universe and thus guests—to broker wider alliances when circumstances permit. Those circumstances are largely defined by the intrusions of a centralising authority which are perceived by local tribesmen as threatening their independence and autonomy. The language cementing these alliances is religious in character as Islam provides the tribesmen with a broader lexicon allowing them to relate to the wider, non-tribal and non-Muslim world.

In some ways, the Fanatics' choice of a religious idiom for confrontation is unsurprising. Most revolts against colonial authority in the nineteenth century contained some sort of religious idiom to explain and justify their revolt, both to adherents and ostensibly to those they revolted against. The Mutiny was the example par excellence, filled as it was with millenarian intimation. What is particularly interesting in the Fanatics' case is not their use of religion as an idiom of resistance, but their adaptations of that idiom over time to meet changing circumstances and maintain their relevance. Thus the "Wahabis" of the mid-nineteenth century found themselves aligned with Sikh nationalists and Soviet Bolsheviks in the 1920s. By 1947, they were actively spreading Muslim League propaganda in the tribal areas. As important as the idiom of expression was the rhetorical value of violence to the Fanatics; for adherents of a "jihadi" culture eager to bring about the downfall of the infidel *sarkar*, the Fanatics' reticence to engage in actual, as opposed to epistemic violence, is noteworthy. Instead, as a community they came to an incredibly durable understanding with the colonial state which, for the most part, exempted both from anything more than verbal posturing. Even those who disagreed with this stance and spilled blood within the *mujahidin* community refrained from attacking the colonial state. The Fanatics thus fashioned a legacy of rhetorical opposition to the state which, arguably, has been taken up by other members of South Asia's Islamic *umma*.

As important as their legacy of opposition to the state is the way in which the Fanatics shaped the attitudes of the colonial state towards its Muslim subjects. Despite the musings of Hunter and those like him who saw Indian Muslims as little more than seditious masses, the colonial state's treatment of and attitude towards the Frontier Fanatics reveals a more nuanced picture too often ignored by later scholars. At times, the Raj acted towards the Fanatics with violent antagonism, while at others it viewed them with decided indifference. The lack of a coherent, over-arching narrative—a discourse of the "official mind"—is important. It indicates a more complex relationship between the Raj and its subjects, even those ostensibly in revolt. Moreover, the Fanatics' presence in Swat reminds us of the central importance of this seemingly peripheral frontier to the fortunes of South Asia, and the Muslim world more generally. Their use of religion as a rhetoric of resistance was one long practiced on the Swat frontier, as well as further afield. By examining and better understanding their experiences here, we can not only better understand Swat today, but also its importance beyond the high mountain peaks which demarcate its geographical limits.

4

KASHARS AGAINST MASHARS

JIHAD AND SOCIAL CHANGE IN THE FATA[1]

Mariam Abou Zahab

Socio-political change in traditional Pashtun tribal society has sped up during the last three decades. Such changes in the society's dynamics go back to the 1970s when tribals started migrating to Karachi and to the Gulf, enabling minor lineages to become rich and to challenge the power hierarchy.[2] The open economy of the 1980s, the boom of smuggling during the Zia ul Haq regime and the tremendous inflow of remittances[3]—which benefited predominantly the disadvantaged and traditionally subordinate segments of the rural society—led to wealth accumulation by emerging classes who invested mostly in construction of huge new houses and shops and also in the purchase of land and weapons. The old inequalities based on Pashtun values of hospitality and manhood were replaced by new inequalities based on money; these transformed the character of tribal society. During the Afghan *jihad* of the 1980s, the flow of US dollars and weapons, as well as smuggling, drug peddling, gun running, car theft and abduction for ransom, became extra sources of money. The consequence was social disruption and polarisation rather than adaptation.[4] Wealth and power started coming from other sources than land and this changed the dynamics of the old system that had existed under the British Raj.

The breakdown of tribal authority began in the 1980s when the agencies marginalised the *maliks* (tribal elders) and used mullahs to unite feuding tribes against the Soviet occupation of Afghanistan. Islam was also seen as a counterweight to the internal threat of Pashtun nationalism. The gradual weakening of traditional rural institutions and the political scenario in Afghanistan led to the empowerment of religious groups who became autonomous as the writ of the Pakistani government was ineffective in the tribal areas.[5] There was virtually no international border between Pakistan and Afghanistan and the settlement of Afghan refugees in the tribal areas affected the demographic balance and the power structure. Moreover, training camps and Deobandi *madrassa*s supported by Arab donors promoted religious militancy in a traditionally secular society.

Most studies dealing with the tribal areas explain the developments of the last three decades by focusing on the external factors without taking local dynamics into account. The importance of external factors should not be underplayed, but they can only work in an atmosphere conducive to their influence.

In this chapter I discuss the change in the sociology and patterns of leadership in the Federally Administered Tribal Areas (FATA) since the arrival of al-Qaeda in the area after 9/11.[6] It must be emphasised that my focus will be on South Waziristan which has become the hub of al-Qaeda and the Taliban—local and Afghan elements—and also of Uzbeks, among other foreign jihadis; this means that the developments in other tribal areas will not be considered here. My key argument is that the Talibanisation of Waziristan might be analysed as the outcome of a social movement among the Wazir tribesmen which started in the 1970s and was accelerated in the post-9/11 context by the emergence of "tribal entrepreneurs" who took advantage of a change in political opportunities and of their access to resources to challenge the traditional tribal leadership. I argue that it is a movement of the *kashar*s (the young, the poor and those belonging to minor lineages or powerless tribes)[7] against the *mashar*s (the tribal elders)[8] and the Political Agent. It is also a movement of the *kashar*s against those who have an interest in the status quo—the so-called "mafia of maliks, transporters and traffickers", in other words the emergent under-class of the new rich.

The first part of the paper will provide an outline of the changes which have occurred in the last three decades in the social structure of the FATA. The second part will look at the social and demographic changes in Waziristan. I will then attempt to analyse the shift in the traditional structure of power—from the political administration to the military and from the *malik*s (elders who are the mediators between their tribes and the Political Agent) to the militants who call themselves the Pakistani Taliban and the emergence of an alternative leadership. Finally I will address the attempts of the old elite to counter the movement. The aim of this paper is modest, but I hope that it can be a starting point to develop the understanding of the internal dynamics of Pashtun tribal society.

Changing patterns of social and political life

Pashtun tribal society, widely considered by earlier ethnographers as classless and egalitarian, has gradually changed and class is now an important dimension of social life and relations. Five categories of class-like social groups can be identified.[9] First, there are the traditional leaders (*mashar*s)—land owning elders and *malik*s—who gradually allied themselves with the administration to pursue their personal interests and have been the sole beneficiaries of the system. They have lost influence over time and are discredited; tribal elders are still respected, but their roles and views are increasingly being questioned. Second, there are the new rich—traders, wholesalers, contractors, timber merchants, transporters, drug/arms traffickers. Many of them have acquired the status of *malik* to contest the elections and register themselves as contractors and suppliers; they are the main beneficiaries of the war economy.[10] Third, the educated and professionals (doctors, engineers, college teachers, journalists, students, NGOs' employees, active and retired members of the military and the bureaucracy) who oppose the status quo and are the self-defined agents of social change. Fourth, the common people (farmers, sharecroppers, landless peasants, artisans, workers in the transport sector, unemployed youth), in other words the *kashar*s who have no civil and political rights and are dissatisfied with the existing political and administrative set-up; the state has not provided people belonging to this group with basic rights—education, health and most important, justice. Fifth, migrants settled in Karachi and the Gulf who, just like the third and fourth categories, are dissatisfied and oppose the status quo and desire to be agents of social change.

The administrative structure

At the Bannu tribal *jirga* (council of elders) in January 1948, Pakistan accepted the autonomous character of the Federally Administered Tribal Areas, FATA, and continued to follow the policy of the colonial rulers towards the tribal areas. There has been little change in the administrative set up of Waziristan since the creation of the agencies of North and South Waziristan during British rule.[11] This area which is geographically, economically and socially at the extreme periphery of Pakistani society has been historically independent of any central authority, owing to its inaccessibility, and has often looked towards Kabul. The Wana Wazir gave much trouble to the British. In 1920 J.M. Ewart wrote: "Their behaviour throughout had been worse than that of any tribe on the Frontier, showing a combination of treachery, lawlessness and fanaticism".[12]

After Partition, partly because of strained relations with Afghanistan, the Pakistani government allowed the FATA administration to become entrenched in its colonial past; it continued to deal with the *malik*s through the Political Agent, and the system of allowances and subsidies has survived.[13] Zulfiqar Ali Bhutto initiated policies aimed at the development of the FATA, but there was no change in the administrative system. He introduced quotas in educational institutions[14] and federal jobs and facilitated the issuance of passports, which had far reaching socio-economic and political implications.[15]

In 1996, the caretaker government of Malik Miraj Khalid introduced universal adult franchise in the tribal areas.[16] A large number of candidates contested elections in 1997 and in October 2002; these elections, however, were held on a non-party basis in the tribal areas. The introduction of local government institutions under the Devolution plan and the FATA reform plan announced in January 2002 by President Musharraf was shelved on account of the War on Terror, as the government thought that a centralised command structure was more suitable for the military operations. The tribals were not given any representation in the North West Frontier Province (NWFP) assembly during the October 2002 election, judicial powers were not separated from executive powers, and the necessary amendments were not made in the Frontier Crimes Regulations (FCR) of 1901.[17]

A reform package was announced in August 2009 lifting restrictions on political parties' activities and excluding women and children from collective responsibility, among other things.[18] These reforms which should be a first step towards bringing FATA into the mainstream have still to be implemented. Two decrees amending the FCR[19] and extending the Political Parties Order (2002) to the FATA were signed in August 2011 by President Zardari. Although some claim that it is too little too late, these steps towards bringing FATA into the mainstream are nevertheless encouraging.

The changing demographic structure of Waziristan

According to the 1998 census, North Waziristan had approximately 360,000 inhabitants, the increase from 1981 to 1998 being 51 per cent, while South Waziristan had 430,000 inhabitants, the increase from 1981 to 1998 being 39 per cent.[20] The unofficial estimated populations of North and South Waziristan are now around 600,000 and 800,000 inhabitants respectively. Tens of thousands of inhabitants of South Waziristan have been displaced by military operations.[21] This has led to forced urbanisation[22] and to the dislocation of whole communities, notably the Burki (Urmar) of Kaniguram.[23]

Half of the population of North Waziristan belongs to the Wazir tribe[24] and one third are Dawar, a minor tribe, a proportion that has been stable for the last three decades. The situation in South Waziristan is very different. Traditionally 75 per cent of the population were Mehsud and 25 per cent Wazir, the most important clan being the Zalikhel, a sub-tribe of the Ahmedzai Wazir which has links with Afghan tribes across the Durand Line.[25] According to the population census of 1972, the Mehsud were about 250,000 and the Wazir 50,000; since 1981 the number of Mehsud has constantly declined while the Wazir population has kept increasing[26] and is now on a par with the Mehsud. The Wazir, who control 70 per cent of business, are more affluent.[27] They also control some of the most fertile valleys and lucrative trade routes along the border. The Mehsud have achieved an impressive literacy rate and produced scores of civil servants and military officers, they have joined mainstream Pakistani society and moved to the settled areas of Tank and Dera Ismail Khan.[28] Many of them have also settled in Karachi where they have opened transport businesses. Well-placed in the power hierarchy of the state, they are inclined towards integration in the state rather than separation from it.

The rivalry between Mehsud and Wazir for control of the resources of South Waziristan goes back to the period preceding Partition. At the turn of the twentieth century, colonial administrators noted that "The relations of the Darwesh Khel with the Mahsuds have never been cordial, and now they might be best described as being distinctly strained."[29] Although they were the largest tribe in South Waziristan, the Mehsud are described in colonial literature as the junior lineage among the main Wazir tribes, therefore having the worst land—largely barren mountains—and living in the most crowded conditions, which partly explains why they looked southwards.

The Mehsud have long been in dispute with the Wazir over the ownership of the Gomal Pass:

> The Gomal Pass […] has always been considered as belonging to the Mahsuds. Actually it is outside the limits of their country. The claim of the Mahsuds to the Gomal Pass is based on the fact of their using it from time immemorial as raiding ground which supplied them

with a source of livelihood. The pass has been used for generations by the Powindah caravans that trade between India, Afghanistan and Central Asia.[30]

Although they inhabit two-thirds of South Waziristan the Mehsud are isolated geographically, having no direct access either to Afghanistan or to the settled areas.

In the 1950s, at a time when the Wazir were in the minority, a peace deal was struck and the political administration introduced the *nikat*[31] (loss and profit sharing) system on the basis of population. The Mehsud were given three quarters of the share of resources and development funds and the Wazir one quarter.[32] The government continues to follow this system in spite of the Wazir tribe's demand to do away with it. In December 2004, an Ahmedzai *jirga* denounced the elections to the Agency Council (two thirds of the seats were allocated to the Mehsud and one third to the Wazir according to the *nikat*) as being anti-democratic, while the Mehsud defended the status quo.[33] The administration is indifferent to the problem and has been seen by the Wazir as supporting the Mehsud. These claims are not new. A movement was launched among the Wazir in the early 1970s by Maulana Noor Mohammad who "mobilized Islam to activate specific tribal ideology into a political movement against the Mehsud, accusing the administration of supporting them."[34] The army moved into South Waziristan in May 1976 and dismantled the parallel administration he had set up; some 1,500 shops in the bazaar of Wana were destroyed, Noor Mohammad and his key followers fled to Angoor Adda but were arrested and jailed. He spent several years in jail and later joined the Jamiat-e Ulama-e Islam (JUI). He received Arab money and weapons in the 1980s which enabled him to build a *madrasa*.[35] Maulana Noor Mohammad was not only a cleric but also a respected tribal leader. He was elected to Parliament in 1997 and after 9/11 he kept a low profile and was seen by the local Taliban as pro-government. Opposed to suicide attacks and to attacks targeting the Pakistani army, he was killed on 23 August 2010 when a suicide bomber—a Mehsud affiliated to the Tehrik-i-Taliban Pakistan (TTP)—blew himself up inside a mosque in Wana.[36] He was delivering a sermon at the time.

The emergence of an alternative leadership after 9/11

The introduction in 1996 of adult franchise—although without political parties—was meant to bring tribal areas into the mainstream and to answer a longstanding demand from the emerging middle class. The participation of the tribals in the general elections of 1997 further eroded the power and authority of tribal elders.[37] Before, members of parliament were chosen by the *jirga*, and the *malik*s had political influence and could get rich.[38] The political system was centred on them and its effectiveness was linked to the competency of the Political Agent; the system was strong as long as the institution of the *malik* was strong, but *malik*s are no more the representatives of the tribes. An alternative leadership, more charismatic and with access to considerable resources, has emerged from the war and filled the vacuum. The October 2002 elections, which coincided with the re-emergence of the Taliban, saw the destruction of the base of the *malik*s' power as mullahs linked to the JUI-F (Fazlur Rehman) were elected as members of parliament and transformed their religious authority into political power.[39] But the Muttahida Majlis-e Amal (MMA) disappointed, or indeed betrayed, the rural poor.

After the American intervention, foreign militants, Afghan Taliban and others who fled Afghanistan entered the tribal areas, and a sizeable number of foreigners settled in Waziristan where they developed deep links with Ahmedzai Wazir. From 2003 Waziristan, described by Ahmed Rashid as "al-Qaeda central", became the focal point of the militant activities. Afghan Taliban and foreign fighters, mostly Uzbeks, were hosted in Wana by the Yargulkhel, a sub-clan of the Ahmedzai Wazir. Prominent among the Wazir who hosted them was Nek Mohammad who had been recruited by the Afghan Taliban in the mid-1990s, had ascended rapidly through the hierarchy and was promoted to lead a Waziri contingent in Bagram.[40] He built links with the Afghan Taliban and the foreign fighters to whom he provided safe passage and support after 9/11; he was generously rewarded by those who made it to the FATA.

After the arrival of al-Qaeda, unemployed locals—"tribal entrepreneurs"—discovered the lucrative business of harbouring foreign militants, which became a source of extra money. They rented compounds for shelter and training camps and provided food at inflated prices, which was a way of gaining influence. Criminals have joined them because of the tremendous influx of Arab money. The disintegration of the institutional structure provided them an open space; they borrowed Taliban rhetoric and contributed to the territorial expansion of the Taliban movement.

Almost every tribe supported al-Qaeda, actively or passively, as guests.[41] In the eyes of the Pashtuns standing by the weak reinforces one's honour. But Pashtunwali is intended to protect the weakest members within the tribe. For outsiders the rules have limits: if a foreigner is a cause of war, he has to leave. *Melmastia* (hospitality), which is one of the stronger Pashtun traditions, has lost its meaning. It is no more a free hospitality but a way of acquiring wealth and influence.

The army and the Frontier Corps moved into Waziristan in June 2002 after long negotiations with the tribes, who agreed, reluctantly, to allow the military's presence on the assurance that it would bring in funds and development works.[42] After the traditional approach of using carrot and stick and tribal *lashkar*s to persuade the tribals to hand over the foreign militants failed, from 2003 onwards, under intense American pressure, the army conducted military operations in the Wazir areas of South Waziristan.[43] The military raids have weakened the already eroded power of the tribal elders who, locked in negotiations with the political administration, saw it as a betrayal and a violation of the traditions and lost whatever influence they still had on the tribes.

The military operations also created conditions for the emergence of new actors who have deep influence on the society: charismatic young men who fought in Afghanistan and are not tribal leaders by lineage, and whose power and legitimacy are based on their recently acquired wealth—either Arab money or the exorbitant compensations paid by the army—as well as their ability to fight, filled the power vacuum.[44] They capitalised on the hostility towards the presence in the area of Pakistani forces, seen as American proxies, and used both reinvented Pashtun values and resistance narratives as mobilisation tools.[45] This dynamic is similar to the situation in Afghanistan in the 1980s, where the mullahs gained autonomy in the Pashtun rural areas after the elimination, or the marginalisation, of the khans and the absence of the government's writ. This led in the 1990s to the emergence of the Taliban as a social movement.

The debacle of Kalusha in March 2004 changed the dynamics, forcing the army to sign peace deals with the militants who have been empowered. Two deals were signed between the army and the militants, in Shakai in April 2004 with Nek Mohammad and in Sararogha in February 2005 with Baitullah Mehsud.[46] The tribal elders were sidelined and the Political Agent was made redundant by the army. Maulana Meraj Qureshi and Maulana Abdul Malik Wazir, both members of the National Assembly, acted as mediators between the militants and the army. The militants had refused to strike a deal through tribal *jirga*s that had attempted to make them surrender to the military authorities in exchange for amnesty.

Changing dynamics

Between 2004 and 2007 the centre of gravity of the Pakistani Taliban moved progressively to North Waziristan as the Pakistani intelligence establishment tried to exploit traditional tribal rifts to split the pro-foreigner front and gain proxies within the Taliban movement.[47] Tribal allegiances, which had given the Taliban an invaluable network to develop their organisation, were also the cause of their fragmentation along tribal faultlines.

In December 2007 the Tehrik-i-Taliban Pakistan (TTP), an umbrella of some 40 groups aimed at bypassing the tribal factor in the insurgency, was created around Baitullah Mehsud. The TTP was established on the basis of an anti-tribal or pan-tribal agenda after the assault on the Lal Masjid (Red Mosque) in Islamabad in July 2007, which led to the proclamation of a "defensive jihad" against the Pakistani army.

Soon after this, a new group named the Maqami Taliban, aimed at "defending the Wazir tribe's interests in North and South Waziristan," was formed by Uthmanzai Wazir of North Waziristan and Ahmedzai Wazir of South Waziristan. The leader, Maulvi Nazir,[48] made clear that the movement was opposed to Baitullah's "defensive jihad" against the Pakistani army and would continue to support the Afghan *jihad* from the FATA. This group was reported to have been devised by Pakistani intelligence as a proxy which could be controlled to stem the growth of the TTP.

Ahmedzai Wazir had a strong interest in playing the anti-Mehsud card and instrumentalising an external actor to challenge the domination of the Mehsud. The Wazir, who have stayed neutral since the launch of the Rah-e Nejat offensive in Mehsud populated areas in October 2009, have been rewarded for their pro-government position.[49] The US has sanctioned $55 million for quick impact projects in South Waziristan, including the construction of a road and the provision of water. In February 2010 General Kayani inaugurated the Wana-Tank road which allows the Wazir to avoid travelling through Mehsud territory. The Mehsud accepted the construction of the road with the condition that they be given three quarters of the Gomal land for construction of houses. The Wazir objected, arguing that the Mehsud wanted to keep them enslaved, as passing through a rival territory means that you have to accept that tribe's dominance.[50]

In February 2010, an Ahmedzai Wazir *jirga* demanded a separate administrative status for areas under their control. This demand was not new, and in fact it was reported in December 2007 that the government planned to divide South Waziristan into two zones to give the Ahmedzai Wazir a separate entity and end their dependence on the Mehsud. Some officials argued that the construction of the Gomal Zam road to allow unhindered access to Wazir and the creation of a separate Wazir tribal agency would end the Mehsud's nuisance value. The Mehsud are opposed to such a measure, which will allow access to Afghanistan via Wazir territory for trade.[51]

According to a senior government official: "The Wazir are satisfied with the government. Development projects are being implemented and three small dams are being constructed."[52] In brief, the *nikat* has become irrelevant and by manipulating an external political actor the Wazir have, at least temporarily, achieved what they had been fighting for.

The redefinition of the jirga *and the new role of the mullahs*

While claiming to be the defenders of Pashtun values, the Taliban have attacked three key bastions of Pashtun male culture: the *hujra*, the mosque and the *jirga*.

Traditionally, every member of the tribe can participate in the *jirga*, the *malik* dominates the proceedings but everyone has a chance to speak. It takes place in the open, participants sit in a circle which symbolises and materialises their equality. There is no place for the mullah, he sits on the side and prays for the success of the *jirga*.

The concept of *jirga* has changed since the 1980s; it has lost its credibility after becoming a tool in the hands of the political administration and is riddled with corruption. The *jirga* is now artificial, it is no more egalitarian and has been converted into a state-manipulated gathering. Membership is restricted to men from powerful tribes, it does not provide justice to the poor and in most cases it favours the richer or more influential party.

Traditionally, the mosque was not used for tribal political activity. The mullah, who had a low status in Pashtun society, was subordinated to the tribal elders who had the monopoly of political activity conducted in the *hujra*, which acted as a counterweight to the mosque. The mullah acted as a mediator between parties in conflict but he did not handle the gun. When the threat came from a non-Muslim enemy, the mullah came to the front line and preached *jihad*, but once the conflict was finished, he went back to the mosque. New opportunities have enabled him to reject his traditional role and to move from the mosque to the *hujra*, or rather they have merged the mosque and the *hujra*. Mullahs participate in the "new *jirga*" and guarantees which were given by the tribe are now given by the mullahs. *Jirga*s, which were traditionally held in the open, have been held inside *madrasa*s and addressed by mullahs.

In the traditional system mullahs could not sustain a network of political patronage as they lacked financial means, but now they have access to money and have created a space for themselves in society. There are now two sets of competing elites: the *malik*s whose power has declined and the mullahs whose power has soared.

KASHARS AGAINST MASHARS

Jihad as a means of social empowerment

The shift in the structure of power—from the political administration to the army and from the *malik*s to the militants—and the new status of the mullahs as arbitrators between the tribes and the state gave assurance to the local Taliban who became an alternative leadership. The deals with the army gave the militants an upper hand. The Shakai deal was not a surrender: in tribal tradition, surrender means that you approach the rival group and meet it on its territory.[53] In Shakai, the army came to meet Nek Mohammad in a JUI-F *madrasa*: "I did not go to them, they came to my place. That should make it clear who surrendered to whom."[54] The militants described the deal as a "reconciliation", which means, according to tribal logic, accepting the other group as equally powerful and legitimate. By signing the deals with the militants, the army has given them legitimacy and allowed them to consolidate themselves. Nek Muhammad emerged as a hero who had put up a tough fight against the army and forced it to strike a deal on his terms. He obtained the release of 163 local tribesmen and Afghan refugees who had been arrested by the army during the Wana operation of March 2004, compensation for all tribesmen whose houses had been destroyed or damaged, and the promise of more money for development work in South Waziristan.[55]

In a society where power is related to tribal identity, age and kinship, the militants' charisma, jihadi credentials and access to resources compensated for both their youth and their lack of tribal and religious legitimacy. Tribal society has been reshaped around the militants who succeeded where the government and the traditional institutions had failed and have been able to carve out enclaves of alternative power. They capitalised on the local anger at the general lawlessness and gangs of bandits and, in doing so, they became an alternative moral authority. The tribal structure has been replaced by a superimposed religious structure based on a local interpretation of the sharia which gives importance to *riwaj* (local custom).[56] The Pakistani Taliban have established alternative centres for the administration of justice and the settling of disputes. The role of the tribal elders was buried when the implementation of sharia was announced by Mullah Nazir in March 2006 in South Waziristan.

Attempts to restore the old order

The tribal social contract is broken, and the collapse of the *malik*s is one of the most important changes in the FATA. Over 200 *malik*s have been assassinated in South Waziristan since 2004 on suspicion of spying for the USA or for the government, and many others have left Waziristan to find shelter in the cities. Some members of the Pashtun elite who are in denial of social change argue that the tribal social fabric is intact[57] and that once the Taliban alternative model is eliminated, the old tribal order will be restored.[58] This is not realistic. The colonial model worked because the tribes were isolated and could tolerate poverty as long as their autonomy was respected. They are no longer isolated and austerity is no more a value. The system is discredited and has been unable to respond to social change. It enhances poverty and denies people access to opportunities of upward social mobility.

To prevent the collapse of the old system, the military is "collaborating with the maliks to form *lashkars* to counter the movement waged by the rural poor under the guise of Islamism and led by the so-called Taliban."[59] *Lashkars* are a way for dominant tribes or clans to get access to modern weapons and money.[60] The sociology of these *lashkars* is telling: they are raised by the dominant tribes who just want to crush the ordinary poor people.[61] And this leads to further polarisation: *lashkars* could get out of control, cause further violence and unending tribal feuds. They might also turn against the state once the elders have re-established their power over the people. By arming the tribes, the state is part of the process of its own marginalisation, and rather than mainstreaming the FATA the state is trying to keep it and its people apart, thereby only exacerbating the problem. The state cannot protect the people against social change.

Conclusion

This chapter has attempted to demonstrate that the dynamics of the insurgency in South Waziristan are not very different from those that characterise other social movements both within and beyond the Pakistan-Afghanistan borderlands. Islamist militancy in the FATA, as well as in South Punjab, retains a strong element of class conflict. There is a need to engage the tribals who have been alienated and have turned towards the Taliban, and particularly to create jobs to reduce social inequality and to implement political reforms aimed at ensuring participation of marginalised groups in the decision-making process. This is the only way to help them overcome their frustrations and to respond to their aspirations in terms of security, justice, political empowerment and socio-economic development.

Before the military operations, about half of the tribal population lived, temporarily or permanently, outside the FATA. Hundreds of thousands of people have been displaced since 2003. About 200,000 people were displaced from Waziristan in January 2008 during Operation Zalzala (earthquake) against Baitullah Mehsud's Taliban. According to Khalid Aziz, the displacement was "one of the biggest in tribal history" and the human cost of the conflict in Waziristan "has gone unrecorded". From June 2009, the Pakistan army launched a massive operation to eliminate Baitullah Mehsud's Taliban. Kaniguram, Sararogha and Laddah were devastated in the fighting. The army declared victory in South Waziristan in December 2009. Owing to the blockade of South Waziristan in 2009 and the huge displacement it and other events created, a new Pashtun diaspora is in the making.[62] A process of re-invention of a Pashtun identity can be observed with particular clarity in Karachi. The old system cannot be restored and the FATA might not exist any more a few years from now. But as J.E. Ewart wrote in 1929: "No man can say what the morrow will bring forth. But this after all is nothing new on the Frontier."[63]

SECTION 2

LOCATING FRONTIER WORLDS

5

A HISTORY OF LINGUISTIC BOUNDARY CROSSING WITHIN AND AROUND PASHTO

Shah Mahmoud Hanifi

The history of any language necessarily involves consideration of that language's relationships to other languages. The history of the Pashto language, for example, is heavily inflected by cross-boundary interaction with Persian as well as a variety of Indian and Turkic languages. In addition to historic boundaries and relationships between languages, there are also historic boundaries and relationships within languages to reckon with. The profile of Pashto is similar to that of hundreds if not thousands of other languages across the globe insofar as there are distinctions and relationships between spoken, handwritten, industrially printed, and computer generated forms of the language in question.

It should also be recognized that multiple historically conditioned intra-language distinctions and connections are affected in distinct ways by divisions and relationships between them and particular forms of other languages. To continue with our case study of Pashto, then, it is important to appreciate historical and structural relationships between spoken and written forms of the language, as well as the interaction between those articulations of Pashto, on the one hand, and written and spoken expressions of Persian, among other languages including Urdu today, on the other hand.

The following survey of Pashto's textual history provides a brief account of Pashto's relationships "within itself" so to speak, as well as attending to Pashto's relationships to other languages and the power structures that surround them. As a broad review, the success of what follows will be determined primarily by the extent to which it generates future substantive inquiries into the areas and issues that are addressed here only in abbreviated form.

The analytical path navigated here is organized around the concept of boundaries. The approach draws particular inspiration from Fredrik Barth's pioneering work on ethnic boundaries and interaction across them. Barth's anthropological writings on Pashto-speaking Pathans have inspired generations of students across the globe in anthropology and other disciplines. His work on the Pathans is still regularly used in university classrooms and therefore continues to animate lively scholarly exchanges across the social science disciplines. The following discussion of the textual history of the Pashto language is designed to engage Barth's treatment of Pashtun ethnic identity, particularly the social and cultural exchanges and dialogues occurring along the ethnic boundaries where Pashtuns and Pashto are found.[1]

Fredrik Barth on the Pashto language

A few words on the place of the Pashto language in two of Professor Barth's books will set the stage for our historical survey of Pashto language texts. On page 11 of the "Introduction" to *Ethnic Groups and Boundaries* (Barth 1969) a shared field of communication is referenced as one of four ethnic group characteristics, and of course language is primary here. On page 119 of *Ethnic Groups* in the chapter titled "Pathan Identity and its Maintenance," Pathan custom is viewed as articulated through language; however, and this is most critical, language alone is not sufficient to actualize Pathan identity. In the same chapter, on page 128 we learn that Pashto is the *lingua franca* in the stratified society of Swat and that merely speaking Pashto (*Pashto wayel*) but not doing Pashto (*Pashto kawul*) devalues the motivation to claim Pashtun-ness and may lead to a "sloughing off" of Pashtun identity. Finally, on page 140 there are a number of observations about the use of Pashto in domestic and public situations in Swat Kohistan. In the crudest of schematizations Professor Barth's analysis of Pashtun identity in *Ethnic Groups* explores four cross-boundary ethnic contact situations where divergent public expression of three core components of Pashtun identity—seclusion (*purdah*), decision by councils (*jirga*) and hospitality (*melmastia*)—are contextualized by ecological, demographic, class, and other variables.

In *The Last Wali of Swat* (Barth 1985), on page 51, readers find the Wali's father's scribe asked to "go and learn to write a bit of Persian" in Thanna because the "official language of correspondence was then Persian," only later shifting to Urdu. On the same page we learn the Wali's father "introduced Pashto" and that the Wali "continued using it" but that all correspondence with the British and Pakistani Governments was in English. Page 51 of *The Last Wali* also indicates that the most trusted messenger of the Wali's father was a converted Sikh who adopted Islam and near fluent Pashto. Finally, on page 101 there is the statement that the political agents in Swat all spoke Pashto up to the level of Governor, and the tantalizing phrase that those officials were "all made to learn it" first before being sent there. At the very least *The Last Wali* draws attention to the strategic value of spoken Pashto, the power of Persian language literacy, and the role of the colonial language examination system.

The theoretical framework surrounding spoken Pashto and Pashtun identity, found in *Ethnic Groups and Boundaries*, is complemented by a brief but rich historical narrative about the writing of Pashto and its bureaucratic adoption in Swat, offered by *The Last Wali of Swat*. Through these two works, at least, Barth provides a set of concepts and useful historical data to help organize an investigation of Pashto language speaking, writing, printing, and computing. Boundaries, both

A HISTORY OF LINGUISTIC BOUNDARY CROSSING

internal and external, will be the clues and themes followed on our historical tour within and around the Pashto language.

While today Pashto's core home territory may lie within the quadrilateral zone bounded by the cities of Kabul, Peshawar, Quetta and Qandahar, there are certainly speakers of Pashto found immediately and far outside that area. As our historical narrative commences, beyond noting the fundamental problem of associating Pashto and Pashtuns with urban locations, readers will do well to think well outside any geographic box and begin to conceive Pashto's history with fluid spatial parameters, a great deal of internal dynamism, and a broad range of external exposures to other languages.

Aryan migrations, Gandhara, and Islam: the enigmatic prehistory and deep history of Pashto speech and writing

The wide variety of competing academic and popular claims about the origin of Pashtuns are collectively undermined by the lack of known ingredients and innovations entailed by the first utterances of Pashto. A lack of data will always make it difficult to prove precisely when Pashto first emerged as a spoken language, but it is possible to reach a rudimentary understanding of the major historical processes at work in the development of spoken Pashto in its own right and in relation to the linguistic world around it. A basic starting point towards understanding Pashto's origin and development is a chart of languages found in the *Encyclopaedia Iranica* that highlights the large number of languages to which Pashto is historically and structurally related.[2]

The genealogical organization of this language family tree model has Pashto representing something in the order of a single complex "leaf" of the eastern Iranian "stem" of the Indo-Aryan "branch" of the Indo-European language "tree" trunk. This chart is the cumulative result of an extensive comparison of grammars, vocabularies, and a wide variety of other linguistic evidence and theory. The idea and methodology behind this fundamentally genealogical and ultimately migration-based approach to the history of languages and linguistic interaction—which subsequently came to be known as comparative philology and historical linguistics, among other disciplinary and cross-disciplinary labels—were in large measure developed by Sir William Jones. Jones' ideas on the Indo-European language, and through it Aryan identity, have had a significant influence on the study of Pashto.[3] Jones's conclusion about the historical significance of Pashto hinged upon a hypothesis about its genealogical relationship to the Chaldaic language (see below for more on Jones and his work on Pashto).

The history of writing in the area we now know as Afghanistan is a vexing subject. If we begin the conversation with Alexander the Great in the fourth century BC, we are left with more questions than answers about the bureaucracies he and his armies encountered. Alexander's presence helps explain the use of Greek and Aramaic by a subsequent ruler in the region where Pashto would later emerge, namely, the Mauryan King Ashoka the Great (ruled c. 269–232 BC). Ashoka left approximately 30 rock inscriptions for posterity, including one in Greek and Aramaic that was discovered in Qandahar in the 1960s. Among the earliest texts written in an Indic language is a set of birch bark scrolls etched in

65

Table 5.1
IRANIAN AND INDO-ARYAN LANGUAGES OF AFGHANISTAN

INDO-IRANIAN

IRANIAN

	West	East
OLD IRANIAN (to the 3rd cent. BC)	SW Old Persian *dṛd-	F. Evestan *zṛd-, zərəd-
MIDDLE IRANIAN (2nd cent. BC)	SW Middle Persian dil NW Parthian zīrd	NE Sogdian NE Khotanese (or Saka) NE Chorasmian NE Bactrian
NEW IRANIAN (from the 8th cent. AD)	SW Persian del NW Balūčī (del, dil)	NE Šuġnī zārδ NE Rōšānī zārδ NE Eškāšmī (av͜zók) NE Sanglēčī (av͜zuγ) NE Wāki (pəzīv) NE Munji zil(ǵ) NE Paštō zṛə
		SE Parāčī zōr, zör SE Ōrmuṛī zle, zlī

INDO-ARYAN

	OLD INDIAN	MIDDLE MAN	NEW INDIAN
	Vedic Sanskrit hṛd-, hṛdaya-		
		Gāndhārī — Pakrits haḍak(k)a-, hiaa-, hitaa-	
		Pāri haday-	Panjābī hiāū Sindhī hio Gojrī Inku hā

NŪRESTĀNI

Kati	zirā
Waygalī	zô
Aškūn	žídi, žédi
Prasūn	zir, zər

DARDIC

Pašai	(h)ār
Tirāhī	wuṛə
Gawar-batī	hiṛa

the Gandhari language using the Kharosthi script that appeared roughly three or four centuries after Alexander, in approximately the first century AD.[4]

The Ghaznavid era, historically anchored around 1000 AD, marks the appearance of durable Islamic state structures in the area now known as Afghanistan. The bureaucracies and chanceries associated with the Ghaznavid and other Islamic polities that proliferated during the medieval period routinely used both Arabic and Persian, a pair of languages then intertwined in the writings of cosmopolitan intellectuals such as al-Beruni, who helps us appreciate the growing importance of writing throughout the medieval Islamic state system.[5]

The high profile of Turkish populations and languages in the emerging Islamic *ecumene* is increasingly apparent during the medieval period, most notably for our purposes in the context of the Delhi Sultanate. The integration of Turkish slave populations in the Delhi Sultanate "naturally" complicated what appears as mere Arabic-Persian hybridity with a number of additional linguistic elements from Central Asia.[6] It is important to bear in mind that the interaction of these Islamic languages was occurring in an environment that also included a larger number of Indian languages.

In the Delhi Sultanate we stand on comfortable historical ground imagining spoken Pashto—no matter how developed on its own evolutionary terms—being audible in commercial, political and military settings throughout the Himalayan foothills and the Ganges plains. In this area an expanding and demographically diversifying Indo-Persian Islamic state was taking shape through a series of migrations between South and Central Asia.[7]

During Babur's passage from Turkistan to Hindustan through Kabul and the Hindu Kush in the early sixteenth century, Pashto could be rather routinely encountered over a wide area between roughly Herat and Calcutta.[8] This expanse was composed of various dynamic zones of linguistic interaction. On the historical cusp of its textualization, spoken Pashto existed in a very diverse environment where Persian, Arabic, Chaghatai and other Turkish languages and dialects, as well as multiple local (as far as local can be determined in a world where movement was ordinary) Indian languages and dialects were present in spoken and written form.

From the Mughals to the British: the writing of Pashto and early Pashto dictionaries and grammars

Leaving aside the contested claims about the *Tazkerat al-Awlia* that is alleged to have been authored by Sulaiman Maku in the early thirteenth century, as well as the non-extant writings of Shaikh Mali from the early fifteenth century, at present the consensus remains that Pashto was first written during the Mughal period.[9] It is generally understood that Bayazid Ansari's *Khair al-Bayan* and Akhund Darweza's *Makhzan al-Islam* are the first two Pashto language texts. The *Khair al-Bayan* is an innovative religious treatise produced on the western frontiers of the Mughal polity in the late sixteenth century, and the *Makhzan al-Islam* is a refutation of the alleged heresy of the earlier text, produced at the Mughal imperial center in the early seventeenth century.[10] Beyond the theological boundaries between innovation and heresy raised by these two texts, it is important to highlight the interactions across cultural, linguistic and perhaps proto-ethnic boundaries involved in their production.

It is significant that neither of these authors, nor any subsequent authority, attached Pashtun identity to either Bayazid Ansari or Akhund Darweza.[11] More relevant is the fact that neither the *Khair al-Bayan* nor the *Makhzan al-Islam* is a Pashto language text exclusively; rather, each contains a significant number of phrases from the Quran and other Arabic passages, as well as abundant Persian translations of the Arabic and extensive Persian commentary. Ansari's text also contains Indian language passages. In the Pashto portions of these two texts, different forms of Pashto writing were used in the original manuscripts and in the subsequent copying of each.[12] The major distinction is that innovations captured in the *Khair al-Bayan*, involving the use of as many as thirteen letters beyond the four Persian letters appended to the twenty eight Arabic letters, are not captured in the *Makhzan al-Islam* that was produced subsequently.[13] Akhund Darweza's contributions to the development of the Pashto script are less substantial than Bayazid Ansari's. However, it should not be assumed that Bayazid Ansari in the late 1500s was the first or sole engineer of thirteen "new" Pashto letters, or that Akhund Darweza in the early 1600s did not influence the development of the Pashto language or script.

Through the opaque history of this formative period of Pashto writing it should be made clear that the writings of Khushhal Khan Khattak (1613–89) also left a considerable mark on the history of the language.[14] Khushhal Khan is historically significant for being the first Pashtun to write in Pashto, for celebrating the language and its speakers, as well as for critiquing his own society. However, while Khushhal Khan Khattak certainly advanced the textualization of Pashto through his scriptural innovations and the sheer volume of his writings, the innovations themselves reflect a different dialect of Pashto than that used by Bayazid Ansari in the *Khair al-Bayan*. Khushhal's Khan's script was somewhat cryptic by design in that its use appears confined to only a handful of his sons, grandsons, and other family members.[15] One view, then, is that Khushhal's innovations were restricted to a small group of authors. From another perspective, the Khattak family writings also served to unify multiple dialects in the Indus plains and the Punjab and Himalayan foothills, and thus produced a substantially expanded range for a new standardized dialect of Pashto through the circulation and re-copying of these writings.[16]

In a sense, Khushhal and Bayazid each solved the "problem" of writing Pashto in a different way. Each developed different characters and graphemes for Pashto phonemes, many of which exhibited and continue to exhibit a range of allophones across a spectrum of dialects spread out over a wide area. The writings of Khushhal and Bayazid together mark an era when Pashto speech firmly crossed into the realm of Pashto writing, but they are separated by roughly one hundred years, and by hundreds of miles between the points of production that can be deduced in the absence of either original manuscript. The texts produced during this formative period reveal varied relationships between at least two Pashto dialects of speech and multiple malleable writing systems. This formative period of Pashto writing is directly related to the emergence of an identity or set of identities cohering in new ways around new forms of an old language. The period of approximately one hundred years between the late sixteenth and late seventeenth centuries is important for transfers across "internal" boundaries between Pashto speech and Pashto writing, which formed an important linguistic synergy within the process of Pashtun ethnogenesis congealing on the territorial and temporal frontiers of the Mughal empire and the modern era.

Pashto's textual emergence involved a number of historically and structurally distinct "external" interactions with Persian, Indian and Turkic languages, and the exchange of loanwords is a primary articulation and index of these varied boundary crossings. In terms of documented lexical exchange, Pashto appears as a borrower rather than a donor language, and this displacement is an important reflection of the language's subordination to the power of neighboring languages and the power structures associated with them. During this period Pashto and Pashtuns were found within and between the Safavid and Mughal empires, and while it is essential to appreciate that both imperial bureaucracies were predicated on the Persian language, there are significant asymmetries in Pashto's incorporation of vocabulary from Persian on the one hand and Indian languages on the other hand.[17]

Through stylistic mimicry, in-text translations and—most importantly for our purposes—nearly half of its total lexicon, Persian language and Persianate influences formed a significant stratum of Pashto writing in the seventeenth and eighteenth centuries.[18] In general terms, the high volume of Persian words incorporated intact in Pashto writing, and prominent unaltered textual elements such as titles and subheadings, are key indices of this imperfect rule concerning the Persian influences on Pashto. In contrast to the rather grafted Persian vocabulary, smaller numbers of loanwords from Indian languages were more intimately incorporated into Pashto. Unlike their stable "cousin" Persian loanwords from the west, these Indian loanwords from the east were subject to orthographic modification and morphologic transformation upon ingestion into Pashto.[19]

In the late sixteenth and the seventeenth centuries Mughal imperial policies heavily influenced the production of Pashto texts including the *Khair al-Bayan*, the *Makhzan al-Islam* and Khushhal Khan Khattak's oeuvre. Similarly, Pashto writing in the eighteenth and early nineteenth centuries was substantially affected by British Indian colonial policies. During the colonial period there was an exponential increase in the volume of Pashto textual production within which there is a considerable amount of lexicographical and grammatical work.[20] No matter how incomplete or rudimentary they may be, dictionaries and grammars represent linguistic boundaries. It is possible to argue that dictionaries articulate "external" boundary crossings between languages, and grammars impose "internal" boundaries between local popularly spoken vernaculars and elite-centered, literate high-culture standards.

Kushev (2001) discusses a number of Pashto lexicographical and grammatical works produced during this period. Two of these works deserve special notice for their production under the dictates of an emerging set of British colonial interests in the Pashto language, its speakers, and their territories. The *Riyaz al-Mahabbat* was written c. 1806–7 by Nawwab Mahabbatallah Shahbaz-e Jang, a son of the Rohilla Chieftain Hafiz Rahmat Khan. This work has two parts, the first being an extensive discussion of verbs and their various forms, and the second a Pashto-Persian dictionary. The *Riyaz* was produced while Mahabbatallah was in British captivity, through the patronage of John Ulric Collins and Georg Hilario Barlow. Mahabbatallah appears to be the first person to describe Pashto sounds using examples from other languages, and the *Riyaz* appears as the first "scientific" lexical-grammatical study of the eastern dialect of Pashto. The *Ajaib al-Lughat* is a four-language dictionary for Pashto, Persian, Arabic, and Hindustani composed in 1813 by another son of Hafiz Rahmat Khan, Ilahyar Khan. Ilahyar notes that he used twenty-six Persian dictionaries published between 1220 and 1736 in compiling his impressive work.[21] Ilahayar also produced his work while in British custody.

Militarizing the study of Pashto through colonial printing and neo-colonial computing

The colonial era is important for a transition across the historical boundaries between scribal manuscript production and industrial mass printing. During the nineteenth century Henry George Raverty was clearly the most accomplished British colonial authority on the Pashto language.[22] The *Riyaz al-Mahabbat* and the *Ajaib al-Lughat* were the primary lexicographical sources he consulted on Pashto, and he notes that both texts "are explained in Persian."[23] In the Introductions to his monumental *Dictionary* (1982 [1860]) and *Grammar* (1987 [1855]) of the Pashto language Raverty exhibits a serious and careful concern for the methodology of historical philology. This colonial scientific practice was in many ways inaugurated by Sir William Jones' pronouncement from the high profile platform of the Asiatic Society of Bengal (1786 in speech and 1788 in print) that Sanskrit, Persian and Greek share a common origin in what is now commonly understood to be a proto-Indo-European language. It is likely that Jones was the first person to print a specimen of the Pashto language in 1788 in the Society's house journal, known then as *Asiatick Researches*.

In British India during the nineteenth century printing became an increasingly widespread, profitable, and politically charged business at the popular and state levels.[24] Early in the century the material ingredients and technical expertise necessary to print Pashto were concentrated around but not fully monopolized by the Baptist Missionary Press that produced a Pashto translation of the New Testament in the year of its founding in 1818.[25] It is unclear how much circulation of personnel and technical resources existed between the Asiatic Society, the Baptist Missionary Press, and the British East India Company's College at Fort William, established in 1800, which was designed around the colonial power's need to engage and desire to control Indian languages and through them Indians and their history.

Raverty's career captures the challenges of printing Pashto, particularly the expense and the language's subordinate status to Persian and Hindustani *cum* Urdu. The production of his Pashto language learning texts involved legal trials and professional tribulations for Raverty. To print his Pashto language writings in costly specially cut metal type Raverty went into considerable debt and became embroiled in a number of legal cases about subscriptions or advanced purchases of his work. These financial and technical imbroglios combined to bring Raverty into a number of court cases that put his career in jeopardy. The litigation at first resulted in his dismissal from colonial service on charges of bribery and corruption, although he was ultimately reinstated after a number of additional legal filings and judicial proceedings.

Raverty designed his Pashto *Grammar* and *Dictionary* in part for educated Orientalists and the interested reading publics in India, England and Russia, at least, but his primary target audience was the colonial military establishment. Military schools such as the College at Fort William were places for British officers to study Indian languages, but these institutions also attracted other groups of students and a large number of Pashto instructors who together constituted a large, growing and lucrative reading audience market. The cause of Raverty's disaffection with the marketing of and remuneration from his Pashto language material was a rapidly expanding colonial military language exam system.

Raverty's detailed and authoritative works were weighty intellectual exercises and were never incorporated into the language examination repertoire. Raverty alleged that the first Pashto language work incorporated into the colonial exam system did not undergo scrutiny by competent authorities prior to adoption.[26] The work released immediately after Raverty's was formatted along the lines of a popular Hindustani textbook following the author's conviction about Pashto's affinity with Sanskrit. Hindustani was the emerging *lingua franca* of colonial India, and the work in question here, Henry Walter Bellew's *Pushto Instructor*, used only twenty of the forty Pashto characters Raverty used in his work. Prominent Pashto language pedagogical works produced in conjunction with the exam system in the late nineteenth century, such as Plowden's 1893 *Kalid-i Afghani*, and in the early twentieth century, such as Zain al-Abdin Khan Abid's 1917 *Pushtu Made Easy*, did not even use Pashto characters, instead opting for full English letter transliteration. Clearly, Raverty's intense philological orientation and his rigorous attention to indigenous linguistic and textual details resulted in highly academic rather than widely popularized Pashto language-learning materials, and they were not adopted as official textbooks or sanctioned study aides in the lucrative and expanding market for those materials that responded to the developing needs of the British colonial military exam system.

Three works of Pashto language pedagogy produced in Afghanistan in the first half of the twentieth century were designed for a Persian speaking and Persian reading audience.[27] The production of these texts was not motivated by military considerations, but rather by a growing sense of Pashtun identity in Afghanistan, particularly but not exclusively in and around Qandahar. The market for Pashto language pedagogy in Afghanistan was, in terms of the sheer volume of texts produced, vastly smaller than the market generated by the British colonial military establishment and its ever-evolving language exam system that continued to be the primary propellant for Pashto language learning well into the twentieth century.[28]

Although Afghanistan and British India/Pakistan combined to form the major audience bloc for Pashto language materials, industrial printing affected the two zones, and the various local and regional markets and networks within them, in structurally different ways, at different historical moments in time, and in divergent ways through time. Most relevant here is that Pashto language printing occurred in relation to distinct but interactive and highly asymmetrical state presences that were articulated in at least two different languages: Persian in Afghanistan and English, as well as Hindustani and then Urdu, in British India and Pakistan. In the twentieth century there were ebbs and flows in Pashto's relationships with other languages in and between these two qualitatively different state contexts. Although it is at present difficult to quantify with precision, it appears that across all genres of Pashto language textual production in Afghanistan and British India between 1900 and 1947, the proportional representation of pedagogical work increased most substantially.[29] The expanding military market for Pashto language material fueled this pedagogical production, and English was the primary language interacting with Pashto in that context.

It is possible to follow the historical trails of Pashto printing in twentieth-century Afghanistan and Pakistan, and in doing so the differential place and treatment of Pashto in each political setting becomes immediately apparent. Tariq Rahman's work is a logical starting point for the much more voluminous literature on the historical presence of Pashto literature in the British Indian and Pakistani educational and political systems in the North-West Frontier Province, and to a lesser extent in the overall Pakistani state structure. Rahman also provides an introduction to the identity politics surrounding Pashto in the context of Pakistani state formation, and there is of course a large body of work on Pakistani nationalism that references the Pashto language and Pathan identity. Regarding Afghanistan, James Caron considers the place of Pashto oral poetry and printed *tazkira*s in the rural eastern zone and draws attention to the Pashto Tolena, or Pashto Society, the unit within the Afghan state structure responsible for producing Pashto language texts.[30]

The histories of Pashto in Afghanistan and Pakistan involve a variety of oral and textual articulations of the language in various regional, class, and bureaucratic locations within each state setting. This general observation re-focuses our attention on the multiple boundary crossings that spoken and written versions of Pashto have with other forms of other languages, in these cases with spoken and written Persian and Urdu. The wide range of Pashto's boundaries with other languages draws attention to the great expanse of intercultural communication that occurs along and across them.

Pashto's relationships with local and global state structures since 2001 have generated a new historical and material layer of pedagogical works for the language that represent emerging transnational geographies of production and consumption. For more than a decade now the Pashto language has been surrounded and affected by highly Anglicized, militarized and technologized frontiers that have transformed the way the language is used and the way it relates to other languages.

Liberal funding through a complex web of national security-based legislative and military initiatives has recently made the United States a thriving center of Pashto language instruction, but there are historical and institutional predicates for the study of Pashto in the twenty-first century. We can at the very least note the existence of Pashto language-focused theses in graduate level linguistics programs in the United States academy during the Cold War, with Master's Degrees earned by the Afghan nationals M. Rahim Elham and Habibullah Tegey at the University of Michigan, and Doctorates earned by M. Ehsan Entezar, Mohammad Esmael Burhan and M. Alam Miran at the University of Texas. The first regular offerings of the Pashto language as a distinct course of study were developed in the late 1980s at the University of Pennsylvania under the direction of Benedicte Grima (now Santry) with Wilma Heston among other faculty administrators and supporters of that unique initiative. There was a noticeable increase in attention to Pashto language materials at the US Government level in the 1990s, as evinced by combined works of Habibullah Tegey and Barbara Robson.[31]

The rapid transformation that occurred after 2001 in the US regarding the study and teaching of Pashto reflects in the first and most obvious instance a military motivation for engaging the language, but also a pedagogical trend towards computer technology and electronically mediated instruction. As of 2010 there are approximately ten universities offering Pashto language courses, with the Universities of Indiana, Pennsylvania, and Wisconsin-Madison receiving US Department of Education Title VI Foreign Language Area Studies funding to sustain programs through 2013.[32] The US military overwhelms the US academy in terms of personnel employment and production of instructional resources.

The primary locus of the US military's Pashto language engagement is the Defense Language Institute Foreign Language School in Monterrey, California. Despite restricted public access to its records, programs and resources, as well as a perpetual web-cleansing regime, it is clear the Defense Language Institute has ingested British colonial, Afghan and Pakistani textbooks and pedagogical techniques. This is not to say the Defense Language Institute has not produced a considerable amount of its own language learning material using its own techniques for an array of US Government officials, including an inter-service military officer corps and the Human Terrain System.[33] Much of the Defense Language Institute's Pashto language material is computer based. The large public market for computer-based Pashto language aids goes far beyond the widely known Rosetta Stone program to include, for example, battery run electronic audio tapes designed for on-duty foot soldiers.[34]

The critical relationship between the academic, military, and public markets for Pashto language learning cannot be explored here, but it is important to draw attention to the demographic and technological overlap between these sectors. In the present global colonial moment, the online and publicly available evaluation mechanism at Indiana University returns our attention to Raverty's encounter with the British Indian military exam system, and a further comparison between colonial eras lies in the very visible web-based translations of the Bible into Pashto.[35] In the first paragraph of his article titled "Computing in Pashto" Craig Kopris (2005) states that "for the most part, the computer age has passed this language by." Kopris goes on to describe a number of challenges in writing Pashto on a computer, including the "problem" of Pashto's multiple versions of the Arabic letter *yey* (ی) that posed similar complications for Bayazid Ansari and Akhund Darweza five hundred years ago when Pashto was first written on paper.

Conclusion: the Pashto differential among Afghans, Pashtuns, and Pathans

Pashto was first textualized within a Persian language template that was framed by the Mughal empire. During the colonial period Pashto encountered English in the British Indian military exam system, among other bureaucratic locations such as the judiciary. Today the American imperial apparatus is robustly engaging Pashto through its military institutions with a clear emphasis on computer-based learning techniques. While the military, the academy, and the private sector are also producing Pashto language learning texts of the traditional paper sort at a high rate, an ever proliferating swarm of non-governmental contractors and other profiteers follow, as pilot fish to sharks, the immense sums of resources attached to industrial and post-industrial warfare. Hordes of self-identified Pashto language "headhunters" actively recruit diaspora Afghans in the United States, particularly in northern Virginia and northern California, to serve as oral translators who can earn well over $200,000 a year.[36] The high rate of defection from US military sub-contracted Pashto translator jobs has been constant and helps to explain these high sums. The endemic lack of competency in Pashto among the Pashto translator corps is now well documented.[37] We can deduce that inefficient translators have strong enough English to make it through encounters with English speaking employers and colleagues, so that the incompetence of Pashto translators that ultimately emerges is predicated on much greater degrees of knowledge of spoken Persian and Urdu that in the end could not effectively mask lesser degrees of command of spoken Pashto.

Today Pashto is nested within a complex moving web of oral, paper/textual, and electronic/computer relationships with Persian, Urdu, and English, at least. These many cross-boundary relationships with other languages affect the way Pashto relates to itself in terms of the incorporation of new loanwords and the creation of new forms of textual and technical representation of the language that are adopted by its speakers. It is unclear precisely how spoken varieties of Pashto and transformations in representation of the language produced in the diaspora are recycled back to any part of the homeland of Pashto speakers. To define that homeland geographically today we may return to the area between Kabul, Qandahar, Peshawar and Quetta mentioned at the outset of this survey. In each city Pashto relates to many different languages and expressions of state-based and locally constituted sources of power. More precisely, many forms of written and spoken Pashto relate to various expressions of many other languages in each city.

In general terms Pashto interacts primarily with Persian in Kabul, Hindko in Peshawar, and Baluchi in Quetta. This leaves Qandahar as the arguable center of Pashto, which in turn raises questions about the mobility of the language and its speakers across any boundaries associated with the city, not to mention yet again the very real problems of associating Pashto with any city or set of cities. Pashto may be a rural language that stands opposed to urban-based states, which then debunks a singular Qandahar-centrist line of inquiry for understanding Pashto. Broadly, then, we may ask if perhaps Pashto represents resistance to states. More specifically, perhaps spoken Pashto is a form of resistance to the literate and textual states of Afghanistan and Pakistan where Persian and Urdu, respectively, prevail today. English was inherently entrenched in the Pakistani state bureaucracy because of its colonial heritage, and English is currently being forcefully inserted into the Afghan state because of its neo-colonial construction. In general boundary terms, is it possible to read Pashto resistance to English into the current local-global relationship between these two languages? In more complex and specific linguistic boundary analysis, is it possible, in Afghanistan at least, that spoken Pashto is historically opposed to printed Persian?

A HISTORY OF LINGUISTIC BOUNDARY CROSSING

Figure 5.1

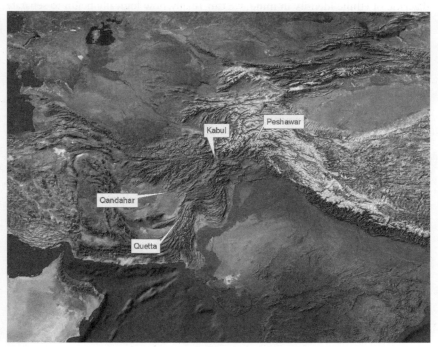

The relevance of positing a quadrilateral region with urban nodes as bounding the Pashto language homeland today is that this vision can be compared with Barth's quadri-differential boundary-based rendition of Pathan identity expressions in his ethnographic present. In a somewhat exculpatory but nevertheless rich paragraph on page 129 of *Ethnic Groups and Boundaries*, Barth draws attention to how, in Kabul and other cities in Afghanistan, expressions of class make it difficult to "consummate a Pathan identity" in those urban locations without reference to Persian and Persianate characteristics.

The importance of Barth's work for the formulation of academic understandings of ethnic identity generally and the ethnicity most proximately packaged around the Pashto language is large, durable, and cannot be underestimated. Barth's work is simultaneously problematic for the explicit equivalence given to the categories or labels *Afghan*, *Pashtun*, and *Pathan* as the ethnic group/s representing speakers of Pashto. One meager contribution of this essay is to highlight the great confusion that the triangulated syllogistic metonymy of Afghan = Pashtun = Pathan has caused students, professors and "analysts" alike. The historical record demonstrates these words arose in distinct contexts and therefore cannot represent the same thing. The ethnographic component of the historical record prompts questions about language. In that regard, Pashtuns, Afghans, and Pathans clearly have differential relationships to the Pashto language. With that critical linguistic diacritic of ethnic identity in mind, we can, finally, now logically begin to separate the categories Afghan, Pashtun and Pathan, no matter how politically uncomfortable the ramifications of such an intellectual maneuver may be.

6

THE ROAD TO KABUL

AUTOMOBILES AND AFGHAN INTERNATIONALISM, 1900–40

Nile Green

"If we compared a country to a living being, it would be no exaggeration to say that its roads are its veins and its bridges its muscles."

Siraj al-Akhbar newspaper (Kabul, 24 October 1911)

While clichés of Afghanistan standing at the "heart of Asia" have long abounded, they have only recently begun to be examined closely enough to reveal the genuine scale and contours of Afghan connectivity with the wider world in different periods.[1] In the nineteenth century, 'Abd al-Rahman Khan (r. 1880–1901) famously chose to keep the Russian and British Indian railways at bay, and by the turn of the twentieth century the trade caravans that reached Kabul still relied on the animal transport methods of previous centuries. Yet in the following three decades, Afghanistan rapidly opened itself to the global motor transport revolution, a shift of policy signalled firstly by the motoring enthusiasms of 'Abd al-Rahman's successor, Habibullah Khan (r. 1901–19). Distinct from the state and company dominated railway in its liberation of the individual traveller, the motorised transport that proliferated through Afghanistan in the period between 1900 and 1940 would have important consequences as the following decades saw Afghan cross-border political and paramilitary mobilisation build on the global motorised transport revolution that reached Afghanistan in the period covered by this essay.[2] While the travel anecdotes discussed here are not the familiar recent tales of Taliban in Toyota pick-up trucks, they are nonetheless part of an historically continuous sequence that connected the construction of motorable roads, the importation of European, American and later Japanese vehicles, and the flow of personnel and ideologies across the border from India/Pakistan and elsewhere. The contention of this essay is that this "speeding up" of intellectual and religious exchange with India/Pakistan as well as Europe was partly a product of the motor age.

In order to reconstruct something of the detail and texture of the early period of motor travel, this essay draws on source materials in Persian, Urdu, German and French that hail from the various directions that motor transport linked Afghanistan. The essay first reconstructs the outlines of the introduction of cars and the construction of motorable asphalt roads during the reigns of Habibullah Khan, Amanullah Khan (r. 1919–29) and Nadir Shah (r. 1929–33). After examining the travel accounts of the European visitors whose entry was also made possible by the motor transport revolution, and Persian accounts of motor cars from Afghan journals of the period, the essay then turns to three Urdu travelogues written by some of India's earliest automotive intellectuals. Together, these German, Persian and Urdu travel writings are used to assess the contribution of motorised transport to the new forms of internationalism that were to reshape Afghanistan's state and society in the twentieth century.

Along with European—particularly German—travel accounts of the period, Urdu travelogues point to the increasing interaction between not only the mercantile spheres of Afghanistan and India, but also their intellectual and artistic spheres. This intellectual and artistic fascination with motoring was echoed in writings by Afghans of the period themselves, particularly in the extraordinary illustrated history of motor cars discussed below that was published by the Kabul Literary Society (*Anjoman-e Adabi-ye Kabul*) in the mid-1930s. Eased by the coming of the motor car, the period's more varied profile of travellers and their intellectual or ideological imports also helped shape the religious transfers analysed by Benjamin D. Hopkins's essay in this volume. For if the genre of the Urdu travelogue had first expanded on the back of the steamship and railway revolutions of the Victorian era, the opportunities that the motor car opened for individualised land travel to destinations with neither ports nor railways saw a considerable body of Indian *littérateurs* and intellectuals venture along the route through the Khyber Pass that few others than merchants and soldiers had trodden before 1900. The emergence of the travelogue as the key literary marker of modernity was therefore dependent itself on the development of the new technologies and infrastructure of travel that rendered new kinds of interaction between Muslims of different regions feasible. For while merchants and camel caravans had travelled through the Khyber Pass since time immemorial, the safe and more commodious movement of poets, intellectuals and statesmen with which this essay is concerned belonged to distinctly twentieth century modes of travel.

The automotive opening of Afghanistan

In the opening years of the twentieth century, Afghanistan's abundant trade with India remained predominantly the business of mule and camel caravans, with urban transport relying on the two-wheeled horse-carriage known as the *baggi*, the latter itself introduced from India.[3] However, Kabul's close connections with the Indian towns of Jamrud and Peshawar and from there with the road and rail networks of British India enabled the introduction of the first motor cars into

Afghanistan. The first cars to reach Kabul were brought from India in December 1904 as part of the special mission of the British Indian Foreign Secretary Sir Louis William Dane (1856–1946), and one of them was presented as a gift to King Habibullah.[4] A steam-powered car (*motar-e bukharî*), it was valued at eight hundred pounds and, in view of the problems of fuel supply in Kabul, had been adapted to burn wood rather than coal. Strange as it now seems, such steam-powered vehicles competed with petrol-engined vehicles worldwide well into the 1920s, and as we will see below, were still used in Afghanistan during the reign of Amanullah.

The cultural dimensions of this first opening of Afghanistan to the new technologies of travel can be traced in the Urdu travelogues that celebrated King Habibullah as the modern technological traveller par excellence. The earliest details can be found in Khaksar Nadir 'Ali's contemporary account of King Habibullah's tour of India in 1907, itself supplemented by the Urdu memoirs of the exiled Afghan soldier Muhammad 'Abdullah Khan 'Azar, who was appointed to the King's Indian entourage.[5] From beginning to end, Khaksar Nadir 'Ali's travelogue celebrated the King's relationship with mechanical forms of mobility from trains to speedboats and motor cars.[6] Crossing the Afghan border, the King was described making his first ever train journey from the Indian town of Jamrud, and throughout the rest of the travelogue his presence on trains and railway platforms was emphasised over and again.[7] Yet it was Habibullah's car journeys during this Indian tour—described as taking place in Calcutta and Lahore—that were to prove more important to the subsequent pattern of Afghan transport development, which would from this point focus on the construction of motorable roads rather than on railways.[8] In linguistic terms at least, the entry of motor transport to Afghanistan from British India would be preserved even to the present day in the English loanword *motar* ("motor") used in Afghan Persian for the car.

After his return to Kabul with two more cars presented as gifts from the Government of India, Habibullah's infatuation with the new transport technology grew further. Fond as he was of new technologies, and a keen photographer, Amanullah took numerous photographs of his cars and popularised them among court circles. Hoping to use trucks to bring passengers, freight and mail across the Khyber Pass from India, around 1910 Habibullah established the Afghan Motor Company (Shirkat-e Motar-e Afghaniyya) with a collection of thirty-seater buses and large vans, though apparently these were frequently sequestered for the whims of his courtiers.[9] By December 1911 the newspaper *Siraj al-Akhbar* was able to report the King being driven to his palace at Jalalabad in a "caravan" of six cars.[10] The potential of motorised goods transport was already realised; in 1913 Habibullah established another transport company (*shirkat-e barbari*), and by 1915 new roads had been built from Kabul eastwards through the Khyber Pass, westwards to Herat, northwards into the mountains as far as Jabal al-Siraj, and southwards as far as Qandahar and thence Quetta in British India.[11] New bridges were also constructed, including an iron bridge of around two hundred feet across the Kabul River outside Jalalabad on the crucial road connecting Kabul with India.[12] While the bridge-building technology came from India—the commission for the iron bridge appears to have been that contracted by Habibullah in 1907 with Messrs Brown & Co. of Calcutta—the hard labour of road-building fell in many cases on the shoulders of Afghan Hazaras under corvée from their mountain villages.[13]

Unfortunately, the quality of many of the new roads was so poor that they would need to be reconstructed only a few years later in the reign of Amanullah during the 1920s.

These early stages in the development of Afghan motor transport were also captured by the German visitors who during Habibullah's and especially Amanullah's reigns came as technical and commercial advisers, as well as journalists.[14] Writing around 1921, the German travel writer Otfrid von Hanstein (1869–1959) reported that Habibullah built the country's first asphalt road between two of his palaces, a development pattern that echoed the King's short-lived railway project.[15] A few years later the roving American reporter Edward Alexander Powell (1879–1958), who in the early 1920s toured the region by motor car himself, journalistically described Habibullah "roaring up and down the narrow mountain roads in a great red motor-car which stampeded the camel caravans".[16] When King Amanullah set off from his capital towards India on the first leg of his tour of Europe in 1927, the Urdu account of the journey opened with a serene drive from Kabul to Qandahar in a "princely red motor car", and the furthest reach of his European tour would appropriately be the Rolls Royce motor works at Derby in England.[17]

More important for Afghan development than such royal jaunts was the construction of new roads suitable for motor vehicles, and this road construction programme gathered pace under Amanullah in the 1920s and continued under Nadir Shah and Zahir Shah in the early 1930s. Describing the new roads of the late 1920s, the Manchester-raised *Daily Mail* correspondent Roland Wild (1904–89) drew a contrast that would become familiar to many later travellers through the Khyber pass: "the camels would amble… straight as a die through the valleys, while the new motor road curled on the flank of the hills."[18] In a Persian article on trade conditions from the Afghan journal *Kabul* from 1935, good roads were described as linking Kabul with Gardiz, Qandahar, Mazar-e Sharif, Herat, Khanabad and the Indian city of Peshawar (via Jalalabad).[19] Notably, the article only mentioned one inter-provincial road that did not tie a provincial city to the capital, namely the road linking Herat with Mazar-e Sharif and Khanabad. Another article in the magazine described the increases in bridge construction in these years, with 1934–35 seeing four new bridges in the district of Kabul, two in Qandahar, two in Farah, and one each in Mazar-e Sharif, Badakhshan and Jalalabad.[20] The close links between road and state were publicised in photographs that appeared in these journals, such as that published in 1936 showing the Minister of War inspecting the new road between Gardiz and Khost, a region that rebelled under both Habibullah and Amanullah.[21]

In joining Kabul with such major provincial centres as Herat, Qandahar and Mazar-e Sharif, the road-building project was at one level an exercise in binding the provinces to the capital. But the decision to extend roads to the borders (towards Peshawar in particular) would not only enable trade but also ease and increase the flow of intellectuals and ideologies, including the very people who have left us their travel accounts. Road-building in this way had inherently conflicting outcomes, both stabilising and undermining the nation-building project, a danger which the state attempted to avoid by policing road borders through the introduction of visas with the opening of Afghan foreign consulates after 1919. Yet roads were not only practical, they were symbolic and their construction served as a means of marking the project of modernising Afghanistan with hard lines inscribed all across the nation. This visual sense of the simultaneous making of road and nation could be seen in the new maps that appeared in such government-sponsored outlets of the new intelligentsia as the journal *Kabul* published by the Kabul Literary Society (Anjoman-e Adabi-ye Kabul). One such map from the *Kabul* journal in 1936 showed the new roads linking Kabul with the other Afghan cities in bold red and black lines; with few other details on the map, the roads were the most visible cartographic feature of the nation.[22]

This road-building initiative reflected developments directly to the west in Iran, where from the 1920s Reza Shah's modernisation programme had similarly initiated investment in motorable road construction, which proved to be a far more cost-effective booster of trade than the Iranian railway built in the same decade.[23] As with the earlier British-sponsored Bakhtiyari Road completed in 1900 that opened the towns of central Iran to British commerce, such road-building projects were by no means free of imperial interest.[24] But compared with the railway projects of Russian Central Asia and British India whose expansion the earlier Afghan ruler 'Abd al-Rahman had firmly opposed, the new motor roads of both Iran and Afghanistan were national rather than imperial projects.[25] As such, the new roads were designed to tie the nation together internally by binding the provinces to the capital rather than linking the latter to more distant imperial territories. These better-connected imperial neighbours were themselves to be used as resources for the nation itself through providing more reliable routes for post and news, the importing of much-needed machinery and the export of Afghan trade goods, a situation that in many respects echoes the contemporary situation discussed by Magnus Marsden's chapter in this volume. Designed for the purposes of national development, the new roads connected Kabul to the more technologically developed cities of colonial India and to a lesser extent Soviet Central Asia, while also opening Afghan society to interactions with the new kinds of travellers who arrived with the motor car.

As in neighbouring Iran, then, it was only during the 1920s and 30s that motorised travel expanded in Afghanistan beyond the circles of the court elite, with the spread of lorry transport for passengers and goods. During the 1920s and early 1930s, King Amanullah and his successor Nadir Shah established a more extensive road-building programme and these years saw the introduction of lorries onto the country's roads, which then, as now, served as human as well as goods transport.[26] With lorries following the pioneering private cars onto Afghan roads, one source records the first regular lorry route as being between Kabul and Charikar, some ninety kilometres north, the price of the journey being seven Afghanis for each of the fifteen passengers.[27] However, it seems more likely that this occurred on the main Kabul-Peshawar route, and data collected in the late 1920s recorded considerable motor activity on this route as an Afghan business concern with government ties, the Shirkat-e Baradaran-e Afghan ("Afghan Brothers Company"), was granted a monopoly on the transport of heavy goods between Kabul and Peshawar, while the Afghan-German Company used diesel-powered lorries or steam-powered Sentinel trucks to carry other goods between the two cities.[28] In running on coal rather than diesel, the Sentinels were the more economical option at this time, with coal more easily available in Peshawar and even further towards the border, owing to massive amounts available for the Indian railway.[29] The existence on Afghan roads of such steam-powered lorries is itself an extraordinary testimony to the internationalism of Afghanistan's motor transport revolution. For these "Sentinels" (most likely the successful Sentinel "Super" of 1923) were manufactured at the Sentinel Waggon Works established in 1920 in the English Midland town of Shrewsbury on the assembly line model of Henry Ford's factory in Highland Park, Michigan.[30]

The Sentinel Works was not the only player, and other European transport companies sought contracts with the Afghan government. While during Amanullah's European tour of 1928 the Krupp Works at Essen in Germany presented him with a gift of one of their newest trucks, it was instead to the Italians that he turned, placing an order for a hundred lorries with the Fiat motor company of Milan.[31] Keen to maintain their own stake in the country, the British presented Amanullah with his favourite "wonder chariot", a black Rolls Royce.[32] The increasing number of petroleum-powered vehicles on Afghan roads increased the need for a fuel that was harder to source than coal, and once again it was the state which sought to lead the way with the establishment of the Shirkat-e Pitrul ("Petroleum Company") by Nadir Shah in the early 1930s.[33] Even so, the vehicles themselves had to be shipped through India, which remained the key mediator of Afghanistan's entry to the motoring age. Echoing the shipping route of the cars and lorries themselves, Ram Prasad, Amanullah's personal driver and head of the royal garage, was himself Indian, having been "specially imported… from British India" in the words of his acquaintance, the journalist Roland Wild.[34] Nor was Ram Prasad the only human import related to the motor trade; Wild also described the Italian mechanics responsible for looking after the Italian transport vans ordered for the Afghan army during Amanullah's reign.[35]

Being the products of travelling middle class intellectuals, the written accounts of motorised travel discussed below relate to the relative comforts of car rather than lorry travel. Even if the written sources in this way lean towards the higher end of the market for motorised transport, the spread of lorries as a form of both human and goods transport in the 1920s was an important development, setting a precedent as it did for the later pick-up trucks of the Taliban. From rare royal perquisites to rough peasant road trips, as with every other aspect of Afghan society the development of motorised travel was sharply marked by class and status.

Motoring and the travelling intellectual

The journeys with which we are concerned in this essay marked a transforming moment in both the act and the writing of travel. For in the structuring of their narratives around the pace and spaces of motorised land transport rather than the languorous steamship journeys and predictable train rides of the Persian and Urdu travel writings of the previous few generations, the Afghan travelogues written in the 1920s and early 1930s by such mobile intellectuals as the educationalist Hajji Shams al-Din (fl. 1900–30), the biographer and erstwhile Pan-Islamist Sulayman Nadwi (1884–1953) and the Sufi nationalist and journalist Khwaja Hasan Nizami (1879–1955) carried their readers into the new era of swift individualised movement that motorised transport made possible. The very fact that their journeys were made—indeed, unlike the merchant or military expeditions of the previous century, undertaken with minimal planning and preparation—was underwritten by Afghanistan's opening to a distinctly twentieth century mode of travel and so to the experiential rhythms that this quickened world brought with it.

While such motorised transport made new kinds of interaction possible by carrying savants and intellectuals across routes previously trod almost exclusively by merchants and soldiers, then Indian Muslims were not the only intellectuals to take advantage of this automotive opening of Afghanistan. One of the most important European instances was the beginning of archaeological excavation in Afghanistan in the early 1920s through the representatives of the Délégation Archéologique Française en Afghanistan, whose journeys from the Musée Guimet in Paris were made in French-manufactured Citroëns.[36] The 1920s was a decade of several classic narratives of the speed age, such as *Im Auto durch zwei Welten* ("Through Two Worlds by Motor Car") of Clärenore Stinnes (1901–90), the German female motor racer who between 1927 and 1929 made the first circumnavigation of the world by car, including a drive through Iran and Central Asia.[37] Riding further south to Afghanistan four years earlier in 1923–24 was Stinnes's compatriot Emil Trinkler (1896–1931), whose account of a breakneck drive from Germany to Kabul provided a motorcyclist's counterpart.[38] Like the French archaeological drivers, Trinkler was no mere tourist; he was a geologist employed by Amanullah to help develop the new nation, once again tying motor transport to Amanullah's larger project of using imported experts and products for the purposes of national development. Indeed, it was only Trinkler's motorcycle that allowed him to conduct the off-road geological survey that produced for Amanullah his detailed map of the nation's geology.[39]

A few years later, in 1933, the Austrian geologist Herbert Tichy (1912–87) followed Trinkler by likewise riding by motorcycle from central Europe to Kabul and on to India.[40] Fascinated by the aesthetics no less than the geology of the Hindu Kush and Himalaya on which he had earlier written his dissertation, Tichy marked the entry into Afghanistan not only of technocrats but also of European artists and visionaries. As small parties of intellectuals rather than caravans of merchants or diplomatic missions travelling under armed escort, the journeys of the French, German and Austrian experts were followed by the more artistic tours of such aesthetes as Robert Byron (1905–41), whose 1933 journey to Herat coincided with the first major motorised expedition of Sven Hedin (1865–1952) further east into Central Asia.[41] Byron's anecdotes about Iranian lorry drivers and Hedin's account of his "Auto-Expedition" along a Silk Road now being traversed by American-made Ford trucks belong to this same transformative moment in which the motor road replaced the railway as the acme of national development and trans-national connectivity. In a short period of coinciding arrivals, motor transport carried such savants from all directions: Tichy, Byron and Hedin all drove from Europe in the same year that the Indian intellectual Sulayman Nadwi and the great Urdu poet Muhammad Iqbal drove by car from Peshawar to Kabul.

By the early 1930s, the motorable road from Peshawar to Kabul was opening Afghanistan to adventurous European and even American tourists. As the *Daily Mail* correspondent Roland Wild scoffed in his closely-observed account of Amanullah's reign:

For many years the Khyber has been included in the itineraries of the tourist bureaux of New York, Paris and London. Round-the-world travellers.... travel up to the north of India, take one swift look at Afghanistan without leaving their cars, and rush back for the evening train to Bombay... Afghanistan was open to the world.[42]

The 1929 revolt that brought Amanullah's rule to an end also halted some of his reform projects, but it did nothing to slow the number of motor visitors to the country. In 1933, the same year as Robert Byron and Muhammad Iqbal's journeys, the pioneering French archaeologist Joseph Hackin and his wife Ria published a French tourist guide on the Buddhas at Bamiyan, with a German edition following in 1939.[43] Among the guidebook's historic details was more practical advice on roads: Bamiyan could now be reached in six to eight hours by car from Kabul (longer by lorry) by taking the new Kabul-Mazar road until twenty-nine kilometres before the turn off into the Bamiyan Valley.[44] By 1939, European women such as the Swiss Annemarie Schwarzenbach (1908–42) and Ella Maillart (1903–97) were able to make the journey on their own from Geneva to Kabul in an elegant black Ford Model 18 Deluxe Roadster.[45] The products of Dearborn, Michigan had reached the roads of Kabul.[46] If the cars themselves have a varying presence in the writings of the Europeans—played down by Byron, celebrated by Stinnes—then for Afghan intellectuals they were objects of fascination and desire, seen as purchasable symbols of modernity itself. In one of the most extraordinary Afghan writings of the period, the Pashtun intellectual Sayyid Qasim Khan Rishtiyya provided to fellow members of the Kabul Literary Society a Persian account of "The Motor Car and its Global Importance". Not only giving a detailed history of the development of motoring in Europe and the United States (including the development of steam cars and the first car accidents), Rishtiyya's long essay also reached in the opposite direction in time to portray in both prose and fantastical illustrations the motor cars and motor cities of the future.[47] Through streamline Art Deco illustrations, readers in Kabul were able to picture the *sarak-ha-ye ayanda*, the "roads of the future", on which finned feline sports cars wove through mountains like their own.

Driving from India: motor vehicles in Urdu

Yet these motorised developments were not unique to European travellers, numerous Indian and Iranian intellectuals were also carried in by car. As with the literary concern with motor transport expressed in such German works as *Im Auto durch zwei Welten*, Urdu writers were also concerned with cars and roads as a topic in their own right. Among the many genres of text which flourished in Urdu, the most valuable for reconstructing the new networks of Muslim exchange generated by the new travel technologies of the industrial era is the *safarnama* or travelogue. As steamships, rail networks and the opening of the Suez Canal in 1869 afforded easier routes between Europe and Asia, the years between around 1870 and 1930 witnessed a tremendous explosion of travel writing in Urdu as well as Persian and Arabic.[48] Printed as monographs or serialised in journals, along with the new genre of the newspaper report such travelogues formed the most effective means by which the Muslim reading public not only became aware of modernity but domesticated it to their own needs and idioms. For these reasons, the extensive *safarnama* literature that emerged in this period serves not merely as a database on Muslim engagements with the wider world, but also as a window into the cultural processes by which those engagements were rendered meaningful in Muslim idioms. Nowhere was the interplay between literature, travel and technology more visible than in the motorised opening of Afghanistan—landlocked and surrounded by forbidding mountains—in the first decades of the twentieth century. For between around 1920 and 1940, a series of Urdu travelogues was composed that allow us to chart the social and cultural ramifications of the distinctly twentieth-century mode of transport that was the motor car. Although written for Indian audiences, the Urdu travelogues were the product of cross-border interactions between Afghan and Indian Muslim modernists, and with their recorded conversations with Afghan high officials and practical accounts of travel conditions they afford insight into Afghan road-building agendas. This cross-border profile of Urdu, which also saw Urdu newspapers and journals regularly imported to Afghanistan, reflected the similarly mobile status of Pashto in this period, as discussed by Shah Mahmoud Hanifi's chapter in this volume.[49]

As they were first and foremost accounts of road trips, one of the most recurrent themes of the Urdu travelogues of the mobile Indian intellectuals of the 1930s was Afghanistan's infrastructure of travel—a theme no less apparent in the aestheticised travelogues of Byron and Schwarzenbach from the same years—and anxieties about the state of Afghanistan's roads were a common feature of the Urdu texts. Writing in the late 1920s for a readership of fellow teachers who might follow him to find work in the modernising Afghan schools of the period, the Indian educationalist Shams al-Din devoted three sections of his travelogue to the topics of the road from India, security along it and the progress of a new road being laid by King Amanullah to improve the route to the Indian border.[50] We are able to surmise something of the increasing number of cars plying the road between Peshawar and Kabul by the falling fare: while in 1927 Shams al-Din paid two hundred rupees, when Hasan Nizami travelled the same route four years later the price had fallen to 130 rupees.[51] Yet if it was through India and the British gift of a princely Rolls Royce that Afghanistan entered the era of motorised transport, it was through the introduction of mass-produced American cars and Italian lorries to the region that the heightened trans-border traffic into India was made possible.[52]

By 1931, even a Sufi preacher such as Hasan Nizami could describe in admiring Urdu prose the *buwik* ("Buick") that carried him from Peshawar to Kabul.[53] Each aspect of the opening of Afghanistan was underwritten by new forms of international connectivity, both at the motorised level of individualised transport and the bureaucratic level of state regulation. From the rapid postal delivery of an invitation from Kabul to Sulayman Nadwi in the provincial Indian town of Azamgarh to the requirement of a passport and the dispatching of an assistant by overnight train to collect the necessary documentation, the opening pages of Nadwi's *Sayr-e Afghanistan* recount a distinctly modern tension between the technological possibilities for individual travel and the state regulation of those same opportunities. Such regulation was not merely from the British Indian side, for the Indian migrant "Hijrat" fiasco of the mid-1920s in which up to 50,000 rural Indian Muslims migrated to the "free Muslim nation" of Afghanistan had made both Afghan and British Indian officials extremely wary of cross-border movement. In effect, they began to bureaucratically control the border at the same time that automotive technology rendered it more accessible. A car ride alone was therefore no guarantee of crossing the Afghan border.

Having obtained the necessary passport from the Indian side within twelve days of receiving his invitation from King Nadir Shah, the well-known *littérateur* Sulayman Nadwi was understandably surprised when he was delayed in Peshawar by Afghan officials insisting that he complete the paperwork for the new bureaucratic invention brought into the Urdusphere by means of an easy loanword: the *viza*.[54] The control of foreign affairs won by King Amanullah in the Anglo-Afghan war of 1919 and the border regulations issued as part of his reform policies through the 1920s were clearly in force. For Nadwi described the route from Peshawar to Kabul as one of frequent stops to check the travellers' papers, until at the outskirts of Kabul the number plate of their car was logged, the names of all passengers noted and a screening telephone call made from the government customs house in the hills above the city.[55] Throughout this section of the travelogue, Nadwi's rhetoric of a free Muslim nation sailed unsteadily through the military outposts that controlled movement both into and around Afghanistan. This same tension between the technological opening of borders and the concerns of both the British and Afghan governments to control the traffic passing through them was also registered in the travelogues of Shams al-Din and Hasan Nizami. For Shams al-Din, the inspection of the novel document of the *paspurt* (the word again borrowed from English into Urdu) was sufficient to deserve a special description in his account of the journey.[56] Until he reached the passport checkpoint, the section of Hasan Nizami's travelogue dealing with his departure from the Indian city of Peshawar was a paean of transport triumphalism: after an enjoyable series of train rides between Delhi and Peshawar, Nizami noted the ease with which a car and driver had been arranged to drive his party across the border from Peshawar to Kabul.[57] Yet despite having been invited by the Afghan government, on reaching the Indian border checkpoint at Torkham, Nizami was dismayed to learn that he also required exit permission from the colonial Indian authorities. As in Nadwi's account, we gain a clear sense of a technologically monitored border, with telephone calls made from the high mountain pass at Torkham to the border officers' superiors in Peshawar.[58] Yet like most colonial institutions, the border was managed by Indians and Nizami's fame ensured that the Muslim senior border police allowed him to continue his journey, even though they insisted his companions turn back by hitching a ride in a passing lorry from the direction of Kabul.[59]

While the high sanction of Hasan Nizami's and Sulayman Nadwi's visits as personal guests of the Afghan government saw them drive successfully through these checkpoints, there was still the more basic matter of road conditions to consider. From start to finish, their accounts were of motorised road travel punctuated by anxieties about punctures and shortages of petrol, which itself had to be carried across the border by truck or even camel. Despite selecting what looked like a sound car and driver for his journey to Kabul, the educationalist Shams al-Din found that the car suffered mechanical failure and a puncture before even reaching Jalalabad. By the time he reached Jalalabad, the city gates had been locked for the night and he was forced to spend a freezing and frightening night in the car, relying no longer on technology for his safe delivery but instead chanting through the night the ritual "remembrance of God" (*zikr-e khoda*).[60] There was also the problem of the roads themselves. Despite the Afghan government's road-building efforts, by the early 1930s the roads were still frequently in a "broken condition" (*fitri halat*) since the combination of topography and the new mode of transport also required strong modern bridges; unlike camel trains, lorries and particularly motor cars made poor crossers of rivers.[61] When faced on the road to Jalalabad with a collapsed bridge that had presumably succumbed to the weight of the lorries now plying the route, Nadwi's driver attempted to drive their car on through the rivulet, only to find that the icy mountain water immediately flooded the engine.[62] Nadwi's prose captured the tension well, as repeated turns of the handle failed to restart the engine and the hour passed eight and the sun sank down behind the "high wall of mountains".[63]

Two years earlier, the same dangers befell Hasan Nizami, whose driver Jan Muhammad narrowly avoided various obstacles on the road to Kabul, whether rocks and ravines or racing truck drivers.[64] After almost crashing the car on one occasion, the driver gave his pious passenger the poor excuse of having been awake all night because he attended the last performance of a Parsi theatre troupe.[65] Yet Nizami's descriptions of his driver Jan Muhammad, who had purchased his Buick for 6,000 rupees, cast valuable light on the cultural dimensions of the entrepreneurs of the new age of motor transport on the Afghan frontier. Not only fond of the travelling Parsi performers who spread around colonial India from Bombay, Jan Muhammad was also a constant smoker of the cigarettes that Nizami compared distastefully to the indigenous betel nut or *pan* which he chewed instead.[66] Imported cars were clearly part of a larger cultural package of commodity consumption, though Jan Muhammad chose to localise his smokes with the addition of hashish. Despite his imported car and cigarettes, the resourceful driver was not detached from the cultural traditions of his milieu. When his one-handed cigarette-smoking driving almost caused him to crash into one of the trucks hurtling from the opposite direction, he defused the argument with the Pashtun truckers by assuring them that in surviving they had actually all been blessed by the *barakat* or grace of Hasan Nizami, his saintly Indian passenger.[67] Even motor cars were subject to older and higher forces than fuel and gravity.

Despite his complaints about broken roads, Sulayman Nadwi was much more complimentary on other dimensions of the infrastructure of road travel. While Afghan road-building did not exactly create the culture of "motels" that emerged from American motoring of the same period, the new roads were certainly accompanied by a state-sponsored series of guesthouses. Nadwi enthusiastically recalled the new government-constructed guest house in the "Garden of the Martyr" (*bagh-e shahid*) at Jalalabad as a large modern building of a style that was aptly distinct from the architecture of British India.[68] Set in attractive gardens fed by streams from surrounding mountains, the guesthouse was crowned with a dome and entered through a large gateway leading to a wide hall and individual guestrooms furnished with clean beds and blankets, writing desks and comfortable armchairs.[69] Hasan Nizami also recuperated there after his terrifying drive through the Khyber, comparing in his travelogue the newness of the guesthouse and the tomb of the martyred moderniser King Habibullah with the nearby ruins of the pre-Islamic Shaka dynasty.[70] The royal guesthouse in Kabul appears in these travel memoirs as grander still, set likewise in a garden but this time amid the model town of Dar al-Aman built for Amanullah by engineers brought in from Europe.[71] Hasan Nizami too described the smooth long road lined with poplar trees that lead up to Dar al-Aman and the buildings there designed by engineers from Germany.[72] During their visit to Kabul, Nadwi and his companions toured the new districts and institutions of the capital and his travelogue provides a rare glimpse into the transport infrastructure of Afghan modernisation. This ranged from the airport (described as simply a cleared space or *maydan* set aside for plane landings) and the efficient governmental garage (*motar-khana*) to the postal service that despatched letters to Peshawar with stamps printed in French and Dari on a twice-weekly truck service, and the new shops built with entirely glass fronts so that passers-by could see their goods displayed even when the shops were closed.[73] It was a notable change for a city where glass was such an unusual sight that twenty years earlier the British engineer Frank Martin had remarked of the bazaars that "there are no glass doors or windows, for glass is too rare and costly except for the Amir's palaces".[74] Not all such new developments were helpful to the larger cause of Muslim unity and Nadwi noted with a blend of frustration and amusement how the Afghan adoption of the metric system from the French left travellers from India confused as to how far was meant by a *kilomitar*.[75]

Caravans of cars: roads in the modernist Muslim imaginary

The concerns expressed about Afghan roads in the writings of the mobile Indian intellectuals were not merely the petty memoirs of fussy travellers and uncomfortable rides. They were the fruits of thoughts and discussions on the centrality of motorable roads to the Muslim "progress" or *taraqqi* to which they and their Afghan interlocutors were committed. Motor cars and roads in this way belonged to a new and distinct Muslim imaginary to which the travelogues lend rare access. For the educational reformist Shams al-Din, for example, roads themselves became the main metaphor for progress as he titled a section of his travel memoir "Afghanistan on the Highway of Progress" (*Afghanistan shahrah-e taraqqi par*).[76] We gain another glimpse into the distinct imaginary to which road-building belonged in the impassioned speech that Nadwi described being made in Kabul by Muhammad Iqbal (1877–1938), the poet and high priest of Islamic modernism who travelled to Kabul by car ahead of Nadwi in 1933.[77] Starting with an overview of the rise of British power (*taqat*) and the progress (*taraqqi*) it afforded as being based on a system of oceanic control and maritime trade binding Asia to Europe, Iqbal then presented a manifesto for a new age of travel in place of the sea routes of European imperialism, with the old "dry road" (*khushki ka rasta*) through Central Asia reopened to "caravans" (*qafila*) that now comprised motor cars, lorries and trains, with aeroplanes connecting Muslims in the skies overhead.[78] Such a road, allowing the liberated nations of Asia to trade among themselves, would trigger a revolution (*inqilab*) that would bring the Muslims back to their old position of global power. And at the centre of this grand design, Iqbal proclaimed, lay Afghanistan, which was nothing less (or more?) than the *shah-rah* or highway joining all of Asia together. In this heady period, such optimistic visions were far from the sole preserve of Indian poets like Iqbal, and as the subtitle for his Afghan travelogue the German visitor Otfrid von Hanstein chose the phrase "A Land of the Future" (*ein Land der Zukunft*).[79]

The Indian party's comparison of their discomforts on the route to Kabul with their easier travel experiences in India, Europe, the Middle East and Japan led them to press this vision of a motorised Silk Road on Afghan ministers who had invited them to Kabul on the strength of their expertise in education rather than roads. Even so, on meeting the Afghan Chief Minister (*sadr-e a'zam*) Sardar Muhammad Hashim Khan (1886–1953), Nadwi's other fellow motor traveller the Vice-Chancellor of Aligarh Muslim University Sir Ross Mas'ud (1889–1937) also launched into a lecture on the importance of road building. New roads, he promised, would open up possibilities of exploiting the mineral wealth and (with an eye to Iran and Saudi Arabia) the potential oil wealth of Afghanistan; Muslim scientific experts from his university at Aligarh could be arranged to help in this, he hinted.[80] After the Chief Minister testily responded that the Afghan government was already replacing the old road between Kabul and Peshawar, building a new route through the heart of the nation between Kabul and Mazar-e Sharif, and to oversee these projects was employing a Japanese expert who had already driven alone in safety throughout the whole country, Iqbal took over from Mas'ud to remind the minister of the importance of an overall grand international design in which all such roads must serve to revive the trade through Central Asia as a whole.[81] The same concerns preoccupied other Indian visitors, far more exposed as they were to the transformative potential of industrialised travel (we should recall that Nizami, Nadwi, Iqbal and Mas'ud had all used steamships, trains and even aeroplanes in their wide travels in the Middle East and Europe no less than Japan). When Hasan Nizami met the Turkish Ambassador and several Afghan officials in Kabul, it was again the importance of good roads—most especially a motorable trunk road connecting Kabul with Delhi—that he and the Ambassador pressed on the Afghans.[82]

While Nadwi's perpetual remarks on road conditions, petrol stalls and the furniture of government rest houses reflect the prosaic preoccupations of the traveller, his sense of the venture of this "free country" (*azad mulk*) and the verses of Persian poetry that the scenery summoned to mind raise his account from a mere compendium of on-the-road banalities to a sustained meditation on the fabric of modernisation.[83] The state of the roads not only remained a practical concern throughout subsequent road trips of Nadwi's party (onward to Kabul, and thence to Ghazni, Qandahar and Quetta) but became a matter of theoretical debate about what routes should be constructed and what place lorries or trains had in the "progress" of the Afghan nation. New roads were crucial, Nadwi noted, for the increase of Afghan trade with India; on passing through the Khyber Pass, he had noted that this trade was still largely conducted through a twice-weekly camel train using rough trails unsuitable for modern transport.[84] As a former leader of the Pan-Islamist Khilafat movement, Nadwi was anything but a champion of British rule, but he felt no compunction in describing the railway on the Indian side of the Khyber Pass as the "most wondrous miracle" (*hayrat-angiz karamat*) of British engineering.[85] For Hasan Nizami, by contrast, the littering of British army vehicles along the road through the Khyber through which Mahmud of Ghazna had once ridden to conquer India served only to rob an old Muslim thoroughfare of its romance and remind him bitterly of the contrast between the colonial rule over his own country and the independence of the nation next door.[86]

Yet neither the ideologies nor the practicalities of progress robbed Indian travellers of the romance of their journeys to a country which, like other Indian Muslims of their generation, they had greatly idealised. Fascinated by the "free valleys" in which every tribe had its own fortress and every fortress holder had its own King (*malik*), Nadwi penned sympathetic portraits of the travelling nomads (*khana-bedosh*) and the rural Pashtuns he saw through the car window and wondered, as he watched Pashtun women dressed entirely in black *kurta*, *shalwar* and *chador* devoid of any kind of decoration, whether the original Muslim purdah of the Prophet's age was so pure and simple.[87] As he passed along the high road between Jalalabad and Kabul, the winding roads and precipitous drops to distant rivers far below brought a Persian verse from Sa'di to Nadwi's mind.[88] For Hasan Nizami, the sight of beautiful nomad women glimpsed as he motored along the road from Kabul triggered playful recollections of the literary tale of Leila and Majnun, leading him to joke in his journal that had Majnun known that thousands of Leilas could be found on the road between Kabul and Ghazni, then he would never have become the worshipper of just one Leila's looks.[89] In such ways, the new mechanics of travel had distinct repercussions for the literary imagination by transforming the interactions of travellers with the nomads—with whom they had previously had much dealing as the chief suppliers of the logistics of animal transport—into fantasising and nostalgic glimpses through the windows of a passing motor vehicle. Through the unprecedented privacy that it offered to travellers, the motor car thus marked a breaking down of interactions during the act of travel at the same time as it allowed the formation of new interactions between points of arrival and departure. And in the solipsistic interstices between these broken points of interaction wandered the daydreaming minds of the automotive era, imaginaries into which the journals of such literary passengers as Sulayman Nadwi and Hasan Nizami provide a tantalising glimpse.

Conclusions

In recent years scholars have increasingly pointed to the diasporic and transnational dimensions of Afghan history as a feature of the geographical and cultural *longue durée*.[90] What we have seen in the previous pages is how the arrival of motorised transport and its attendant project of road-building in Afghanistan marked off a distinct period with new forms of interaction characterised by the mobility of artists, intellectuals and statesmen, and not only such professional itinerants as merchants and soldiers who dominated pre-industrial forms of cross-border movement. While in certain respects Afghanistan's state-sponsored road-building projects of the early twentieth century draw comparisons with the impact of the motor car on such other regions of the world as America, in the Afghan case the impact was all the more sudden through the absence of any railway construction in the previous century.[91] The changes were by no means absolute: motor cars, trucks and buses did not replace the biological transport of camels and mules, and our chief informants Nadwi, Nizami and Shams al-Din all described the novel and jarring experience of driving past the caravans of nomads and merchants. But motorised transport did allow different sections of society—urban women and the intelligentsia not least—to travel both within and beyond Afghanistan's borders in ways that had previously been extremely uncommon. Moreover, unlike many other commodities and technologies, motor vehicles were supremely culturally adaptable. When Western goods and other symbols of European influence were rejected during the nativist turn that followed the rebellious overturning of Amanullah's reforms in 1929, motor cars were one of the few exceptions. Having described the disappearance of the foreign goods and experts of the previous decade, in the early 1930s the journalist Roland Wild noted how cars had been exempt from this cultural cleansing, so much so that "there are more motor cars in Afghanistan than ever before."[92] That situation would be repeated in the years of Taliban rule.

If the state of Afghanistan's roads still remains a high developmental priority in the twenty-first century, then in the previous pages we have seen how between 1900 and 1940, both Afghan and Indian modernists regarded roads as the symbolic no less than the practical acme of Afghan modernisation. In Afghanistan, as in other regions of the world at the same time, motor cars that were themselves imported from the factories of America and Europe served as both the means and the end of modernity. The Islamic connections of motorised transport in Afghanistan are more usually associated with the Taliban's effective deployment of Japanese pick-up trucks and motorbikes. But in the road-building high rhetoric of such ideologues as the Afghan Qasim Rishtiyya and the Indian Muhammad Iqbal, we have seen that in spite of the clichés of Afghan primitivism, the alliance of Islam and technology has been a potent force in modern Afghan history.[93]

7

BEING A DIPLOMAT ON THE FRONTIER OF SOUTH AND CENTRAL ASIA

TRADE AND TRADERS IN AFGHANISTAN[1]

Magnus Marsden

During conversations with Afghans in their country and elsewhere, I am often told that everybody in Afghanistan has become a trader (*har kas tojir shudand*) and that the only thing that goes on there is trade (*tijorat*). Trade is talked about as both moral concept and economic practice. At one level, the importance of trade to Afghan life is invoked to index the immorality of the country's current political culture: the "*jihad*" being fought by the Taliban has no "point" (*adaf*), it's just about trade. As one London-based Panjshiri trader told me: "our people's eyes have opened, we think about luxury, unlike the days of jihad when our eyes were closed (*phut*), and we fought for the homeland". For others, "the Taliban are the only ones who fight with a point, the rest of us are just squabbling for the sake of money and trade". At the same time, my informants also talk about trade's importance to Afghanistan's economy, the types of skills required of traders, and the wider contributions that such people make to life in the country. They recognise that after the collapse of the government of Najibullah thousands of Afghans became traders and merchants, a trend affecting the country's urban populations in particular, and one that spawned varying trading routes and trajectories of economic life, as well as distinct geographies of regional and transnational interaction between different contexts.[2] In the north, where I have been working, the cities of Mazar and Kunduz became central hubs for the markets of the Central Asian Republics, especially Turkmenistan, Uzbekistan and Tajikistan. These markets were especially critical to the everyday lives and livelihoods of many families from these two cities and across northern Afghanistan more generally; they are also now home to important communities of Afghan traders.[3]

Given Afghanistan's historic importance as a trade corridor between the markets of southern and Central Asia, surprisingly little is known about the social worlds of its traders (*tojirha*) today.[4] Afghanistan's economy is largely analysed in terms of "war" and drugs, its merchants depicted as the "cronies" of warlords[5] and even its small scale traders as "profiteers".[6] Some studies emphasise that a new class of militia-trader-entrepreneurs, while cynically profiting from a range of licit and illicit economic activities that bring suffering to the "vast majority", also contribute in important ways to the fashioning of state structures.[7] More generally, however, Afghan markets are considered to be interesting for their imperfections—largely, the degree to which access to them is determined by economic inequalities. There are some attempts to historicise changes in the sociological make-up of Afghanistan's merchants, yet these often make binary distinction between an older class of apolitical merchants and a newer assemblage of brash and politically compromised militia-trader-entrepreneurs.[8]

Such approaches to understanding trade and traders in Afghanistan and the wider region build on the analytical models that anthropologists have developed in their attempts to understand society across the Afghanistan-Pakistan frontier region. Ashraf Ghani noted in his remarks for the "Rethinking the Swat Pathan" conference how merchants frequently appear in anthropological accounts of the Afghanistan-Pakistan frontier as largely inconsequential actors, both to society and processes of state-making, especially by comparison with the attention given to self-defined saints, khans and, more recently, mullahs and warlords. David Edwards, for instance, argues that the vindictiveness and violence of Afghanistan's first "communist" leader, Nur Muhammad Taraki, was a product of his experience of working as a trader for the Pashtun Trading Company's office in Bombay.[9] According to Edwards, Taraki's experiences in Bombay, combined with his tribe's "age-old association with South Asian trade", remained with him throughout his life: they rendered him a "middleman, a broker in foreign goods who operated on the margins between different social worlds, never fully committing himself to anyone, never being fully accepted in any place".[10] For Edwards, this deracinated cultural broker looked for new types of identity security in "the party" (*hizb*) of the pro-Soviet People's Democratic Party of Afghanistan, behaving viciously towards those who objected to his vision of Afghan society: trade is alien to "mainstream" Afghan culture and society. This point is also often made in anthropological depictions of the traders' positions within Afghan moral universes. Excellent studies of Pukhtun villages and nomadic communities demonstrate how exchange is widely associated by villagers in Swat and amongst Durrani nomads with poverty and unequal relations, dangerous aspects of daily life in a world where egalitarian ideals should reign supreme: "all relations of direct exchange are suspect if conducted with potential equals, for the equality of shared descent is fragile and exchange poses questions of rank divisively".[11] The figure of the "obsequious trader" or "violent and vindictive" money-dealer is, in short, the counterpoint to Pakhtun ideas of morality and honour.[12]

More recent studies of Afghan traders have treated trade as a product of war and social breakdown—a force that reflects ruptures and not continuities in the moral universes of Afghans. Anthropologists have explored the nature of trading networks that involve Afghans, noting the important role that these have played in maintaining people's livelihoods over the past thirty years of war. Alessandro Monsutti has documented how trade, war and population dispersal have affected a particular ethnic community, the Hazaras, spawning and reinvigorating networks that traverse the frontiers of Iran, Afghanistan and Pakistan. Mobility, Monsutti demonstrates, is a normal feature of Hazara livelihood strategies, and is connected to important formal and informal institutions, including the *hawala* system and the centrality of friendship to the making of business relationships.[13] In a comparable study, Edwina Thompson explores the business practices of largely Pushtun money-lenders: these people's economic activities are global in scope yet have their centres in Kabul and Peshawar. Less well understood, however, are the changing nature of the lifestyles, outlooks and identities of traders, their connections with diaspora Afghans and other "communities on the move" in the arenas within which they live and work, the nature of their shifting alliances with power-holders both in Afghanistan and in the countries to which they travel, and their role in the production and emergence of urban culture, urban-rural relations, as well as local, national and transnational identity formations. These, however, are all parts of being a trader that anthropologists and historians have addressed in other comparable regional settings. Elizabeth Picard analyses how a class of new "militia entrepreneurs" emerged in Lebanon: their success was based on "identity, faith and group solidarity"[14] and this did not simply lead to the demise of an older class of Christian Syrian merchants; these rather, continue to play an active role in the forging of a transnational "Ottoman space" that straddles the Syria-Lebanon border and is forged through interactive ties of marriage and business. New and old geographies, and the people involved in the construction of these, exist side-by-side. China specialists also explore the role played by merchants in the fashioning of distinctly Chinese forms of urban cosmopolitanism today and in the past, noting the relationship and tensions between such forms of behaviour and new modes of expressing wealth through consumption. These studies point towards traders' role in the fashioning of ethical standards that seek to combine making profit with the ongoing expansion of morally nurturing personal networks.[15] Traders and merchants play important agentive roles in the production of a wide range of varying, contested and often apparently conflictual moral, cultural, and political worlds. If merchants are treated as profiteers and small-scale traders as the hapless victims of improperly functioning markets, it is difficult to grasp the significance of the complex normative worlds they create, the forms of moral and economic agency they exert, and the range of sensibilities, attitudes, and debates with which these are also interlaced.[16]

Between Dubai and Dushanbe: trading across unstable regions

Those who inform this chapter are mobile Afghan traders whose lives and work connect both urban spaces and rural areas of northern Pakistan, Afghanistan and Tajikistan. I have known some of them for over 15 years, having first met them as Afghan refugee-traders (mainly from Badakhshan and Panjshir) while conducting fieldwork in a village and a small town in Chitral. I have interviewed and travelled with these men and others I have since met after starting to conduct research in Afghanistan and Tajikistan in 2005. They identify with different ethno-linguistic and socio-economic backgrounds, yet, importantly, all also identify with the category "Afghan", and refer to themselves as being traders (*tojir*).

Some are very wealthy "principal merchants" who are involved in trading activities requiring investments of up to 5 million US dollars, such as the import of fuel to Afghanistan from Russia. Others trade on a much smaller scale: they work as "percentage workers" (*commission kar*) for wealthy merchants—it is their job to find, for a percentage charge, a buyer for the products of the merchants for whom they work. The extreme mobility of these percentage workers often contrasts with the relative immobility of the merchants they work for: if based in Kabul, merchants will almost certainly assess that travel outside their houses is dangerous, and this is likely to limit their mobility very considerably.[17] Some of these commission workers go on to become eventually the representatives "*namaindagon*" of companies, especially those that are Afghan and Iranian registered, in the Central Asian countries to which they export their goods. In this role, they open factories for companies that produce products ranging from soap and cosmetics to bakeries and confectionery. Still more are independent petty traders involved in the sale of Pakistani tangerines (*kinu; mandarin*) in Tajikistan: these are transported through Afghanistan by Afghan traders based in Kabul. Some Kabul-based traders travel to Dushanbe each winter when the construction business is slack in Kabul, combining pleasure and business in their visits to the city. Others live permanently in the city as "refugees"[18] (*gurizondah*): they buy tangerines from Afghan importers, distribute these across the country's markets, while also running small shops selling basic food items. Finally, other Afghans are engaged in trading activities that they also talk about as being long-important to their collective identities: the collection and processing of animal products—sheep intestines (*ruda*) and wool (*pashum*), for example—are trading professions that are important to Turkic-speaking Uzbek and Turkmen traders, especially from Andhkhoy, Shiberghan and Maimana in northern Afghanistan; men from these Afghan towns can be found collecting wool and animal products across Tajikistan.

These men's working lives are made up of a complex combination of mobility and immobility, as well as a strong orientation towards both trading centres and to disparate networks of trade and exchange. Their lives are also framed in relation to rich yet fraught relations between merchants, commission workers, and more petty or small-scale traders, as well as those who live in or travel to Afghanistan frequently, and others who are part of a wider, transnational Central Asian Afghan diaspora. Given their very internationally oriented lives, and the importance of mobility to them, it is not surprising that many refer to themselves as "*diplomats*": "diplomacy" (a skill or sensibility that they also refer to as *siyasat* or politics) is deployed for economic purposes, and is critical to their ability to move across the multiple borders that criss-cross their world. Yet, as "diplomats," they must also represent and stand at the behest of the interests of the merchants, investors, and companies for whom they work.[19]

Most of the men currently hail from urban settings in Afghanistan (especially Kabul, Mazar-i Sharif and Kunduz). The wealthier and more established of them have been living in cities since the 1950s, although most of the people with whom I speak are from families who moved to the cities over the course of the last three decades. Some came to embark on a life of trade when they or their fathers ceased to be employed by the Afghan state as the struggle with the Mujahidin intensified. Many, indeed, talk of the difficulties they faced at the end of the

1980s, having both served the state yet also traded goods across the multiple boundaries that divided the country during this period. They talk about how they had both served as state officials and been traders in ways reminiscent of the experience of professionals in other places in the wider socialist world.[20] Their life histories offer important insights not only into the worlds of Afghan traders and entrepreneurs, but also the moral and social transformations that have affected Afghan society more generally. Many of them have spent much of their adult life outside of Afghanistan, as refugee-traders in one, many or all of the post-Soviet Muslim-majority states, and frequently, too, in Russia and Pakistan. Some lived in Europe (London, Hamburg and Amsterdam) and continue to "keep" their families there (for security and education), while saying they prefer to live and trade in Dushanbe or Kabul, places where they can work and earn money.

All my informants are multi-lingual, speaking both "regional" (Turkish, Uzbek, Dari, Pashto, Turkmen, Tajik, Chitrali) and "international" (English, German, and Russian) languages, although in a variety of combinations, and to differing levels of proficiency. The older of them (those in the late forties and above) were educated as far as college and university level in Afghanistan and often the USSR. Younger traders might have only been through intermittent schooling, sometimes studying in schools for Afghan refugees (for example in Tajikistan), elsewhere being educated in the state-education sector (in Pakistan, for example). They interact and work with one another regardless of the linguistic, ethnic and class markers that distinguish them, often actively denying the significance of these markers to their everyday lives as traders or to the normative values that shape their worlds. When I asked one Panjshiri man in Kunduz whether the people who procured him cement in Pakistan were also Panjshiri he commented to me, "we are not bothered by stories of ethnicity" (*ma dar qissa-i millat nistim*). Another trader, in his thirties and originally from Badakshan although now based in Dushanbe, tells guests in his house that they may say what they wish, but are never allowed to talk about differences in *millat*, or ethnicity. By focusing on spaces of trade, hospitality and even entertainment, rather than a particular "community" or ethnic "network" of traders, I have come to appreciate the lived complexity of relations between people who identify with different ethnic identity markers.

Makers of Islamic reform and Persianate modernity

A growing body of anthropological work on Muslim entrepreneurs emphasises the ways in which, in the context of neo-liberal economic systems, such people seek to make money according to both colonially-derived ideas of "social responsibility" and Islamic normative conventions. Reform-minded Islam occupies the heart of these merchants' understanding of the moral forms of agency they hold; this is also embodied in their efforts to finance schooling that is both modern and Islamic. The efforts they make to bring together market entrepreneurship and commitment to Islamic ethical values add important shades and textures to the study of contemporary forms of capitalism: new forms of social solidarity and community have emerged in the context of neo-liberalism, and charity and social-mindedness have risen in significance in spaces of social life from which the state has retreated: entrepreneurship, material success, and moral connectedness are increasingly seen as exemplary aspects of being a modern Muslim.[21]

"Market Islam" is a significant feature of Afghanistan's moral landscape today. This is especially the case for companies that are based in the Gulf, which, over the past decade, have established internationally significant operations that produce and package in the Gulf products such as tea and cooking oil for export to countries across Asia and Africa. In Afghanistan, these companies have now been awarded international funding to establish centralised carpet production lines for export to the United States and Europe; they have demonstrated their commitment to "socially responsible" business by doing so. The managers of these family companies relate how their businesses donate to charity, yet in secret rather than in public, commenting on how this distinguishes them from their country's other, brasher and more politically influential merchants. Such morally-minded merchants are also establishing schools for the children of the women who work for them in their carpet-making centres in Kabul, as they also continue to invest in Afghanistan's private security market. It is tempting to treat the more publicly "ethical" sides of their businesses as evidence of their hypocrisy. As the Osellas argue, however, doing so involves making a moral judgment about the intentions of such people, and this is beyond the scope of anthropology; more important, such a move fails to ask more interesting and complex questions about actors' own understandings of the importance of belief and moral integrity to their working lives.

Not all the merchants with whom I spend time, however, are centrally preoccupied with attempts to ensure that their economic activities reflect Islamic teaching. This does not mean that these people are not practicing Muslims, or that Islam is not a topic of conversation or something of importance to their everyday lives and also business practices; it often is both of these. Yet, rather than Islam forming the underlying spine of people's evaluations of their moral self worth, its importance emerges and recedes in relation to particular events: such as the loss of a vehicle of goods and ensuing debates about whether or not the transport company should pay the client for damaged goods according to the sharia. Reflection on Islam's importance to their professional activities also varies according to the places to which they travel: merchants in Tajikistan often say it is especially important to choose trading partners in that context who have reconverted to Islam and given up drink, as they are more likely to speak the truth and work hard than their less scrupulous compatriots. Even in realms of personal and collective decision-making, like for example the choice to "plump for" a relationship with a trader in Tajikistan who has openly embraced "reform-minded" forms of Islam (he prays, claims not to drink vodka, and has grown a beard), is often publicly spoken about in terms of the power of Islam to cement bonds of trust between Muslims. In private, however, such relations are also said to reflect little if anything about the actual behaviour, trustworthiness or moral substance of the trader. One way of explaining this attitude towards Islam amongst the traders I know is to argue that Islam's place in Afghan moral universes continues to exist as a form of unthought Geertzian "religiousness" as opposed to a more modern and self-reflective "religious-mindedness".[22] Many young Afghans have joined the Tablighi-Jama'at, however. Still more call themselves Salafis, having read Salafi texts rather than merely being affiliated to a Salafi organisation or movement. In my experience, such people are more likely to work for NATO as translators than to be good traders: they often shirk their family occupations as traders, not because they say trading is an immoral way of making money, but, rather because it is for them a "boring" and "unmindful" way of spending time: "not another conversation about cement", young men complain, as they listen to their brothers' business talk over the course of an evening. Here as elsewhere in the Muslim world, there is no strict division between Afghans who are self-reflective and modern and others whose ways of being Muslim are unthinking and traditional. Such differences in attitudes towards Islam signal, rather, the need for more comparative analysis of the relationship between the domains of economy, politics and religion in this context.

The context in which my Afghan trading friends and informants work offers especially interesting possibilities for exploring the relationship between political, economic and religious transformations. Doing so also helps to explain why Afghan traders bring to light articulations between Islam, cultural identity and politics that differ from those that anthropologists have written about elsewhere in the Muslim world. On the one hand, as I suggested above, a form of Gulf-oriented "market Islam" is now an important feature of the Afghan moral landscape. Afghans, moreover, not only travelled to the Gulf to do business, they also became expert entrepreneur-traders in the complex post-command economies of post-Soviet Central Asia. In these contexts, new markets and new categories of trader have flourished over the past twenty years as Soviet black markets evolved into rent-seeking and mafia-like operations. Yet these economic factors and the people who work for them have also been fiercely regulated as state officials in the independent republics continue to be influenced by Soviet ideas of trade and the market as being a source of chaos.[23] In Tajikistan, Afghan traders played a critical role in supplying the country's Soviet-era black market, especially in jeans and clothes. They also imported and distributed food in the country during and after its bloody civil war. Afghan trading worlds straddle and transcend both the Gulf and Central Asia, as well as other contexts beyond, and traders are required to be familiar with forms of discourse and comportment that are suitable across these settings.

Afghan traders and merchants might easily be assumed to be central to the fashioning of new forms of piety-minded Muslim identity in post-Soviet Central Asia.[24] Yet Afghan merchants are often more visibly important to the production of global and Persianate forms of "modernity". In Tajikistan, for example, they are now major—if hidden, given restrictive legislation in Tajikistan on business activities by foreign investors—players in Dushanbe's burgeoning restaurant scene, a key site for the display of modernity here as elsewhere. Afghans have introduced post-Soviet Tajik consumers to global food types, notably Afghan-style pizzas, burgers and fried chicken; the success of these enterprises is the source of much discussion amongst Dushanbe's traders, who are surprised to see the swift trade in Afghan juice bar joints. Afghans are also critical as investors in and consumers of new expressions of "Persianate modernity". This is something embodied in restaurants that cater to groups of merchants visiting Dushanbe from Iran, Afghanistan and the diasporas of both these countries. Evenings at these restaurants involve live musical performances of older and newer Persian-language songs, both Afghan and Iranian, suggesting the important role that Afghan merchants are playing in the fashioning of transnational identities and imaginaries in Central Asia, rather than just those related to "being Muslim". They also organise concerts in Dushanbe at which Afghan musicians perform alongside their counterparts from Tajikistan and Uzbekistan. And the same merchants involved in financing these concerts also bring the same performers to the stages of London and Toronto, where they play before mixed audiences of Afghans, Iranians and, albeit relatively few, Central Asians. This "Turko-Persian modernity" is informed by tussles, hierarchies and contests between different political spaces in the region, rather than being a concerted attempt to smooth these over: Afghans and others assert the authenticity of their forms of language and culture above those of other "Persianate" nation-states; Persianate modernity takes the form of an "assemblage" or "heterogeneous collection of elements", rather than a "bounded culture".[25]

Such restaurants are the places to which Afghans visiting Dushanbe are taken by their hosts as soon as they arrive in Tajikistan, usually after a long car journey from Afghanistan or a flight from the USA, Dubai or Australia. It is simultaneously a source of surprise and embarrassment to these men that their compatriots are the most visible of all restaurant-goers in Dushanbe: "go to any restaurant", one Uzbek trader in Iranian-produced milk from Maimana told me, "and you will find that at least 40 per cent of the people there are Afghans, and most of them are spending money that they do not have". Afghan, Iranian and Tajik traders and merchants gather together on tables to watch "floor shows" that include the songs of both 1970s-era Ahmad Zahir and the US-based diaspora musician Farhad Darya. These songs are performed as women from Tajikistan—dressed in Pashtun clothing—dance on a podium. The audience is likely to include one-time Parchami (from one of the former communist regime factions) Afghan officials visiting from Australia, former Afghan cultural attachés, and even Hizb-i Islami ideologues or Panjshiri traders who have recently come from Afghanistan and are on their first visits to Tajikistan. However, in the context of the restaurant, most traders claim that they were "never part of a *hizb*" (*ma hich waqt hizb na doshtam*): assertions of political neutrality are widely held as being critical to a man's success in the trading world, and are an important aspect of their professional identities.

In the everyday worlds of traders, participation in such forms of Persianante modernity is recognized as having risks attached. The temptations of this world are known to be too much for some traders to resist—after a few months of fun, some, having spent the savings of those who had "invested" in their trading business back in Afghanistan, find themselves with no other option than applying to the government of Tajikistan for refugee status in the country—without the money to pay back their creditors, they know that on return to Afghanistan they face kidnapping for ransom at the very least. Fathers in Afghanistan have asked me how their sons managed to go to Tajikistan, spend all of their savings ($10,000 or more) and come back so poor that they needed to work as taxi drivers plying the road between Kunduz and Kabul, before sighing and saying "luxury (*ayashi*), of course".

Diplomats across Central and South Asian Frontiers

Afghan traders and merchants are playing an important role in the production of a wide range of collective identity markers and moral sensibilities that relate in complex and contested ways to one another. These, we have seen, are framed both in terms of their being "Islamic" and in relationship to other cultural schemes and motifs, such as Turko-Persian modernity. What, however, is the nature of the moral debates, tensions and conflicts that shape the inter-subjective lives of these men? Having lived with these merchants in their rented accommodation in Dushanbe and spent days with them at the city's main bazaars, as well as in their homes and trading offices in Mazar and Kunduz, I have come to see how discussions about the importance of politeness, civility and humanity to being a merchant, as much as debates on Islam or ethnic identity, animate their thinking and self-presentation.

Merchants and traders, far from presenting themselves as abject folk who have been forced to embarked on a degrading way of earning money by the circumstances of their country, often reflect in complex ways about how, even if they have been rendered into the lowly status of "shopkeepers" (*dukanadar*) by war in their country, they are still morally superior to Afghan politicians and commanders. On asking what a particular man is like or whether he is to be trusted, I am often told, "he is a trader, and therefore a good man". This general judgment recalls Montesquieu's famous remark that "wherever there is commerce there the manners of men are gentle".[26] Traders also often talk openly about the types of decisions they have made that led them to become traders in Central Asia rather than something else, somewhere else. Many, for example, continued to trade in Central Asia even after they were given documents that allowed them to travel as refugees to the West. They often relate their "decision" to stay to their family ties in Afghanistan: commitment to the family, indeed, is a critical aspect of their moral worlds. Yet others relate it to the lifestyle they have achieved in Dushanbe, and their ability to trade in prestigious goods—"I have a car, a flat, respect, and I import sugar from Poland, why would I go to London and drive a taxi or, more likely, become a dog-washer (*sag shu*)", one trader told me.

At the same time, a great deal of discussion concerns more abstract moral issues, especially the nature of humanity. Men discuss this question throughout the night. Some couch their arguments about what it is that ultimately distinguishes animals from humans in terms of the body; others advance theories about the uniqueness of human sentiments and emotions, such as those of love and compassion. Such debates often focus on the need to act in such a way as to ensure that humanity is sustained, rather than just taking its presence for granted. One of the most popular ways to index such forms of humanity-producing work is to highlight the refusal to talk about the divisive matter of ethnicity or *millat*. Discussions about *millat* are widely held by traders to have the capacity of turning humans into wild animals and thereby destroy the fragile peace of their everyday relations with one another. It is important, indeed, that many of these traders live temporarily in flats in Dushanbe that are ethnically mixed—one I know well housed a "Tajik" from Badakhshan, a "Pushtun" from Pagham who now lives in Kabul and a "Turkmen-speaker" from Maimana, as well as all their guests, for six months in the winter of 2010.

A further way in which morality is indexed and talked about by the traders is in relation to the values they hold about commitment to and success at their work. Such commitment and success are a major source of moral self worth. Success at work is talked about both in terms of providing for the family and, simultaneously, also as embodying commitments conflicting with those associated with family life: traders must work without thinking of immediate material gain, but for the sake of trade alone.[27] A whole range of skills are central to this endeavour, ranging from a complex mixture of self-discipline (avoiding throwing too much money away in unthinking acts of excess hospitality), risk-taking, the ability to be a dedicated trader, and, if a commission worker, being loyal yet never unthinkingly deferential to one's principal merchant (*tojir*). All of these dimensions of a trading life might lead to situations in which the family is left out of pocket or loyalty to the principal merchant is rated more important than family. Yet such courses of action, duly thought about and considered, are also important dimensions of traders' understanding of their own moral worth.

Anxieties about class and social mobility are a palpable dimension of these men's social and moral worlds. Relations between business partners, fragile at best, often come undone with questions about the so-called *kalan kari* (arrogance) of one partner in relation to another; the term *kalan kari* is often used by men to talk of a felt sense of being treated in a demeaning and servile manner by their partners. At the same time, however, anxieties about failed social mobility are also often critical to men's self-narratives: the aim for many is to stop working as a lowly *commission kor*, and instead to have one's own trading company and become a more sedentary type of merchant. Yet setbacks along the way, and powerful mafias of trading bosses and powerful politicians who request a cut of all profits made in their cities, mean that the aspiration to become a sedentary merchant is a mere dream for many, who complain that they are likely to finish life where their fathers left off: as lowly commission workers.

Such anxieties—especially acute in the off-season for mandarin trading when there is little to sell or trade in Dushanbe, or when a trader's business partner runs off to Moscow with his new wife leaving debts behind—are manifested in longrunning bouts of drinking, aggressive behaviour with flatmates, and even insulting the sacred guest. These moments of despair also often lead to fantastic talk (*khali gap*) about future dealings with millionaire Russian businessmen who will arrive in Dushanbe from Moscow any day soon with suitcases full of cash and lucrative contracts to export dried fruit to the Ukraine. At such times, the hastily established friendships of Afghan traders who have been sharing living spaces together for months break down as rumours spread that trader X thinks there is no other path left for his survival than to bring a consignment of heroin: a course of action that could compromise the business activities of all of those known to him, especially his flatmates. The response to such forms of behaviour by friends and associates often indicates how far a person's moral worth is considered in terms of his success at work: "he is crying and drinking and putting himself in a worse situation, but everybody's situation is difficult and behaving like this will be of no help to him".

These anxieties about moral self worth are deeply reminiscent of conflicts between "old-timers" and the "up-and-coming youth" in other contexts and professions.[28] There is much talk in Afghanistan and amongst Afghan traders in Dushanbe of a new legion of young men in shiny suits who are picked up by powerful merchants to represent their companies because they can speak English and go *tak tak tak* on the computer. Yet this new generation of traders are also said to know little of the practicalities of trade. There are also accused of being incapable of making those all-important connections with government officials and local populations: unlike the old guard who would not sleep for days on end in order to ensure that the products of "my merchant" crossed the region's multiple borders, the youngsters are unwilling to sacrifice much for trade.

Such changes in practices and the anxieties they produce cannot, however, be put down to a generational conflict alone: they reflect changes in the nature of trading in this space, and signal transformations, here as elsewhere, in the relationship between work and moral character. Some of my older informants, now in their forties, talk of trade as being run by young men who find information about the market through telephone conversations and the Internet rather than by speaking a wide variety of languages, keeping rigorous accounts, and using innate skills to "sense" the corrupt official who will take the bribe and allow the goods to pass. In contrast to older traders who speak fluent Russian, and have or had Russian girlfriends or wives and children in Moscow and Ashghabat to boot, these youngsters are dismissively said to have lived and traded in Tajikistan, Uzbekistan, Turkmenistan, and Kazakhstan without even having bothered to learn a word of Russian: "they get by in Uzbek and Kazakh, only speak with locals, but not deal with others". A sense of nostalgia exists, thus, for a more open or cosmopolitan past way of doing trade.

Conclusion

Afghan traders and merchants are playing an important and critical role in a wide variety of fields—political, economic and social—both in Afghanistan and in the wider region. These range from their importance to the emergence of Gulf-influenced market Islam in Kabul to the simultaneous construction of a transnational form of Persianate modernity in Tajikistan. Both these strands of the forms of cultural production in which traders are playing an important role are made possible by a constellation of Afghan merchants' wealth and their diasporic connections. They are also consumed by, and become markers of identification and cultural life for a transregional class of traders, entrepreneurs and businessmen that includes people from Pakistan, Iran and Central Asia. The thinking and identities of these men offer a unique glimpse into some of the complex dynamics currently shaping life in and around Afghanistan. They underscore the need to understand ethnicity in this context not simply in terms of the performance of difference, but in relation to people's socio-economic activities. Many traders seek to deny ethnicity's importance to their thinking and daily lives. They also see this attitude towards *millat* as being critical to their understandings of humanity. Afghan trading is something produced and adopted as a form of economic activity by people in the context of war. Yet it also builds on a very large pool of collective historical experience, and is now implicated in the production of new modes of identity, moral selfhood and standards of measuring self worth.

SECTION 3

CLASS, PATRONAGE AND THE STATE: BEYOND THE EXCEPTIONAL PASHTUN?

8

CLASS, PATRONAGE AND COERCION IN THE PAKISTANI PUNJAB AND IN SWAT

Nicolas Emilio Martin

Factional politics and military rule

Owing largely to efforts by successive military governments, class-based political mobilisation has not taken place in Pakistan since the 1970s when Zulfikar Ali Bhutto rose to power.[1] Through "divide-and-rule", by placing restrictions on political parties and opponents, and by undermining the impartiality of state institutions such as the judiciary and the police, military governments ensured the entrenchment of factional politics where elite-led political coalitions, whose membership cuts across ties of caste and class, compete for appropriation of the spoils of power. This type of politics was described by Barth for Swat but was by no means unique to the valley, or to the Pakhtuns. Alavi described similar political arrangements for the Punjab, and Nicholas, Bailey, and Brass for different parts of India.[2]

These accounts written in the 1960s and 70s described situations where political contests were power struggles within a ruling class that had monopoly control over key political and economic resources. This monopoly allowed leaders to exercise the power and patronage necessary to obtain the political allegiance of members of dependent social groups. In this chapter I use ethnography from the Punjab to argue that Pakistani elites continue to have monopoly control over key political and economic resources, but the patronage relations and hierarchies that kept vertical factional alliances together have been undermined by the Pakistani state and by capitalism. Because these changes are due to broader state structures and economic changes affecting all of Pakistan, I suggest that the ethnography from the Punjab can shed light on political trends in Swat. I argue that because political parties have not stepped in to replace traditional patrons, militant Islamic outfits have started to do so in their stead. Thus this chapter, like those by Abou Zahab and Nichols, show that the rise of Islamic militancy has more to do with the breakdown of traditional hierarchies and patronage relations than with something inherent to Pakhtun culture or ethnicity.

The ethnography of the Punjab shows how the Pakistani state has played a salient role in consolidating the power of its landed classes and prevented the emergence of class-based political movements that might challenge them.[3] I argue that it has given members of the landed classes greater scope to exploit labourers, sharecroppers and artisans. I suggest that the antagonistic class relations between Pakhtuns and their clients posited by Asad[4] in his critique of Barth only really start to emerge with the emergence of broader state structures.[5] Prior to the emergence of the state, Asad's critique of Barth's emphasis on hierarchy tempered by mutuality in relations between patrons and clients does not entirely hold, because Pakhtuns depended on clients to protect their land and fight rivals, and this set limits both to exploitation and to the emergence of overt class antagonism. A Pakhtun who was excessively exploitative risked losing his clients, and therefore eventually his land, to rivals. According to Barth[6] this was less true with the advent of the state because Pakhtuns no longer needed to gain the allegiance of clients to secure their landownership but could instead rely on the state security apparatus. This led him to argue that the relationship between Pakhtuns and their clients became restricted to the "purely economic contract".[7]

This chapter broadly agrees with Barth's verdict and shows how the ties of patronage that once mitigated the exploitation of clients by landlords in Pakistan have been replaced by more impersonal and contractual ones.[8] I argue that various factors in addition to the Pakistani state contributed to this. These include the mechanisation of agriculture, the decline of village crafts, and the increasingly urban and middle class lifestyles of landlords. Such capitalist transformations are global, and increasingly contractual relations between landlords and clients have also been reported by anthropologists studying neighbouring India.[9]

These transformations mean that erstwhile village craftsmen and tenants can earn their livelihoods independently of landlords. They also allow landlords to spend less time in their home villages supervising agricultural tasks and more time pursuing consumerist lifestyles in towns. As a result their relationship with villagers has become increasingly impersonal and restricted to key times in the agricultural cycle, and to election times when they seek people's votes by bribery or the use or threat of coercion. In this paper I suggest that these developments have deprived the majority of the rural population of access to key state institutions controlled by an absentee landed elite. This, combined with insecurity of life and property resulting from violent conflicts between rival leaders, has exacerbated grievances fuelling movements such as the Taliban in Swat or the Sipah-e Sahaba in the Punjab.

At least part of the reason why socially marginalised groups have resorted to violence is that they have no institutional means to redress their grievances. Pakistan's political parties basically represent different factions within the landowning and industrial classes. This is shown in the widespread phenomenon of politicians switching back and forth between parties, and families fielding their members to different political parties in order to assure themselves parliamentary seats.[10]

Evidence suggests that the only time in Pakistan's history when political parties did represent popular aspirations and interests besides those of the landed elites was when Zulfiqar Ali Bhutto obtained his popular mandate in 1970. At the time, vertical factional political coalitions comprising landlords and their clients were briefly replaced by horizontal ones comprising landlords on one side and the landless on the other. In rural areas Bhutto's promise of land and homestead reforms and the abolition of corvée labour enlisted the support of tenants, landless labourers and artisans. These groups hoped that the Pakistan People's Party would pursue their interests against "the classes and institutions that had weighed upon [them] so heavily and for so long—the zamindariat, the police, the bureaucracy and the courts".[11] Accordingly, Jones shows how tenants and the landless, emboldened by the mass support generated by Bhutto, voted for the PPP in villages across Pakistan, against the instructions of the dominant landlords. Jones further shows that many landlords, faced with a challenge to their political and economic hegemony, set aside the violent rivalries and feuds between them in order to defeat the PPP. It is therefore clear that, regardless of the degree to which Bhutto really did represent the interests of the working classes, his rise to power did briefly create class politics (in distinction to factional politics) and a challenge to the ruling landed class (see also Nichols in this volume for an account of how the rise of the PPP affected patron-client ties in Swat).

Subsequently, under the US-backed dictatorship of General Zia ul Haq, the political and economic dominance of the landed elite was reasserted. Class struggle was subdued and politics reverted to its previous elitism. Under Zia's regime landlords were protected from a second round of land reforms, and courts reverted to being unsympathetic to the claims of tenants. The military regime prevented the sort of mass mobilisation that had occurred in Bhutto's time through a large-scale repression of the PPP-led political opposition, and by holding non-party local body elections. Like Pakistani military rulers before and after him (General Ayub Khan and General Musharraf), Zia used the pretext of devolving power to revert to a "colonial" mode of politics, whereby politicians were elected on the basis of local ties of caste, tribe, faction and tenurial relations. By fragmenting the political landscape, Zia succeeded in forestalling the emergence of large-scale popular movements such as the one witnessed during Bhutto's rise to power. Zia's divide-and-rule tactics also coincided with the influx of heroin and cheap weapons during and after the Afghan Jihad. The combination resulted in a highly fractious polity teeming with deadly factional, ethnic and sectarian conflicts.

Middle-aged Punjabi labourers and tenants whom I interviewed recalled Bhutto's rise to power as a time of great hope. These hopes were subsequently dashed, and the plight of the rural poor was made worse both by the growing criminalisation of politics and by the fact that landlords ignored their obligations as patrons once they took up increasingly removed urban middle class lifestyles. Absentee landlords with control over armed toughs, and working in collusion with the police, increasingly used coercion rather than patronage in order to obtain the labour and votes of the rural population. Often they also added the murderously competitive business of heroin trafficking to their various predatory activities. The failure to challenge the local fiefdoms of powerful landlords working with the police and local officials in a symbiosis of private interest, the repeated undermining of the judiciary by authoritarian governments which manipulated it to harass whomever happened to be in the political opposition, and the widespread availability of cheap weapons and drugs all created a fertile environment for the proliferation of crime. Drug trafficking combined with the availability of cheap Kalashnikovs also made traditional village rivalries—often between agnates—more bloody than ever. As will be argued, landless villagers suffered greatly from these conflicts, not least because they were often the ones fighting on behalf of the landlords. Moreover, addiction to the heroin that landlords and their allies peddled also ruined many of their lives. In combination, all of these factors have come to make people's lives and livelihoods chronically insecure, and have arguably fuelled militant Islamic movements that promise to bring impartial Islamic justice and government.

The politics of enmity and dependence in Bek Sagrana

Many politicians who rose to power in Pakistan from the 1960s belonged to middle-ranking landed castes that benefited from the "Green Revolution" and from state patronage under Ayub Khan. Although they did not necessarily own much land at first, they had influence over the local arms of the state, which they used to great personal advantage.[12] Some of the most influential politicians in the Punjabi district of Sargodha—where I carried out my fieldwork—had started their political careers in the 1960s with little more than ten acres of land, but thirty years later owned hundreds of acres as well as factories, petrol stations and sugar mills. They achieved this by using their local muscle-power and influence to usurp the political power of the older class of aristocratic landlords (locally the Makhdooms). Although the latter owned vast tracts of land they had in many cases ceased wielding significant political power because they were unwilling to use force to maintain their political influence. Besides political influence, these aristocratic families also started losing their land to the new class of predatory politicians and their allies.

In the central Punjabi village of Bek Sagrana the Gondal landlords (*zamindars*) were the dominant lineage and some of its members belonged to this upwardly mobile category of politicians. Members of the lineage in the village all shared a common apical ancestor four generations back, and they generally married endogamously, with first and second cousin marriage being very common.[13] They made up fourteen of the 120 households in the village and owned most of its land. The Bek Sagrana Gondals not only controlled formal and informal institutions at the village level, several of them had also become politically influential at district, provincial and even national levels.

Their rise to regional political prominence had taken place in the 1970s when Zulfikar Ali Bhutto rose to power. Prior to the 1970s a lineage of Makhdoom saints (*pirs*), who owned thousands of acres in the neighbouring village of Daulatpur, had controlled both provincial and national assembly seats in the area. During this time the Bek Sagrana Gondals had been united in opposition to them, but it was only with Bhutto's rise to power that they overtook them in terms of political power and influence. People like the Gondals, who constituted an intermediate-ranking landlord class, were not the target of the PPP's anti-feudal rhetoric, and were in fact able to benefit from its popular appeal. They did this by presenting themselves as populists who shared the interests and cultural outlook of locals, and by distinguishing themselves from the more cosmopolitan Makhdooms who preferred the air-conditioning in Lahore to the heat, dust and rustic company of village life. More than thirty years later the sons and grandsons of the Gondals who had risen to power in the 1970s regarded village life much as the Makhdooms had earlier. They too now lived in Lahore and only returned to Bek Sagrana to supervise the citrus and wheat harvests, or to run in elections when it suited them. Political office made them, their relatives, friends and close supporters rich.

One Gondal, Chowdri Mazhar Ali, started his political career in the 1980s with 70 acres of canal-irrigated land; by 1999 he owned over 400 acres, several petrol stations and two houses in Sargodha. Political office provided Chowdri Mazhar Ali and his relatives and friends with various opportunities for illegal self-enrichment. It also gave them the influence over the police necessary to engage in heroin trafficking, bootlegging and buffalo theft without hindrance.[14] During their time in office, Chowdri Mazhari Ali and his elder brother provided friends and relatives with government building contracts, government jobs and favour with the police and the courts. Although the village of Bek Sagrana acquired a school, a water tower, a basic health unit, a wedding hall and a post office through their political influence, the average villager in fact gained little from these public infrastructure projects. Not surprisingly, the main beneficiaries of them were the Gondals and their friends. Other than the school, no one of the buildings and facilities was used for its original purpose. The doctor in charge of the basic health unit, who was given the job by his uncle Chowdri Mazhar Ali, claimed his wages but spent his days running a private clinic in town; he only occasionally came to the unit to make fake entries in the attendance register. The government bungalow built next to the basic health unit was used by one of the village landlords to host private parties, where guests were entertained with dancing girls and alcohol. The water tower was unused because people preferred to have free water from their hand-pumps. The post office was used to store the wheat of a Gondal landlord, and Chowdri Mazhar Ali's younger brother turned the communal wedding hall into his personal residence.

The case of the Bek Sagrana Gondals illustrates the importance of understanding the political and economic fortunes of local chiefs and leaders with reference to the Pakistani state. Even though the Gondals had not been particularly powerful prior to Bhutto's rise to power, it was their influence over local state institutions that had allowed them to emerge as powerful politicians. This influence dated back to colonial rule, when the British entrusted the Gondals with key aspects of the delivery of public services within the area of Bek Sagrana. These included administration, revenue collection, policing, dispute resolution and general intermediation between the state and villagers. Chowdri Mazhar Ali and his family provide a good example of this sort of insider involvement and positioning: before entering provincial level politics in the 1970s, Chowdri Mazhar Ali was a lawyer with plenty of connections in the local judiciary, his younger brother worked in the district administration and one of his half-brothers worked in the land revenue department. Influence over state institutions such as the judiciary and the land revenue department was useful to politicians because it helped them conclude the court cases and land disputes of their close friends and relatives favourably, and thereby gain their votes and political loyalty.

Such influence was more important for the acquisition of clients than landownership. Land alone could only provide landlords with the support of direct dependants working and living on it, whereas influence over state institutions gave them power over a much broader range of people through the ability to grant and withhold patronage strategically. Most significantly, this strategic granting and withholding of patronage allowed them to influence landowning relatives and friends, who could deliver the political allegiance and votes of their own labourers and tenants.

Part of the reason for politicians' ability to appropriate the powers of the state relates to the way the authoritarian central governments rewarded political supporters. The Gondals particularly benefited from the unprecedented levels of patronage doled out by Nawaz Sharif when he was Chief Minister of the Punjab under Zia and later Prime Minister.[15] In the manner typical of this patronage, the Gondals obtained profitable licenses for the extraction of sand, and contracts for various infrastructure building projects (the school, hospital, post office, water tower and communal wedding hall mentioned above were all gained during Nawaz Sharif's terms in office). Moreover, Nawaz Sharif was known to have frequently ordered the transfer of police officers who hindered or failed to cooperate with corrupt party members. Accordingly, police officers who did not want to be transferred to remote posts had to turn a blind eye to, or actively participate in, illegal activities such as land grabbing, cattle rustling and drug trafficking.

Conversely, landlords who failed to get involved in politics or others who remained in the political opposition tended to see their fortunes diminish as rivals and enemies with power used their influence to deprive them of patronage and mire them in bureaucratic processes (especially by entangling them in court cases). The idea that people who were out of office were deprived of patronage was frequently illustrated by the Pakistani saying that if you wanted to know if the leader of a village was in office, all you needed to do was look at the state of its roads. If they were potholed and crumbling it meant that the village chief was either in the opposition or simply not involved in politics. However, potholed roads were arguably less of a worry for opposition politicians than the risk that their rivals in power might snare them in fabricated court cases or grab their land. Through the power opportunities that politics provided (including easy access to and influence over the courts and police) the state was implicated not only in the making and unmaking of ruling elites but also in the political conflicts between them.

In the village of Bek Sagrana infighting among the Gondals started once the Makhdooms had been politically displaced, and the two main Gondal rivals for village leadership—who shared a great-grandfather—took turns putting each other in jail as they took turns in power. At the time of my fieldwork, Abdullah Gondal had been affiliated with Musharraf's government and had managed to get the National Accountability Bureau to bring corruption charges against his rival, Mazhar Ali Gondal, and to have him jailed for a year. The main charge against Mazhar Ali Gondal was that he had illegally occupied the government-built communal wedding hall. At the same time Abdullah Gondal also managed to deprive Mazhar Ali Gondal of access to a World Bank-funded irrigation project in Bek Sagrana. However, things turned around dramatically when Musharraf's government fell in 2008 and Abdullah Gondal suddenly found himself in the opposition against Mazhar Ali Gondal, who had close ties with Nawaz Sharif and the new ruling coalition. Abdullah Gondal soon found himself entangled in a court case and prosecuted for illegally cultivating rice on government land, which resulted in his being jailed for several months. In both cases Abdullah Gondal and Mazhar Ali were guilty as charged, but the only reason they were prosecuted was that they happened to be in the opposition to successive governments. So long as they had been aligned with the ruling coalition, whoever that happened to be, they had enjoyed virtually complete impunity against investigation and prosecution.

By taking turns undermining the impartiality of the judiciary and the civil bureaucracy in order to attack rivals and strengthen supporters, authoritarian civilian and military central governments contributed strongly to sharp reversals of local fortune and exacerbated rivalries. When General Musharraf tampered with the constitution, repeatedly ordered the transfer of uncooperative judges and used the judiciary to prosecute members of the opposition selectively, he was following in the footsteps of his predecessors. His anti-corruption watchdog, the National Accountability Bureau, was like Nawaz Sharif's Ehtesab Cells in that it was used to prosecute political opponents, and it was well known for letting pro-government politicians with proven track records of crime and corruption off the hook. In at least one instance the National Accountability Bureau even dropped its corruption charges against a powerful landlord-politician when he agreed to abandon the opposition and join Musharraf's ruling coalition. Moreover, like Nawaz Sharif and Benazir Bhutto, Musharraf also ordered the large-scale transfers of uncooperative bureaucrats and police officers in order to benefit supporters. This happened particularly before elections, when pro-government judges, police officers and bureaucrats where strategically deployed in order to ensure electoral success.[16]

In this political environment, landlord politicians like Mazhar Ali and Abdullah Gondal, along with their close followers, faced a great deal of personal insecurity. When out of power they faced the prospect of being sent to jail or of having their land encroached upon by rivals. They also risked being killed in gunfights that readily erupted over land disputes and elections. Abdullah's youngest brother was killed in a gunfight and his second brother walked with a limp as a result of a bullet wound suffered during elections in the 1990s. On the other side of the feud, Mazhar Ali's nephew, one of his uncle's faithful supporters, also walked with a limp as a result of a bullet wound gained in similar local warfare.

While for landlord politicians violence and insecurity were the high but nevertheless productive cost of riches and power, this was not true for the majority landless population. Violent factional conflict affected the rural poor more than it did their overlords. When factional strife amongst the Gondals of Bek Sagrana reached its peak in the 1990s it was poor villagers acting as gunmen who suffered the greatest number of casualties in the violence. Gunmen complained that their masters stayed indoors watching Bollywood films in air-conditioned rooms while they fought at their behest. Moreover, villagers who had nothing to do with these conflicts lived in fear of stray bullets and of gunmen who got drunk and became abusive towards them. Unchecked by their masters, some gunmen took on attitudes of haughtiness and arrogance typical of landlords. They coerced villagers, sent them on errands, and some even took people's livestock.

The heads of the two village factions were able to escape the stray bullets and fighting by moving to newly built farmhouses amidst their citrus orchards, but such a move was not an option for the majority of villagers. The village leaders' move out of the village was in fact emblematic of their growing distance from local affairs and dereliction of their obligations as patrons. Since the 1970s influential Gondals were spending more time in the towns and cities of the Punjab than in the village. The men's community meeting house of the village, where patrons and clients had once gathered in the evenings—much as they did in the men's community meeting houses described by Barth (1959) in the case of Swat—was now mostly empty. Unlike their parents and grandparents, the youngest generation of Gondals no longer went to school in the village, so that they never acquired the same intimacy with villagers that their predecessors once had. Members of the artisan and menial castes, the *kammi*s, complained that it was now very difficult to obtain patronage from the Gondals because the Gondals rarely came to the village; and, they said, even when the Gondals were around they ignored their problems. One *kammi* related that if a poor man knocked on a Gondal's door because his child was dying the servants would turn him away, claiming their master was either ill or away; the reason, the *kammi* said, was that the Gondals had become greedy and were now solely concerned with material things and status. The *kammi*s claimed that the Gondals only showed concern for their welfare during election times, when they needed votes.

Various factors contributed to this growing distance between landlords and villagers. To begin with, the large-scale introduction of tractors in the 1960s meant that landlords who had once begged sharecroppers to cultivate their land could now cultivate it with a single tractor driver.[17] Secondly, the introduction of citrus orchards in the 1970s, similar to the introduction of mango orchards in rural Indian Gujarat,[18] meant that the Gondal landlords could pursue urban middle class lifestyles which involved spending as little time in the fields supervising labourers as possible. Because citrus orchards required far less labour than crops such as sugar cane, cotton and maize, the Gondals were able to get away with minimal supervisory responsibility and could spend increasing amounts of time in town, where they dealt in property and sent their children to expensive private schools. Thirdly, the introduction of cheap mass-produced goods replacing goods traditionally produced by artisans also meant that landlords employed fewer villagers for the production of things such as shoes, clay pots or clothes. And finally, the fortunes that many Gondals gained through power politics obviously further facilitated their move to the cities, and out of the village, for long periods.

Although many villagers welcomed the possibility of no longer having to work directly for frequently abusive and exploitative landlords, their lives came to be marked by greater economic uncertainty than in the past. It became common for a growing population of labourers to seek work outside the village during low periods of agricultural activity. Labourers from Bek Sagrana lived like wage hunter-gatherers, often spending some months of the year working in construction, a few more months working in some factory and the rest working in the fields in and around the village during the citrus and wheat harvests. On top of this, even though the Gondal landlords were no longer the direct principal employers, they nevertheless continued to expect the deference, loyalty and labour of the villagers, and they retained the political and economic influence necessary to extract these. Most labourers continued to live on land owned or claimed by the Gondals.[19] This meant that they could be evicted by Gondal landlords if the latter felt they were insufficiently obedient. House tenants and sharecroppers were expected to perform errands and odd jobs for their landlords free of charge, and they were often expected to vote according to their landlord's wishes during elections. In some cases they could even be expected to pick up arms and fight against their landlord's rivals. In the very worst cases some Gondal landlords were known to use the threat of eviction to coerce sexual favours from female tenants.

The Gondals' control over access to key state institutions such as the police, the judiciary, the land revenue and irrigation departments, hospitals and even schools also contributed crucially to their power over villagers. For example, through their influence and connections with the Punjab police, landlords could free people from jail and have charges against them dropped. They could even protect people from the police itself, a force of law and order known more popularly for its involvement in extortion rackets and other criminal activities. Similarly, if people needed to be treated in a hospital they needed to go through a Gondal landlord to obtain their treatment. Many doctors, including the one at the Basic Health unit in Bek Sagrana, did not attend to their jobs because they were running their own businesses and private clinics. In order to see one of these absentee doctors villagers generally required the backing of a Gondal landlord; he would write a short note to a doctor who owed him a favour or was a friend, asking for a client to be seen.

Those local people who showed excessive independence from the landlords were likely to face great difficulties obtaining protection, justice, healthcare and loans. Without the patronage of a Gondal landlord ordinary villagers needed to pay significant bribes even to have an interview with a police officer, and to pay expensive fees to get medical treatment at private clinics.[20] It was also very difficult for people to obtain small consumption loans or larger loans without a landlord patron. Because the introduction of citrus orchards had created long periods of slack demand for agricultural labour there were times when labourers temporarily pledged their labour to landlords in exchange for small consumption loans.[21] These small loans rarely equalled more than three months' worth of wages and were repaid within a matter of months. On the other hand, wedding or medical expenses often equalled several years' wages, and without the help of able-bodied siblings labourers could spend their entire lives repaying them.

Thus it is clear that, even though labourers were often no longer under the direct control of their absentee Gondal landlords, they were still subject to them in various ways. Patronage, which had previously enjoyed some reciprocity on both parties, however unequally, was now even more of a one-way relationship of benefit to the landlords with scant obligation attached. One reason was that the landlords were far less involved in dealing with village problems and disputes than in the past, because they spent more and more time in town. Their distance from the village meant that they were less aware of the local situation and could more easily ignore problems there. In addition, their increasingly urban orientation meant that many Gondals preferred spending their time and money on activities and entertainments in the cities rather than in the villages. They now viewed these as places from which they could extract incomes and votes in order to fund their urban lifestyles and the costs of sending their children to prestigious schools and universities abroad. One outcome of this distance was that the landlords began to discharge their formerly more complex local obligations to labourers and villagers by simply paying them for their labour, so that they themselves could ignore their broader traditional responsibilities as patrons. Even in the sphere of politics, villagers complained that the Gondals' newly acquired practice of paying for votes meant that they limited their political duties towards the electorate to a one-off payment; having paid for people's votes, the Gondals believed that they had no further obligation towards them.

The progressive withdrawal of the landlords from village life, and the increased difficulty for villagers to gain favourable treatment and have their grievances heard through the previous reciprocities of patronage, had direct and ongoing local effects as well. The withdrawal of the landlords from everyday village life left a power vacuum that allowed a variety of petty tyrants involved in bootlegging and drug dealing to bully and harass villagers. These were either poorer landlords who had not been able to move out of the village and who acted as power brokers for more powerful Gondals, or landless villagers who occasionally acted as gunmen for the more powerful Gondals. These people typically played cards, drank and dealt drugs from the men's community meeting house (*darra*), where the village chiefs had once gathered to resolve village disputes, gossip and smoke hookahs. Ordinary villagers now feared walking past the *darra* because they risked being insulted and pressed into performing various menial services. People claimed that in the past the Gondal chiefs would never have allowed such disorder and vice to flourish in the village. Nostalgic old men frequently told me that the Gondals of old would never have tolerated drugs and public drunkenness, and had even ensured that men always wore their turbans and that women did not linger to talk to men in the streets. Although these claims may have been tinged by nostalgia for a safer, more predictable village life, it is logical to assume that it had been in the landlords' own interest to maintain order and harmony in the village when they lived in the village themselves.

Conclusions

Since the rural elite's capture of the state at the local level, and its increasingly urban orientation, are phenomena that are common throughout Pakistan—because they are the result of national state structures and global capitalist transformations—the Punjab ethnography presented in this chapter can help shed light, and raise questions, about the present day political sociology of Swat. Although further research on contemporary politics in Swat is necessary, the available evidence suggests that similar processes of state capture and elite withdrawal are at play there. In fact the evidence suggests that the failure of landlords to act as patrons for the poor is contributing to the rise of Islamic militancy in Swat as it is in parts of the Punjab.

Following Barth I have argued that the advent of the Swat state, followed by that of the Pakistani state, transformed relations between Pakhtun chiefs and their clients. It basically made the security of Pakhtun chiefs less dependent on their ability to mobilise clients, meaning that they could spend less time trying to attract clients through the exercise of patronage. Subsequently, because democracy never gained a secure foothold in the country, the rural electorate was unable to force landlords to act as patrons. Had democracy and popular political parties established themselves more securely, landlords would have been under pressure to share some of the spoils of power with the poor; those who did not would have risked losing their elected positions and maybe even their government jobs.[22] Instead, authoritarian rule allowed them to continue treating the state as their private fiefdom.

This chapter has illustrated how, by treating the state as their private property, landlords deprived people of access to healthcare, communal spaces, justice and a decent education. Instead of government services, landless villagers got small amounts of cash in exchange for their votes. Less fortunate villagers were told whom to vote for; failure to comply could result in the loss of employment and housing. In both instances patronage as an ongoing relation of reciprocity between landlords and clients was absent. This chapter also illustrated how elite appropriation of the state generated violence, crime and political instability because politicians manipulated the police and the judiciary in order to pursue criminal activities and victimise rivals. I showed how those who suffered the most from all this were the rural poor who were left at the mercy of local toughs who trafficked drugs and harassed them.

Given the virtual absence of leftist political parties after General Zia-ul Haq's decade in power, Islamic militant groups became a channel for the expression of popular grievances. This was the case particularly, but not solely, in the Pakhtun areas, because of their proximity to Afghanistan as well as their historical association with state-backed *jihad*s in Kashmir and Afghanistan. In the Punjab, and particularly in the south of the province, class grievances were channelled by sectarian Sunni organisations, such as the Sipah-i-Sahaba, that decried the abuses of the predominantly Shia rural magnates.[23] One cause of the Sipah-i-Sahaba's popularity in the district of Jhang derived from the fact that it gave people access to justice of which the landed elites had effectively deprived them. Thus Haq-Nawaz Jhangvi, the leader of the organisation, used his influence to obtain justice for people both through the elite dominated official judicial system and through informal sharia courts. Similarly the Tehrik-i-Nifaz-i-Shariat-i-Muhammadi (TNSM), otherwise referred to as the Swat Taliban, channelled popular grievances by decrying the elite controlled official justice system and calling for the implementation of sharia law. When the TNSM took over the Swat valley in 2009 it gained some popular support by putting landlords to flight and encouraging sharecroppers and labourers to cut down their masters' orchards and sell the wood for personal profit. Although the Taliban are reported to have subsequently taken the place of the landlords and pressed the tenants into work for them, they are also said to have acquired a degree of popularity by scrapping the elite-dominated official justice system and replacing it with rough-and-ready sharia courts. However, neither the Sipah-i-Sahaba's policies nor the TNSM's indicate that they are replacing vertical forms of solidarity with horizontal ones; rather than offering the disaffected poor a platform for empowerment, they offer them alternative channels of patronage.

In conclusion, a thorough consideration of the dynamics of class interaction, and the ways that the state has been and continues to be involved in creating and sustaining them, is central to understanding the political situation in both the rural Punjab and Swat. Such a focus helps shed light on the causes of violent factional politics, and also helps to elucidate the grievances that are fuelling the breakdown of stability, and facilitating militancy, at the local level in both regions.[24]

9

EXCEPTIONAL PASHTUNS?

CLASS POLITICS, IMPERIALISM AND HISTORIOGRAPHY

Nancy Lindisfarne

Distanced, top-down political analyses dominate the recent literature on the Taliban, while much of Middle East social science writing has focused on ethnicity or tribalism or has been imbued with Islamophobia. This work diverts attention from the old story of imperial over-reach in three ways. First, Pashtuns are made to seem exceptional and incomparable; second, class analyses disappear; and thirdly, a coherent theory of imperial competition is hidden by the powerful discourse of the War on Terror. Yet to understand the anthropology of Swat and the Taliban resistance in Swat and Afghanistan, it is important to return to questions of class, and to what Asad has called "ethnographies of imperial hegemony"[1] via attention to the lives of ordinary people, understood holistically, and in intimate, complex detail.[2]

Anthropology and the Middle East

The ethnography of the Middle East,[3] compared with that of other regions, has always been rather poor. By 1995 Lindholm went so far as to describe Middle Eastern ethnography as in "deep crisis".[4] Historians of the Middle East, political scientists and investigative journalists all seem to cope rather better, probably because, unlike anthropologists, they are not professionally committed, as anthropologists are, to analyses from below.[5]

One problem for anthropologists is that the old imperial politics of the Cold War, and the new imperial politics between China and India and the US, are not remote from the field. Oil and strategic geography bring imperialism very close to people's everyday lives—and so to the very stuff of ethnographic descriptions. Folk models of the region are about local groups, but also about class, money, land, local tyranny, state power and imperialism—all of them understood in quite secular terms. Should anthropologists give accurate ethnographic accounts of how ordinary Middle Easterners see the world, they are likely to end up writing sophisticated, radical critiques of Western European and American imperialism.

For many anthropologists, this is just too near the bone. So they have tended to focus on the topics which seem "to belong" to the discipline. This has made "tribes", "sects" and "ethnic groups" disproportionately important. Others are rightly concerned about what it is safe to say without bringing harm to informants. Or they worry about being thrown out of the field, or having difficulties getting published or finding an academic job.

Certainly, there is a deep reluctance among many anthropologists to acknowledge their personal politics as an integral part of their theories and ethnographies.[6] In part, this is because, as professionals, anthropologists are expected to be politically agnostic: a holistic approach is the *sine qua non* of the discipline, while cultural relativism, in its weak form, is a source of much-vaunted disciplinary pride. But equally, such radical local critiques are likely to impinge closely on the anthropologist's own politics and class position at home. These contradictions leave anthropologists in an awkward spot and prone to dissembling. In the case of Afghanistan, in recent decades this tension has been particularly acute.[7]

There is, of course, a tradition of resistance in the Middle East, but it results in few academic publications taking an oppositional stance.[8] This means that anthropologists too can find themselves isolated, at which point speaking truth to power becomes not just fraught but frightening. By comparison, managing the relation between folk models, local politics and the anthropologist's personal politics is much easier for foreign and Indian anthropologists writing on India. This is because India is a democracy, with a strong radical traditional of opposition, among intellectuals certainly but also, more important, in the popular politics of the unions, communist parties, Dalits, *adivasi*s and others. Or, consider Latin America, where local folk models often are, as amongst Afghans, remarkably clear-sighted about material wealth and political control. In both India and Latin America there is an established academic, and often explicitly Marxist, left, and both foreign and local anthropologists have consistently produced vibrant, challenging ethnographies. These examples suggest that in the Middle East there is less space, and far less tolerance, for critiques of state power from below.

Another problem lies in the history of the discipline. Early anthropologists were concerned to demonstrate ethnographically that the "natives" were fully human "like us", and the disciplinary disposition remains. Anthropologists continue to focus on difference, then use comparison to reconcile differences into sameness. However, if such efforts are to be useful today, they need to go beyond what was apparently exotic (kinship systems, witchcraft and the Kula) and instead consider those people, such as Islamists and the Taliban, whose beliefs and practices are now at best treated as exotic, and at worst demonised and to be suppressed. But to explain the Taliban in terms of what they say and do requires anthropologists to engage with the explicitly political debates of the world we all share. Otherwise anthropology risks irrelevance and is emptied of credible intellectual or moral content.[9]

Because of the disciplinary commitment to understanding the lives of ordinary people, it is likely that today a majority of anthropologists are left-leaning. This is clear from the collective outcry from the profession against an association between anthropology and the Human Terrain Teams in Iraq and Afghanistan,[10] but it is certainly not inevitable. Anthropologists come in all political stripes and whatever their politics, as anthropologists they do not necessarily have cogent or compelling explanations of the global economic and political systems that are more accurate, or moral, than other, competing explanations. This leaves many anthropologists confused about taking sides. So they often ignore issues of class and empire, which have implications for their own professional and private lives, while losing themselves in explorations of difference—as construed in exotic tribal, ethnic, sectarian, cultural and gendered terms.

Class analyses and resistance to imperialism

While virtually every anthropologist writing on Afghanistan mentions the "Great Game", for most it is a blocking metaphor, one that seems to say it all and thus stifles further inquiry. Beyond the problems of taking sides, studies which marry theories of imperialism with ethnography are quite rare, compared with those with an historical bias.[11] The cross-disciplinary skills and confidence needed to bridge seemingly incommensurate differences of scale are daunting. But there is also a confusion whereby colonialism and imperialism are treated as synonymous. Yet clearly a study about social relations in a settlement occupied for economic gain differs fundamentally from one which investigates how the global economic system impacts on the lives of ordinary people around the world. Colonialism is just one aspect of an imperial system, and studies can reproduce an exoticising distance between the metropolitan rich and the far-flung poor. Theorising imperialism obliges the student to consider the nexus of global inequality in causal terms.

Both right and left wing theories of imperialism owe a considerable debt to early Marxist thinking.[12] Later accounts in their different ways build on three basic ideas which are key to understanding imperialism: centralisation, competition and resistance.[13] Let me outline them briefly.

Centralisation is fundamental: capital tends towards monopoly and capitalists increasingly turn to the state to further their interests. In this way different sections of the ruling class become intimately intertwined, and with this process comes militarisation. The aim is to compete for control of the world economic system, in terms of both resources and markets. The growth of the arms industry is part of the same centralisation that fuels the war in the Congo, and allows Coke and the dollar to dominate world markets.

However, this process is never straightforward because of competition between rival centres of capital accumulation. Rivalries between major powers resulted in the devastation of the First and Second World Wars. Then the Cold War between the US and the Soviet Union led to the horrors of Vietnam and the Soviet war in Afghanistan. In the last decade rivalry has shifted to that between three centres, the US, the EU and East Asia. To overcome its economic weaknesses in the world setting, the US government has capitalised (literally) on its military ascendancy and systematically militarised economic competition, especially for oil and gas. As Gilles Dorronsoro suggests, "It could also be asked whether the increasing militarisation of American politics is not primarily a reflection of the relative decline of the United States in the international scene".[14]

In short, there is an intrinsic connection between domestic and foreign policy. A good place to begin understanding resistance to imperial domination is to consider exploitation *within* each centre of capitalist power as well as between them. This requires a class analysis—that is, a relational understanding of how the interests of the ruling class differ from those of middle and working class people whose labour is the source of profit.

In this respect, it is at least as important to understand the American state, economy and society as it is to understand Afghans and Afghanistan. Equally, to make sense of resistance to imperial competitions we need to understand the link between imperial elites and the national elites of even the poorest countries on earth, and the shared conditions and interests of the working women and men in wealthy and poor states alike. We cannot explain the International Brigade in the Spanish Civil War, foreign fighters in Afghanistan, Stop-the-War demonstrations around the world, protests in the German parliament over the bombing of civilians in Kunduz,[15] the 11,000 British soldiers who have gone AWOL since 2003,[16] or the WikiLeaks revelations,[17] if we don't make connections between imperial and national elites, and the related connections between workers under pressure—whether these workers are college professors, construction workers or soldiers in the US, the UK, Afghanistan and Pakistan.

We know about the weapons of the weak.[18] We also know about strikes and demonstrations for social justice, better working conditions and health care. People can also choose other forms of defiance, including non-violent and armed resistance. In the English and French Revolutions, and for the Communists in Afghanistan, the targets were the King and the aristocracy. In other settings, workers and national elites together have fought to end an imperial occupation, as happened in the American Revolution and with the Congress in India, and is happening in complex new variations in Afghanistan and Iraq and during the Arab Spring of 2011.

Unclarity about resistance leads to a confusion that is easily exploited via the dominant discourse of empire today—Islamophobia and the rhetoric of the War on Terror. When this happens, Iraqi fighters or the Taliban are portrayed as aberrant, isolated and exceptional. But no war is ever only one-sided. To understand present resistance in Iraq and Afghanistan, it is important to hold on to two different ideas at the same time. Bush, Obama and American imperialism are undoubtedly bad for most people around the world; but the tyranny of Saddam, and the oppression of the Taliban, were also bad for most of the people of Iraq and Afghanistan. The Taliban are a response to imperial competition, just as the War on Terror is a response to Taliban resistance. The relation is best explained in terms of class and the imperial process itself.

How imperial conflicts end depends on imperial competition. Certainly the Karzai government "exists solely as a consequence of international military and financial aid, the continuation of which depends on considerations beyond the control of Afghans themselves".[19] It also depends on the character of class struggle at home. Thus the possible success of the Taliban is connected to the economic meltdown in Europe and America, its effect on class politics and on public commitment to the war, as well as the class character of the resistance in Afghanistan and Pakistan.

EXCEPTIONAL PASHTUNS?

Questions of similarity and difference

One problem with class analyses of Afghanistan and Pakistan is that there are just not many around. Dorronsoro argues strongly against interpretations of the political violence in Afghanistan in terms of "ethnic conflict" as a criterion of analysis which is sometimes taken "as an alternative paradigm to that presented by Islamism". He also notes the "frequent confusion between the two ideas, with Pashtun being equated with Taliban".[20] González offers a stunning critique of the "tribal" discourse in the US military.[21] Equally, an anthropological disposition to focus on Pashtuns and ethnicity is misleading, and anything but politically innocent.

As Marcus Banks puts it, ethnicity is constantly produced as an explanation: the reason why the A's are slaughtering the B's, the reason why the C's are "clannish" or "dirty", or "unreliable".[22] Using "ethnicity" as a frame for *both* description and analysis is tautological, yet the widespread commitment to this circularity suggests that much is at stake. In 1988, Richard Tapper wrote, "The descriptions of 'ethnic groups' are political acts that create order and facilitate control, whether for academic or for governmental purposes,"[23] to counter the enthusiasm for ethnic mapping among some historians and anthropologists of Iran and Afghanistan. Yet Giustozzi offers us one of these very same, 1988, ethnic maps.[24]

We are all both different and the same; we all know this. Yet, where differences are marked, more or less strongly, they create and sustain hierarchy. Some people have greater access to and control of resources than others. Such differences may be marked in class terms, or in others which essentialise and divide people by categorising them in terms of gender, ethnicity and under the guise of "fundamentalist" Islam. As a corollary, the more differences are marked—by choice or imposition—the greater the inequality they serve to hold in place. And because competition fuels capitalist imperialism, hierarchy and inequality are everywhere, though not uniformly so.[25]

Marking sameness increases equality. Some familiar universalising discourses—which emphasise similarity and downplay difference—are inspired by Islam, others by Christianity. Yet others, including Marxism, derive from Enlightenment accounts of human potential. These last rely on notions of rationality, secularism, human equality and democratic forms of government; they attend to the materiality of human lives. And there is another, unnamed, universalising discourse which is enormously important in the world. This allows people all around the world to shrug and say: "There are good people and bad people, all kinds of people everywhere, but in the end, we are all human beings". This offers scope for great decency in human relations.[26]

The universalising discourses share much history and common ground. Because they emphasise sameness and can appeal to the majority of the people at any one time and place, they are powerful ways to contest authority and confront power. In major confrontations, the balance of forces between popular opposition and elite power determines the outcome: in electoral contests, social movements, civil wars and revolutions. How you judge the outcome—as progressive or conservative—depends on whose side you are on.

The tensions and contradictions between universal ideals and marked inequalities are everywhere the stuff of everyday life. In the 1970s, Durrani Pashtuns of northwestern Afghanistan cared greatly that as tribespeople and Muslims they were all equal. Yet their egalitarian ideals were contradicted daily as they sought to survive in an increasingly competitive environment in which notions of ethnicity and tribe became more marked to legitimise growing feudal and class inequality.[27]

As I argue below, the Taliban combine Islamist ideals and class politics to emphasise egalitarian feeling and mobilise support. In the brief for *Decoding the New Taliban*,[28] contributors were asked to describe the Taliban as a new social movement. This required attention to the internal dynamics of the movement: to "command and control" structures, negotiation, compromise and how unity is sustained, personally, institutionally and ideologically. The book asks how people manage, or do not manage, to work together to effect change in the world. Yet so too people can be sold out and endlessly betrayed by others at the top, leaving no trust and no ideals untarnished. Panjshiri entrepreneurs understand this very well: "all this talk of Taliban and al-Qaida is senseless. Afghanistan is today made up of two types of al-Qaida: the *al-guida* [the fucked] and the *al-fida* [the seekers of profit]".[29] A class analysis if ever I heard one!

And there is one similarity that unseats all the accounts of difference. If the US, the UK or France were invaded and occupied, we would all hope we had the courage to follow whichever leaders, and join whatever organisations, were consistently fighting the occupation. American revolutionaries, the French Resistance, the Viet Cong and SWAPO all fought to end imperial occupations. In this the Taliban are just like "us" in their struggle against occupation. However, to deny the normalcy of violent resistance, imperial spin exoticises "cultural" differences.[30]

Why the emphasis on difference?

The pull to treat social relations in terms of difference is very strong. So strong that it is easy to forget that *analyses* in terms of "ethnicity" and "identity politics" are new. They grew out of uneasy compromises between the American elite and the leadership of the radical social movements of the 1960s,[31] when divide-and-rule politics were used to tame the movements for civil rights, peace and women's liberation. And it was not long before the fashion for postmodernism, also new, began to dominate the social sciences and a third overlapping discourse of alterity (and the ideas of "self and other") gained credence. By the 1980s this new ideology, with its divisive ways of describing sociality, swept all before it.

In effect a previously strong movement for equal rights and human liberation was fragmented into hyphenated minorities like African-Americans, and competing interest groups, such as "women" and "gays", which greatly weakened class politics in the United States.[32] The process was shrewd and worked through co-option. The American establishment admitted small numbers—often only the top tenth—of blacks, Latinos and women to their number, while the lives of other blacks, Latinos and women became significantly harder. As Gary Younge suggests, "Black presidents and women MPs do not alone mean equality and justice".[33]

The radical legacy of the 1960s made overt racism and sexism illegal and ensured that US did not dare invade another country for more than twenty years (if you don't count Grenada and Panama). Yet because notions of ethnicity and identity politics hide class relations and confuse many who would oppose elite power, in most respects the divide-and-rule strategy has worked for the elite.

This new strategy has had imperial as well as domestic implications. American imperialism was developed in Latin America as a system of indirect domination, not direct colonisation. For 150 years, US foreign policy was versatile, and forwarded US imperial interests economically. It was generalised after 1945. In the Middle East, the American government sought control in Saudi Arabia via Aramco and military aid, supported right-wing dictators in Iran and Pakistan and funded the Israeli state, while opposing Cold War enemies like Syria and competing with the Soviet Union to give development aid to Afghanistan.

Then, after the shocks of the Islamic revolution in Iran and the communist revolution in Afghanistan, there was a noticeable shift to add the new US domestic ideology of divide-and-rule to foreign policy—a strategy that had not been used previously in Latin America. This was evident in the sinister play between Sunni and Shi'ite in US support for Saddam's Iraq in the Iran-Iraq war, and in American support for the Pashtun mujahidin in Afghanistan.

Under Clinton, the rhetoric of division, including ethnicity, sectarianism and nationalism, became even more marked during the Balkan wars. As Syrians joked at the time: "Last week President Clinton was very angry and told the Serbs if they didn't behave, he'd bomb Saddam Hussain".[34] In Afghanistan, after the Soviet withdrawal, there was a move towards an alignment of the distribution of ethnicities and political affiliations on the ground. It should be understood, however, that the ethnicisation of the parties was a consequence of the war. Finally, the focus on ethnicity excluded the consideration of other dynamics, both social and ideological, which were equally significant. The new political equilibrium which had its origin in the American intervention tended to favour a new interpretation of the war as "ethnic", since this was the only language which the foreign powers understood without difficulty.[35]

Whereas racism was part and parcel of colonial expansion, since 9/11 Islamophobia has become a dominant discourse of the US and UK and other EU governments. Islamophobia uses "culture" as a gloss for religious difference marked superficially by beards and veils. Such differences are understood to be unalterable and more than skin deep. They arise from a concatenation of emotion and unreason to include visceral hate and fanatical belief. Islamophobia is a racism which combines colour, ethnicity and religion. Domestically, Islamophobia justifies increased government control over ordinary lives and scapegoating of the most vulnerable people at home—migrants, refugees and Muslims. Internationally, Islamophobia has become part of the US armoury, and Islamists the enemy.

I have written elsewhere about Islamophobia and the gendering of the American wars in Afghanistan and Iraq.[36] A crucial difference is that "freeing women" remains, for many, an acceptable pretext for the war in Afghanistan. And "freeing women" is the trope that most effectively exoticises the Taliban and turns them into barbarous fanatics.

But "freeing women" was not a credible reason for opening a second front in Iraq, nor for the Israeli war in Lebanon, nor the bombardment of Gaza. To link all these, Islamophobia has been ramped up and generalised. For instance, the French national debate on veiling gained considerable momentum at the time of the Iraq war. Eight years later the French legislated against fully veiled Muslim women in public places. And, over the same period, the threat of an American or proxy war with Iran grew.[37]

Case studies

Following these general remarks, let me now turn to the anthropology of Swat as an example of how class and empire disappeared in ethnography of the region, before considering the Taliban resistance in Swat and Afghanistan.

Barth's monograph on Swat, as we all grew up knowing, was based on fieldwork in 1954. However, the thrust of the book is to extrapolate back to describe an acephalous political system as it might have been in Swat in the 1920s. As an example of transactional analysis, the book had a considerable theoretical impact, while for a long time it remained one of very few ethnographies of the area.[38]

Talal Asad's important critique of the book came later.[39] Three points from Asad are particularly important here. First, the Yusufzai protagonists of the ethnography make up a small proportion of the population, variously between one-fifth and one tenth across Swat. Moreover, the large landlords, the elite Yusufzai khans, are very few indeed. So Barth's account is top-down. The majority of the peasantry do not get much of a look-in as ethnographic subjects in their own right.[40] And Barth's account also loses the British.

Secondly, the study offers no cadastral material on Swat, past or present, yet Barth's analysis of Yusufzai power would seem to require a detailed understanding of the system of land tenure and its manipulation.

Thirdly, although Barth certainly understands politics as a *relationship* between leaders and followers, his transactionalist approach misses the systemic inequalities of, and resistance to, the feudal state. Rather, his discussion individuates landless peasants and tenant farmers, posits a virtually free labour market, and emphasises rational choice to offer a deeply capitalist understanding of peasants who can chose how and when to align themselves with competing khans. His description cries out for a class analysis.[41]

Barth reconsidered his Swat material in 1981, acknowledging Asad's critique. In places he seemed to accept that the system he described in Swat "can be characterized as a structure of agrarian exploitation".[42] But he did not otherwise engage with Asad's historical and class interpretation. Perhaps this is not surprising, because by the 1980s the anthropology of the Middle East had taken on a very particular shape, in large part because academic fashion mostly follows and reinforces dominant political trends.

By this time the idea of Area Studies, driven by American policy considerations, had penetrated the academy. The region—from north Africa to south west Asia—was often framed ethnographically in the west by Ernest Gellner's *Saints of the Atlas*,[43] which is rather similar to Barth's description of Swat in the east.

Apart from bits of China, the Middle East is the home of the oldest class societies in the world, yet class analyses and urban studies hardly figured at this time. There were of course exceptions, such as Gilsenan's study of practised Islam in Cairo. But it is also important to understand the political pressures which for more than twenty years made it difficult for Gilsenan to write and publish his prior, and much more audacious, study of local and state politics in Lebanon.[44] Though Edward Said's *Orientalism* appeared in 1978,[45] the imperial competition of the Cold War was hardly mentioned in contemporary ethnographies. Indeed, theories of imperialism were notably absent. Rather, most anthropologists concentrated on making sense of "tribalism" (and its apparently less primitive friend, "ethnicity")[46] and/or "honour and shame".[47] Among them were two important critiques of Barth's *Swat*, by Akbar Ahmed and Meeker. Of these Ahmed's is more valuable, not least because it includes an historical account of relations between Swat and the Raj. At this time Lindholm's detailed ethnography of the Yusufzai Pashtuns in Swat also appeared. This amplifies and updates Barth's account. Lindholm, like Barth, writes from the point of view of the powerful, and offers little insight into the lives of the poor and landless, yet dismisses Asad's class critique as "oversimplistic".[48]

Swat and the Taliban

With this ethnographic history in mind, let us consider what has since happened in Swat, first under Zulfiqar Ali Bhutto and then, when Swat became the focus of global interest, with the rise of the Taliban and their suppression in May and June 2009. My interest is to draw together issues of class, social movements, state politics and imperialism. It is a point of view that complements others, such as that of Nichols, in this volume.[49]

When Swat was fully absorbed into Pakistan in 1969 it was a feudal state, much as Barth described it a decade before.[50] The population was divided between a small elite, mostly Yusufzai Pashtuns, led by large landowning khans, some smallholders, and the rest of the population, most of whom worked for the khans as sharecroppers.

In the same year, 1969, there was also a mass peasant upheaval all across the NWFP.[51] In Swat too, landless peasants occupied the land they cultivated and "accquired up to 42 per cent of land in some villages".[52] This uprising was part of the much larger movement when "Maoist groups organized peasants to fight for the eradication of feudal taxes and a more just tenancy system".[53] The peasants believed that Bhutto, President (1971–73) and then Prime Minister (1973–77) of Pakistan, meant them to get the land. In Swat, as elsewhere, "the struggle turned violent, with significant loss of life and property, and thousands were arrested".[54] The land disputes of this period continue to be contested in the courts.

The uprising was quelled when the military took power, executed Bhutto and put a stop to the class-based mass movement. In Swat too the military coup had this effect, while, as Ali argues, the landowners succeeded in dividing the peasant struggle "partly on the basis of identity politics, raising the issue of Pashtun solidarity".[55]

In the following decade, a middle class began to emerge in Swat. Increasingly, peasants became labour migrants, and sent home remittances from the textile mills of Karachi and from the Gulf. "But the men left behind, disproportionately unskilled and ill-educated, [faced] grim economic prospects indeed"[56]—although after 1978 some made good money from the war in Afghanistan and from trade and smuggling.[57] In the early 1990s, there was a real-estate boom, and the new middle class, including labour migrants and border entrepreneurs, sought to challenge the landowning elite. Meanwhile, the landlords, many now absentee, turned to cash-cropping tobacco, sugarcane and cotton, but the agricultural oppression remained, and "the large landlords [were] also likely to hold concessions for the timber forests and the contracts to operate the gemstone mines that also employ the working class of Swat".[58]

In 1992, the landowning khans were being squeezed between the poor and the new middle class. These two quite different forces opened a space for the rise of the TNSM, the Tehrik-i-Nifaz-i-Shariat-i-Muhammadi. This movement "presented sharia law as an answer to the public grievances, most significantly the rapid settlement of land disputes".[59] After 9/11, the TNSM also mobilised support to fight the Americans in Afghanistan, and their leaders were swiftly jailed. Meanwhile, Swati peasants and most other Pakistanis became increasingly hostile to the American war in Afghanistan, American bombing and American political interventions in Pakistan. Support for the Taliban increased across the NWFP. In 2002, a coalition of moderate Islamists won the elections and continued to allow the Taliban a safe haven. The Islamists stayed in power in the NWFP until the elections in 2008.

Throughout this period, "[c]lass interests could be disseminated in the name of Islam and sharia. That is how Mullah Fazlullah, the leader of the Swat Taliban, appeared on the scene".[60] Initially, the man also known as the Radio Mullah because of his FM broadcasts "enjoyed support from all sections of society … in the name of "[q]uick justice and efficient government".[61] As the Radio Mullah gained influence, the movement grew more radical, and became a party of the rural poor: taxing the khans, then targeting them and the police and administration which supported them. The Swati elite responded by demanding that Musharraf quell the Taliban militarily.

By September 2006, the Pakistani government was forced to do a comprehensive deal with the Taliban across the NWFP and effectively surrender control in Waziristan.[62] From 2007, there was increasing violence between the Taliban militia and the Pakistani army and paramilitary, but by the autumn of 2008, the Taliban had gained control of a number of villages in Swat.

In the elections of 2008 the voters in the NWFP changed sides again, and supported the Awami National Party of Pakhhtun nationalists. The Awami National Party was led by Asfandyar Wali, a grandson of Abdul Ghaffar Khan, the founder of the Khodai Khidmatgar, the Servants of God, also known as the Red Shirts, the secular, anti-khan, pro-peasant, pro-land reform and sometime Pakhtun nationalist movement which had dominated politics in the NWFP from 1925 until 1948.[63]

In 2008, the Awami National Party—without its earlier progressive stance—was allied to the national government of the Pakistan People's Party. In the eyes of the people, the PPP represented the left in Pakistan. However, voters seem to have switched sides not because they favoured the party, but because it was the least objectionable choice when none of the politics on offer addressed their concerns. They continued to fear the khans, and to feel solidarity with the Afghans suffering the American occupation, but they were repelled by the terrorist targeting of civilians in Pakistan, and above all they did not want war in their own country.

In February 2009, the Taliban gained control of the major towns in Swat and forced the provincial government, led by the Awami National Party, to negotiate an "accord". This was an agreement to a ceasefire in return for the surrender of all state control of a vast area of Pakistan's northwest frontier with Afghanistan. It ceded "judicial, administrative and security authority, including police functions, to the local Islamic groups"[64] under the leadership of Sufi Muhammad, Mullah Fazlullah's father-in-law and the previously jailed leader of the TNSM. The big landowners left Swat as the Taliban gained control[65] and their tenants no longer had to pay rents. In that moment there was a revolution in class relations in Swat.

It is clear that the "impetus for the accord came from the state",[66] just as earlier in Waziristan. With the Swat "accord" in place, the Taliban advanced to within sixty miles of Islamabad. The earlier deal with the Taliban in Waziristan, and the Swat "accord", both deeply disturbed the American government. They wanted the Pakistani army deployed to secure NATO transport routes and regain control of the frontier territory which had become a safe haven for the Afghan Taliban. The concern of the Pakistani elite was different. Their fear was that the Taliban advance in Swat would set off risings in the Punjab[67] and elsewhere and they would seize power in Pakistan, an ambition that Taliban spokesmen did not deny.[68] "The Taliban have advanced deeper into Pakistan by engineering a class revolt that exploits profound fissures between wealthy landlords and their landless tenants in a strategy that may help militants make broader inroads in the populous heartland."[69]

By April 2009 the Americans were making it clear that they would attack the Taliban in Swat if the Pakistan government did not itself act. In early May, Afghanistan's President Karzai and Pakistan's President Zardari met Obama at the White House, just as the Pakistani military and paramilitary, with American support, mounted a massive operation. By 1 June, after heavy bombing and death squads on the ground, the army retook Mingora city in Swat. Many Taliban and others were killed, though the onslaught was less horrific than it might have been because more than half the civilian population of Swat became refugees, creating one of the greatest flights from military violence in history. Of a population of two million, perhaps 500,000 people fled the state in the first week of May.[70] They joined others who had left earlier, and yet others followed. Mercifully, many were able to find refuge with relatives elsewhere in Pakistan and avoided ending up in the camps.

By August, as hundreds of thousands of refugees were returning to their devastated homes, there were nonetheless fears that the Swat valley would be destabilised because wealthy landowners were "refusing to return, handing the insurgents a significant victory".[71] The legacy has a class character: some fear and hate the Taliban, others loathe the Pakistani military, and the Americans, for their reprisals.

Near Mingora, a year after the Taliban took control of the city, some 200,000 were still being fed daily by the World Food Programme,[72] and a million people were still displaced when the devastating floods hit in August 2010.[73] Meanwhile the Taliban and the people who support them are still there. The Taliban were quick to offer flood relief to the people in Swat and elsewhere,[74] and they are likely to reappear as a political force if the army leaves.

The Afghan Taliban

Let me now draw on insights from Swat to consider how attention to class, and the universalising ideology of the Taliban, can help us to understand the present resistance to American occupation. Certainly what is happening in Afghanistan is similar, and intimately connected, to what has occurred in Swat. But as Azerbaijani Moghaddam points out, focusing on the south and east of Afghanistan and the Pashtun-ness of the Taliban misses much concerning the extreme "poverty" (that is, class relations) and resistance of non-Pashtuns throughout the country.[75]

David Edwards' account of the Afghan Taliban illustrates Azerbaijani Moghaddam's point. Although Edwards himself laments the practice, his "Learning from the Swat Pathans: Political Leadership in Afghanistan, 1978–97" is a discussion of global politics framed through the lens of anthropology. Edward's project is to understand why, given the conflict in Afghanistan, "the Swat literature has been so widely ignored".[76] He approaches this apparent conundrum by seeking to discover how much, or little, of Afghan politics up to 1997 conforms to the ethnographic contributions of Barth, Asad, Ahmed and Meeker. In this context, what he adds from his own interesting ethnography has a limited explanatory range.

Because none of his chosen anthropological experts were describing revolutionary politics or a civil war, the lives of impoverished, fearful peasants, dictatorships and resistance movements in Saudi Arabia and Pakistan, the Chechen Islamists' fight against Soviet occupation or oil politics and imperialism, all these topics are absent. Yet the Taliban, the foreign fighters in Afghanistan and many other ordinary Afghans knew a great deal, and had strong opinions, about these things.

Edwards denies any great virtue to class-analyses (*pace* Asad), though he sees some mileage in Ahmed's notion of "charismatic leadership". Indeed, Edwards ascribes Taliban success to three things: the link between their purist Islam and "village identity", war exhaustion, and the invisibility of their leadership. Edwards' account is narrowly focused on ethnicity and sectarianism, so much so that he ends on a most curious note. He writes of the Taliban in 1997, "While Pakhtuns made up something under 50 per cent of the prewar population and are traditionally the most powerful ethnic group in Afghanistan, they are also famously fractious, and no party or movement had previously managed to bring so much of this large and disparate population under one political umbrella"[77]—a statement which ignores the entire history of the Afghan state from Abdur Rahman Khan on.

Let me now draw out a few points from the important work on the neo-Taliban by Giustozzi, whose strategic study is essentially pro-government, and not at all class oriented.[78] This makes my suggestive shortcut all the more potent.

But first, a few contextualising remarks. In Afghanistan there was, as in Swat, a class of feudal landlords, some of whom remain powerful today. Gregorian, writing of the 1930s, describes a situation which remained little changed until the coup in 1973:

For the most part, the feudal tribal chieftains and big landholders owned the country's water rights and controlled the great bulk of the agricultural product. According to the estimates of Soviet Afghanists, some 70 per cent of the cultivated land and a great percentage of the irrigation facilities and water rights belong to the big and moderately well-to-do landowners. The peasants, who represented an estimated 90 per cent or more of the population of Afghanistan, owned less than one-fifth of the cultivated land. About 30 per cent of them were landless, and most of the others cultivated at least part of their lands as tenants.[79]

During the Soviet war, few landlords became leaders of the resistance. A few fighters were committed Taliban, but most leaders were members of the new educated middle class. They were engineers and the like, people who shared a class position with the leading Afghan communists.[80] After the Soviets left, these leaders emerged as a new elite, of "new khans", warlords and druglords.[81] Meanwhile, "The Taliban's seizure of power was among other things a class struggle, in which the urban bourgeoisie were for the moment losers".[82] Then, after 2001, others around the Karzai government came to occupy this position.[83] Far removed from the Karzai elite in class terms are the Taliban, including Mullah Omar and other leading figures, who look like and talk like the small peasant farmers and share-croppers who follow them.[84]

In the first years of the American occupation, Afghans were quiescent and hopeful: for an economy which would allow them to support their families and a reconstruction which would bring safe roads, clinics and education back into their lives. Joining the resistance, or at least tacitly supporting it, came later. As a Pakistani official from South Waziristan put it: "Military actions and policy have contributed to the anarchical situation that pro-Taliban militants are more than happy to fill. Their demonstrated ability to restore order, prosecute criminals and dispense speedy justice was welcomed by many civilians fed up with violence and insecurity."[85] Or, as another analyst said, "fear of the militants, combined with resentment against a corrupt administration and draconian laws, has contributed to local acquiescence of Taliban-style governance."[86]

The pattern is the same as that associated with the rise of the Taliban in the 1990s. It has been repeated in Uruzgan, in Helmand and among "disenfranchised communities" elsewhere.[87] The resistance has grown as the local government has been increasingly undermined and the occupation has become more violent, with air strikes causing more civilian deaths and internal refugees.[88] The process is organic. A mullah and Taliban commander in Kunar delivered a funeral eulogy for "an insurgent" and an unnamed woman and her nursing infant: he told the people they needed to be angry at the Coalition Force and the Afghan National Security Forces for causing these tragic deaths and invited "everyone who wants to fight to join the fighters who traveled with him".[89]

Giustozzi describes the neo-Taliban movement in terms of a small hard core and much larger numbers of local insurgents. He notes that from 2003, "the pattern according to which local communities divided up into pro-government and pro-Taliban did not follow a strict tribal logic. The Taliban were ready to accept anybody who shared their views and accepted their rules, regardless of ethnicity and tribe,"[90] as Uzbeks and other non-Pashtuns have done.

With respect to Taliban recruitment, of equal significance is the fact that Afghan government figures put unemployment at 33 per cent of the workforce or higher.[91] Some 56 per cent of the people employed work in the agricultural sector, and of the total population some 28 per cent are literate.[92] In one of the very poorest countries in the world, that means the majority of people—the locals—are likely to be quite hostile to those with wealth and power, whether criminal, inherited or acquired through corruption and/or government patronage. Corruption is a class issue. And as the former Taliban Ambassador to Pakistan has described, the occupation is failing, not least because "poverty and unemployment are at their peak and the roots of the economy are drying up" and America has "exploited the poverty of Afghans to the utmost".[93]

Giustozzi's description of the origins and growth of the Afghan Taliban is detailed and convincing. His focus on Pashtuns in the south and east has been broadened in his edited volume which includes descriptions of local responses to the vicissitudes of the war and important insights into the lives of ordinary Afghans.[94] Yet, Giustozzi's study of the warlords, Dostam in the north and Ismail Khan in the west, in spite of its formidable detail, is limited by a theoretical formalism. We learn almost nothing about who controls the land, or how the majority of Afghans gain their livelihoods.[95] And although he says warlords may be susceptible to "ideological contamination" to gain legitimacy and followers,[96] he does not explore ordinary Afghans' beliefs, class sentiments and opposition to warlordism.

Until now, what has been most obviously missing from scholarly discussion and political analyses are ethnographic accounts of the universalising rhetoric and practice of resistance and the class politics on which it draws. A class discourse has been an important part of the politics of the NWFP since the Red Shirts of the 1930s. In Afghanistan, although explicit class politics was utterly discredited by the violence of the communist regime, class relations have not ceased. Smallholders, sharecroppers and agricultural workers remain the majority in the countryside. The urban poor work for wages as cleaners, hairdressers, watchmen and drivers, while other workers are in the pay of warlords, the occupation and the Afghan government.[97] Even Karzai must have garnered some popular support with his threat to "join the Taliban" in an effort to protect Qandahar from an American surge in the summer of 2010.[98]

Locating resistance

The expanding "enlightened" European, and later American, empires often met armed resistance framed in religious terms: from the benighted "fuzzy-wuzzys" of the Sudan to the mad mullahs of the NWFP and the ghost dancers at Wounded Knee. After the middle of the twentieth century, Western imperial hegemony became more vulnerable. People who were in favour of the national independence movements in Africa and Asia saw themselves as supporting leftist political resistance against imperial capitalism. Yet now, when the hypocrisy of Western secular democracies is widely understood, the political left is confused about the religious banner under which Hizbollah, Hamas and Taliban resistances fight.

The twist that demonises religious resistance movements also creates political paralysis. Many people deplore the American occupation of Afghanistan, but can find little sympathy for a resistance movement led by the right-wing Taliban. This contradictory middle position, which is both anti-American and anti-Taliban, is immensely unsettling to inhabit.

Some who adopt it are pro-Muslim but conservative in class terms.[99] Others are secularists. On the extreme right are secular fundamentalists like Ayaan Hirsi Ali, the former Dutch MP, and Gita Sahgal, recently of Amnesty International.[100] Other secularists are left-leaning. Some, like RAWA (the Revolutionary Association Women of Afghanistan) feminists, are on the far left. Other progressive secularists may support the ideal of national liberation, but have little interest in the lives, and choices, of the people actually involved. Often they are uninformed about, or dismissive of, the class dynamics of the Taliban resistance and focus on the Taliban religious bigots. In this process, many middle and working class people end up, by default, supporting the occupation and the interests of the imperial and national elite.

Instead of seeing the occupation as the problem, not the solution, those holding this middle position retreat to the right. First, some assume that ordinary Afghan working people are unable to govern themselves, a latter-day version of the "white man's burden". Second, others are convinced that the Muslim (but not Christian) religious right is invariably autocratic, in spite of the democratic elections of Hamas in Palestine and the present government in Turkey. Third, most do not think in military terms and are unable to see the Taliban resistance as a new form of guerrilla warfare in circumstances of immense military inequality. For instance, Taliban attacks on schools, roads and government offices are of tactical and strategic importance in weakening the Karzai government and as a response to the Americans' increasing use of drones and targeted killing.[101] It is notable that when the Taliban have gained control of an area, as in the case of Musa Qala, they have then shown themselves willing to relax their ideological strictures.[102] Finally, for some, the bias is categorical and an aspect of class war: middle class women are particularly vociferous opponents of the Taliban, yet they resist comparing abuses of women's rights with the numbers of women (and men and children) killed, maimed, and made homeless by the war and occupation itself.[103]

A guerrilla war can only be sustained with local support. The Taliban are locals, while the majority of Afghans of whatever gender or ethnic background want an end to the American occupation. I share their wish. At present the Taliban are the only force with the express aim of achieving that result. The Taliban and the Americans have been in contact and looking for a settlement for some time.[104] What the future bodes is hardly clear: perhaps a return to the *status quo ante*, in a country now further brutalised and impoverished by the past decade of war.

Treating what is happening in Afghanistan in terms of class analyses and theories of empire invites academics and others to consider their own class and political loyalties. A wider focus also makes it easier to point out that when people ally themselves with an invader, they soon find themselves hated by those who oppose the occupation. This is what has weakened secularists and feminists in Afghanistan since the Soviet 1980s. And although the argument is a powerful one—that being (or supporting) the invaders has exacerbated the "security threat" and generated great hostility and anger around the world against the US and UK governments—in reality it ignores stronger arguments about global capitalism and resistance to imperial power. The echoes reverberate. At the end of the second volume of his history, Kaye writes of imperial over-reach and the disgrace of the British retreat from Kabul in 1842: "For the Lord God of recompenses shall surely requite".[105]

10

CLASS, STATE, AND POWER IN SWAT CONFLICT

Robert Nichols

This paper draws upon scholarly and non-academic literature about the last century of social, political, and religious dynamics in Swat[1] and the Pashtun areas of Pakistan and the region. Three broad points about scholarship, power, and history frame the analysis. First, nominally competing anthropological interpretations of Pashtun and Swat society, including the choice-based modeling of Barth and the class sensibility of Asad, are viewed as representing different aspects of evolving, but enduring, social processes of power competition and distribution, operating at both elite and non-elite levels.[2]

Second, although certain relationships of political power changed in Pakistan after independence in 1947 and in Swat after integration into Pakistan in 1969, leading interests maintained and adapted many previous practices of elite control over economic resources, especially land, and elite access to education, health care, and employment opportunities. Resulting notions of social injustice, economic inequity, and illegitimate authority were mobilized by Islamist activists, including Sufi Muhammad, in Swat from the 1990s onward.[3]

Third, through an examination of the details of recent events in Swat, this paper draws connections between two levels of my previous historical research; first, local studies of the Peshawar region, including of Sufi Muhammad's 1990s Tehrik-i-Nifaz-i-Shariat-i-Muhammadi movement in Swat,[4] and second, broader inter-regional work on migration and circulation, including post-1970 labor migration to the Gulf.[5] Both registers of history reveal alternate, occasionally overlapping, responses to unresolved imbalances of power and access to resources.

In Swat and Pakistan, the history of the last sixty years has traced the adapting and restructuring of hierarchies of political and economic control during the Swat State period and in the early postcolonial decades of the Pakistan nation-state. In Swat, after 1969, as control of land, income, and politics widened to include new business and political party elites, historically familiar idioms of political leadership and religious authority were drawn upon by old and new leaders contesting claims to secular and religious legitimacy and authority. This history generated a variety of responses, especially from the young, the ambitious, the disaffected, and the disenfranchised. As studied in neighboring Chitral, individuals in Swat made personal evaluations and judgments as they negotiated the psychological and emotional consequences and stresses of their time.[6] Responses included political competition and fragmentation, resistance from below, and migration to Pakistani cities and abroad. Others, as Marsden's essay in this volume more broadly notes, had identities shaped by merchant and business activities, especially in the Swat valley's tourist economy of hotels and restaurants. This history also included the polemics and initiatives of ideological advocates, both political and Islamist, offering alternative visions of order, legitimate authority, and justice.[7]

This discussion argues that local, provincial, and national elites, including Pakhtun khans and politicians, merchant and urban elites, and several dozen major landlords in Swat, still competed at the highest levels for formal political power and more informal social control. It is also argued that recent decades of regional flows of migration and circulation, including within the Swat valley, and to and from Karachi, Dubai, Bradford, and Malaysia reflected the continued reality of limited opportunities for social and economic mobility for the majority. In addition, especially after the Iranian revolution and the Soviet invasion of Afghanistan, both in 1979, alternative sharia-based models of social and economic organization emerged in new ways to recruit followers from this unsettled society. An important argument here is that, despite decades of failing to provide swift justice or development, by 2010 the centralizing policies of the state of Pakistan proved to be an ever more decisive factor in Swat, if not yet across the wider border region.

Recent individual life histories embodied many of these different themes. A most symbolic figure was Muslim Khan, who once migrated to the United States. He worked but did not particularly prosper, and eventually returned to Swat. In spring 2009 he emerged as the media spokesman for the Swat Taliban movement led by Fazlullah, son-in-law of Sufi Muhammad. The claim of the movement, and of Muslim Khan, to status and legitimacy was temporary. Later in 2009 he was taken into custody by agents of a nation-state claiming a monopoly over coercive power in Swat and Pakistan. An equally symbolic institutional marker of this recent period was the post-conflict planning of permanent military bases in Swat by the consolidating Pakistan state, perhaps the most important political result of recent years of turmoil.

To summarize, in Swat after 1969 market-driven social hierarchies and economic inequality became important realities that contributed to later political instability, a crisis of nation-state legitimacy, and the consolidation of Islamist political alternatives. Nevertheless, in Swat after 2009, both recently challenged local and provincial political elites and aggressive Islamist and subaltern agendas would be, for the moment, subordinated and marginalized as the heavily militarized nation-state, through military intervention and occupation, made claims to dominance, with or without having established the hegemony of a state-building ideology.[8]

Scholarship

Written by an historian among the anthropologists, this discussion draws only upon useful relevant scholarship and offers no systematic evaluation of political anthropology or the disciplinary literature on Swat. Accepted is Professor Barth's argument that the rulers of the Swat State (1915–69) diminished the political power of Pakhtun landowners, whether or not this consolidated a land-based class hierarchy. Also important is his point that the disappearance of the Swat State in 1969 and the earlier decline of Pakhtun landed clan leadership weakened previous social and policy constraints on the exploitation of the weak and landless.[9] The inequality that developed in Swat in the last forty years, unmitigated by inadequate nation-state provisions for law, order, or development, was an underlying factor in the recent Islamist mobilization and conflict in Swat.

About five hundred years ago the Swat valley was settled by a dominate Yusufzai Pakhtun population who, with allied Pakhtun clans and religious adjuncts, occupied the best, often irrigated, main and side valley agricultural sites. Allied Shinwari and Tarkanri Pakhtun clans claimed the Sebujni area on the west bank of the Swat river.[10] The Pakhtuns ruled over a majority population of subordinated village service and artisan populations (barbers, smiths, carpenters, potters, muleteers) and non-Pakhtun tenant farmers and herders (Gujars, Ajars) who occupied higher slopes and upland pastures.

Swat society was transformed over the last century as the heavily agrarian stateless population was shaped by a new indigenous state, then by incorporation into the nation-state of Pakistan, and by ongoing regional and global economic and political dynamics. However one defines the communities and occupations of Swat, as *quam*, caste, or class, one might still benefit from Professor Barth's analysis that the most important institutional changes affecting Swat society have been "changes in the land tenure system", "monetization and commercialization", "population growth", and "the development of the state".[11] These factors contributed to social change, tensions, and unresolved problems—problems that highlighted failing government policies and provided issues for critique by religious activists advocating the need for sharia-based alternatives.

Power

The literature describing Swat history and politics traces the decline of Pakhtun customary political and social dominance during the indigenous Swat State rule of Miangul Abdul Wadud, the Badshah, and his son Miangul Jahanzeb, the Wali of Swat. The Mianguls gradually subordinated elite Pakhtun khans who for generations had used a monopoly over landholding, crop surpluses, and patron-client relations to dominate the three quarters of the population who were non-Pakhtun agrarian laborers, service providers, and herders. The Mianguls consolidated their state by slowly eroding the independent political and economic autonomy of the biggest khans who had historically competed with each other for land, clients, prestige, and power.

The Mianguls subordinated the most powerful Pakhtun khans to the state, in part, by pursuing policies that gradually favored a group of allied landlords who were allowed to accumulate economic resources even as they were pressured to give up political autonomy. A subordinated aristocracy was consolidated by Miangul Abdul Wadud's key change in the land tenure system: the ending, between 1925 and 1929, of periodic customary land exchanges between Pakhtun clans, *wesh*, and the permanent settlement of land ownership, still generally among ethnic Pakhtun elites.[12]

Though cast in terms of a reform that would lead to progress and development, the abolition of *wesh* left certain clans in control of the best agricultural lands and of income producing houses and shops in developing urban areas. One political motive attributed to Miangul Abdul Wadud for abolishing *wesh* was to favor political allies. Akbar Ahmed stated that "to further consolidate the support of loyalist khans he implemented numerous 'reforms' such as the abolition of the custom of 'wesh' whereby his enemies were permanently deprived of their lands and his allies permanently obligated". The political dimension of the land settlement was, according to Sultan-i-Rome, "a commonly known fact".[13]

The Miangul state portrayed this land settlement as a method to end land disputes, bring security to small holders, and encourage investment.[14] Also, Miangul Abdul Wadud and his son Miangul Jahanzeb claimed that their ability to swiftly adjudicate disputes, in part, justified their authority. The issue after 1969 and the end of the Swat State administrative structure was the weakened state of both Pakhtun customary patron-client obligations and the expedient Swat State conflict resolution process. Both may have limited the absolute exploitation of the weak and dependent. Market driven dynamics turned clients into wage workers and surplus grains were sold off to fund elite consumption. By "1977 only a very few important exchanges resisted monetization."[15] New agrarian methods and technologies and cheap imported goods led to migration to Mingora and unemployment. Population pressure continued as the "1972 census claimed 935,444 people in the district; an increase of 49.7 percent in eleven years", all this in a watershed of rough highland landscape having only "16.45 percent as farmland".[16]

This led to "the massive exodus of cheap labor out of Swat," including migration to Peshawar and other Pakistani cities and overseas to construction sites in Gulf oil states.[17] Before the 1990 downturn in oil prices, a single town, Barikot, with a population of 12,000, had up to 723 migrants working in the Middle East. Chain migration through the 1980s sent numbers of residents from specific villages in Buner to work sites in Malaysia.[18] Better off residents could afford the often steep expenses of securing overseas work. Many Kabal residents, with adequate connections and resources, continued to find employment as merchant seamen.[19] Across Swat, the new functionaries from the Pakistan administrative services allowed services to drift and disputes to remain tied up in backlogs of court cases. Power holders gained, and lack of opportunity and inequality increased.

In Talal Asad's re-reading of Barth's 1954 study, horizontal economic separations were more significant that the vertical dynamics of khan and bloc political competition: "… in re-analyzing some of the material within a class framework, we found it necessary to make the distinction between immediate choice and collective life-chances, between class interest and individual motive. We saw that though the motives of individual Pakhtuns and non-Pakhtuns might be convergent, their class interests were opposed." As numbers of smallholding Pakhtuns lost their land after 1969, sometimes to newly wealthy non-Pakhtun shopkeepers and merchants, *paracha*s, ethnic distinctions faded as an absolute marker of hierarchy and difference.

Whether or not one agreed that Barth suitably answered Asad's challenge,[20] the issue of class in Pakistan and Swat was raised in the 1970 national election campaign as Z.A. Bhutto deployed a populist appeal and advocated social welfare, labor protection, and land reform. Bhutto's rhetoric "affected the courts which, besides being flooded beyond capacity with complaints and conflicts, were unsure and reluctant to act decisively,..."[21] Populist resistance in Swat was dramatic. Tenants, anticipating land reform, stopped paying rent. Leaders from below emerged, and "For the very first time, collectivities of tenants have also engaged in armed confrontation and battle against landlords (and their followers) in some areas, particularly Sebujni."[22] The west bank of the Swat river, including the Shamizai, Sebujni, and Nipki Khel areas, had been an intermediary zone contested by state-building local rulers in Dir and Swat. In the pre-1969 elite political competition, "The most intransigent area of Swat was Shamizai/Sebujni...Here the khans had large private armies of dependents,...".[23] After 1969, weakly incorporated into the nation-state and with a growing population of non-Pakhtuns, including Gujars, the alienated, and the poor, the west bank of the Swat river was where the TSNM movement would settle and organize in the 1990s.

History

After 1970, the policies of the PPP government under Bhutto "acted to accelerate the growing separation between the landless and the landed classes", with rhetoric and efforts towards land reform and "a new emphasis on tenant rights and an end to compulsory labor." In Swat, Gujar herdsmen and tenants claimed and fought over land. "From a society dominated by the vertical splits of the *dala* system, in which clients joined their patrons in battles against other patron-client groups, Swat moved towards horizontal cleavages and class conflict."[24] In the 1977 national election, resistance to the Bhutto reforms came from Swat landlords and a religious party, the Jamaat-i-Ulema-i-Islam (JUI), which defended the rights of private property. A conservative religious ideology, one protecting property rights, was proclaimed by General Zia when he overthrew the Bhutto regime after contested election results.

The 1979 Soviet invasion of Afghanistan resulted in the West supporting Zia's patronage of Islamist political parties in a "*jihad*" to liberate Afghanistan. After the fall of the Afghan communist government in 1992, radicalized Islamist political factions rejected constitutional state models as they fought over the establishment and control of a polity operating under sharia law. Transnational Islamist activists supported the Afghan resistance and then the post-1994 rise of the Afghan Taliban movement. In this era, massive numbers of Afghan refugees moved into the Pakistan border areas, with many transiting or trying to subsist as refugees in the Malakand areas. Militant ideas, personalities, and armaments circulated freely.

In 1989, Sufi Muhammad left the Jamaat-i Islami party (JI) and settled in the Maidan area of lower Dir in the Malakand Division. He began organizing a movement to replace state systems of justice and authority with sharia law derived from the Quran and Sunnah. The earlier Swat State had allowed parties in dispute to agree whether their case was to be resolved by customary law or sharia.[25] After incorporation into Pakistan in 1969, Dir and Swat were administered under the

Pakistan Criminal Procedure Code.[26] In 1975, the NWFP government passed new Provincially Administered Tribal Area (PATA) criminal and civil codes. The Pakistan Penal code was split into two schedules with one set of criminal charges to be decided under the state code, while a second schedule listed "tribal" crimes to be decided by local, officially appointed councils nominated by the political division executive officer.[27]

The PATA laws were opposed by some for too closely resembling the authoritarian colonial era Frontier Crimes Regulations used to control the border regions. In 1990, the Peshawar High Court found the PATA laws unconstitutional, a decision appealed and upheld in 1994 by the Pakistan Supreme Court. During the years of appeals, thousands of civil and criminal court cases accumulated and remained unresolved. Sufi Muhammad seized on this issue and demanded that sharia courts replace the PATA laws. The provincial government allowed the issue to drift and by November 1994 Sufi Muhammad's TNSM movement had agitated and coerced the NWFP into agreeing to the enforcement of sharia law in the Malakand division.[28] Disputes over the interpretation of sharia law and control of sharia court judges remained unresolved over the next fifteen years. Sufi Muhammad's movement continued through the 1990s. After 11 September 2001 he led hundreds of followers into Afghanistan in a failed effort to support the Taliban. Later in the decade the movement would be revived by Fazlullah, Sufi Muhammad's son-in-law, now in alliance with a Pakistani Taliban movement.

Without denying the Islamist political agendas of individuals or specific religious parties, or the worldwide effects of American foreign policy choices after 11 September 2001, this paper argues that the militancy in Swat over the last decade cannot be understood solely in terms of religious ideology. Instead, there could be recognized a much more complex historical pattern of resistance to colonial and postcolonial state institutions perceived to be oppressive, illegitimate, and lacking moral authority. This resistance, as in the 1890s fighting around the Malakand pass, was often more tactical and contingent than reflective of absolute ethnic, class, or subaltern consciousness or solidarity.[29]

On a wider scale, during the 1990s, in South Asia, "the lingering inertia of old ruling institutions and hierarchies"[30] led one observer to note "…that without some sort of restructuring of the present equations of dominance and privilege, the subcontinent as a whole,…seems inexorably poised for greater conflict along the myriad lines afforded by its class, caste, communal, regional and linguistic divisions."[31] Indeed, in 2007–09, in Swat and the other districts of the Malakand Division, the followers of Sufi Muhammad, Fazlullah, and the Pakistan Taliban movement cultivated class resentments within Swat residents by specifically targeting landlords and calling for the redistribution of their land to the tenant tillers. Could such events be discussed beyond discourses of ethnic character, fundamentalism, fanaticism, and terrorism?[32] To what extent did such militant phenomena, including those in Swat and FATA and Afghanistan, represent Islamic political movements? To what extent might such activism and resistance be better seen as reflecting social movements in Muslim societies?[33]

Indeed, after 1969, much of Pakistan and Swat represented the reality of a "post-colonial 'strong society and weak state', a state which fundamentally exercised only a 'fragmented social control' over tribal clans long delegated as the

CLASS, STATE, AND POWER IN SWAT CONFLICT

responsibility of privileged intermediaries and political dependents who thrived in subordinated relationships of hierarchy and patronage structured in the colonial era".[34] Both General Musharraf's authoritarian government (1999–2008) and the following elected coalition government struggled to convince Pakistanis to place national identities and agendas above regional, ethnic, and sectarian loyalties.

More immediately, the Swat crisis of 2009 could be traced to events after 11 September 2001, when the government of President Musharraf allied with the United States and began to rein in militant jihadi groups, especially those active in Kashmir. In August 2004, two militants were arrested in Swat for involvement in a 2003 attack on Musharraf in Rawalpindi. The two were released in November 2006, returned to Matta sub-district (*tehsil*) on the west bank of the Swat river in the Sebujni area of Swat, and organized rallies to re-mobilize supporters of Sufi Muhammad, who had been held in custody after his failed effort to lead local fighters against the Americans in Afghanistan. The revived movement helped set up illegal FM radio stations around Swat, including one for Sufi Muhammad's son-in-law Maulana Fazlullah, the so-called Radio Mullah. Militant activities and violence continued.

From October 2007 to January 2008, General Musharraf actively deployed the Pakistan army across Swat in response to a request by the NWFP government. In May 2008 a peace accord was signed between the militants, including the wider Tehrik-i-Taliban Pakistan (TTP) movement of Baitullah Mehsud, and the NWFP government. The ceasefire broke down and sporadic fighting continued in Swat from mid-2008 until it wound down in the winter of 2008–09. By February 2009 a new accord calling for sharia law in Malakand, the Nizam-e-Adl 2009 pact, was agreed between the two sides. Sufi Muhammad was later released from prison, apparently to act as a moderating influence on Fazlullah.

The reality of the militancy in this period could be traced in the treatment of women in Swat. Bakht Zeba was a woman who had served on the Swat District Council and worked with the Swat Child Rights Committee. On 20 November 2008, Global Children's Day, she criticized the Taliban for destroying schools and keeping children, especially girls, from an education. On 26 November 2008 militants dragged her from her Mingora home, shot her dead, and left her body in the public square where they routinely dumped corpses of executed opponents.

The symbolic violence of the Taliban was exemplified in December 2008 when the body of Pir Samiullah, a Barelvi religious leader and government supporter, who had died in an October clash with the Swat Taliban, was exhumed from its grave and hung in a square.[35]

By early 2009 the previous eighteen months of conflict had generated many thousands of refugees. The Taliban had damaged, destroyed, or forced closed hundreds of schools. Perhaps 80,000 female students and 8,000 female teachers were deprived of education and employment.[36]

Taliban social policies banned "un-Islamic vices" such as music and dancing, especially in Mingora's entertainment district, the Banr Bazaar. On 2 January 2009 a defiant dancer, Shabana, was dragged to the public square and shot dead for refusing to retire from performing. The Taliban threw money and copies of her CD recordings and album photos on her body.

The Pakistan national reaction to the TTP abuses in Swat and international pressure on the central government after the Taliban moved into neighboring

Buner in April 2009 spurred the decision to launch a serious military effort. By the end of 2009 the military had displaced the Taliban from the core areas of the Malakand Division and Swat.

Lost in the obvious headlines and narratives was the reality of the Taliban's ability to mobilize large numbers of Swat Valley residents across social and economic categories. In negotiations with the state, militants used the rhetoric and idioms of Islamic solidarity, especially in demands for the imposition of sharia. But often militant recruitment at the local level quite directly addressed issues appealing to class resentments and hopes for social revolution. Significantly, after the displacement of the Taliban from Swat by late 2009, it was also clear that threatened power holders recognized these efforts and identified and targeted local individuals who had joined the militants.

The Malakand Division, as a Provincially Administered Tribal Area, had the NWFP government as immediate political authority over the region. The provincial government and ruling politicians often had different interests and agendas from the ruling coalition at the national center in Islamabad. Within the Swat valley, local politicians, businessmen, and community and landed elites had their own interests and relationships that might or might not link to provincial and national agendas. And, after years of interaction, agents of the local and provincial authorities were often in close communication and even sympathy with different Islamist personalities. Finally, the Swat Islamists had their own interregional links to wider networks in the FATA, Afghanistan, and Pakistan.

In this complex political environment of fragmented authority, evidence from 2007–09 revealed the social composition of a growing Swat Taliban movement that raised support through Islamist proselytizing, but also through the mobilization of the disaffected and disenfranchised. In mid-May 2009 a retired school teacher observed that:

> The Taliban are strange characters. Not long ago we knew Tor Mulla and Muslim Khan. They were not associated with any group or party. All of a sudden, as if recruited by some organisation, they became known people.
>
> So were many others who either held small pieces of land or worked part-time, as transporters, shopkeepers or fruit and cattle stock-holders etc.; their sudden strength came from the blue, and now our people are scared of these shady characters to their bones. No authority ever spoke of how these people became so influential. That is very strange.[37]

If Tor Mulla, perhaps a simple village prayer leader, had become "Taliban commander in Malakand," Muslim Khan had taken a less obvious, more cosmopolitan path to becoming "Taliban spokesman". By mid-May 2009 after the first three weeks of the government military offensive to displace the Taliban from Swat, "the grey-bearded Muslim Khan had been the public face of the Taliban, enthusiastically courting local and international media in jovial telephone conversations."[38] In one interview he told CNN "how he had spent four years living in the United States, working as a painter in the Boston area."[39] A migrant for employment and opportunity, Muslim Khan had not secured work beyond a manual trade, and had returned home. Though he had English language skills and enjoyed a new public status, his transnational experience had made him critical of the West and local official authorities. As fighting developed, Muslim Khan demanded the resignations of national and provincial assembly members from the Malakand Division, "Otherwise, we will arrest all their families. We will destroy all their buildings."[40] Under the Frontier Crimes Regulations, official authorities were authorized to make collective punishments and arrests and target family homes for demolition.

Through this period, with the Pakistan army engaged in numerous locations across the Federally Administered Tribal Areas and with inadequate NWFP security or political resources, officials pressured Swat landowners and political elites to raise community militias, *lashkars*, and confront the militants. Here played out the micro-politics of Taliban efforts to mobilize older sentiments about land, justice, and social hierarchies. In April 2009 one observer noted, "Preaching class warfare, as well as *jihad*, they have seized hundreds of houses and landholdings, including many of Swat's prized orchards. Half of the district's police officers and many administrators have fled, as have most landlords."[41]

A July 2009 analysis counted that, "About four dozen landlords were singled out over the past two years by the militants in a strategy to foment a class struggle. In some areas, the Taliban rewarded the landless peasants with profits of the crops of the landlords".[42] Individual estates were targeted and landowners pressured into exile. Landed elites complained that the army and the authorities asked them to fight, but provided little support during immediate confrontations. Provincial and national political party members were marked for assassination. Militants were particularly active on the west bank of the Swat river, including in the Kabal and Matta areas.

In July 2009, American political advisors were well aware of the dynamics. "If the large landowners are kept out by the Taliban, the result will in effect be property redistribution," Mr Nasr said. "That will create a vested community of support for the Taliban that will see benefit in the absence of landlords."[43]

The military displacement of the Swat Taliban continued through 2009, though most refugees returned to their homes by the end of the year. Military sweeps and operations continued into 2010, with continued clashes, targeted killings of government supporters, and slow reconstruction of often extensive damage. Naseem Akhtar, "a senior official in the civil administration" recognized the unresolved nature of the social problem he labeled "class war". "There is a need for a new social contract between the haves and have-nots."[44] One UN estimate counted 1,576 schools in Swat, with 175 destroyed and 226 damaged. The related story said the army was supervising school repairs, though "none of those razed has been rebuilt" yet. Though USAID had budgeted $36 million for Swat, "including $25 million to rebuild around 50 schools", in April 2010 a USAID official "conceded that not a single school had yet been fully rebuilt."[45]

The Islamist agenda of Sufi Muhammad, Fazlullah, the TTP, and the wider regional Taliban parties was straightforward enough. On 19 April 2009, Sufi Muhammad had been allowed to address a crowd of 40,000 gathered on the "Grassy Ground" in Mingora. Reinterpreting a ceasefire agreement just settled with the NWFP administration, Sufi Muhammad rejected Pakistan's constitution and said democracy was for infidels;[46] sharia was to follow for the whole country. Within a few days of this speech the Swat Taliban had moved into Buner.

The political problem for Islamabad in April 2009 reflected the dynamics of "state in society" arguments made by Joel Migdal and others who critiqued claims of "overvalued ideas of state power and autonomy… analyzing why often apparently powerful, centralized official institutions had less than their intended influence or legitimacy at the local level." By Migdal's discussion, the Pakistan nation-state achieved success or failure because of particular linkages to the NWFP and Swat. Indeed, the Pakistan state, especially in regards to the politics of the TNSM movement and Swat, "was not a monolithic entity, but a congeries of local, provincial, and federal bureaucratic and political interests".[47]

Islamabad had certain powers and asserted authority, but often had limited regional influence and legitimacy. The Pakistan military had massive coercive capacity and used heavy artillery, helicopter gunships, and jet aircraft within the boundaries of Pakistan. But many NWFP politicians and administrators, including ruling provincial governments, had for years supported or been sympathetic to many of the policies and individuals connected to claims for sharia-based systems in Swat and Malakand. Over the years, different NWFP provincial governments had rotated different senior administrators through the Malakand Division's several levels of offices to use pressure or cooperation alternately so as to influence Sufi Muhammad, Fazlullah, and their movements. In spring 2009, as the crisis in Swat came to a head, it was charged that the leading Malakand Division political officer, Syed Muhammad Javed, appointed by the NWFP government for his close ties to Sufi Muhammad since the early 1990s, had misused his authority in early April to convince Buner clan leaders to end resistance to Swat Taliban efforts to enter the valley. Unopposed, the Taliban quickly traveled over connecting passes and occupied key Buner towns and villages.[48] This was the final event that triggered the national military response and refugee crisis of 2009. The sympathetic Malakand Commissioner was relieved and later taken into custody.[49]

By mid-2010 the Pakistani military controlled the core areas of Swat. But local representatives of provincial political parties and the NWFP and Malakand administrative services remained insecure or absent. By the end of April 2010, a series of attacks had killed several anti-Taliban community group leaders, including Sajjid Khan, ANP politician and former Mingora *nazim*. The national government left the security forces and pro-government interests to secure fringe areas, but also conducted systematic neighborhood sweeps and arbitrary detentions. Few, if any, landlords moved back to their estates. Six months after the November 2009 killing by suicide bombing of Dr Shamsher Ali Khan, ANP member of the provincial assembly from Dherai, all nine Malakand provincial and national political representatives lived outside of Swat and the Malakand Division.[50]

The extent of local recruitment to the Taliban effort, and a fierce reaction, were revealed by reports of hundreds of extrajudicial arrests and reprisal killings around the Swat valley attributed to "security forces and law enforcement agencies", from July 2009.[51] By different estimates there were up to 2,500 or more prisoners held in detention.[52] Multiple cases were reported of tradesmen, shopkeepers, workers, and villagers, apparently identified by informants, being picked up by security personnel and later found dead.[53] One story revealing social origins said security forces had just "hunted down and killed several militants, including Commander Sher Gujjar, in parts of Kabal and Matta."[54]

The attempt to restore an unreformed status quo was exemplified by the coercive measures used to identify and capture hundreds of local Taliban supporters.

CLASS, STATE, AND POWER IN SWAT CONFLICT

Map from Fredrik Barth, *The Last Wali of Swat, An Autobiography as told to Fredrik Barth* (1985), Bangkok: White Orchid Press, 1995, p. 20.

BEYOND SWAT

One official notice posted at the end of April 2010 gave Swat residents accused of militancy a 15 May deadline to surrender or "they will lose their property and their families will be expelled from Malakand".[55] A Nepkikhel community "peace committee" in Kabal demanded that named "absconding" militants surrender by 20 May 2010 or their families would be expelled from Swat. By 20 May, 115 men had come in to district authorities, but most remained at large.[56] On 23 May, a first group of twenty-five families, about 130 people, were exiled to a refugee camp just outside of Swat. One "security man" admitted it was illegal action, even as he justified the relocations.[57] Extrajudicial punishments deterred many from surrender.

By summer 2010 the ANP party website listed dozens of party member "martyrs" killed by the militants. Any resistance from below had gone under cover as the Taliban guerrillas fled into the border regions. In June 2010 Kabal area residents complained that the government was offering only one percent of the market value for land being acquired for expansion of the Saidu Sharif airport and a cantonment.[58] In early July, the military mentioned that four different cantonments were planned around the Swat region.[59]

The Swat situation was analyzed within larger critiques of the legitimacy and authority of the postcolonial nation-state. A newspaper polemic stated, "The basic cause of the current turmoil is a feudal system that robs the common man of all hope of escape from his miserable existence while the privileged few continue to pocket national wealth".[60] One academic explained that "the decline in the ability of the Pakistani state to govern effectively and in accordance with its own formal constitutional parameters between the 1950s and the 1990s" was a regression to a pre-colonial method of despotic rule.[61]

Local and national processes and relationships controlling power and access to resources, while they were challenged, had not been transformed. From 2010, American sponsors needing allies in a larger confrontation with political Islam offered Pakistan $1.5 billion a year in social and development aid in the five-year Kerry-Lugar package. On 15 August 2011, an American official said that in Swat more than 230 hotels had been repaired with USAID funds. There would be no call for fundamental changes in Swat hierarchies, inequality, or access to resources. The west bank of the Swat river would remain unstable. The unemployed, the alienated, and the disaffected would continue to migrate to Pakistani cities, Gulf oil state construction sites, and Taliban *madrasa*s and camps. Over time many would circulate back to Swat, including advocates of continued conflict.

SECTION 4

THE TALIBAN, PASHTUNS AND SWAT

11

THE SWAT CRISIS[1]

Sultan-i-Rome

The historic Swat is situated in a geo-strategically important region of the world, where three significant regions of Asia—South Asia, China and Central Asia—meet. Swat, which at present is part of the Provincially Administered Tribal Areas (PATA) of the Khyber Pakhtunkhwa province of Pakistan, has been a politically prominent site throughout its known history, and periodically invaded by great armies. The deployment of a significant number of the Pakistani security forces there since 2007 is just the most recent example.

During the years 2007–09, the world saw the upheaval in Swat that shook the fabric of the Pakistan government in Swat and its writ to rule there, and, at the same time, put the wider world into a state of alarm. This chapter deals with this crisis in historical perspective, exploring the factors that stimulated the unrest and disaffection against the prevailing system and government in Swat, and also presenting a blueprint for a permanent solution to the political crisis in the district and beyond.

Historical Background

The Yusufzai Afghans migrated en masse to the Peshawar Valley; by the mid-sixteenth century they had occupied Swat and emerged as the dominant segment of society there. The Yusufzais, however, did not establish a government and a state, and lived according to the logics and dynamics of "tribal" society. In the last quarter of the nineteenth century, some portions of Swat came under the authority of the neighbouring ruler of Dir, while some came under the loose control of the British; others remained independent.

Weary of the constant internal faction fighting and excesses of the Nawab of Dir, as well as the high-handed behaviour of his agents and officials, some sections of the Swatis made common cause against the Nawab's occupation of Swat in early 1915 and were successful in their attempts to achieve independence from

Dir. A *jargah*[2] installed Abdul Jabbar Shah as the King of Swat in April 1915, but replaced him with Miangul Abdul Wadud in September 1917. On coming to power, Abdul Wadud (alias Bacha Sahib) continued to expand, consolidate and develop the Swat state. Its boundaries were extended both within and outside the Swat Valley.

Developmental works and schemes were undertaken by the Swat state during this period. Modern education and healthcare services were introduced and developed with the establishment of educational institutions and hospitals. Peace, order and the authority of the state were established with considerable success in the context of an illiterate society and tribal set-up. The state became a model of tranquillity and progress in Pukhtun tribal society more generally.[3] The changes were brought by developing a model of state authority, which was based on a mixture of traditional values and Islamic laws, while also being reflective of modern norms and modes of "development".

Miangul Jahanzeb, alias Wali Sahib, replaced his father as ruler of the state on 12 December 1949. He gave impetus to further developmental works and schemes. Priority was given, in particular, to the communication, education and health sectors. With the passage of time, considerable changes emerged in the social set-up of the region.

During the Swat state era, policies and decisions were made and implemented locally. There was no red-tape or bureaucratic file work. Multi-faceted developmental works were implemented. In 1969, however, Swat state was brought to an abrupt end. The areas of the former state were given the status of a district and a Deputy Commissioner was put in charge of the region's administration. The Kalam area, formerly an Agency administered by the Wali of Swat state as "Administrator" on behalf of the government of Pakistan, was made part of the Swat District.

The change in the mode of ruling, that came with the end of the state, slowed if not completely halted new development work in Swat. A decade later, however, in the 1980s and afterwards, a number of development projects were once again launched and undertaken. For example, the number of educational and healthcare institutions was increased, and the chain of the communication system extended. But the standard and quality of these services quickly deteriorated, while the civic amenities, such as free healthcare facilities, also faded away. The new officers' and bureaucracy's main concern was, and indeed largely continues to be, making money and "passing time" as best as they can. They were and are, on the whole, not concerned with solving the problems and redressing the—growing—grievances of Swat's populace.

And so, the end of the Swat state by the government of Pakistan resulted in drastic changes. A new and alien administrative apparatus was installed, characterised by federal and provincial centralisation and much red tape. Decisions on priorities, developmental schemes and the allocation of funds passed to the federal and provincial levels of the Pakistan state and the implementation of these is carried out by the bureaucratic hierarchy—a new and alien thing for Swati people.

Against this backdrop, I now outline the main factors that stimulated the unrest and dissatisfaction, and contributed to the crisis and insurgency in Swat (2007–09).

Constitutional issues

The tribal social organisation and set-up of Swat were altered radically by the rulers of the state, and hence the "tribal" nature of Swat society underwent drastic changes.[4] Nevertheless, the area's constitutional status as a tribal area is very significant.

The area is part of the Provincially Administered Tribal Areas (PATA), under article 246 of the Constitution of 1973. Accordingly, no laws made and passed by the federal and provincial legislatures apply here unless these are extended by the Governor of the province with the approval of the President of Pakistan. All this is stipulated under article 247(3) of the Constitution of 1973.

Additionally, the area's constitutional status has created a sort of dyarchy. The area is a Provincially Administered Tribal Area and hence under the control of the provincial government, which is responsible for the maintenance of law and order; yet the provincial government has no authority to make and promulgate laws for the area on its own. Laws are extended under article 247(3) of the Constitution, or are made under article 247(4) of the Constitution, with the consent of and by the Governor of the province with the prior approval of the President of the country, neither of whom is part of the provincial government or answerable to it; nor, more importantly, are they answerable to the people.[5]

Judicial issues

The commonly held belief that the Swat state's judicial system was "Islamic" and hence that disputes were settled swiftly, as per Islamic law, is unfounded.[6] However, the judicial system during this period was effective. Trials were quick and cheap; judgments and verdicts properly executed; and decisions on cases were usually made on either the first or second hearing. Moreover, "some of the shortcomings of the Western judicial system—technicality, delay, and high costs"[7] did not exist.

This situation, however, changed with the merger of Swat state in the province: initially in the then province of West Pakistan and later in the North-West Frontier Province. The government gradually started to extend Pakistan's laws but simultaneously failed to address the grievances of Swat's people that grew in strength and importance with each passing day. Although for most of the post-Swat state era the judicial mechanism has remained largely different from that in the rest of the province owing to special procedures being applied, it did not deliver a decent legal system to local people.

Geopolitics of Swat

Swatis regularly compare the period of the Swat state with their present situation. They rate the latter dismally in relation to the former, most notably in the areas of law and order, health, education, communication, peace and security.

In the post-Swat state period the indifferent and repressive behaviour of the police towards the common populace and the way they deal and interact with them, and their involvement in bribery, severe torture, high-handedness and collaboration with and assistance to criminals, embittered and alienated most people in Swat.

The political parties and leaders behave in the same manner as the officers and bureaucracy. They have often failed to take concrete steps to remove the anomalies, solve the problems and redress the grievances of the people.

Pakistani and American intelligence agencies (with blessing and support also from European and Arab countries) organised and trained jihadi organisations (forerunners of the Taliban) for armed jihad (*qital*)[8] to counter the Soviet Union in Afghanistan.[9] A new jihadi mindset and culture were created to counter the Soviet Union in Afghanistan which continued to work after the withdrawal of the Soviet forces.[10]

In the 1990s, the new elements, described as the Taliban, emerged in Afghanistan and took control of most of that country. But following the 9/11 incidents in the US, Pakistan backtracked from supporting the Afghan Taliban under American pressure; the Afghan Taliban's Pakistani supporters and counterparts (now called Pakistani Taliban) resented this U-turn and vowed to fight against the US and its allies, including the Pakistani security forces. As a result, the wider impact of the Afghan war on Pakistan has been enormous. Additionally, America's multifaceted interests in the region alarm Russia, China, Iran, and Pakistan, adding fuel to the fire to play out their war on Pukhtun soil, including in Swat.[11]

There has been an influx of outsiders into Swat (from other parts of the country, especially the province and the tribal areas like Dir, Bajawar, Mohmand and Khyber as well as Afghanistan) for business, trade, industry, tourism, labour, and services. Besides, the emergence of a new wealthy class and their desire for a change in the power structure and the choice for some sections of the un-privileged class to take revenge on the khans and malaks,[12] the federal government's operations in the FATA (Federally Administered Tribal Areas), the Lal Masjid (Red Mosque) operation in Islamabad in 2007 (especially the manner in which it was carried out), and the government's failure to enforce and implement Islamic laws in the courts with determination—as demanded by the TNSM and promised by successive governments—are some of the other broad reasons behind the 2007–09 armed struggle and upheaval.[13]

Mismanagement on the part of the government, an inefficient administrative system, and the failure of almost all the government departments in delivering services caused it to lose credibility in Swat. More importantly, these deficiencies also disappointed the masses or *awam*, who no longer have faith in the governments or their departments or the prevailing system.

The TNSM factor

In 1989, a movement was started in Dir District, neighbouring Swat, called the Tahrik Nifaz-e-Shariat-e-Muhammadi (TNSM), meaning Movement for the Enforcement of Islamic Law; it produced an organisation of which Sufi Muhammad was declared the Head.[14] The objective of the organisation was to compel the Pakistani authorities to enforce Islamic laws in the judicial arena and make the judiciary conform to the Islamic system in the Malakand Division. The organisation gradually extended the movement to Swat.[15] Prolonged legal procedures (after the merger of Swat state), undue delay, heightened expenditure, bribery, misuse of *riwaj* or customary laws, and the complicated nature of PATA Regulations[16] had already aggrieved most of the people of Swat. A judgment of the Peshawar High Court, on 24 February 1990, and then of the Supreme Court of Pakistan, on 12 February 1994, declaring the PATA Regulations *ultra vires* to articles 8 and 25 of the Constitution, worried the executive circles in Malakand Division: it meant a dilution of their unbounded power. Therefore, they allowed a free run to the TNSM and tacitly approved and supported its activities.[17] All of this resulted in an increased momentum for the TNSM in Swat (though at first Swatis were passive towards the movement and its organisers faced difficulties),[18] which led to the uprising and armed struggle in Swat in 1994.

The promulgation of the "Provincially Administered Tribal Areas (Nifaz-e-Nizam-e-Sharia) Regulation, 1994", as a result of the 1994 insurgency, and the purported changes it brought about did not satisfy the TNSM, and so the organisation started "Jeel Bharo Tahrik" (the movement to fill jails by offering self-arrests/court arrest) in June 1995. Local resentment continued, and a new regulation titled 'Shari-Nizam-e-Adl Regulation, 1999' was promulgated, yet it too failed to bring about any practical change in the workings of the legal system. And while Sufi Muhammad and his organisation were busy in the struggle for the enforcement of Islamic laws and for change in the judicial system, the 9/11 events unfolded and America invaded Afghanistan shortly afterwards. Sufi Muhammad along with tens of thousands of his supporters crossed into Afghanistan in November 2001 to fight on the Taliban's side against the Americans and their allies. After losing a large number of his supporters and being unable to counter the US assault, he, along with his son-in-law Fazlullah, made their way back to Pakistan, where they were caught by security forces and subsequently incarcerated.

Sufi Muhammad remained in jail, but Fazlullah was released in 2003. After his release, he started preaching a purity campaign on an FM radio channel. Since his father-in-law was in prison, he was supported by TNSM activists and sympathisers and with the assistance of the radio channel he quickly progressed with his activities. Later, he started the construction of a *madrasa* (seminary) and *markaz* (centre) in his home village Mamdherai (also known as Imamdherai). People from all sections of society generously made donations (*chandah*) on his orders; they would reach the venue in crowds of thousands of people at short notice. He was greatly promoted in and by the local media, although some opposition did exist.

His growing power and popularity emboldened him and his supporters to challenge the writ of the government. To counter this challenge, the government needed to make a show of force. These developments, however, were brought under control each time because certain agreements were reached between the provincial MMA government and Fazlullah. The policy and course of action adopted by Fazlullah, however, became a source of dissension within the rank and file of the TNSM. Though the TNSM disavowed his policy and officially severed connections with him, his power and popularity continued to increase rapidly and significantly. And in December 2007, a breakaway faction, led by Fazlullah, became part of the newly-established organization Tahrik Taliban Pakistan, at that time headed by Baitullah Mahsud, an alliance or umbrella organization of different groups.[19]

Musharraf's tussle with the judiciary

President Musharraf's tussle with the Chief Justice of the Supreme Court, Justice Iftikhar Muhammad Chaudhry, and the judiciary started in March 2007. This provided space for Fazlullah to continue his activities unhindered and expand his sphere of influence, as both the federal and provincial governments were involved (one way or the other) for or against the parties'/sides' activities, and all the political parties and non-state actors/civil society turned their guns in that direction and focused on that issue.

Security forces' conduct

Although they were sent into Swat in July 2007 to curb Fazlullah's activities and growing power, and to restore the government's writ, the security forces remained dormant and a spectator to his activities. It was in the army's presence that he for the first time, came out of his village, in person, heavily armed and guarded to offer the Eid prayer in the Kabal ground, kilometres away from his home and centre. Ironically (and to the further surprise of the masses) the army, deployed at Kabal Golf Course, sought Fazlullah's permission and offered the Eid prayer with and behind him. Afterwards, the operation against the Swat Taliban from November 2007 to February 2009 was carried out in a way that apparently did not target the Taliban, but rather innocent civilians.[20]

These events and the way the security forces interacted with the civilians more generally, as well as the damage and destruction their activities brought about during the three phases of the Operation Rah-e-Haq (Operation the Righteous Path), generated distrust and resentment against the security forces among the civilian populace, and created and increased support for the Taliban.

Taliban policies and works

Some of the Taliban policies and actions were abominable to the standards of local people, yet this was not the whole story; some of their policies and works generated sympathy and support. For example, unlike the NGOs and the government functionaries, they addressed the people in simple Pashto, their mother tongue; what they said was easily comprehended and absorbed by educated and non-educated people alike, and went to the hearts of many.[21]

They also constructed new roads and paths; opened up irrigation water courses that were covered and brought within the houses in many places; disposed of cases and disputes quickly without any costs to the parties; solved some age-old disputes and issues; tried to effect conciliation among enemies; stressed women's right to inheritance; decreased doctors' and pathological laboratories fees; compelled PESCO[22] and PTCL[23] employees to repair and restore the lines without delay; and ended electric power load-shedding in Swat.

Besides, police high-handedness and oppression were brought to an end, after the police became increasingly ineffective in carrying out their basic duties. A number of dacoits and habitual murderers (*ujrati qatilan*) who committed murders for others and took money for carrying out the task, perished; and *charas* or hashish, heroin, alcohol and other intoxicants and narcotics were banned. The Taliban also banned the direct flow of toilet waste to the drains and made septic tanks compulsory.[24] These and other such works of public utility and policies of the Taliban generated local support and sympathy.

The present scenario

As both the government and Fazlullah refused to budge from their respective positions, by October 2007 the situation had become extremely volatile. So the government deployed more security forces in the area and started an operation named Operation Rah-e-Haq. Overtly some armed clashes occurred, but simultaneously the government seemed willing to find a peaceful solution to the problem, the provincial Governor declaring that any army operation would be the last option. President Musharraf, however, on the same day asked the Taliban to lay down their arms.[25] The Taliban also showed flexibility and expressed their desire for a peaceful solution of the issue through negotiations.[26] Despite speaking of reconciliation, however, they also demanded the withdrawal of the security forces, enforcement of Islamic laws, and the release of Sufi Muhammad.[27]

The overt clashes and the security forces' heavy shelling of Swat continued, using helicopter gunships, artillery and mortars that mostly hit not the Taliban and their bases but the civilians and the hills. However, after some days, Fazlullah and his *shura* (consultative body or aides) ordered their fighters to pull back from the roadside bases to avoid further losses to the civilians, and they went underground.[28] They said this was not flight from the fight, but a change of war strategy.[29] While the situation seemed to have calmed down by January 2008, heavy and indiscriminate shelling by the security forces caused heavy losses to the lives and property of innocent civilians; a large number of people inside Swat were also displaced. Monetary losses worth billions of rupees were incurred.

In February 2008, general elections were held in Pakistan and an Awami National Party (ANP)-led coalition government was formed in the NWFP (now Khyber Pakhtunkhwa). As the ANP contested the elections on the slogan of restoring peace and order and bringing normalcy to the province, the provincial government negotiated with Sufi Muhammad's and Fazlullah's organisations. Agreements were made and Sufi Muhammad was released. Besides other things, the government promised the enforcement of Islamic laws as per the demands of the TNSM, who in turn agreed to support the government in its righteous endeavours and in the restoration of peace and the maintenance of law and order.[30]

Differences, however, soon emerged between the parties on particular points. Each side blamed the other for not fulfilling the agreements, which, once more, strained relations and resulted in fresh armed clashes. The security forces embarked on the second phase of their operation, and the Taliban organised their own strategies. All of this, however, again brought misery and great losses—to both human beings and property—for the region's civilians. Additionally, the unprecedented curfew imposed by the army, lasting 22 consecutive days during the month of Ramadan,[31] and the severance of electricity and telephone lines caused further serious problems for the local population. While the militants resorted to decapitation, slaughter, targeted killing and the destruction of government installations (especially educational institutions, bridges, police posts, and police stations), the Pakistan army resorted "to carpet bombing and massive shelling as invading armies do."[32] The targeted blowing up and destruction of residential houses and bungalows, shops and commercial markets by both sides became routine. If the course adopted by the Taliban generated resentment and brought misery and worry for the people, the actions of the army compelled the people to look upon it "as an occupying force rather than a protector."[33]

The security forces' actions managed to generate sympathy for the Taliban and resentment against the government and the army, because it was "the people of the area who" were "suffering as innocent civilians" were "being killed in the army action".[34] Delawar Jan observed, in November 2008:

> The military operation was welcome with a hope that the militants would soon be eliminated. They [the army men] were garlanded and hugged when Taliban were routed in the major towns in their initial action. However, with the passage of time, the military lost control and the militants bounced back strongly. Now one year on, the people find them back to square one, as the militants still rule the roost.
>
> Today, despite their continuing sacrifices for bringing peace to the valley, the army's intention to crush militants is being doubted and instead of winning hearts and minds, the military is alienating people of the valley due to continuing civilian casualties and problems triggered by the military operation. The alienation is caused by the fact that the military could not protect the life and property but instead added to their problems. This is high time to prove this growing perception wrong by defeating, and too quickly, the militants to secure people. For it, the action must be visible and difference felt, not claimed.[35]

Even the ANP parliamentarians and ministers showed their reservations about the security forces' conduct and the credibility of the operation. Haji Adeel, ANP Senior Vice President and senator, observed: "What will be the credibility of the military operation in Swat when houses of ministers are destroyed and their family members are queued up for shooting." He admitted that "the people have lost confidence in the government and the army".[36] The provincial government publicly raised the issue "after an unusually long session of the Cabinet" and the Provincial Information Minister Mian Iftikhar Hussain conveyed "the concern of his government over the rising number of civilian casualties during the military operation". He said the security forces should carry out the operation in a manner that would help restore the confidence of the people in Swat. He was also quoted as saying that "the military should take effective action against the militants so that peace is restored in Swat Valley."[37] And in a resolution that was passed by a majority, the provincial assembly "asked the federal government to immediately restore peace in Swat".[38] President Asif Ali Zardari held meetings, on four separate occasions, with the high-ups of the provincial government, members of the Provincial Assembly (MPAs) from Swat and the *jargah* of Swat in Islamabad and Peshawar. All the time he was apprised of the situation on the ground and the reservations over the army's actions in Swat. The provincial ministers and MPAs also lodged their protests with the Corps Commander Peshawar and the provincial Governor.[39]

The violence continued and the army conducted phases two and three (which was claimed as the fastest one) of the Operation Rah-e-Haq. These had the effect of spreading and expanding the power, control and authority of the Taliban with each passing day and shrinking and waning that of the government. The tragedy was that there were "many players involved" (at both the state and global levels), each with "its own agenda".[40] However, Swat and its civilians continued to be victimised.

While the government continued to press for an unconditional laying down of arms as a precondition to a dialogue and settlement, the Taliban were also adamant that their demands, including the withdrawal of the security forces, implementation of Islamic laws as they demanded, compensation for their losses at the hands of the security forces, and an unconditional release of their arrested associates, must be met as a precondition for pulling back.

Swat was at the crossroads. At last the provincial government, compelled by the circumstances,[41] entered into a fresh agreement with Sufi Muhammad on 15 February 2009 and the clashes subsided. Amazingly, and to the surprise of the Swatis, the reactions of India, America and Afghanistan to the peace deal were extremely negative. This testifies to the involvement and stakes, one way or the other, of the external elements and forces in the affair, upheaval and destruction in Swat. Even countries like France, thus far unheard on the issue of militancy and the upheaval in Swat, expressed reservations over the "Talibanisation" of Pakistan. France's new special envoy to Afghanistan and Pakistan, while talking to reporters in New Delhi, said: "The Swat agreement 'has a worldwide resonance'."[42] Ironically, President Asif Ali Zardari was not giving his approval to the new proposed Nizam-e-Adl Regulation. Without his prior approval—under article 247(4) of the Constitution—the regulation could not be promulgated, though under the agreement signed between the representatives of the provincial government and the TNSM it had to be promulgated and implemented. That was why the ANP-headed provincial government was "growing impatient over" his "reluctance" to sign the regulation and was "desperately urging him to do so at the earliest".[43]

At the peace agreement Sufi Muhammad came to Swat, established his camp and made peace marches to various areas of the valley. Outwardly the situation was moving back to normalcy and tempers were cooling. Sufi Muhammad, however, was pressing the government to speed up the process of implementing the Islamic laws. Otherwise, he threatened to wind up his camp and go back; later on this is what he practically did. It was expected—following verbal commitments made between the provincial government and the TNSM—that Sufi Muhammad would not only restore peace in Swat but also denounce, in a public meeting, militancy and fighting against government forces as being un-Islamic.[44] Instead, he denounced different organs of the state, which created a great mess in the region and led the situation to worsen.[45]

Interestingly, Fazlullah and the Swat Taliban ruled the roost through their FM radio from 2007 till April 2009. The broadcasts not only continued uninterrupted at a fixed frequency and according to a timetable with no attempt made by the army and government to interrupt them. The frequency was also continuously upgraded, enabling the Swat Taliban to extend their influence and to keep control over Swat and parts of Dir, Shangla, and the Malakand Protected Area.[46]

Another development in the post-peace agreement days was the release of an old video-clip by a women activist, Samar Minallah, to the media. The clip shows the Taliban lashing a girl, allegedly for her "immorality". This was not the sole case of lashing of allegedly guilty persons/criminals. There were reported to be four cases of the lashing of females and some twenty four cases of the punishment being meted out to males, for allegedly different crimes by the Taliban at the zenith of their power.[47] A number of these acts were recorded on CD by the Taliban themselves and made available in the market. Yet both the national and the international media took this particular video-clip and used it to campaign vigorously against the peace agreement. Both the provincial government and the Taliban termed the release of the video-clip "as a conspiracy to sabotage the 16 February peace deal."[48] Interestingly, a year later government agencies claimed that the video-clip was fake and had been financed by some non-state actors so as to defame Pakistan.[49]

While the ceasefire was effected in February 2009 and peace was restored, inwardly both sides of the conflict—the Taliban and the army—were making their positions stronger and flexing their muscles for a fresh and decisive round of fighting. As well as making their position stronger in Swat, the Taliban made inroads into Dir and Buner, with the blessings of the Commissioner Malakand Division, Muhammad Javaid.[50] Their inroads into Dir and especially Buner were sensationalised by the media, and were perceived as a march towards and a prelude to taking over Islamabad and Pakistan's nuclear weapons. Interestingly, the issue took a crucial turn and was further sensationalised when Fazlur Rahman (Amir/chief of Jamiatul Ulama-e-Islam-F, that is, the Jamiatul Ulama-e-Islam faction led by him) said on the National Assembly floor that the Taliban had reached Tarbela and that there were only the Margalla Hills between them and Islamabad, the country's capital city.[51]

The government claimed that the inroads into Dir and Buner were violations of the peace agreement made between the provincial government and TNSM on 15 February 2009, and hence embarked on a military operation in those areas. On the other hand, Sufi Muhammad said that by launching these operations, "the government had violated the Swat peace agreement"[52]; and a Taliban commander, using the alias of Tahir, said that the "peace agreement with the NWFP government has practically been scrapped but we are waiting for a word from Maulana Sufi Muhammad for taking a decision."[53]

Against this backdrop, "in a meeting of the Joint Chiefs of Staff Committee," held on 30 April 2009, "Pakistan's top military leaders resolved to support the government in showing 'zero tolerance' towards militancy in Malakand division."[54] Though the operation was already in progress, Prime Minister Yusuf Raza Gilani announced in a broadcast to the nation on 7 May 2009 that a fresh military operation against the Swat Taliban was being launched. This led to the military Operation Rah-e-Rast (Operation the Straight Path) in Swat. An Indian analyst, Brig Gurmeet Kanwal (retd.) had already cautioned "the senior leadership of the Pakistan army" in October 2008:

It needs to understand that artillery barrages and helicopter and air force bombings of civilian villages and towns are inherently counterproductive. The field commanders must be taught to discriminate between innocent civilians and armed combatants and must demonstrate concern for senior citizens, women and children instead of treating them with disdain.[55]

Completely disregarding this advice, and to the dismay of the civilians whose fears and apprehensions proved true, the security forces resorted to indiscriminate bombardment and shelling by jet aeroplanes, gunship helicopters and artillery and the use of force targeting civilians. This caused great civilian casualties, the destruction of houses, buildings and the infrastructure, and the displacement of hundreds of thousands of people, bringing distress to all Swatis in one way or another.[56] Even at this critical juncture, the policy of containment and not elimination of the TNSM/Taliban was followed. Ironically, the catastrophe and calamity brought to the land and people of Swat was not natural but man-made. And it is a pity that the federal and provincial governments and the security forces have since sought to absolve themselves of the responsibility for this disaster.

The government and the security forces claimed success and, in late July 2009, the return of the internally displaced persons (IDPs) was allowed in a stage-by-stage manner. The grip of the Taliban weakened, yet the distress of the region's civilians continued owing to the mass destruction caused to the land and people of Swat. Moreover, the security forces, on the whole, interacted with the civilians like foreign occupation forces and failed to uphold local values and traditions, most especially by violating the sanctity of the *chadar* and *chardiwari*.

Of the two main actors, the Taliban and the security forces, the Taliban seemed uprooted and, amid the blackout of free media coverage, the security forces and governments issued statements/news according to their own preferences. But while not visible on the streets, the Taliban have maintained their presence in other ways. Besides, the security forces' success may not mean that the Taliban's ideology and mindset have changed or faded away. The Taliban are defeated physically, but their ideology, mindset and ideals still remain.

Therefore, all the forces and actors involved directly and indirectly, need to behave sanely and address the core issues that contributed to and prepared the ground for the Taliban and militancy and generated local support for them. The security forces need to further reform their ways of interacting with the masses, so that Swat may not once again become a flashpoint. The mere presence of the security forces will never be sufficient for the Taliban's permanent removal from the Swat scene, and is equally never a guarantee of durable peace.[57]

At the defeat of the Taliban, the security forces compelled the civilians to form *lakhkars* (or *lashkars*),[58] and some *jargahs*[59] by the name of "peace *jargahs*" have also been formed by and at the behest of the army.[60] Moreover, the security forces have also compelled the civilians to patrol and conduct "watches" (especially at night-time) and search operations against the Taliban. Yet it is not the duty of the civilians to patrol, conduct watches and protect themselves. They have agriculture, trade and other works and services to occupy them. It is the responsibility of the security forces to perform patrols and watches, to ensure the smooth running of life and provide security and a working environment for the civilians and also a sense of honour and respectability to their lives. Forming the *lakhkars* and *jargahs* in the post-Taliban scenario, and patrolling and watches by the civilians, are steps that take Swati society back to a latter-day form of "tribalism" that is neither a positive nor an encouraging development for its people.

The resentment against the destruction caused by the security forces during their operations in Swat is high. This is because of the delay in and the failure to record all the losses—great or small—experienced by local people during these operations. Moreover, while the damage was being assessed (in 2009), the decision was made not to give full compensation but instead uniform and meagre sums of 160,000 and 400,000 rupees for partially and fully damaged buildings respectively. At the same time, no compensation was awarded for damage to household items and other articles and crops. In addition to issues arising out of compensation policy, the manner in which some of the security forces' personnel interact with the civilians, notably their lack of respect for *chadar* and *chardiwari*—sanctity of the veil and privacy of houses—especially during the search operations, led to local anger. Added to this disregard for the local values and traditions is the occupation of private residences and other buildings by the security forces, which has compelled the owners of these to reside elsewhere in rented houses, while receiving no payment in return. All of this and more led to mistrust, abhorrence and resentment against the security forces and provincial and federal governments more generally.

In addition, the security forces ruthlessly cut down the trees standing on the paths and road sides and also standing in the fields (grown with great labour, and seen as asset not only to landowners and the people of Swat but also to the country and humanity at large) on the grounds of security concerns.[61] In addition the cultivation of particular crops like maize (which is a source of livelihood for many, and not only a cash crop but also a food grain and source of wet and dry fodder and fire-fuel) was banned in some areas, on security grounds. Furthermore, in some areas ordinary people were compelled to carry security passes (issued by the army), which they must display over their necks or chests and, in addition, to have vehicle passes[62]; this, and the number of check-posts which create hurdles in the smooth running of life even two years after the defeat of the Taliban, and the news of targeted killings and militants' encounters with the security forces, are other matters of concern for the civilians at large.

All these issues and factors might possibly spark a further stage in the conflict, if the grievances of the people of the area are not properly addressed and the reconstruction and developmental works are not embarked upon without delay. Preferably the reconstruction efforts should be carried out by the civil administration and the concerned departments so as to shift the responsibility to the government and establish their writ once more.

A permanent solution

While calling the Taliban fanatics and rebels is justified by some standards—H.G. Raverty said sardonically in the nineteenth century that "all are 'fanatics,' rebels, or dacoits, who fight against us according to some people"[63]—and provides a reason for military action against them, it has not proved and will not prove a durable solution to the region's problems.

Although the Swat Taliban have been defeated, dispersed and made vulnerable, they are not completely uprooted, nor have their ideology and mindset changed. Their defeat and disappearance from the scene may not be deemed to have erased their ideology, mindset and ideals from this space. As a result, bringing them back to the mainstream of the political, social and religious dynamics of the region is now imperative.

THE SWAT CRISIS

If talks with the Afghan Taliban are imperative for a political solution—the Head of the UN mission in Afghanistan, Kai Eide, has said it is "high time" a political solution is found with the Taliban to resolve the ten-year-old conflict[64]—then why is this not so in Pakistan as well?

Prime Minister Yusuf Raza Gilani conceded in Peshawar, on 4 March 2010, while addressing members of the NWFP PPP parliamentary party, that a "military operation was no solution to terrorism and extremism".[65] He even told the National Assembly, on 19 January 2009, that "military operations are not a solution to all the problems in the Tribal Areas and Swat, and vowed to come up with a 'political strategy' to deal with the situation";[66] and while talking to journalists, on 13 February 2009, he said that "a military operation is not the only solution to the Swat situation".[67]

Being citizens of Pakistan, the Taliban need to be brought back to the mainstream. To this end, a general amnesty might be announced, and workshops and courses for their debriefing and de-brainwashing arranged and conducted. If not all, then the majority of them can certainly be brought back to the mainstream and made peaceful citizens with minimal efforts, the precedents of which are found in Indonesia and Saudi Arabia.[68]

Further complementary and essential steps needed for defusing the situation permanently are the implementation of Islamic laws and a concerted attempt to make the judicial system responsive, efficient and effective; addressing the core local issues contributing to the disaffection and unrest; friendly interaction by the security forces with the people; strengthening the civil administration; and the withdrawal of the army in a step-by-step way over the course of the year. The withdrawal of foreign forces from Afghanistan and Iraq, and resolving the Kashmir and Palestine issues, are also imperative. Combined, all of this will reduce the jihadi organisations' importance in Pakistan and defuse the anti-Western and anti-America sentiments that are found there.

12

PRODUCING CIVIL SOCIETY, IGNORING *RIVAJ*

INTERNATIONAL DONORS, THE STATE AND DEVELOPMENT INTERVENTIONS IN SWAT

Urs Geiser

Until the war between the Pakistan army and the "Swat Taliban" escalated in late 2007, the valley of Swat was almost unknown to the general public in the outside world. If reports did emerge, they portrayed a remote and isolated spot amidst snow-covered mountains (often termed the Switzerland of Asia) that was inhabited by proud but militant tribes living within a timeless and rigid social order.[1] Within academia, though, Swat became an important anchor for differentiated insights into, and theories of, tribal structures, social organisation and state-making. In addition, Swat was also an important site for early attempts to conceptualise agency and structure. Fredrik Barth[2] and Charles Lindholm,[3] among others, carefully analysed Pushtun social norms as well as the room for manoeuvre that these allowed, and seemingly egalitarian tribal structures; they detailed power rivalries and the emergence of an indigenous princely state within the wider context of the British Raj and the first decades after formal decolonisation.

It was, however, after 9/11 and the War on Terror that Swat entered daily newspapers and TV channels around the globe. They showed how in late 2007 Taliban fighters became active in Swat and thus beyond the context of Afghanistan. The media showed images of heavily armed militias and there were also many reports in the world's press about how these brutally enforced a rigid social order. Later, images followed the Pakistan army's fight against the "Swat Taliban", the drama of IDPs (internally displaced persons) and the army's eventual declaration of victory in 2009.

Journalists and many academics made connections between the Taliban uprising and the military suppression of this in terms of received wisdom about the nature of the region as deeply entrenched in a rigid and highly masculine Pushtun culture, and also as a spillover of the "War against Terror" in nearby Afghanistan which was seeping into North-West Pakistan's Pushtun belt. According to these interpretations of the events, the militant confrontations in Swat were explained as the unintended consequences of the encounter between local culture and global politics; at their core was a struggle for "identity".[4]

There is no question that 9/11, the War on Terror, elements of Pushtun "culture" and the extension of this across national boundaries were, indeed, important factors that shaped the events of 2007. But this focus on "static culture" and "global politics" falls short of appreciating dynamics beyond those that are "cultural" and defined in terms of grand global politics. Local dynamics also play a role in the emergence of militancy as well, though these are not as easily identifiable and are less suitable for offering simple, causal explanations. The focus on global politics and Pushtun culture does not inquire into the potential complexities of "the local", such as social heterogeneities within Swat (Swatis are treated as being all Pushtun, and either as villains or victims), or the nature of people's everyday economic lives and livelihood struggles, including contested access to resources. Instead, they are just depicted as living "tribal lives". The conventional narrative about the conflict reduces the encounter to one that took place between a homogeneous Swat and a "global" factor, the War on Terror. And it does not address the importance of the Pakistan state and its varied entities as being active but complex mediators between the local and the global. Instead, the Pakistan state is depicted either as a liberating force or as the power behind the Taliban. Some of these shortcomings of conventional modes of analysing the events in Swat since 2007 are discussed by observers who seek to explain the Swat conflict in terms of it being a classical class struggle, a conflict between bourgeois khans and their proletarian tenants.[5] As I will show in this chapter, this form of analysis is also a reductionist reading that fails to account for a great deal of local social and economic complexity.

This chapter seeks to understand Swat not as a stagnant social space constrained by the culture of Pukhtunwali[6] and recently exposed to unsettling singular global forces. It attempts, rather, to bring attention to the differentiated agency of Swat's people, the multiplicity of structures that they have reproduced, and have to deal with, or challenge during the course of their lives. This chapter calls, in short, for closer attention to relations between diverse dimensions of Swati peoples' lives, including the legal system of the modern state, customary land rights, practices of forest usage, the judiciary, civil society and "social movements".

In order to contribute to a more nuanced understanding of Swat, the chapter focuses on a little known aspect of Swat's recent history that also involves an encounter between the "local" and the "global", and is in addition explicitly connected to the mediating role of the modern state in this: ideas and practices of the global phenomena of "development". "Development" encompasses ideas, among others, about "better lives" and "good societies", and the role of the modern state in the fashioning of these. "Development" is often guided by a specific reading of existing realities, a reading that is predominantly deployed in order to justify practices of social and economic transformation. The development industry and its fringe of "applied researchers" seek to change the "under-developed" into something new and "developed". Indeed, I will argue, "development" led many in Swat to confront global ideas—ideas they directly experienced in a way that often clashed with the routinised practices of everyday life. Some welcomed these ideas and practices; others responded critically; some even resisted them. The encounter I refer to started in the early 1980s. At that point, Swat and its surrounding districts (roughly the Malakand Division) in the North-West Frontier Province (NWFP)[7] experienced a sudden boom in "modern development". The region was chosen by an array of international aid donors for the implementation of development interventions. Among them were the Dutch, the Swiss, the European Union, the Italians, and multilateral donors such as the FAO and the ADB (see table 12.1).[8]

The fact that Swat, on the one hand, experienced a high density of modernising development projects and, on the other, became an arena for brutal confrontation between "anti-modern" forces and states represents a puzzle to be reflected upon; it also offers the opportunity for a more differentiated inquiry into the developments that led to the conflict in 2007. How did the encounter between modern development and local realities take place in Swat? How did it influence this political space? How far did it contribute, often in the most subtle of ways, to the emergence of resistance and militancy? And what can we learn from these encounters in relation to other recent events in this part of the world?

In order to discuss these issues, the following section describes the peculiar meaning of "modern state" in the context of Swat. As I will show, people in Swat experience "the state" in a highly complex manner, replete with many contradictions and also potential lines of conflict. It is important that we describe the details of "the state" and its relation to Swat in as "thick" a manner as possible, for this represents the context into which the boom of international donor aid fell.

The next section then illustrates how these donors started to support the Pakistan state, especially the provincial government of the NWFP. This section highlights how far donor initiatives and "development" as such cannot be studied in isolation, as mere expressions of economic concerns or altruistic intentions. They need, rather, to be analysed, again through thick description, as political acts, more specifically in the context of the efforts by the new nation state of Pakistan to expand its control over Swat. The following section describes the strategies and interventions of aid (perceived by aid workers as apolitical "participatory strategies"), and the new forms of social organisation that these initiated. I call this the "new civil society", made up mostly of non-governmental organisations (NGOs), many of them instituted by international aid.

While the second, third and fourth sections focus on the state and aid donors—and, thus, are "seeing like a state"[9]—the fifth section attempts to understand how these interventions were experienced by different sections of Swat's people, and, therefore, how they "see the state" and "the global", predominantly in terms of these being mediated and experienced through development projects.[10] I suggest three main fields of articulation: (i) In spite of their participatory approach, projects strengthened state control over natural resources, ignoring locally existing forms of regulating access (routinised institutions or "customs" or *rivaj*); (ii) projects actively created new forms of social organisation that competed with existing forms of political organisation such as the council of elders (*jirga*); and (iii) concerns central to many people in Swat, especially contestations around land rights and the related state judiciary, were ignored and not addressed by these interventions.

The sixth section argues that donor-supported projects were not in a position to increase the modern state's legitimacy in the political space of Swat, and that the "civil society" they caused to emerge had shallow roots in this locale. These points, though, became part of the anti-state discourse and practice of the radical Tahrik Nifaz-e-Shariat-e-Muhammadi (TNSM)—a movement that (at least until mid 2007) promised a more vernacular development path. The section details how exponents of the TNSM skilfully framed local concerns into an anti-state and anti-"modernisation" discourse—offering Islamic rules and regulations (sharia) as a logical alternative that was also justified as being vernacular, though in a way that recalls Hobsbawm and Ranger's arguments about "invented traditions".

In the final, seventh section I explore the potential entanglements between the modern state's approach to Swat after the merger, development projects' attempts at modernisation, and the discourse of factions of the TNSM up to mid-2007. I argue that there are no simple causalities, but that some consequences of state and donor practices did feed arguments that suited the TNSM factions in their venture of "other"-isation—in other words, the portrayal of the state and donors as being responsible for problems faced by Swatis—and the offering of sharia to them as the only alternative. I identify a few issues that, I suggest, interlink the development enterprise with the resistance of the TNSM. The arrival of modern civil society (NGOs, CBOs) in Swat, for example, bypassed and challenged established forms of political power such as the *jirga*; the modern nation state did not take into account issues of *rivaj* that inform actual on-the-ground and everyday relations of controlling natural resources but instead, introduced legislation that was "alien" to many; further, donor-supported development ventures did not address issues of land rights and related concerns about inefficient judiciary services. All these points figured prominently in the discourse of the TNSM factions, and there was no surprise that this discourse resonated in powerful ways among vast sections of Swat's population. However, by mid-2007 this more locally informed dimension of the discourse perished in other forms of militancy fuelled by events beyond Swat; I will specifically refer to the Lal Masjid incident.

Empirical insights underpinning the arguments presented in this chapter are based on my earlier involvement in the region as "utilitarian researcher"[11] for several aid projects (1985 to the mid-1990s),[12] and later as a university-based researcher involved in highly stimulating joint research ventures with Pakistani scholars (late 1990s to the present).[13]

"Seeing like a state"

To recall:[14] In 1849, the British colonial power conquered the north-west of the Indian subcontinent up to the plains of Peshawar to establish its colonial state structures, which included land settlement. In 1901 the North-West Frontier Province (NWFP) was created. The mountainous areas beyond the plains, and thus the NWFP, remained under independent tribal control. Fearing a takeover by the British, Pushtun tribes in the Swat valley began to join hands.[15] Around 1917, a new leader (invested with the title Wali) started to build the new and independent state of Swat. This process included the gradual evolution of a coherent administration and the re-formulation of land and inheritance rights. Swat did not pro-

PRODUCING CIVIL SOCIETY, IGNORING *RIVAJ*

perly become a part of Pakistan when this country emerged as an independent, modern nation-state in 1947; it was only in late 1969 that Swat, together with adjacent areas, was merged into the nation state of Pakistan.

For Swat proper, the merger meant the abolition of administrative rules and regulations that existed under the state of Swat, and their replacement by the rules and regulations of the new state of Pakistan—however, not in full. Through specific legislation, the new districts of Swat, Dir, Chitral, the Malakand Agency and a few other areas[16] were brought together to form a new Malakand Division. This Division was to maintain a special status different from the settled areas of the NWFP—a status designated as "Provincially Administered Tribal Area" or PATA. One important characteristic of the PATA is that modern state legislation (that of the settled regions of the NWFP in the context of federal legislation) does not apply automatically, but its extension to the PATA needs to be sanctioned by the Governor of the NWFP and the President of Pakistan.[17] Regarding civil administration, the former Head of Swat state was replaced by a Deputy Commissioner, responsible to the provincial capital of Peshawar. People in Swat thus experienced the new regime through a new civil administration, a new police, a new judiciary—and in addition through a series of (new) governmental departments ranging from civil works (roads, power) to health to education and rural development. In the following, I focus on entities of the modern state that are mandated with bringing progress and development—the "Nation-Building Departments"[18]—with special reference to forestry and agriculture. In order to grasp the importance of these agencies, I first discuss their relation to Swat prior to the merger.

In November 1947, the ruler of the Swat state and the Governor-General of Pakistan signed the "Instrument of Accession". Through this document, the Swat ruler handed over control of "External Affairs, Defence and Communication" to the State of Pakistan, but maintained and even expanded control over internal affairs.[19] Therefore it appears that none of modern Pakistan's nation-building departments became active within the jurisdiction of the Swat state after 1947—except the Forest Department. As a matter of fact, it was already the colonial forest officials that regularly tried to influence forest management in Swat. The Wali agreed that colonial forest officials carried out inventories and wrote forest management plans; however, he also maintained strict control over actual forest use.[20] With the Instrument of Accession, the Wali further expanded his control over forest resources vis-à-vis the NWFP Forest Department. For this purpose, he established his own forestry service.

The merger of Swat into modern Pakistan in late 1969 gave the nation-building departments the long-awaited opportunity to expand their sphere of influence to this region as well—only, however, under the condition that they followed the complex legal procedures as defined for the PATA. To enable government departments to operate in Swat, respective legislation had first to be established or extended to Swat. It took time for such legislation to arrive. Regarding forestry, modern state laws reached Swat only around 1974. Other state agencies followed, such as the Department of Agricultural Research, Department of Agricultural Extension, Department of Livestock, etc.[21] By the late 1970s, these departments still had limited staff and operational budgets. As explored below, a key argument deployed to get support from international donors was to further strengthen the capacities and spatial reach of the modern state's agencies.

An important change in the working of line departments took place with the most recent attempt at decentralisation. Pakistan has seen several efforts at improving the interlinkages between its "citizens" and the state's developmental administration. Earlier examples included Basic Democracies and Union Councils.[22] The "Devolution of Power" process announced by General Musharraf in late 1999 (and formally operational by mid-2001) represented a new attempt, by introducing a three-tier political system with elected Union Councils, a body at *tehsil* level, and elected District Councils. The level of Division (in our example, Malakand Division) was abolished.[23] Government field staff now became accountable to the new district administration. However, it was only the Forest Department that did not follow this arrangement—it continued its old hierarchical structure with full control vested in the Peshawar head office. This highlights the specific strength and political power of this agency that is in charge of dealing with an economically highly valuable natural resource in Swat, something to which I return below.[24]

Supporting the developmental state

So far, I have indicated the efforts undertaken by the authorities of the province to expand their structures, reach and power throughout Swat. As a result, a complicated system to declare and operate state rules and regulations emerged, many of them being new and unknown to the people of Swat.

I also mentioned that during the 1970s, financial and manpower resources were limited, which resulted in a very limited presence of the modern state at local level. But this changed in the 1980s with the arrival of donor-supported development projects. It is difficult to determine whether this was a planned strategy of the NWFP government (to pro-actively acquire foreign funding and project support) or whether it followed more supply-driven dynamics. In many Northern countries, the early 1980s saw an enormous increase in budgets allocated to "development of the South", which in turn required the creation of projects to spend funds on. There were almost no donor-supported projects in Swat prior to 1980.

In the early 1980s, the category of "state" still had considerable credibility within global development circles. In the mainstream discourse, it was the modern, post-colonial nation state and its expert staff that were to deliver development.[25] In line with this view, emphasis was given by the mid-1980s to strengthening the field-level capacities of the state: area-based and integrated rural development projects were born. In order to establish these, most donors entered into agreements with one (for sectorial projects) or several departments (for integrated projects) of the NWFP government through planning procedures and mechanisms as established within the modern state administration. Upwards, they were responsible to the Secretary of the respective state agency and the donor's head office. There was, though, no formalised "downward" accountability.

Indeed, Swat can be described as a hot-spot of the global development industry. There were some donor-supported projects in the Hazara region (for example, German forestry projects in Kaghan and Siran) and the Peshawar plain (such as German support for integrated rural development in Mardan, or ADB-funded irrigation projects), and very few in the southern districts of the NWFP. But

PRODUCING CIVIL SOCIETY, IGNORING *RIVAJ*

proportionally many more were attracted to the Swat valley and its surrounding mountains (see table 12.1).

However, in the perception of aid experts, there was considerable reluctance on the side of "local people" in Swat to interact and collaborate with governmental staff. In addition, the projects' spread was limited. There was an urgent need to find new ways of reaching and winning "the people",—and it was here that the emerging global paradigms of "participation", "empowerment" and "civil society" became influential.

Producing civil society

Indeed, the second half of the 1980s witnessed the emergence of a new global development paradigm—participation. It argued that state agencies alone are not

Table 12.1: Some area-based donor supported projects in the Malakand Division

Name of project	Area covered	Main Donors	Duration
Kalam Integrated Development Project (KIDP)	Kalam and Behrain Tehsils of Swat district	Swiss SDC	1981–1998
Range Management Project (RMP)	Swat, Dir	Dutch	1989–1992
Dir-Swat Watershed Management Project (WMP)	Swat, Dir	Dutch	1980–1992
Malakand Social Forestry Project (MSFP)	Malakand Agency, southern Swat	Dutch	1987–1992
Social Forestry Project Malakand-Dir (SFP)	Malakand Agency, Dir	Dutch	1992–1999
Dir-Kohistan Environment Rehabilitation Project (ERNP)	Dir	EU, IUCN	1997–2003
Fruit and Vegetable Development Project (MFVDP)	Swat	Swiss	1990s
PATA irrigation project	Swat, Malakand Agency	Dutch	late 1980s
Fruits Project		Italian	mid 1980s
Pakistan-Swiss Potato Development Project (PSPDP)	Upper Swat	Swiss	late 1980s
Dir District Development Project (DDDP)	Dir	UNDCP	early 1990s
Malakand Rural Development Project (MRDP)	Swat etc.	ADB	late 1990s
Buner Agricultural Project	Buner	World Bank	1980s

ADB: Asian Development Bank; EU: European Union; SDC: Swiss Development Cooperation; IUCN: International Union for the Conservation of Nature; UNDCP: United Nations Drug Control Programme.

in a position to tackle rural poverty, but need the close cooperation of their "target groups". In Pakistan, the Aga Khan Rural Support Programme (AKRSP) was one of the first that put this emerging discourse into operation.[26] The AKRSP initiated "Community-based Organisations" (CBOs in project language) in the form of "Village Organisations" (VOs). Village communities were asked to establish such a "VO" (including a President, Secretary, etc.) at the village level which accommodated all of the villagers and was to form the local partner for the project. During meetings between project representatives and the VO, development priorities were discussed and activities planned. Aid experts from Swat went to visit the AKRSP and its charismatic leader, and took the idea of "VO" back to Swat.[27]

In order to establish VOs or other forms of CBOs, staff with specific skills were required—staff that was usually not available within state agencies. Having donor funds at their disposition, projects started to hire people, preferably with a background in social sciences (such as anthropologists, students of social work, largely trained in Peshawar University). To give them an institutional home, separate units within projects were created (a Social Organisation Unit, for example) for dealing with community organisation and interaction. In the course of the 1990s, this approach became mainstream—reflected, for example, in the developmental language of a later ADB-supported Malakand Development Project:

> The main steps are the (i) identification of village activists for community mobilization, (ii) training and support of village activists in community mobilization, (iii) first dialogue with the community to identify community needs and project responses, (iv) second dialogue to prepare the village development plan, (v) third dialogue to appraise the village plan, (vi) implementation of the village plan, and (vii) monitoring and evaluation of village development. The VOs and WOs are formed after the first dialogue. At that time, terms of partnership (TOP) are signed by heads of participating households and the Project Director in the case of VOs, and by women members and the Project Director in the case of WOs. All line agencies will use the forum of the VO/WO meetings for service delivery.[28]

In the early 1990s, an array of such projects were active in Swat. Many of them had their head offices in Saidu Sharif/Mingora, and this was a time when around a dozen foreign experts, many with their families, lived in this locality. However, in the late 1990s, the boom in area-based projects in Malakand ended. There was a growing frustration with their performance—"communities" did not react as expected, and state officials hesitated to support the participatory paradigm. Foreign experts gradually left Swat, and the projects were closed as they did. This had two specific consequences.

First, many of the aid donors considered their project-based social organisation units with their hired and job-insecure staff of Social Organisers as an important asset, but state departments were not in a position to continue these units after project closure. Therefore, several donors either directly encouraged staff to transform their units into independent non-governmental organisations (NGOs, to be registered under the respective state rules), or initiated NGOs that were to support these more fragile and still inexperienced groups through "capacity building". NGOs that have roots in donor projects include CARVAN (having roots in the KIDP), Hujra (emerging out of the Dutch Environment Rehabilitation Project) or TVO (Trust for Voluntary Organisations, established 1992 with USAID support). As a third option, international NGOs opened local branches in Peshawar. Indeed, very few of the organisations in this new and modern civil society "between household and the state"[29] emerged independently.[30]

Second, many international donors shifted their support to the provincial level, as this was expected to have a broader impact.[31] Still, many were interested to work at the local level, whether for the development of "model" procedures or to test new development approaches. For this, they interlinked with the emerging NGO scene in Swat. As a consequence, the importance within Swat of these NGOs in the sphere of "modern development" further increased, as they now also had access to considerable resources.

"Seeing the state"

So far, I have been looking "like a state", focusing on the state's own development administration, and on how international aid donors closely collaborated with this set-up to support "development" and "empowerment". How, then, is state-led and donor-supported development experienced in Swat? How has it impinged on prevailing social relations, and what have the consequences of this been? In this section, I focus on three issues that warrant specific attention, because, as I argue below, they fed arguments into the TNSM's "anti-modernisation" discourse: (i) expanding state control over natural resources; (ii) new forms of social organisations; and (iii) the ignoring of central concerns of people in Swat.

Expanding state control

As mentioned above, the NWFP Forest Department is the strongest department in Swat and deals with the financially most interesting resource, so I take it as an example of state-society relations. The relationship between the state's forest authorities and local routines of forest use can be described as ambiguous, conflicting and shaped by legal pluralism. To explain this, first a closer understanding of locally dominant forms of resource control is due. This vernacular governance of forests is closely related to land rights. These in turn are governed by customary law (*rivaj*). There are regional differences in *rivaj*[32] but they encompass most of the facets described in the following. It is also important to recall that customary law is not static, and its forms have undergone major transformations.[33] But what I describe below did, indeed, have a certain endurance, and it framed the vernacular understanding of rights and non-rights for a considerable period of time. In general, those who owned land as private property (*dawtar* lands) had a share in adjacent forests and pasture areas. Thus, while agricultural land was held as private property, adjacent forest land was jointly owned by the owners of arable land. Owners of agricultural land cum "shareholders" in forests were also "shareholders" of *shamilat* lands.[34] This group of people—usually the influential khans described by Fredrik Barth and Charles Lindholm—controlled forest use, regulated access, and made arrangements for the distribution of forest resources. Even after 1947 and up to the present day, landowners claimed forests as their joint ownership. They accepted, though, that the Wali undertook the harvesting of trees against the payment of royalty "to the forest owners".[35] Things changed after the merger with

Pakistan. The government of the NWFP declared all the forests of Swat as provincial government property subject to the payment of some royalty to local "right holders" (note the change in legal wording). In 1975, the Pakistan Forest Act of 1972[36] was extended to Swat, declaring forests as "protected", and trees as "reserved".[37] With this, no forest produce was to be taken out of the forests without prior sanctioning by the forest authorities. This expansion of state control through legislation required an enforcement apparatus on the ground—which, however, was not available. Although the Forest Department was the strongest agency, it still lacked sufficient staff at the local level. And the field level Foresters and Range Forest Officers were exposed to a local elite that maintained the legitimacy of *rivaj*.[38] As a consequence, a legal vacuum and a linked room for manoeuvre emerged that triggered uncontrolled forest use. It was this context that made the notion of "Timber Mafia" popular. It refers to a network of influential people (khans, state officials, businessmen, politicians) established with the single purpose of making money from cutting and selling timber illegally, using practices like networking, bribing, buying royalty, and "foreignising" timber (that is, exporting the timber to, and re-importing it from, Afghanistan). Many in Swat started to mistrust the modern state, as the Forest Department was accused of playing a key role in the timber mafia, and the "timber mafia" is also well known. I argue that this contributed to people hesitating to develop an identity as "citizens", and many started to view "the past" as a better period. Elderly people talked about the strict forest protection under the Wali, and his acceptance of forest ownership by *dawtar* land holders (I will return to this point later).

The new "civil society"

Ambiguities characterised the relationship between people of Swat not only with the modern state, but also with the participatory approaches of donor-supported projects and the emerging new "civil society" of NGOs. Many community-based organisations were created, and they became the link between villagers and aid projects, and thus the conduits to project resources as well. Interaction between project staff and "local people" was informed by the perception of social realities in Swat as egalitarian "communities of place". But access was not for all. Social realities differed from project assumptions—and that is where the scholarly writings of Barth and Lindholm would have provided excellent insights had they ever been consulted. Swat society was and is highly stratified, and this finds its expression in the spheres of agriculture and forestry through the difference between *dawtar* land owners, their tenants, *gujars*, etc. As a consequence, "community-based organisations" tended to be controlled by locally influential persons—mostly, although not only, khans. There was also a category of people—"brokers"[39]—who were more exposed to, and familiar with, the arguments, logics and language of the modern state and aid donors. They were among those better equipped to use CBOs to access project resources. Often, a good many of the locally influential elders were sceptical of the emerging CBOs, as they might compete with the established organisation of village politics—that is, the council of elders, or *jirga*. Aid projects in turn fuelled scepticism as *jirgas* were rarely consulted, equating them with "tradition", backward social relations (or underdevelopment), and exploitation.[40]

Zooming into the example of forestry can provide further insights. Realising the tension between local forest users and state forest authorities, some aid projects linked up with the global discourse on "joint forest management". To develop "confidence-based approaches" (to quote yet another influential development paradigm), a specific village-based organisation was created: "Joint Forest Management Committees" (JFMCs). Village representatives and state officials were to jointly agree on forest use plans and their implementation. In some cases, separate "Women's Groups" were formed. However, scholarly studies revealed that often only local elites (such as khans and emerging new elites) were included in or controlled such JFMCs, that "Women Groups" existed on paper only, and that forest officials had full control over the committees in spite of the participatory language. They, for example, had the power to dissolve them.[41] As a not so unexpected consequence, JFMCs did not foster trust.

In other ventures, community groups were encouraged to reafforest "barren land" (in the terminology of project forest experts)—*shamilat* in the language of the vernacular. As a consequence of unequal power relations within the assumed egalitarian community groups, there have been instances of *de facto* privatisation of *shamilat*. That is, certain *dawtar* land owners were in a position to use afforestation schemes and their influence in CBOs to establish control over land that they previously had to share with other land owners and specifically with tenants.

Specific challenges emerged around the new NGOs. For some in Swat, they became important local development agents in the absence of the state; others perceived them as too closely related to the state and especially "foreign" donor interests. On top of that, suspicion that these NGOs had other agendas, or represented the interests of some alien elite, was nurtured through symbols such as posh "Pajero cars" or "work-shopping at Swat Serena".[42] A specifically sensitive issue emerged around the "progressive" ways in which NGOs dealt with gender topics, such as women's health or girls' schooling. In the early periods of participatory endeavours, donor-supported projects hired female Social Organisers who came from Islamabad or Lahore, and who did not follow local gender norms and dressed, rather, "like Westerners". In sum, a powerful sense of unease crept into the relationship between NGOs and their "target groups".

Neglected priorities

A great many of the aid projects focused on natural resources. This was based on a perception that agriculture, grazing and forest use continued to form the backbone for people's livelihoods; that, in short, Swat was an agrarian, rural society. Forests are indeed of crucial importance, but agriculture less so. The economy of Swat had changed since the 1960s and 70s when Fredrik Barth and Charles Lindholm conducted the bulk of their fieldwork. Additional income sources emerged through the enormous increase in tourism, leading to a mushrooming of hotels and related services (and a new class of influential people). But more important than the emergence of a mercantile class were remittances. Though no official statistics are available, a huge number of people from Swat (usually young to middle-aged males) work outside the Valley—in Karachi, Baluchistan, the Middle East, or on Greek ships. In many regions it is the women, the very young, and

173

the old that remain. As a consequence, and especially so in the mountainous parts of Swat, agriculture functions (again) more as part of subsistence activities; cash income is supplied through remittances.[43]

Land, though, remains an important family asset, and control over land is an often seriously contested issue among relatives, between landowners and tenants, and between all of these people and the state. In this field, the state judiciary plays a crucial role, at least in principle. However, access to and the "timely dispensation" of justice[44] increasingly became a sensitive issue. I illustrate this with the following case: During an interview, a man from Swat held a bundle of chits in his right hand, and a letter in his left one. A kinship-based dispute over land could not be settled within the concerned families, and was thus brought before the modern state's courts in Saidu Sharif in 1999. In fact the case was still ongoing by end of January 2008, when this interview was conducted. Each of the chits held by the man in his right hand referred to a call to appear before the court for a next proceeding. All in all, he showed 124 chits—124 calls to courts since 1999—with each visit involving financial and time costs, often other troubles and further uncertainties. In his left hand, he held a piece of paper referring to an earlier dispute over land, again within the larger kinship, that took place in the early 1960s, and thus during the period when the state of Swat still existed. The case was detailed on this very letter and then brought before the court of the Wali. In the course of one or two sessions, the court decided the case, and marked the decision taken on the back of the letter in handwriting.

Indeed, the judiciary in Swat is a highly complex sphere of its own, and is an expression of the complicated translation of the modern state's authority onto the former princely state (see above). From the early 1970s and the creation of the PATA structure, there were a series of modifications and attempts to reform and re-reform it, but none improved the highly inefficient judicial procedures, or brought about "speedy justice".[45] It is this sphere of legal procedures that is of great concern to many in Swat, a sphere of underlying contestations that was unseen and ignored by development projects—projects that by definition take less interest in the existing everyday, and instead look forward to an imagined new future. The existing everyday was, however, addressed explicitly by the TNSM.

The TNSM

I have described above how Swat became a hot-spot of "Western" development projects. Still, local people's experience of the modern nation state and "the global" (mediated through international aid projects and materialised through foreign experts, NGOs, Pajeros and new laws of resource access) was one characterised by poor road connections, a lack of teachers in village schools, poor quality health infrastructure, a lack of employment opportunities outside agriculture, and a judicial system that was not in a position to adequately handle their cases. These issues, though, were to become part and parcel of the agenda of a very different type of "development agent". Around 1990, a "social movement" called Tahrik Nifaz-e-Shariat-e-Muhammadi (TNSM, Movement for the Enforcement of Sharia) under the leadership of Sufi Muhammad made skilled use of people's dissatisfaction with living conditions. The TNSM linked this dissatisfaction with the poor performance of the "modern" state, and instead started to advocate implementation of the sharia as a way forward to supply "speedy justice". It claimed that the sharia much better reflected vernacular traditions. The TNSM became known to a wider public in mid-1994, when it was able to mobilise thousands of people, who started to block main roads in order to attract attention. Police and security personnel reacted, and this led to several casualties. Towards the end of 1994, militant sections of the TNSM tried to take control of Saidu Sharif airport, and this again led to a number of dead. After these incidences, there was quiet around the movement.

In the wake of 9/11, the TNSM was proscribed as a terrorist outfit in January 2002,[46] and its leader Sufi Mohammad was imprisoned. By early 2007, one Fazlullah launched a new campaign for the introduction of sharia laws in Swat. As he was the son-in-law of the imprisoned Sufi Muhammad, Fazlullah's efforts were associated with a revival of the TNSM. He also stylised the dissatisfaction with the performance of the modern nation state—even as this "modern state" was governed at the provincial level by an alliance of religious parties called the Muttahida Majlis-e-Amal (MMA).[47] Things, however, radically changed after the Lal Masjid incident in Islamabad. Between 3 and 11 July 2007, Pakistan's security forces besieged a mosque and *madrassa* in the heart of the country's capital Islamabad, where a radical teacher with his followers (including women) resisted state demands to stop the harassing (including kidnapping) of residents of Islamabad and to vacate the premises; it ended in the deaths of an unknown number of people, among them many from Pushtun areas of the NWFP, including Swat. In this context, Fazlullah's TNSM intensified relations with other "Taliban" groups in the Frontier[48] and called for open militancy against the state, which reacted with military means. After the 2008 elections and the coming into power of the Awami National Party at provincial level, the new Chief Minister announced a ceasefire and offered negotiations. As a gesture of confidence building, Sufi Mohammad was released from prison. He denounced violence and expelled Fazlullah from the TNSM. However, negotiations collapsed, and this triggered a new military offensive. The subsequent drama of the "internally displaced people" (IDPs) is well-known, as is the brutal regime of Fazlullah's "Swat Taliban" and the military offensive. By mid-2009, the military declared the Swat Taliban to be defeated.

Discussion

Swat experienced a high density of development projects and witnessed a brutal confrontation between the state and its opponents, presenting a puzzle indeed worthy of reflection. Are there relations between the recent spread of militancy in Swat and the ventures for "modern development" by state and (global) aid donors? In this concluding section, I reflect on some of the facets of this puzzle that are especially pertinent. While doing this, I keep in mind what I have detailed so far: the very complicated relations between the varying parts of the modern nation state (expressed through the complex rules and regulations that link Swat to the province and the federal state), the enduring and even increasing social heterogeneity in Swat, the emerging tension between "old elites" (such as khans and landowners) and "new elites" (including development brokers and people that gained power and wealth through trade and tourism), the tension between routinised resource control and the tendency of the modern state to ignore these and bring in "alien" laws instead, and the emerging conflict between established organisations of social control (*jirgas*) and the "new civil society" of NGOs.

Like his father-in-law, Fazlullah skilfully exploited people's dissatisfaction and made the state, NGOs and the judiciary some of the scapegoats for these. Of course, the emergence of the TNSM has various causes, among them an attempt to spread the Wahhabi school of thought into the Swat and Malakand region—a region that predominantly follows the Barelvi school—and vested interests of sections of the bureaucracy,[49] the influence of other Taliban groups after Fazlullah's group had joined their alliance, and so on. Nevertheless, it appears that at least initially (that is, in early 2007), Fazlullah was able to tap into people's socio-economic dissatisfactions. Through his references to religious codes, I propose that to some extent he advocated a different "development paradigm", based on a radical critique of the paradigm of "the others". This critique targeted among others the new civil society of NGOs and CBOs. Fazlullah's deputy, Muslim Khan, stated that NGOs "come and tell us how to make latrines in mosques and homes. I'm sure we can do it ourselves. (...) NGO is another name for vulgarity and obscenity. They don't want us to remain Muslims and want to take away the veil from our women."[50] Fazlullah accused NGOs operating in the region of having an "American agenda".[51] Such statements are in line with other critiques of NGOs voiced by religious circles, for example:

those [NGOs] spreading the Western culture and working according to their global agenda would be dealt with an iron hand and those who really worked for the welfare of the people would be encouraged. However, (...) there is a wide difference between Western and Islamic cultures and the NGOs should give priority to the latter. [They] would extend help to all those (...) who wanted progress of the country and its standing on its own feet.[52]

State corruption provided food for arguments as well. In an interview given to pressmen in May 2007, Fazlullah stated that people are "fed up with (the) corrupt system in which smugglers, murderers and rascals are considered the nobility."[53] In other contexts he explicitly referred to the timber mafia, which, in turn, is linked by most people in Swat to corrupt officials of the modern state's Forest Department.

Dissatisfaction and feelings of resistance are also nurtured by things not done. I have referred to the development industry's general blindness regarding land rights issues and the state's continuously changing judiciary. Here, Fazlullah found rich ground for meeting expectations hitherto not addressed. To overcome perceived problems and to expedite judicial procedures, Fazlullah advocated the introduction of sharia. In this context, he often recalled the earlier period of the Wali's Swat state as an example. During a debate on one of Pakistan's new TV channels, a group of journalists and lawyers from Swat argued that "the common people of the area are disappointed from the state authorities of Pakistan, and the period of Wali was better because of justice and honesty. The people anticipate a society based on justice and equality under the 'Islamic State' based on the principles of sharia."[54] Such statements had appeal, as they resonated with what younger Swatis had learned from the elders about the past. And it did not matter that the claim was false and not based on evidence. As research conducted by Sultan-i-Rome shows, linking the state of the Wali with an Islamic regime is but an "invented tradition". Civil and criminal cases were handled by the Swat state's own legal administration, which made reference partly to *rivaj* (and its varying local manifestations), partly to the strategic and political needs of the autocratic Wali. There existed some *qazis*, who practiced Islamic law as well, but people were free to choose the legal system for their cases.[55]

But Fazlullah even went a step further in the sense that the sharia overruled *rivaj*; as I have shown elsewhere,[56] he argued that "[we] strongly preach [...] about women's rights given in Quran and Sunnah. Our Pukhtun culture does not recognize the share of women in inheritance. In this connection the result [...] is that people consult us to give the due shares of sisters in the inherited property." Women from Swat were quoted as stating that "[for] the first time, someone is talking of women's rights as spelled out in the Holy Quran. He talks of our right to inheritance, (...) asking fathers to get the consent of their daughters before contracting their marriage etc." Indeed, under *rivaj*, "as a rule, only the males could own and inherit land and the womenfolk held no right to own and inherit land. The land passed only to the patrilineal male heirs or the near agnates in case of having no male descendant. The Islamic right of women to own and inherit land was, as a rule generally not recognized."[57]

Fazlullah started the construction of a huge *madrasa* close to the Swat district's capital of Saidu Sharif. Visitors reported huge crowds gathering at the site in the early months of 2007 to help with the construction, and on the amount of donations received, especially from women.[58] The enormous success of Fazlullah in mobilising people led a Mingora-based Pakistani colleague of mine, working in an aid project supported by international donors, to state that projects should "learn from him how to mobilize people".

My argument is not merely to blame international development projects for what happened in Swat. Many of them tried to address the actual "felt needs" of poorer Swat people, and project staff worked hard and were dedicated to achieving their visions. For the present analysis, though, it is important to understand that foreign aid becomes part and parcel of local social and political dynamics, including the dynamics that exist between "the local" and "the state"; projects work with some people and not with others, projects favour a certain "future", not another, and projects also choose particular avenues to reach these futures, and not others. Most development projects took the side of "the poor" and tried to bring "good governance" into the practices of state agencies and staff. But they took the role of the modern state in Swat as granted, and most donors were unaware of the uneasy post-merger relations between the state and the complex vernacular tradition. In addition, development interventions are also manifestations of "the global". They translated into practice the more abstract (global) modernisation discourse, producing events that were directly experienced by some in Swat and heard about (often as distorted and distorting rumours) by others. As a result, some benefited but more became sceptical, and receptive to TNSM's discourse of other-isation.

I conclude by arguing that my thick description of the encounter between local complexities, the state's practices specifically at local level, the aid projects, and the "movement" of the TNSM shows the urgent need for a more nuanced reading of the local political space. It shows that an explanation of the Swat conflict through "Pushtun culture" and "grand global politics" fails to do justice to the dynamics involved. But still more facets of these dynamics have to be understood to allow an appreciation of the intertwining of aspects of "resistance" with outright greed for absolute power, and this within the complex nestedness of the heterogeneous "local", the multi-faceted modern state and the diverse "global". At one level, the TNSM's discourse indeed represents a contestation of what "development" encompasses, and for whom. Taken at its face value, it invites further reflection on the tensions between "global dominance"—locally experienced as a complex mix of grand politics (the War on Terror) with grand discourses (development)—and local contestations and aspirations. References to theorising on multiple modernities or subalterns would offer neat entry points. In another and contrasting reading, however, the state's and donors' actions simply supplied "vested interests" with welcome arguments to seduce the public, to construct antagonism, and to expand and consolidate exclusive power. This reading in turn could be justified with references to Foucauldian discourse analysis. Unfortunately, Swat has become a very sensitive place for scholarly analysis, and "evidence-based" theorising poses a major challenge.

13

CRISIS AND RECONCILIATION IN SWAT THROUGH THE EYES OF WOMEN

Anita M. Weiss[1]

The Valley of Swat has endured many challenges and transformations in its recorded history, but none may have such a lasting impact on space and society as the occupation of the area by the Pakistan Taliban in the mid-2000s and the subsequent invasion by the Pakistan military to root them out in May 2009. In January 2010, I traveled to three areas within Swat to meet with women and hear their stories of what they endured during that period. Whether I was meeting with returned refugees or a group of widows in Saidu Sharif, or women who remained during that time despite horrific living conditions in Manglawar, or displaced teachers and healthcare workers in Matta in Upper Swat, the message that emerged was similar: confusion over the causes of the crisis combined with an eagerness to share their ideas on how to move past it. A woman captured this sentiment when she said to me, "We're still afraid: afraid of the unknown, and we don't know how it all happened."

I was able to travel to Swat and conduct this research through personal ties I have in Swat. Of greater relevance, however, is that the woman who helped make my arrangements, although from the late Wali's extended family (which could have skewed the discussions among the women I interviewed), also enjoys enormous credibility among women in Swat as she too was widowed because of the conflict. In addition, despite her own personal difficulties now as a single parent of three children, she mobilized people and resources to assist women in the wake of the May 2009 military offensive, and women throughout the area were aware of this. Regardless, we agreed she would just help me make the initial arrangements and to offset potential biases, would not participate in the interviews. Instead, I was accompanied wherever I went by two young local women, Saniya and Sobia, whose middle class family had remained in Swat during the crisis period. Their Pashto translating helped supplement my Urdu discussions with women, thereby further facilitating open, animated conversations with women and girls wherever we went.

This research is situated in the larger theoretical arenas that question the relation between gendered citizenry and the modern state, particularly in Muslim contexts, and how local transformations have global underpinnings. I am positing the construction of what can be termed "gendered modernity," manifested as a compelling social dilemma in an area such as Swat. When women first engaged with the Tehrik-i-Taliban Pakistan (TTP) in Swat, it was through listening to Maulana Fazlullah's sermons transmitted via FM radio through their mobile phones. For these mostly illiterate women, this was an act of modernity, using global technology to learn about religion. Yet the thrill of the early engagement soon dissipated into fear, disappointment and trauma.

In various parts of Swat, I met with a total of roughly 150 women in groups ranging from ten to twenty-five. In these public conversations, women bantered back and forth, reminding each other of events and animatedly engaged in discussions with one another, sometimes to the point where my presence was even forgotten. My conversations with women focused on eight issues:

i. What the local Taliban told people they wanted when they first arrived.
ii. What the local Taliban said or did, in particular, that affected women.
iii. Specific stories about events that happened to women after the Taliban's influence had grown.
iv. Particular instances and events of the Taliban's interactions with women that were positive, when they were particularly helpful towards women, or women (and women they know) personally enjoyed them.
v. How the participants' lives had changed in the past year (2009–2010).
vi. When the army arrived in Swat [in May 2009], how were they different from the Taliban towards the participants?
vii. What will it take for Swat to recover and, in particular, for the women of Swat to move on with their lives?
viii. What are their dreams and expectations for the future?

The majority of women with whom I met were uneducated, largely illiterate, yet enthusiastic to share their stories with me. They responded with a clear need for the state to maintain security, for income opportunities, investment in schools, and especially to enable them to facilitate their own empowerment. I trust I have represented them well in these pages.

Backdrop to the crisis

As I drove up the winding road to Swat, up through the Malakand Pass in the Provincially Administered Tribal Area (PATA) of the Khyber Pakhtunkhwa province (KP, formerly NWFP), the physical landscape seemed no different from that I have observed for decades on that route. Here a road barrier—to prevent buses from flying down into the ravine below while overcorrecting on a sharp turn—was broken, there stood an orange seller with distinct Mediterranean features, a legacy of Alexander the Great's invasion, hawking his goods which are grown in the surrounding villages. But just as we approached the very first village, I knew

CRISIS AND RECONCILIATION

Figure 13.1: "Welcome to the Pakistan Army".

something was very different: a Pakistani flag and some writing on the village wall said "*Pak fauj ko salaam*" (Welcome to the Pakistan Army). Such writing and flags have become common throughout the Valley, in marked contrast to the way most Swatis viewed the Pakistan military in previous years.

Swat remained a semi-autonomous princely state, along with Dir and Chitral, until 1969 when it finally acceded to Pakistan. Its ruler, the Wali of Swat, governed the area through a combination of sharia and paternalistic decrees. When Field Marshal Ayub Khan, whose two daughters had married two of the Wali's sons, was removed from office in 1969, Swat's fate was sealed as well. The Wali and his family realized they could not contest the Pakistan military, and finally acceded, thereby ending their royal state.

For roughly twenty years, Swat underwent a period of adjustment. The two most significant changes included the arrival of numerous government bureaucrats—people not indigenous to the area, who did not know the local people and practices, took seemingly forever to effect change, and could be bribed, in contrast to most of the Wali's retinue—and of the British-based system of law, a legacy of the Raj used throughout Pakistan. The key reason why people in Swat resort to the formal legal system is to settle property disputes, but it is slow to adjudicate matters. Gradually, Swatis began to miss the "speedy justice" of the days of the Wali's rule, although it had been autocratic and paternalistic. The longer land disputes remained unresolved, the more they festered and prompted violent clashes between groups.

Sufi Mohammad and a small group of supporters (as discussed more extensively in Sultan-e-Rome's chapter earlier in this work) founded the Tehrik-i-Nifaz-i-Shariat-i-Muhammadi (TNSM) in the adjacent former princely state of Dir in 1989 with the goal to reinstate sharia as the primary legal system in Malakand Division and the Kohistan District of the PATA. Within a few years, the movement had gained support in Swat and was beginning to destabilize governance in the area. In response to the TNSM's provocations, the government promulgated new regulations twice in the 1990s—in 1994 and 1999—to enhance the scope of the sharia courts in the PATA, but with limited impact. Legal delays remained incessant and outcomes became widely perceived as influenced more by bribery and intrigues than by justice.

The crisis in Swat

Two years later, in October 2001, in the wake of the US invasion of Afghanistan, Sufi Mohammad and many of his supporters left for Afghanistan to fight alongside the Taliban government there. Both he and his son-in-law, Maulana Fazlullah, were imprisoned upon returning to Pakistan in January 2002; while Sufi Mohammad remained in jail until 2008, Fazlullah was released in 2003. Notably, this was shortly after a coalition of Islamist political parties, the Muttahida Majlis-e-Amal (MMA), had won the provincial election in the NWFP (now Khyber Pakhtunkhwa) in October 2002.[2] This was the first time in Pakistan's history that an Islamist party had come to power through an election. Indeed, the presence of the MMA government in the NWFP from 2002 to 2007 played an important role in opening a space for groups such as the TNSM and related "Taliban" factions to gain a foothold and build upon their influence in the province.

Fazlullah, a cable operator (someone who transports people across rivers via a cable for a fee) in the Mamdherai/Imamdherai area of Swat, took up the leadership of the Swat faction of the TNSM. He began broadcasting programs on Islam and how to live "as a good Muslim" via FM radio in 2004. Women, in great numbers, tuned into Fazlullah's programs; I was told that many women would say their prayers before doing so. For many, this was a legitimate form of entertainment, and it connected them to a kind of global modernity where people use mobile phones and listen to the radio. While speaking to them through their mobile phones, Fazlullah was telling women new things about Islam which they had not previously known. Women became his most enthusiastic supporters, allegedly donating large quantities of gold jewelry to help build Fazlullah's *madrasa* (religious school). Fazal Khaliq Fazal (2009:39), an eyewitness to the turmoil in Swat, writes that this was possible because "They convinced the people that whoever spends a single penny in the way of God will receive virtues and a place in paradise in return. So people donated generously—not just their money but their jewelry as well."

Women with whom I spoke confirmed that many had been early supporters of Maulana Fazlullah and had supported his efforts by donating jewelry. They had been deeply influenced by his message at the outset:

"Maulana Fazlullah? He was mesmerizing, a great orator. We can't speak like him."

CRISIS AND RECONCILIATION

"FM[3] said don't watch TV, so we stopped watching. We just spoke about religion. It said to stop doing bad things, *fashion mut karo* [don't be concerned with clothes and such things]. We stopped listening when the message turned to killing the police."

"We thought they came to tell us about the *shariah* but they *ulta kar liya* [turned it upside down]. Their goal wasn't to show us the right path."

Within a few years, the TNSM was targeting police stations and other official offices for violent attacks. Decapitations, especially of police in outlying areas, became a primary, formidable tactic in their quest to get the sharia declared the legal system in Malakand district. People were confused about the seemingly mixed messages emanating from the FM station, and were reluctant to act against Fazlullah; as a woman said, "Everyone listened to FM, so we could learn more about Islam. We never expected what would result from this. Because men were afraid of having their heads cut off, they did nothing."

Key leaders within the TNSM are said to have disagreed with Fazlullah's violent activities and officially disowned his policies, although some members, mostly from Swat, remained with him. In December 2007, he and his followers helped found the Tehrik-i-Taliban Pakistan (TTP, often referred to as "the Taliban" by Swatis), headed overall by Baitullah Mahsud but headed locally—in Swat—by Fazlullah.

As the influence of the Taliban and Maulana Fazlullah grew, three things occurred: the *bazaar*—all public trading areas—was closed; the Taliban demanded that women had to be in full purdah; and girls were discouraged from going to school, especially past grade 4 (age 10). Swat's economy was hit particularly hard as tourists were now avoiding the area because of the unrelenting violence perpetrated by the TTP. The Taliban asserted their power by interfering in the bazaar, threatening goods transporters and shopkeepers to demand support, and almost completely shutting down trade. A woman explained to me how the local Taliban destroyed commerce in Swat, uncomfortably smiling as she pointed out how happy she and her family were at first that they could now buy things cheaply: "The Taliban forced the *bazaaris* (shopkeepers) to lower their prices. We consumers were happy, but it hurt the *bazaaris*."

As the economy condensed it was essentially only the TTP who could supply jobs: "Here in Matta, the only people the Taliban gave jobs to were young recruits: Rs. 300 ($4) daily for ordinary workers or *chowkidars* (watchmen), Rs 600 to be a gunman, and the families of suicide bombers were given Rs. 25–30 *lakhs* [$31,000–$37,000], afterwards."

The orchards of Upper Swat, especially those in Nul and Matta known for apples, peaches and various nuts, were left to lie untended. The Taliban prohibited people from working in the orchards as a way to pressure the government to give in to their demands.

The second result of the growing influence of the TTP in Swat was its impact on women's mobility, through their insistence on women wearing the "shuttlecock" *burqa*, a garb not indigenous to this area, and giving up paid employment. Many women resisted wearing the shuttlecock *burqa* as they were used to wearing a *chador*, more like a long sheet draped around them. A woman explained how she felt when forced to wear the *burqa*: "It was not our habit to wear the *burqa*. The

Figure 13.2: Swati woman in a shuttlecock *burqa*.

chador is less revealing. We were ashamed to lift the front of the *burqa*. The Taliban didn't allow the regular *burqa*, I think because their men could sneak around in *burqa*s. The *burqa* was *besharam* [shameless]."

The local Taliban were seemingly relentless in their pursuit to get all women to wear *burqa*s:

They would look into cars, they would look wherever they could, to check if women were in full purdah. If you were not in a *burqa*, they would ask "why not in burqa?" There was a woman in a car—she was over 50—and they grabbed her from the car and asked why not in *burqa*. She said she's not a girl, so doesn't need to wear a *burqa*. They [the Taliban men who grabbed the woman] cut her hair saying, "I'll make you a girl, now wear a *burqa*."

A schoolteacher recounted to me an incident that happened to her one day,

We four teachers were in a rickshaw. I was in a *burqa*, the other three women were in *chador*s. The Taliban made the other three girls get off the rickshaw and said, "if your husbands can't afford to buy burqas, we'll give you the money." And then they beat the rickshaw driver, why did he pick up women not in *burqa*s? "If we see you drive women not in burqas in the future, we'll cut off your head."

She doubted that rickshaw driver would ever again offer a ride to any woman not wearing a *burqa*. Another female teacher remembered, "We were standing by the school gate. We were five teachers. Two Taliban with big hair and beards came with long knives. They grabbed a teacher and said, 'If you ever come back we'll cut off your head.' Then they broke the school's door."

Figure 13.3: The destroyed Sangota Pubic School and its remaining boundary wall.

A seven-year-old girl I met in Matta, Upper Swat, told me what had happened to her the previous year, "A Talib grabbed me on my way to school and said 'wear a *burqa*.' I ran home crying." As she told me this, the other women present were all cursing the local Taliban for treating a young girl this way, and shouting that Islam does not require a six-year-old girl to cover herself.

The TTP very deliberately targeted girls' schools. This met with resistance in Swat, which has higher female literacy levels than surrounding areas, in large part due to the Wali's largesse; he adamantly believed in the value of educating girls and helped establish and maintain a number of schools for them. The Afghan Taliban's ideology of discouraging female education was adopted by Maulana Fazlullah's followers. A Principal of a girls' school in Saidu Sharif recounted to me how the FM station was used to discourage sending daughters to school despite numerous *hadith* which support educating females: "They would announce over the radio that a girl quit school in grade 5, and that she and her parents now have a direct route to heaven."

But this period of merely discouraging girls from going to school was short-lived; in early 2009 the TTP turned to destroying their schools. Three teenage girls in Manglawar told me that their school, Sangota Public School, which had been established by Irish nuns and later donated to the people by the Wali, was completely destroyed; only the school wall and sign remain. They said they missed their school; they now attended a nearby boys' school in late afternoons, after the boys were dismissed.

When I asked them why the Taliban razed their school, they were incredulous with the reason that had been given: "The Taliban said we were drinking wine at our school, and that we were dancing, so they destroyed our school." It was preposterous to these girls, pious as most people are in Swat, that anyone could ever think they had been consuming alcohol or dancing.

Boys' schools did not fare much better, although they were not destroyed. Instead, parents had to watch out for their sons' safety. While women were telling me stories they had heard of boys who had been kidnapped, I felt it important to establish first-hand accounts (of which, it turned out, there were many). Immediately a woman came up to me and said, "They closed the schools and kidnapped children, up to 15 year old boys, for their training. They came and took my brother's son." She didn't break down crying until she finished; she wanted his story to be told. She never saw her nephew again, nor does she know what happened to him.

A climate of fear had clearly been created; in this environment, people were fearful of attracting the Taliban's attention. Between the beheadings, school bombings and the closing of most bazaars, somehow the impetus to fight back eluded the Swatis. A woman described to me the most horrific scenario that could happen to a Muslim, when body parts are not buried together (therefore leaving the soul unable to stand in front of God on the Day of Judgment): "One girl's uncle was killed in Sair [an area in Swat]. They buried one head and a different body. We've been to hell and back."

The fear of beheading led many people to give up activities the Taliban disallowed, despite their utility for the larger society. This was true for schoolteachers, police, and healthcare practitioners: "My brother and his friend were threatened with beheading for giving polio drops. They said there was urine in the polio drops, and they would hurt people. So under such psychological pressure he gave this up." Someone else explained to me that they thought the Taliban opposed polio drops because they saw them as a "conspiracy against the *umma* [Muslim community] because they make women barren."

In addition to the psychological pressure there was the physical devastation wrecked by the Taliban. Their power had built up over a period of roughly three years. On 16 February 2009, the federal government capitulated and drew up a five-point agreement, the Malakand (*Nizam-e-Adal*) Accord. It called for an end to both military operations and Taliban operations in Swat, and for sharia to be imposed in the districts of Malakand, Swat, Shangla, Buner, Dir, Chitral, and Kohistan. The signatory for the TTP, however, was Sufi Mohammad, Fazlullah's father-in-law, who had recently been released from prison to try to broker an agreement between the state and the Taliban. His credibility among the Taliban, therefore, was very low.

Elsewhere in Pakistan, the Malakand Accord was widely criticized as being akin to "giving into the terrorists' demands," and the government backpedalled to reverse the decision. When the Taliban launched a cavalcade from Swabi through Buner heading towards Swat on 21 April 2009, openly brandishing all sorts of weapons, the government now had no option but to act. Swat, previously nicknamed "the Switzerland of Pakistan," was devastated; and now the Taliban were openly challenging the writ of the state.

CRISIS AND RECONCILIATION

The Pakistan military made periodic incursions into Swat to rout out the Taliban in the years leading up to its wholesale attack against them in May 2009. One woman reflected on the destruction when she told me, "The Taliban took over hotels, and the army shelled them. They also bombed little bridges to keep the army out. But most of the physical destruction was done by the army, trying to destroy the Taliban."

There were food shortages, gasoline shortages, and medicine was scarce. Women were disproportionately affected, in part because of the traditional gender segregation in this area and in part because many male family members were now absent, either killed by the Taliban or having joined them: "Women died a lot because there were no tablets or injections that could be given. There was no proper *ilaj* (medicines); people are still sick because of what happened then."

Trying to grapple with the reason why local people had not risen up on their own to fight against the Taliban, I had to ask the women with whom I met to explain this to me. I found the response very sobering when a woman said to me, "We had become *kamzoor mureez* [weak patients]; we never thought the government could help. The police were the initial targets, so how could they help anyone? Everyone left their services [jobs]."

Yet there were everyday forms of resistance by women against the Taliban. When I met with a group of *dais* (midwives), one of them recounted the following event to me,

> They told us to stay home now, and when their rule comes, they would give the dais more salary. Maulana Fazlullah said, "we ourselves will help with the births." When Taliban Commander Muhammad Alim later came to us for help when his wife was about to give birth, we midwives had not received our salaries. We refused to help her and said to him "you help her."

Merely a month after she told me this story, Muhammad Alim was killed (1 March 2010) in Bahrain, Swat.

Another evident form of resistance was hiding things so that the Taliban could neither take nor destroy them. The Taliban had taken foreign books and set them on fire in a few places. One woman recalled that she had a tape recorder and enjoyed listening to music. In April 2009, the Taliban came to her house and told her family to stop playing it. They later returned to take it, but she told the Taliban she had given it away. She hadn't; she had only hidden it. A teenage girl told me what she did to hide her books to ensure their safety when her family fled to Peshawar in the wake of the army's onslaught against the Taliban in May 2009: "I buried my books so they wouldn't take them. I put them under the wood floor, by the lawn. I retrieved them after I returned from Peshawar three months later. They were not in bad shape." She had not put them under the wood floor inside the house, out of fear of losing them if the Taliban burned the house down.

By early May the crisis had escalated, and the army told the local people to leave, virtually overnight. On 4 May the Taliban occupied the main buildings of Mingora; the army began its attack on 5 May. However, pushing the Taliban out of the Valley proved to be harder than the government had anticipated. People told me that the destruction caused by the military onslaught against the Taliban was even more devastating than that launched earlier by the Taliban. What had been a nightmare was now escalating further, and people were fearful of being caught in the crossfire of fighting between the Taliban and the military; "Some people left because of the Taliban. Even more people left because of the army."

There were many pregnant women who walked out of Swat. They gave birth on the roadsides and often lost the babies: "We slept on the ground. One woman—she was pregnant—walked out of Swat with one small daughter and had a miscarriage on the way."

For many, it was as difficult to stay as to leave: "When the army finally came, there was nothing in the bazaar—no vegetables, no *atta* (flour). The price of tomatoes rose overnight from Rs. 25 to Rs. 180 per kilo." Those who opted to leave Swat had a difficult journey before them. Many relocated to live with relatives in Mardan or Peshawar. Some 1.7 million people are reported to have fled Swat to escape the military offensive. Those who had nowhere else to go were put up in makeshift refugee camps, organized by myriad organizations which sprang up overnight in Mardan, Nowshera and nearby locales. But how to get there? An elderly woman whose son was alleged (according to other women, although she disputed this) to have been one of the Taliban, had a particularly difficult journey: "Everyone just walked and we reached Mingora in a day; we walked for two more days. The chairlift was Rs. 1400 so I paid a *mazdoor* (worker) to carry me. I was afraid they would kill me for running away." She never clarified who "they" were, although I surmise she meant the Taliban who considered that her family had joined them. She has since never heard from her then 30-year-old son, and his wife subsequently ran away and is said to have remarried.

Extended families generally walked down the mountains together, as another woman recounted, "We twenty-three people, including my six children, walked over the mountains to Jambil. Then someone helped us—we paid them Rs. 100 for each person to sit in their truck—to get to Yar Husain Camp in Mardan."

These are mountain folk who live in Swat, which has long been a destination retreat for Pakistanis to escape the plains of Punjab and the frontier region during the heat of the summer. Suddenly the new refugees found themselves in sweltering heat within ill-prepared tent camps: "There was no water, no electricity and the camp was extremely hot. I gave birth to my baby there. We returned to Swat three days before the *roza* [month of Ramadan] began." This woman was similar to many other illiterate women I have met in over thirty years of conducting research in Pakistan. She did not demarcate her life by dates on a calendar but rather by religious festivals observed: the Ramadan fast, Eid, the martyrdom of Imam Hussain on Ashura, and the like.

Another woman who was then pregnant when the military onslaught began told me how she traveled with her family to a refugee camp she found repulsive. It was hot, overcrowded, and then the camp doctor suggested she have a caesarian delivery. "I was pregnant, and walked with my three children for two days. My feet were badly swollen and I cried, 'God, what is going to happen?' It was very hot there." Instead of having the caesarian birth in late August, as recommended by the doctor at the refugee camp, she gave birth to a healthy son in Swat in December. She remains proud that she was able to endure the stress and discomfort and wait until the child was full term before giving birth.

There were others who stayed, most because they lacked the means or resources to leave: "The roads were blocked and we didn't have money for transportation, so we stayed. I tried to walk but it was too dangerous to keep going. The helicopters were flying overhead; there was no electricity at all. My house was hit. My five children and I survived by eating the pumpkins from our field." I assumed she might have been nostalgic that her family had survived because of the pumpkins in those turbulent times, but showing her resilience—and retention of a sense of humor—she categorically stated, "I don't want to eat pumpkins ever again."

In hearing such stories of daily survival while the Pakistan army was battering the Swat Taliban, I could picture how the women were able to withstand the onslaught; how they were able to deal with the stress of trying to keep their children safe was harder to comprehend. The strategy used by one woman apparently was typical of many: "I have seven sons, between ages 6–22. I could not let them go from one place to the next; I was afraid they'd be picked up either by the Taliban or the army, so I locked them in the house." Her sons remained locked within her home for seven months. But staying within one's home was not necessarily safe either. I heard numerous accounts of people killed by shrapnel falling in their yards; one woman recounted to me that shortly after the death of her husband,

My mother also died in the shelling, nine months ago. She was crossing the courtyard to go to the toilet when mortar hit her back, and she died instantly. We had to bury her at once, but didn't have either a coffin or white cloth because of the curfew. So we buried her in her own clothes. My son, age six, is now in an orphanage. I live with my brother, but he has two wives and six children so it's a big problem. My in-laws don't ask about me at all.

Bakht-i-Saywa—who *wanted* me to use her name to underscore the real people behind these accounts—stayed in Manglawar with no electricity, no water, fighting going on all around her, and a curfew for the three months while the army actively sought out the Taliban. She showed me a full box of various kinds of shrapnel she had recovered inside her yard, noting that uncannily, no one in her extended family had been harmed by the shelling.

What is sobering is not only the large number of widows now in Swat, but that most of the widows are very young and have children. Husbands in the army or the police had been killed in the years leading up to the May 2009 assault. A 19-year-old woman told me how her husband, a soldier, had died four years earlier, in 2006, in Gilgit fighting against the Taliban there. She was 13 when married, 14 when widowed—they had only lived together seven months—and now has a five-year-old daughter:

Another husband won't want my daughter, so I cannot remarry. I was afraid: we're an army family, and my two brothers are also in the army. I am also afraid my in-laws will force my remarriage with my brother-in-law who is a drunkard and a glue-sniffer. I know how to sew. I can teach other women sewing, and how to be a tailor, but I have no resources to do that.

Another woman told me she was married at age 15, and is now a widow at age 22. She has three boys, aged eight, five and three. Her husband was killed by the army: "He went out to get water" and was killed by shrapnel in May 2009.

What this community has endured was poignantly summed up by a woman exclaiming to me, "We've seen so much pain and misery that just survival is *janaat* [heaven]."

rooms for free to bring tourists back, have been unsuccessful. Trade and commerce, especially in goods necessary for building reconstruction, has been picking up somewhat, but has a long way to go to get back to pre-Taliban levels.

Various official and non-government organizations provided food relief to Swat, which ended 15 March 2010. The women with whom I spoke recognized the usefulness of such efforts when they had immediately returned from the refugee camps, but now were clamoring for jobs and other kinds of employment support efforts instead of food handouts, "We don't need food; we need jobs. And salaries paid for doing those jobs."

For these women in particular, many of whom no longer have male family members for support, programs to help them earn an income are crucial. Many have skills such as sewing, midwifery, tutoring, and cooking (which used to feed into the tourism industry) but need help to get started in these efforts:

"We would share sewing machines in the past. Now, we don't have one for anyone to use."

"There is nothing here—no groups for women at all. We need help to start groups. We have teachers and nurses—we can help each other."

"We were so scared for 3–4 years. We now need guidance and help in how to start."

The kinds of "women-friendly centers" begun by SUNGI, Shirkat Gah and other NGOs in the vicinity following the devastating earthquake of October 2005 could be replicated here quickly, given the relatively high female literacy rates in Swat.

Pakistan's "Super Flood" of the summer of 2010 devastated parts of Swat further. Entire areas of Upper Swat, especially near Kalam in its northeast, again had crops and orchards devastated, this time by the natural disaster of water overflowing the Swat River. Mingora, near the district's capital of Saidu Sharif but lying lower than it, also suffered major structural damage from the flood and commerce came to a standstill. Food insecurity has risen again. Viewing Swat after the Super Flood was sobering:[4] it was not possible to discern if destroyed houses, bridges and aquifers had been destroyed by the Taliban, by the military onslaught, or by the floodwaters and mountain run-offs.

The threat of a return to unbridled militarism is manifested every day, whether by another roadside bombing or by another suicide attack. A truck loaded with men sitting on top drove by in Manglawar; a woman leaving our meeting pointed to it and said, "Who knows where they are today? The Taliban are still among us.[5] They're just waiting for the army to leave."

Pakistan has an arsenal of nuclear weapons, holds an important geostrategic position in Asia, wields political clout in the Muslim world, and the blowback from the October 2001 US invasion and subsequent ongoing occupation of Afghanistan has empowered insurgent militants such as the Swat Taliban throughout the country. It will take generations for Pakistanis to overcome the way their country has been transformed and militarized during this decade. Movements like the TTP exist on fear and repression of the disempowered. Young women in Swat must be able to envision a future, in which they complete their education, get married and remain married, and they and/or their husbands are able to bring in a reasonable income and they do not live in constant fear as women do now.

A young girl, about age ten, not only underscored to me what was at stake but also reminded me of the resiliency and hope that survives in Swat even after the most unimaginable dreadful conditions when she categorically stated, "I'm going to be a PIA pilot. No one can stop me!"

Figure 13.5: "I'm going to be a PIA pilot. No one can stop me!".

14

PUBLIC VISIBILITY OF WOMEN AND THE RISE OF THE NEO-TALIBAN MOVEMENT IN KHYBER PAKHTUNKHWA 2007–9[1]

Sana Haroon

Recent religious intolerance and political and military conflict in the Pakhtun north-west, where it did not directly cause harm to women, at the very least limited opportunities for women to freely come and go outside their homes. It is women's and men's acceptance of these restrictions that I seek to understand. This uneasy acquiescence came to be described in a short-lived space for conversation created by a women's action-research group. In critically reading the texts produced by this organisation, I find myself, like so many other contributors to this volume and to the study of Swat, at an intersection of anthropological and historical methodologies.

In 2007 Shirkat Gah, literally the "Place of Participation",[2] began a long-planned project to investigate the possibilities for women's empowerment in Khyber Pakhtunkhwa, just as the Taliban movement of Pakistan's north-west reached its 2007–09 heights of coercive power. Emerging out of the devastation of the Afghan *jihad*, Pakistan's Taliban movement gradually laid claim to the civil spaces of the Khyber Pakhtunkhwa province.[3] Army action in the FATA after 2001 provoked a wide questioning of the legitimacy of the state and its institutions, and schools, police stations and administrators' offices were openly attacked. Defining their objectives as moral, not only material, the Taliban openly sought to control discursive spaces in the province and across the country.[4] The papers in this work by Anita Weiss, Sultan-i-Rome, Robert Nichols and Mariam Abou Zahab describe how anybody not supportive of the Taliban's agenda was threatened. Journalists, school teachers, university faculty and administrators, workers in non-government organisations, and *malik*s faced extortion, kidnapping and death threats. FM radio stations were set up to support Mulla Fazlullah, reaching into people's homes, beyond *purdah*, to control individual logic and morality.[5] Shirkat

Gah, in creating spaces for women to speak about their concerns, came to be operating in a sphere which the Taliban were intent on controlling, but also one within which dissent, the articulation of disagreement with the Taliban agenda, was theoretically possible. Both the circumstances under which the study was conducted, and the particular interests of the survey, create a unique testimony to the nature of Taliban coercion.

The transcripts of the interviews, translated into Urdu, are textual accounts of the conversations that took place, accompanied by planned observational and mapping exercises also carried out by the interview teams. These mediated, translated documents are far from conforming to the ethnographer's strict methodologies of observation, recording and analysis; they are created by researchers who are intentionally provocative and participant in conversation. But coming from a time now past, I believe that these transcripts may become an historian's document and provide insight into that moment in which they were created.[6]

This study comes up against the discourse on Pakhtun culture as preserved in the notion of Pakhtunwali or "Pakhto". The Pakhto code, greatly romanticised in Pakhtun literature and ethnographic studies of the Pakhtuns, rests on a variety of principles loosely tied to notions of honour and revenge and, consequently, friendship and enmity. These principles are extrapolated to male societal conduct such as providing shelter and protection to guests, even at the risk of one's own life, and exacting revenge for murder or theft even if it spirals into a decades-long enmity. Women are strongly implicated in the code of Pakhtunwali because extramarital liaisons with the women of a family, whether forcible or consensual, are considered a slur on the honour of the men of that family and punishable under the principle of revenge or *badal*. Cultural and (consequently) scholarly discourses rely heavily on the concepts embodied in Pakhtunwali, using oral and textual social records of "traditions" of the Pakhtun north-west to rationalise personal, familial and tribe-based action. Yet Pakhtunwali is demonstrably flexible and continually reinvented, capable of accommodating nationalistic, religious and political tropes into conceptions of honour and rationalising succour for foreign militants on the principles of hosting and protecting guests. This chapter considers the manner in which the threat to women from the Taliban's coercive social agenda meshes with the trope of *ghairat* or *izzat*, a woman's sexual modesty, through the discursive domain.

The study of women in the Pakhtun north-west and action research

There have been very effective studies of women's engagements with patriarchal systems by the feminist scholars Lila Abu-Lughod, in her study of Bedouin women,[7] and Saba Mahmood, in her study of the *Politics of Piety* among the women of Cairo. These works frame a new discourse for the study of women in Muslim societies, one that does not resort to the limiting conceptual framework of resistance, subversion, or "false consciousness". Mahmood in particular has theorised the efforts of women to absorb and enact the ethical norms defined in Islam as agency, in an attempt to challenge the dominant Western suppositions about feminist issues.[8] Mahmood argues for an understanding of the agency of Muslim women, expressed within an Islamic ethical framework through displays of piety. She has deeply influenced anthropological work on the Pak-Afghan region, from the study of the Al Huda women's school[9] to Magnus Marsden's study of Chitral[10] and Julie Billaud's study of Afghan women.[11]

These works consider responses and agency within the cultural code that restricts women's appearances in public, highlighting the engagement with and challenge to these principles structured through the ethical language of Islamic reformism. But in cases where the psychological and subjective rationale for acceptance of religious-cultural principles is not an ethical one, how do we understand acceptance of norms which are understood to restrict the freedoms of women and even threaten their safety?

Shirkat Gah ran its project in three provinces of Pakistan through male and female research teams. The Shirkat Gah Peshawar office managed the project in the Khyber Pakhtunkhwa province by convening single-sex focus groups of eight to fifteen participants. Using a standardised and pre-planned action research methodology which involved bringing a group of women or men together and initiating a dynamic conversation around specific contemporary issues, Shirkat Gah's action-research trained, Pashtu-speaking employees led and transcribed conversations across Khyber Pakhtunkhwa. Others of their colleagues carried out similar research in Sindh, Punjab and Balochistan, aiming to understand the nature of women's concerns from a culturally nuanced, yet broad national perspective.

Unlike scholarly investigators in the Pakhtun regions, these action-researchers work from an acute nationalist and feminist commitment to and camaraderie with the communities with which they engage. Their work in the Pakhtun regions is not without political and social complexities: Urs Geiser's sensitive study "Producing Civil Society, Ignoring Rivaj" describes the interventions of NGOs as attempts to "develop and empower" which have been roundly condemned by the Swat Taliban as attempting to produce a Western culture and working for American imperialism. At a time when Fazlullah was himself determined to reform Pakhtun "*rivaj*" or custom, these transcripts become a fascinating interrogation of culture by virtue of the stresses and the questioning that they subject it to.

By engaging with local communities at a time that the Taliban were actively targeting NGOs, and by encouraging women to speak about their freedoms at a time when these were under attack from the Taliban, Shirkat Gah created a position in alliance with group participants. And in creating a space for discussion about women in conditions of suspicion and danger, the forums provoked participants to articulate the nature of their fears of the Taliban. This "alliance" makes extensive reading of social and cultural imperatives in Pakhtun society impossible because action researchers see themselves as participants in and influencers of culture. They provoke reflections on individual intent and desire, and encourage participants in their forums to reflect on their personal agency. Because of this intentionality, these interventions are records of the ways in which individuals may, for a time, distance themselves from dominant "culture".

The Shirkat Gah interviewers created new but short-lived spaces, privately arranged and populated with people who are similar yet possibly strangers to one another. These were transient spaces, created in people's living rooms, or occasionally in the offices of NGOs where these were available. Meetings were organised with the intention that they should go unnoticed by others who might be watching, and usually through a local contact in the neighbourhood. The researchers recorded the responses of individuals by hand because participants often refused to allow the sessions to be recorded, afraid that the Taliban would find out what had been said. This overwhelming fear, shared by the interviewers and the local participants in a time of conflict and violence directly targeted at women and at NGOs, influenced conversation to a point that the societal and cultural space that the Taliban were occupying in Khyber Pakhtunkhwa itself became a subject of inquiry.

Women's visibility and allegations of immorality

While women rarely appear in Pakhtun gathering places such as *masjid*s, *hujra*s and the old traders' bazaars, they have for long visited shrines, local vegetable, meat, fruit and cloth sellers, and more recently hospitals and schools as well. Women's public appearances are therefore restricted, but culturally permissible. When Shirkat Gah interviewers opened up the discussion on whether women should leave the house, both male and female participants argued that there were good reasons and financial exigencies that sometimes made it desirable for women to participate in a public world. Among women, discussions of acceptable jobs and reasons for leaving the house included teaching in a school, opening a school, or becoming a doctor (interestingly, professions linked to the moral objectives of the modernising state).[12] Emulating the Afghan Taliban, and attacking the institutions of the Pakistan state, the Taliban insisted that women moving outside their homes wear the *burqa*, a demand that Anita Weiss explores in this volume as an instance of invented tradition which was a cause of discomfort and anger for Swati women.

In the Shirkat Gah interviews, when women talked about claiming their rights to leave the house, they used a language of moral responsibility to do the "right thing" and not to do "wrong things" (translated by the interviewer as *ghalat kaam*), thereby assuming the moral burden thrust upon them. "Some girls pretend to go to school but actually go and do *ghalat kaam* instead," said twenty-year-old Naseem. "If my sister [who studies very hard and is only interested in her school work and takes no interest in housework] was to do *ghalat kaam* then she would no longer be allowed to go to school." "*Ghalat kaam*", coming up repeatedly in conversation, was used as a euphemism for any sort of involvement with men. In one case, the interviewer specifically framed discussion to address the question of *ghalat kaam* with the underlying assumption that involvement with men was indeed a bad thing. A group of women brought together in Lahori Gate Peshawar were asked, "Why do girls take 'steps in the wrong direction?'" (*larkiyan ghalat qadam kyun uthati hain*?) The following are a selection of the comments that followed:[13]

Shaista, 25, Seamstress and Embroiderer: "I think that educated girls do jobs, and they run away with boys."

Fatma, 26, Seamstress and Embroiderer: "It was not like this before. It happens now. Money has come [to people]. Bad intentions have come. There are boys in our neighbourhood who look at other people's sisters as they would their own, but there are those who think "wrongly" (*ghalat sochtay hain*). Now I have gathered girls together for you for this group, and people in the neighbourhood must be saying, "She met up with girls to discuss *yaars* (boyfriends.)"

PUBLIC VISIBILITY OF WOMEN

Syeda: "Those who are bad (*kharab*) themselves have bad thoughts about others."

Fatma (in agreement): "This is the wrong (*ghalat*)-thinking of the people of the neighbourhood. They think 'other people must leave their homes to get up to the same things which we leave our houses to do'."[14]

On provocation, comments by some women certainly displayed notes of subtle resistance to the charge of *ghalat kaam* or wrongdoing. While no one denied that such liaisons may occur, they questioned the social assumption that women's appearances in a public domain implied that they would engage in sexual misconduct. In a subtle push back against use of the term against women, the definition of *ghalat* was broadened to *kharab* ("bad" as in rancid or corrupted) to refer to the minds of those casting of aspersions on women's moral characters.

There was similarly a great deal of sympathy expressed for women who might be punished for sexual "misconduct". Lailah, a participant in a focus group with young unmarried women in Dargai Khas, said that girls were often forced into marriages when they were in love with someone else. If that happened, the girl could only concede, commit suicide or run away with her boyfriend to another town or province. Naseem had added that if they picked the latter option, which girls sometime did, it was better to "hide, otherwise they [would] be murdered".[15]

Violent punishments for women suspected of impropriety are condoned in the discourse of Pakhtunwali or *Pakhto* (the code of appropriate behaviour). For women, the link between their sexuality and male honour threatens their personal safety, and correspondingly women subjected to violence were described by other women as being "unfortunate", not the embodiment of a cultural ideal. Despite the apparent acceptance of principles of sexual virtue by women, there was no discernible sense among the women who were interviewed that the restrictions and punishments imposed on them were merited. What was agreed was that women seen in public were exposed to rumination about their sexuality—sometimes merited, sometimes unmerited, but which put them and other women within their families in a great deal of danger.

Principles governing women's sexuality were substantially articulated by men as well, and their discussions hinged on the concept of male *izzat* or honour as embodied in their women. Islamic scripture and religious principles were rarely invoked except on provocation. Because the phenomenon has been studied in great detail by anthropologists I choose not to dwell extensively on the notional value of *izzat* here, but rather on the ambivalence that underlies it. Men tended to describe social mores governing women as emanating not from themselves, but from others in a shared discursive space which exerted great pressure.

A men's group in Dargai Khas had a short and charged conversation which we can consider as representative of the most extreme sorts of opinions held about women seen outside the house. The report of the session takes on some of the qualities of the "untethered" voice: stories of unknown authorship, widely shared in an anonymous collective voice, which Veena Das identifies to explain how the "unsayable" is said.[16] Women sitting in close proximity to men in public transport vehicles were likened to "known" prostitutes in bazaars. Through vague allusion in a single conversation to what is known about different sorts of women seen in public, it was "anonymously" suggested that women who frequented bazaars did so to engage in prostitution.

Akbar: "There is a market close by here. It is always full of women. Men leave their houses and women come to the market."

Sayyid: "Don't be angry, but I know all about your [the interviewer's] Charsadda [city] and Peshawar. Men and women are sat facing each other in Suzuki [vans]. As much sexual licentiousness as there is in Charsadda ..."

Interjection from Muzaffar: "Particularly in Ghaffuria Market—not really anywhere else."

Interjection from Mustafa: "And particularly in Swabi [city]. There is one fact which is well known. But you [the interviewer] will be offended if I say."

Interviewer: "No, *yaar*. Speak openly. No one will be offended."

Mustafa: "If you have money then girls will come from even so far as Kalabat. Kalabat is an area in Swabi."

Interviewer: "Isn't Thana [district] also quite well known [for prostitution]?"

Mustafa: "Yes. Thana which is in Malakand district. Forty per cent of girls who run from their homes are there. That is a very well known place."[17]

The unsayable, that women who were visible in public were indistinguishable from prostitutes, or perhaps were venturing out to engage in prostitution, was suggested through the structure of the conversation: that some women go out to bazaars when they choose, they do so to prostitute themselves, and this is established by the fact that there is prostitution in the bazaars of Charsadda, Peshawar and Thana. And yet the men managed to distance themselves from such base and undignified accusations which implicated their own moral selves by never stating the implication as personal conviction or experience. No man said "I have been approached by prostitutes in the bazaar". The knowledge of prostitutes was plucked from a societal knowledge where "it is well known", where "they say", where it is "fact".

The collective voice, in its anonymity, in its subtle nuance, allowed speakers to distance themselves from a complicating condemnation of women's intentions, yet use it to assert a perceived social reality. In the formulation of these young men, the disembodied and dangerous voice of "society" which spreads rumours, casts aspersions and defines social worth is both autonomous and employable by individuals. This device is the mechanism by which men manage a societal expectation of women alongside their intimate relations to them, allowing them to contribute to a widespread social formulation of the sexuality and position of women while morally distancing themselves from its inequities and brutalities towards women. In describing a voice of "society" which they had no control over and were at the mercy of, it became possible for men to critique the behaviour of women and yet articulate the empathy that comes from the close personal relations with wives, sisters, mothers and daughters.[18] This duality was expressed as follows by Akbar: "What do we do? To tell you the truth, I wouldn't mind if my sister married someone she liked or chose herself. The problem is with 'society' (*muashira*). If someone was to shut the mouth of the world, they would make us all free."[19]

This brings us to the question of how exactly society condemns the social appearance of women while ostensibly recognising the need for, and sometimes even the merit in, a woman being out in public. The balance rests on the discernibility of female sensuality in a manner which could excite the imagination of others. A fascinating example of this was the oft-repeated argument that a girl cannot be "known" to have married out of love because that constitutes a testimony to her sexuality:

Masud, 24, Unemployed: "If it is found out that a girl is refusing [an arranged marriage] because she has connections to [another] boy then no one will ever do what that girl asks."

Fahim, 18, Student: "If [parents and family] suspect for even a moment that she might like a boy, they will marry her to anyone, even a donkey, but not to that boy…"

Muhammad Jamaluddin, 27, *Galukar:* "If it is discovered that a girl has connections to a boy, [the parents and family] are even ready to murder her. And such a matter has resulted in murder many times."

In very few instances did individuals suggest that Islamic values guided their public or private lives. In one conversation with married men in Dargai Khas the interviewer asked, "so what is the face of a 'good woman'?", to which Usman (a 26-year-old student) replied, "that woman who is 'Islamic',[20] who wears the clothes of *purdah*: she is a good woman." In the lively unmarried-men's group in Dargai Khas, one of the participants suggested the following:

Everything is in a woman's hands. … I have three brothers and the wife of [one] brother has made everyone in the house her follower… because she is graceful. She speaks little and does not interfere in anyone else's business. She keeps her own children very clean and even oversees the homework of the children of my other sisters-in-law. … Even my father does not interfere in her affairs. She has taken responsibility for the whole house. When my brothers come back from Malaysia they do not bring as much for their own wives and kids as they bring for my *bhabhi*. She is an "ideal" woman. My other sisters-in-law can neither take care of their children nor of themselves.

Even though the entire discourse of womanhood is a domain of principles, questions of right and wrong, good and bad or the pure and the corrupted, the set of ideals being described here is not to do with a moral code. Good parenting, good housekeeping and personal deportment are not moral values, but domestic ones. The best sort of girl stays firmly put at home and takes good care of the rest of the family. The sense that a woman's greatest control and safety were in a domestic world was articulated by men and women across the different groups. The critical feature of the domestic space for our study is that it is out of public sight, populated and frequented only by women or male family members. The outside can be understood as having the qualities of opposition to this realm. It is full of unknown people who can see women while going undetected themselves. In it, women are transformed as their grace and love become sexuality and any relations of affection with men are lewd. In public, women become construed through the gaze and the musings of the *ghair*: he who is not of the family.

Women's sexuality, men's fear and the Taliban

At the end of the 1979–89 Afghan war, as the battle of succession began in Kabul, a new movement was launched in the Malakand division of what was then named the North-West Frontier Province (NWFP), by Maulana Sufi Muhammad, a one-time member of the Jamaat-i Islami. The movement was referred to as a "neo-Taliban movement" because of its emulation of the Afghan Taliban's efforts to reform and police society. Sufi Muhammad aimed to establish sharia law in Malakand through his organisation called the Tehrik-i-Nifaz-i-Shariat-i-Muhammadi (TNSM).[21] His movement waxed and waned through the 1994–2000 period. In 2001 Sufi Muhammad came to national attention when he led a *lashkar* into Afghanistan to support the Afghan Taliban's fight against the coalition forces in the post-9/11 War on Terror. As Robert Nichols explains, by 2007 Sufi Muhammad's son-in-law Fazlullah drew the movement into an alliance with groups referring to themselves as the Tehrik-i-Taliban Pakistan. It is for this reason that the religious extremism in Malakand has come to be referred to as "Taliban" in both the official and a general public discourse.

The language and ideology of the Taliban in Afghanistan, despite being rooted in purist notions of Islam and the Quran, were developed through a campaign of war in the 1990s. Similarly the Tehrik-i-Taliban Pakistan and associated groups see themselves as being at war with the state and imperial power. Residents of the region equally see themselves trapped in a terrain of war, marked by frontier constabulary posts and military installations and the geographic location of the fighting between the Afghan Taliban, the neo-Taliban and the Pakistan army.[22] As Mariam Abou Zahab effectively argues, rather than thinking about the Taliban and the neo-Taliban movements as only representing religion, we should understand them as equally rooted in local culturally and politically intoned concerns.

Without an articulated position on what women's morality entailed for the Tehrik-i-Taliban, their *de facto* position can be assumed to be akin to the Afghan Taliban's stance in Afghanistan, as the TTP was of course modelled on the social and political model of the Taliban. Ahmed Rashid's appraisal of the Taliban's concern with women's sexual morality quotes Mullah Qamaluddin who led the Department of Amr Bil Maroof wa Nahi Anal Munkir (the Department for the Promotion of Virtue and Prevention of Vice) in Kabul in 1997. Rashid focuses on the gendered prohibitions just put in place by the Department of ABM—banning women from wearing makeup and from walking in a manner that makes a noise (the latter injunction was extended to a ban on high-heeled shoes). This edict also formalised prohibitions on women working in any field except the medical sector, and if they worked in the medical sector they were prohibited from riding in the front of a vehicle with a man.[23] When Rashid questioned Qamaluddin about the logic behind these prohibitions, Qamaluddin replied:

> We will be blamed by our people if we don't educate women and provide education for them eventually, but for now we have serious problems... There are security problems. There are no provisions for separate transport, separate school buildings and facilities to educate women for the moment. Women must be completely segregated from men. And within us we have those men who cannot behave properly with women.[24]

In this discussion is a crucial linking of three ideas—the *insecurity* of the region, the *impropriety* of men and the threat to the virtue of women. Women are in danger of being raped or molested by criminals, or of attracting improper attention from men. Hence their movements and appearance are closely governed. Even without the intent to assert their sexual charms, women are sexual beings

PUBLIC VISIBILITY OF WOMEN

and their presence in public spaces endangers a very fragile order of sexual morality. In more secure times, Mullah Qamaluddin said, such restrictions would not be necessary, but these were terrible times in Afghanistan.

When Sufi Muhammad's imitative neo-Taliban movement was launched in the mid 1990s in Swat, he used the same concepts of reclaiming state and governance, but in his case specifically through enforcing the sharia and the dispensation of justice through special Qazi courts created by him. Sufi Muhammad's ambit of power was in Swat, part of the Malakand region but on the other side from where Shirkat Gah conducted its research. Sufi's movement grew in the 2000–2010 period under his son-in-law Fazlullah, emulating the Taliban principles of segregated public spaces, advocating the *burqa* and condemning women who were seen unaccompanied outside the house.

In 2007–09 Fazlullah came to have virtual control over Swat. Girls' schools, people accused of being government informers, barbers and music shop owners were attacked by his supporters who were coming to be widely referred to as "Taliban". Women were warned not to come to the bazaars or hospitals or even leave their houses alone. In the bordering area of Dargai Khas and Kharkai in Malakand, fewer and fewer women were visible in public spaces as they came to have fewer reasons for being there.[25] Women who were seen out unaccompanied or not wearing the *burqa* were threatened, or in some cases attacked with acid.[26] Fazlullah created alliances with other groups calling themselves the Tehrik-i-Taliban Pakistan (the movement of the Taliban in Pakistan), with headquarters in Waziristan. In the manner of the Afghan Taliban, the TTP carried out a public flogging of a woman who had violated the rules of chastity in at least one highly publicised and dramatic incident in Swat in 2009. Copy-cat attacks on women were carried out in other districts of the NWFP as well, and as far away as Islamabad women accused of prostitution were threatened or kidnapped.[27]

Participants in Shirkat Gah's focus groups made innumerable references to how "*draowny*" (scary) the Taliban were, how dangerous they were, and how powerful their networks of informers were. Non-Governmental Organisations (NGOs) had been specifically targeted as agents of foreign (American) interests, and local employees of NGOs were asked to quit, or else be treated as enemies. The power of the Taliban, operating outside Swat as militias, was rooted in a politics of fear exercised through the possibility that an informer might be watching. The Taliban are a phantom presence in the areas where interviews took place, but although they did not have actual governmental control, they were understood to have a murderous political will and the potential to wreak vengeance on both public and private critics. It was in this environment that the Shirkat Gah team carried out its investigations.

Many of the men and women who were interviewed were clearly and boldly unsympathetic to the Taliban movement by virtue of maintaining, under great threat, a working relationship with the NGO. Other groups were deeply uncomfortable with the circumstances of the meetings, apparently because of the dangers posed to them by the Taliban and by the state looking for allies against the growing influence of the radical group. All were concerned about the Taliban "finding out" about the meetings. One men's group, convened in Kharki at the same that an anti-Taliban army operation had begun in another part of Malakand, was noted as being deeply uneasy. Investigators described the response as follows:

The people present in the groups were suspicious of us, as to who we were and what our purpose was. "Why are we making this map of the village? For what purpose will it be used?" On the excuse of bringing water in, two men went outside and asked our driver who we were... We felt how nervous and unsettled they were throughout.[28]

References were repeatedly made by interviewers and by respondents to how the working groups had been convened at great personal risk to all present. In Lahori Gate, participants were part of a community *friendly* to organisations working for women's health, education and public safety, when girls' schools, women's health clinics and women's public presence were being threatened by the Taliban. Yet participants' narratives should not be considered voices of resistance, or the meetings a politics of secret subversion. Whenever mention of the Taliban came up, it was with disdain tinged with worry and in the hope that those in attendance would not come to the notice of the militants. Participants attended because they felt it was still possible to dodge bullets and detection in the ongoing and as yet unconcluded war, and the discretion with which focus groups were convened allowed some social rumination about the Taliban and their gendered social perspective to take place.

During this period, one of the interviews in Dargai Khas provoked a young man to try to explain the link between sexuality, the control of women through fear, and the Taliban:

Mahmood: "If men do something who is to know? If a *ghair mard* entered a woman's house, everyone would know."

Interviewer: "But then isn't this an issue of fear, not doing right or wrong?"

Mahmood: "Well that is exactly what fear is—that which prevents [someone] from doing right or wrong. if you gave these men and women freedom they would all be having sex like animals in the streets and in buses."

Interviewer: "Well, doesn't religion forbid this as well?"

Mahmood: "Yes, religion forbids it, but far greater than [observance of religion] is the fear of the Taliban."[29]

This discussion, which took place in 2008, established how far the link between the Taliban agenda, the control of female sexuality, and the threat of *public* punishment was linked in public discourse. Mahmood went on to describe the overpowering sexuality of women, backing this up with quotation of a "*hadith*" that "women have been given nine times the sex [drive] of men". Mahmood saw some discrepancy between the treatment of women and men, but suggested that perhaps fear was the only thing that could adequately control women's aberrant sexuality.

So the logic of the control of women through fear took on the following structure: women have a much greater sexual energy and if allowed to exercise it would cause mayhem. The Taliban were merely enforcing the logic of religion which would otherwise be ineffective if left to personal morality, and they did so by making public examples of licentious women. No one denied that the power of the Taliban lay in their ability to threaten. Yet no one disputed the right of the Taliban to try to control women's sexuality through force. A men's group in Kharki denied that any attacks had been made on women in that town, or that girls were prevented from going to school (a fact not disputed by the investigator in his report): "Girls go to school he said. Only now they wear *burqas*."[30] The logic of this demand, in a place where girls had been going to school up until the previous year wearing *chador*s, was accepted unquestioningly. The Taliban's assumption of the right to regulate the bodily appearance of girls and women in public spaces was not challenged because it merged with the preexisting conviction that women should be covered.

The threats made against women were not only of rationalised punishment. They included implied sexual threats to women seen on the streets. Public discourse about the "danger" of the Taliban ascribed to them the potential to molest, rape or abduct women seen outside. That the guardians of women's virtue should threaten it is the essential paradox of popular opinion about the Taliban. While women were encouraged to stay out of public sight to restrict their appeal to men, their appearances could be punished by the very violation which the Taliban claimed to be protecting the women from. The Taliban of Swat and their networks of informers through the surrounding regions were viewed with terror for what they could do to those defying their rules. One man said: "families do not let their girls go to school. My own parents say, what is worth doing for the education of our daughters when if God forbid one of the Taliban were to lay a hand on our daughter we would die right there". Another said: "now the Taliban's influence is very strong. Girls don't go to school, they don't go to work. [It has reached the point that] if they go to participate in [occasions of] joy and sorrow, they have to come home before evening otherwise they can be endangered by two or four on the street on their way back."[31]

On the one hand, the Taliban posited themselves as resolvers of the political and social crisis of insecurity and injustice. Defenders of the Taliban (numbering very few among those interviewed as the participants in the surveys were, by virtue of their presence there, friendly to NGOs) did not deny that the group had targeted girls' schools, or carried out attacks on people, schools and hospitals. One man in Kharki, Malakand suggested, "If the Taliban have stood up then that is not wrong. The entire society is fallen in filth."[32] On the other hand, the Taliban were seen by many as a symptom of the insecurity and criminality which endanger women. References to the dangers to women when outdoors were interwoven with mentions of louts among the Afghan *muhajireen* (new migrants from Afghanistan) who smoked hashish and ogled women, and talk of abductions carried out by Taliban or their sympathisers.[33] The danger they posed to women took on the language of wartime conditions in which women's bodies become the terrain on which politics of anarchy, possession and control are played out.

The complexity of the fear-morality and protector-violator paradigm stemmed from the general assertions that the Taliban were part of the composite of regional and local society. Although there were occasional mentions of Afghans living in local *masjid*s or loafing in the streets,[34] there was never a reference to members of the Taliban being from other places. The acceptance that local realities had thrown up the Taliban went hand in hand with the references to their politics, their abuses and their morality being symptomatic of those of society at large. So although they offered a response to state and imperialism, the Taliban were seen as being themselves a threat to the peace and security of the region and the safety of women in a visible public realm.

It is in no way a new or radical supposition that the Taliban force social complicity with their gendered project by inspiring fear, but it is important to understand the manner in which they have engaged and altered societal principles. The Taliban dictates mirror those of society, yet they are the inversions of norms that favour familial control over women's sexuality and punishment. The Taliban have been permitted to enter a private familial domain. In villages where families have dared to defy Taliban dictates and send their daughters to school or allow their sisters to work, the Taliban have been permitted to speak the unspeakable—to name a particular man's wife, sister or daughter and accuse her of shameful things. Among women, where once the pressure to conform to cultural obligation had once begun and ended with the family, the Taliban could now stoke fear and carry out punishments. In one exchange in Kharki, Zar Bibi said, "If my husband doesn't bother me then I would not be afraid of anyone else in all of Pakistan," to which Savira, a 54-year-old housewife, answered jokingly, "If the Taliban came, then you would be afraid."

The Taliban were said to sexually assault women in a cultural environment which avenges such crimes with blood, and assumed patriarchal dictate over issues of family concern in familial units which jealously guard the hierarchy and authority of the oldest male family member. Despite this, there was neither widespread resistance to the Taliban, nor explicit condemnation voiced in the group discussions.

I posit the following: that instead of meeting recrimination, the coercive power of the Taliban merged with a preexisting perception of malignant and dangerous societal ruminations. An unknown yet widespread membership, the possibility that anyone anywhere could be a Taliban informer, echoed the sense that unknown, unrelated people anywhere could be watching women and casting aspersions on their character. Descriptions of the "seeing eyes" and listening ears of the Taliban and their network of informers echo the untethered voice of society which was described by men in relation to the moral restrictions of women's freedom. Through penetration into the public domain—the bazaars, *masjid*s and broadcast and print media—the Taliban could generate visual testimony about the lives of men and women and tap into preexisting fears about who might "see" and caste aspersions on their women. With their added control over mosques and bazaars and membership across villages and regions, the Taliban became, for that time, a dominant voice of "society". Men became unable to respond to this control which approximated a popular opinion, because their own rationale for the control of women was precisely that opinion and not an ideological premise.

Society, coercion and the public

Mariam Abou Zahab's work on the changing systems of relations in Waziristan, Sultan-i-Rome's descriptions of the growth of *jihadi* organisation in Swat, and Robert Nichols' work on class describe the fractures in family and community life which have emerged over thirty years of militarisation and economic impoverishment. Magnus Marsden's study of Afghan traders working between the Gulf and Central Asia describes their ability to "develop forms of public discourse and comportment suitable to both these settings", exploring Salafi Islam because they are "bored" with conversations about cement. This path-breaking body of work impresses upon us that we must account for change in our references to Pakhtun culture, in the very way that we understand culture. And because we have actors who engage in entirely new ways with the meaning of "tribe and state", we must think more deeply about where and how culture and society are constituted.

In the discursive formulation, society functions as a rhetorical device, expressing a cognitive duality: the experience as opposed to the perception of the self through the gaze of the other. In the sets of interviews described here, "society" also occupies a space where the individual cannot advocate for himself or herself, and his or her behaviour will be critiqued on the basis of a shared set of assumptions about appropriate individual conduct.[35] These assumptions are, to all intents and purposes, cultural norms: those directives to individual behaviour which are not rooted in a personal logic, but in a widely shared set of assumptions about what is appropriate. The individual is a participant in the persistence of those assumptions by anticipating them, but does not necessarily agree with them at all times. The cultural space where the individual cannot influence another's judgment of his or her actions is a location where coercive norms are produced and asserted.

Despite the fact that the Taliban are Pakhtun, use language and history to lay claims to ethnic belonging, and in many cases belong to the communities within which they exercise their violent and misogynistic power, they are not negotiating their place as arbiters of a cultural morality through "traditional" institutions such as the *hujra*, the clan or the family. Rather they assert this power through bazaars, *masjid*s, streets and open *maidan*s. This brings us to reflect on the nature of the public in the formulation of contemporary Pakhtun society: despite the importance of the tribe or clan, the definition of society includes those who operate outside genealogical systems, and rather than being named members in the hierarchy of the clan, are unknown and unidentifiable.

Personal resistance, social activism or ideological decisions which may or may not have subsequently been offered by the participants in this survey will remain unknown to us by the methodology I have employed in this study. But we can understand, through this chance record of social rumination, how a form of religious coercion can find a place in culture and society. In the case of the Taliban's gender politics, the intersection came because of their connection to a "societal" imagination by occupying physical spaces in the towns and cities of Khyber Pakhtunkhwa which made it possible for them to observe others.

There is a tendency with the study of Islamic societies to use paradigms of either ideological conviction or forced subjection to explain societal acceptance of prohibitions on women. But it should also be accepted that social complicity can stem from less acute convictions than those generated by dogma or visceral terror. Transcripts of conversations in the Pakhtun north-west exhibit a rationalising of the prohibitions on women provoked by fear, but also by the integration of the Taliban into a public domain. Thus, their dogma finds a place despite challenging other norms which privilege family and clan-based patriarchies.

SECTION 5

TRIBES, CONFLICT AND STATE-BUILDING IN AFGHANISTAN AND PAKISTAN

15

CUSTOM AND CONFLICT IN WAZIRISTAN

SOME BRITISH VIEWS

Hugh Beattie

Waziristan makes an interesting contrast with other parts of the North-West Frontier region such as the Swat valley. On the whole land in Waziristan is less productive than in Swat, its ownership is less concentrated, and society is, or was, more egalitarian. Nor, it appears, has Waziristan ever had a ruler like the Wali of Swat. Nowadays, unlike Swat, it forms part of Pakistan's Federally Administered Tribal Areas (FATA). This chapter looks briefly at some of the ways in which, in the late nineteenth and early twentieth centuries, British officials imagined the Frontier tribes. It goes on to focus on Waziristan, exploring two contrasting understandings of the socio-political organisation of the Mahsuds in particular, and the way they were associated with different strategies for controlling them. In conclusion the chapter draws a few comparisons and contrasts between the situation in the early twentieth century and the present day.

Nowadays most of Waziristan is in Pakistan, though the Afghan district of Birmal is usually considered to be part of it as well. About sixty miles across at its widest point, Waziristan extends roughly in the shape of a parallelogram from the Gumal river in the south about ninety miles north as far as the Kaitu river and across it to Thal. On the east it is bordered by Bannu and Tank and to the west it extends through Birmal to the Afghan plateau and the provinces of Paktia, Khost and Paktika. The southern half is mainly mountainous, while the northern half is more open with wider valleys separated by ranges of lower mountains.[1] It is inhabited largely by Pashtuns, usually thought of as being divided into "tribes" or "tribal confederations" on the basis of supposed shared descent from a common ancestor.[2] The principal ones are the Mahsuds (or Mehsuds), the Darwesh Khels Wazirs (referred to from now on simply as Wazirs), the Bhittanis and the Dawars. The Bhittanis live to the east between the administered areas and the Wazirs and Mahsuds. The Dawars live in Dawar in the lower Tochi valley. The Mahsuds live

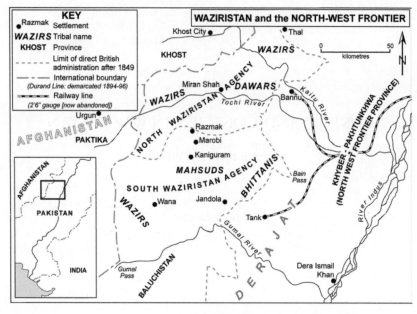

Map 15.1.

in the centre, and the Wazirs in an arc extending across the north and north-west towards the bottom left-hand corner of the parallelogram. The Wazirs are further divided into Utmanzais and Ahmedzais, and the Mahsuds into three main groupings: Alizais, Bahlolzais and Shaman Khels. Waziristan's population is now reported to be more than 800,000, but it was much less than this in the mid-nineteenth century, perhaps as low as 100,000.[3]

The GOI and the "tribes"

During the First Anglo-Afghan War (1839–42), the British Government of India (GOI) had dealings with the Afridis who lived around the Khyber Pass (and to a limited extent with the Orakzais and Shinwaris). However, it only began to come into sustained contact with the other tribal groups living along the North-West Frontier after 1849, when it annexed the Punjab. Though they did not all take part in these activities, men from some of these groups had a tradition of raiding in the settled areas to the east and looting caravans passing to and from Afghanistan. This might not have mattered so much, but the border along which these groups lived was regarded by the GOI as a particularly strategic one, and the majority view came to be that the stability of British rule in India required the establishment of British influence over it. The question of how best to achieve this therefore became increasingly important. Until the 1920s permanent military occupation was not a practical proposition for various reasons, so it was a matter of trying to influence the behaviour of its inhabitants by other means. As well as the intermittent use of force, these included encouraging them to trade in British territory, enlisting them in various military units, paying them allowances, and sometimes offering them land on which to settle in British territory. To facilitate this, the British had to try to understand the culture and social organisation of this stateless society. As a result a complex discourse developed which comprised a number of debates and incorporated different, even contradictory, ideas and models. British administrators who dealt with Waziristan made a significant contribution to this.

In administering the people they conquered, Europeans often found it convenient to privilege some identities rather than others. In areas where political structures were weaker this sometimes involved the foregrounding of some kind of "tribal" identity. In dealing with the North-West Frontier British administrators undoubtedly placed a great deal of emphasis on what they referred to as the "tribal constitution of society".[4] They saw that the inhabitants of Waziristan, for instance, identified themselves as belonging to different groups—Wazirs, Mahsuds, Bhittanis, Dawars and so on—membership of which was supposed to depend on shared patrilineal descent from a common ancestor. They appreciated that this identity had some significance. The problem was to work out what it meant in practical terms, and whether they could make any use of it.

Recognising that the groupings which they referred to as tribes were in genealogical terms further subdivided, British administrators began to draw up intricate tables and charts, listing different subdivisions and showing the supposed relationships between them. However, they did not necessarily agree about the terms they used to refer to these subdivisions. For instance, the Derajat Commissioner, Reynell Taylor (Political Officer during the Ambela expedition in 1863, mentioned in Chapter 3) referred in 1861 to the different "sections" of the Mahsuds.[5] A little later, with reference to the Frontier tribes in general, the Kohat Deputy-Commissioner, Trevor Plowden, used the terms "divisions", "clans", "sections" and "subsections".[6] Sir Denzil Ibbetson, the administrator and author of *Outlines of Punjab Ethnography* (1883) referred to "clan" and "sept".[7] Another administrator, Sir Charles Tupper, suggested that "we should speak of the tribe of a race, the clan of a tribe, the section of a clan, the branch of a section, and the house of a branch ... generally, *zat* or *kaum* would be translated "race" or tribe"; and *got*, "tribe" or "clan" according to circumstances ... Thus, we should have the Massozai section of the Zaimusht tribe of the Afghan or Pathan race ...".[8]

Inconsistent use of these terms sometimes led to misunderstandings between officials. More important, however, was the question of how far these tribal groups were, or could be turned into, corporate ones. If they were indeed corporate, then their members could justifiably be regarded as responsible for each other's actions, and it would be legitimate and effective to punish some for the crimes of others, in other words to impose collective punishments.[9] According to Ibbetson for instance, "(t)he frontier tribe whether within or beyond our border has almost without exception a very distinct corporate existence".[10] As he saw it,

(t)he territorial distribution of the frontier tribes in the fastnesses of their native mountains is strictly tribal. Each clan of each tribe has a tract allotted to it; and within that the families or small groups of nearly related families either lead a semi-nomad [*sic*] life, or inhabit rude villages round the fields which they cultivate and the rough irrigation works which they have constructed".[11]

One difficulty with this model was that—as those British officials who dealt with Waziristan recognised—there was not always the close correspondence between clan and a particular territory suggested by Ibbetson. In the Mahsud case in particular, people from different sections might live quite close to each other. So, for example, it was noted in 1901 that "(t)he Mahsuds do not live each clan collected within its ring fence as do Afridis, Mohmands and others, but the clans, sub-sections and smaller divisions live intermixed in an extraordinary way".[12] Another problem was that tribal responsibility was not an idea with which the tribes themselves were necessarily familiar or happy. As Taylor commented in 1860, the Mahsuds were "unused to the idea of being bound to control every member of the tribe and be responsible for his acts".[13] At the same time, it is worth noting that one respect in which the Wazirs and Mahsuds do seem to have seen themselves as having a kind of overall tribal identity concerned the distribution of benefits acquired from, and any losses suffered at the hands of, outsiders. Associated with the idea of a thread or link, *sarishta*, linking the different groups was *nikkat* (from *nikka*, grandfather). *Nikkat* was a tariff according to which profits and losses were to be shared in fixed proportions both between Wazirs and Mahsuds, and then between the three main Mahsud divisions, Alizais, Bahlolzais and Shaman Khels, and their sub-sections.[14]

Having agreed that it was appropriate to impose some kind of collective responsibility, the next question for the officials was which segmentary "level" should be regarded as the critical one.[15] Some wanted to focus on smaller subdivisions. Others wanted to extend this responsibility quite widely, to whole sections or tribes. However, in the Mahsud case in particular, because of "the intermingling of tribes" referred to above, it was very difficult to impose responsibility on one section rather than another.[16] British policy was inconsistent here. After 1861 the local officials tended to argue that it would be better to demand collective tribal responsibility from the Mahsuds rather than from each of the three main sections—Alizais, Bahlolzais and Shaman Khels. However this was resisted by the Punjab government until 1876 when Charles Macaulay, the Dera Ismail Khan Deputy-Commissioner, was given permission to impose a blockade on the tribe as a whole.[17]

Different approaches to controlling the Mahsuds and the Mullah Powindah

For the first 30 or 40 years after 1849, collective tribal responsibility was seen as vital in Waziristan because the British thought of the people as being particularly "democratic or anarchical".[18] A typical comment was that:

> The social condition of the tribes is anarchic. The so-called maliks are only men who have got a little more property, better arms and stronger family connections than their neighbours. But any half-starved tribesman thinks himself the equal of any one of these maliks, and where the tribe is collected in any numbers it at once becomes apparent that these so-called headmen, instead of possessing any influence to control the others, dare not give offence even to the poorest clansmen.[19]

The Mahsuds especially were regarded as "extremely democratic in their ways. If ten men are wanted to do a bit of business, a hundred will come".[20]

The fact that there were no real leaders helped to make the Mahsuds especially difficult to handle. In 1879, for instance, they came down in force and looted and burned the town of Tank. However in the later 1880s Richard Bruce, who had previously worked with Sir Robert Sandeman in Baluchistan, thought he had found the answer. In the 1870s and 1880s Sandeman had successfully extended British influence into Baluchistan by paying allowances to selected chiefs and backing them with force when necessary.[21] In 1888 Bruce took over as Deputy-Commissioner Dera Ismail Khan, and suggested that it would be possible to apply Sandeman's approach to Waziristan.[22] Claiming that before 1849 the Mahsuds, like the Baluchistan tribes, had had effective chiefs, he argued that British policy was responsible for their anarchic condition. By changing this it would be possible, he said, to recreate an oligarchy of influential men through whom the tribe could be managed. After the Russian takeover of Merv in 1885, the threat of a Russian invasion of India had again begun to concern many British officials. To enable it to meet a possible Russian advance as effectively as possible, in 1887 the GOI had written to the Punjab government calling for independent tribal territory between India and Afghanistan to be brought under British control.[23] Bruce's proposals seemed to offer the prospect of achieving this aim in Waziristan and he was given permission to take them forward.

He therefore identified men who seemed to him to have some authority among the Mahsuds, however informal, and tried to form them into what he called a "manageable representative *jirga* on a sound basis". At a meeting in 1889 with what he called "a large and thoroughly representative tribal assembly", it was agreed that Rs. 1,264 would be distributed to fifty-one *malik*s. In return for this men were to be provided for irregular military service.[24] In 1890 the Mahsud *malik*s among others were given further subsidies for providing levies to maintain the security of the Gumal Pass in particular.[25] The *malik*s were also supposed to control the rest of the tribe and hand over wanted men to the government.

It appears that Bruce did not choose his *malik*s very carefully. A few years later the Wana Political Agent, F.W. Johnston, suggested that most of them had actually been nominated by Azim Khan Kundi, a landowner living in British territory, who since the early 1870s had been an influential intermediary between the Mahsuds and the government.[26] Nevertheless, for three or four years the policy seemed to work. The security of the Gumal Pass improved, and when a British official was killed by Mahsuds in 1893 the *malik*s handed over the men responsible to the authorities. However, in revenge three *malik*s were killed by the men's relatives; the other *malik*s left for British territory. It proved impossible to capture the murderers. The Punjab Government recommended a punitive expedition, but the GOI would not allow one. After this episode the remaining *malik*s cooperated only reluctantly with Bruce and did not do much to help him.[27]

At the beginning of this chapter the point was made that Waziristan appears to have differed from Swat in various significant ways. However, as in Swat, the obvious alternative to *malik*s or khans was religious leadership. Islam was central to Pashtun identity in Waziristan (if for most people in the form of "an unthought Geertzian "religiousness", as Marsden puts it in Chapter 7). Opposition to the British could easily be presented as resistance not just to external interference but also to Christian intrusion, and therefore a religious duty. So the more assertive

213

British policy in Waziristan, as elsewhere on this border, helped religious leaders to play a more important political role than they had done before. Those with some influence in Waziristan at this time included Lala Pir, based across the Durand Line in Khost, and Mullah Hamzullah, who had links with the Wazirs living in north Waziristan. However the most prominent was Muhiy-ud-Din, a (Sultanai) Shabi Khel Alizai Mahsud; the British referred to him as the Mullah Powindah.[28] After studying at a *madrasa* in Bannu, he had built up a following of *shaikh*s (deputies) and *taliban* (religious students). He set up his headquarters at his home in Marobi between Razmak and Kaniguram, and became the major rival to the *malik*s.[29]

The Mullah first attracted the GOI's attention in the autumn of 1894. The British effort to secure control of the Gumal Pass was followed by the demarcation of the Durand Line in the mid-1890s, designed to delimit Afghan and British spheres of influence along the Frontier. Bruce was appointed to mark out the new boundary in southern Waziristan with an Afghan counterpart. It was also decided to establish a garrison of regular troops at Wana. In November 1894, supported by 2,000 soldiers, Bruce began to set up camp there. Only a few days later the Mullah Powindah organised a night attack on the troops by as many as 2000 men, mostly Mahsuds, and the British force was withdrawn. This was followed by another British punitive expedition into Waziristan in 1895, after which the North and South Waziristan agencies were set up with their headquarters at Miran Shah and Wana respectively.

At this point Bruce, admitting that he had got things wrong the first time, drew up another list of *malik*s, 270 of them this time. He divided them into five classes, and paid each class at a different rate, according to how much influence he judged them to have.[30] Bruce left the Frontier in 1896, and his successor Anderson continued with his policy, without, it would seem, much success. Some Mahsuds continued to rob and murder in the Tank and Bannu districts; they began to intimidate and even try to assassinate the local officials. In July 1899, for instance, there was an attempt to kill the South Waziristan Political Agent.[31] The *malik*s may have been, as Anderson reported, "sensible responsible men", but it was clear that Bruce's system—the so-called "maliki system"—was not working.[32] Even had they been willing to try, it would have been almost impossible for the *malik*s to control their fellow tribesmen. In fact their ability to do so decreased as they grew closer to the British; "in some cases it would seem that by becoming our men whatever little influence they would otherwise have with the tribe is weakened".[33]

In 1900 Anderson was replaced as Commissioner by William Merk, who had experience of working with other groups without chiefs or leaders, the eastern Mohmands and the Afridis.[34] In the summer of 1900 Merk wrote to the Punjab Government outlining and advocating a new approach to the Mahsuds. Once upon a time, he suggested (more or less correctly, it would appear), general *jirga*s of the whole Mahsud tribe, the *ulus* (*wolus*) had been held, and had kept order by appointing *chalweshti*s or tribal militias to enforce the tribal will; now *chalweshti*s were no longer appointed, and there was "political paralysis". Like Bruce, he accepted that "(c)ontact with a settled Government like our own" had had "a disintegrating effect" on them.[35] However, it was not earlier British efforts to manage the Mahsuds that were to blame, as Bruce had argued, but Bruce's own attempts to deal with them through *maliks*.[36] The Mahsuds, he maintained, constituted "an independent little republic", in which some men had some influence but "little real power".[37] Bruce, he said, had failed to understand that behind the *maliks* were "the many yeomen who constitute the real republic, and with whom obviously the ultimate power rests".[38] Presumably by referring to the Mahsuds as yeomen, Merk meant to suggest that they were mostly small independent farmers like those of pre-Enclosure England. Making another European comparison, he also suggested that, because of their ability to disrupt any settlement, individual tribesmen possessed something like the *liberum veto* of pre-partition Poland.[39] In any case, he said, "with a democracy of this kind, it is fatal to deal with individuals, however powerful they may be".[40]

According to Merk, "in a democratic republic, like that of the Mahsud community ... [the old tribal *jirga*] was the natural, and indeed the only possible, governing agency."[41] His aim therefore was to revive "internal self-government" by paying allowances to the heads of families, rather than just to a relatively small number of *maliks*.[42] Whereas under the "Maliki system only a few individuals, perhaps small sections, [were] ... concerned in restrictive action", the Mahsuds as a whole would be held collectively responsible for any crimes committed by any of their members.[43] In this way he hoped gradually to rebuild the tribal *jirga* and regenerate a sense of tribal cohesion.[44]

Merk was therefore given permission to abandon Bruce's *maliki* system and reintroduce tribal responsibility. Firstly he wanted the Mahsuds to pay compensation for raids and various fines. The *maliks* refused to take any responsibility for this; "they abdicated".[45] As no progress was being made, Merk imposed a blockade on the tribe in December 1900, aimed at preventing anyone from entering or leaving their territory. An agreement was reached in May at a large *jirga* held at Jandola but soon broke down. Rivalry between the Mullah Powindah and the *maliks* made a settlement difficult. "The two, Mulla and Maliks, just balance each other. I do not think we find this phenomenon anywhere else on the frontier," commented Merk, "two political parties of about equal strength, and a tribe now leaning to one, now to the other".[46] To increase the pressure on the Mahsuds, a series of surprise attacks by small bodies of troops was launched in the autumn of 1901. A number of Mahsuds were killed or taken prisoner, towers and mills destroyed, animals slaughtered or taken away, and grain and fodder seized. "The pressure of the offensive blockade rapidly matured," Merk said, "what had been silently growing—the authoritative tribal *jirga*".[47] In January 1902 the leading men and others finally submitted. They actually appointed *chalweshti*s to collect a fine of Rs.25,000. Merk was optimistic, reporting that "We have now the *jirga* in full strength and successfully at work in its task of controlling the tribe".[48] In March they agreed to accept full tribal and sectional responsibility and the blockade was raised.[49]

Merk now drew up a plan for the distribution of Rs. 54,000 equally between the three sections—Alizais, Bahlolzais and Shaman Khels; an additional Rs. 7,000 was set aside for the influential men.[50] The new allowances were distributed on 5 April 1902 "among the heads of families according to houses", 1,565 men in all.[51] However, these arrangements were soon modified because Johnston, the Political Agent at Wana, drew attention to several difficulties. These included the fact that Merk's scheme had not included most of "Bruce's maliks" nor a large class of men he called *mu'tabar*s ("elders"). Johnston also thought that it was impractical and expensive to distribute the allowances in the way that Merk had envisaged.[52] Certainly these large *jirga*s, attended by thousands of men, must have been difficult to organise.

Johnston was therefore allowed to modify Merk's arrangements. Each tribal section was to elect *wakil*s (representatives), who would include Bruce's *malik*s (the "old maliks") and the *mu'tabar*s, and they would distribute the allowances of Rs.54,000 to the rest of the tribe. In return for this the *wakil*s would receive a share of the special payments set aside for influential men, and these were raised to Rs.16,000. However it appears that the number of men through whom allowances were paid was only reduced to 1,334, and it began to grow again.[53] This new system remained in operation for two or three years. Some officials, including the Chief Commissioner of the newly-created North-West Frontier Province, Sir Harold Deane, thought it worked as well as could be expected.[54]

In 1905, however, a new Political Agent, L.M. Crump, took over responsibility for relations with the Mahsuds, and a further change was made. Crump argued that Bruce had been right all along, and the "old maliks" were after all the tribe's "natural leaders".[55] Dealing with the Mahsuds through these large *jirga*s was, he said, inefficient and expensive, and he persuaded the government to allow him to adjust the allowances again. They continued to be distributed to the tribe as a whole, but the number of *wakil*s who received an extra payment was reduced to around 300 men. These men were to form what he called "a wieldy *jirga* for working purposes".[56] These changes, which were introduced against the advice of the Chief Commissioner, had an unsettling effect. As Deane commented, the 1,200 or so men affected would not only be upset to lose their "small but steady income", but would also be even more annoyed to lose "the prestige that being in receipt of an allowance gave them".[57] Indeed in November 1907 the Mullah Powindah sent a petition on behalf of "the poor people of the Mahsud tribe" to the Chief Commissioner in which he called on the government to send Crump away.[58] Hardly surprisingly, Crump's arrangements were no more successful than Johnston's. In fact a *malik* commented in 1909 that "their country was now a regular hell and in utter chaos and confusion ..."[59] Either the British should occupy Waziristan themselves, he continued, or they should withdraw from Wana, in which case they should allow the Amir of Afghanistan to occupy it. In 1908 Crump left and in 1910 the government reverted to Johnston's system, to "the principle of internal distribution by the republic itself".[60] There were no major revisions until after World War I.

Ultimately, none of these different approaches was very successful, and the British supplemented the system of allowances and political agents with a form of military occupation. This followed the insurrection which broke out in May 1919, towards the end of the brief Third Anglo-Afghan War. In December a large British force advanced into Waziristan to crush it, but it took nearly two years to force all the Mahsuds to surrender. New roads were constructed and a permanent garrison of as many as 15,000 troops was located at Razmak, in a commanding position on the border between Utmanzai Wazir and Mahsud territory. However, even this did not pacify Waziristan for very long. In particular it did not prevent Mirza Ali Khan, the Faqir of Ipi, emerging to lead a major rebellion in northern Waziristan, in which some Mahsuds played a part, in the late 1930s.[61]

CUSTOM AND CONFLICT IN WAZIRISTAN

There were other reasons for the problems experienced with the Mahsuds besides the British officials' failure fully to appreciate the complexities of their socio-political organisation (and to pursue a consistent policy). Firstly, a division between a minority of better-off *mashar*s (elders) and a larger group of poorer *kashar*s (young men) was already becoming apparent in the 1880s.[62] The injection of new resources widened the gap. During the 1900s, in addition to paying allowances, the British also for a time recruited Mahsuds for the South Waziristan militia and the Indian army. Men were also employed on public works, such as the railway line from Kalabagh to Bannu and the branch line to Tank, and on road-building. Often this employment was organised by Mahsud contractors. As a result some men became considerable wealthier than others, and this exacerbated existing tensions.

As Tapper reminds us in the next chapter, we should always expect to find "beside and within … cultural boundaries … a multiplicity of inconsistent voices and values". However, it does seem that many Mahsuds regretted the loss of much of their independence, and the fact that non-Muslims were responsible for it rubbed salt in the wound. These feelings were expressed and exploited by the Mullah Powindah. The rise of the Mullah was a significant new development in Mahsud politics. Before the 1890s factional groupings had existed in the tribe, but they had been "secular" ones, organised by different would-be leaders without any claim to religious authority. In fact, at one stage the British also paid the Mullah an allowance, and gave him some land in British territory. Though he accepted this, he continued to encourage the Mahsuds to resist the British and try to increase his influence vis-à-vis the *malik*s.[63] He encouraged his supporters to kill British soldiers and officials. Deane actually referred to "the system of Mahsud terrorism" and the climate of fear this created in the administered areas.[64]

Thirdly, Waziristan's frontier location obviously made it more difficult to control. In response to the British forward policy the Afghan government increased its efforts to promote its influence in Waziristan by paying its own allowances to *malik*s and religious leaders. The Mullah Powindah several times visited Kabul, obtaining money and ammunition from the Afghan government.[65] This naturally contributed to tribal disunity. Afghanistan also provided a base for Mahsud outlaws who towards the end of the nineteenth century began to carry out raids into British territory.[66]

If we want to understand the way the relationship between the Mahsuds and the British (and the Afghan government) developed in the early twentieth century these factors should not be ignored. Even so, the difficulties the British encountered in getting a grip on the Mahsuds were partly due to their particularly unstructured political organisation. Other frontier groups, the Afridis and some of the Mohmands for instance, had little in the way of institutionalised political authority, but this "democratic" tendency was most marked among the Mahsuds (the Afridi *malik*s, for example, were stronger than the Mahsud ones).[67] In Waziristan there was certainly nothing like the relatively enduring bloc organisation which developed in Swat, the hereditary chiefs of some of the other Mohmand groups, the khanate which emerged in Dir in the nineteenth century, or the state which was created in upper Swat between 1917 and 1926 by the Miangul Abdul Wudud.[68]

Bruce and Merk both recognised that contact with the British had had a significant impact on Mahsud political organisation.[69] Bruce, however, failed to appreciate how much most of the Mahsuds (and some of the Wazir groups as well) valued their independence, not just from the British (or the Amir of Kabul), but from each other. For his part Merk overestimated the Mahsuds' willingness, and in the changed circumstances of the early twentieth century their ability, to recreate the system of *jirgas* that appears to have existed for much of the nineteenth century. As noted above, during the twentieth century some men did become much better-off than others and this did give them a certain amount of influence in the tribe. However, as late as 1945 the Report of the Frontier Committee pointed out that among the Mahsuds, "'so kaleidoscopic is the structure, so loose the organisation that an infinite variety of alliances is possible, negotiations with them are difficult and treaties seldom binding".[70]

Some subsequent developments

In the years since Britain withdrew from Waziristan in 1947, there have been enormous social, economic and political changes. Many people from the region have moved into the administered areas of Pakistan; many men have worked in the Gulf States. Mahsuds, for instance, have established truck and bus networks and a significant presence in Karachi in particular. However, although in 1947 regular troops were withdrawn from Razmak, the administrative arrangements remained largely unchanged, and the post-World War I allowance system was extended.[71] In military terms, during the 1970s the government began to pursue a cautious forward policy, partly in response to developments in Afghanistan. Razmak for instance was reoccupied by Frontier Scouts, as were forts like Datta Khel and Ladha.[72] New Scouts' posts were established near the Durand Line. However, the Soviet occupation of Afghanistan and the civil war which followed the Soviet withdrawal created new difficulties; for instance some 80,000 Afghan refugees camped near Wana.[73] In fact the war in Afghanistan stimulated the local economy and brought money into the region, reducing people's dependence on government allowances, and contributing, it has been suggested, to the "(t)he state-condoned, increasing independence" of Waziristan (and the other Tribal Areas).[74] Continuing a trend which, as we have seen, began in the British period, the influence of religious leaders has grown, with mullahs and *madrasa*-educated men playing an increasingly significant role since the 1970s. Events since 9/11 have created further difficulties. Hundreds of thousands of people have become refugees thanks to successive interventions by the Punjabi-dominated Pakistani army.[75] The system of Political Agents and payment of allowances which developed since the late nineteenth century has been seriously weakened, and many pro-government *maliks* have been killed in recent years by the Tehrik-i-Taliban and members of al-Qaeda who fled to Waziristan in the autumn of 2001.[76]

However, particularly since 9/11, some parallels with the British period have become apparent. These include, in the first place, the use of some traditional tactics by the government of Pakistan in its attempts to deal with the Taliban insurgency in Waziristan. For example, before its invasion of South Waziristan in 2009 the army imposed a blockade and closed many businesses in the town of Tank on the edge of the district.[77] The invasion itself recalls the last major British incursion when, as we have seen, a British army occupied central Waziristan for nearly two years (1919–21). Secondly, there are some resemblances between the current Tehrik-i-Taliban insurgency and the Mullah Powindah's and other mullahs' resistance to the extension of British influence in Waziristan in the late nineteenth and early twentieth centuries. Thirdly, the rivalry between two competing elites in Waziristan today, the *malik*s and the mullahs, highlighted by Mariam Abou Zahab (Chapter 5), re-enacts that between the Mullah Powindah and the *malik*s referred to by Merk in 1901. The murder of *malik*s in recent years echoes the killing of "Bruce's maliks" by the Mullah's supporters in the 1890s. Moreover, recent suicidal attacks reportedly organised from Waziristan, particularly those aimed at Pakistani troops and army bases, recall the suicidal attacks by individual Mahsuds on British administrators and troops before 1914.

Conclusion

To sum up, we have seen that British officials usually saw the people of Waziristan and the Frontier as a whole as belonging to tribes. They usually maintained that, where strong leaders were not in evidence, the tribes or their subdivisions formed, or could be turned into, corporate groups on which collective responsibility could be imposed. They did not always agree, however, on to which level it was best to focus. In the Mahsud case, sometimes the tribe as a whole was made collectively responsible, sometimes each of the three main sub-groups, Alizais, Bahlolzais and Shaman Khels. The need for the British to establish their authority over the particularly "democratic" Mahsuds seemed to grow more urgent as fears of a Russian invasion of India from the north-west re-emerged towards the end of the nineteenth century. In the late 1880s Bruce persuaded the Punjab Government to allow him to introduce a different approach, one that did not rely in the same way on collective tribal responsibility. He argued that before 1849 the Mahsuds had accepted the authority of chiefs or *malik*s, and their unstructured and anarchic organisation was actually the result of contact with the British. It should be possible therefore to recreate *malik*s, and manage the tribe through them. However, his efforts to do so were unsuccessful. Twelve years later Merk suggested, somewhat more plausibly, that the Mahsuds had once formed a kind of democratic republic which had managed its affairs through *jirga*s. He tried to reconstitute this kind of organisation by paying allowances to a much larger number of men, and reimposing tribal responsibility. Particularly in the changed circumstances of the early twentieth century, this was almost equally unrealistic. Ultimately neither the *malik*-centred nor the tribal approach was very successful, and the GOI supplemented the allowance system with a kind of military occupation.

Although a great deal has changed in Waziristan since 1947, arguably developments in the late nineteenth and early twentieth centuries still have relevance. The difficulties the British encountered were due partly to the value most Mahsuds attached to individual autonomy and freedom from both external and internal authority, and the resulting absence of strong leaders. Other important influences included growing economic inequality, the region's frontier location, and religious loyalties. Recently the Tehrik-i-Taliban, one of whose founders was the late Baitullah Mahsud, has been the most prominent opponent of the government of Pakistan in Waziristan. However, as in the British period, resistance to the state is not driven simply by religious imperatives. As well as being a response to insecurity and economic hardship, it appears that for many it still expresses a wish, in the face of external pressures of various kinds, to maintain their distinct identity and determine their own future.

16

STUDYING PASHTUNS IN BARTH'S SHADOW

Richard Tapper

A personal journey

For the first decade or so of my anthropological career I worked in the shadow of Fredrik Barth. I did fieldwork among Pashtuns in Afghanistan some 15 years after his work in Pakistan, but I had also studied nomads in Iran only a few years after him. Barth's publications were, and remain, the most significant corpus of anthropological analyses relating to all three countries—let alone the others where he has worked.

My first fieldwork was among the Shahsevan, a major nomadic tribal group in northwestern Iran. When I began, about all that was available by way of ethnographic background reading was Barth's recently published monograph *Nomads of South Persia*, based on fieldwork in 1958 among the Basseri.[1] I took my copy of *Nomads* with me to the field in the summers of 1963 and 1964, when I was still an undergraduate at Cambridge, and on my more extended field trip in 1965–66 as a SOAS doctoral student. In 1970, when my then wife Nancy and I went to live among Durrani Pashtuns in northern Afghanistan, among the few available ethnographic studies of Pashtuns was Barth's *Political Leadership among Swat Pathans*.[2]

Not coincidentally, my theoretical interests also followed Barth. In Cambridge, I was exposed to the dominant doctrines of the time: the orthodoxy—later to be known as "structural-functionalism"—purveyed by Fortes and others, and largely focused on research in Africa; and the more exciting new structuralism of Lévi-Strauss, as introduced and mediated by Leach. In 1964 I moved to the SOAS to study for a PhD; in the London anthropology of the mid-1960s, further alternatives were on offer. At the SOAS, Adrian Mayer had pioneered the study of networks and "quasi-groups", Abner Cohen was developing the "Marxism" of Manchester in his focus on the politics of culture, while others approved Evans-Pritchard's historical turn. Like many SOAS anthropology research students, I also attended Raymond Firth's seminars at the LSE, and was exposed to his interests in social organisation, economics and individual choice.

I was keen to try out all these approaches when working among the Shahsevan, but particularly structuralism. It was easy to find binary oppositions and "totemic thought", as well as "segmentary lineages", but it was hard to see their relevance to the important things going on in Shahsevan life. When analysing my field materials, indeed, I found greater inspiration in Evans-Pritchard's insistence on the importance of history, but particularly in Barth's "generative models" approach, explicit in his new *Models of Social Organization* and his analysis of Robert Pehrson's material on the Marri Baluch,[3] but also implicit in his earlier studies of both the Swat Pathans and the Basseri.

Several of my earlier writings on the Shahsevan included Barth-style regional comparisons, seeking to explain differences between the Shahsevan, the Basseri, the Baluch and other nomadic groups. In the course of these exercises I found a number of minor lacunae in Barth's account of the Basseri nomads, which were perhaps not surprising given the short period of fieldwork he was able to do. But in the long run I found much more significant the ways in which his text was read and misread. Thus, two anthropologists of Iran, neither of whom had worked among nomads, portrayed and attacked *Nomads of South Persia* as a study of segmentary lineage organisation.[4] Barth himself has mildly but effectively rebutted this misrepresentation.[5] I have also criticised several historians for using the Basseri tribe (in Barth's account) as a prototype of tribal politics and pastoral economies of southwest Asian mountain nomads, not just in the twentieth century but in mediaeval times: ill-fated and methodologically unsound extrapolations that ignored Barth's own analyses of differences between the Basseri and several of their neighbouring tribal groups.[6]

Few commentators, however, have acknowledged what is for me the major analytical contribution of *Nomads*: the separation of the pastoral nomadic from the tribal levels of organisation, the former closely following adaptive ecological strategies, the latter explicable by involvement with the state, settled society and neighbouring tribes. Differences between tribes (over time as well as space) could be explained with reference to either different ecological conditions or relations with neighbours and the state. The usefulness and validity of this analysis have been demonstrated again and again by later anthropological work in Iran and Afghanistan, notably among nomadic groups that had no chiefs or discernible centralised tribal organisation, and not least among Pashtun nomads—as Barth himself had pointed out.[7]

For many reasons, Nancy and I did not expect the social organisation of the Durrani nomads and villagers in northern Afghanistan in 1971–72 to replicate that of Yusufzai landowners in Swat earlier in the century. Barth, having also encountered Pashtuns in Baluchistan and elsewhere, was well aware of the wide range of cultural and social forms among Pashtuns, and had examined this as an analytical problem in his recent edited volume *Ethnic Groups and Boundaries*.[8] This hugely important collection became one of my guiding texts in the field, figuring prominently in our grant proposals, not least because a preliminary visit to northern Afghanistan in summer 1968 had revealed ethnic identity and difference to be a central issue. My own fieldwork brief was to apply Barth's insights on ethnic boundary maintenance to the multi-ethnic environment of the Durrani Pashtuns we studied. At the same time, other central analytical elements in *Political Leadership*—notably the relations between chiefly and saintly leaders, and the roles of choice and transaction in political allegiances—proved eminently applicable in the northern Afghan context too.

Barth's writings on Pakistan, including his "ghost-writing" of Pehrson's 1966 Baluch monograph, have become classics in social anthropological theory, but, like his book on the Basseri, and like all foundational texts, have proved open to very different, motivated readings. In a wide-ranging and sustained reconsideration of his Swat analysis, in which he sought to account for some misinterpretations of *Political Leadership*, Barth wrote of his "disaffection [in the 1950s] with the structural-functional paradigm, and the structuralist alternative that was beginning to take shape".[9] He disliked the notion of a society as a thing or a system, or of treating idea(l)s as determinants of behaviour, as essentials of culture and society. He sought to study practices, accumulated choices, as themselves determinants of structure and of change; and to construct generative models consisting of the factors involved in choices, such that, in a location where variability was the norm, one could identify the constants that underlay the variation. Barth clearly and effectively disposed of his chief critics, some of whom appear to have sought to boost their own reputations by what had become the fashionable practice of ancestor-killing. As with later misreadings and criticisms of *Nomads*, Barth had to point out that these critics were guilty of numerous "factual errors and unsustainable conjectures".[10] At the same time, he admitted that he might not have made his intentions clear; and I am not alone in having found some of his arguments, however carefully constructed, to be somewhat dense and compressed. A case in point is the "Introduction" to *Ethnic Groups and Boundaries*. Barth's approach to ethnic identities and cultural difference, despite using rather different terminology, coincided closely with that of Abner Cohen in his analysis of *Custom and Politics in Urban Africa*, published the same year.[11] Both constituted what came to be called an "instrumentalist" approach to ethnicity. Cohen himself did not recognise this, but read Barth's conception of ethnicity as "primordialist".[12]

Pashtuns and others: perspectives from northern Afghanistan

Barth's writings on Pashtuns and on ethnicity were thus of central importance to my research on Afghanistan. I have not myself visited the Swat valley, nor is my field experience in the region recent. However, I have had several decades—tragic ones for Afghanistan—in which to reflect on my field materials, little of which has yet seen publication. I shall devote the rest of this chapter to suggesting ways in which my materials, and insights drawn from Barth's work, might throw light on the political actions and fortunes of Pashtuns in recent years, not least their connection to the Taliban movement.

I take my cue from two sentences in the original call for papers for this volume. First, "Ethnicity has emerged as a key cleavage point in Afghan society over the past thirty years." This is, I think, misleading. Ethnicity, in the sense of the perception and construction of cultural identities and differences, has always been central to Afghan society. What has changed is the focus of attention of observers, particularly anthropologists, and the political rhetoric of actors, particularly governments of Afghanistan. Anthropologists of Afghanistan did not begin to focus on ethnicity—in its "post-primordial" sense—until Barth's *Ethnic Groups and Boundaries* sparked a burst of interest by fieldworkers in the 1970s, including myself. Afghans themselves have long argued about whether or not ethnic differences are relevant to understanding the present or future of their country. In the 1970s, when ethnic identities were still marked in ID cards, government "nation-building" priorities led to official denial of such distinctions. Proponents of this denial were predictably almost all Pashtuns, the historically dominant group: they claimed to regard all others as their brothers and sisters, to respect the Persian language, and so forth. This sentiment was accepted by educated non-Pashtuns who felt that admission of ethnic distinctions would only perpetuate them and what they saw as the consequent cultural and political backwardness of the country. At the same time, there were then, as now, vociferous proponents and opponents of Pashtun chauvinism.

The second sentence that I shall address is the question: "How can the coexistence of seemingly contradictory ideologies be explained?"—referring to the history in Swat of "both violent religious militancy as well as of left-wing labour activism". In my view, anthropologists familiar with the work of Barth and others of our noted precursors should be surprised if they came across a people or a place where there was only *one* unchallenged ideology.

In an unpublished 1998 paper on the rise of the Taliban, I argued for analyses in terms of two well-established anthropological premises: first, that cultural boundaries and definitions are constructed by politicians (both actors and observers), academics and the media, and by the interplay of perceptions; and secondly, that besides and within such cultural boundaries we should expect a multiplicity of inconsistent voices and values, varying according to gender, class, age, ideological persuasion and so on, and that these should be evident in relationships of dominance and subordination, in oscillations between competing alternative parties, or simply in incoherent coexistence, all of which lead to, allow, or even are essential for adaptability and change.

Dichotomous or multiple competing values, ideologies, ideal types, or modes of organisation have been the stuff of social theory at least since Marx, Weber and Durkheim, while analyses of their operation within single social formations have a genealogy in anthropology going back to Leach, and coming to us via Ernest Gellner's reading of Ibn Khaldun's *Muqaddima*, developed in various analyses of "tribe-state" relations in the 1980s by myself among others.[13] In my own analysis, I suggested that "tribe" and "state" in Iran and Afghanistan should be viewed as actors' idea(l)s, corresponding broadly with two of Weber's ideal types of domination, the traditional and the bureaucratic/legal, with a historical dynamic provided by charismatic-religious leaders and movements. Put most simply, this approach argues that all social formations are "two(or multi)-party" systems, where dominant ideologies alternate between opposed extremes, as a result of either a clash between inevitable internal contradictions, changing external pressures or opportunities, or some catalytic, dynamic third factor.

Both features (the constructedness of boundaries, inconsistent ideologies) are counter-intuitive, in that politicians and other agents commonly present their own ideologies as definite, determined and internally coherent, and often paint their opponents in similarly stark lines. Some recent observers of both Pashtuns and Taliban have accepted such self-presentations at face value, but there have been a series of studies, following Barth's analysis of the interplay between khan and saint in *Political Leadership*, showing the contrasting and competing ideologies that are part of Pashtun culture.[14]

When Nancy and I studied northern Durrani—mainly nomads and villagers from the Ishaqzai tribe—we found a complex and changing society in which the strongest cultural values, most often invoked in situations of conflict and crisis, were those associated with Islam and Pashtun ethnicity and tribalism, all of which trumped the rather weak nationalist ideology of the Afghan state; we were also struck by a general tolerance and curiosity about other people's values and practices. As regards Islam, the Durrani seemed to us, by and large, motivated by other values than rigid fanaticism. A year or so after leaving Afghanistan, I wrote:

Durrani are remarkably conscientious in observing the formal duties of Islam: prayer, fasting, alms, pilgrimage. Every Durrani settlement has at least one mosque, built by common effort and expense, with a resident mullah who leads prayers and other rituals there, performs general Islamic offices, and conducts classes for boys of wealthier families. Collective prayer sessions, including the Friday prayers, are not obligatory nor generally attended, but senior men usually gather in the mosque to perform the last two daily prayers. Even nomad camps commonly have a small place nearby marked out with stones for the men to pray in, and many have a resident mullah from a leading family ... Durrani Islam is a religion of moderation, piety and sobriety. At formal religious gatherings, at funerals or prayers in the mosque, extreme emotion or ecstasy are never displayed. Durrani Islam is also a religion of the powerful and successful, which culminates for them in the performance of the ultimate duty, pilgrimage to Mecca, which frequently marks the retirement of an active leader from competition. Such men of power and wealth take no part in, and adopt an ambivalent attitude towards, the involvement of less successful men and many women in a complex of activities and beliefs relating to Sufism, shrines and spirit possession ... Sufi leaders (*aghas*), both local and visiting, lead Sufi zikrs and exorcism rituals, and also mediate and make peace in local inter- and intra-tribal conflicts.[15]

Ethnic and tribal identity (*qawmi*) provided the basic framework and language of social and political interaction, while elements of class formation cut across both tribal and ethnic boundaries and were reinforced by the state and its local representatives. "Class" as a concept was not explicitly recognised except by newly educated urban youth; there was no term equivalent to "class" in common speech, but other terms for collectivities and statuses had strong class connotations. People contrasted the *qawmi* mode of association and of conducting political business with the *rasmi* (official, governmental) mode.

The dominant tension was between a strongly-articulated local tribal egalitarianism and state-fostered inequalities, both among different ethno-linguistic groups and between rich and powerful and poor and weak. Powerful and wealthy Durrani khans were feared for their oppression (*zulm*) of the poor of all local ethnic groups. Mullahs as a class were identified most often with their wealthy patrons and with the oppression of the khans and the corruption of government representatives, not least the law courts, which people avoided. By contrast, the Sufi leaders, who provided much-wanted physical and spiritual healing during their regular visits, were closer to the religious values of the ordinary people and epitomised the notion of the *wolus*, the tribal community. Durrani often used the term *wolus* when talking of the power of united community effort against the oppression of both khans and the government, especially in the maxim, *da wolus zur da khuday zur*, literally "people's power is God's power".[16]

This was undoubtedly a patriarchal society; whatever Islam and state law granted women in theory, they had few rights, were treated as legal minors, and sometimes suffered cruelly. Durrani men, despite great inequalities of wealth and power, considered each other equals by virtue of their common descent (ultimately from a companion of the Prophet), their Sunni faith and law, their Pashto language, and their refusal to allow their women to marry non-Durrani.[17] They regarded their values as Durrani and as Muslims as a consistent whole. They regularly articulated these criteria and ideals when evaluating or negotiating the meanings of behaviour in situations of crisis. At the same time, they volunteered disappointment that their practices so often fell short of their values. When pressed, they would also concede that there were at least some "fuzzy" areas in their values, where tribal priorities might not square with known Islamic precepts; they would sometimes present their practices as a compromise between tribal values and Islamic values. In a crisis the former might prevail over the latter.

The traditionally conservative, but moderate and humanistic Durrani religion that we encountered was combined with prejudices against local non-Pashtuns: they charged their fellow-Sunni but Persian-speaking Tajiks and Turki-speaking Uzbeks with religious extremism, for example in their over-meticulous observance of women's seclusion. They recalled how they had been joined by the local Shi'ite, Persian-speaking Hazaras in opposing Uzbeks and Tajiks who supported the short-lived Saqawi revolt in 1929;[18] but they found the sectarian aberrance of the Hazaras both horrifying and fascinating. They also directed prejudice and hostility towards non-Durrani Pashtuns, particularly those they called "Parsiwan" (literally: Persian-speakers): Pashto-speakers who looked and talked like Durrani, but couldn't produce authentic genealogies. They accused them of being secret Persian-speakers, of marrying Shi'ites, even of being crypto-Shi'ites or recent converts to Sunnism. The only "foreigners" they knew were Soviet citizens (usually associated with oil and mineral exploration) whom they occasionally encountered in both town and countryside; they were shocked by their atheism and alcohol consumption, and suspected them of unspeakable sexual practices.

Our recordings of conversations with rural Durrani in northern Afghanistan include some striking texts on ethnic difference. In an article published in 1997 I reproduced one such text from 1971, in which a young man, reacting to a recent scandal in which a Durrani woman eloped with a Hazara man, reveals attitudes that by current Western "politically correct" standards are both "racist" and "sexist"; he is otherwise very tolerant of cultural difference. Interestingly, the young man does not articulate Islam as a prime consideration in his account of Durrani identity: he introduces religious sanctions only at the end of the text, when discussing sexual relationships among Durrani themselves. But even here, when he talks about violence and adultery among Durrani—admitting that, though regrettable, they are not uncommon—his priority is forgiveness and compensation. For Durrani, he says, the actor's true intention, his "heart", matters far more than what he may say. Forgiveness of someone who has offended you, and the repentance of an adulterer, only count if sincerely intended.[19]

The young man's father, Hajji Ibrahim, our host and sponsor, recorded the following apocalyptic remarks in 1972:

I don't know, perhaps it's the end of time. Our books say, we shan't reach the year 1400 ... The mullahs can't agree on whether it's the solar or lunar calendar[20] ... Such rotten mullahs, they're no use, they just don't know, and there are no true saints or sheikhs any more ... The sheikh of today, curse him, is no sheikh. If he can find lies, he'll never tell the truth; if he can find sin, he'll never do what's right; if he can find *haram*, he won't eat *halal*. That's where we've got to. Now, when you and I talk with each other, it tastes very good on the tongue, but God knows what's in our hearts. That's how it is, I swear! With you people, your words are at one with your conscience. As for the people of Afghanistan, as I said, these sheikhs say one thing but have another in their hearts. Only God knows what's in their hearts. That's how it is; it's the end of time!

Our books say that ... at the end of time truth will be lies, people will abandon right and do wrong, brothers and fathers and sons will fight each other. That is the way things *will* be, they say—but look around now! Not ten in a hundred pray. I don't call it prayer, if you pray just once a week, or if you're obliged to do your ablutions because you see someone else doing it, that's not prayer. That's just fear of what people will say. Such a person doesn't say, God created us, sent us a Prophet who commanded us "Pray five times a day, repent your sins, tell the truth, don't tell lies, don't steal other people's property, give alms and tithes, stay on the Right Path ..." There's none of this left. It's all gone to ruin.

The survivors and descendants of Hajji Ibrahim's large family and his fellow-villagers are now, to the best of my knowledge, back in the south where their ancestors originated, in Helmand province, or in refugee camps near either Qandahar or Quetta. Some of them, quite likely, joined the Taliban, whose rank and file supporters were largely drawn from Durrani tribespeople.

Taliban, media and boundary marking

After the communist revolution in 1978, the new rulers declared that ethnic differences, along with tribalism and feudalism, were over and done with, that the dominant cleavage in society was now class, and that politics was class conflict. Religion was associated with feudal backwardness and ignored until the successes of the Mujahidin forced a revision of policy. In the 1980s, the Pakistan-based Mujahidin groups that resisted the PDPA and the Soviet army all more or less identified with Islam. Analysts argued about whether there was still a tribal or ethnic dimension to either Kabul politics or the rivalries among the Mujahidin, both during the Soviet occupation and after their withdrawal in 1989. In the 1970s and 1980s class difference and conflict did have an increasing importance, but ethnic identities continued to play a major part in the constitution of the Mujahidin factions that tore the country apart—still in the name of Islam—in the early 1990s.

When the Taliban emerged in the mid-1990s, one of their platforms too was the abolition of ethnic difference in favour of religious unity; but again, their own actions, and popular perceptions, meant that Pashtun ethnicity remained central both to local understandings of persons and politics, and to outsiders' attempts to explain them.

The emergence and composition of the Taliban, and the balance sheet of their measures up to their defeat in 2001–02, have now been the subject of numerous studies. Here let me just note that their ranks contained many different strands: certainly not just rural Durrani like Hajji Ibrahim's family, but other Pashtuns and non-Pashtuns also. But it is fair to see one aspect of their rise as "*la revanche des Pachtounes*",[21] the revenge of the Pashtuns, especially the Durrani, who had been out of power since 1978 after 250 years of dominance in Afghanistan. Roy also speaks of "*la logique profondément ethnique du mouvement taliban, laquelle a toujours été niée par les talibans eux-mêmes*".[22] Official Taliban statements indicated their programme to be—like that of the PDPA—anti-feudal (anti-khan) and "anti-tribal": for example, replacing the "payment" for women with the payment of money to resolve disputes among men,[23] and insisting on daughters receiving half-shares of a father's inheritance.[24] There was also a class dimension: Taliban leadership and ranks were overwhelmingly of rural tribal and peasant origins; they presented themselves as a grass-roots movement, offering to bring peace and justice and to alleviate the suffering of the rural poor. They were despised as country bumpkins by their Mujahidin opponents, many of whom had educated, urban, professional backgrounds, while others were a middle class of new land-owners and warlords, who remained dominant in Kabul and the north, and implacably opposed to Taliban.

In their early years the Taliban leadership proved sensitive to their portrayal in foreign media. Pashtuns or Pathans, let us recall, have had a fairly prominent—but shifting—image in Western, especially British media, for nearly two centuries, as numerous scholars have analysed at length. In the nineteenth century and the first half of the twentieth, independent-minded Pathan tribal warriors on the frontiers of the British Empire were much-discussed actors in the Great Game of Central Asia. In recent decades this image, or its Kipling version, has been a gift to journalists looking for copy, who ignore the very different strand in Pathan culture represented by the non-violent Khudai Khidmatgaran analysed recently by Mukulika Banerjee. Then, in the 1980s, the Mujahidin played the role of gallant freedom-fighters on the Western front-line against Soviet imperialism and communism. Much of the fighting was done out of sight inside Afghanistan by non-Pashtuns (Tajiks, Uzbeks, Hazaras), but the most vocal and active Mujahidin based in Pakistan (where the media circus was located) were Pashtun groups and leaders, hence the perpetuation of a slightly transformed image of the Frontier Pathan.

After the Soviet forces departed in 1989, Western political and military support—and media interest—melted away. For several years feuding warlords plagued the Afghan countryside, while party rivalries and corruption among the Mujahidin destroyed much of Kabul; rival leaders and their forces were from all the main ethnic groups. The second half of the 1990s brought a further transformation of the image of frontier Pathans, in the shape of the Taliban, who emerged as a band of religious students; they were supported and imitated by extreme Islamist elements in Pakistan and elsewhere who approved their firm "sharia" solution to corruption and modernisation (Westernisation), which they perceived as threats to Islamic and traditional values. Western governments came to identify them as the front-line threat to their new interests in Central Asia, and they conveniently (but in the uncomfortable company of Iran) fell into the role abandoned by the Soviets, as the chief menace to Western civilisation. For some people, it seemed that the "clash of civilisations" was shaping up nicely.

The Taliban rose, as they never failed to point out, to cleanse the country of the disorder and corruption it had suffered after the fall of Kabul and Najibullah to the Mujahidin, and to purify Islam. Horrified by the practices of the PDPA communists (and their masters, the "godless" Soviets), the Taliban saw the Mujahidin and their successors in the United Front/Northern Alliance as worse, as responsible for unimaginable atrocities, and as having betrayed the Islam they professed.

The Taliban leadership was split from the beginning, as it has been increasingly since, between more moderate, pragmatic traditionalists, led by Mullah Omar, and their extremist guests and sponsors, particularly Osama bin Laden and the Arabs, Pakistanis and others associated with the al-Qaeda network.[25] The official Taliban rhetoric and programme[26] revealed an ideology of religious fervour, justifying every action in relation to textual sources, including prophetic traditions. But there was also considerable evidence, over the years, of a willingness to be flexible and pragmatic, to respond to world opinion, and to attempt to justify their actions, not least in order to win recognition as the legitimate government of Afghanistan. They hoped to be respected for their restoration of peace, justice and order to the country, and they did receive popular acceptance in many parts of the countryside for quite a time in the 1990s.

Pragmatism and willingness to change policy were evident in the ways in which the original Taliban constructed their identity by marking their boundaries.

Gender marking: treatment of women

It is an anthropological commonplace that such boundary marking tends to focus on regulations regarding sex/gender and food/drink. A case in point was the Iranian revolution, in which redefinitions of gender roles in law and in society, and in particular dress codes for men and women, went hand in hand in the early years with the ban on alcohol. The Taliban notoriously focused on gender definitions, on dress-body codes for men and women, and in particular on restricting women's appearance in public.

Traditional (pre-1978) custom in Afghanistan provided a context in which gender, ethnicity, educational level, class and other individual and social identities could be "worn" and "read" on the body: country people would claim to be able to identify, for example, an Uzbek women, or a Hazara man, by appearance (dress, hair, physiognomy), unless they were urban, middle class and educated, in which case a man would likely wear a suit and a karakul hat and a woman would go unveiled or wore only a headscarf. It is notable that the full *chadri/burqa* was, by the 1970s, a declining, lower-middle-class urban custom, while young, rural Pashtun men traditionally "veiled" their (beardless) lower faces.

The Taliban, referring to such traditional local practices, replaced all "ethnic markers" of dress, facial hair, etc. and imposed standardised body marking and dress for men and women: all Muslim men must let their beards grow (the Prophet's practice) and wear turbans and trousers above the ankle; Muslim women were not

229

allowed out of the house unless totally covered in the *chadri* and accompanied by a male relative.

The Taliban thus officially denied any differentiations except by gender and religion: this of course made it both difficult to distinguish anything other than men and women and "good" or "bad" Muslims, and much easier for a man to "pass" ethnically, while the *chadri* covered not only all aspects of a woman's identity but even a possible male in disguise.

Western media (newspaper reports, cartoons, TV footage) represented the Taliban as bearded fanatics, engaged in the complete oppression of women and the banning of fun. Here, the media tended to be selective in their evidence. Context gives a rather more complex picture of Taliban measures.

The media highlighted the Taliban ban on women's education and employment, and their compulsory veiling, as abuses of their human rights. Once the West (meaning the US State Department) had decided (in 1997–98) to abandon support of the Taliban, the treatment of women became their excuse for doing so. This began the Taliban campaign to justify themselves and create an Islamic image. Their websites (in 1999) were dominated by (sometimes plausible) justifications of their treatment of women. Despite twentieth-century campaigns to increase education for girls, it had always been very limited in Afghanistan, largely confined to Kabul and other cities. It was most successful under the communists in the 1980s. In 1993, the overall participation rate in education for girls was estimated as 3.7 per cent, and a 1995 UNICEF report, finalised well before the Taliban takeover of most of the country, found girls "largely excluded from education". However, reports from NGO experts in 1998, under the Taliban, indicated, for example, that "there are parts of the Afghan countryside where there have never been more girls being educated."[27]

As regards the dress code for women, Western media focused on the *chadri*, which became known as *burqa*, a complete body covering. Strangely, cartoons and other representations showed this covering as black: yet TV footage (and Makhmalbaf's 2001 film *Safar-e Qandahar*) showed *chadris* to be almost invariably brightly coloured. For that matter, Taliban men's clothing—and beards—were often highly coloured too. Doubtless Western media were influenced by the colour coding in the official dress codes of Saudi Arabia and particularly the Islamic Republic of Iran, where men's clothes and beards remained black or white, while women's covering (whether *chador*, *maghnaeh*, *ru-sari* or other scarves) should be black, particularly in official contexts (white for weddings). In Iran since the Revolution, women have worn coloured scarves widely as a sign of resistance. In Afghanistan, coloured and patterned clothing has always been normal, even under the Taliban.

Further, despite the media focus, it seems that the dress code was not an issue for most Afghans: "the tactic of capitalizing on American horror of the Muslim veil, while it may work well in drawing attention to the heartbreaking plight of women in Afghanistan, has now been undeniably uprooted from reality."[28] Not surprisingly, following the retreat of the Taliban, most urban women, even in Kabul, continued to wear the *chadri*. Village and nomad women never did.

STUDYING PASHTUNS IN BARTH'S SHADOW

Oppression and massacres of Shi'i Hazaras

Taliban gender policy attracted far greater attention than their actions against non-Pashtun minorities. The most atrocious of these were their massacres of Hazaras in late 1998 and 1999, in Mazar-e Sharif, Bamyan and Yekawlang. Evidence that came to light (in UNHCR and other reports) indicates that these actions were not a simple matter of extreme sectarian bigotry; there were elements of *badal* or revenge, in true Pashtun tribal tradition. Pashtuns and other Sunnis had a long history of oppressing the Shi'i minority, notably the Hazaras of the central provinces. In the battle for Kabul in 1995, the Hazaras in the city had allied with the Taliban and other Pashtuns in an effort to resist the northern forces led by Ahmad Shah Massoud (who had been responsible for a pogrom of Kabul's Shi'is two years before), but they blamed the Taliban for the subsequent death of their leader Abdul Ali Mazari, and were implacably opposed to them thereafter.[29] There followed a cycle of revenge killings, of which these massacres were the latest and most extreme instances.

In addition Taliban atrocities were undoubtedly prompted by their Arab guests, with their extreme Salafi antagonism to the Shi'a, and to Iran in particular. A number of Iranian "diplomats/agents" were assassinated in Mazar and the killers were never brought to justice, an incident that nearly led to war in 1998.

World media coverage of all these events was very thin. Western media ignored the available reports, because—one is forced to assume—the victims were "only" Shi'ites, and only Iran cared.[30]

Destruction of the Bamyan Buddhas

By contrast, there was extensive international media coverage—as the Taliban indeed intended—of their destruction of the Bamyan Buddhas in early 2001. By then they were disillusioned. In their more idealistic and responsive early stages, as they imposed "sharia" punishments and restrictions on women in pursuit of their higher aim of restoring Islam and order, they spent much effort to justify these to the world's media, in press conferences and on their website. They were careful to order the protection of pre-Islamic heritage sites like the Buddhas of Bamyan. Moreover, they offered to hand over Osama bin Laden to the Americans if they could produce evidence of his involvement in terrorist attacks.

But the more flexibility they showed, it must have seemed, the more the world's media were blind to the virtue and morality of what they were doing. The world (notably the USA and the UN) refused their requests for the lifting of sanctions and for international recognition. So the Taliban leadership, increasingly influenced by their Arab guests, changed policies and learned to use the media. There is evidence that the destruction of the Buddhas was at least in part an expression of their frustration. The explicit reason was the Islamic ban on images and idolatry, as promoted by their Wahhabi guests, even though this had been refuted or rejected as irrelevant to this case by numerous Islamic scholars from around the world, including several Afghan jurists. Their original teachers, the Deobandi Muslims, had long put up with the Hindu and Buddhist statuary of South Asia. It seems the Taliban may also have been covering up a previous despoiling of the

231

statues; also significant was the fact that the Buddhas were in the land of the Hazaras, who remained the Taliban's main internal enemy. But the destruction also succeeded not only in antagonising the world's Buddhists but in further alienating the rest of world—and other Afghans—for whom the statues were a world-class heritage monument.[31]

Yellow cloth for Hindus—but not Sikhs

The next measure came in mid-May 2001, when the Taliban announced plans for the Hindu population of Afghanistan. In 1995 there were perhaps 50,000 Hindus and Sikhs together in Afghanistan; then, following looting by Mujahidin, many Hindus moved to India and Pakistan. Some returned under the Taliban. Despite a history of conflicts between Sikhs (often fighting for the British army in India) and Pashtuns in both the North West Frontier and Afghanistan, Taliban maintained good relations with the Sikhs in Afghanistan, where they were commonly traders in cloth (including the women's *chadris* ... as the Sikhs joked themselves) and cosmetics. They lived especially in the city of Jalalabad, where they numbered several hundred; many appear to have returned after the difficult 1980s period of Soviet control. Already distinguished by their turbans, Sikhs were regarded as *ahl-e kitab* (people of the book), and *dhimmi* (a protected minority), and shared the Taliban antipathy to Hindu idol-worship.

As for the Hindu minority, the Taliban proposed to compel women to wear a yellow cloth piece, and men a yellow armband. Hindus were to dwell separately from Muslims, and a two-metre yellow flag was to be hung outside each Hindu household. No temples were to be built or reconstructed.

There was immediate world media outrage, starting with reactions from India, where the press once more castigated Taliban (Pakistani, by implication) backwardness and discriminatory policies. As an Afghan opposition radio programme stated: "For several generations, Hindus, Sikhs and even Jewish families have lived in harmony with Muslim Afghans. Their rights were respected and they feel as much an Afghan as a Hazara, Pashtun, Tajik or Uzbek born and raised in that country. To make them wear an identity patch or ribbon is an insult to humanity and decency."[32]

Foreign media saw the proposal as marking the Hindus out for persecution and worse. Western commentators immediately recalled histories of iconoclasm and of ethnic/religious marking in Europe, and referred particularly to the Nazi imposition of yellow stars for Jews. But Taliban spokesmen presented the measure as a convenience, even a right; a marker, not to single Hindus out for persecution, but to prevent their prosecution under laws that apply only to Muslims: compulsory beards, compulsory prayer. Non-Muslims, they said, had full legal protection under the Taliban government. "For example, a Muslim thief, whether he stole from Muslims or from Hindus, would receive the same punishment—the amputation of his hand."[33] They said that the idea came from the Religious Police (*Amr-e be Maaruf va Nahi az Munkar*); later, that it came from Hindus themselves. Dress codes had been talked of in the past, but were only now to be confirmed, though the regime gave no details or date for their implementation.

The underlying motive, on this occasion, appears to have been to antagonise India, which was supporting the United Front opposition against the Taliban, who were backed by Pakistan. India, along with Russia, USA and Tajikistan had signed up to the sanctions on the Taliban. India's Prime Minister Vajpayee had visited his ally Iran the month before, when they jointly denounced the Taliban destruction of the Buddhas. Meanwhile, Pakistan's response was guarded and indirect: it said the deed was "against the spirit of Islam" and the Human Rights Declaration—the furthest it had gone in criticising the Taliban.[34]

By mid-June, modification of the new measure seemed likely, in the direction of special ID cards. Something was needed, the Taliban said, since "some of the Afghan Muslims pretended to be Hindus in order to escape on-the-spot punishments for not observing the Islamic code of conduct."[35] At the end of June, apparently under US-induced Pakistani pressure, the Taliban abandoned the measure; the end result was a propaganda victory for the United Front and India, and a defeat for the Taliban and Pakistan.

Arrest of Christian NGO workers

Finally, Christians: in early August 2001 twenty-four persons of different nationalities (including sixteen Afghans) working for Shelter Now International, a German-based Christian NGO, were arrested in Kabul and detained on charges of preaching Christianity in the guise of relief work. The Taliban authorities claimed to have evidence (Persian-language Bibles, thousands of tapes and computer disks) that they were attempting to convert local Muslims, including boys at a school they were running. If convicted, the foreigners would be expelled, but the Afghans in the group were subject to the death penalty.

In the days that followed, there was extensive international media coverage, and representatives of the UN and the governments concerned sought to engage the Taliban, who went to great lengths to explain the legal process involved. It also emerged that the Taliban were investigating other international aid groups they suspected of propagating Christianity, including the UN World Food Programme.

The Afghan workers, having affirmed that they had not abandoned Islam, were released, while the trial of the eight foreign workers began on 8 September. Following the 11 September attacks on the USA, their trial was suspended, and after the fall of Kabul the Taliban removed the foreigners to the south, until US special forces rescued them and flew them to Pakistan.

To judge from the sources I have seen, these various Taliban boundary-marking measures in the first half of 2001, like other religious policies of the leadership, owed more to pressure from their Arab guests than was at first apparent. But the Taliban themselves were determined to be seen to be different, as following the "true Islam", and to mark publicly what they saw as significant differences between their Islamic *ummah* and their religious and political others/enemies. Western commentators, in turn, were determined to recognise this difference: to demonise the Taliban—and Islam. Other Islamic authorities meanwhile protested against the "distortions" of Islam evident in policies such as these.

Anthropologists and others have compared the Taliban movement variously with religious revivalist and millennial movements, prophet cults, and peasant revolts. All generalisations about the Taliban and their ideals and policies since 2001 have run up against the very obvious heterogeneity of the movement since it became an "insurgency"; yet heterogeneity has been there since their emergence in the 1990s.

Tribalism, ethnicity and religion among the Taliban

In my early understanding of the northern Durrani, as outlined above, there was an interplay between religion, tribalism and ethnicity, in a context where the state played a growing but still remote role in maintaining order, but at a cost (conscription, taxation, bribery) to the people. Each dominant value was full of ambivalence and potential inconsistency: religion was both the strict rules and punishments prescribed by mullahs and administered in courts, and the spirituality and peace-making of the Sufi Aghas; tribal identity was a source of both *wolusi* solidarity and punitive violence; ethnic identity both included and excluded. Boundaries in each case were clearly marked in theory, yet open to negotiation and accommodation in practice.[36] My initial analysis of Taliban ideology and practice in the light of these dominant values found elements of continuity, as well as radical differences.

Some commentators on the rise of the Afghan Taliban, and their revival following the US-led invasion of 2001, have sought monocausal explanations in religious fanaticism, Pashtun ethnicity or Pashtun tribalism. One argument is that, in a tribally and ethnically divided country where the state had failed and Mujahidin factions, warlords and khans had brought chaos, the Taliban restored order by reintroducing traditional Pashtun tribal norms and values. Another version of this argument maintains that the Taliban were an extreme manifestation of an Islamic "alternative" (Barth's Saint model), but this was only one element in their Pashtun cultural background, whose emergence was facilitated by nearly two decades of war, plus foreign resources and support. Sooner or later, because of internal contradictions, or external pressures, or some other catalyst, the pendulum would swing back the other way, to some more moderate, liberal regime, representing alternative Pashtun values.

To my mind, there is some plausibility in both versions of the argument. The original Taliban warriors, drawn from refugee camps and *madrasa*s in Pakistan and from among the tribes around Qandahar, were a movement of Pashtuns, and not unnaturally brought with them elements of Pashtun culture, however distorted or unbalanced: notably an honour code extreme in its treatment of women. But again, despite some ethnic hostilities and misunderstandings, they welcomed "good" Sunni Muslim non-Pashtuns from the beginning, and were even prepared—as Pashtuns always have been—to make alliances with Shi'ites to further their political or military ends. Many explicit Taliban values would have been familiar to rural Pashtuns, though they have rarely in history been so strictly put into practice as they were under Taliban rule between 1996 and 2001.

In my 1998 paper I explored the apparent contradiction between the moderate, humanistic Islam that I associated with the Durrani of 1971–72 and the puritan revivalism that the media portrayed as the beliefs, policies and behaviour of the Taliban of a generation or more later. I could recognise elements of Taliban Islam in the Durrani I had known—they are there in Hajji Ibrahim's musings quoted above, and he might well have welcomed the emergence of the Taliban leader Mullah Omar as a "true saint" or "shaikh". Many commentators (such as Johnson and Mason 2006) have recognised Mullah Omar as the latest manifestation of what the British used to call "Mad Mullahs", Sufi leaders who led revivalist revolts on the Frontier against foreigners and un-Islamic influences. At the same time, the Taliban ideology surely echoed the northern Durrani concept of the righteousness and power of the *wolus* community. But I felt sure that Taliban fanaticism was, first, only an extreme version of one strand in Durrani culture and society, and second, a temporary response to an extreme crisis. This was supported by Taliban apologists, as reported in the press and set out on their original websites.

In the absence of state authority, where warlords dominated the local scene, the Taliban offered—to Pashtuns—tribal unity, strong and historically exemplified claims to ethnic superiority, and the uncompromising application of an Islamic legal code. The Taliban leadership, whether deliberately or through ignorance, were opposed to existing models of state, and when in power themselves they failed to form an effective government. But if they wished to establish a viable Islamic state in a country of Afghanistan's ethnic and regional heterogeneity, they had to relax some of their declared rules; and their actions showed that, like all Islamist movements, they were prepared to adjust their policies to achieve their political aims. Thus they learned that an Islamist appeal, through a very strict and distorted version of the law, did not attract most people in the country.

After their defeat and disintegration in 2001–2, the Taliban successfully reorganised and revised both their ideology and their strategies. Their old opponents, the warlords, were back in power in Kabul, supported by new occupying forces, which over the years following the invasion managed to alienate much of country through ignorance of the people and their values and by causing a horrific toll of civilian casualties. Apart from the support they continued to receive from abroad, the Afghan "Neo-Taliban" had no difficulty recruiting young warriors in most parts of the country. Taliban self-representation changed.[37] The explicit and unifying ideology was still predominantly Islamic, but it also included strong tribal and nationalist appeals: eagerness for revenge and for the expulsion of the occupying forces. They also sought to appeal to urban, educated classes as well as the rural and urban masses. Several of the earlier regulations—for example the prohibition of television and other items of modern technology as well as music, dog-fighting and kite-flying, the ban on female education (which always continued in the east) and the insistence on beards for men, and the opposition to both Shiism and Sufism—were eased.[38]

The Afghan Taliban consist, as before, of a core of die-hard followers and associates of Mullah Omar and a highly varied periphery of local "insurgents". Given that Taliban too have been responsible for many civilian casualties, it is hardly surprising that this periphery—as always with Pashtun tribes—is liable to "change sides", often privileging local feuds and rivalries over "national" or ideological commitments. Inter-tribal rivalries too have played an important part, both between the major Durrani and Ghilzai confederations and between their component tribes.[39]

Some analysts have argued that there is nothing "tribal" about the Taliban. Not only have Afghan rural culture and society changed radically and irreversibly since the war against the Soviets, but the Pashtun tribal system has broken down and gone for good, as a result of widespread assassinations of tribal elders, the strictly limited worldview of the young warriors (many of them born and brought up in refugee camps in Pakistan), and the acquisition of modern armaments and electronic technology.[40]

In my view, such arguments are often based on an idealised notion of tribal society, drawn from dated anthropology texts, in which tribes are egalitarian descent groups, operating according to principles of segmentation and complementary opposition. Actual tribal groups in much of Afghanistan and Iran never did conform to such an ideal; reality was much more fluid, and has always been complicated by other political processes, from shifting alliances and blocs to political centralisation and class formation, not to mention the emergence of Sufi leaders. Elphinstone, the first to write in detail about the Pashtun tribal system, acknowledged its complexity nearly two centuries ago.[41] Of course the Taliban are not (only) a tribal organisation, any more than any of the nineteenth or twentieth century Frontier movements were; but Taliban members, including the leadership, belong to tribes, and tribal values and principles are part of their lives. I would argue that the Pashtun tribal system has always been "tribal (in the ideal type sense) plus", and has always adapted to changed circumstances, as it continues to do in the twenty-first century.

Tribalism and ethnicity both have a bad press in the West. Tribalism is commonly presented as the antithesis of rational "modernity", a dark, destructive, primeval force that corrupts civilisation. In recent decades, its place has been taken by ethnicity. "Ethnic cleansing" and genocide have been established as the scourge of our times; and whenever an "ethnic" dimension is apparent in any of the world's conflicts, it is conventionally identified as the "root" of the conflict, whose complex material and economic roots are rarely examined or publicised.

There is another perspective on this. As I wrote in 1983: "Tribalism has its faults and limitations, but its provision of social security and its long-term survival value should recommend it as no anachronism in the last decades of the twentieth century."[42] It remains true that, in conditions of insecurity and crisis such as Afghanistan has experienced since 1978, people naturally seek security in families, tribes, ethnic communities, and religious leaders. The tragically changed circumstances of so many Afghan communities have of course radically affected their constructions of identity, and religion has certainly come to play a larger part in Afghan official and political discourses than before, just as it also now figures more prominently in academic analyses of events. Only if and when a strong state is founded, and security, justice and services to the people are established, are ethnic and tribal identities likely to diminish in importance.

In the early 1970s, ethnic, tribal and religious ideologies were all important to the Pashtuns in Afghanistan as guides to action and frameworks for evaluating the actions of others. But it seems clear to me that, however catastrophic the ensuing three to four decades, and however radically changed the circumstances now, the same ideologies, in all their complexity, ambivalence and mutual inconsistency, have not lost their influence among Pashtuns, whether or not they are part of the Taliban movement; that is, a convincing analysis of Taliban practices must take account of them all. In effect, Barth's analysis of politics and ethnicity among the Swat Pathan remains a foundational text for us all.

17

IF ONLY THERE WERE LEADERS

THE PROBLEM OF "FIXING" THE PASHTUN TRIBES

Antonio Giustozzi

From the perspective of an historian trying to write a history of state-formation and state-building in Afghanistan, the anthropological debate over tribes and states is important but needs to be turned upside down: how did the political centre reshape communities in order to create the foundations for state making in Afghanistan?

Despite many ups and downs, the region today known as Afghanistan has by no means been a stateless territory throughout most of its known history. Ruling elites were repeatedly able to establish sets of social relations with both social groups and local elites, and these have enabled them to exercise control and influence over people, territories and resources, as well as to obtain recognition from neighbouring states. These activities fit pretty well with at least some definitions of the state.

Where does a state begin and end? Elsewhere I have argued that the monopolisation of *large scale* violence marks the formation of the state; I have also argued that such monopolisation is not merely a military process, but in fact is primarily a political one.[1] The description of the monopolisation of large scale violence should therefore deal with not just the formation of large armies, but the shaping of political settlements and of the structures developed to manage them. States usually emerge out of the competition of groups for control over population and resources; it is a strategy of control, an attempt to stabilise a political environment to avoid continuous war and the risks associated with it.

In its most basic form, a state combines a military superiority of some kind with a set of political structures aimed at preventing the mobilisation of armed power in opposition to the state. Small armed retinues at the service of local leaders are of little consequence if they can be prevented from coming together in opposition to the state. The power tools utilised to this aim include co-optation of local leaders, divide-and-rule, selective repression, etc.

Within the anthropological debate on tribes and states it has been recently pointed out that if we define the state as a social relation, it does not need to adopt a centralised structure; classes or social groups could use a series of tools, of which kinship is one, to exercise power and influence in a headless way. Examples of this include the Mongol state, but also, possibly, the Bakhtiari confederation in Iran.[2] Even more so with the emergence of centralised polities, the manipulation of kinship and tribes for political purposes can be expected to play a major role in how tribes have evolved. Assuming the existence of tribes as autonomous entities, therefore, could be a major misinterpretation of how they function.

Until Abdur Rahman, we cannot really speak of a centralised Afghan state: what we saw was the periodical emergence of tribal confederacies around a charismatic leader, who had some coercive power but never managed to establish a monopoly of large scale violence for more than one or two generations. This was mainly because the leading figures within the Afghan state commanded only a comparatively modest power and their bargaining position was weak. Only when able to lead the tribes towards conquest and looting were they able to keep the polity somewhat united. As the environment surrounding Afghanistan changed during the nineteenth century, that model of state formation became increasingly difficult to maintain. Under pressure from the empires surrounding Afghanistan, Abdur Rahman set out to create a centralised state in Afghanistan; the demand for such a state was weak or non-existent inside Afghanistan, but its formation met the desire for order and for an interface with which to negotiate among the neighbouring empires, particularly the British one.

What made Abdur Rahman different? Two things mainly: he imported methods of state-making from the British and Tsarist empires and made deals with external powers to secure his domain from external interference. He also obtained British external support in the form of subsidies. Such techniques were in part already in use before Abdur Rahman. As an early twentieth century British observer reported about the Atsakzai nomads when they were still under the Afghan kingdom, "…it was usual in Afghan times to appoint one of a particular family […] to supervise the tribe on the part of the government and probably to be responsible that their notoriously predatory propensities were kept within moderate bounds."[3] And, as pointed out by Glatzer, Elphinstone had already noted that "when tribes formed viable constitutencies, [this] was instigated by the royal court's policy of trying to extend its influence by organising local populations along tribal lines by promoting local big men as tribal chiefs".[4] Abdur Rahman, however, went further in establishing a system of divide-and-rule which served the purposes of the monarchy better.

The state established by Abdur Rahman remained in operation in its general outlines until the late 1970s. What follows is a schematic description of the system in terms of its relationship with communities and tribes. The purpose is to highlight implicit elements of instability in the system, which explain its rapid collapse from the late 1970s onwards and the difficulties in rebuilding the system after 2001.

Glatzer pointed out how state formation and state consolidation were different matters in Afghanistan's tribal kingdoms: "once such leaders had ascended to the highest power, the tribal structure had little more to offer in terms of sustaining power and running the state, and the rulers had to find or to create alternative institutions outside the tribal network".[5]

As Hasan Kakar explains, after coming to power Abdur Rahman moved to eliminate community elders everywhere in the country. After the pacification of the rebellious communities, an order was created in which the relations of the elders with the government and with their own districts were fixed on a new footing. The outstanding feature of this new order was the dependence of the elders on the state. Indeed, the institution was reinforced, and the number of elders, paradoxically, increased during the reign of the Amir. These new elders were given allowances and visited the Amir at frequent intervals.[6]

In essence, Abdur Rahman's action after having established himself as a ruthless leader at the centre of the chaotic Afghan polity was to break up the autonomous communities, whose self-governance capability represented an obstacle for state consolidation. It is important in this context to understand that the establishment of a monopoly of large scale violence as the primary foundation of the state needs to be understood not just in terms of concentration of coercive power, but also in terms of the political ability of the ruling elite to prevent collective action/mobilisation in the periphery. The monopoly of large scale violence is therefore acquired without the complete disarming of the population or the complete elimination of local leaders with their retinues of armed men; what matters is that those armed men are not able to mobilise collectively to mount a strategic threat to the centre.[7]

In this optic, there are two dimensions worth discussing in this assertion of state power: regulating relations among communities and acquiring a degree of control over single communities. Abdur Rahman's state needed to divide-and-rule over communities, not only among them but also *within* them, as will be explained in greater detail below. In general the attitude of the Afghan state was focused on creating a stratum of pliable (and dependent) local leaders, which it could call on for service, information gathering and information distribution. In order to do so the state administration manipulated existing features of the various communities to its advantage, in the process changing the internal structure of many communities. As a general rule, the more remote a community the more likely it was to be more lightly affected by state manipulation. Another general rule was that communities which had challenged central rule were punished, among other things, with the imposition of a new set of government-appointed elders. Some very remote mountain communities were probably not affected at all, at least not directly.

There was pragmatism in the way Abdur Rahman and his successors ruled over communities. The south-eastern tribes, for example, were left relatively autonomous, because of their remote location, which made them difficult to coerce, and because of political deal-making. There was also some value in leaving their ability to mobilise intact for use against external enemies. By contrast, within the eastern tribes the state operated to weaken tribal power and split the tribes internally.

Among the non-Pashtun communities of the north, north-east, centre and west, in most cases relatively strong local leaderships were already there (although one should not generalise); sometimes the government would co-opt such local leaders, but more often it tended to create an alternative stratum of government representatives running parallel to local leaders or elders. The former were indigenous leaders (*bay*s) with local support and the latter were the so-called *arbab*s, the villages' official leaders. As Barfield notes, "real tribal leaders had often no connection with the government, but were continually sought out by their people to resolve disputes and mediate problems." This in part was due to the fact that although the *arbab*s were supposed to be chosen by people and approved by government, in practice they were often chosen by government without consultation. While it could happen that *bay*s (local notables) could become *arbab*s, that was rather the exception than the rule. The result was that the *arbab*s were in Barfield's assessment "useless" as enforcers of general policy. A *bay arbab* would put the interests of his people first. An *arbab* had no independent support and could do little.[8] Other authors are not as dismissive of the influence of the *arbab*s; Azoy, for example, mentions that there could be several *arbab*s in each village, each with his own clients,[9] and the Centlivres noted that the *bay*s often manipulated or influenced the appointment of the *arbab*s.[10]

Divide-and-rule among existing local elites was another aspect of Kabul's strategy of power and influence. For example, some big Uzbek landlords, who had maintained good relations with the Afghan state from the beginning, were co-opted and received political support from Kabul; others who resisted the expansion of state power in the north were targeted for expropriation, to the benefit of Pashtun migrants who received their lands. This pattern of divide-and-rule continues to this day. For example, Qazi Kabir, a big Uzbek landlord in the northern part of Takhar province, refused to join the Uzbek lobby of other former militia commanders in Takhar province which was formed in 2002 with the aim of obtaining the appointment of Uzbeks to positions of power within the provincial administration. Qazi Kabir was then appointed Governor of the province. His family was one of those that had been spared in the land redistributions of the previous 120 years.[11]

Arguably the Pashtun tribes were affected more heavily in their internal structures than most other communities, because their tribal structure, which originally was relatively egalitarian, made them impervious to state control. The tribal *jirga*s were taking decisions by consensus, except for a few tribes already heavily affected by state intervention in Ahmad Shah's time (largely in the south), and arguably had lost their tribal character at that point. For Afghan rulers to mobilise and control the tribes it had proved very complicated historically, as witnessed by the constant ups and downs of Pashtun confederacies; the dilemma of the Afghan state-maker was how to make communities dependent on the state, so that they would have to obey orders coming from the top, at least to some extent. There was in principle plenty of room for government manipulation. The khans were seeking out government contacts in order to "add to their armament of dispensible favours". Soon a new environment arose in which "no little of a khan's power inhere[d] in what might be called his Kabul connection".[12]

As mentioned at the beginning of this chapter, it is difficult to be certain of the extent to which government manipulation was the work of individual officials or part of a pre-conceived plan. It is worth quoting Anderson at length here;

At various times different tribal groups have received special privileges of attention from the government that, by their indivisible character, reinforce the jointure of interests. […]

IF ONLY THERE WERE LEADERS

In other areas the government interferes, in local estimations, to consolidate or dissolve specific combinations by recognizing or not recognizing them, most commonly through the requirement that each "village" have a headman (malik) for official communication with the civil authorities. Intentional or not, manipulation is often suspected by the tribesmen, because access to government services to influence their distribution is a resource which the adept, well-connected or outright agents can mobilize in local affairs.[13]

As explained above the actual form of the manipulation of the internal structure of the tribe varied from place to place, but for the sake of simplicity I have selected here one "median" example, the Shinwari tribe of eastern Afghanistan. The Shinwari live mostly in Nangarhar province, between Jalalabad city and Torkham, as well as in Kunar and across the border in Pakistan. Before Abdur Rahman, the tribe was led collegially by a tribal *jirga* of approximately 10–12 elders, the most influential and experienced among the Shinwari elders. The process of selection took place among the "respectable" families of the Shinwari and was consensual. The actual power or influence of individual elders varied, but none of them were even remotely in a position to dominate the *jirga* by coercing their peers or by buying their support. Hence collegial leadership was necessary. The *jirga* had extensive powers to take decisions and enforce them. This does not mean that the elders always had good personal relations with each other; in fact the tribe was ridden by blood feuds, rivalries and animosities, but the *jirga* was able to contain them by punishing excesses. The rather scant historical evidence suggests that it was common even before Abdur Rahman for tribal khans and *maliks* to form factions within the tribe, but there does not seem to be any indication of permanent alignments between one particular tribal faction and the central leadership.[14]

From Abdur Rahman onwards the state intervened to destroy or weaken this system of self-government, in order to make the population dependent on the state for security, justice and leadership. What is particularly important is the analysis of how exactly this was achieved. In some cases, the old leadership was exterminated or banned; in others, it was marginalised; in others still, it was co-opted, as in the case of the Shinwari tribe, which I have chosen so as to illustrate how even the least coercive option (co-optation) could profoundly alter the tribal structure. Figure 17.1 shows a simplified scheme of how the tribal leadership looked before state intervention. Figure 17.2 shows how state intervention affected it. The pre-existing factional divisions were greatly reinforced by state intervention; the appointment of government representatives (government *maliks*) was not so important in this case. In my view the formation of political alliances with elements of the tribal leadership was more important.

The state administration arbitrarily selected one of the components of the tribal *jirga* as its ally within the tribe; he was not necessarily the most influential or the wealthiest, but he would have been the leader of one of the two factions/parties (*gund*). By the very fact of selecting him, the state immensely increased his power and influence within the tribe. He would also be in a position to dispense favours, rewarding his supporters and hurting those least friendly to him, because of privileged access to the state administration and because of government subsidies, which Abdur Rahman established. This would in turn snowball into a further increase of the influence of this "government khan", who could consoli-

Figure 17.1

Before the intrusion of government

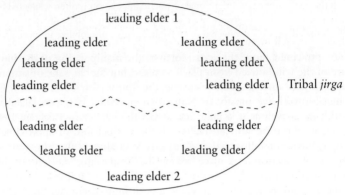

The example of the Shinwari tribe

Figure 17.2

After intrusion of government

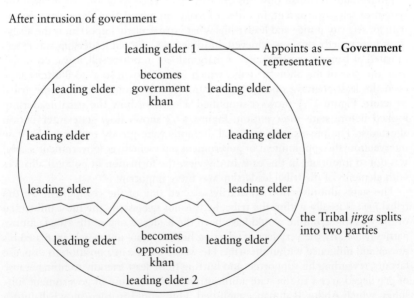

The example of the Shinwari tribe

IF ONLY THERE WERE LEADERS

date or establish an alliance with a majority of the leading elders and therefore assert a relative dominance over the tribe. The end result is shown in Figure 3: the tribal *jirga* as a governance institution is weakened to the point that a bipolar system of governance emerges and tendentially replaces it. The "government khan" assumes a dominant position and gathers around himself a number of loyal elders, with whom he probably had good relations from the start. He also gathers the support of a number of not-so-friendly elders, who may have issues with him personally (old feuds, disputes…) or with some of his closest allies. They might have been members of the opposite faction before the state's intervention strengthened his ability to distribute patronage. These "opportunistic" elders side with the "government khan" because of the high risk/cost of opposing him and because of the benefits associated with cooperation: the "government khan" decides about conscription, taxation, etc. At the same time, among the remaining elders who cannot cooperate with the "government khan" because of a number of issues (feuds, rivalry, competition over resources, diverging interests), the pre-existing faction, significantly weakened, turns into the opposition party (*gund*), built around the most respected, charismatic and/or wealthiest khan (the "opposition khan", or if you like a paraphrase from the British parliamentary system the "shadow tribal leader").[15]

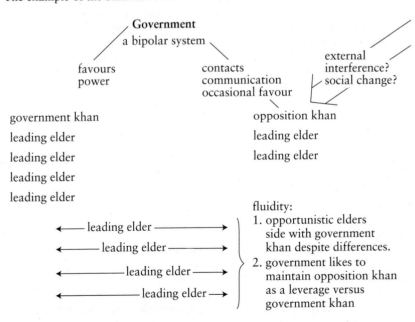

Figure 17.3
After the introduction of government
The example of the Shinwari tribe

The system as described above maintains a high degree of fluidity, mainly because of three factors:

1. The opportunistic elders have reluctantly sided with the government party, in order to benefit personally, but are ready to switch sides should the opportunity arise.
2. The government is disinclined to strengthen its ally (the "government khan") beyond a certain point; it certainly does not want the "government khan" to assume total control over the community, because the government is not certain about his long-term loyalty. Particularly if the central government were to squeeze communities in terms of taxation and conscription, or were to decide an increase in state penetration into the area of the tribe, the loyalty of the government khan might be tested. Either because of his own decision or because of pressure from tribesmen and tribal elders, he could be tempted to reject the orders of the government. As a result the central government has a vested interest in keeping the "opposition Khan" and his *gund* alive, even if in a weak position. This can be achieved by preventing the "government khan" from eliminating his rival altogether, and also by the occasional dispensation of some patronage.
3. The closer the khans become to the government, the greater the distance between them and their clients. As a result, they would tend to gradually lose influence among the villagers and risk being challenged by the opposition khan or by others—though the process was not as pronounced among the khans as it was among the *malik*s, who in many areas showed a tendency to become "quasi-permanent officials".[16]

As can be seen, the fluidity in the system is functional to the implementation of divide-and-rule from the centre; it is indeed essential to make the system work in the government's interest in the long run. This fluidity, however, is also the key weakness of the system. It can only work in the government's interest if it has an unchallenged monopoly of large scale violence and external interference does not occur. Indeed this was a key feature of the system created by Abdur Rahman: turning Afghanistan into a buffer between the British and Russian empires, hence motivating the two empires to abstain from interfering and in specific periods even supporting the new Afghan state. What, however, if such non-interference was to come to an end, for whatever reason? The system then becomes very vulnerable, as the "opposition party" is always susceptible to be co-opted into a rebellion if assured of lasting support and offered sufficient incentives (Figure 3).

This was indeed the experience of the late 1970s onwards, which continues to this day. The best that the system can achieve in the presence of strong external interference is to keep the "government khan" on its side. Keeping both parties on the central state side becomes very difficult, as the local leaders now have greater leverage than the state: the offer of large rewards to the opposition khan in order to lure him away from alliance with external/anti-state powers ends with the defection of the "government khan" to the opposition. The system needs to favour one party over the other to function effectively and cheaply.

In the case of the Shinwaris this dynamic was observed both in 1928–29 and in 1980–92. During the revolt against Amanullah, the "government khan" switched his support to Habibullah Kalakani, while the "opposition khan" instead offered his support to Amanullah. In the 1980s Wakil Azam, who had been "government khan" under Daud, went into opposition in 1980 and joined Hizb-i Islami. In 1988 he joined Najibullah's government, which appointed him as Governor, but that did not translate into government control over the six Shinwari districts of Nangarhar as the situation within the tribe remained fluid.[17]

In sum, the hypothesis that emerges from this discussion is that the Afghan state needed local leaders loyal to itself to have a degree of control over the communities, but at the same time to limit their control because its ability to create dependency on the state by means others than divide-and-rule was limited. It is difficult to tell apart what was the result of deliberate, planned government policy and what was the result of pragmatic interaction between government officials at the provincial and district level and the communities. A full-scale research project, exploring patterns of relations between state and local communities in various parts of the country, could establish to what extent this was a planned policy or improvisation at the local level. Whatever the case, the result was that in the presence of external interference, the system of governance created by Abdur Rahman is not really feasible. The state needs communities with leaders dependent on the state to control the population, but that inevitably creates opposition because local leaders sidelined by the state try to mobilise support within the communities by offering to address their grievances. As long as a monopoly of large scale violence (note the definition) is there, the risk of a successful rebellion is modest, but if the monopoly is challenged, the potential for rapidly spreading rebellions is huge because it is built into the system. In the past the Afghan state has not been able to afford a transition towards a different system; with generous external support or with increased internal revenue, such transition becomes possible in principle, but the problem remains how to contain chaos in the interim.

This chapter has also illustrated how looking at tribes in isolation from the wider political context and in particular from their relationship with the state is highly problematic, and likely to produce misunderstandings more than anything else.

18

LESSONS ON GOVERNANCE FROM THE WALI OF SWAT

STATE-BUILDING IN AFGHANISTAN, 1995–2010

David B. Edwards

Some years ago, I wrote an essay entitled "Learning from the Swat Pathans" that considered the relevance of Fredrik Barth's work on the Swat Pathans to understanding the political situation in Afghanistan from the first period of anti-Soviet militancy in the late-1970s through the initial ascendency of the Taliban in the mid-1990s.[1] I noted in that essay that it was a telling commentary on the fate of anthropology as a discipline that, at a crucial juncture, when the political currents swirling in Afghanistan and northwest Pakistan were so difficult to navigate, Barth's insightful analysis of Pakhtun political leadership that had been so influential within anthropology itself, at least for an earlier generation of political anthropologists, was so little referred to or recognized. Often termed "the handmaiden of colonialism" for its earlier association with colonial administration (and indeed much of the formative ethnographic research on the Pakhtuns of Afghanistan and northwestern Pakistan was carried out by British civil and military officers), anthropology had become encysted within its own parochial debates and was little noticed outside the corridors of academia.

The value that I saw in Barth's work then I see now even more strongly, and in this essay I will attempt to update my analysis of why Barth's analysis of the Swat Pakhtun matters and is of continuing relevance to the politics of the new millennium. In my earlier essay, I considered the relevance of Barth's insights on "methodological individualism" to understanding the competition for power among tribal and Islamic political factions. While Barth's analysis of the dynamics of Pakhtun political competition is still relevant, the specific focus of this essay is Barth's work on the rise of the Swat state and what it might tell us about efforts to secure and develop a viable apparatus of state rule in Afghanistan under both the Taliban and Karzai regimes. The importance of understanding the process of

249

state formation is particularly pressing because of the tendency among Western policymakers to assume that the state model with which they are familiar is the only possible model that might exist. Before you can fix "failed states," however, you have to understand where particular states come from and how they are viewed by the people who come under their sway, as well as by those who oppose them. Westerners have difficulty in this regard because they have always lived within the confines of, and with the certainties provided by, a particular kind of viable centralized state that has existed in their countries of origins for centuries. Wars have come and gone, governing systems have been re-imagined and modified, alliances have prospered and declined, sovereignties have been transgressed, borders have shifted, but through it all the bounded, centralized, bureaucratic state has endured.

The same is not true in the region comprising Afghanistan, where until the second half of the nineteenth century there were no stable borders, and instead of states one found a shifting landscape of expanding and contracting kingdoms and khanates, displaced dynastic rivals, predatory tribes, commercial networks of merchants and caravan traders, all interwoven by networks of Sufi *khanqa*s that could themselves become the basis of new political formations of varying size and duration. Of all the areas of Central Asia, the steep, forbidding mountain valleys of present-day Nuristan, Kunar, Paktia and Ningrahar Provinces in Afghanistan and Mohmand, Bajaur, Chitral, Dir, Swat, Malakand, and the Northern Territories of Pakistan have constituted over the last several hundred years one of the most dynamic laboratories of political evolution that we know of, a kind of Galapagos of independent political evolution. In this region coexisted all manner of political formations of varying size, ideological pretense, organizational logic, economic underpinning, and historical duration. Based on the work of insightful British observers like Elphinstone and Bellew, we can reconstruct at least some of what was going on up through the first half of the twentieth century, but the only part of this region for which we have sufficient information to form larger generalizations about indigenous processes of state-building is Swat, and that is largely thanks to the work of Fredrik Barth.

It is fair to say that Barth's appreciation of the importance of the state in Swat developed gradually and only came to the center of his attention after the first phase of his Swat research had been concluded. In *Political Leadership among Swat Pathans*, Barth's classic work of political anthropology published in 1959, the state is in the background. Barth's short historical chapter in *Political Leadership* contains a non-analytical chronological summary of events leading up to the formation of the state, which has the appearance of an afterthought and, presented as it is without any description of the regional framework, is mostly just a list of names, places, and events. Barth's main point in this chapter is that the state is largely irrelevant to the analysis he is presenting in his monograph. Perhaps anticipating the objection that there exists a contradiction between a portrait of a political system in "dynamic equilibrium" and the historical reality that state systems emerged in Swat twice between 1840 and 1917, Barth argues that in all of its essentials,

the traditional system of opposed blocs, maintaining balance by occasional changes in allegiance, continues. None of the factors contributing to it are removed by the State organization. The pre-requisites for local dominance are the same as in the acephalous system. The centralized system is merely superimposed on this, presupposing rather than attempting to replace it. The description of the bloc organization thus remains valid and accurate within the area of the Swat state as well as outside its boundaries.[2]

While appreciating Barth's dismantling of the static determinism of structural functionalism, many critics saw in Barth's "methodological individualism" a projection of the Western market system, a turning of Pakhtuns into Norwegian entrepreneurs in the words of one critic. In his analysis of *Political Leadership*, Talal Asad proposed from afar to account for the rise of the Swat state via a more or less Marxist analysis of class formation and a world systems approach to colonial intervention. In Asad's words, "a class perspective reveals the political structure to be a complex, developing reality, and not a logically closed system which happens to be located at a point in linear time."[3] Asad argued that "an adequate analysis of Swat structures of domination ... requires a historical perspective in which the developing political system of Swat is set within a wider imperial framework."[4]

Asad's contribution to the development of such an historical perspective, however, was limited to speculative assertions, for example about the "possible political implications of population growth and changing patterns of property distribution"; and his inclusion of imperialism as contributing to the rise of the Swat state amounts, again, only to a few suggestive comments on how "the presence of the British may have significantly influenced such factors as the rate of population increase (through, e.g., access to cheap modern medicines), and the scope for intimidation (through, e.g., access to expensive modern firearms)."[5] The elaboration of these possibilities was not Asad's object, and he admitted that "until the appropriate historical research has been carried out such questions must remain largely matters for speculation."[6]

Presumably inspired by such critiques, Barth addressed the question of foreign influence in his "Swat Pathans Reconsidered" essay published in the volume *Features of Person and Society in Swat*, but only to reject its significance to his model:

... the state was an indigenous, not a colonial creation; it reasserted previously unsuccessful efforts of centralization during the nineteenth century and seems to have arisen without external support and subsequently to have relied only marginally on colonial and postcolonial national establishments. This autonomy perpetuated a distinctive feature of the preceding acephalous organization of Swat: through a turbulent history of contact with civilizations and empires, Swat itself had long constituted an independent region. It was never conquered by Moghuls or Sikhs; and despite British penetration on all sides it was never so much as seen by European eyes till 1895–7.[7]

At the same time, Barth devoted some consideration to elaborating what had been left undeveloped in his monograph: the means by which the state was "superimposed" on the traditional bloc system. According to Barth, the Swat state was achieved by the ruler seeking influence rather than land and by developing "a new kind of relationship" with individual contract-holders organized to serve as his army. The nature of this relationship remained somewhat murky in "The Swat Pathans Reconsidered," but Barth returned to the topic four years later in his extended epilogue to *The Last Wali of Swat*, in which he provided the first substantial analysis of state-building in Swat based on the Wali's own testimony.[8] Elaborating on his earlier assertions, Barth argued that "the creation of Swat state was in no way the establishment of an offshoot of a pre-existing state" and that the centralization of power was based not on control of land but on adroit manipulation of political dynamics within the Valley.

According to Barth, the principal means by which the ruler succeeded in breaking down the factions that were at the root of Swat political culture was the creation of a centralized military force capable of providing unified military defense against external threats. Traditionally, in responding to outside threats, Swatis, like others in the region, could fall back on the alternative of *jihad*, so long as they had the support of religious authorities to do so. This alternative worked best, of course, in situations in which the threat posed was by non-Muslims and also when the danger was of short duration. However, some threats, notably that posed by a fellow Muslim, the Nawab of Dir, were "too close and too persistent to be withstood on such an *ad hoc* basis...The only way they could see to break out of this systemic weakness was by reconstituting the political organization around a central King."[9]

In discussing the development of a proto-military force under the command of the Swati ruler, Barth noted that the army provided the double advantage of ensuring the security of the state at the expense of traditional factions, by drawing men at various levels, who might have become embroiled in local factional politics, to the more stable employment of the central administration:

Commissions provided officers with a highly valued source of legitimate authority and command, and thereby with the outer forms of the influence and status—the "glory"—so eagerly sought in Swat society. Among the poorer households of the population at large, ordinary soldier contracts provided a significant marginal addition to subsistence, and thus a valued source of commitment to the regime.[10]

Once in place, the army provided not only a permanently constituted force protecting the Valley from outside aggression, but also a cohort of individuals, in the pay of the ruler, who could do his bidding in other spheres, be it punishing local troublemakers or providing a pool of corvée labor for state-sponsored projects such as the building of roads.

Maintaining a standing army required, of course, reliable means for ensuring the inflow of adequate resources to provide for the continuing functions of the state and to deprive potential rivals of the means for challenging state supremacy. The solution arrived at helped keep local-level khans secure within their own domains while also augmenting the treasury of the central administration:

...at the cost of one third of the fines imposed by the Tahsildars' courts, the State obtained the services of the local Khan in collecting such fines, provided a reward for acting as Khan and an incentive for him to involve himself in reporting breaches of State law by locals to the State's officials, and divided the authority of imposing fines from that of collecting them and thereby prevented abuse.[11]

Beyond the problem of unified defense against external enemies, an even more persistent and immediate problem was that of dealing with internal factionalism brought about by the unchecked operation of *della* or bloc politics. One path by which the founders of the Swat state sought to help cement their burgeoning authority and regulate local-level politics was the settlement of disputes:

LESSONS ON GOVERNANCE FROM THE WALI OF SWAT

The "cases" to be settled by the Ruler and his officials are precisely the stuff of *della* politics: land disputes and disputes between persons variously aligned in factions. Thereby, the Ruler achieves two purposes: (1) the State increasingly invades and takes over those function which *della* activities previously served, and thereby reduces the importance of the patronage which local leaders provide, on which they based their authority; and (2) by influencing the outcomes of disputes, the Ruler can variously strengthen and weaken competing leaders and thus affect their alignment and the patterns of local and regional power. By this crucial process the Ruler was able to practise an essential economy of force: whereas each *della*, unopposed, would through much of the history of Swat have commanded a force considerably stronger than that of the State apparatus, the power of Khans was perpetually balanced mainly by the power of *other* Khans, and the State only needed to command the marginal force always to hold the balance of power between the *dellas*.[12]

Over time and as power moved to the center, the ruler's approach shifted from one of balancing opposed blocs to that of "progressively localizing and pulverizing" factions,[13] in the process making small landowners "maliks of their own land".[14]

The gradual creation of a centralized state was not simply a matter of a strategic skillful ruler outflanking mid-level khans by turning the smallholders below them into independent operators. To that extent alone, the ruler would reinforce the egalitarian and independent tendencies already very much alive and well in Swat. As Barth and many others have demonstrated, a basic assumption of Pakhtun culture is that "other people's political relations were their separate concerns, not a collective responsibility" and that "independence and personal sovereignty were highly, perhaps inordinately, valued."[15] Consequently, a central prerequisite to state-building in Swat was to modify operative cultural assumptions to such a degree that people would be willing to accept centralized authority as not only a valid way to settle disputes, but also a legitimate way to manage political affairs more generally. One way the ruler was able to do this was simply by demonstrating the practical benefits of the people sacrificing some portion of their independence and resources to the state:

The most frequent form of praise heard in Swat concerning the Badshah's and the Wali's rule refers to the functions and services provided by the State, and it is in the emphasis on these services that we come closest to an explicit legitimatization of state organization and rulership. *Roads* are used, both by the common man and by the Wali, as a concrete symbol of progress and achievement: the bridges; the penetration of communications into all parts of Swat…Educational and health facilities are praised. Personal security under the State is contrasted to insecurity under pre-State conditions, in the stateless tribal areas, and even in neighbouring administered areas.[16]

Constructing an Afghan state

In changing venues from Swat to Afghanistan and time frames from the late nineteenth and early twentieth centuries to the late twentieth and early twenty-first, one must exercise considerable caution, of course. To begin with, there is the problem of scale. Swat consists for the most part of a single, extended valley, while Afghanistan is a geographically and ethnically varied country with a land mass roughly equivalent to that of Texas. Beyond this, if we accept Barth's assertion, the Swat state was an indigenous construct and not a secondary product of contact

253

with larger state systems, Moghul, Sikh, or British; but the same cannot be said of Afghanistan, whose history has largely been determined by its position betwixt and between powerful and expansionary imperial states. Nevertheless, the principles of state-building in Swat developed by Barth from his study of Swat are at least as useful as, and perhaps a good deal more pertinent than, those brought with them by contemporary outside experts whose experience is with states built on European foundations. From its origins in the late nineteenth century, the Afghan state has been an amalgam of local and imported ideas of what a state should be, one indigenous expression of which is a map that was published and distributed throughout his kingdom by Amir Abdur Rahman in 1898.

I have analyzed this map and its associated proclamation in depth in my book *Heroes of the Age: Moral Fault Lines on the Afghan Frontier*.[18] Here, I would just point out the way in which the image literally melds two models of state rule. The first is embodied in the central tower, with its ascending rows leading up to the uppermost pavilion in which stands the ruler, each row representing hierarchically stratified and ranked subjects of the King, the humblest on the bottom rung, and

Figure 18.1: Proclamation and Map issued by Amir Abdur Rahman, late nineteenth century.[17]

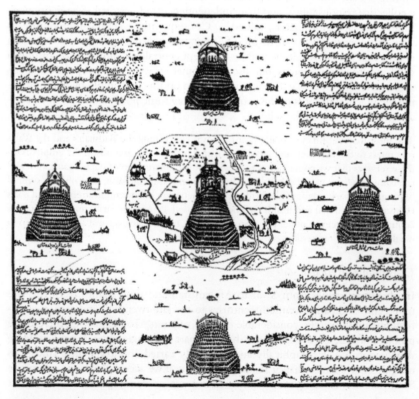

each higher rung representing a higher degree of status, but all ultimately subordinate to the King himself, from and in relation to whom all power derives. The second model is embodied in the dotted circular line, representing the "for-its-time-and-place" novel idea of a border designating the territorial extent of the state. Prior to this time, kingdoms in the region had been centers from which power radiated outward, decreasing the further one went from the center itself and contested where one ruler's influence intersected with another's.

The existence of this graphic representation of a border circumscribing the limits of Afghanistan reflects both a concession on the part of the Afghan King to the demand of his neighbors, Britain in particular, that he accept a formal border and a recognition that such a border, while it cut into his territory and denied him certain subjects he considered rightfully his (especially the Pakhtun tribes on his eastern border), also provided a degree of protection for his own claims. That is to say, the representation of the Afghan ruler as sovereign within his territory and on a par with the rulers of neighboring states (Persia, Russia, China, and British India), each with its governing edifice (of more or less equal height to Abdur Rahman's tower of state), demonstrated the control exercised by the King within his domain (there are no little fiefdoms, khanates, warlords or tribal chiefs depicted on the map, only peasants tilling their fields and tending their animals) and his status as the equal of his neighbors. One fact the map does not show is that the border was imposed on the Afghan ruler at the insistence of the most powerful of his neighbors (Britain); another is that, far from presiding over his domain as the sort of absolute ruler represented by the map and far from interacting as a peer with his neighboring rulers from atop his lofty perch, the Afghan King in fact ruled a fractious nation in which local warlords and tribes sought to maintain their independence from central government control, and was incapable of supporting the operations of state rule without the financial support of his British patrons.

However it is represented on the map, Abdur Rahman's image is as much wishful thinking as the present-day imaginings of policy planners trying to redesign the Afghan state in ways amenable to Western political ideals and funding priorities. Just as Abdur Rahman wanted to impose a hierarchical order on Afghanistan, to turn it into a neatly stratified society in which power and command would emanate from him down through the ranks, those in charge of reinventing Afghanistan likewise want to impose a strong central government, though one patterned on Western notions of democracy and rational management in which authority and accountability are neatly distributed to relevant nodes within the governmental bureaucracy. Just as the domestic political situation faced by Abdur Rahman was a good deal more complicated than the model he presented to his people, so it is with Hamid Karzai who, even more than the so-called "Iron Amir," is dependent on the largesse and patronage of outsiders whose very presence undermines the authority he seeks to consolidate for himself.

My purpose here is not to attempt a history of Afghan state-building. It is merely to offer a consideration of the utility of Barth's analysis of state-building in Swat to state-building in Afghanistan. In presenting this analysis, however, it is necessary to remind ourselves that the Afghan history of state-building, from the start, has been one in which more powerful states have pressured Afghanistan into becoming what they wanted it to be, and these efforts, predictably, have led to the creation of bastard political formations, golem-like amalgams of various notions of state authority, incapable of standing on their own or of reproducing themselves without the ongoing support of outside benefactors.

Thus, under the sway of the Soviets in the late 1970s, the Marxist government that came to power via a military coup d'état tried to overcome its weakness and lack of connection to the people nominally under its jurisdiction by creating an improvised political movement composed of landless peasants, women, and other "oppressed" groups. Meant to stand in for Afghanistan's absent industrial working class, the formation created by the Afghan Marxists represented a concerted attempt by party leaders to dismantle local society in order to rebuild it in a way that would make it more amenable to Marxist theory and their own political longevity. In one respect at least, these efforts were successful, though not at all in the ways intended. Local social structures that had over decades of royal administration accommodated themselves to varying degrees to central administration were largely destroyed or marginalized, as party leaders had hoped, but what rose in their place were novel politico-military structures associated with and financed by counter-revolutionary political parties based in Pakistan and advocating various forms of more or less strict Islamic governance, which—like the Marxist political forms—had no footing in Afghan society. In this way, a new social organization was indeed created, but one inimical to the vision of its progenitors.

Rather than moving Afghanistan boldly forward, the Marxist revolution and the counter-revolution it spawned created conditions in Afghanistan by the mid-1980s that were arguably closer to those of the mid-nineteenth century than to those of 1978 when the Marxists first began the process of refashioning the Afghan nation and state. In the wake of the Soviet withdrawal in 1989, nearly twenty years of war had decimated the very idea of governance, while the political party leaders formerly based in Pakistan after their triumphal return to Afghanistan assumed the role formerly played by royal pretenders. In this zero-sum game of political advantage, each would-be *amir* conspired to best his rivals, but any advantage gained by one claimant led to his rivals banding together to forestall his rise to the top.

Meanwhile, the capital city itself was subjected to frequent shelling; roads were beset by bandits; local potentates set up their own miniature fiefdoms, turning the arms that had been used to expel the Soviet invaders against their own people to ensure their continued domination. Instead of the sort of cavalry Amir Abdur Rahman led before he took the reins of power in 1879, former *jihad* leaders commanded light brigades of Datsun and Toyota pickups, each containing a squad of Mujahidin armed with AK-47s and RPGs. In his autobiography, Amir Abdur Rahman speaks of the Afghanistan he inherited as a house full of scorpions, and much the same thing could be said of Afghanistan on the eve of the Taliban takeover in 1996, where highway banditry had again become endemic and people were often afraid to leave their homes.

One question that arises in considering the early success of the Taliban is the one Barth considers for Swat, namely what "propelled the assemblies of autonomous tribesmen to give up at least some of their autonomy to a central power." There is no doubt that the majority of Afghans, most particularly the Pakhtun populations of eastern and southern Afghanistan, were willing to give up a substantial degree of their autonomy to the Taliban, and they did so for at least one of the reasons cited by Barth in his discussion of the rise of the Swat state: "the urgency of united military defense." In this case, however, it was not defense against foreign aggression but defense against the local predations of former Mujahidin commanders. The Taliban promised, and at first delivered, safer roads and freedom from harassment and the regular shakedowns that women and men alike experienced at the hands of the former Mujahidin-turned-bandits. What the Taliban did not provide was the second of Barth's considerations, "a different polity capable of new functions."[19] Thus, where the Taliban state failed was in creating an armature of administration that could provide basic services to the people once a degree of security had been established. Providing for the physical safety of its citizens is the most essential service any government can provide, but over time other needs become important, and it was in the provision of these basic services that the Taliban lost the confidence of the people and fell back on ever more draconian measures to control the population.

In answering the question of how the transition to state rule occurred in Swat, Barth points to the existence of "*two* basic modes of establishing regional hegemony, one representing a stateless pattern, the other through state-building."[20] The Taliban can be seen as a representative of the first of these modes. Their focus was never on state-building in itself, but—as in Swat in the middle of the nineteenth century under the Akhund—on "setting up Shariat courts and monopolizing judicial functions within a territory," without much consideration to the other functions which states in other contexts fulfill.[21] Such uni-dimensional political formations do not tend to last long. As the threat to physical security recedes, people begin to expect something more in exchange for the autonomy they have given up. Even in Afghanistan, where there is little tradition of state-sponsored social services, the government is still looked to, at the very least, for patronage and employment. In this respect, the Taliban never managed to deliver, except insofar as they provided employment to *madrasa* students as shock troops for their military campaigns against non-Pushtun Afghans and as patrolmen for their morality police units in Kabul and other urban centers.

To the extent that they were staffed at all, ministries drew their manpower from the ranks of administratively inexperienced *madrasa* teachers. Although they had the consequences of drought and massive dislocation to deal with, the Taliban never ventured far into the realm of social services, largely relegating responsibility for meeting the basic needs of the most destitute to Western humanitarian organizations. The focus of their governance never pushed far beyond the sort of judicial concerns with which they were familiar by virtue of their background in Islamic law. As opposition mounted internally and abroad, the Taliban focused their efforts on eliminating ethnic blocs of dissent within the country and vilifying foreign critics of their regime, principally the United States.

Barth observed for the "stateless" model in Swat that, "there seem to have been at least seeds of a whole theory or vision of a polity in these Saintly efforts to establish the rule of law through spiritual influence—an alternative realization of Islamic society in a stateless version".[22] In the case of the Taliban, efforts to realize an Islamic society centered around ongoing and continuous efforts to recruit and deploy young adherents to put down oppositional threats throughout the country and the establishment of a puritanical rule of law, principally through the relentless exertions of the Bureau for the Propagation of Virtue and Suppression of Vice against corrupting influences, whether in the form of weekly shrine visitations by rural village women or taxi drivers listening to Bollywood film music. Such defense and reform efforts were certainly not unique to Afghanistan or to recent history, but in the hands of the Taliban, these efforts resembled nothing so much as the campaign mounted by the Red Guards in China to institute permanent revolution, nominally to suppress forces of counter-revolution but at least equally to cover up failures of the state to meet basic human needs.[23]

The second model outlined by Barth was that of a state established not on the basis of spiritual force but rather by the consolidation of key social and economic functions through the person of the ruler. As noted previously, the success of the rulers of the Swat state who succeeded the Akhund in the twentieth century derived from their ability to constitute "a different kind of polity capable of new functions," the most important of which were a centralized and rationalized military force capable of expelling foreign invasion, as well as building roads and a bureaucratic organization for collecting revenues, such that the central administration was able to pay for itself and the new roles it intended to carry out, upon which the local population would become increasingly dependent. These were not simply technical changes. They involved fundamentally recasting the structure of political relationships in Swat. In the case of consolidating force in a centrally controlled army, the Badshah and Wali had to realign traditional cultural values in such a way that the sort of glory and prestige that Pakhtun men had always sought through personal use of arms could now be legitimately attained through association with the state military apparatus.

In the matter of revenues, the central administration gradually moved from a situation in which it parlayed its association with local khans to collect revenues in a cooperative fashion to one in which the central government, as it gained greater and greater power, gradually cut the local khans out of the action, "progressively localizing and pulverizing" factions and gaining the support of small landowners. Throughout this operation, the state had to shift operative cultural assumptions to a sufficient degree for people to be willing to accept centralized authority as a legitimate way to manage political affairs and look to the state instead of their own devices for the fulfillment of their aspirations and the resolution of their problems.

While the first-generation Taliban government was never able to make an effective transition to this model of state-building during its time in power because of its administrative incompetence, the Karzai administration has failed because of its administrative corruption. The origins of the Karzai government, of course, are very different from those of the Taliban. The blueprint for the Afghan state that took power on an interim basis in the spring of 2002 was devised by a group of Afghan exiles and international foreign policy planners in conference rooms in Bonn, Germany, far from Afghanistan. Karzai was chosen by this group to assume the leadership of the new government, in part because of his Qandahari Pushtun tribal pedigree, in part because of his interstitial position—the fact that he had spent most of the preceding twenty-plus years in

Pakistan and Afghanistan, while still developing important political, economic, and media contacts in the West.

In considering Karzai's route to power, it is worthwhile comparing him to another ruler who emerged as top dog after a period of foreign invasion and civil strife—the aforementioned founder of the Afghan state, Amir Abdur Rahman. Abdur Rahman's ultimate success after years of hard struggle came about as a result of tenacity, ruthless political calculation, no small amount of luck, and foreign backing. Karzai's main talents, by contrast, were that he spoke fluent English, was from an influential family and had extensive connections, and had never been taken seriously as a threat by anyone, which had allowed him to float along the surface of the changing political currents of the 1980s and 90s. In this sense, Karzai was not so much the best candidate as the least objectionable, and the very fact that he had never been more than a third-tier figure in any earlier political organization was one of his most important qualifications in gaining the acquiescence of the various parties involved in the creation of the interim government, even if his inexperience and lack of clear political vision have not, in the long run, served him or his country well.

For his part, Karzai seems less insistent on the importance of instituting rational structures of administration and accountability than on consolidating authority in his own hands and undercutting potential rivals, which is, of course, exactly what the Wali of Swat did. The Wali, however, managed affairs far more adeptly than Karzai. For one thing, while the Wali undercut potential rivals in order to strengthen his position in the long term, Karzai's reputation is for buying off his opposition for short-term gain. In this sense, the President's ultimate goal appears to differ from that of the Wali in that he does not appear so much intent on undermining his rivals as on *satisfying* them (or distracting them from the pursuit of their own power) by enabling their access to the for-now-bottomless trough of foreign largesse, in the process transforming his country into what some have taken to calling "Corruptistan."[24]

In an earlier age, Amir Abdur Rahman—who, like Karzai, was dependent on Western patrons for the bulk of his resources—sought to solidify his rule by recruiting this or that tribe or ethnic group to attack some other tribe or ethnic group, sometimes turning a recalcitrant foe into a nominal ally by the fact of their mutual collusion in the destruction of a third group that each saw as inimical to its interests. The hoped-for effect of this strategy was to gain victories over and/or to neutralize enemies, thereby eliminating rivals and buying time for the government to consolidate its power. In fact, many would argue that whatever short-term successes Abdur Rahman might have achieved, the long-term effect of this strategy was to embitter his subjects and deepen their distrust of central authority.

The Taliban, during their period of rule, practiced a variant of Abdur Rahman's confrontational policy, when they used oppressive actions against refractory Hazaras as a means of retaining Pakhtun loyalty to their cause, and while this might have helped sustain support in the Pakhtun heartland, especially around Qandahar, it also exacerbated ethnic tensions in other parts of the country. For his part, Karzai's strategy of divide-and-rule is less focused on the stick and more on the carrot, neutralizing his rivals not through force of arms, but through the seductions of wealth. At the same time, in addressing various Afghan audiences, Karzai is quick to blame the patrons providing the largesse for most of the country's manifold problems, thereby taking another short-term gamble that the US and its allies have no alternative but to keep the spigot open.

One factor previously mentioned in the development of the Swat state was the ability of the rulers to rise above local factional conflicts and create a different sort of army with its own *esprit de corps* that provided tribal Pakhtuns with, in Barth's words, "the outer forms of the influence and status—the "glory"—so eagerly sought," and poorer ranks with a significant source of income and "thus a valued source of commitment to the regime."[25] As of early 2012 and despite the concerted efforts of the US military command, the Afghan government has managed to inject little semblance of "glory" or status for those serving in the military, and salaries for all ranks have been variously too small in size, too sporadically distributed, and too inadequate to prevent police and army from seeking alternate sources through bribes, extortion and other forms of corruption corrosive to the prestige and legitimacy of the government.

The neo-Taliban, on the other hand, have been able to revive with at least some success the claim that they represent, if not tribal honor, Islamic *jihad*. The imperative of responding to the "summons" (*dawat*) of *jihad* was muted by the abuses of the previous generation of Mujahidin, but the legitimacy and urgency of that summons have been revived, at least to some extent and for some audiences, because of the government's mistakes and its continuing dependency on foreign troops for its survival. In this regard, it is also worth pointing out that the "summons" of the neo-Taliban has been substantially aided by the fact that—perhaps counter-intuitively—they have been far more successful than the Karzai government and its Coalition partners in winning the so-called "information war." I say "counter-intuitively" because of the Taliban's notorious rejection of all forms of media technology and the content they contain. The current Taliban, however, have evolved and learned from their defeat, to the point that they consistently outmaneuver the Western allies in their command of cellphones, video imaging, and general management of the press, through which they masterfully "spin" events to their advantage, bringing public attention to civilian casualties caused by Coalition errors and casting their own abuses and violence as legitimate acts by courageous martyrs determined to defeat the enemies of Islam who have occupied their homeland. Thus, while the Taliban twitter, Karzai and the Coalition dither, and many hard-won victories by the Coalition have gone for naught.[26]

State-building depends on revenues, and here again the neo-Taliban have proved more adept than the Karzai government, for while Karzai, like so many of his predecessors, is dependent on foreign aid, much of which is siphoned off by contractors long before it ever reaches Afghanistan, the Taliban have found a relatively reliable source of home-grown income in poppy production, as well as their own sources of covertly provided foreign aid coming from the Arab states and Pakistan. These sources of aid have enabled the neo-Taliban to create a shadow government with a provincial administrative structure, to sustain troops in the field in most of the provinces of Afghanistan and reportedly to provide those troops with better salaries than the salaries of regular Afghan troops, and even to provide some social services. Thus, the Taliban, which in their first incarnation were unable to transform themselves from a social movement into a state, have begun, in the context of guerilla warfare against an ineffective state apparatus, to finally take on the appearance and some of the functions of an effective state.

LESSONS ON GOVERNANCE FROM THE WALI OF SWAT

Finally, one of the most important component of state-building, Swat-style, was the role that rulers played in resolving local level disputes. In recent years, at least in the Pushtun regions of the south and east, the neo-Taliban have managed to interject themselves in local conflicts, through the establishment of impromptu courts, sometimes from the back of a pickup truck, to handle the sorts of local dispute cases that the national government has often proved incapable of handling:

By mid-2008, the Taliban were operating 13 guerrilla law courts throughout the southern part of Afghanistan—a shadowy judiciary that expanded Taliban influence by settling disagreements, hearing civil and criminal matters, and using the provisions of Islamic sharia law and their own Pashtun code to handle everything from land disputes to capital crimes. Local communities often cry out for external mediation in settling local disputes: along with security for person and property, dispute resolution is the public service that tribal and community leaders…most ardently wish for.[27]

While the international community has invested heavily in building the legal system,

local judges, prosecutors, and police are often known for their love of bribes, and locals see them as giving phony "justice" to whoever can pay most handsomely. The Taliban may be cruel—everyone acknowledges this—but they are seen as fair. Too often, local people who are asked "If you had a dispute with a neighbor, to whom would you turn to resolve it?" answer, if they are being honest: "The Taliban".[28]

As Barth demonstrated, dispute resolution was perhaps the single most important building block of state-building in Swat, through which the Badshah and Wali succeeded in making themselves indispensible and local khans irrelevant. In many of the flashpoint provinces of Afghanistan, however, it has been the neo-Taliban that have intervened in this way, more often than the government, which is becoming famous more for creating than for ending disputes.

Conclusion: The Not-so-Great Game

Seeking parallels between Swat and Afghanistan has to be undertaken with considerable caution. The Badshah and Wali rulers built the state in Swat at a time when the British were winding down their involvement in the subcontinent and the people of Swat and other outlying regions were left largely to their own devices. Afghanistan, in contrast, has been embroiled in a three-decade-long war directly involving the most powerful countries and armies in the world. Barth insisted that the developments in Swat had to be understood as an expression of indigenous processes, and one thing we can say with some certainty is that the process of state-building in Afghanistan has been unsuccessful partly because there has been a fundamental inconsistency in whose state this is and whose understanding of how a state should be formed holds sway. Thus, we see the tension between our notion of what it means to "build" a state and Karzai's, first in the priority given by the US and its Coalition partners to "democratic elections," despite the fact that there was little evidence that this was a central concern of the Afghan people and the fact that elections in Afghanistan in the past had not been notably successful at establishing functioning institutions.

261

The notion that democracy and elections were an unambiguously good thing was simply assumed, and at first this assumption seemed to be borne out by the sight of Afghans lining up to go to the polls despite threats of disruption by the Taliban. In the end, however, it is difficult to say what their value has been, particularly given the fact that the winner of the presidential elections held so far has been the man the West put in power in the first place, while a large percentage of the parliamentary deputies elected have come from the ranks of warlords and former Mujahidin who created much of the turmoil in Afghanistan in the first place. The extent to which early popular aspirations for democracy have been dashed can be gauged by the fact that the term "democracy" itself has become a virtual synonym for immorality and license, so much so indeed that politicians have had to come up with neologisms so that they don't have to use the term.

What we can say is that in prioritizing elections, the United States was acting in accord with its own unexamined idea of what a nation-state is, how it should be established, and how legitimacy should be ensured. In this sense, our export of democracy to Afghanistan in the last decade—irrespective of the conditions on the ground and the preparedness or lack thereof among Afghans for democratic elections—can be seen as a logical follow-up to the West's earlier intervention in the decade of the 1980s. Then the West supported and funded political parties it referred to as "freedom fighters," many of whom were fighting not for freedom but for the establishment of a fundamentalist Islamic regime tightly controlled by a political elite—an elite that was little different, except in the specifics of its ideological pronouncements, from the Marxist elite it was trying to overthrow.

It is no surprise that the chief beneficiary of the emphasis on elections has been a product of the 1980s. While Hamid Karzai, in his years working with the Peshawar Mujahidin parties, never associated with the ideological extreme, he does carry the other virus propagated in that era—dependency on foreign aid for which there was no expectation or system of accountability—and that is a disease that, whatever good intents might be behind US and international assistance to Afghanistan, has continually undermined efforts to create a semblance of an independent, functioning state. While the West can bemoan that it does not have a leader more to its liking, the fact remains that Karzai is in an extremely vulnerable and difficult position that is in large part the result of ill-advised efforts by Afghanistan's international patrons.

It might be argued that the West has given billions of dollars in aid to Karzai with little to show for it; the bulk of that aid has gone to a multitude of predatory contractors and far too little has made it to the people who need it most. Beyond the ineffectiveness of much of the aid, Karzai's perilous position owes a great deal to the fact that, like so many Afghan rulers before him, he has few resources of his own to deploy, and so long as he is dependent upon outsiders to provide resources to him, he also provides ammunition to his enemies who will call him (as they have called so many Afghan rulers in the past) a "puppet" of more powerful outside forces. As Barth notes, this was a stigma that the rulers of Swat were largely able to avoid, but Afghan rulers have not been so fortunate. From the foundation of the Afghan state under Abdur Rahman, through the Cold War and the Soviet invasion and the Mujahidin counter-invasion, up to the present, Afghan rulers have had to rely on foreign sources of funding, and this has always been more of a curse than a blessing.

LESSONS ON GOVERNANCE FROM THE WALI OF SWAT

Whether the West believes in him or not, the game is largely Karzai's to win or lose, and if he or any future ruler is ultimately to be successful, he must learn to operate on much the same basis as the Wali of Swat, even if the population with which he must contend is ethnically, linguistically, culturally, economically, and structurally far more diverse. While the Wali proved himself to be a master tactician on the single game board of Swat, he was able to do so because he developed over time a close, personal knowledge of all the players with whom he had to contend and knew first-hand the context and background of virtually every problem with which he was confronted. Karzai, for his part, seems to want to play the game that the Wali in Swat and various earlier Afghan rulers played so well—that of playing factions off against each other, supporting a weaker party in a given region in order to undermine the influence of a stronger and potentially more threatening party, directing resources in ways that build credit in his account, all the while keeping his distance from the foreigners upon whom he depends but whose embrace, if it ever seems too close, can quickly erode the small modicum of legitimacy he still retains. However, after two terms in power and the expenditure of vast resources, Karzai is still more intent upon avoiding antagonizing warlords and buying friends than upon "pulverizing" his corrupt opponents, which buys him time in the short run but in the long run has created a climate of favoritism, non-accountability, and corruption that by now has sunk deep into the bureaucratic and popular culture of the country.

Whether this situation will change and the Afghan state will prove itself capable not just of defeating the Taliban militarily but of competing effectively with them in the political arena remains to be seen. If that is to happen, however, one prerequisite will be that those who are nominally trying to help "stand up" the Afghan government recognize that the process by which this can be done might look very different from the way they imagine it should be done. Ultimately, it must be their game and not the West's. In the end, the state that arises in Afghanistan must be an Afghan state built on Afghan understandings of how political relations are formed and how they are sustained.

NOTES

INTRODUCTION: RETHINKING SWAT: MILITANCY AND MODERNITY ALONG THE AFGHANISTAN-PAKISTAN FRONTIER

1. Throughout this introduction, we use "the Frontier" to refer to a wider arena—part conceptual, part real—that includes bordering regions of Afghanistan-Pakistan, as well as other geographically proximate locales connected to them through patterns of movement and mobility. For a more in-depth discussion see Magnus Marsden and Benjamin D. Hopkins, *Fragments of the Afghan Frontier*, London: Hurst and New York: Columbia University Press, 2012.
2. See Akbar Ahmed, *Millennium and Charisma among Pathans*, London: Routledge & Kegan Paul, 1976; Talal Asad, "Market Model, Class Structure, and Consent: A Reconsideration of Swat Political Organization," *Man* (NS), 7/1, 1972, pp. 74–94; Michael Meeker, "The Twilight of a South Asian Heroic Age: A Rereading of Barth's Study of Swat," *Man* (NS), 15, 1980, pp. 682–701; Charles Lindholm and M. Meeker, "History and the Heroic Pakhtun," *Man*, 16/3, 1981, pp. 463–8. See also Fredrik Barth, *Features of Person and Society in Swat: Collected Essays on Pathans*, London: Routledge & Kegan Paul, 1981.
3. While the legacy of British ethnographic inquiry along the Frontier is well known, a lesser known but important strain of scholarship is that of Scandinavian ethnographers of the region, of whom Barth is the most prominent. Barth himself was a student of the Norwegian linguist Georg Morgenstierne, who authored a number of important works on the region. See for example G. Morgenstierne, *Report on a Linguistic Mission to Northwestern India*, Cambridge, MA: Harvard University Press, 1932.
4. For a self-reflective, autobiographical overview of Barth's intellectual life, see Fredrik Barth, "Overview: Sixty Years in Anthropology," *The Annual Review of Anthropology*, 36, 2007, pp. 1–16.
5. Akbar Ahmed, "Swat in the Eye of the Storm: Interview with Akbar Ahmed," *Anthropology Today*, 25/5, October 2009.
6. We use the terms Pukhtun, Pashtun/Pushtun, and even Pathan interchangeably throughout this introduction. We recognize the importance of naming and the long history and meaning each of these terms carries; our use of these terms is not meant to endorse any single one and is intentional.
7. Scott Atran, *Talking to the Enemy: Violent Extremism, Sacred Values and what it Means to be Human*, London: Allen Lane, 2010, p. 262.

8. This distinguishes the volume from other scholarly works which have been more narrowly focused. See for example Robert Crews and Amin Tarzi, *The Taliban and the Crisis of Afghanistan*, Cambridge, MA: Harvard University Press, 2009.
9. On the policy background to such forms of scholarship and their implications for anthropology, see Jonathan Spencer, "The Perils of Engagement: A Space for Anthropology in the Age of Security?" *Current Anthropology*, 52/2, 2010, pp. 289–9.
10. Thomas Barfield, for example, writes about the importance of hospitality in customary law in Pashtun tribal society as follows: "With a nuanced approach that would have done credit to any Pashtun tribal *jirga*, the assembled clerics told Omar that he must indeed protect his guest, but that a guest should not just cause a host problems, Osama should be asked to leave Afghanistan voluntarily as soon as possible. It is notable that the question Omar tabled was not one of sharia jurisprudence, but rather an issue of Pashtunwali. Very fittingly, the last major policy decision of the Taliban before they were driven from Afghanistan was based on good customary law standards in which religious law provided only window dressing": quoted in Atran, *Talking to the Enemy*, p. 257.
11. See David Edwards, "Counterinsurgency as a Cultural System," *Small Wars Journal*, December 2010. Available at http://smallwarsjournal.com/jrnl/art/counterinsurgency-as-a-cultural-system.
12. For a critical overview of the varying quandaries faced by anthropologists when asked to provide "expert knowledge" to policy makers and public audiences in the context of the War on Terror see Pnina Werbner, "Notes from a Small Place: Anthropological Blues in the Face of Global Terror," *Current Anthropology*, 51/2, 2010, pp. 193–221.
13. Magnus Marsden, *Living Islam: Muslim Religious Experience in Pakistan's North-West Frontier*, Cambridge University Press, 2005.
14. Sensitivities amongst Afghan intellectuals to the depiction of the country in the wider world have long existed. See, for example, Muhammad Aziz and Ahmad Jamal-ud-din, *Afghanistan: a Brief Survey*, Kabul: Dar-Ut-Talif, 1934/1313AH.
15. Charles Lindholm, *Frontier Perspectives: Studies in Comparative Anthropology*, Karachi: Oxford University Press, 1996; Paul Titus, "Honour the Baluch, Buy the Pashtun: Stereotypes, Social Organisation and History in West Pakistan," *Modern Asian Studies*, 32/3, 1998, pp. 689–716; M. Jamil Hanifi, "Editing the Past: Colonial Production of Hegemony Through the Loya Jerga in Afghanistan," *Iranian Studies*, 37/2, 2004, pp. 299–322; Mukulika Banerjee, *The Pathan Unarmed: Opposition and Memory in the Khudai Khidmatgar Movement*, Oxford: James Currey, 2000.
16. See Timothy Mitchell, *Rule of Experts: Egypt, Techno-politics, Modernity*, Berkeley: University of California Press, 2002.
17. See Heonik Kwon, *The Other Cold War*, New York: Columbia University Press, 2010.
18. Talal Asad, *On Suicide Bombing*, New York: Columbia University Press, 2007; D. Richards, *The Savage Frontier: A History of the Anglo-Afghan Wars*, London: Macmillan, 1990.
19. See Antonio Giustozzi, *Koran, Kalashnikov and Laptop: the Neo-Taliban Insurgency in Afghanistan, 2002–2007*, London: Hurst, 2007.
20. It is important to note that Swat was home to several peasant and worker movements in the 1970s, although the nature and significance of these have been under-studied, not

least because the Frontier's modern political history has so often been located within a history that explains the rise of its status as an Islamist "stronghold". On the paucity of scholarly coverage of the left in Pakistan, see Humiera Iqtidar, "Jamaat-I Islami Pakistan: Learning from the Left" in Naveeda Khan (ed.), *Beyond Crisis: Re-evaluating Pakistan*, London: Routledge, 2009; K. Ali, "Strength of the State Meets Strength of the Street: The 1972 Labor Struggle in Karachi" in Naveeda Khan (ed.), *Beyond Crisis: Re-evaluating Pakistan*, London: Routledge, 2009. More generally see S. Toor, *The State of Islam: Culture and Cold War Politics in Pakistan*, London: Pluto Press, 2011.

21. Rory Stewart, *The Places in Between*, London: Mariner Books, 2006.
22. Robert Nichols, *A History of Pashtun Migration*, Karachi: Oxford University Press, 2008; Alessandro Monsutti, *War and Migration: Social Networks and Economic Strategies of the Hazara of Afghanistan*, Patrick Camiller (trans.), London: Routledge, 2005.
23. On anthropological reflections on the political significance of the ways in which "the region" is written and theorised see Richard Fardon, *Localising Strategies: Regional Traditions in Ethnographic Writing*, Edinburgh: Scottish Academic Press, 1990.
24. Charles Lindholm, *The Islamic Middle East: Tradition and Change*, Oxford: Wiley-Blackwell, 2002; Fredrik Barth, *Balinese Worlds*, Chicago: University of Chicago Press, 1993; Akbar Ahmed, *Journey into Islam: The Crisis of Globalization*, Washington: Brookings Institution Press, 2007.
25. For a discussion of the idea of "falling in between" see Willem van Schendel, "Geographies of Knowing, Geographies of Ignorance: Jumping Scale in Southeast Asia," *Environment and Planning D: Society & Space*, 20, 2002, p. 647.
26. For an overview of these debates see Lindholm, *Frontier Perspectives*.
27. Robert Canfield, *Turko-Persia in Historical Perspective*, Cambridge: Cambridge University Press, 1989; Robert Canfield et al., *Ethnicity, Politics and Power in Central Asia: Games Great and Small*, London: Routledge, 2010; M. Djalili, A. Monsutti and A. Neubauer (eds), *Le Monde turco-iranien en question*, Geneva: Karthala, 2008.
28. Michiel Baud and Willem van Schendel, "Toward a Comparative History of Borderlands," *Journal of World History*, 8, 1997; Ainslie Embree (ed.), *Pakistan's Western Borderlands: the Transformations of a Political Order*, New Delhi: Vikas Publishing, 1977.
29. Nile Green, "Diaspora and Sainthood in Afghan History," *Journal of Asian Studies*, 67/1, 2008.
30. See generally Marsden and Hopkins, *Fragments of the Afghan Frontier*.
31. Bruce Grant, "Shrines and Sovereigns: Life, Death and Religion in Rural Azerbaijan," *Comparative Studies in Society and History*, 53/3, 2011, p. 658.
32. Faisal Devji, *Landscapes of the Jihad: Militancy, Morality, Modernity*, London: Hurst, 2005; Faisal Devji, *The Terrorist in Search of Humanity: Militant Islam and Global Politics*, London: Hurst and New York: Columbia University Press, 2008.
33. See for example http://www.khurasansrc.org//index.php/english/
34. See also Madeleine Reeves, "Introduction: Contested Trajectories and a Dynamic Approach to Place," *Central Asian Survey*, 30/304, 2011, pp. 307–330.
35. One young man from Kunduz who had been born and brought up in Peshawar reported to Marsden that he was so appalled by the state of the roads in Afghanistan that he told his mother he would never again visit the country until they were

improved. He now lives and works in Badakhshan, and says he has learned to enjoy and respect the rough nature of road travel in his home country.

36. Shah Mahmoud Hanifi, *Connecting Histories in Afghanistan: Market Relations and State Formation on a Colonial Frontier*, Palo Alto, CA: Stanford University Press, 2011; B.D. Hopkins, *The Making of Modern Afghanistan*, Basingstoke: Palgrave Macmillan, 2008.

37. The notion of the peasant society free of market and capitalist logics was challenged by Jonathan Parry and M. Bloch, *Money and the Morality of Exchange*, Cambridge: Cambridge University Press, 1989.

38. Hopkins, *The Making of Modern Afghanistan*, pp. 11–33.

39. Conrad Schetter, *Ethnizität und ethnische Konflikte in Afghanistan*, Berlin: Dietrich Reimer Verlag, 2003; G. Rasuly-Paleczek, "Alignment Politics and Factionalism among the Uzbeks of northeastern Afghanistan" in R. Canfield and G. Rasuly-Paleczek (eds), *Ethnicity, Politics and Power in Central Asia: Games Great and Small*, London: Routledge, 2011; Thomas Barfield, "Afghanistan is not the Balkans: Central Asian Ethnicity and Its Consequences" in R. Canfield and G. Rasuly-Paleczek (eds), *Ethnicity, Authority and Power in Central Asia*, pp. 95–109.

40. Lisa Wedeen, *Peripheral Visions: Publics, Power and Performance in Yemen*, Chicago: University of Chicago Press, 2007.

41. For a critique of the ways in which the notion of an unruled region as deployed by the US spatializes government in an over simplistic manner and assumes that territory is central to all ways of thinking about order, see Conrad Schetter, "Ungoverned Territories: Eine konzeptuelle Innovation im War on Terror," *Geographica Helvetica*, 65/3, 2010, pp. 181–8.

42. Nir Rosen, "Western Media Fraud in the Middle East," 18 May 2011, http://english.aljazeera.net/indepth/opinion/2011/05/201151882929682601.html. For an example of the type of approach that Rosen challenges see Akbar Ahmed, "Code of the Hills," *Foreign Policy* http://www.foreignpolicy.com/articles/2011/05/06/the_code_of_the_hills

43. Cf. James Ferguson, *Kandahar Cockney: a Tale of Two Worlds*, London and New York: Harper Perennial, 2004.

44. See for example "Afghanistan: The Problem of Pukhtun Alienation," *ICG Asia Reports*, Kabul/Brussels: International Crisis Group, 2003. Compare Stephen Rittenberg, "Continuities in Borderland Politics" in Ainslee Embree (ed.), *Pakistan's Western Borderlands: the Transformations of a Political Order*, New Delhi: Vikas Publishing, 1977, pp. 67–84.

45. David Miliband, "How to end the war in Afghanistan," *New York Review of Books*, 29 April 2010.

46. See generally R.J. González, *American Counterinsurgency: Human Science and the Human Terrain*, Chicago: Prickly Paradigm Press, 2009.

47. Richard Tapper, *The Conflict of Tribe and State in Iran and Afghanistan*, London: St Martins Press, 1983. This key text was reprinted by Routledge in 2011, see Richard Tapper, *Tribe and State in Iran and Afghanistan*, London: Routledge, 2011. For a recent crtitique of the key terms of the debate see David Sneath, *The Headless State: Aristocratic Orders,*

Kinship Society, and Misrepresentations of Nomadic Inner Asia, New York: Columbia University Press, 2007.

48. See for example Hanifi, *Connecting Histories in Afghanistan*; Hopkins, *The Making of Modern Afghanistan*; C.A. Bayly, *Imperial Meridian*, London: Longfellow, 1989.

49. Alessandro Monsutti, "The Impact of War on Social, Political and Economic Organisation in Southern Hazarajat" in R.D. Djalili, A. Monsutti and A. Neubauer (eds), *Le Monde turco-iranien en question*, Geneva: Karthala 2008, pp. 195–209.

50. Sanjay Subrahmanyam, "Iranians Abroad: Intra-Asian Elite Migration and Early Modern State Formation," *The Journal of Asian Studies*, 51/2, 1992, pp. 340–63; Sanjay Subrahmanyam, "Of Imarat and Tijarat: Asian Merchants and State Power in the Western Indian Ocean, 1400 to 1750," *Comparative Studies in Society and History*, 37/4, 2003, pp. 750–80. For a comparative perspective on the role of merchants in the formation of political structures in South India, see M. Mines, *The Warrior Merchants: Textiles, Trade and Territory in South India*, Cambridge: Cambridge University Press, 1984.

51. See Hanifi, *Connecting Histories in Afghanistan*; Hopkins, *The Making of Modern Afghanistan*.

52. For one recent study of Afghan trading practices, see Edwina Thompson, *Trust is the Coin of the Realm: Learning from Afghanistan's Money Men*, Karachi: Oxford University Press, 2011.

53. On the importance of businessmen and merchants to the fashioning of new political dynamics in the Malakand agency of Pakistan's Pakhtunkwha province, see Mohammad Ayub Jan, "Contested and Contextual Identities: Ethnicity, Religion and Identity among the Pakhtuns of Malakand, Pakistan," PhD thesis, University of York, 2010.

54. A. Belasco, *The Cost of Iraq, Afghanistan, and other Global War on Terror Operations since 9/11*, Washington: Congressional Research Service, http://opencrs.com/document/RL33110/2011-03-29/. This amount has no doubt increased substantially since this report was published in March 2011. See also the detailed report, "Costs of War", produced by Brown University, http://costsofwar.org/.

55. See Anatol Lieven, "Insights from the Afghan Field," Open Democracy, October 2010, http://www.opendemocracy.net/anatol-lieven/insights-from-afghan-field.

56. For one recent contribution to the anthropological literature on consipracy, see Harry West and T. Sanders (eds), *Transparency and Conspiracy: Ethnographies of Suspicion in the New World Order*, Durham, NC: Duke University Press, 2003. See also C.A. Bayly, *Empire and Information: Intelligence Gathering and Social Communication in India*, Cambridge: Cambridge University Press, 2000.

57. J. Risen, "US identifies vast mineral riches in Afghanistan," 13 June 2010, *The New York Times*, http://www.nytimes.com/2010/06/14/world/asia/14minerals.html?pagewanted=1.

58. As in other comparable regional contexts defined by political and economic flux, rumours of wealth stored in shrines point to the "threat of spiritual damage" in case of theft and outside intervention: Jane Guyer, *Marginal Gains: Monetary Transactions in Atlantic Africa*, Chicago: University of Chicago Press, 2004, p. 81.

59. Barth, *Political Leadership among Swat Pathans*, p. 2.

NOTES

1. SWAT IN RETROSPECT: CONTINUITIES, TRANSFORMATIONS AND POSSIBILITIES

1. Charles Lindholm, *Generosity and Jealousy: The Swat Pukhtun of Northern Pakistan*, New York: Columbia University Press, 1982.
2. All selections are from *Poems From the Diwan of Khushal Khan Khattack*, D. MacKenzie (trans.), London: Allen and Unwin, 1965.
3. A masterful account of this pattern is provided in Fredrik Barth, *Political Leadership Among Swat Pathans*, London: Athlone Press, 1959. I am grateful and privileged to have had the opportunity to follow in Barth's footsteps.
4. For a detailed account of this election, see Charles Lindholm, "Contemporary Politics in a Tribal Society," *Asian Survey*, 19, 1979, pp. 485–505. An updated version was published in Charles Lindholm, *Frontier Perspectives: Essays in Comparative Anthropology*, Karachi: Oxford University Press, 1996.
5. As I argued in the first article I ever wrote: see Charles Lindholm, "The Segmentary Lineage System: Its Applicability to Pakistan's Political Structure" in Ainslee Embree (ed.), *Pakistan's Western Borderlands*, Durham, NC: Carolina Academic Press, 1977.
6. For a recent ethnography of these urbanized Swati elite, see Amineh Ahmed, *Sorrow and Joy among Muslim Women*, Cambridge University Press, 2006.
7. This is not to say that all these preachers and teachers renounced the values of Pukhunwali. In particular, they shared the Pukhtun insistence on strict female seclusion. Their main preoccupation was the overthrow of the *dullah* system.
8. My wife Cherry's work with village women balanced my all-male perspective. Without her help, I would have never known the female/household side of village life.
9. See *Selections from Rahman Baba*, J. Enevoldsen (trans.), Herning, Denmark: Poul Kristensen, 1977. In recognition of the conciliatory power of his poetry, Rahman Baba's shrine was blown up in 2009 by militants.
10. For an ethno-history of this movement, see Mukulika Banerjee, *The Pathan Unarmed: Opposition and Memory in the North West Frontier*, London: James Currey, 2000.

2. THE ABDALI AFGHANS BETWEEN MULTAN, QANDAHAR AND HERAT IN THE SIXTEENTH AND SEVENTEENTH CENTURIES

1. Christine Noelle, *State and Tribe in Nineteenth-Century Afghanistan: The Reign of Amir Dost Muhammad Khan (1826–1863)*, Richmond: Curzon Press, 1997, p. 230.
2. For a more comprehensive treatment of this question, see Christine Noelle-Karimi, *The Pearl in its Midst, Herat and the Mapping of Khurasan from the Fifteenth to the Nineteenth Centuries*, Vienna: Verlag der Österreichischen Akademie der Wissenschaften, 2012.
3. Francisco Pelsaert, *Jahangir's India: The Remonstratie of Francisco Pelsaert*, Cambridge: W. Heffer & Sons, 1925, pp. 13–15, 31; Comte de Modave, *Voyage en Inde du Comte de Modave, 1773–1776*, Paris: Ecole Française d'Extrême Orient, 1971, pp. 336–7. See also Scott Levi, *The Indian Diaspora in Central Asia and Its Trade, 1550–1900*, Leiden: Brill, 2002; Chetan Singh, *Region and Empire: Panjab in the Seventeenth Century*, Delhi: Oxford University Press, 1991; Niels Steensgaard, "The Route through Qandahar: The Signifi-

NOTES pp. [32–34]

cance of the Overland Trade from India to the West in the Seventeenth Century" in S. Chaudhury and M. Morineau (eds), *Merchants, Companies and Trade: Europe and Asia in the Early Modern Era*, Cambridge University Press, 1999, pp. 55–73.

4. Judasz Tadeusz Krusinski, *The History of the Revolutions of Persia Taken from the Memoirs of Father Krusinski*, New York: Arno Press, 1973, vol. I, pp. 144–5; George Forster, *A Journey from Bengal to England through the Northern Parts of India, Kashmir, Afghanistan and Persia, and into Russia, by the Caspian Sea*, London: R. Fauldner, 1798, vol. 2, pp. 72, 103.

5. Amir Mahmud b. Khvand Amir, *Iran dar ruzgar-i Shah Isma'il-i avval va Shah Tahmasb-i safavi*, Tehran, Bunyad-i Mauqufat-i Duktur Mahmud Afshar Yazdi, 1991, p. 244.

6. Iskandar Beg Munshi, *Tarikh-i 'alamara-yi 'abbasi*, Tehran: Dunya-yi Kitab, 1998, pp. 150, 1161.

7. Muhammad Ibrahim b. Zain al-'Abidin Nasiri, *Dastur-i shahriyaran salaha-yi 1105 ta 1110 h.q.*, Tehran: Bunyad-i Mauqufat-i Duktur Mahmud Afshar Yazdi, 1994, p. 105. Please note that this author refers to "Patans" and "Afghans" as separate categories.

8. Muhammad Tahir Vahid Qazvini, *'Abbasnama*, Arak, 1951, pp. 117, 132–3.

9. Nicolas Sanson, *Estat présent du royaume de Perse*, Paris: Jacques Langlois, 1694, pp. 164–5.

10. Surendranath Sen (ed.), *Indian Travels of Thevenot and Careri*, New Delhi: National Archives of India, 1949, p. 80.

11. Muḥammad Khalil Mar'ashi, *Majma' al-tavarikh dar tarikh-i inqiraz-i ṣafaviya va vaqayi'-i ba'd ta sal-i 1207 hijri qamari (1207/1792)*, 'Abbas Iqbal (ed.), 2nd ed., Tehran, 1362/ 1983; Christine Noelle-Karimi, "Historiography xi. Afghanistan," *Encyclopaedia Iranica*, vol. 12, New York: Encyclopaedia Iranica Foundation, 2004, p. 391.

12. Bernhard Dorn, *History of the Afghans. Translated from the Persian of Neamet Ullah*, 2nd ed., London: Susil Gupta, 1965, Part I, pp. 37–8. For an in-depth discussion of the *Tarikh-i Khan Jahani* and its role in shaping Afghan identity in the Indian setting, see Nile Green, "Tribe, Diaspora, and Sainthood in Afghan History," *The Journal of Asian Studies*, 67/1, 2008, pp. 171–211.

13. Imam al-Din al-Husaini, *Tarikh-i ḥusainshahi* or *Tavarikh-i ahmadshahi* (1213/1798), National Archives Kabul, pp. 5–7. See also 'Aziz al-Dīn Vakili Fofalzai, *Tīmūr Shāh Durrānī*, repr. Kabul: Anjuman-i Tarikh, 1967, pp. 303–4.

14. Unfortunately, the original version of *Tadhkirat al-muluk-i 'alisha'n* was not at my disposal. The following account is based on the information reproduced by Umar Kamal Khan in English and 'Ashiq Muhammad Khan Durrani in Urdu: Umar Kamal Khan, *Rise of the Saddozais and Emancipation of Afghans (1638–1747)*, Multan: Bazm-i Saqafat, 1999; 'Ashiq Muhammad Khan Durrani, *Tarikh-i Afghanistan*, Lahore: Sang-i-Meel, 1999.

15. Sultan Muhammad b. Musa Durrani Barakzai, *Tarikh-i sultani*, Bombay: Karkhana-yi Muhammadi, 1881, pp. 8–52. Aside from the *Tarikh-i Firishta*, Sultan Muhammad Khan alternately names the *Makhzan-i afghaniyya* and the *Mirat-i afaghina* by Navvab Khan Jahan Lodi as his source for Pashtun genealogy and the developments from the "rise of the sun of Islam to the leadership of Lodis and Surs" (pp. 8, 52). Both titles refer to the *Tarikh-i Khan Jahani*, which was written under the auspices of Khan Jahan Lodi (d. 1040/1631) (Green, "Tribe, Diaspora, and Sainthood", pp. 183, 200–1). The impact of

the Indian discourse is also apparent from the fact that Sultan Muhammad refers to Qais 'Abd al-Rashid as "Pathan" (Sultan Muhammad, *Tarikh-i sultani*, p. 52).

16. Mar'ashi, *Majma' al-tavarikh*, pp. 2–3.
17. Ibid., p. 19.
18. Kamal Khan, *Rise of the Saddozais*, pp. 52–5.
19. Ibid., pp. 64–6. Also see Humaira Dasti, *Multan, a Province of the Mughal Empire*, Karachi: Royal Book Company, 1998, pp. 127–9; Durrani, *Tarikh-i Afghanistan*, p. 12; Riazul Islam, *Indo-Persian Relations: A Study of the Political and Diplomatic Relations between the Mughul Empire and Iran*, Tehran: Iranian Culture Foundation, 1979, vol. I, p. 251.
20. Kamal Khan, *Rise of the Saddozais*, p. 75. See also Qazvini, *'Abbasnama*, pp. 128–9; Sir Jadunath Sarkar, *History of Aurangzib*, Bombay: Orient Longman, 1973, pp. 74–5.
21. Kamal Khan, *Rise of the Saddozais*, pp. 69–92. See also Dasti, *Multan, a Province*, pp. 148–9; Durrani, *Tarikh-i Afghanistan*, p. 13. The notion of a close relationship between Khudadad Khan and the Safavid governor of Qandahar is not corroborated by the Safavid sources.
22. Durrani, *Tarikh-i Afghanistan*, p. 13. Also see Muhammad Hayat Khan, *Hayat-i afghani*, Lahore, 1867, pp. 139–41. According to some sources, Shah Husain Khan also received a *jagir* in Sialkot from Shah Jahan (*Gazetteer of the Mooltan District, 1883–84*, Lahore: Punjab Government, 1884, p. 26; Kamal Khan, *Rise of the Saddozais*, p. 78).
23. Dasti, *Multan, a Province*, pp. 162–3. Also see Ahmad Nabi Khan, *Multan: History and Architecture*, Islamabad: Institute of Islamic, Culture & Civilization, 1983, p. 112.
24. Kamal Khan, *Rise of the Saddozais*, p. 141.
25. Durrani, *Tarikh-i Afghanistan*, pp. 16–17; Kamal Khan, *Rise of the Saddozais*, pp. 102–7.
26. Mar'ashi, *Majma' al-tavarikh*, p. 19. According to the *Tadhkirat al-muluk-i alishan*, Hayat Khan was accompanied by 500 adherents (Kamal Khan, *Rise of the Saddozais*, pp. 108, 111–13).
27. Dasti, *Multan, a Province*, pp. 168–9; Kamal Khan, *Rise of the Saddozais*, p. 109; Nabi Khan, *Multan: History and Architecture*, p. 112.
28. Dasti, *Multan, a Province*, pp. 163, 248.
29. Jos Gommans, *The Rise of the Indo-Afghan Empire c. 1710–1780*, Leiden: E.J. Brill, 1995, p. 35.
30. Dasti, *Multan, a Province*, pp. 197; Kamal Khan, *Rise of the Saddozais*, p. 108.
31. Another case in point are the Khvishgi Afghans, who accompanied Babur to India and received *jagirs* including expansive grazing areas in Qasur in exchange for their military services under the Mughals (Muhammad Shafi, "An Afghan Colony at Qasur," *Islamic Culture* 3, 3, 1929, pp. 454–5). Also see Gommans, *The Rise of the Indo-Afghan Empire*, pp. 109–10.
32. Noelle, *State and Tribe*, p. 282.

3. A HISTORY OF THE HINDUSTANI "FANATICS" ON THE FRONTIER

1. See for example "Pakistan-Taliban deal: Islamic law for peace in Swat Valley," *Christian Science Monitor*, 16 February 2009, seen at: http://www.csmonitor.com/2009/0216/p99s01-duts.html, accessed 3 March 2009; "Pakistan makes a Taliban truce, creating a

haven," *New York Times,* 17 February 2009, seen at: http://www.nytimes.com/2009/02/17/world/asia/17pstan.html, accessed 3 March 2009.

2. See for instance "Taleban's stranglehold brings fear to Swat," *BBC,* seen at: http://news.bbc.co.uk/1/hi/world/south_asia/7851790.stm, accessed 3 March 2009.

3. D.S. Richards, *The Savage Frontier: A History of the Anglo-Afghan Wars,* London: Macmillan, 1990.

4. See Robert Nichols' chapter in this volume.

5. The worst example drawing a direct line between the Frontier Fanatics and today's terrorists is C. Allen, *God's Terrorists: The Wahabi Cult and the Hidden Roots of Modern Jihad,* London: Abacus, 2006.

6. "Swat," *Encyclopaedia of Islam,* 2nd edn. Seen at: http://www.brillonline.nl/subscriber/uid=1368/entry?result_number=1&entry=islam_SIM-7229&search_text=swat#hit, accessed 4 March 2009.

7. See for example F. Barth, *Political Leadership among Swat Pathans,* London: Athlone Press, 1959.

8. For a history of the Swat state, see Sultan-i-Rome, *The Swat State,* Karachi: Oxford University Press, 2008.

9. Maulana Fazlullah's core group of fighters are reported to be Uzbek members of the Islamic Movement of Uzbekistan. See Miriam Abou Zahab's essay in this volume.

10. For a good recent treatment of Sayyid Ahmed and his ideas, see A. Jalal, *Partisans of Allah: Jihad in South Asia,* New Delhi: Permanent Black, 2008, Chapter 2.

11. A.H. Mason and W.H. Paget, *A Record of the Expeditions against the North-West Frontier Tribes, since the Annexation of the Punjab,* London: Whiting & Co. Limited, 1884, p. 82.

12. Melvill to C. Allen, Officiating Secretary of the Government of India, 15 October 1852, *Foreign Department, Political,* No. 87, National Archives of India (henceforth NAI), New Delhi.

13. For a detailed statement about the composition and state of the colony's recruits, based on the testimony of three captured Fanatics, see Lylle to Mackeson, 24 March 1853, *Foreign Department, Secret,* No. 116, NAI, New Delhi. This connection would be at the centre of the so-called "Wahabi" trials of the 1860s and 1870s.

14. See for example the Copy of a letter from Commissioner and Superintendent of Peshawur Division to Secretary to Government of Punjab, No. 165 dated 10 September 1863, December 1863, *Foreign Department, Political A,* No. 150, NAI, New Delhi.

15. J. R. Carnac to W. T. Tucker, Officiating Magistrate of Patna, 15 October 1852, *Foreign Department, Political,* No. 86, NAI, New Delhi.

16. Mackeson to Melvill, 28 January 1853, *Foreign Department, Secret,* No. 163, NAI, New Delhi.

17. The breakaway faction established themselves at a place called Mangal Thana. The faction, led by Maulvi Inayat Ali, included roughly 150 of the 500 Hindustanis present in Sitana, along with 30–40 Company Sepoys of the 55th Native Infantry who had mutinied at Rawalpindi in 1857. This internal strife and fracturing would become a central feature of the *mujahidin*'s subsequent history. Edwardes to R. Temple, 31 October 1856, *Foreign Department, Secret,* No. 5, NAI, New Delhi. For a description of their site, see also Edwardes to H. B. Urmston, 31 October 1856, *Foreign Department, Secret,*

No. 5, NAI, New Delhi; Mason and Paget, *A Record of the Expeditions against the North-West Frontier Tribes, since the Annexation of the Punjab*, p. 86.
18. Ibid., p. 95. Amongst the dead the British were reported to have found down-country Indians from Rampur and Bengal. "Brief chronology of the Hindustani Fanatics, October 1915," *Foreign & Political Department, Frontier B*, No. 83, Enclosure, NAI, New Delhi.
19. For a discussion of the bureaucratic manipulation of the "man on the spot" which led to this expedition, see M.D. Kasprowicz, "1857 and the Fear of Muslim Rebellion on India's North-West Frontier," *Small Wars and Insurgencies*, 8/2, 1997.
20. See for instance Maj. Hugh James, Commissioner and Superintendent of Peshawar Division, to R.H. Davies, Secretary to Government, Punjab, March 1864, *Foreign Department, Political A*, No. 15, NAI, New Delhi.
21. Taylor to H.R. James, March 1864, *Foreign Department, Political A*, No. 164, NAI, New Delhi.
22. Sir Charles Wood, the Secretary of State for India, was outspoken in his criticism of the Ambela campaign. He wrote to John Lawrence, the Viceroy, that "[W]e never have seen any account of the reasons for doing anything beyond a general statement of necessity of expelling the Sitana fanatics and compelling the tribes to exclude them from our frontier.... Montgomery [Lt. Gov. of Punjab] speaks of a general Mahommedan move against us as a danger looming in the distance, and the course we have taken seems well calculated to accelerate if not to produce it." Secretary of State to Viceroy, 23 December 1863, *Wood Papers*, No. f86, India Office Records (henceforth IOR), London, Mss. Eur.F/78/LB15.
23. The Fanatics also took up arms in 1891, although according to the British, this was done apparently under duress. "After the lesson taught them at Towarra in the former expedition of 1888, although they were bound by the exigencies of their peculiar position as a band of 'irreconcileables' settled among foreigners to take the lead again in opposing the expedition in 1891, they did not dare another open attack by daylight, but resorted to an attempt to effect a night surprise." "Report on the Punjab Frontier Administration for the Year 1891-2, 16 July 1892," *Punjab Administration Reports*, IOR, London, V/10/369B. See also Cunningham to Maj. Gen. W.K. Elles, Commanding Hazara Field Force, September 1891, *Foreign Department, Frontier A*, No. 189, NAI, New Delhi; Note by the Private Secretary to His Honour the Lieutenant-Governor of the Punjab, dated 10 July 1893, *Foreign Department*, No. 494, NAI, New Delhi.
24. Peter Hardy, *The Muslims of British India*, Cambridge: Cambridge University Press, 1972, p. 69.
25. Notes 1870, *Mayo Papers*, No. 109/83, Cambridge University Library (henceforth CUL), Cambridge, Add.Ms.7490.
26. C.U. Aitchison, the Foreign Secretary to the Government of India, wrote, "[t]he very interest that we exhibit in trying to suppress the colony, helps, to my thinking, to keep up a sort of enthusiasm for them among certain classes of our own subjects. They are looked upon as martyrs, men suffering for religion at the hands of the infidel. It therefore becomes meritorious to keep them. The greater the danger incurred, the greater the merit." Aitchison to Burne, 12 August 1870, Mayo Papers, CUL, Add. Ms.7490, ff. 109/84.

27. Extract translation from a report by Raja Jehandad Khan, K. B., Extra Assistant Commissioner, Hazara, May 1883, *Foreign Department, Political*, No. 37, NAI, New Delhi.
28. Extract from Abstract of Intelligence, Punjab Police, dated 14 April 1883, No. 15, May 1883, *Foreign Department, Secret E*, No. 30–7, K.W., NAI, New Delhi.
29. The Assistant Commissioner, Mardan, to the Deputy Commissioner, Peshawar, May 1883, *Foreign Department, Secret E*, No. 35, NAI, New Delhi.
30. Translation of a letter from Nawab Muhammad Akram Khan of Amb, to the Commissioner and Superintendent, Peshawar Division, dated 20 January 1884, June 1884, *Foreign Department, A Political E*, No. 185, NAI, New Delhi. See also Extract from Abstract of Intelligence, Punjab Police, dated 14 April 1883, No. 15, NAI, New Delhi.
31. Maulvi Abdullah was approached by the Mian Gul, son of the then late Akhund of Swat, to support him against the British. "The Maulvi is said to have replied that he was unable to put much trust in the people of Swat and Bajour, who might, if the Hindustani fanatics joined them, suddenly make peace and leave them (the Hindustanis) to bear the brunt of the fight, but if Swat and Bajaur really intended to fight, of course he and his party would join." Peshawar Confidential Diary, No. 6, dated 29 March 1888, April 1888, *Foreign Department, Secret F*, No. 73, NAI, New Delhi.
32. "Brief chronology of the Hindustani Fanatics."
33. Dean to Capt. A. H. McMahon, July 1899, *Foreign Department, Frontier A*, No. 89–90, K.W., NAI, New Delhi.
34. They apparently ignored an entreaty from the Mulla of Hadda, one of the leaders of the revolt. Peshawar Confidential Diary No. 19(a), dated 8 October 1897, November 1897, *Foreign Department, Secret F*, No. 745, NAI, New Delhi.
35. "Brief chronology of the Hindustani Fanatics."
36. C. Bunbury to F. D. Cunningham, November 1895, *Foreign Department, Secret F*, No. 98–9, K.W. 2, NAI, New Delhi.
37. "Brief chronology of the Hindustani Fanatics." There were various estimates of the strength of the colony during this period, ranging from roughly 500 to upwards of 1,000 fighting men. In 1898, it was reported they numbered 900 and were "not happy." Diary of the Political Agent for Dir, Swat and Chitral for the week ending 14 November 1897, January 1898, *Foreign Department, Secret F*, No. 190, NAI, New Delhi.
38. The Commissioner and Superintendent of the Peshawar Division to the Chief Secretary to the Government of the Punjab, July 1899, *Foreign Department, Frontier A*, No. 98, NAI, New Delhi.
39. "Administration report of the Northwest Frontier Province from 9 November 1901 to 31 March 1903," 1903, *NWFP Administration Reports*, IOR, London, V/10/370.
40. By 1912, their numbers were estimated at 800 fighting men and over 1,200 women and children. Extract from North-West Frontier Provincial Diary No. 15 for the week ending 10 April 1915, October 1915, *Foreign & Political Department, Frontier B*, No. 81–3, NAI, New Delhi.
41. See Chief Commissioner, NWFP, to the Foreign Secretary to the Government of India in the Foreign and Political Department, January 1916, *Foreign & Political Department, Secret F*, No. 53, NAI, New Delhi.
42. Extract from North-West Frontier Provincial Diary No. 15 for the week ending 10 April 1915.

43. Chief Commissioner, NWFP, to the Secretary to the Government of India in the Foreign Department, October 1915, *Foreign & Political Department, Frontier B*, No. 81–3, NAI, New Delhi.
44. Most of these students eventually went on to Kabul, where they were received by the Amir. Ibid.
45. Roos-Keppel to the Viceroy, 13 February 1915, *Roos-Keppel Papers*, IOR, London, Mss. Eur.D/613/1.
46. Chief Commissioner, NWFP, to the Secretary to the Government of India in the Foreign and Political Department, January 1916, *Foreign Department, Secret F*, No. 279, NAI, New Delhi.
47. Baha, "The Activities of the Mujahidin 1900–1936," pp. 104–05. See also "Afghanistan: the Silk Letter Case, 1916–18", *Political & Secret*, IOR, London, L/PS/10/633.
48. Lt. Col. Roos-Keppel, Chief Commissioner, NWFP, to A.H. Grant, Foreign Secretary to GOI, 9 May 1917, *Political & Secret*, No. P2405/1917, IOR, London, L/PS/11/111.
49. For a reprint of his letter to Sir George Roos-Keppel, Chief Commissioner of the North-West Frontier Province, see Baha, "The Activities of the Mujahidin 1900–1936," pp. 156–9.
50. Translation of a letter from Niamatullah, Amir-i-Mujahidin to the Nawab of Amb dated Asmast, the 22nd Rajab 1333 Hijri (corresponding to 15 May 1917), 15 May 1917, *Political & Secret*, No. P2647/1917, IOR, London, L/PS/11/111.
51. For a copy of the settlement, see Lt. Col. Sir George Roos-Keppel, Chief Commissioner of the NWFP, to the Foreign Secretary to the GoI, 1917, *Political & Secret*, No. P1395/1918, IOR, London, L/PS/11/111.
52. Cleveland to Grant, 1917, *Political & Secret*, No. P3036/1917, IOR, London, L/PS/11/111.
53. One of the conditions of the peace settlement between Niamatullah and the British was the recall of the Chamarkand *mujahidin*. This was not the only other outpost of the Hindustani Fanatics; they also had a small colony in Tirah which sought to stir up trouble amongst the Afridis, as well as a colony established at Makin in Waziristan to cause trouble. North-West Frontier Province Intelligence Bureau Diary No. 21 for the period ending 19 November, 15 December 1926, *Political & Secret*, No. P4335, IOR, London, L/PS/10/1137; Chief Commissioner, NWFP, to the Foreign Secretary to the Government of India, 1923, *Foreign & Political Department, Frontier*, No. 22, NAI, New Delhi; Mujahidin: Hindustani Fanatic Colony in Waziristan, 1930, *Foreign & Political Department, Frontier*, No. 14-F, NAI, New Delhi. As late as 1946, internal rifts within the *mujahidin* led some to establish a breakaway colony "at Dandar (Surai-Amazai) on the south bank of the Chamla River, about 1 1/2 miles south west of Asmas." Weekly summary no. 30, dated Peshawar the 27 July 1946, *Political & Secret*, No. 5616, IOR, London, L/PS/12/3200.
54. Chief Commissioner, NWFP, to the Foreign Secretary to the Government of India, January 1916, *Foreign & Political Department, Secret F*, No. 39, NAI, New Delhi.
55. Chamarkand was a colony in Bajuar on the Afghan border. The first mention of the *mujahidin*'s presence there, though not by name, is in November 1916 when it was estimated there were 290 *mujahidin* present. Extract of the North-West Frontier Pro-

vincial Diary No. 45, for the week ending 4 November 1916, April 1917, *Foreign & Political Department, Secret—Frontier*, No. 137, Notes, NAI, New Delhi.

56. It was thought these weapons passed through Asmas. The British thought it unlikely that "established members" of the colony were either active in or profiting from such activity, and believed that "a considerable number of them appear to be seriously thinking of abandoning the role of 'Mujahidin' and seeking opportunities to settle down in British territory." Supplement to the Intelligence Bureau Dairy No. 8 for the week ending 21 January 1924, *Foreign & Political Department, Frontier*, No. 33, Notes NAI, New Delhi.

57. North-West Frontier Province Intelligence Bureau Diary No. 23 for the week ending 15 June 1922, *Political & Secret*, No. P207/1923(V), IOR, London, L/PS/11/111. For a description of the various *mujahidin* factions along the Frontier, see North West Frontier Province Intelligence Bureau Diary No. 12 for week ending 23 March 1922, *Political & Secret*, No. P207/1923(IV), IOR, London, L/PS/11/111.

58. Copy of a report dated 6 July 1925 by the Officer in Charge, Intelligence Bureau, North-West Frontier Province, Peshawar, *Political & Secret*, No. P3035/1925, IOR, London, L/PS/11/111/P4261/1916. See also North-West Frontier Province, Intelligence Bureau, Diary No. 4, for the period ending 18 February, 28 March 1928, *Political & Secret*, No. P1455, IOR, London, L/PS/10/1137.

59. Supplement to North-West Frontier Province Intelligence Bureau Diary No. 11 for the period ending 7 May, 2 June 1925, *Political & Secret*, No. P1732, IOR, London, L/PS/10/1137. See also Extract from the North West Frontier Province Intelligence Bureau diary No. 42, for the period ending 28 October 1931, *Foreign & Political Department, Frontier*, No. 584-F, NAI, New Delhi. The Soviet legation was said to have attempted to supply the *mujahidin* colony in Waziristan with £300 in gold in 1927, which was intercepted by Afghan authorities. North-West Frontier Province Intelligence Bureau, Diary No. 23 for the period ending 20 November, 28 December 1928, *Political & Secret*, No. P6967, IOR, London, L/PS/10/1137.

60. On British efforts to interfere with attempts by the Chamarkand *mujahidin* to collect subscriptions in British India, see North-West Frontier Province Intelligence Bureau Diary No. 18 for the period ending 24 September, 20 October 1926, *Political & Secret*, No. P3593, IOR, London, L/PS/10/1137.

61. The Fanatics were promised Rs. 10,000 by the Afghan Amir. Supplement to North-West Frontier Province Intelligence Bureau Diary No. 1 for the period ending 7 January 1926, 10 February 1926, *Political & Secret*, No. P498, IOR, London, L/PS/10/1137. Separately, the Afghan Interior Minister, Abdul Azizi Khan, gave them Rs. 24,000. Note, 1927, *Foreign & Political Department, Frontier*, No. 558-F, NAI, New Delhi. On the suspension of the Afghans' regular subsidy, see Weekly summary no. 13, dated Peshawar the 31 March 1945, *Political & Secret*, No. 1826, IOR, London, L/PS/12/3199.

62. North-West Frontier Province, Intelligence Bureau, Diary No. 8, for the period ending 11 April, 23 May 1928, *Political & Secret*, No. P2591, IOR, London, L/PS/10/1137.

63. Weekly summary no. 9, dated Peshawar 3 March 1941, *Political & Secret*, No. 2185, IOR, London, L/PS/12/3195.

64. Copy of a report dated 6 July 1925 by the Officer in Charge, Intelligence Bureau, North-West Frontier Province, Peshawar.

65. Supplement to the North-West Frontier Province Intelligence Bureau Diary No. 8 for the week ending 26 March, 16 April 1925, *Political & Secret*, No. P1431, IOR, London, L/PS/10/1137.
66. Supplement to North-West Frontier Province Intelligence Bureau Diary No. 30 for the period ending 10 December, 12 January 1926, *Political & Secret*, No. P140, IOR, London, L/PS/10/1137.
67. Secret note by Intelligence Bureau on the proposal contained in Political Agent, Malakand's Confidential Letter No. 105, dated 30 March 1925, *Foreign & Political Department, Frontier*, No. 86, NAI, New Delhi.
68. Supplement to North-West Frontier Province Intelligence Bureau Diary No. 7 for the period ending 26 March 1926, *Political & Secret*, No. P1455/26, IOR, London, L/PS/11/111.
69. North-West Frontier Province Intelligence Bureau Diary No. 26 for the period ending 29 October, 30 November 1927, *Political & Secret*, No. P5460, IOR, London, L/PS/10/1137. These numbers remained fairly consistent, though the distribution with regard to the *mujahidin*'s origins changed. In 1928, it was reported the colony numbered forty-five, with twenty-nine Punjabis and sixteen Bengalis: North-West Frontier Province Intelligence Bureau, Diary No. 21 for the period ending 19 October, 21 November 1928, *Political & Secret*, No. P6193, IOR, London, L/PS/10/1137. In 1936, the colony was reported to have between thirty and sixty occupants: Weekly summary no. 19, dated Peshawar, the 11 May, 1936 *Political & Secret*, No. P.Z.3942, IOR, London, L/PS/12/3192, Weekly summary no. 11, dated Peshawar, the 16 March, 20 April 1936, *Political & Secret*, No. P.Z.2492, IOR, London, L/PS/12/3192.
70. One was in Swat and the other in Bajaur. Minute: NW Frontier—The Chamarkand and Samasta colonies, 23 April 1923, *Political & Secret*, No. 1422, IOR, London, L/PS/11/111; North West Frontier Province Intelligence Bureau Diary No. 12 for week ending 23 March 1922, March 1922, 1923, *Political & Secret*, No. P207/1923(IV), IOR, London, L/PS/11/111/P4261/1916. Schools appear to have been a perennial concern of the *mujahidin*. As late as 1947, they were soliciting Afghan contributions for a school in the Chamarkand colony itself. Weekly summary no. 9, dated Peshawar, 1 March 1947, *Political & Secret* No. 5914, IOR, London, L/PS/12/3201.
71. Supplement to North-West Frontier Province Intelligence Bureau Diary No. 11 for the period ending 7 May.
72. Weekly summary no. 18, dated Peshawar the 29 April 1940, *Political & Secret*, No. P.Z.2909, IOR, London, L/PS/12/3194.
73. North-West Frontier Province Intelligence Bureau Diary No. 18 for the period ending 24 September.
74. The issue for 10 December 1927 held up the Albanian fight for independence as a model to be emulated by the Frontier tribesmen. North-West Frontier Province, Intelligence Bureau, Diary No. 7, for the period ending 31 March, 2 May 1928, *Political & Secret*, No. P2129, IOR, London, L/PS/10/1137.
75. Extract from North-West Frontier Province Intelligence Bureau Diary No. 40 for the week ending 1 November 1923, *Foreign & Political Department, Frontier*, No. 11, Notes, NAI, New Delhi.

NOTES pp. [47–52]

76. Sir John Maffey, Chief Commissioner, NWFP, to the Secretary to the Government of India in the Foreign and Political Department, 25 April 1923, *Political & Secret*, No. P3044/1923, IOR, London, L/PS/11/111.
77. Baha, "The Activities of the Mujahidin 1900–1936," pp. 112–13.
78. Weekly summary no. 36, dated Peshawar, the 7 September 1942, *Political & Secret*, No. 6465, IOR, London, L/PS/12/3196.
79. Weekly summary no. 17, dated Peshawar, the 22 April 1940, *Political & Secret*, No. 2751, IOR, London, L/PS/12/3194.
80. Weekly summary no. 14, dated Peshawar the 5 March 1947, *Political & Secret*, No. 6331, IOR, London, L/PS/12/3201.
81. Weekly summary no. 25, dated Peshawar the 21 June 1947, *Political & Secret*, No. 7282, IOR, London, L/PS/12/3201.
82. Rauf, "The British Empire and the Mujahidin Movement in the N.W.F.P., 1914–1934," p. 420, n. 42.

4. *KASHARS* AGAINST *MASHARS: JIHAD* AND SOCIAL CHANGE IN THE FATA

1. I am indebted to the editors and to Hugh Beattie for their comments and advice on an earlier draft of this chapter.
2. "There is evidence that junior, or depressed, lineages saw employment abroad and the economic opportunities at home as an avenue of escape from their positions in society": Akbar S. Ahmad, *Resistance and Control in Pakistan*, Cambridge: Cambridge University Press, 1991, p. 97.
3. For instance, in 2010 there were about 350,000 Pakistani Pashtuns in Dubai alone, more than half of them belonging to the FATA.
4. For an analysis of social change among Pashtuns, see Inam ur Rahim and Alain Viaro, *Swat: An Afghan Society in Pakistan: Urbanisation and Change in a Tribal Environment*, Karachi: City Press, 2002. Although the local dynamics in Swat and Waziristan are very different, similar trends can be observed in the transformation of society since the mid-1970s.
5. "From the regime of General Zia ul Haq onward, the state started to fund the mullas directly, giving them financial independence. Over the years the mullas took on an enhanced political role in the tribal community and gradually became more powerful than the malik. With new resources and status, the local religious figures were able to emerge." Marvin G. Weinbaum, *Counterterrorism, Regional Security, and Pakistan's Afghan Frontier*, Testimony to the U.S. House of Representatives Armed Services Committee, Washington DC, 10 October 2007.
6. This paper draws from my research in the region since the 1980s, from interviews with residents from Waziristan and from written material on the FATA. Owing to the inaccessibility of the field since the start of military operations, interviews took place in other parts of Pakistan as well as in Europe and the USA.
7. In South Waziristan this refers to Suleimankhel and Dotani.
8. A *mashar* has influence and command over the tribe and is member of the *jirga*. Although generally speaking *mashar* connotes *spin giray* (white beard), a *mashar* may be young.

9. *Traditional Structures in Local Governance for Local Development: A Case Study of Pakhtuns Residing in NWFP & FATA, Pakistan*, World Bank, 2004.
10. The misuse of the Afghanistan Transit Trade (ATT) by the tribals and Afghan traders created a new class of businessmen in the FATA. Moreover, from the 1980s transport became a major source of income for the tribals.
11. The Wazir resisted the demarcation of the Durand Line in 1893, which brought Waziristan, with the exception of Birmal, under the British sphere of influence. A *lashkar* led by the famous Mulla Powindah, a Shabikhel Mehsud who assumed the title of Badshah-e Taliban, attacked the British army camp in Wana. A punitive operation was launched and in 1895 Political Agents were posted to Miranshah and Wana; North Waziristan and South Waziristan were thus constituted.
12. J.M. Ewart, *Story of the North West Frontier Province*, Lahore: Sang-e-Meel, 2000 (reprint of the 1929 edition), p. 53.
13. For details about the FATA reform plan and the role of the Political Agent and the law enforcement system, see Pervaiz Iqbal Cheema and Maqsudul Hasan Nuri (eds), *Tribal Areas of Pakistan: Challenges and Responses*, Islamabad: Policy Research Institute/Hanns Seidel Foundation, 2005.
14. The beneficiaries were mostly the children of the *malik*s who are settled in cities outside the FATA.
15. Pashtuns started migrating in great numbers to the Gulf from the mid-1970s.
16. Before 1996, a college of about 35,000 *malik*s and other tribal elders would cast their votes on behalf of the population.
17. Cheema and Noori, *Tribal Areas of Pakistan*.
18. See for details *Pakistan: Countering Militancy in FATA*, International Crisis Group, 21 October 2009.
19. The Frontier Crimes Regulation was promulgated in 1901 by the colonial administration. For a detailed study of the FCR, see Khalid Aziz, *The Reform of the Frontier Crimes Regulations (FCR) and Administration of the Tribal Areas of Pakistan*, 22 November 2005, http://www.khalidaziz.com/art_detail.php?aid=51.
20. For detailed statistics on the FATA, see http://www.nwfpbos.sdnpk.org/fds/2000/6.htm. Official estimations for 2002 gave a figure of 401,000 for North Waziristan and 467,000 for South Waziristan.
21. "Over 100, 000 uprooted by military operations in Waziristan: UN," *The News*, 12 September 2009.
22. Apart from the conflicts with the local population (particularly in Karachi and Dera Ismail Khan), urbanisation is a disorienting process. Many tribals who took shelter in the settled areas or in Karachi will probably never go back to South Waziristan, particularly because there is no compensation process for the people who suffered "collateral damage". They risk lapsing into chronic poverty and their sense of deprivation is likely to increase.
23. Kaniguram suffered large-scale destruction during the military operations in 2009. There is a real risk that the language (Urmuri) and the culture of the displaced Burki will disappear as their children will speak only Pashto.
24. The Wazir and Mehsud claim to have originated from a common ancestor: Wazir son

of Suleiman who had three sons, Musa, Mubarik and Mahmud. Musa, known as Darwesh because of his religious piety, is the ancestor of the Wazir and Mahmud of the Mehsud. For years, the Mehsud were a Wazir sub-tribe and they were sometimes referred to as the Wazir Mehsud in colonial literature.

25. Just like the Mehsud, the Zalikhel are famous for their resistance against the British. They were instrumental in Nadir Shah's success in capturing Kabul in 1929, they were used to crush a rebellion in Kohistan in 1930, and they laid siege to Khost in 1933 when the partisans of Amanullah wanted to use them to get rid of Nadir. The monthly stipends they received from Kabul government were stopped after 1992 and restored by President Karzai in 2006. Iqbal Khattak, "Karzai restores monthly stipend to FATA elders," *Daily Times*, 26 September 2006. Wazir and Mehsud were part of a tribal *laskhar* which entered Kashmir in 1948; the memory of *jihad* in Kashmir is very strong among them, and they are also proud of their support to the Pakistan military in the 1965 war with India.

26. According to the 1981 census, the Mehsud numbered 234,000 and the Wazir 61,000.

27. Mehsud are settled in East and Central Waziristan and Wazir in West and South. Wana has a Wazir majority.

28. When the Hindu traders left Tank after Partition in 1947, most of their shops were taken over by Mehsud.

29. F.W. Johnston, "Notes on Wana (Recorded in 1903)" in Robert Nichols (ed.), *Colonial Reports on Pakistan's Frontier Tribal Areas*, Karachi: Oxford University Press, 2005.

30. *Report on Waziristan and its Tribes*, Lahore: Sang-e Meel Publications, 2005 (reprint of the 1901 edition).

31. *Nikat* derives from *nika* (grandfather). It takes the meaning of hereditary rights and obligations. The *nikat*, which is not based on current population figures, appears unfair to the Wazir. *Nikat* had been in existence for quite a long time and the colonial administration had to take it into account. Akbar Ahmed refers to it as "an inviolable law of tribal division" (*Resistance and Control in Pakistan*, p. 18).

32. Iqbal Khattak, "Wazir tribesmen want independent agency," *The Friday Times*, 17–23 October 2003.

33. Iqbal Khattak, "Wazir elder demands proportionate council seats," *Daily Times*, 5 December 2004.

34. Akbar S. Ahmed, *Pakistan Society: Islam, Ethnicity and Leadership in South Asia*, Karachi: Oxford University Press, 1986, p. 77.

35. He also opened a private school for girls in Wana bazaar.

36. Hafizullah Wazir, "Ex-MNA among 26 killed in Wana blast," *Daily Times*, 24 August 2010; Iqbal Khattak, "South Waziristan tense after cleric's killing," *Daily Times*, 25 August 2010.

37. Irfan Ghauri, "Adult franchise system in FATA put clerics in Parliament: ISPR DG," *Daily Times*, 27 July 2006. Eight MNAs were elected, seven of them for the first time. Maulana Noor Mohammad was elected in South Waziristan.

38. In the 1973 Constitution, about 37,000 *maliks* were entitled to vote and elected members of the National Assembly.

39. For details about the JUI-F connection in Waziristan, see Khalid Aziz, *Causes of Rebellion in Waziristan*, Peshawar: RIPORT, 22 February 2007.

40. For an interesting profile of Nek Mohammad, see Tanvir Qaisar Shahid and Naim Mustafa, "Nek Mohammad kaun tha? [Who was Nek Muhammad?]", *Pakistan*, 19 June 2004, and Mohammad Ilyas Khan, "Nek Muhammad Wazir," *The Herald Monthly*, June 2004.
41. Local conflicts were played out in the context of army operations. The tribes made alliances of opportunity with the government or with the militants in order to gain advantage in local conflicts. In Pashtun society, "duality structures all relationships. Betrayal is always a threat and alliances can shift, one is never defeated, except by death. While allied, Pashtuns are reliable until the point at which it is in their advantage in local disputes to no longer be reliable'. Haroon Akram Lodhi, "Attacking the Pakhtuns," *The Global Site*, October 2001.
42. Maqbool Wazir, *Waziristan Chronology*. www.waziristanhills.com
43. It was perceived as a war against the Wazir. The Mehsud stayed neutral.
44. Nek Mohammad, Baitullah Mehsud and Maulvi Nazir are the archetype of *kashars* challenging the tribal system of power from below.
45. The army presence in Waziristan was described as a violation of the purdah of Pashtun territory. Invading tribal space is considered as penetrating private space and is an affront to tribal honour.
46. A third peace deal was signed in September 2006 in North Waziristan.
47. In June 2006, Sirajuddin Haqqani issued a decree that it was no longer Taliban policy to fight the Pakistan army. This marked the end of significant fighting in South Waziristan. Maqbool Wazir, *Waziristan Chronology*.
48. Ahmedzai Wazir, belonging to the Zalikhel clan, was born in Birmal (Paktika) in 1975; Mullah Nazir studied in a *madrasa* in Wana and joined the Afghan Taliban from 1996. He came back to Pakistan after the fall of the Taliban and fought the Pakistani military until he surrendered in 2004. He was appointed emir of the Taliban's Wazir faction in South Waziristan in 2006, and joined forces with the Pakistani military in March 2007 to defeat the Uzbeks. He refused to join the TTP and has been maintaining an ambiguous position playing both sides since 2008. Chris Harnisch, "Question Mark of South Waziristan: Biography and Analysis of Maulvi Nazir Ahmad," *Critical Threats*, 17 July 2009.
49. Iqbal Khattak, "Maulvi Nazir decides to stay neutral," *Daily Times*, 19 October 2009.
50. Iqbal Khattak, "Mehsud unhappy over construction of Wana-Tank road," *Daily Times*, 2 March 2010. There are two roads going from Wana to Jandola: one through Mehsud territory which was paved a long time ago, and the other going through the Gomal Zam dam area and bypassing Mehsud territory. Construction work is also underway on a Tank-Makeen road in Mehsud area.
51. "Army close to winding up first phase of operation," *Dawn*, 5 November 2009.
52. Personal communication, October 2009. See also "Army working towards development of S. Waziristan," AFP, 8 July 2010.
53. Weapons were not surrendered but "offered". The militants presented gifts—an old sword, Waziri daggers, prayer mats, *miswak* (toothbrush made of wood) and *tasbeeh* (prayer beads)—to the Corps commander and the civil and military officials accompanying him.

54. Iqbal Khattak, "I did not surrender to the military, says Nek Mohammad," *The Friday Times*, 30 April—6 May 2004.
55. Nek Muhammad promised not to fight the army or harbour foreigners, in return for amnesty. He claimed later that no promise to deliver the foreigners to the government had been made (which is consistent with Pashtun values). The deal broke down and Nek Muhammad was killed in a drone attack in June 2004.
56. *Riwaj* is a body of social customs which has over time become the prevailing law. While Pashtunwali is universal, practices dictated by *riwaj* vary from tribe to tribe and from place to place. Abiding by *riwaj* is considered obligatory. There is a clash between *riwaj* and sharia in many matters, particularly concerning women; the sharia gives more rights to women than *riwaj*, Pashtuns generally give precedence to *riwaj* over the sharia which is more an ideal of social justice. See also Geiser's chapter in this volume.
57. Some even claim that the "most aggressive sons of *malik*s who have been killed" can be trained to take over and restore the old system.
58. For example, the aim of the Report of the President's Task Force on Tribal Reform submitted in April 2006 was the revival of the authority of the Political Agent.
59. Sartaj Khan, "Changing Pashtun society," *The News*, 14 January 2010.
60. This is a reinvention of the *lashkar* which traditionally was not backed and armed by the state.
61. Good examples are the Salarzai *lashkar* in Bajaur and the Shinwari and Mullagori *lashkar*s in Khyber.
62. Repatriation of displaced Mehsud families was announced from July 2010, but many tribals were reluctant to go back to Waziristan owing to the destruction of infrastructure and the lack of security.
63. J.M. Ewart, *Story of the North West Frontier Province*, p. 66.

5. A HISTORY OF LINGUISTIC BOUNDARY CROSSING WITHIN AND AROUND PASHTO

1. For the purpose of this essay see Fredrik Barth, *The Last Wali of Swat: An Autobiography as Told to Fredrik Barth*, Oslo: Universitetsforlaget AS and New York: Columbia University Press, 1985; Fredrik Barth, *Political Leadership among Swat Pathans*, London: Althone Press, 1965 [1959]; and Fredrik Barth (ed.), *Ethnic Groups and Boundaries: The Social Organization of Cultural Difference*, Boston: Little, Brown, 1969. For additional essays on Pashtuns and Swat that are not engaged here see Fredrik Barth (ed.), *Features of Person and Society in Swat: Collected Essays on Pathans*, London: Routledge & Kegan Paul, 1981. Barth's deployment of the term Pathan and his use of it as a synonym for Pashtuns and Afghans will be addressed below. This paper is a revised version of "A Combined History of Pashto Printing and Resistance to Print," presented at the "Rethinking the Swat Pathan" Conference held at the University of London's School of Oriental and African Studies in June 2010 (See http://www.soas.ac.uk/events/event56771.html [accessed 2 July 2011]). I would like to thank Ben Hopkins, Magnus Marsden, and Jane Savory for their collective hospitality during the conference and all of their help before and after it.

2. This table appears in Charles M. Kieffer, "Languages in Afghanistan," *Encyclopaedia Iranica* online edition http://iranica.com/articles/afghanistan-v-languages (accessed 4 July 2011).

3. For more on the influence of Sir William Jones on the study of Pashto in the context of British colonialism see Shah Mahmoud Hanifi, "Henry George Raverty the Colonial Marketing of Pashto" in Cythnia Talbot (ed.), *Knowing India: Colonial and Modern Constructions of the Past*, New Delhi: Yoda Publishers, 2011. For more on the wider influence of Sir William Jones see Thomas R. Trautmann, "The Lives of Sir William Jones" in Alexander Murray (ed.), *Sir William Jones 1746–1794: A Commemoration*, Oxford University Press, 1998, pp. 93–121, and Thomas R. Trautmann, "Indian Time, European Time" in Diane Owen Hughes and Thomas R. Trautmann (eds), *Time: Histories and Ethnologies*, Ann Arbor: University of Michigan Press, 1995, pp. 167–97.

4. Frank G. Salomon, "A Preliminary Survey of Some Early Buddhist Manuscripts Recently Acquired by the British Library," *Journal of the American Oriental Society*, 117/2, 1997, pp. 353–8. See also http://www.bl.uk/onlinegallery/sacredtexts/gandhara.html (accessed 2 July 2011).

5. Abu Rayhan al-Beruni, *Alberuni's India*, Eduard Sachau (trans. and ed.), London: S. Chand, 1964 [c. 1020]; C.E. Bosworth, *The Ghaznavids: Their Empire in Afghanistan and Eastern Iran, 994–1040*, Edinburgh: Edinburgh University Press, 1963; and Marshall Hodgson, *The Venture of Islam: Conscience and History in a World Civilization, vol. 2, The Expansion Of Islam in the Middle Periods*, Chicago: University of Chicago Press, 1974.

6. Wolseley Haig (ed.), *The Cambridge History of India, vol. 3, Turks and Afghans*, New York: Macmillan Co., 1928.

7. D.N. Marshall, *The Afghans in India Under the Delhi Sultanate and the Mughal Empire: A Survey of Relevant Manuscripts*, C.J. Brunner (ed.), New York: Afghanistan Council of the Asia Society, 1976.

8. Zahiruddin Muhammad Babur, *Baburnama: Part II*, W.M. Thackson Jr. (trans. and ed.), Cambridge, MA: Harvard University, Department of Near Eastern Languages and Civilizations, 1993 (Persian translation c. 1757–58 of Chaghatai Turkish text c. 1530).

9. On the *Tazkerat al-Awlia* see Abd al-Hai Habibi http://www.alamahabibi.com/English%20Articles\Memoirs_of_Saints.htm (accessed 5 July 2011). For a reference to Shaikh Mali's text see Barth, *Political Leadership*, p. 9 (on the authority of Henry George Raverty, *A Grammar of the Puk'hto, Pus'hto, or Language of the Afghans*, New Delhi: UBS Publishers, 1987 [1855], p. 32).

10. Both of these texts have been printed and republished many times. See, for example, Bayazid Ansari, *Khayr al-Bayan* (commentaries by Abd al-Hai Habibi, Abd al-Raouf Benawa and Abd al-Shakur Rashad), Kabul: Da Adabiyato aw Bashari Ulummo Pohanzai, 1974, and Akhund Darwezah, *Makhzan al-Islam* (introduction by Muhammad Taqwim al-Haqq Kaka Khel), Peshawar: de Pashto Academy, de Peshawar University, 1969. It is important to note that neither a specific location nor a specific date/time frame of production is known for either text. For restricted attention to Bayazid Ansari and the *Khair al-Bayan* see Muhammad Shafi, "Bayazid Ansari," *The Encyclopedia of Islam; 2nd Edition*, vol. 1, 1960, pp. 1121–4. For combined attention to Bayazid Ansari's *Khair al-Bayan* and Akhund Darweza's *Makhzan al-Afghan*, with an emphasis on the

NOTES p. [68]

former, see D.N. MacKenzie, "The Xayr ul-bayan," in *Indo-Iranica: Mélanges présentés à Georg Mongenstierne à l'occasion de son soixante-dixième anniversaire*, Wiesbaden: Otto Harrassowitz, 1964, pp. 134–40, and Georg Morgenstierne, "Notes on an Old Pashto Manuscript Containing the Khair ul-Bayan of Bayazid Ansari," *New Indian Antiquary*, 2/8, 1939, pp. 566–74. For a survey of Pashto that also addresses the two texts in question, see pages 59–61 of Alessandro Bausani, "Pashto Language and Literature (translated from Italian into English by Bernard Blair)," *Mahfil: A Quarterly of South Asian Literature*, 7/1–2, 1971, pp. 55–69.

11. For use of Bayazid Ansari's *Hal Nama*, a Persian source that resembles an autobiography and describes the author's affiliation with the Barki (Burki, Baraki, etc.) community in the village of Kaniguram (in contemporary South Waziristan, Pakistan) see Joseph T. Arlinghaus, "The Transformation of Afghan Tribal Society: Tribal Expansion, Mughal Imperialism and the Roshaniyya Insurrection, 1450–1600," Ann Arbor: University Microfilms International (PhD Dissertation, Department of History, Duke University), 1988, p. 256. In a note on page 225 of volume one of Zehir-ed-Din Muhammad Babur, *Memories of Zehir-ed-Din Muhammad Babur* (translated from Persian and Turkish manuscripts by John Leyden and William Erskine in 1826; annotated and revised by Sir Lucas White King in 1921), London: Oxford University Press, 1921, King cites Sir George Grierson, the authoritative author/editor of the monumental *Linguistic Survey of India*, who identifies the Barki language as Urmuri, which is described as "a curious linguistic island…(with no) connexion whatever with Pashtu…" Akhund Darweza's identity is less well defined, but Persian appears to be his first and primary language and he is often described as a Tajik.

12. Although no original version of either text is presently available, the oldest known copy of the *Khair al-Bayan* is from 1651; it is held at the University of Tübingen in Germany. The oldest known copy of the *Makhzan al-Islam* dates to 1703, and as of at least 1997 it was held in the Library of the Press Department (of the Government of Afghanistan) in Kabul. See pages 138–41 in D.N. MacKenzie, "The Development of the Pashto Script," in Shirin Akiner and Nicholas Sims-Williams (eds), *The Languages and Scripts of Central Asia*, London: School of Oriental and African Studies, 1997, pp. 137–43. Portions of the *Makhzan-i Islam*, also known as the *Makhzan-i Afghan* and the *Makhzan-i Pashto*, appear in Bernhard Dorn (ed.), *A Chrestomathy of the Pushtu or Afghan Language, to which is Subjoined a Glossary in Afghan and English*, Saint Petersbourg: Imperial Academy of Sciences, 1847, and Henry George Raverty, *Gulshan-i Roh, Being Selections, Prose and Poetical, in the Pus'hto or Afghan Language*, London: Longman, 1860.

13. See page 8 in V. Kushev, "The Dawn of Pashtun Linguistics: Early Grammatical and Lexicographical Works and Their Manuscripts," *Manuscripta Orientalia*, 7/2, 2001, pp. 3–9, and D. N. MacKenzie, "The Development of the Pashto Script" in Shirin Akiner and Nicholas Sims-Williams (eds), *The Languages and Scripts of Central Asia*, London: School of Oriental and African Studies, 1997, pp. 137–43.

14. For discussion and translation of some of the Pashto writings of Khushhal Khan Khattak and his descendants see pages 27–30 of Raverty's *Grammar* and pages 149–289 in Henry George Raverty, *Selections from the Poetry of the Afghans: From the Sixteenth to the Nineteenth Century, Literally Translated from the Original Pushto; with Notices of the Different*

285

Authors, and Remarks on the Mystic Doctrine and Poetry of the Sufis, Peshawar: De Chapzai, 1981 [1867].

15. For reference to *zanjiri*, or a "chained" shorthand script "known only to [Khushhal] and family", see page 28 of the Introduction to Raverty's *Grammar*.
16. See especially D.N. MacKenzie, "A Standard Pashto," *Bulletin of the School of Oriental and African Studies*, 22, 1959, pp. 231–5, but also MacKenzie, "Languages and Scripts," pp. 140–1, and page 161 of V. Kushev, "Areal Lexical Contacts of the Afghan (Pashto) Language (Based on the Texts of the XVI-XVIII Centuries)," *Iran and the Caucasus*, 1, 1997, pp. 159–66.
17. For more on the impetus to use Persian in the Mughal empire see Muzaffar Alam, "The Pursuit of Persian: Language in Mughal Politics," *Modern Asian Studies*, 32/2, 1998, pp. 317–49.
18. For attention to the Persianate concept see Said Amir Arjomand, "Evolution of the Persianate Polity and Its Transmission to India," *Journal of Persianate Studies*, 2/2, 2009, pp. 115–36; Said Amir Arjomand, "Defining Persianate Studies," *Journal of Persianate Studies*, 1/1, 2008, pp. 1–4; and Kushev, "Areal Lexical Contacts," especially p. 160 for the metaphor of a Persian stratum within Pashto.
19. See Kushev, "Areal Lexical Contacts," particularly pages 159 and 161 for reference to the organic incorporation of Indian loanwords in Pashto. In this article Kushev does not significantly distinguish the variety of Indian languages from one another. For a brief notice on the presence of Persian and Arabic, as well as Hindi and Punjabi vocabulary in Pashto see J.L. Vaughan, *A Grammar and Vocabulary of the Pooshtoo Language (as Spoken in the Trans-Indus Territories Under British Rule, &c. &c.)*, Calcutta: Thacker, Spink and Co. and R.C. Lepage and Co., 1864 [1854], pages viii and ix. The important and complex relationship between Arabic and Persian, on the one hand, and Indian languages such as Sanskrit, Khari Boli, Hindustani, and Urdu on the other are beyond the scope of this paper. For the British colonial impact on the evolving relationships between and textual histories of Indian languages see chapter two of Bernard S. Cohn, *Colonialism and Its Forms of Knowledge: The British in India*, Princeton: Princeton University Press, 1996; David Lelyveld, "Colonial Knowledge and the Fate of Hindustani," *Comparative Studies in Society and History*, 35/4, 1993, pp. 665–82; Rama Sundari Mantena, "Vernacular Futures: Colonial Philology and the Idea of History in Nineteenth-Century South India," *Indian Economic and Social History Review*, 42/4, 2005, pp. 513–34; Farina Mir, "Imperial Policy, Provincial Practices: Colonial Language Policy in Nineteenth-Century India," *Indian Economic and Social History Review*, 43/4, 2006, pp. 395–427; and Richard Steadman-Jones, *Colonialism and Grammatical Representation*, Oxford: Blackwell Publishing, 2007.
20. James Fuller Blumhardt, *Catalogue of the Marathi, Gujarati, Bengali, Assamese, Oriya, Pushtu and Sindhi Manuscripts in the Library of the British Museum*, London: The British Museum, 1905; James Fuller Blumhardt, *Catalogues of the Hindi, Panjabi, Sindhi, and Pushtu Printed Books in the Library of the British Museum*, London: B. Quaritch, 1893; and James Fuller Blumhart and D.N. Mackenzie, *A Catalogue of Pashto Manuscripts: in the Libraries of the British Isles*, London: The British Museum, 1965.
21. Kushev, "The Dawn of Pashtun Linguistics," pp. 4–5. Other relevant manuscripts noted

in this article include a teaching and conversation manual prepared for Ahmad Shah Durrani's son Sulayman by Mulla Pir Muhammad Kakar titled *Marifat al-Afghani* (c. 1773), and the anonymous *Amadnama-ye Afghani* and *Kitab-e Khiyalat-e Zamani dar Lughat-e Zaban-e Afghani* that are combined dictionaries and grammars compiled during the reign of the Durrani monarch Shah Zaman (r. 1793–1801).

22. Hanifi, "Henry George Raverty," from which the following paragraphs are largely distilled.

23. Henry George Raverty, *A Dictionary of the Pukhto, Pushto, or, Language of the Afghans: With Remarks on the Originality of the Language and its Affinity to the Semitic and Other Oriental Tongues, Etc. Etc.*, Karachi: Indus Publishers, 1982 [1860], page xv, and Henry George Raverty, *Grammar*, p. 34.

24. See, for example, Anandita Ghosh, *Power in Print: Popular Publishing and Politics of Language and Culture in a Colonial Society*, New Delhi: Oxford University Press, 2006, and Miles Ogborn, *Indian Ink: Script and Print in the Making of the East India Company*, Chicago: University of Chicago Press, 2007.

25. http://www.wmcarey.edu/carey/bib/works_bible.htm (accessed 3 July 2011).

26. John Vaughan appears to have captured the emerging colonial market for Pashto language material. See J.L. Vaughan, *A Grammar and Vocabulary of the Pooshtoo Language (as Spoken in the Trans-Indus Territories Under British Rule, &c. &c.)*, Calcutta: Thacker, Spink and Co. and R.C. Lepage and Co., 1864 [1854].

27. These are Salih Muhammad, *Lumra Kitab da Pashto I*, 1917, Kabul: Matba' Mashin Khana (http://afghanistandl.nyu.edu/books/adl0146/index.html [accessed 3 July 2011]), Muhammad Abd al-Wasi Qandahari, *Lumray Mashar da Marki da Pashto*, 1923, Kabul (http://afghanistandl.nyu.edu/books/adl0144/ [accessed 3 July 2011]), and Majlis-e Talif-e Pashtu, *Mu'allim-e Pashtu Kitab Duvvum*, 1935, Qandahar: Majlis-e Talif-e Pashtu (http://afghanistandl.nyu.edu/books/adl0180/ [accessed 3 July 2011]). For more on Salih Muhammad and Muhammad Abd al-Wasi Qandahari see James Caron, "Cultural Histories of Pashtun Nationalism: Public Participation, and Social Inequality in Monarchic Afghanistan, 1905–1960" (PhD Dissertation, South Asian Regional Studies, the University of Pennsylvania), 2009, chapters 2 and 3 (see http://gradworks.umi.com/33/81/3381504.html [accessed 3 July 2011]). On the subject of printing and the printing press in Afghanistan see Shah Mahmoud Hanifi, "The Combined History of Pashto Printing and Resistance to Print," paper delivered at the 2010 SOAS "Rethinking the Swat Pathan" Conference http://www.soas.ac.uk/cccac/swat-pathan/file59663.pdf (accessed 3 July 2011), pp. 14–16, which relies on primarily on Caron, *Cultural Histories*; Willem Floor, "*Chap* (printing)," *Encyclopaedia Iranica* online edition http://www.iranica.com/articles/cap-print-printing-a-persian-word-probably-derived-from-hindi-chapna-to-print-see-turner-no (accessed 4 July 2011); Vartan Gregorian, *The Emergence of Modern Afghanistan: The Politics of Reform and Modernization, 1880–1946*, Palo Alto, CA: Stanford University Press, 1969; Vartan Gregorian, Mahmud Tarzi and Saraj-ol-Akhbar, "Ideology of Nationalism and Modernization in Afghanistan," *Middle East Journal*, 21/3, 1967, pp. 345–68; May Schinasi, *Afghanistan at the Beginning of the Twentieth Century: Nationalism and Journalism in Afghanistan: A Study of Seraj ul-Akhbar (1911–1918)*, Naples: Istituto Universitario Orientale, 1979; and G.W.

Shaw, "Matb'a (printing) in Afghanistan," *Encyclopedia of Islam*, 2nd Edition, vol. 6, 1991, pp. 806–7. As indicated, Salih Muhammad, Qandahari and Majlis-e Talif-e Pashto are available on-line at the Afghanistan Digital Library (http://afghanistandl.nyu.edu/index.html [accessed 4 July 2011]) where to my knowledge the only example of Pashto language textual production during Abd al-Rahman's reign can also be found: Mulla Ghulam Jan Lomqani, *Su'al wa Jawab-e Dawlati wa Band wa Bast Salatini*, Kabul: Dar al-Saltanah, 1886 (http://afghanistandl.nyu.edu/books/adl0190/adl0190-fr01.html [accessed 4 July 2011]). The text in question contains the minutes of Abd al-Rahman's meeting with the British Indian Viceroy Lord Dufferin in the spring of 1885; on its frontispiece Mulla Ghulam Jan is identified as a Pashto Writer for the Afghan state. I have been unable to secure any Pashto language military texts (that may have been) produced in Afghanistan in the nineteenth century.

28. See, for example, George Olof Roos-Keppel and Qazi Abdul Ghani Khan, *A Manual of Pushtu*, Bombay: Oxford University Press, 1937 [1901]. Roos-Keppel was President of the Central Committee of Examination in Pushtu when this work was first published in 1901.

29. My use of the word pedagogy in this essay incorporates teaching by an instructor and individual self-instruction.

30. Tariq Rahman, "The Learning of Pashto in North India and Pakistan: An Historical Account," *Journal of Asian History*, 35/2, 2001, pp. 158–87; Tariq Rahman, "The Pashto Language Movement in Pakistan," *Contemporary South Asia*, 4/2, 1995, pp. 151–70; Tariq Rahman, "The Teaching of Pashto: Identity versus Employment," http://www.tariqrahman.net/language/Teaching%20of%20Pashto.htm (accessed 4 July 2011), James Caron, *Cultural Histories*; Tariq Rahman, "Reading the Power of Printed Orality: Popular Pashto Literature as Historical Evidence and Public Intervention," *Journal of Social History*, 45, forthcoming. For more on the Pashto Tolena see Wali Ahmadi, "Kabul Literary Society," *Encyclopaedia Iranica* online edition http://www.iranica.com/articles/kabul-literary-society (accessed 4 July 2011), and Wali Ahmadi, "Kabul Magazine," *Encyclopaedia Iranica* online edition http://www.iranica.com/articles/kabol-magazine (accessed 4 July 2011). It would be valuable for a future researcher to historically excavate and ethnographically situate the place of Pashto and language materials in the Afghan and Pakistani militaries in the later half of the twentieth century.

31. For citations and access to Tegey and Robson's work, and many other Pashto language teaching and learning works, see the Afghanistan Analyst Website http://afghanistan-analyst.org/PashtoTextbooks.aspx (accessed 4 July 2011).

32. http://afghanistan-analyst.org/UniversityPashtoLanguagePrograms.aspx (accessed 4 July 2011).

33. See http://www.dliflc.edu/LangPortal/index.html (accessed 4 July 2011) for the gateway to DLI's Pashto language materials. For the Human Terrain System, see http://humanterrainsystem.army.mil/Default.aspx (accessed 4 July 2011) and Roberto J. Gonzales, *American Counterinsurgency: Human Science and the Human Terrain*, Chicago: Prickly Paradigm Press, 2009.

34. http://www.rosettastone.com/learn-pashto/level-1 and http://library.playaway.com/product/12516/accent-on-afghanistan-pashto (both accessed 4 July 2011).

NOTES pp. [73–79]

35. http://www.indiana.edu/~celcar/evaluation_pashto.html and http://www.pashtozeray.org/bible/en/ (both accessed 4 July 2011).
36. http://www.indiana.edu/~celcar/language_textbooks.html# (accessed 4 July 2011), Nicholas Awde and Asmatullah Sarwan, *Pashto: Dictionary and Phrasebook*, New York: Hippocrene Books, 2005 [2002], and http://www.washingtonpost.com/wp-dyn/content/gallery/2010/07/10/GA2010071003106.html?hpid=topnews (accessed 4 July 2011).
37. See, for example, http://www.economist.com/blogs/johnson/2010/09/military_translators, http://www.languageonthemove.com/recent-posts/the-monolingual-mindset-goes-to-war, http://www.guardian.co.uk/world/video/2008/jun/11/afghanistan.johndmchugh, and http://www.npr.org/templates/story/story.php?storyId=129396818 (all accessed on 5 July 2011).

6. THE ROAD TO KABUL: AUTOMOBILES AND AFGHAN INTERNATIONALISM, 1900–40

1. Shah Mahmoud Hanifi, *Connecting Histories in Afghanistan: Market Relations and State Formation on a Colonial Frontier*, New York: Columbia University Press, 2008, and Robert Nichols, *A History of Pashtun Migration*, Karachi: Oxford University Press, 2008.
2. Dietrich Reetz, *Hijrat: The Flight of the Faithful: A British File on the Exodus of Muslim Peasants from North India to Afghanistan in 1920*, Berlin: Das Arabische Buch, 1995.
3. Bruno Markowski, *Die materielle Kultur des Kabulgebietes*, Leipzig: Verlag Asia Major, 1932, pp. 109–112 and Abdul Wahed Malekyar, *Die Verkehrsentwicklung in Afghanistan*, Cologne: W. Kleikamp, 1966, pp. 39–43. On the introduction of the *baggi*, see Carl Rathjens, "Karawanenwege und Pässe im Kulturlandschaftswandel Afghanistans seit dem 19. Jahrhundert" in Adolf Leidlmair and Hermann von Wissmann (eds), *Hermann von Wissmann-Festschrift*, Tübingen: Geographisches Institut der Universität Tübingen, 1962, p. 217.
4. Habībullāh Rafī', *Armaghān-e Tamaddun: Tārīkhcha-ye Vurūd-e Vasā'i-e 'Asrī beh Afghānistān*, Peshawar: Siyār Arīk, 1378/1999, p. 43. I am grateful to James Caron for supplying me with this book. On the gift, see also Angus Hamilton, *Problems of the Middle East*, London: Eveleigh Nash, 1909, p. 261.
5. Khāksār Nādir 'Alī, *Al-Habīb, jis-mēn A'lā-Hazrat Hiz Majestī Amīr Habībullāh Khān kē Sayr ō Siyāhat-e Hindustān kē Vāqa'āt*, Agra: Sādiq Husayn, n.d. [c.1908]. A facsimile and translation of the Urdu manuscript have been published as Shaikh Muhammad 'Abdullah Khan 'Azar, *My Heartrendingly Tragic Story*, ed. Alberto M. Cacopardo and Ruth Laila Schmidt, Oslo: Novus Press, 2006; for the sections treating Habibullah's tour, see pp. 96–101 (translation), pp. 125–35 (Urdu text).
6. For a fuller study of the royal travelogue, see Nile Green, "The Afghan Afterlife of Phileas Fogg: Space and Time in the Literature of Afghan Travel," in Nile Green and Nushin Arbabzadah (eds), *Afghanistan in Ink: Literature between Diaspora and Nation*, London: Hurst and New York: Columbia University Press, 2012.
7. Khāksār Nādir 'Alī, *Al-Habīb*, p. 35.
8. Ibid., pp. 64, 70.
9. A.C. Jewett, *An American Engineer in Afghanistan, From the Letters and Notes of A. C. Jewett*, ed. Marjorie Jewett Bell, Minneapolis: University of Minnesota Press, 1948, p. 220.

289

10. Cited in Rafi', *Armaghān-e Tamaddun*, p. 43.
11. Rafi', *Armaghān-e Tamaddun*, p. 43. Details on roads and bridges were also recorded in the letters of Habibullah's employee, the American engineer and eyewitness, A.C. Jewett, *An American Engineer*, p. 225. However, Malekyar (1966, p. 43) states that no "motorable road-building" (*Autostrassenbau*) was carried out in Habibullah's reign.
12. Jewett, *An American Engineer*, p. 226.
13. Ibid. and Khāksār Nādir 'Alī, *Al-Habīb*, pp. 64–5, 67–8.
14. On the beginnings of German contact, see Thomas L. Hughes, "The German Mission to Afghanistan, 1915–1916," *German Studies Review* 25/3, 2002, pp. 447–76.
15. Otfrid von Hanstein, *Im wilden Afghanistan: Reisen, Abenteuer und Forschungen*, Leipzig: Verlag Deutsche Buchwerkstätten, 1923 [1922 edition], pp. 175–6. Hanstein received this information from the earlier German envoy Werner Otto von Hentig.
16. E. Alexander Powell, "A Modern Magic Carpet," *The Century Magazine*, 104/2, 1922, p. 204. On the gift of the cars, see Jewett, *An American Engineer*, pp. 24 and 225. Also E. Alexander Powell, *By Camel and Car to the Peacock Throne: Syria, Palestine, Transjordania, Arabia, Iraq, Persia*, New York: Century Co., 1923.
17. Mawlānā Zāhid al-Qādirī, *A'lā-Hazrat Shāh Amānullāh Khān Ghāzī Tājdār-e Afghānistān kā Safarnāma*, 2 vols, Delhi: Qurēshī Buk Depō, 1928, pp. 5–6.
18. Roland Wild, *Amanullah: Ex-King of Afghanistan*, London: Hurst & Blackett, 1932, p. 73.
19. "*Vasā'il-e Hamal va Naql: Tijārat: Rāh-hā*," *Sālnāma-ye Kābul* 1313/1935, qismat-e avval [part 1], pp. 198–9.
20. "*Ta'mīr-e Pul-hā*," *Sālnāma-ye Kābul* 1313/1935, qismat-e avval [part 1], p. 110.
21. *Sālnāma-ye Kābul* 1314/1936, qismat-e avval [part 1], photograph opposite p. 91.
22. *Sālnāma-ye Kābul* 1314/1936, qismat-e dovvum [part 2], map opposite p. 246.
23. Ghulam Jailani Arez and Andreas Dittmann (eds), *Kabul: Aspects of Urban Geography*, Peshawar: s.n., 2005, p. 17 and Patrick Clawson, "Knitting Iran Together: The Land Transport Revolution, 1920–1940," *Iranian Studies*, 26/3–4, 1993.
24. Arash Khazeni, *Tribes and Empire on the Margins of Nineteenth-Century Iran*, Seattle: University of Washington Press, 2010, pp. 99–110.
25. On early Russian rail and road construction in Central Asia, see François Lantz, "Mouvement et voies de communication en Asie centrale: L'avènement d'une colonie," *Cahiers d'Asie Centrale*, 17–18, 2009.
26. Malekyar, *Die Verkehrsentwicklung*, p. 64.
27. Ibid., p. 43.
28. Markowski, *Die materielle Kultur*, p. 112.
29. Ibid.
30. William J. Hughes and Joseph L. Thomas, *A History of Alley & MacLellan and the Sentinel Waggon Works: 1875–1930*, Newton Abbot: David & Charles, 1973.
31. *Motor Transport*, 46, January-June 1928, p. 393.
32. Wild, *Amanullah*, p. 146.
33. *Sālnāma-ye Kābul* 1313/1935, qismat-e avval [part 1], p. 234, with a progress report in *Sālnāma-ye Kābul* 1314/1936, qismat-e avval [part 1], p. 109.
34. Wild, *Amanullah*, pp. 146, 177. Ram Prasad was murdered in the 1929 rebellion when Habibullah Kalakani's rebels stormed the royal garage and slit his throat; ibid., pp. 225, 241.

35. Wild, *Amanullah*, pp. 136–7.
36. Annick Fenet, *Documents d'archéologie militante: La mission Foucher en Afghanistan (1922–1925)*, Paris: Académie des Inscriptions et Belles-Lettres, 2010.
37. Clärenore Stinnes, *Im Auto durch zwei Welten*, Berlin: Reimar Hobbing, 1929.
38. Emil Trinkler, *Quer durch Afghanistan nach Indien*, Berlin: K. Vowinckel Verlag, 1925.
39. Emil Trinkler and Paul Langhans, *Geologie Afghanistans und seiner Randgebiete: Orographie von Afghanistan* [map], Gotha: Perthes, 1928, and Emil Trinkler, *Afghanistan: eine landeskundliche Studie auf Grund des vorhandenen Materials und eigener Beobachtung: mit 3 Textabbildungen, 4 Bilder- und 4 Kartentafeln*, Gotha: Perthes, 1928.
40. Herbert Tichy, *Zum heiligsten Berg der Welt: auf Landstraßen und Pilgerpfaden in Afghanistan, Indien und Tibet*, Vienna: Seidel, 1937, and Herbert Tichy, *Afghanistan: das Tor nach Indien*, Leipzig: W. Goldmann, 1940.
41. Robert Byron, *The Road to Oxiana*, London: Macmillan, 1937, and Sven Hedin, *Die Seidenstraße*, Leipzig: F.A. Brockhaus, 1936.
42. Wild, *Amanullah*, pp. 78–9.
43. Joseph Hackin and Ria J. Hackin, *Le Site archeéologique de Bāmiyān: Guide du visiteur*, Paris: Les Éditions dArt et d'Histoire, 1933; Joseph Hackin and Ria J. Hackin, *Bamian: Führer zu den buddhistischen Höhlenklöstern und Kolossalstatuen*, Paris: Les Éditions d'Art et d'Histoire, 1939.
44. Hackin and Hackin, *Bamian: Führer zu den buddhistischen Höhlenklöstern*, p. 8.
45. Ella Maillart, *The Cruel Way*, London: W. Heinemann, 1947, and Annemarie Schwarzenbach, *Alle Wege sind offen: die Reise nach Afghanistan 1939/1940*, Basel: Lenos, 2000.
46. In 1926 the English intelligence officer Reginald Teague-Jones ("Ronald Sinclair", 1890–1988) similarly drove from Beirut through Iran to Indian Baluchistan in a Ford Model-A with the name Zobeida written on its side in white paint. Recommending Fords highly for such journeys, he wrote that "the extra high clearance of this particular model and its light weight were big advantages in rough country". See Reginald Teague-Jones, *Adventures in Persia: To India by the Back Door*, London: Victor Gollancz, 1990, p. 22.
47. Sayyid Qāsim Khān Rishtiyyā, "*Mōtar va Ahmiyyat-e ān va Dunyā*," *Sālnāma-ye Kābul 1314/1936*, *qismat-e dovvum* [part 2], pp. 354–72.
48. On the history of the Urdu travelogue, see Vahīd Qurēshī, *Urdū Adab main Safarnāma*, Lahore: Qawmī Prēs, n.d. On the intersection of the travelogue with technology transfer, see also Nile Green, "Journeymen, Middlemen: Travel, Trans-Culture and Technology in the Origins of Muslim Printing," *International Journal of Middle East Studies*, 41/2, 2009.
49. On Afghan use of Urdu and the sharing of Indian Muslim and Afghan modernism, see Nile Green, "The Trans-Border Traffic of Afghan Modernism: Afghanistan and the Indian 'Urdusphere'," *Comparative Studies in Society and History*, 53/3, 2011.
50. Hājjī Mīr Shams al-Dīn, *Siyāhat-e Afghānistān, Mushtamil bar Kawā'if-e Ta'līmāt*, Lahore: Rafīq-e 'Ām Prēs, 1347/1929, p. 17. I am grateful to May Schinasi for providing me with a copy of this rare text.
51. Khvāja Hasan Nizāmī, *Safarnāma-ye Afghānistān*, Lahore: Ātash Fishān, 2007 repr., p. 22, Shams al-Dīn, *Siyāhat-e Afghānistān*, p. 6.

52. For early statistics on US car exports to South Asia, see the data collected by the American trade commissioner C.C. Batchelder, *American Automotive Products in India*, Washington: Government Printing Office, 1923.
53. Nizāmī, *Safarnāma*, p. 27.
54. Sayyid Sulaymān Nadvī, *Sayr-e Afghānistān*, Lahore: Sang-e Mīl, repr. 2008, p. 9.
55. Ibid., pp. 9, 10, 11, 15, 19.
56. Shams al-Dīn, *Siyāhat-e Afghānistān*, p. 6
57. Nizāmī, *Safarnāma*, pp. 18–20 on trains and p. 22 on the motor car.
58. Ibid., p. 25.
59. Ibid., pp. 25–7.
60. Shams al-Dīn, *Siyāhat-e Afghānistān*, pp. 6–7.
61. Nadvī, *Sayr-e Afghānistān*, p. 10.
62. Ibid., p. 12.
63. Ibid.
64. Nizāmī, *Safarnāma*, pp. 28–9.
65. Ibid., p. 28.
66. Ibid., pp. 27, 31.
67. Ibid., p. 31.
68. Nadvī, *Sayr-e Afghānistān*, p. 13.
69. Ibid., p. 14.
70. Nizāmī, *Safarnāma*, p. 29.
71. Nadvī, *Sayr-e Afghānistān*, pp. 19–20. On parallel model town construction across the border in Punjab in the same period, see William J. Glover, "Objects, Models, and Exemplary Works: Educating Sentiment in Colonial Punjab," *Journal of Asian Studies*, 64/3, 2005.
72. Nizāmī, *Safarnāma*, p. 35. On other Germans in Kabul at this time, see Antoine Fleury, *La Pénétration allemande au Moyen-Orient, 1919–1939: le cas de la Turquie, de l'Iran, et de l'Afghanistan*, Leiden: Brill, 1977.
73. Nadvī, *Sayr-e Afghānistān*, pp. 32, 61–2. On Kabul's shopkeepers during the early 1900s, see Sūfī Pāyanda Muhammad Kūshān, *Bā Kābul-e Qadīm Āshnā Shavīd*, Peshawar: Markaz-e Nashrāt-e Sa'īd, 1384/2006, pp. 15–21.
74. Frank A. Martin, *Under the Absolute Amir*, London: Harper & Brothers, 1907, p. 49.
75. Nadvī, *Sayr-e Afghānistān*, p. 15.
76. Shams al-Dīn, *Siyāhat-e Afghānistān*, p. 15.
77. Various accounts Iqbal's Afghan and European travels have been collected in Haq Nawāz (ed.), *Siyāhat-e Iqbāl*, Lyallpur [Faisalabad]: Kitāb-e Markaz, 1976.
78. Nadvī, *Sayr-e Afghānistān*, pp. 26–7.
79. Otfrid von Hanstein, *Im wilden Afghanistan: ein Land der Zukunft: Reisen, Abenteuer und Forschungen*, 2nd edition, Leipzig: Verlag Deutsche Buchwerkstätten, 1928.
80. Nadvī, *Sayr-e Afghānistān*, pp. 36–37. On Muhammad Hashim Khan, see Ludwig W. Adamec, *Historical and Political Who's Who of Afghanistan*, Graz: Akademische Druck und Verlagsanstalt, 1975, p. 160.
81. Nadvī, *Sayr-e Afghānistān*, p. 37.
82. Nizāmī, *Safarnāma*, p. 39.

83. Nadvī, *Sayr-e Afghānistān*, p. 10.
84. Ibid., pp. 11, 15, 17. Also Nizāmī, *Safarnāma*, pp. 65–6.
85. Nadvī, *Sayr-e Afghānistān*, p. 9.
86. Nizāmī, *Safarnāma*, pp. 24–5.
87. Nadvī, *Sayr-e Afghānistān*, pp. 11–12.
88. Ibid., p. 18.
89. Nizāmī, *Safarnāma*, p. 66.
90. Nile Green, "Tribe, Diaspora and Sainthood in Afghan History," *Journal of Asian Studies*, 67/1, 2008; Hanifi, *Connecting Histories*; Nichols, *A History of Pashtun Migration*.
91. Cf. Owen D. Gutfreund, *Twentieth-Century Sprawl: Highways and the Reshaping of the American Landscape*, Oxford: Oxford University Press, 2004.
92. Wild, *Amanullah*, p. 268.
93. Cf. David B. Edwards, "Print Islam: Media and Religious Revolution in Afghanistan" in June Nash (ed.), *Social Movements: An Anthropological Reader*, Oxford: Blackwell, 2005.

7. BEING A DIPLOMAT ON THE FRONTIER OF SOUTH AND CENTRAL ASIA: TRADE AND TRADERS IN AFGHANISTAN

1. The research upon which this chapter is based has been made possible with the help of support from the British Academy and the Leverhulme Trust. It would also not have been possible without the support of many friends in the region.
2. See Edwina Thompson, *Trust is the Coin of the Realm: Lessons from the Money Men in Afghanistan*, Karachi: Oxford University Press, 2011.
3. The precise nature of these trading geographies varies, of course, in relation to the specific part of Afghanistan; some regions and places being especially tied to the bazaars of Iran, and the free ports now found there, and others intricately related to the emergence of Dubai and other spaces within the United Arab Emirates as a focus for Asian trade.
4. B.D. Hopkins, *The Making of Modern Afghanistan*, London: Palgrave Macmillan, 2008; Shah Mahmoud Hanifi, *Connecting Histories in Afghanistan: Market Relations and State Formation on a Colonial Frontier*, Palo Alto, CA: Stanford University Press, 2011.
5. Antonio Giustozzi, *Empires of Mud: War and Warlords in Afghanistan*, London: Hurst, 2009, p. 139.
6. E.g. Conrad Schetter, "The "Bazaar Economy" of Afghanistan" in Christine Noelle-Karimi, Conrad Schetter and Reinhard Schlagintweit (eds), *Afghanistan—A Country without a State?*, IKO-Verlag fur Interkulturelle Kommunikation, 2002, p. 121.
7. Jonathan Goodhand, "From Holy War to Opium War?: A Case Study of the Opium Economy in North Eastern Afghanistan," in Christine Noelle-Karimi et al. (eds), *Afghanistan—A Country without a State?*, pp. 139–60; Jonathan Goodhand, "Afghanistan in Central Asia" in M. Pugh, N. Cooper and J. Goodhand (eds), *War Economies in a Regional Context: Challenges for Transformation*, Boulder, Colo.: Lynne Rienner Publishers, 2004, pp. 45–91.
8. Adam Pain and S. Lister, "Markets in Afghanistan" in A. Pain and J. Sutton (eds), *Reconstructing Agriculture in Afghanistan*, Rugby: Practical Action Publishing, 2007, pp. 235–50. Paula R. Newberg, "Surviving State Failure: Internal War and Regional Conflict in

Afghanistan's Neighborhood" in C. Arnson and I. W. Zartman (eds), *Rethinking the Economics of War: the Intersection of Need, Creed and Greed*, Washington: Woodrow Wilson Center Press and Baltimore, MD: Johns Hopkins University Press, 2005, pp. 206–233. For a situated exploration of the importance of drugs to Afghanistan's economy, see Jonathan Goodhand, *Bandits, Borderlands and Opium Wars: Afghan State Building Viewed from the Margins*, DIIS Working Paper, Copenhagen, 2009. These are, indeed, perspectives shared by Afghan merchants influential in the country before the Soviet invasion of 1979, who, at weddings in Dubai where wealthy merchants gather, berate their fellow traders for being loud and publicly drunk, reminding them that they are "new to the game" and to strive for its full respect.

9. David Edwards, *Before Taliban: Genealogies of the Afghan Jihad*, Berkeley: California University Press, 2002.

10. Ibid., p. 45.

11. Paul Dresch, "Mutual Deception: Totality, Exchange and Islam in the Middle East" in W. James and N. Allen (eds), *Marcel Mauss: A Centenary Tribute*, New York: Berghahn Books, 1998, p. 125. The money changing bazaar in Kabul until the 1970s was, indeed, dominated by first Jewish and then Hindu and Sikh traders. See Maxwell Fry, *The Afghan Economy: Money, Finance, and the Critical Constraints to Economic Development*, Leiden: Brill, 1974.

12. See also Thompson, *Trust is the Coin of the Realm*.

13. Alessandro Monsutti has explored the importance of literacy to Hazara migration and trade in Iran, Pakistan and the West. Alessandro Monsutti, *War and Migration: Social Networks and Economic Strategies of the Hazaras of Afghanistan*, P. Camiller (trans.), London: Routledge, 2005. See also Alessandro Monsutti, "Afghan Migration Strategies and Three Solutions to the Refugee Problem," *Refugee Survey Quarterly*, 27, 2008, pp. 58–73, and Alessandro Monsutti, "Migration as a Rite of Passage: Young Afghans Building Masculinity and Adulthood in Iran," *Iranian Studies*, 40, 2004, pp. 167–85. Cf. Kirsten Harpviken, *Social Networks and Migration in Wartime Afghanistan*, London: Palgrave Macmillan, 2009.

14. See Elizabeth Picard, "Trafficking, Rents and Diaspora in the Lebanese War" in C. Arnson and I.W. Zartman (eds), *Rethinking the Economics of War: the Intersection of Need, Creed and Greed*, 2005, pp. 23–51. Picard offers an excellent analysis not just of the emergence of a class of "militia entrepreneurs" on the Lebanese political scene, but also of the importance of "identity, faith and group solidarity" for understanding the agency of these actors.

15. This scholarship raises important questions about the identities of Chinese middle class merchants today, and their role in this ongoing historical process: are they enacting "mercantile agendas" repressed in the communist era, or does such an interpretation downplay the centrality of local officials plugged into the state to China's new "modernising elite"? H.F. Siu, "The Grounding of Cosmopolitans: Merchants and Local Cultures in South China" in Wen-Hsin Yeh (ed.), *Becoming Chinese: Passages to Modernity and Beyond*, Berkeley: University of California Press, 2000, p. 216.

16. An expanding body of anthropological work explores the importance of work routines for instilling moral attitudes and sensibilities. See, for instance, Charles Stafford, "Two

Stories of Learning and Economic Agency in Yunnan," *Taiwan Journal of Anthropology*, 2, 2004, pp. 171–94. See also Trevor Marchand, "Preface and Introduction: Making Knowledge," *Journal of the Royal Anthropological Institute*, 16, 2010, pp. 1–21.

17. Historians have debated extensively the types of structures and relations informing long-distance trading relations in the Muslim world. See for example Avram Udovitch, *Partnership and Profit in Medieval Islam*, Princeton University Press, 1960; Timur Kuran, "The Islamic Commercial Crisis: Institutional Roots of Economic Underdevelopment in the Middle East," *Journal of Economic History*, 63, 2003, pp. 414–46. For an excellent historical account of the nature of trading relations and practices in one historic region, the Sahara, see Ghislaine Lydon, *On Trans-Saharan Trails: Islamic Law, Trade Networks, and Cross-Cultural Exchange in Nineteenth Century Western Africa*, Cambridge: Cambridge University Press, 2009.

18. I agree with a wide body of literature which argues that the term refugee is as much a category of global governance as an accurate term of political or sociological analysis. I use the term here only as an indication of the degree to which the men I talk about in this article as traders and merchants are also often categorised by the Tajikistan state and, in particular contexts, by themselves as "refugees". On the problematic term "refugee" see, programmatically, Lissa Malkki, *Purity and Exile: Violence, Memory and National Cosmology among Hutu Refugees in Tanzania*, Chicago: University of Chicago Press, 1993.

19. For a comparative study of another type of work that also involves complex relations between more and less mobile employees, see Hannerz's discussion of the world of foreign correspondents, Ulf Hannerz, *Foreign News: Exploring the World of Foreign Correspondents*, Chicago: University of Chicago Press, 2004, especially pp. 82–4.

20. Susan Bayly, *Asian Voices in a Postcolonial Age: India, Vietnam and Beyond*, Cambridge: Cambridge University Press, 2007.

21. Filippo Osella and Caroline Osella, "Muslim Entrepreneurs in Public Life between India and the Gulf: Making Good and Doing Good," *Journal of the Royal Anthropological Institute*, 15, 2009, pp. 202–221. See also Daromir Rudnyckyj, "Spiritual Economies: Islam and Neoliberalism in Contemporary Indonesia," *Cultural Anthropology*, 24/1, 2009, pp. 104–141.

22. See, generally, Thomas Barfield, *Afghanistan: a Political History*, Princeton: Princeton University Press, 2010.

23. On mafia, violence and protection costs in post-Soviet contexts see, especially, Caroline Humphrey, *The Unmaking of Soviet Life: Everyday Economies after Socialism*, Ithaca: Cornell University Press, 2002. For an ethnographic consideration of trading spaces in Mongolia, see Morten Pedersen, "From "public" to "private" markets in post-socialist Mongolia," *Anthropology of East Europe Review*, 25/1, 2007, pp. 72–84.

24. Johan Rasanayagam, *Islam in post-Soviet Uzbekistan: the Morality of Experience*, Cambridge: Cambridge University Press, 2010.

25. Stephen Collier and Aiwa Ong, "Oikos/anthropos: Rationality, Technology, Infrastructure," *Current Anthropology*, 44/3, 2003, p. 423.

26. E.g. Albert Hirschman, *The Passions and the Interests: Political Arguments for Capitalism before its Triumph*, Princeton: Princeton University Press, 1982.

27. "Commitment and dedication" to work and labour are powerful dimensions of per-

sonal and collective identity amongst urban communities in northern Afghanistan. Ingeborg Baldauf suggests that "holding a positive, affirmative attitude" towards a "specific type of labour" is perhaps even more important to a person's individual and group identity than "notions of decency, locality, or shared historical memory and social goals": Ingeborg Baldauf, "The Dāyi—Kārgil of Andkhoy: Language, History and Typical Professions. Discourse on Local Identity," *ASIEN*, 1004 S, 2007, p. 149. On the degrading of social-professional identities in the West in the context of late-capitalism, see Richard Sennet, *The Corrosion of Character: the Personal Consequences of Work in the New Capitalism*, New York: W.W. Norton, 1998.

28. See, for example, Elizabeth Picard's discussion of the changing role of mobile Syrian merchants in relation to war and conflict and the making of an "Ottoman space" across the Lebanese-Syria border: Elizabeth Picard, "Managing Identities among Expatriate Businessmen across the Syrian-Lebanese Boundary" in I. Brandell (ed.), *State Frontiers: Borders and Boundaries in the Middle East*, London: I.B. Tauris, 2006, pp. 74–100. Like other literature on economic actors in comparable contexts, Picard contrasts older, elite Syrian merchants in Beirut, who maintained a distance from formal politics and were both wealthy and discreet, with a newer group of merchants who lived luxurious lives and were openly tied to both the regimes of Syria and Lebanon. These transformations are also pertinent to understanding the nature of trading peoples' identities elsewhere, even those of futures traders in London and New York. See Caitlin Zaloom, *Out of the Pits: Traders and Technology from Chicago to London*, Chicago: University of Chicago Press, 2006.

8. CLASS, PATRONAGE AND COERCION IN THE PAKISTANI PUNJAB AND IN SWAT

1. See Ayesha Jalal, *Democracy and Authoritarianism in South Asia*, Lahore: Sang-e-Meel Publications, 1995 and Muhammad Waseem, *The 1993 Elections in Pakistan*, Lahore: Vanguard Books, 1993. See also Rasool Baksh Rias, "Elections in Pakistan: Is Democracy Winning?," *Asian Affairs*, 12/47, 1985, pp. 81–102.

2. Hamza Alavi, "The Politics of Dependence: A Village in West Punjab," *South Asian Review*, 4/2, 1971, pp. 111–28; Fredrik Barth, *Political Leadership among Swat Pathans*, London: The Athlone Press, 1959; Frederick Bailey, *Stratagems and Spoils: A Social Anthropology of Politics*, Oxford: Westview Press, 2001 [1969]; Paul Brass, *Factional Politics in an Indian State: The Congress Party in Uttar Pradesh*, Berkeley: University of California Press, 1965; Ralph Nicholas, "Factions: A Comparative Analysis" in K. Banton (ed.), *Political Systems and the Distribution of Power*, London: Routledge, 1965. pp. 21–9.

3. I refer to the landed classes in the plural because this is a diverse group, and different segments of it have gained political and economic prominence at different times since independence. Thus although the aristocratic feudal elite that dominated the Muslim League at independence still plays an important role in politics, members of intermediate ranking landed families are increasingly prominent.

4. Talal Asad, "Market Model, Class Structure and Consent: a Reconsideration of Swat Political Organisation," *Man*, 7/1, 1972, pp. 74–94. Fredrik Barth, "Swat Pathans Reconsidered," in A. Kuper (ed.), *Features of Person and Society in Swat: Collected Essays on Pathans*, London: Routledge & Kegan Paul, 1981, pp. 121–81.

5. In the case of Swat this means first the princely state and only subsequently the Pakistani state.
6. Ibid.
7. Barth, "Swat Pathans Reconsidered", p. 143.
8. I agree "broadly" because although it is true that these relations have become more contractual and monetised, it does not mean that they are purely "economic", since landlords are extensively involved in politics and wield significant political power over clients.
9. See Jan Breman, *Patronage and Exploitation: Changing Agrarian Relations in South Gujarat, India*, Berkeley: University of California Press, 1974.
10. The fickle loyalty of politicians towards political parties is sometimes popularly referred to as "*lotaism*". The *lota* is most commonly a metal jar with a curved spout that is used for ablutions and for cleaning oneself after going to the toilet. A single *lota* is generally used by several people. I was told that the reason why politicians were like *lotas* was that they were constantly switching hands.
11. Phillip E. Jones, *The Pakistan People's Party: Rise to Power*, Oxford: Oxford University Press, 2003, p. 362.
12. See Syed Reza Vali Nasr, *Islamic Leviathan: Islam and the Making of State Power*, Oxford: Oxford University Press, 2001 for a discussion of how the Ayub Khan regime sought to create a constituency among the middle ranking landed classes in order to bypass and weaken the power of the traditional feudal elite.
13. Hamza Alavi, "Kinship in West Punjab Villages," *Contributions to Indian Sociology*, 6/1, 1972, pp. 1–27.
14. The police were in fact widely held to cooperate actively in these activities.
15. Andrew Wilder, *The Pakistan Voter, Electoral Politics and Voting Behaviour in the Punjab*, Karachi: Oxford University Press, 1999.
16. See International Crisis Group, *Pakistan's Local Polls: Shoring up Military Rule*, Islamabad and Brussels: International Crisis Group, 2005.
17. Saghir Ahmed, *Class and Power in a Punjabi Village*, London: Monthly Review Press, 1977.
18. See Breman, *Patronage and Exploitation*.
19. The land upon which the village had been built was technically government land since Bhutto's reforms in the 1970s, but the Gondals treated it as if it was theirs. Villagers told me that the Gondals and their gunmen could evict them from their village homes if they wanted to. See Shahnaz Rouse, "Systematic Injustices and Inequalities: Maliki and Raiya in a Punjab Village" in H. Gardezi and J. Rashid (eds), *Pakistan, The Roots of Dictatorship: The Political Economy of a Praetorian State*, London: Zed Press, 1983, pp. 311–25.
20. In one instance the driver of a Gondal landlord spent 1500 rupees in multiple trips to the police station, and paid bribes to clerks and officers, in order to file a First Information Report against someone. Had his employer intervened he would not have had to spend anything.
21. For a discussion of bonded labour in the Pakistani Punjab see Nicolas Martin, "The

Political Economy of Bonded Labour in the Pakistani Punjab," *Contributions to Indian Sociology*, 43/1, 2009, pp. 35–59.

22. This is arguably what happened in neighbouring India where the upper castes lost their traditional monopoly over political power, and were forced to partially relinquish their control over government jobs because of reservation policies that guaranteed jobs to members of the lower castes.

23. For an account of sectarianism in the southern Punjab see Mariam Abou Zahab, "Sectarianism as a Substitute Identity: Sunnis and Shias in Central and South Punjab" in S. Mumtaz, J.L. Racine and I.A. Ali (eds), *Pakistan: The Contours of State and Society*, Oxford: Oxford University Press, 2002.

24. See Syed Reza Vali Nasr,"The Rise of Sunni Militancy in Pakistan: The Changing Role of Islamism and the Ulama in Society and Politics," *Modern Asian Studies*, 34/1, pp. 139–80 and Qasim Zaman, *The Ulama in Contemporary Islam: Custodians of Change*, Princeton: Princeton University Press, 2002.

9. EXCEPTIONAL PASHTUNS?: CLASS POLITICS, IMPERIALISM AND HISTORIOGRAPHY

1. Talal Asad, "Afterword: From the History of Colonial Anthropology to the Anthropology of Western Hegemony" in George W. Stocking Jr. (ed.), *Colonial Situations: Essays on the Contextualization of Ethnographic Knowledge, History of Anthropology*, Madison: University of Wisconsin Press, 1991, pp. 314–24.

2. My great thanks to Ruard Absaroka, Miriyam Aouragh, Anna Laerke, Iftikhar Malik and Pablo Mukherjee for their thoughtful comments and suggestions on earlier drafts of this paper. I thank especially Jonathan Neale for his support and wisdom as we have struggled to understand the Afghan tragedy.

3. There has been much debate about where Afghanistan and Pakistan fit into area anthropologies of the Middle East, Muslim Southwest Asia and/or Central Asia, and of Islam. This discussion is symptomatic of some of the problems I address here.

4. Charles Lindholm, "The New Middle Eastern Ethnography," *Journal of the Royal Anthropological Institute*, 1/4, 1995, pp. 805–820, cf. 805, 812, 817.

5. Part of this difference is disciplinary. History is about the past: an historian's work can be discounted if it challenges current hegemonies, and most informants are beyond temporal punishment. Moreover, most historians, and other scholars, write of elites and public figures. This, and a range of writing conventions, affords them and their sources a degree of protection. And there is an expectation that such accounts will be polemical.

6. Compare Heidi Armbruster and Anna Laerke (eds), *Taking Sides: Ethnics, Politics and Fieldwork in Anthropology*, Oxford: Berghahn, 2008; Alisse Waterston and Maria D. Verperi (eds), *Anthropology off the Shelf: Anthropologists on Writing*, Oxford: Wiley-Blackwell, 2009; and Nancy Scheper-Hughes, "Making Anthropology Public," *Anthropology Today*, 25/4, 2009, pp. 1–2.

7. Compare Asraf Ghani, "Impact of Foreign Aid on Relations Between State and Society" and "The Future of the Past," International Seminar on Social and Cultural Prospects

for Afghanistan, Peshawar, *Journal of Afghan Affairs* (5/4, Special Issue, October–December 1990), Writers Union of Free Afghanistan (WUFA), Association of Professors of Universities of Afghanistan, 1990, pp. 115–33, 155–90, with Asraf Ghani and Clare Lockhart, *Fixing Failed States: A Framework for Rebulding a Fractured World*, Oxford: Oxford University Press, 2009. Also see, for example, Antonio Giustozzi's coy and confusing note on the Sandinistas of Nicaragua in *Empires of Mud: Wars and Warlords in Afghanistan*, London: Hurst, 2009, p. 301, n.1.

8. There are exceptions which prove the rule: e.g., the strong oppositional academic literature on Israel/Palestine, and on Iran, mostly written in exile. On Afghanistan and Pakistan, see, for instance, Aijaz Ahmed, *Iraq, Afghanistan and the Imperialism of Our Time*, New Delhi: Left Word, 2004 and Tariq Ali, "The Perils of Islamophobia," Recorded talk, *Marxism 2010: Ideas to Change the World*, 2 July 2010.

9. Cf. Carolyn Nordstrom's brave, wide-ranging anthropology of war, *Shadows of War: Violence, Power and International Profiteering in the Twenty-First Century*, Berkeley: University of California, 2004. The case of the Taliban resistance is in some ways comparable to that of the Mau Mau uprising in Kenya in the 1950s, when few anthropologists dared face the tyranny of empire then or afterwards. See David Anderson, *Histories of the Hanged: The Dirty War in Kenya and the End of Empire*, London: Weidenfeld & Nicolson and New York: W.W. Norton, 2005; Caroline Elkins, *Imperial Reckoning: The Untold Story of Britain's Gulag in Kenya*, New York: Henry Holt Elkins, 2005.

10. David Price, "Past Wars, Present Dangers, Future Anthropologies," *Anthropology Today*, 18/1, 2002, pp. 3–5; Robert J. González, "Human Terrain: Past, Present and Future Applications," *Anthropology Today*, 24/1, 2008, pp. 21–6; M. McFate and S. Fondacaro, "Cultural Knowledge and Common Sense. A Response to González in this Issue," *Anthropology Today*, 24/1, 2008, p. 27; Robert Albro, "Anthropology and the Military: AFRICOM, 'Culture' and the Future of Human Terrain Analysis," *Anthropology Today*, 26/1, 2010, pp. 22–4; cf. Robert Young Pelton, "The New War for Hearts and Minds," *Men's Journal*, 18/3, 2009, pp. 78–83, 98.

11. There are of course admirable exceptions, as mentioned in Note 9.

12. Nikolai Bukharin, *Imperialism and the World Economy*, London: Bookmarks, 2003; Rosa Luxemburg and Nikolai Bukharin, *Imperialism and the Accumulation of Capital*, Harmondsworth: Penguin, 1971; V.I. Lenin, *Imperialism, the Highest Stage of Capitalism, Collected Works*, XXII, Moscow: State Publishing House, 1964.

13. On these debates, see Andre Gunder Frank and Barry K Gills (eds), *The World System: Five Hundred Years or Five Thousand?*, Abingdon: Routledge, 1993, and John Darwin, *The Empire Project: The Rise and Fall of the British World System, 1820–1970*, Cambridge: Cambridge University Press, 2009; for recent Marxist critiques, see David Harvey, *The New Imperialism*, Oxford University Press, 2003; Alex Callinicos, *Imperialism and Global Political Economy*, Oxford: Polity, 2009; Gilbert Achcar, "Rethinking Imperialism: Past, Present and Future," *International Socialism*, 126, 2010, pp. 187–95.

14. Gilles Dorronsoro, *Revolution Unending: Afghanistan: 1979 to the Present*, London: Hurst, 2005, p. 317, n.12.

15. Christine Buchholz and Jan van Aken, *Afghanistan: Das wahre Gesicht des Krieges*, Berlin: Fraktion Die Linke im Bundestag, 2010.

16. Joe Glenton, "Experience. I went to prison for going awol," *The Guardian Weekend*, 14 Aug, 2010, p. 10.
17. Judy Dempsey, "Afghan leaks add to Europe's doubts'," *International Herald Tribune*, 29 July 2010, p. 3.
18. James Scott, *Domination and the Arts of Resistance: Hidden Transcripts*, New Haven, CT: Yale University Press, 1990.
19. Gilles Dorronsoro, *Revolution Unending*, p. 355.
20. Ibid., pp. 13–14.
21. Robert J. González, "Going "Tribal": Notes on Pacification in the 21st Century," *Anthropology Today*, 25/2, 2009, pp. 15–19.
22. Marcus Banks, *Ethnicity: Anthropological Construction*, London: Routledge, 1996, p. 190.
23. "Ethnicity, Order and Meaning in the Anthropology of Iran and Afghanistan," in J.-P. Digard (ed.), *Le Fait ethnique en Iran et en Afghanistan*, Paris: CNRS, 1988, p. 22.
24. Antonio Giustozzi, *Koran, Kalashnikov and Laptop: The Neo-Taliban Insurgency in Afghanistan*, London: Hurst and New York: Columbia University Press, 2008, p. 240.
25. Richard Wilkinson and Kate Pickett offer an unequivocal demonstration of how inequality harms not only the poor, but the vast majority (*The Spirit Level: Why More Equal Societies Almost Always Do Better*, London: Allen Lane, 2009). Their statistics relate to citizens of single states, yet the argument also has global implications. For example, the gross inequalities introduced by the occupation and the rich expatriate community in Afghanistan give impetus to both the egalitarian discourse of Islamist resistance and anti-war sentiment in Euro-America.
26. Cf. Marsden, this volume.
27. Nancy Tapper, "Direct Exchange and Brideprice: Alternative Forms in a Complex Marriage System," *Man* (NS), 16, 1981, pp. 387–407; Nancy Tapper, *Bartered Brides: Politics, Gender and Marriage in an Afghan Tribal Society*, Cambridge: Cambridge University Press, 1991.
28. Antonio Giustozzi (ed.), *Decoding the New Taliban: Insights from the Afghan Field*, London: Hurst and New York: Columbia University Press, 2009.
29. Magnus Marsden, "Talking the Talk: Debating Debate in Northern Afghanistan," *Anthropology Today*, 25/2, 2009, p. 22.
30. Jonathan Neale, "Afghanistan: the Case Against the 'Good War'," *International Socialism*, 120, 2008, pp. 31–60.
31. Cf. Banks, *Ethnicity*, pp. 32–3, *passim*.
32. Along with the new ideology came other assaults on class politics in the economic downturn of the 1970s and 1980s. Thatcher broke the miners' union, so too the American government systematically attacked the unions. Elsewhere too class analyses are discredited. For example, anti-Stalinist critiques of dictatorship in the Soviet empire or Cuba often slide into right-wing critiques of Marxism as a whole.
33. *The Guardian*, 15 March 2010, p. 27.
34. Nancy Lindisfarne, *Dancing in Damascus: Stories*, Albany: State University of New York, 2000, p. 143.
35. Dorronsoro, *Revolution Unending*, p. 15; cf. Neamatollah Nojumi, *The Rise of the Taliban in Afghanistan: Mass Mobilization, Civil War and the Future of the Region*, New York:

Palgrave, pp. 60 ff. Even as senior diplomats, like Sir Sherard Cowper-Coles, believe the time has come to discuss a power-sharing government with the Taliban (Richard Norton-Taylor, "The wait for talks to start," *The Guardian*, 29 June 2010, p. 30; Richard Barrett, "Taliban put to the test," *The Guardian*, 21 July 2010, p. 28), the impetus to divide-and-rule remains. Karzai has apparently approved a plan for new local militias which the Taliban believe is "an attempt by the United States to split up Afghanistan ahead of the withdrawal of its troops" (Richard A. Oppel, Jr. and Taimoor Shah, "Attack killed 52, Afghans report," *International Herald Tribune*, World News Asia, 27 July 2010, p. 6).

36. "Starting from Below: Fieldwork, Gender and Imperialism Now," *Critique of Anthropology*, 22/4, 2002, pp. 403–423; "Culture Wars," *Anthropology Today*, 24/3, 2008, pp. 3–4.
37. In a rare admission, Obama's main military adviser said, "US 'will attack if Iran poses nuclear threat'," (Ed Pilkington, *The Guardian*, 2 August 2010, p. 11).
38. Fredrik Barth, *Political Leadership among Swat Pathans*, London: Athlone, 1959. See also Fredrik Barth, "Segmentary Opposition and the Theory of Games: a Study of Pathan Organization," *Journal of the Royal Anthropological Institute*, 89, 1959, pp. 5–21.
39. Talal Asad, "Market Model, Class Structure and Consent: A Reconsideration of Swat Political Organization," *Man* (NS) 7/1, 1972, pp. 74–94; cf. Banks, *Ethnicity*, pp. 13 ff. and especially Akbar S. Ahmed, *Millennium and Charisma among Pathans*, London: Routledge & Kegan Paul, 1976.
40. Barth also divides the peasantry into a timeless hierarchy of "castes": Pakhtún (landholding tribesman), farmer (*zamidār*), agricultural labourer (*dehqān*) (*Political Leadership*, p. 17). A class analysis would have invited comparison with peasant societies elsewhere instead of making Pakhtuns appear exceptional, and it would have better explained Barth's numerous examples of individuals and groups moving between these occupations—thus, "they used to be herders, but now they are farmers", or "they were really Pakhtuns, but ate up all their lands, and now they are smiths." (ibid., p. 21)
41. Asad also points out that Barth's account also has curious implications for the stereotyping of Pakhtuns, and that the "maleness" of the chiefs, and their aggression, may be artifacts of Barth's agonistic description itself.
42. Fredrik Barth, *Features of Person and Society in Swat*, London: Routledge & Kegan Paul, 1981, p. 151.
43. Ernest Gellner, *Saints of the Atlas*, Chicago: University of Chicago Press, 1969.
44. Michael Gilsenan, *Saint and Sufi in Modern Egypt: An Essay in the Sociology of Religion*, Oxford: Oxford University Press, 1973; Michael Gilsenan, *Lords of the Lebanese Marches: Violence, Power and Narrative in an Arab Society*, London: I.B. Tauris, 1995.
45. Edward Said, *Orientalism*, New York: Pantheon, 1978.
46. It is important to note that Barth's introduction to his edited volume (*Ethnic Groups and Boundaries*, London: George Allen and Unwin, 1969, cf. Banks, *Ethnicity*, pp. 14ff.) bucked the then new ideology of division by focusing on the persistence of boundaries between named categories of people in spite of the osmosis of personnel across them. This approach admits an historical perspective on the material bases and structural constraints to individual and collective negotiation and strategies. For a relational approach to tribes and the state, see Richard Tapper (ed.), *The Conflict of Tribe and State in Iran and Afghanistan*, London: Croom Helm, 1983.

47. Barth describes honour and shame as idioms used to manage economic conflict and political competition (*Political Leadership*, pp. 82ff.), as do C. Lindholm and C. Lindholm ("Marriage as Warfare," *Natural History*, October 1979, pp. 11–20) and Nancy Tapper, *Bartered Brides*. These writers offer an approach which is very different from those essentialising accounts of Pashtunwali and honour and shame (which often reify Ahmed's ideal types, *nang* and *galang*: *Millennium and Charisma*, pp. 73 ff.) that continue to appear regularly in the literature (e.g. David Kilcullen, "Taliban and Counter-Insurgency in Kunar" in Giustozzi (ed.), *Decoding the New Taliban*, pp. 231–45 (234ff.) and Ann Jones, *Kabul in Winter: Life without Peace in Afghanistan*, New York: Picador, 2006, pp. 40ff. For a radical approach to discourses of honour and shame in the Middle East, see Nancy Lindisfarne ("Variant Masculinities, Variant Virginities: Rethinking 'Honour and Shame'," in Andrea Cornwall and Nancy Lindisfarne (eds), *Dislocating Masculinity: Comparative Ethnographies*, London: Routledge, 1994, pp. 82–96).
48. Ahmed, *Millennium and Charisma*; Michael Meeker, "The Twilight of a South Asian Heroic Age: A Rereading of Barths Study of Swat," *Man* (NS), 15, 1980, pp. 682–701; Charles Lindholm, *Generosity and Jealousy: The Swat Pukhtun of Northern Pakistan*, New York: Columbia University Press, 1982, p. 92 and compare Lindholm, this volume.
49. And compare Anatol Lieven's *Pakistan: A Hard Country*, London: Penguin, 2011.
50. Fredrik Barth, *The Last Wali of Swat: An Autobiography as told to Fredrik Barth*, New York: Columbia University Press, 1985.
51. The North West Frontier Province was renamed Khyber Paskhtunkhwa in April 2010.
52. Sartaj Khan, "Imperialism, Religion and Class in Swat," *International Socialism*, 123, 2009, pp. 21–6, p. 23.
53. Kamran Asdar Ali, "Pakistan's Troubled 'Paradise on Earth'", *Middle East Report Online*, 29 April 2009, p. 4. http://www.merip.org/mero/mero04909.html (accessed 20 May 2010).
54. Ibid.
55. Ibid., p. 5.
56. Ibid., p. 4.
57. And see Asad's excellent ethnography on poppy production in NWFP. During fieldwork, he relied on his own kin as bodyguards and played the dynamics of local feuds to protect him (Amirzada Asad and Robert Harris, *The Politics and Economics of Drug Production on the Pakistan Afghanistan Border: Implications for a Globalized World*, Aldershot: Ashgate, 2003).
58. Ali, "Pakistan's Troubled 'Paradise on Earth'", pp. 5–6.
59. Khan, "Imperialism, Religion and Class in Swat," p. 24.
60. Ibid.
61. Ibid., pp. 24–5.
62. See Abou Zahab, this volume.
63. Cf. Vartan Gregorian, *The Emergence of Modern Afghanistan: Politics of Reform and Modernization, 1880–1948*, Palo Alto, CA: Stanford University Press, 1969, pp. 323 ff.; S. Rittenberg, *Ethnicity, Nationalism and the Pukhtuns: The Independence Movement in India's NWFP*, Durham, NC: Carolina Academic, 1988; Mukulika Banarjee, *The Pathan Unarmed*, Oxford: James Currey, 2000.

NOTES

64. Ali, "Pakistan's Troubled 'Paradise on Earth'," p. 2.
65. Cf. Lindholm, and Weiss, this volume.
66. Ali, "Pakistan's Troubled 'Paradise on Earth'," p. 6.
67. See Martin, this volume. "In south Punjab, the class factor is quite crucial in understanding the purist-militarist ideology as the local mullahs seem to be trying to assert themselves as mouthpieces for the have-nots against the feudal dynasts" (Iftikhar Malik, Personal Communication).
68. Declan Walsh, "Pakistani troops continue assault on Taliban near Swat valley," *The Guardian*, 27 April 2009, www.guardian.co.uk/ .../Pakistan-troops ... (accessed 20 May 2010). Cf. Akbar S. Ahmed and Gustaaf Houtman, "Swat in the Eye of the Storm," *Anthropology Today*, 25/5, 2009, pp. 20–22.
69. Jane Perlez and Pir Zubair Shah, "Taliban exploit class rift to gain ground in Pakistan," 16 April 2009, http:www.vuw.ac.nz/~caplabtb/dprk/US_world09.htm#april09 (accessed 20 May 2010); cf. "The Taliban's latest tactic; Class warfare. Inroads are being made in Pakistan by playing poor against the wealthy," *International Herald Tribune*, 17 April 2009.
70. Declan Walsh, "Humanitarian Crisis in Swat," *The Guardian*, 7 May 2009, Theage.com.au/world/humanitian crisis in Swat valley, 20090506 avaf.html (accessed 20 May 2010).
71. Jane Perlez and Pir Zubair Shah, "Landowners still in exile from unstable Pakistan aread," 28 July 2009, http:www.vuw.ac.nz/~caplabtb/dprk/US_world09.htm#august09 (accessed 20 May 2010); cf. "Lack of landowners could destabilize Swat valley," *International Herald Tribune*, News, 7 August 2009.
72. J. Malcolm Gracia, "A Year Later, Life Resumes in the Swat Valley," 21 January 2010. http://www.allvoices.com/contributed news/5086650-a-year-later-life, etc.
73. Riaz Khan, "More than 1,100 dead as Pakistan floods wash away whole villages," *The Guardian*, 2 August 2010, p. 12.
74. *The New York Times*, Editorial, "Rage and floods in Pakistan," 4 August 2010, p. A18.
75. Sippi Azerbaijani Moghaddam, "Northern Exposure for the Taliban" in A. Giustozzi (ed.), *Decoding the New Taliban*, pp. 247–68. Cf. A. Klaits and G. Gulmamadova-Klaits, *Love and War in Afghanistan*, New York: Seven Stories, 2005.
76. David Edwards, "Learning from the Swat Pathans: Political Leadership in Afghanistan, 1978–97," *American Ethnologist*, 25/4, 1998, pp. 712–28, p. 712; yet compare Edwards' own far-reaching history, *Heroes of the Age*, Berkeley: University of California Press, 1996.
77. Ibid., p. 725.
78. Antonio Giustozzi, *Koran, Kalashnikov and Laptop: The Neo-Taliban Insurgency in Afghanistan*, London: Hurst and New York: Columbia University Press, 2008.
79. Gregorian, *The Emergence of Modern Afghanistan*, pp. 319–20.
80. Neale, "Afghanistan: the Case".
81. Giustozzi, *Empires of Mud*, pp. 35ff.
82. Dorronsoro, *Revolution Unending*, p. 288.
83. On how this shift affected the lives of ordinary people, see Said Hyder Akbar and Susan

Barton, *Come Back to Afghanistan: My Journey from California to Kabul*, London: Bloomsbury, 2006; Deborah Rodriguez, *The Kabul Beauty School*, London: Hodder, 2008.
84. Abdul Salam Zaeef, *My Life with the Taliban*, London: Hurst, 2010.
85. Giustozzi, *Koran, Kalashnikov and Laptop*, 2008, p. 39
86. Ibid.
87. Ibid., pp. 66, 68.
88. Cf. J. Rico, *Blood Makes the Grass Grow Green: A Year in the Desert with Team America*, New York: Ballantine Books, 2007; Tom Coghlan, "The Taliban in Helmand: An Oral History" in Giustozzi (ed.), *Decoding the New Taliban*, pp. 119–53; and Christopher Reuter and Borhan Younus, "The Return of the Taliban in Ander District, Ghazni," in Giustozzi (ed.), *Decoding the New Taliban*, pp. 101–118.
89. *International Herald Tribune*, "The Afghan war logs," World News, 26 July 2010, 1, 6–7, p. 6.
90. Giustozzi, *Koran, Kalashnikov and Laptop*, p. 47.
91. Ibid., p. 209.
92. Ibid., p. 36.
93. Zaeef, *My Life with the Taliban*, pp. 238, 240.
94. Giustozzi (ed.), *Decoding the New Taliban*.
95. Giustozzi, *Empires of Mud*, pp. 138 ff.
96. Ibid., p. 23.
97. Neamatollah Nojumi, Dyan Nazurana and Elizabeth Stites, *Life and Security in Afghanistan*, Lanham, Maryland: Rowman and Littlefield, 2009.
98. Jon Boone and Ewan MacAskill, "Obama moves to bypass Karzai as drug abuses claim adds to dismay over his behaviour," *The Guardian*, 8 April 2010, p. 27.
99. Akbar S. Ahmed, 25/4/2009http://www.independent.co.uk/opinion/commentators/Akbarahmed-lose-lawless-tribal ….; Akbar S. Ahmed and Gustaaf Houtman, "Swat in the Eye of the Storm".
100. Emma Brockes, "Why are Muslims so hypersensitive?," *The Guardian Weekend*, 8 May 2010, pp. 21–6; Mark Townsend, "Gita Sahgal's dispute with Amnesty International puts human rights group in the dock," *The Observer*, 25 April 2010. http://www.guardian.co.uk/world/2010/apr/25/ gita-sahgalamnesty international.
101. Helene Cooper and Mark Landler, "U.S. shifts to targeted killings in Afghanistan," *International Herald Tribune*, 2 August 2010, pp. 1, 8.
102. Giustozzi, *Koran, Kalashnikov and Laptop*, p. 72.
103. Ibid., p. 176.
104. Julian Borger, "Assault deepens Afghan anxieties over what will happen when Nato troops leave," *The Guardian*, 14 September 2011, p. 14.
105. John William Kaye, *History of the War in Afghanistan*, 3 vols. London: Wm. H. Allen, 1878, p. 390. Cf. Simon Jenkins, "A history of folly, from the Trojan Horse to Afghanistan," *The Guardian*, 28 July 2010, p. 31, and Geoff Cowling and John Newsinger, "Failing to learn the lessons of Afghan history,", *The Guardian*, 29 July 2010, p. 29.

10. CLASS, STATE AND POWER IN THE SWAT CONFLICT

1. Swat district had an estimated population of 715,938 in 1981 and 1,249,572 in the 1998 census, a 3.3 per cent growth rate. Iman-ur-Rahman and Alain Viaro, *Swat: An Afghan Society in Pakistan*, Karachi: City Press, 2002, p. 17. Miangul Abdul Wadud estimated a 1969 population of "three quarters of a million" for the larger area of the former Swat State: Fredrik Barth, *The Last Wali of Swat* (1985), Bangkok: White Orchid Press, 1995, p. 112.
2. Fredrik Barth, *Political Leadership among Swat Pathans*, London: The Athlone Press, 1959. Talal Asad, "Market Model, Class Structure and Consent: a Reconsideration of Swat Political Organization," *Man* (NS), 8/1, 1972, pp. 74–94. Also see Charles Lindholm, *Generosity and Jealousy, The Swat Pukhtun of Northern Pakistan*, New York: Columbia University Press, 1982.
3. For the consequences of the failure of representative government and "a ruling class that has monopoly control over key political and economic resources," especially in Punjab, see Nicolas Martin's contribution to this volume.
4. Robert Nichols, "Challenging the State: 1990s Religious Movements in the Northwest Frontier Province," in Craig Baxter and Charles Kennedy (eds), *Pakistan 1997*, Boulder: Westview Press, 1998, pp. 123–42.
5. Robert Nichols, *A History of Pashtun Migration, 1775–2006*, Karachi: Oxford University Press, 2008. Early travelers circulating through the lower Swat valley after traversing the Kunar valley-Bajour route from Afghanistan included Alexander the Great, the armies of Mahmud of Ghazni, and the Mughal Emperor Babur.
6. See Magnus Marsden, *Living Islam: Muslim Religious Experience in Pakistan's North-West Frontier*, Cambridge: Cambridge University Press, 2005.
7. For discussion of the Taliban's effort to "combine Islamist ideals and class politics to emphasise egalitarian feeling and mobilise support" see Lindisfarne's essay in this volume.
8. See multiple texts, including Ayesha Jalal, *State of Martial Rule: the Origins of Pakistan's Political Economy of Defense*, Cambridge: Cambridge University Press, 1990; Ayesha Siddiqa, *Military, Inc.: Inside Pakistan's Military Economy*, London: Pluto, 2007.
9. Important literature for this paper includes Fredrik Barth, *The Last Wali of Swat*; Fredrik Barth, "Swat Pathans Reconsidered," in *Features of Person and Society in Swat: Collected Essays on Pathans*, London: Routledge & Kegan Paul, 1981.
10. Inam-ur-Rahim and Alain Viaro, *Swat: An Afghan Society in Pakistan*, Karachi: City Press, 2002, p. 6.
11. Barth, "Swat Pathans Reconsidered," p. 153.
12. *Wesh* exchanges occurred between the Sebujni and Nikpikhel, Shamizai and Adinzai, Abakhel and Khankhel, Musakhel and Maturizai, Azikhel and Chakaisar, Babozai and Pooran, and Jinkikhel and Kana. See Inam-ur-Rahim and Alain Viaro, *Swat*, p. 129.
13. Akbar S. Ahmed, *Millennium and Charisma among Pathans: A Critical Essay in Social Anthropology*, London: Routledge and Kegan Paul, 1976. See discussion in Sultan-i-Rome, *Swat State (1915–1969), From Genesis to Merger*, Karachi: Oxford University Press, 2008, p. 232.

14. Fredrik Barth, *The Last Wali of Swat*, p. 73.
15. Lindholm, *Generosity and Jealousy*, p. 48.
16. Ibid., p. 6.
17. Ibid., pp. 48, 9–10.
18. Inam-ur-Rahim and Alain Viaro, *Swat*, p. 208.
19. Ibid., p. 207.
20. The chapter "Swat Pathans reconsidered" is a sixty page essay of response to a variety of reviews and critiques. "There is no doubt that there was widespread and clearly expressed discontent: with poverty and toil; with subjugation.... We grasp the form of this discontent truly only if we see it in local cultural terms, not by renaming it class exploitation and class consciousness." Barth, "Swat Pathans Reconsidered," p. 147.
21. Ibid., p. 145.
22. Ibid.
23. Charles Lindholm, "Contemporary Politics in a Tribal Society" in *Frontier Perspectives: Essays in Comparative Anthropology*, Karachi: Oxford University Press, 1996, p. 80. Kabal became the main town of the Nipkikhel clan region.
24. Lindholm, *Generosity and Jealousy*, p. 49.
25. Barth, *The Last Wali of Swat*, p. 56.
26. The Malakand Division would eventually include the districts of Chitral, Dir, Swat, Shangla, Buner, and Malakand.
27. See Nichols, "Challenging the State," pp. 125–7.
28. Ibid., 125–8.
29. See Robert Nichols, *Settling the Frontier: Land, Law and Society in the Peshawar Valley, 1500–1900*, Karachi: Oxford University Press, 2001, Chapter 10.
30. Nichols, "Challenging the State," p. 124.
31. Ayesha Jalal, *Democracy and Authoritarianism in South Asia*, Cambridge: Cambridge University Press, 1995, p. 121.
32. Essentializing discourses are critiqued in Charles Lindholm, "Images of the Pathan: The Usefulness of Colonial Ethnography" in *Frontier Perspectives*, pp. 3–16; David Edwards, *Heroes of the Age, Moral Fault Lines on the Afghan Frontier*, Berkeley: University of California Press, 1996, pp. 181–2; Maira Hayat, "Still 'Taming the Turbulent Frontier'? The State in the Federally Administered Tribal Areas of Pakistan," *Journal of the Anthropological Society of Oxford* (NS) 1/2, Winter 2009.
33. Edmund Burke III, "Islam and Social Movements: Methodological Reflections" in Edmund Burke III and Ira M. Lapidus (eds), *Islam, Politics, and Social Movements*, Berkeley: University of California Press, 1988, pp. 17–35.
34. Nichols, "Challenging the State," p. 128; and see Joel Migdal, *Strong Societies and Weak States, State-Society Relations and State Capabilities in the Third World*, Princeton: Princeton University Press, 1988, Chapter 3.
35. Delawar Jan, "Why did Swat militants exhume Pir Samiullah's body," *The News*, 19 December 2008.
36. Zahid Hussain, "Paradise lost," *Newsline*, February 2009 (online).
37. Ikram Hoti, "The peaceful people of the 'ghost valley' tormented, humiliated," *The News*, 14 May 2009, p. 9.

38. "Taliban want Malakand legislators to quit," *Dawn*, 14 May 2009, p. 12.
39. Ibid., p. 12.
40. Ibid.
41. *The Economist*, 2 May 2009, p. 25.
42. Jane Perlez and Pir Zubair Shah, "Landlords still in exile from unstable Pakistan area," *New York Times*, 28 July 2009.
43. Quote from Professor Vali Nasr, adviser to Richard Holbrooke, "Landlords Still in Exile," *New York Times*, 28 July 2009.
44. "Roots of Taliban conflict fester in Swat," *Dawn*, 19 April 2010.
45. Ibid.
46. *The Economist*, 2 May 2009, p. 25.
47. See discussion in Nichols, "Challenging the State," p. 125. Also see discussion in Joel Migdal, Atul Kohli, and Vivienne Shue (eds), *State Power and Social Forces*, Cambridge: Cambridge University Press, 1994, pp. 1–4, 5–34.
48. A. Ameer, "Taliban influence in bureaucracy," *Dawn*, 18 April 2009.
49. "Commissioner of Malakand being replaced," *Dawn*, 24 April 2009.
50. Umer Farooq, "Enemy Inside the Gates," *Herald*, May 2010, pp. 46–7.
51. Rahimullah Yusufzai, "Extrajudicial deaths in Swat?" *The News*, 19 August 2009.
52. "HRCP sees improvement in Swat law and order," *Dawn*, 28 May 2010, p. 3.
53. Elena Becatoros, "Relatives accuse Pakistan forces in Swat killings," *San Diego Union* (AP), 24 August 2009.
54. Delawar Jan, "Swatis believe army will smoke out Taliban remnants," *The News*, 24 May 2010.
55. "Swat militants told to surrender by May 15," *Dawn*, 30 April 2010.
56. "25 families of rebels expelled from Swat," *Frontier Post*, 22 May 2010.
57. Gohar Ali Gohar, "Expelled Swatis 'confined' to Palai camp," *Dawn*, 24 May 2010.
58. "Kabal elders demand market price for acquired lands," *Daily Times*, 13 June 2010, p. 2.
59. Mohammad Ali Khan, "Four cantts to maintain Swat peace," *Dawn*, 10 July 2010, p. 9.
60. Ezdi, "Drawing the right lesson," *Dawn*, 5 December 2007.
61. Ilhan Niaz, *The Culture of Power and Governance of Pakistan, 1947–2008*, Karachi: Oxford University Press, 2010, Preface, p. ix.

11. THE SWAT CRISIS

1. This is a modified and updated version of an earlier paper, entitled "Swat: A Critical Analysis", published by the Institute of Peace and Conflict Studies (IPCS), New Delhi, as Research Paper No. 18, January 2009.
2. The traditional consultative institution and forum, wherein matters of common interest and communal affairs are discussed and decided.
3. Also see Sayyed Abdul Ghafoor Qasmi, *Hidyah Wadudiah yani Sawanih Hayat Ala Hazat Badshah Abdul Wadud Khan Khudullahu Mulkahu Hukamran Riyasat-e-Yusufzai Swat wa Mutaliqat* (Urdu), Baraily: Matbua Saudagar Press, n.d. [written in 1936], pp. 61–2; Taj Muhammad Khan Zebsar, *Uruj-e-Afghan* (Pashto verse), vol. 1, Peshawar: Printed by Manzur-e-Aam Press, 1360 AH, pp. 234–51.

4. For some detail, see Sultan-i-Rome, *Swat State (1915–1969): From Genesis to Merger; An Analysis of Political, Administrative, Socio-Political, and Economic Developments*, Karachi: Oxford University Press, 2008, chapter 9.
5. See Sultan-i-Rome, "Swat: A Critical Analysis," *IPCS Research Paper 18*, New Delhi: Institute of Peace and Conflict Studies, January 2009, pp. 8–12.
6. For detailed analysis, see Sultan-i-Rome, *Swat State (1915–1969)*, pp. 195–203; Sultan-i-Rome, "Judicial System, Judiciary and Justice in Swat: The Swat State era and the Post State Scenario," *Journal of the Pakistan Historical Society*, 49, 2001, No. 4, pp. 89–100.
7. Wayne Ayres Wilcox, *Pakistan: The Consolidation of a Nation*, New York: Columbia University Press, 1963, p. 155.
8. *Jihad* has several meanings. Fighting in the way of Almighty Allah by means of arms (holy war fought for the cause of Islam against non-Muslims) is one of them and is mentioned as *qital* in the Holy Qur'an. With the tendency of the use the word *jihad* in the context of *qital* alone, the other dimensions and aspects of *jihad* remain obscured.
9. Also see Mohammad Yousaf and Mark Adkin, *Afghanistan—The Bear Trap: The Defeat of a Superpower*, New Delhi: Bookwise (India) Pvt Ltd, 2007; Muhammad Amir Rana and Rohan Gunaratna, *Al-Qaeda Fights Back Inside Pakistani Tribal Areas*, Lahore: Pak Institute for Peace Studies (PIPS), 2007, pp. 12, 24–7, 35, *passim*; Fazal-ur-Rahim Marwat and Parvez Khan Toru, *Talibanization of Pakistan: (A Case Study of TNSM)*, Peshawar: Pakistan Study Centre, University of Peshawar, 2005, p. 2; Emma Duncan, *Breaking the Curfew: A Political Journey through Pakistan*, reprint, London: Arrow Books Limited, 1990, p. 280; Christina Lamb, *Waiting for Allah: Pakistan's Struggle for Democracy*, New Delhi: Viking Penguin Books India (P) Ltd, 1991, pp. 196, 206–42; Khan Abdul Wali Khan, *Bacha Khan au Khudai Khidmatgari*, vol. 3 (Pashto), Charsada: Wali Bagh, 1998.
10. Previously, *jihad*, training for it and jihadi activities were not the concern of the common populace or the talk of the day, as they are today. The change came about because of the role played by the Pakistani, American, European, and Arab countries and intelligence agencies. In spite of their coming from different mindsets and cultural and geographical areas, a shared culture of jihad and mindset of the jihadis was fashioned. Therefore, those countries and their intelligence agencies are responsible in direct and overt, and indirect and covert ways for the upheavals, destructions and sabotage associated with contemporary jihadism.
11. India also is engaged for reasons of its self-interest. Although it was too late, Mian Iftikhar Hussain, provincial Minister for Information and spokesman of the Khyber Pakhtunkhwa provincial government, conceded the point by asserting that America, Russia, China, Iran, India, Pakistan, and Afghanistan play a third World War (i.e. a war for securing their interests) on Pukhtun land: see *Mashriq* (Urdu daily), Peshawar, 9 May 2010, p. 12; *Roznama Azadi Swat* (Urdu daily), Mingawara, Swat, 20 June 2011, pp. 1, 7; *Roznama Express Peshawar* (Urdu daily), Peshawar, 20 June 2011, pp. 1, 5. The Chief Minister of the province, Amir Haidar Khan Hoti, also made a similar contention: see *Roznama Express Peshawar* (Urdu daily), Peshawar, 20 June 2011, pp. 1, 5; *Roznama Aaaj Peshawar* (Urdu daily), Peshawar, 20 June 2011, pp. 1, 10.
12. In Swat, khans and *malak*s were chiefs selected and designated by the people of the respective segment. These were not hereditary posts and designations. The *malak*s were,

on the whole, lesser tribal chiefs compared with khans. After the emergence of the Swat State, the situation gradually changed and the State rulers started to designate the persons they wished to be khans and *malak*s; besides other perks these figures were paid stipends or *muwajib*s from the state exchequer, the precise amount of which represented the status of the khan or *malak* concerned. After the merger of the State this system came to an end, as the people do not designate and select khans and *malak*s, nor does the government. Interestingly, all the families and offspring of the previous *khan*s and *malak*s usually call themselves by these titles, yet they do not have the role those titles gave them either during the pre-Swat State period or in the time of the Swat State.

13. See also Sultan-i-Rome, "Swat: A Critical Analysis".
14. For a consideration of how the movement started, how the organisation came into being and the ways in which Sufi Muhammad was appointed as its Head, see Sayyad Ali Shah, *Da Shariat Karwan: Manzal bah Manzal* (Pashto), Lahore: Mukhtar Ahmad Khan Swati (Idara Nashr al-Maarif), 1995, pp. 10–19.
15. See ibid., pp. 24–27.
16. The Provincially Administered Tribal Areas Criminal Law (Special Provisions) Regulation (Regulation No. I of 1975) was promulgated on 26 July 1975 and was enforced immediately, whereas the Provincially Administered Tribal Areas Civil Procedures (Special Provisions) Regulation (Regulation No. II of 1975) was published on 26 July 1975 but in its section 1(3) it was stated that "it shall come into force on such date as Government [Government of North-West Frontier Province] may, by notification in the official Gazette, appoint in this behalf." Both these regulations are commonly known as PATA Regulations. On 19 March 1976, the date of the enforcement of Regulation No. II of 1975 was set as 25 March 1976. However, amendments were made in Regulations No. I and No. II of 1975—see The Provincially Administered Tribal Areas Special Provisions (Amendment) Regulation, 1976 (NWFP Regulation No. IV of 1976), 29 December 1976—and powers to decide cases, both criminal and civil, were transferred from the judiciary to the executive. The executive referred the cases to *jargah*s (under and in accordance with the PATA Regulations) which did not work properly as their decisions were usually manipulated. Moreover, the cases were not decided quickly, which generated resentment. Instead of redressing the grievances and helping the people the PATA Regulations led the situation from bad to worse.
17. Also see Sultan-i-Rome, *Swat State (1915–1969)*, pp. 310–11; Sultan-i-Rome, "Judicial System, Judiciary and Justice in Swat: The Swat State Era and the Post State Scenario," pp. 96–97. The then Deputy Commissioner Dir, Habibullah Khan, has been praised, between the lines, by the TNSM (see Shah, *Da Shariat Karwan: Manzal bah Manzal*, pp. 11, 14–16), who, it is alleged, even provided financial support from the District Council's funds (*The Friday Times*, 10–16 November 1994, p. 3, quoted in Navid Iqbal Khan, "Functioning of Local Government in N.W.F.P.: A Case Study of Malakand Division (2001–2005)," Unpublished MPhil Thesis, National Institute of Pakistan Studies, Quaid-e-Azam University, Islamabad, 2009, p. 28, and Navid Iqbal Khan, "Tehreek-i-Nifaz-i-Shariat-i-Muhammadi in Malakand Division (Khyber Pakhtunkhwa): A Case Study of the Process of "State Inversion"," *Pakistan Journal of History & Culture*, 31/1, 2010, p. 142.

18. For the Swatis' passiveness towards the movement at the start, see also Shah, *Da Shariat Karwan: Manzal bah Manzal*, pp. 26–28.
19. Interestingly, while outwardly there were differences between the two groups (one headed by Sufi Muhammad and the other by his son-in-law Fazlullah), especially with regard to strategy and course of action, both have the same motto and objective. Sufi Muhammad was reported to have told the media that if sharia laws were implemented as per his demands, he would go to Swat and disarm the other group (headed by Fazlullah); Muslim Khan, the spokesman of the other group, asked that Islamic laws be enforced in full, as per the draft submitted by Sufi Muhammad. See *Roznama Azadi Swat* (Urdu daily), Mingawara, Swat, 22 October 2008, 26 October 2008; *Roznama Aaaj Peshawar* (Urdu daily), Peshawar, 22 October 2008, and 18 October 2008. Also see *Roznama Azadi Swat* (Urdu daily), Mingawara, Swat, 20 October 2008.
20. See also Sayyad Inam-ur-Rahman, "*Aman Koshashayn*" in Ehsan Haqqani (comp.), *Swat ka Muqadimah/The Plea of Swat* (Urdu/English), Mingawara, Swat: Shoaib Sons Publishers and Booksellers, 2009, pp. 38–39; Aqeel Yusufzai, *Talibanization: Afghanistan say FATA, Swat aur Pakistan tak* (Urdu), Lahore: Nigarishat, 2009, pp. 209–15.
21. The government officials and the NGO functionaries speak in English and Urdu or mixed English, Urdu and Pashto, which makes it difficult for the common populace to comprehend and absorb what these people want to say and convey.
22. Peshawar Electric Supply Company supplies electricity, repairs its transmission lines and restores the supply.
23. Pakistan Telecommunication Company Limited supplies the landline telephone connections and repairs and restores the lines.
24. For some instructions issued by the Taliban to the public regarding civic works of such a nature, see a pamphlet titled "*Aama Itla*" (Pashto) [April 2010], Minjanib Tahrik Taliban Swat.
25. See *Roznama Azadi Swat* (Urdu daily), Mingawara, Swat, 30 October 2007.
26. See Abdul Hai Kakar, "*Ghair mulki nahi hay, magar aa saktay hay*," 31 October 2007, http://www.bbc.co.uk/urdu/pakistan/story/2007/10/printable/071031_swat_commander_as.s...
27. See ibid.
28. Announcement made on their FM radio channel. Also see Rifatullah Orakzai, "*Swat: char muqamat par murchay khali*," 27 November 2007, http://www.bbc.co.uk/urdu/pakistan/story/2007/11/printable/071127_swat_areasfree_rzt.sht...; Rifatullah Orakzai, "*Swat: Taliban kay murchay khali*," 27 November 2007, http://www.bbc.co.uk/urdu/pakistan/story/2007/11/printable/071127_swat_operation_updat...; Abdul Hai Kakar, "*Swat: mazeed pachas halakatu ka dawa*," 28 November 2007, http://www.bbc.co.uk/urdu/pakistan/story/2007/11/printable/071128_swat_deads_sen.shtml.
29. See Rifatullah Orakzai, "*Taliban hikmat amli tabdeel, Matta fauj kay pass*," 5 December 2007, http://www.bbc.co.uk/urdu/pakistan/story/2007/12/printable/071205_swat_update_zs.shtml; Rifatullah Orakzai, "*Swat: lugu mayn adam tahafuz barqarar*," 8 December 2007, http://www.bbc.co.uk/urdu/pakistan/story/2007/12/printable/071208_swat_matta_capture_n...; Abdul Hai Kakar, "*Kharija policy mayn tabdili chahiyayn*", 30 November 2007, http://www.bbc.co.uk/urdu/pakistan/story/2007/11/printable/071130_taliban_uniform_sen.s...

30. For texts of the agreements see the monthly *Pukhtun* (Pashto), 3/5, May 2008, pp. 51–52, and No. 6, June 2008, pp. 6–7.
31. Ironically, the curfew in Swat broke the old records as it continued for eleven months, sometimes with breaks of relaxation and sometimes without.
32. Khurshid Alam, "The Second big game & Pashtoons," 15 November 2008, retrieved on 16 November 2008, from http://khyberwatch.com/nandara/index2.php?=com_content&task=view&id=663&...
33. Ibid.
34. "Expats from Pakistan's Swat worry over relatives," retrieved on 12 March 2008, from http:// khyberwatch.com/nandara/index2.php?option=com_content&task=view& id=475&po...
35. Delawar Jan, "Time to act with a difference in Swat," *The News International*, Islamabad/Rawalpindi edition, 15 November 2008, p. 4.
36. Daily Times—Site Edition, http://www.dailytimes.com.pk/print.asp?page=2008\12\07\story_7-12-2008_pg1_2
37. Rahimullah Yusufzai, "Military victory in Swat not in sight," *The News International*, Islamabad/Rawalpindi edition, 22 December 2008, pp. 1, 8.
38. Syed Bukhar Shah, "PA warns India against 'adventurism'", Urges restoration of peace in Swat," *The News International*, Islamabad/Rawalpindi edition, 23 December 2008, p. 3.
39. Yusufzai, *Talibanization*, p. 214 (for detail see, pp. 209–15).
40. Khurshid Alam, "The Second big game & Pashtoons," 15 November 2008, retrieved on 16 November 2008, at http://khyberwatch.com/nandara/index2.php?=com_content&task=view&id=663&...
41. Fazlur Rahman, Chief of the Jamiatul Ulama-e-Islam-F (Fazlur Rahman) faction, later contended in his speech in the National Assembly, on 22 April 2009, that "the Swat peace deal was 'based on defeat, not success'." (Daily Times—Site Edition, http://www.dailytimes.com.pk/print.asp?page=2009\04\23\story_23-4-2009_pg1_4.
42. Daily Times—Site Edition, http://www.dailytimes.com.pk/print.asp?page=2009\05\02\story_2-5-2009_pg1_7.
43. Rahimullah Yusufzai, "Nizam-e-Adl and durable peace in Swat," *The News International*, Islamabad/Rawalpindi edition, 11 April 2009, p. 6. The President later gave his approval but, strangely, only after presentation of the draft to the parliament and parliament's vote for it, which was not a requisite and did not have a precedent. In certain respects, this course of action itself was unconstitutional.
44. The provincial government and ANP people gave this impression in public. There was, however, no such mention or commitment in the declaration signed by representatives of both the provincial government and the TNSM. For the Pashto version of the *ilan* (declaration), see monthly *Pukhtun*, 4/3, March 2009, p. 10; and for the Urdu version, see Yusufzai, *Talibanization*, p. 226. And the fourteen points of the peace accord that remained secret but were later "made available by the concerned sources" to the media-men also have no such mention or commitment or clause. See Hamid Mir, "Swat deal: The long and the short of it," *The News International*, Islamabad/Rawalpindi edition, 11 April 2009, pp. 1, 8.
45. This was his old viewpoint which he expressed frequently. It is, however, believed by

some in Swat that what he was saying was dictated to him by "hidden forces/hands", (i.e.) the intelligence agencies/Taliban, who instructed him to say such things or else face the consequences.

46. Interestingly, while speaking to the media in Islamabad, the ISPR Director General Major General Athar Abbas said, on 22 February 2009, that Pakistan had no facilities/equipment to jam Fazlullah's FM radio broadcasts; he also said that the security forces did not possess the required facilities to cope with the Taliban (Yusufzai, *Talibanization*, p. 214).

47. The number of such cases has not been agreed, as not all of them were reported in the media. According to Rahimullah Yusufzai (a renowned journalist, analyst, and resident Editor of the daily *The News International* at Peshawar): "The Taliban in Swat awarded punishment of public flogging about 25 times to men and twice to women during the past two years as they consolidated their control in the valley and established their own courts." (Rahimullah Yusufzai, "This is not the first time," *The News International*, Islamabad/Rawalpindi edition, 4 April 2009, pp. 1, 8). According to another journalist, Aqeel Yusufzai, the Taliban courts gave flogging sentences to more than about 35 persons during 2008 (Yusufzai, *Talibanization*, p. 218). And according to oral information that spread in Swat during those days there were four cases of flogging or lashing of females by the Taliban. However, only three cases of flogging or lashing of females became public in the media later (see *Roznama Azadi Swat*, an Urdu daily, Mingawara, Swat, 6 December 2010, pp. 1, 7), after which reporting of such cases in the media was allegedly suppressed as they were discrediting the government and security forces.

48. For detail, see Essa Khankhel and Daud Khattak, "NWFP govt, Taliban smell a rat," *The News International*, Islamabad/Rawalpindi edition, 4 April 2009, pp. 1, 8.

49. They claimed that they gathered information, from culprits arrested, in the course of the investigation that the video was fake and was produced on the demand of some non-state actors for which a handsome amount of money was paid. This caused a fresh debate in the media over the subject.

50. It is widely believed that the inroads by the Taliban from Swat into Dir and Buner were part of a planned attempt to sensationalise the issue and situation further, thereby giving additional justification for military action on an even grander scale.

51. See Muhammad Anis, "Militants nearing capital, Fazl tells NA," *The News International*, Islamabad/Rawalpindi edition, 23 April 2009, pp. 1, 8; Daily Times—Site Edition, http://www.dailytimes.com.pk/print.asp?page=2009\04\23\story_23-4-2009_pg1_4.

52. Haleem Asad, "Operation a violation of Swat deal, says Sufi," DAWN.COM, http://www.dawn.com/wps/wcm/connect/dawn-content-library/dawn/the-newspaper/…

53. "Swat Taliban getting active help from Baitullah," *The News International*, http://www.thenews.com.pk/print3.asp?id=21849.

54. Sajjad Malik, "Armed forces vow 'zero tolerance' towards militancy," Daily Times—Site Edition, http://www.dailytimes.com.pk/print.asp?page=2009\05\01\story_1-5-2009_pg1_1.

55. Brig Gurmeet Kanwal (retd.), "Losing Ground: Pak Army Strategy in FATA & NWFP," *IPCS Issue Brief, No. 84*, October 2008, New Delhi: Institute of Peace and Conflict Studies (IPCS).

56. This destruction and displacement took place at the hands of the government security forces who were duty-bound by moral and legal standards to take care of civilians and their property at all costs.
57. As is evident from the case of Peshawar, where the army cantonment is the permanent presence and abode of the army, the government and the army fortify even this sort of space by replacing barbed wire fences and grilles with tall walls, as well as further heightening the existing walls and further fences them by constructing sand embankments. The attack on Rawalpindi's General Headquarters and the army area mosque also reveal that presence of the army is not guarantee of security. In Karachi also, even though it has been a cantonment and had a huge number of security forces, life in the city is routinely disturbed, hundreds of people killed, and vehicles and properties are destroyed and ransacked. Even in Swat, despite the defeat and disappearance of the Taliban, the security forces entrenched themselves for their security. Instead of removing the barricades and the entrenchments around them, they increased their number and fortified them further.
58. *Lakhkar/Lashkar* is a tribal force that takes to the field of battle against the opponents/enemy on its own, providing its own arms and ammunition. It disperses to go home at the close of the fight. The *lashkar* neither is nor has the role of a permanent standing force. Against the backdrop of the operations and security forces actions in the post 2001 scenario in the FATA and PATA, the *lakhkars* are largely not formed by the people of their own free will.
59. *Jargah/Jarga* (erroneously transliterated as *jirga*) is the traditional consultative institution and forum where matters of common interest and communal affairs are discussed and decided. In *jargahs* all the stakeholders are represented; all those attending express their viewpoints and present their arguments freely; the decisions are made by consensus or unanimously, after deliberations. All abide by decisions made in this manner; violators are liable to be fined and punished. The *jargahs* formed in Swat in the post-Taliban scenario are devoid of these dimensions. Hence their decisions lack the essence and spirit as well as the force and legitimacy of the forms of gathering whose name they take and which they seek to emulate.
60. *Lakhkars* and *jargahs* are features of tribal society. Although it is a tribal area constitutionally, being part of the PATA, Swat's society is not tribal by any standard. Swat is advanced and has gone past the tribal stage of its life in the growth of civilisation. By forming these *lakhkars* and the *jargahs*, Swati society ostensibly reverts to previous forms of control at least 70–80 years old. In view of the dynamics of the society, these might lead towards more polarisation, social upheaval, and factional feuds, although in a new way and manner, very different from those in the region eighty years ago. What will be the long-term implications of the *lakhkars'* taking up arms and of the *jargahs'* decisions and steps? These issues raise a number of further questions. Under what laws of the country do these institutions have the authority to take arms and make decisions such as those concerning exile, the burning of houses and the confiscation of property, in the presence of state, federal and provincial governments, as well as a number of institutions and departments? What legitimates their actions, decisions and steps?
61. This act of the security forces was in violation of the Islamic laws of war as well as the Environmental Protection Act 1997, under which Environmental Impact Assessment

of such a step is mandatory. See also Sultan-i-Rome, "Darakht, Taliban aur Fauj," Roznama Azadi (Urdu daily), Mingawara, Swat, 27 May 2010, p. 4.
62. See also Sultan-i-Rome,"Security kay naam par insaniat ki tazlil," Roznama Azadi (Urdu daily), Mingawara, Swat, 3 June 2010, p. 4.
63. Henry George Raverty, *Notes on Afghanistan and Baluchistan*, vol. 1, 2nd edn. Published in Pakistan, Quetta: Nisa Traders, 1982, p. 251.
64. "It's 'time to talk' to Taliban, says US envoy," *The News International*, 5 March 2010, http://www.thenews.com.pk/print3.asp?id=27623; DAWN.COM, http://www.dawn.com/wps/wcm/connect/dawn-content-library/dawn/the-newspaper/internat…; Daily Times—Site Edition, http://www.dailytimes.com.pk/print.asp?page=2010\03\05\story_5-3-2010_pg7_3.
65. "'Military action no solution to terrorism' Gilani urges winning hearts of people; favours uniform local govt system in provinces," *The News International*, 5 March 2010, http://www.thenews.com.pk/print3.asp?id=27621.
66. Zulfiqar Ghuman,"Military action not only solution to Swat: PM," Daily Times—Site Edition, http://www.dailytimes.com.pk/print.asp?page=2009\01\20\story_20_1_2009_pg1_6.
67. "Military operation not the only option in Swat: Gilani," Daily Times—Site Edition, http://www.dailytimes.com.pk/print.asp?page=2009\02\14\story_14-2-2009_pg1_9.
68. For the strategy and models of Saudi Arabia, Indonesia and some other countries, the constraints of developing these in Pakistan, as well as those of the "Swat Model" developed by the Pakistan army, see Muhammad Amir Rana, "Swat De-radicalization Model: Prospects for Rehabilitating Militants," *Conflict and Peace Studies*, 4, 2011, No. 2, pp. 5–12.

12. PRODUCING CIVIL SOCIETY, IGNORING *RIVAJ*: INTERNATIONAL DONORS, THE STATE AND DEVELOPMENT INTERVENTIONS IN SWAT

1. My first encounter with this world was through the Time-Life Book on "the Pathans": André Singer, *Guardians of the North-West Frontier—The Pathans*, Amsterdam: Time-Life Books, 1982.
2. E.g. Fredrik Barth, *Political leadership among Swat Pathans*, London: The Athlone Press, 1959.
3. E.g. Charles Lindholm, *Frontier Perspectives*, Karachi: Oxford University Press, 1996.
4. For a detailed review of mainstream reporting regarding Swat and the Frontier in general, see the introduction to this volume.
5. Sartaj Khan,"Behind the crisis in Swat," *The News International*, 27 November 2008.
6. *Pukhtunwali* refers to the code of honour of Pukhtuns.
7. In April 2010, the name of the Province was officially changed to Khyber-Pakthunkwha.
8. FAO: Food and Agriculture Organisation; ADB: Asian Development Bank.
9. See James C. Scott, *Seeing Like a State: How Certain Schemes to Improve the Human Condition have Failed*, New Haven, CT: Yale University Press, 1998.
10. See Stuart Corbridge, Glyn Williams, Manoj Srivastava and René Véron, *Seeing the*

State: Governance and Governmentality in India, Cambridge: Cambridge University Press, 2005.
11. See the description of knowledge production in the introduction to this volume, and the related tension between utilitarian and scholarly expectations.
12. E.g. Urs Geiser, *Learning from the Kalam Integrated Development Project 1981–1998; Towards Sustainable Land Use and Livelihoods in North-West Pakistan*, Berne and Peshawar: Technical Report to Intercooperation.
13. E.g. Urs Geiser, "The Urgency of (Not Necessarily) Policy-oriented Research—the Example of Power Devolution and Natural Resource Management in North-West Pakistan" in SDPI (eds), *Sustainable Development: Bridging the Research/Policy Gaps in Southern Contexts*, Karachi: Oxford University Press, 2005, pp. 67–76.
14. For more details on this recall see Urs Geiser, "Reading Political Contestation in Pakistan's Swat Valley—from Deliberation to 'the Political' and beyond," *Geoforum* (forthcoming).
15. Sultan-i-Rome, *Forestry in the Princely State of Swat and Kalam (North-West Pakistan): A Historical Perspective on Norms and Practices*, Zurich: NCCR IP6 Working Paper No. 6, 2005.
16. The other areas include Khala Dhaka and Amb.
17. In 2009, this procedure also complicated the introduction of *Nizam-i-Adl* legislation to Malakand.
18. M.M. Qurashi and Z.A. Khan, "Drift and dissipation in rural development—an SOS for Survival" in M.A.K. Beg, H.M. Naqvi and H. Jonathan (eds), *International Conference on Challenge of Rural Development in the Eighties*, Peshawar: Pakistan Academy for Rural Development (PARD), pp. 400–431.
19. Sultan-i-Rome, *Forestry in the Princely State of Swat and Kalam*.
20. Urs Geiser, "Contested Forests in North-West Pakistan: The Bureaucracy between the 'Ecological', the 'National', and the Realities of a Nation's Frontier" in Gunnel Cederloef and K. Sivaramakrishnan (eds), *Ecological Nationalisms: Nature, Livelihoods and Identities in South Asia*, Seattle: University of Washington Press, 2005, pp. 90–111.
21. Geiser, *Learning from the Kalam Integrated Development Project*.
22. Akbar S. Zaidi, *The Political Economy of Decentralisation in Pakistan*, Zurich: Working Paper No. 1, NCCR.
23. The level of Division was reintroduced around 2009. By late 2009, the decentralisation process has been declared a provincial subject, and the government of the NWFP is currently defining further procedures.
24. Urs Geiser and Bernd Steimann, "State Actors' Livelihoods, Acts of Translation, and Forest Sector Reforms in Northwest Pakistan," *Contemporary South Asia*, 13/4, 2004, pp. 437–48.
25. See especially Robert McNamara, "Address to the Board of Governors of the World Bank, Nairobi, Kenya, 24 September 1973" in World Bank (ed.), *The McNamara Years at the World Bank*, Baltimore, MD: Johns Hopkins University Press, 1981, pp. 233–61.
26. AKRSP started its activities in the Northern Areas and partly in Chitral in the early 1980s under the leadership of the well-known rural development expert Shoaib Sultan Khan. See e.g. Shoaib Sultan Khan, *Rural Development in Pakistan*, Mumbai: Vikas Publishing House, 1981.

27. Realising the prevailing gender norms in Malakand, projects started to initiate separate community groups for men (Village Organisations, VOs) and women (Womens' Organisations, WOs).
28. Asian Development Bank, *Report and Recommendation of the President to the Board of Directors on a Proposed Loan to the Islamic Republic of Pakistan for the Malakand Rural Development Project*, Manila: ADB, 1999. The methodology of "dialogues" has been developed by the AKRSP in the Northern Areas.
29. See the popular definition of civil society, e.g. by James Manor, Mark Robinson and Gordon White, *Civil Society and Governance: A Concept Paper*, Brighton: Institute for Development Studies, University of Sussex, 1999. "An intermediate realm situated between state and household, populated by organized groups or associations which are separate from the state, enjoy some autonomy in relations with the state, and are formed voluntarily by members of society to protect or extend their interests, values or identities."
30. One of them is the Environmental Protection Society (EPS).
31. International development discourse switched from local area-based projects to higher level policy-oriented programme approaches (e.g. support to decentralisation, good governance programmes, direct budget support).
32. Sultan-i-Rome, *Forestry in the Princely State of Swat and Kalam*.
33. See the discussion of *wesh* in Sultan-i-Rome, *Swat State, 1915–1969, From Genesis to Merger: An Analysis of Political, Administrative, Socio-Political, and Economic Development*, Karachi: Oxford University Press, 2008.
34. Sultan-i-Rome, *Forestry in the Princely State of Swat and Kalam*.
35. Ibid.
36. This actually is the Indian Forest Act of 1927.
37. Ghaus Muhammad Khattak, *Issues in Forestry: Report to the Kalam Integrated Development Project*, Peshawar, 1987.
38. Urs Geiser and Bernd Steimann, "State Actors' Livelihoods, Acts of Translation, and Forest Sector Reforms in Northwest Pakistan."
39. Thomas Bierschenk, Jean-Pierre Chauveau and Jean-Pierre Olivier de Sardan, *Local Development Brokers in Africa. The Rise of a New Social Category*, Mainz, Germany: Working Paper No. 13. Institut für Ethnologie und Afrikastudien, Johannes Gutenberg-Universität, 2002.
40. In this context we need to recall the considerable influence that gender-sensitive aid experts had in qualifying existing practices.
41. Babar Shahbaz, *Dilemmas in Participatory Forest Management in Northwest Pakistan. A Livelihoods Perspective*, Zurich: Human Geography Series 25, University of Zurich, 2009.
42. Many development projects and often NGOs used modern-looking four-wheel-drive cars like the Mitsubishi Pajero. Swat Serena is a rather expensive hotel in Saidu Sharif, the capital of Swat.
43. Bernd Steimann, "Rural Livelihoods in a Lighland-Lowland Context and the Role of Forest Resources (NWFP, Pakistan)" in SDPI (eds), *Troubled Times: Sustainable Development and Governance in the Age of Extremes*, Islamabad: City Press, 2006, pp. 44–65.

44. This is a very popular notion in Swat.
45. See the details in Sultan-i-Rome, this volume. See also Khadim Hussain, *The Peace Deal with Swat Taliban, the Nizam-i-Adl Regulation and the Military Operation: The Discourse and the Narratives*, Islamabad: Aryana Institute for Regional Research and Advocacy, 2009.
46. Around 2001, Sufi Mohammad led many of his followers to fight in Afghanistan.
47. For details on their term in power see Mohammed Waseem, Mariam Mufti, *Religion, Politics and Governance in Pakistan*, University of Birmingham: Working Paper 27, Religions and Development Research Programme, International Development Department, 2009.
48. An alliance of various "Taliban" groups emerged under the name of Tehrik-i-Taliban Pakistan (TTP).
49. See the case of the Deputy Commissioner Swat Syed Muhammad Javed, accused of facilitating, in early 2009, the access of Fazlullah to Buner, a neighbouring district of Swat.
50. IRIN, "'NGOs should leave Swat'—insurgent leader," IRIN, Humanitarian News and Analysis, UN Office for the Coordination of Humanitarian Affairs, 2009.
51. *Dawn* (International edition), 25 May 2007.
52. From a local newspaper.
53. KhyberWatch, 8 May 2007.
54. Personal communication.
55. Sultan-i-Rome, *Forestry in the Princely State of Swat and Kalam*.
56. Geiser, "Reading Political Contestation in Pakistan's Swat Valley—from Deliberation to "the Political" and Beyond".
57. Sultan-i-Rome, "Women's Right to Land Ownership in Swat State Areas—the Swat State Era and the post-State Scenario," *Pakistan Journal of Gender Studies*, 1, 2008, pp. 105–120.
58. Khyberwatch, 17 February 2007.

13. CRISIS AND RECONCILIATION IN SWAT THROUGH THE EYES OF WOMEN

1. I am deeply indebted to the many people who met and shared their stories with me in Swat. I am thankful to Falak Naz Asfandyar for her help and support, as well as Saniya and Sobia in Saidu Sharif and Bakht-i-Saywa in Manglawar. I am grateful for the unique insights into the Swat state shared with me by Miangul Hassan Aurangzeb and by Sultan-i-Rome. All quotes used are anonymous to protect the privacy of the women with whom I spoke. All photographs used are by the author.
2. For further discussion of the various factions that comprised the MMA, its social reform agenda and its political outlook, see Weiss 2008.
3. "FM" is commonly used to refer to Fazlullah's FM radio station.
4. I returned to conduct two additional stints of fieldwork in November 2010 and January-February 2012.
5. This reference is to the large numbers of Swati men who had joined the Taliban—most Swat Taliban were from Swat—and the prevalent fear that the group will re-emerge.

14. PUBLIC VISIBILITY OF WOMEN AND THE RISE OF THE NEO-TALIBAN MOVEMENT IN KHYBER PAKHTUNKHWA 2007–9

1. This article is an output of the Women's Empowerment in Muslim Contexts programme, funded by the UK Department for International Development (DFID), based on the field research of Shirkat Gah-Women's Resource Centre. The views expressed are not necessarily those of DFID. Thanks to Farida Shaheed for asking me to work on this valuable collection. Thanks also to Deniz Kandiyoti, Robert Nichols and Nausheen Anwar for their comments on earlier drafts of this paper.
2. "Shirkat Gah was formed as a non-hierarchical collective in 1975 by a group of women with a shared perspective on women's rights and development. The organisation's fundamental goal was to encourage women to play a full and equal role in society by promoting and protecting the social and economic development of women already participating in, or wanting to participate in, the national development." http://www.shirkatgah.org/about-us.html.
3. Essays in this volume by Robert Nichols and Mariam Abou Zahab describe the extent to which the Taliban movement has developed into a social movement with claims to arbitrating justice and redefining authority in the region.
4. I will henceforth refer to the Neo-Taliban movement as only the Taliban, as is popular in contemporary discourse. This term does not refer to the Afghan Taliban movement which seized power in 1996 unless specifically mentioned.
5. Robert Nichols, "Class, State and Power in the Swat Conflict," and Anita Weiss, "Crisis and Reconciliation" in this volume.
6. For reading oral testimony as "text" see Sherna Berger Gluck and Daphne Patai (eds), *Women's Words: The Feminist Practice of Oral History*, New York: Routledge, 1991. For new considerations of women's subjectivity see Saba Mahmood, *Politics of Piety: The Islamic Revival and the Feminist Subject*, Princeton: Princeton University Press, 2005.
7. Lila Abu-Lughod, "Romance of Resistance: Tracing Transformations of Power through Bedouin Women," *American Ethnologist*, 17/1, 1990, pp. 41–55.
8. Mahmood, *Politics of Piety*, p. 10.
9. Sadaf Ahmad, *Transforming Faith: The Story of Al-Huda and Islamic Revivalism among Urban Pakistani Women*, Syracuse, NY: Syracuse University Press, 2009.
10. Magnus Marsden, "Women, Politics and Islamism in Northern Pakistan," *Modern Asian Studies*, 42, 2/3, 2008, pp. 405–29.
11. Julie Billaud, "Visible under the Veil: Dissimulation, Performance and Visibility in an Islamic Public Sphere," *Journal of International Women's Studies*, 11/1, 2009. Billaud challenges the ethical framework of study, instead analysing veiling as "performance".
12. Shirkat-Gah, "Shirkat Gah Female and Male Research Activities NWFP," in *Women's Empowerment in the Muslim Context (WEMC) Survey Reports*, Lahore: Shirkat Gah, 2010 (henceforth WEMC-SG); Female NWFP Report Dargai Khas, Malakand: Focus Group Discussion 7–09–07 10.40 am to 12.25 pm.
13. I have changed the names of all speakers quoted in this paper.
14. WEMC Female NWFP Report, Empowerment/Family Laws, Female Unmarried, Lahori Gate Peshawar, 19–11–08, 11.00 am to 12.30 pm.

15. WEMC-SG Female NWFP Report, Dargai Khas, Family Laws, Female Unmarried, 07–09–07, 12.30 pm to 01.40 p.m.
16. Veena Das, *Life and Words: Violence and the Descent into the Ordinary*, Berkeley: University of Calfornia Press, 2006, p. 181.
17. WEMC-SG Male NWFP Report, Focus Group Discussion Empowerment, Dargai Khas, Malakand, 05–08–08, 9.00 to 11.45 am.
18. See also Billaud's reading of the same tension in "Visible under the Veil," p. 123.
19. WEMC-SG Male NWFP Report, Family Laws, Married Men, Dargai Khas, Malakand, 06–06–08, 12.00–1.30 pm.
20. He used the word *Islami*.
21. Farida Shaheed, "Gender, Justice and Civil Society in Unjust Societies," Lahore: Shirkat Gah, 2009.
22. Interviewers' observations from Social Mapping discussions Dargai Khas Malakand 25–10–09 Male NWFP Report.
23. Ahmed Rashid, *Taliban: Militant Islam, Oil and Fundamentalism in Central Asia*, New Haven, CT: Yale University Press, 2000, pp. 105–6.
24. Ibid., p. 106.
25. See WEMC research team Reflective Notes and Transact Walk Female NWFP and Transact Walk Male NWFP for Dargai Khas for 2007 and 2008, Transact Walk Dargai Khas, 31–1–2009; WEMC-SG Male NWFP Report, Social Mapping Kharki Malakand 24–01–09 2.50 to 3.50 pm and WEMC-SG Female NWFP Reports, Governance, Kharki 29–01–09 11.00 am to 1.00 pm.
26. See the 2009 IRIN article: http://www.irinnews.org/Report.aspx?ReportId=82470.
27. Shaheed, "Gender, Justice and Civil Society in Unjust Societies," p. 38. Samar Minallah's documentary film work brought this to public attention.
28. WEMC-SG Male NWFP Report, Social Mapping, Kharki Malakand, General Group, 06–06–08 6.10 pm to 6.50 pm. According to the Director of Shirkat Gah, Farida Shaheed, interviewers are always viewed with suspicion and questioned as to their "actual" motives. In a situation of increased tension, this wariness grew.
29. WEMC-SG Male NWFP Report, Focus Group Discussion Empowerment, Dargai Khas, Malakand, 05–08–08, 9.00 am to 11.45 am.
30. WEMC-SG Male NWFP Report, Social Mapping, Kharki Malakand, General Group, 06–06–08 6.10 pm to 6.50 pm.
31. Saeed, in WEMC-SG Male NWFP Report, Group Discussion of Family Laws, Dargai Khas, Malakand, 06–08–08, 12.00 pm to 1.30 pm.
32. Focus Group Discussion Empowerment Male Unmarried Kharki Malakand 08–08–08 9.30 am to 11.00 am Male NWFP Report.
33. Reports from Father's Colony, Peshawar.
34. In addition to the above reference also see WEMC Male NWFP Report, Group Discussion of Empowerment, Male Unmarried, Dargai Khas Malakand, 05–08–08, 9.00 am to 11.45 am.
35. For theoretical approaches to "society" as a discursive formulation, see John Bowers and Kate Iwi "The Discursive Construction of Society," *Discourse and Society*, 4/3, 1993, pp. 357–93.

15. CUSTOM AND CONFLICT IN WAZIRISTAN: SOME BRITISH VIEWS

1. Lal Baha, *N.-W.F.P. Administration under British Rule 1901–1919*, Islamabad: National Commission on Historical and Cultural Research, 1978, p. 33.
2. The Barakis or Urmurs live, or lived, at Kaniguram in central Waziristan (see Mariam Abou Zahab, Ch. 4 and Shah Mahmoud Hanifi, Ch. 5). They may have left as a result of recent fighting in the area.
3. *The Economist*, 30 December 2009.
4. Griffin, Frontier Memo, no. 150, February 1878, India Proceedings (IP) P1216, India Office Records, British Library (henceforth IOR BL).
5. Commissioner Derajat Division (CDD) to Punjab Government (PG), no. 91, 11 July 1861, in no. 219, March 1862 IP P204/59, IOR BL.
6. Deputy Commissioner Kohat to Commissioner Peshawar Division, no. 35–220, 20 January 1879, in GOI Foreign Department to Secretary of State for India (SofS), no. 79, 31 March 1881, L/P&S/7/24, IOR, BL.
7. H. Beattie, *Imperial Frontier Tribe and State in Waziristan*, Richmond: Curzon, 2002, p. 173.
8. Charles Tupper, *Customary Law of the Punjab*, Calcutta: Office of the Superintendent of Government Printing, 1881, p. 4. Even the word caste was used occasionally (see e.g. Political Agent Wana (PA Wana) to Chief Commissioner NWFP (CC NWFP), no. 759, 25 September 1907, Reg. 2063, L/P&S/10/43, IOR BL).
9. They could also be made collectively responsible for the security of the area in which they lived.
10. Denzil Ibbetson, *Outlines of Punjab Ethnography*, Calcutta, 1883, p. 61.
11. Ibid., p. 22.
12. CDD to PG, telegram, 10 May 1901, in 1902 [Cd.1177] East India (north-west frontier). Mahsud-Waziri operations. *House of Commons Parliamentary Papers Online*, p. 193.
13. CDD to PG, no. 34, 22 March 1861, in no. 215, March 1862 IP P204/59, IOR BL.
14. See e.g. Akbar Ahmed, *Resistance and Control in Pakistan*, London/New York: Routledge, 1991, p. 18.
15. Individual British officials and politicians did often condemn this collective responsibility as unjust and uncivilised. See e.g. Beattie, *Imperial Frontier*, p. 126.
16. Johnson, *Mahsud Notes*, L/P&S/20 B.307, IOR BL.
17. Beattie, *Imperial Frontier*, p. 123.
18. CDD to PG, no. 598, 7 June 1889, in Governor General in Council (GG) to SofS, no. 13, 28 January 1890, L/P&S/7/59, IOR BL.
19. Deputy Commissioner Dera Ismail Khan (DC DIK) to CDD, no. 421, 23 October 1887 in Richard Bruce, Memorandum on Waziristan, in GG to SofS, no. 13, 23 January 1890, L/P&S/7/59, IOR BL.
20. CDD to PG, no. 598, 7 June 1889 in Bruce, Memo., L/P&S/7/59, IOR BL. Commenting on the difficulty of trying to control them by paying allowances to influential men, H.D. Watson, the Political Officer at Wana, suggested that Mahsud men "attain to prominence and notoriety so rapidly that it is quite possible that a year or two later men without allowances will have risen, whose recently acquired influence makes itself

felt in their sections and who will commit offences until their claims are satisfied, as their predecessors did" (PO Wana, Note on the present state of the Mahsud tribe and our relation therewith, 14 May 1900, HofCPPs 1902 [Cd. 1177], p. 136).

21. See e.g. T. Thornton, *Colonel Sir Robert Sandeman: His Life and Works on Our Indian Frontier*, London: John Murray, 1895. Sandeman's approach contrasted with that adopted at this time with some of the Pashtun tribes to the north. In the case of the Afridis for example, the GOI wanted to keep the Khyber pass open, but not to extend British influence over the tribe as a whole. So the tribesmen were only made responsible for the security of the pass, with allowances being paid to the representatives of their different sections. These representatives were selected by the tribesmen themselves, and they arranged for levies to escort caravans through it, and the levies themselves also received a payment from the government (Baha, *N-W.F.P. Administration*, pp. 52–53; R. Christensen, "Conflict and Change among the Khyber Afridis," PhD thesis, Leicester University, 1987, pp. 213–14).

22. Bruce, Memo., in L/P&S/12/3265, IOR BL.

23. CDD to GP, 28 February 1894 [C.8713][C.8714] *Military Operations on the North-West Frontiers of India, vol. 1 Papers Regarding British Relations with the Neighbouring Tribes on the North-west Frontier of India, and the Military Operations Undertaken against them During the Year 1897–1898*, p. 9.

24. CDD to PG, no. 715, 9 July 1889, in Punjab Proceedings P3396 IOR BL.

25. E. Howell, *Mizh A Monograph on Government's Relations with the Mahsud Tribe*, Karachi: Oxford University Press, 1979, p. 18.

26. F. Johnston, "Notes on Wana" in R. Nichols (ed.), *Colonial Reports on Pakistan's Frontier Tribal Areas*, Karachi: Oxford University Press, 2005, p. 49.

27. Ibid., p. 13; C. Davies, *The Problem of the North-West Frontier 1890–1908 Second Edition*, London: Curzon, 1975, p. 126.

28. They all had links with Amir Habibullah's younger brother Nasrullah Khan (see e.g. Tochi Political Diary week ending 22 September 1907, register 2063, L/P&S/10/43 IOR BL).

29. Beattie, *Imperial Frontier*, p. 155; Howell in O. Caroe, *The Pathans 550 B.C.–A.D. 1957*, Karachi: Oxford University Press, 1983, p. 471. So conflict between *maliks* and mullahs, resembling that in contemporary Waziristan to which Mariam Abou Zahab draws attention in Chapter 4, was already evident by the 1890s.

30. See e.g. Howell, *Mizh*, p. 18. It was reported that the second, third, fourth and fifth grade *maliks* were nominees of the first grade ones, and were unable to exert any influence over the rest of the tribe (Political Officer, Southern Waziristan, State of the Mahsud Tribe and relations therewith, 17 July 1900, HofCPPs 1902 [Cd.1177], p. 14).

31. Davies, *The Problem*, pp. 122/3.

32. CDD to GP, Annexure 1, 30 March 1900, HofCPPs 1902 [Cd.1177], p. 63.

33. GP to GOI Foreign Department (FD), no. 997, 6 Aug. 1896, L/P&S/7/88, IOR BL.

34. GP to GOI FD, 17 Aug. 1900, enclosure 12 in no. 2, Foreign Department (GOI FD, 18 October 1902, HofCPPs 1902 [Cd.1177], p. 119). Merk was converted to the idea that Bruce's "maliki system" was not suited to Waziristan by John Lorimer, who had been Political Agent in the Tochi, and was then a member of the Viceroy Lord Curzon's Secretariat (Howell, *Mizh*, p. 29).

35. GP to GOI FD, 17 Aug. 1900, enclosure 12 in no. 2, FD GOI to SofS, 18 October 1902, HofCPPs 1902 [Cd.1177], p. 122.
36. CDD to GP, note, 24 July 1900, ibid., p. 125.
37. CC NWFP to GOI FD, no. 1579-N, register 1811, L/P&S/10/44, IOR BL.
38. Ibid.
39. Com. on Special Duty (CSD) to CC NWFP, 20 March, 1902, in No. 28, CC NWFP to GOI FD, 27 March 1902, HofCPPs 1902 [Cd.1177]), p. 288.
40. Ibid. Harold Deane agreed that Mahsud society was divided into "innumerable petty groups which admit the leadership of no single large Malik, [which] itself necessitates representation by numerous smaller men" (CC NWFP to GOI FD, no. 1142, 9 November 1906, register 2033, L/P&S/10/42, IOR BL).
41. CSD to CC NWFP, 20 March 1902, HofCPPs [Cd.1177], p. 286.
42. Note, CDD to GP, 24 July 1900, ibid., p. 131.
43. Ibid.
44. CSD to CC NWFP, 20 March 1902, ibid., p. 286, also tel., CDD to PG, 10 May 1901, ibid., p. 193.
45. CSD to CC NWFP, 20 March 1902, ibid., p. 287.
46. CDD to CC NWFP, 18 May 1901, ibid., p. 201.
47. CSD to CC NWFP, 20 March 1902, ibid., p. 287.
48. Ibid., p. 288.
49. Ibid., p. 286.
50. Beattie, *Imperial Frontier*, p. 158. This was described as having been the system adopted with Orakzais, Afridis, Mohmands, and the Black Mountain clans (CSD to CC NWFP, 20 March 1902, ibid., p. 289).
51. Baha, *N-W. F.P. Administration*, p. 39, Political Agent (PA) Wana to CC NWFP, no. 693, 18 September 1906, register 1756, L/P&S/10/43, IOR BL.
52. PA Wana to CC NWFP, no. 693, 18 September 1906, register 1756, L/P&S/10/43, IOR BL.
53. By 1906 the number of *wakils* had increased to 1,588 (CC NWFP to GOI FD, No. 1142, 9 November 1906, register 2033, L/P&S/10/42, IOR BL).
54. Ibid.
55. PA Wana to CC NWFP, no. 693, 18 September 1906, register 1830, L/P&S/10/43, IOR BL.
56. Ibid.
57. CC NWFP to GOI FD, no. 1142, 9 November 1906, register 2033, L/P&S/10/42, IOR BL.
58. Translation of a petition in Persian from "Mulla Sahib and the poor people of the Mahsud tribe", 7 Ramzan, 1325 AH (15 October 1907), register 2197, L/P&S/10/43 IOR BL.
59. In Monthly Memo. for June 1909, letter from India, register 1105, 29M, L/P&S/10/44 IOR BL.
60. CC NWFP to GOI FD, no. 1579-N, 1 December 1910, register 1811, L/P&S/10/44 IOR BL.
61. See e.g. A. Warren, *Waziristan, the Faqir of Ipi and the Indian Army: The North West Frontier Revolt of 1936–37*, Karachi: Oxford University Press, 2000.

62. Mariam Abou Zahab refers to contemporary divisions between *mashars* and *kashars* in South Waziristan in Chapter 4.
63. See e.g. Baha, 1978, p. 37.
64. CC NWFP to GOI FD, 2 January 1902, enclosure 116 in GOI FD to SofS, no. 3, 30 January 1902, HofCPPs 1902 [Cd.1177], p. 256.
65. Howell, *Mizh*, p. 22.
66. Ibid., p. 38.
67. R. Christensen, *Conflict and Change*, pp. 212–14.
68. See e.g. F. Barth, *Political Leadership among Swat Pathans*, London: Athlone Press, 1959, p. 128, "Swat Pathans Reconsidered" in *Features of Person and Society in Swat: Collected Essays on Pathans*, vol. 2, London: Routledge & Kegan Paul, 1981, p. 165; Baha, *N-W. F.P. Administration*, p. 67; C. Lindholm, "Models of Segmentary Political Action The Examples of Swat and Dir, NWFP, Pakistan" in S. Pastner and L. Flam (eds) *Anthropology in Pakistan: Recent Socio-Cultural and Archaeological Perspectives*, Ithaca, NY: Cornell University Press, 1982, p. 23.
69. They might be said to have refused to "recognise any leader, indigenous or imposed, and [maintained] a diffuse form of organisation" (R. Tapper, "Introduction", in R. Tapper (ed.) *The Conflict of Tribe and State in Iran and Afghanistan*, Beckenham: Croom Helm, 1983, p. 54).
70. "Report of the Frontier Committee 1945," para. 4, L/P&S/12/3265, IOR BL.
71. Warren, *Waziristan The Faqir of Ipi*, p. 262.
72. Caroe, *The Pathans*, pp. 527–9.
73. *The Economist*, 2 January 2010, p. 4.
74. S. Haroon, *Frontier of Faith, Islam in the Indo-Afghan Borderland*, London: Hurst, 2007, p. 204.
75. Selig Harrison, "Pakistan's ethnic fault line," *The Washington Post*, 11 May 2009. www.washingtonpost.com/wp-dyn/content/article/2009/05/10/AR2009051001959 (accessed 10 September 2011).
76. *The Economist*, 2 January 2010, p. 4; M. Weinbaum and J. Harder, "Pakistan's Afghan Policies and their Consequences," *Contemporary South Asia*, 16/1, March 2008, p. 32.
77. See e.g. *Dawn*, 2 October 2009. Similar tactics were used in Wana in 2004 for instance (Nichols, 2005, p. x). Things appear to have changed since the late 1970s when the Mahsuds were reported as basking in the government's favour and benefiting in various ways from this (see e.g. Ahmed, *Resistance and Control*, p. 77).

16. STUDYING PASHTUNS IN BARTH'S SHADOW

1. Fredrik Barth, *Nomads of South Persia: the Basseri Tribe of the Khamseh Confederacy*, London: Allen & Unwin, 1961.
2. Fredrik Barth, *Political Leadership among Swat Pathans* (LSE Monographs), London: Athlone, 1959.
3. Fredrik Barth, *Models of Social Organization* (Occasional Papers 23), London: Royal Anthropological Institute, 1966; Robert Pehrson, *The Social Organization of the Marri Baluch*, compiled and analysed from his notes by Fredrik Barth, Chicago: Aldine, 1966.

4. Brian Street, "Orientalist Discourse in the Anthropology of Iran, Afghanistan and Pakistan" in Richard Fardon (ed.), *Localizing Strategies: Regional Traditions of Ethnographic Writing*, Edinburgh: Scottish Academic Press, 1990, pp. 240–59; Brian Street, response to Barth, *Man* (NS) 27, 1992, pp. 177–9; Susan Wright, "Method in our Critique of Anthropology: a Further Comment," *Man* (NS) 27, 1992, pp. 642–4; Susan Wright, "Constructing Tribal Identity in Iran; Comment on Burkhard Ganzer," *Man* (NS) 29, 1994, pp. 182–6.

5. Fredrik Barth, "Method in our Critique of Anthropology," *Man* (NS) 27, 1992, pp. 175–7; see also Richard Tapper, "Introduction" in Richard Tapper and Jon Thompson (eds), *The Nomadic Peoples of Iran*, London: Azimuth/Thames and Hudson, 2002, pp. 31–2.

6. Richard Tapper, "Historians, Anthropologists and Tribespeople on Tribe and State Formation in the Middle East" in Philip Khoury and Joseph Kostiner (eds), *Tribes and State Formation in the Middle East*, Berkeley: University of California Press, 1991, pp. 48–73; Richard Tapper, *Frontier Nomads of Iran: A Political and Social History of the Shahsevan*, Cambridge: Cambridge University Press, 1997, pp. 18–24.

7. Fredrik Barth, "Nomadism in the Mountain and Plateau Areas of South West Asia" in *Problems of the Arid Zone: Proceedings of the Paris Symposium* (Arid Zone Research 18), Paris: UNESCO, 1962, p. 349, quoted by Marshall Sahlins, *Tribesmen*, Englewood Cliffs: Prentice Hall, 1968, p. 38; see also Bernt Glatzer, "Political Organization of Pashtun Nomads and the State" in Richard Tapper (ed.), *The Conflict of Tribe and State in Iran and Afghanistan*, London: Croom Helm, 1983, pp. 212–32, Daniel Bradburd, *Ambiguous Relations: Kin, Class, and Conflict among Komachi Pastoralists*, Washington: Smithsonian, 1990.

8. Fredrik Barth (ed.), *Ethnic Groups and Boundaries: The Social Organization of Culture Difference*, Bergen: Universitetsforlaget, 1969.

9. Fredrik Barth, *Features of Person and Society in Swat: Collected Essays on Pathans* (Selected Essays Volume II), London: Routledge & Kegan Paul, 1981, p. 124.

10. Ibid., p. 180.

11. Abner Cohen, *Custom and Politics in Urban Africa: A Study of Hausa Migrants in Yoruba Towns*, London: Routledge & Kegan Paul, 1969.

12. Abner Cohen, "Introduction" in Abner Cohen (ed.), *Urban Ethnicity* (ASA Monographs 12), London: Tavistock Publications, 1974, p. xii; Richard Tapper, "Ethnicity, Order and Meaning in the Anthropology of Iran and Afghanistan" in Jean-Pierre Digard (ed.), *Le fait ethnique en Iran et en Afghanistan*, Paris: CNRS, 1987, pp. 22–3.

13. Edmund Leach, *Political Systems of Highland Burma* (LSE Monographs), London: Athlone, 1954; Ernest Gellner, *Saints of the Atlas*, London: Weidenfeld & Nicholson, 1969; Ernest Gellner, *Muslim Society*, Cambridge: Cambridge University Press, 1981; Richard Tapper, "Introduction" in Tapper, *The Conflict of Tribe and State*, pp. 1–82; see also Philip Salzman, "Does Complementary Opposition Exist? *American Anthropologist* 80, 1978, pp. 53–70; Lila Abu-Lughod, *Veiled Sentiments: Honor and Poetry in a Bedouin Society*, Berkeley: University of California Press, 1986; David B. Edwards, *Heroes of the Age: Moral Fault Lines on the Afghan Frontier*, Berkeley: University of California Press, 1996; G.E.R. Lloyd, *Demystifying Mentalities*, Cambridge: Cambridge University Press, 1990.

14. For example Mukulika Banerjee, *The Pathan Unarmed. Opposition and Memory in the North West Frontier*, Oxford, James Currey, 2000.
15. Richard Tapper, "Holier than Thou: Islam in Three Tribal Societies" in Akbar S. Ahmed and David M Hart (eds), *Islam in Tribal Societies: From the Atlas to the Indus*, London: Routledge & Kegan Paul, 1984, pp. 260–61.
16. I.e. not *vox populi* but *vis populi*; see Richard Tapper, "Ethnicity and Class: Dimensions of Inter-group Conflict in North-Central Afghanistan" in M. Nazif Shahrani and Robert L. Canfield (eds), *Revolutions and Rebellions in Afghanistan: Anthropological Perspectives*, Berkeley: Institute of International Studies, 1984, pp. 230–46.
17. When asked, Northern Durrani stated that they did not use the term Pashtunwali, but they knew it as a term used by their remote cousins in the south and east, and they claimed to adhere to its component principles.
18. For nine months, the Tajik Habibullah Kalakani, known as Bacha-i Saqaw, ruled in Kabul (Robert D. McChesney, *Kabul Under Siege: Fayz Muhammad's Account of the 1929 Uprising*, Princeton: Markus Wiener, 1999).
19. Richard Tapper, "Afghan Articulations of Identity: Text and Context" in Jacques Hainard and Roland Kaehr (eds), *Dire les Autres: Réflexions et pratiques ethnologiques: Textes offerts à Pierre Centlivres*, Lausanne: Payot, 1997, pp. 89–103.
20. The Islamic lunar year 1400 began in late 1979, shortly before Soviet troops invaded Afghanistan.
21. Olivier Roy, "Avec les talibans, la charia plus le gazoduc," *Le Monde Diplomatique*, November 1996, pp. 6–7.
22. Olivier Roy, "Olivier Roy, politologue: 'Les talibans incarnent la revanche des Pachtounes,'" *Le Monde*, 2 April 2001; http://www.radicalparty.org/it/node/5061122, accessed Feb 2011.
23. cf. Nancy Tapper, *Bartered Brides: Politics, Gender and Marriage in an Afghan Tribal Society*, Cambridge: Cambridge University Press, 1991.
24. Pierre Centlivres, "Le mouvement Taliban et la condition féminine," *Afghanistan Info* (Switzerland) 44, March 1999, pp. 11–13.
25. For Taliban ideological positions, and their changes after 2001, see Alia Brahimi, *The Taliban's Evolving Ideology* (Global Governance Working Paper 02/2010), London: London School of Economics, 2010.
26. E.g. on their original, now-defunct, English-language websites: http://www.ummah.net/taliban/taliban/i-taliban.htm and http://www.taleban.com/taleban.htm.
27. Anders Fange of Swedish Committee, quoted in Jan Mohammad Butt, "Girls Education in Afghanistan," *Frontier Post*, 10–11 November 1998.
28. Sonia Shah, "Unveiling the Taleban: Dress Codes Are Not the Issue, New Study Finds," ZCom, 10 July 2001 (also circulated by UNDP Afghanistan, 7 August 2001), accessed February 2011 at http://www.zcommunications.org/unveiling-the-taleban-dress-codes-are-not-the-issue-new-study-finds-by-sonia-shah, commenting on Physicians for Human Rights, *Women's Health and Human Rights in Afghanistan: A Population-Based Assessment*, 2001, accessed May 2011 at http://physiciansforhumanrights.org/library/report-2001afghanistan.html. The original reads: "Despite considerable media attention on the Taliban's dress code requirements for women, PHR's findings indicate that a

majority of participants (82 per cent–88 per cent) did not consider persecution for dress code infractions important. However, these findings do not negate the serious imposition that dress code restrictions represent for educated Kabulese women, as documented in the 1998 PHR study, or for any other women who would not choose to wear the garments." The reference here is to Physicians for Human Rights, *The Taliban's War on Women: A Health and Human Rights Crisis in Afghanistan*, 1998, accessed May 2011 at http://physiciansforhumanrights.org/library/the-talibans-war-on-women.html.

29. See Sayed Askar Mousavi, *The Hazaras of Afghanistan*, Richmond: Curzon, 1998.

30. See reports listed in Rupert C. Colville, "One massacre that didn't grab the world's attention," *International Herald Tribune*, 7 Aug. 1999, esp. Human Rights Watch, "Afghanistan: massacre in Mazar-i-Sharif," 10, no. 7 (C), November 1998, accessed March 2011 at http://www.hrw.org/legacy/reports98/afghan/.

31. See Pierre Centlivres, *Les Bouddhas d'Afghanistan*, Lausanne: Favre, 2001; Pierre Centlivres, "The Death of the Buddhas of Bamyan", *Viewpoints Special Edition, Afghanistan, 1979–2009: In the Grip of Conflict*, Washington: Middle East Institute, 2009, pp. 26–8; Finbarr Barry Flood, "Between Cult and Culture: Bamiyan, Islamic Iconoclasm, and the Museum," *Art Bulletin*, 84, no. 4, December 2002, pp. 641–59.

32. Azadi Afghan Radio, "Afghans against Taliban Gestapo-like actions," 22 May 2001, accessed May 2011 at http://www.afghanistannewscenter.com/news/2001/may/may22c2001.html. There was once a substantial Jewish minority, but mass emigration meant that by the 1990s there were only two individuals left.

33. Mullah Za'eff, Taliban Ambassador to Pakistan, quoted by Kate Clark, Islamabad, BBC 25 May 2001.

34. In early June, several members of US Congress pledged to wear a yellow badge in sympathy if the Taliban decree ever came into law.

35. Report (probably from *Dawn*) in *South Nexus*, 15 June 2001.

36. For examples, see Nancy Tapper, *Bartered Brides*.

37. See the analysis of the Layeha of 2006 and 2009: *Understanding Afghan Culture Analyzing the Taliban Code of Conduct: Reinventing the Layeha*, Program for Culture and Conflict Studies, US Dept of National Security Affairs, Naval Postgraduate School, 6 Aug. 2009, accessed May 2011 at info.publicintelligence.net/Layeha.pdf.

38. See for example Antonio Giustozzi (ed.), *Decoding the New Taliban: Insights from the Field*, London: Hurst, 2009.

39. This subject has been examined at length, with different conclusions, by, for example: Thomas Barfield, "Weapons of the not so Weak in Afghanistan: Pashtun Agrarian Structure and Tribal Organization for Times of War & Peace," Agrarian Studies Colloquium Series "Hinterlands, Frontiers, Cities and States: Transactions and Identities," Yale University 23 February 2007, accessed March 2011 at http://www.yale.edu/agrarianstudies/archive/colloq0607.html; Thomas H. Johnson and M. Chris Mason, "Understanding the Taliban and Insurgency in Afghanistan," *Orbis: A Journal of World Affairs*, 51/1, 2007, pp. 1–19; Graeme Smith, "Talking to the Taliban," *The Globe and Mail*, 22 March 2008; Anand Gopal, "The Battle for Afghanistan. Militancy and Conflict in Kandahar," New America Foundation, Counterterrorism Strategy Initiative Policy Paper, 2010.

40. See Antonio Giustozzi, *Koran, Kalashnikov, and Laptop: The Neo-Taliban Insurgency in*

Afghanistan, London: Hurst, 2007; Joshua Foust, "The myth of Taliban tribalism", accessed March 2011 at http://www.registan.net/index.php/2008/07/15/the-myth-of-taliban-tribalism/; Thomas Ruttig, "How Tribal Are the Taleban? Afghanistan's Largest Insurgent Movement between its Tribal Roots and Islamist Ideology," Thematic Report 04, Afghan Analysts Network, 2010.

41. Mountstuart Elphinstone, *An Account of the Kingdom of Caubul, etc.* 3rd edition, London, 1842 [1815], vol. 2, book 3 *passim*.
42. Tapper, "Introduction," *The Conflict of Tribe and State*, pp. 74–5.

17. IF ONLY THERE WERE LEADERS: THE PROBLEM OF "FIXING" THE PASHTUN TRIBES

1. See A. Giustozzi, *The Art of Coercion*, London: Hurst, 2011.
2. See David Sneath, *The Headless State: Aristocratic Order, Kinship Society and Misrepresentation of Nomadic Inner Asia*, New York: Columbia University Press, 2007.
3. Hugh-Buller, *Gazetteer of Balucistan*, v. 5, 1907, p. 72.
4. Bernt Glatzer, "Centre and Periphery in Afghanistan: New Identities in a Broken State," *Sociologus*, Winter 2002, p. 118.
5. Ibid., p. 119. See Giustozzi, *The Art of Coercion*, for a thorough discussion of this issue.
6. Hasan Kakar, *Government and Society in Afghanistan*, Austin: University of Texas Press, 1979, pp. 62–3.
7. On the political dimensions of the establishment of the monopoly of violence, see Antonio Giustozzi, *The Art of Coercion*.
8. Thomas Barfield, "Weak Links in a Rusty Chain: Structural Weaknesses in Afghanistan's Provincial Government Administration" in M. Nazif Shahrani and Robert L. Canfield (eds), *Revolutions and Rebellions in Afghanistan: Anthropological Perspectives*, Berkeley: University of California Press, 1984, pp. 173–5. See also Pierre Centlivres and Micheline Centlivres-Demont, *Et si on parlait de l'Afghanistan?*, Neuchâtel: Editions de l'Institut d'Ethnologie, 1988, pp. 26–7.
9. Whitney Azoy, *Buzkashi* (2nd edition), Long Grove: Waveland Press, 2003, p. 26.
10. Centlivres and Centlivres-Demont, *Et si on parlait de l'Afghanistan?*, p. 240.
11. Personal communications with UN officials, Uzbek intellectuals and former commanders in Takhar and Kunduz, 2003–2006.
12. Jon Anderson, "There are no Khans Anymore," *Middle East Journal*, 32/2, 1978, p. 170.
13. Jon Anderson, "Tribe and Community among the Ghilzai Pashtuns", *Anthropos* 70, 1975, p. 598.
14. This discussion of the Shinwaris is based on meeting with elders and educated Shinwaris in Kabul and Jalalabad, 2006–08.
15. The term "government khan" is widely used among the Shinwaris themselves.
16. About the *maliks* see Bernt Glatzer, "Political Organisation of Pashtun Nomads and the State" in R. Tapper (ed.), *Conflict of State and Tribe in Iran and Afghanistan*, London: Croom Helm, 1983, p. 230.
17. Antonio Giustozzi, *War, Politics and Society in Afghanistan*, London: Hurst, 2000, p. 173.

18. LESSONS ON GOVERNANCE FROM THE WALI OF SWAT: STATE-BUILDING IN AFGHANISTAN, 1995–2010

1. David B. Edwards, "Learning from the Swat Pathans: Political Leadership in Afghanistan, 1978–1997," *American Ethnologist* 25/4, 1998, pp. 712–28. At the time Barth wrote his first book on Swat, the term "Pathans" was still in usage as a term of reference to the people now more commonly referred to as Pakhtun or Pashtun. In this chapter, I use the term "Pakhtun".
2. Fredrik Barth, *Political Leadership among Swat Pathans*, London: Athlone Press, 1959, p. 132.
3. Talal Asad, "Market Model, Class Structure and Consent: A Reconsideration of Swat Political Organization," *Man* (NS) 7/1, 1972, p. 90.
4. Ibid.
5. Ibid., p. 89.
6. Ibid.
7. Fredrik Barth, *Features of Person and Society in Swat*, London: Routledge & Kegan Paul, 1981, p. 122.
8. *Wali* was the title by which the ruler of Swat was known from 1926, when Swat was incorporated as a princely state within the British Raj, until the dissolution of the Swat state by Pakistan in 1969. Prior to 1926, the Swat ruler went by the title of *Badshah*. Miangul Abdul Haqq Jahanzeb, the last Wali of Swat who was the subject of Barth's book, ruled Swat from 1949 to 1969.
9. Fredrik Barth, *The Last Wali of Swat*, New York: Columbia University Press, 1985, p. 155.
10. Ibid., p. 166.
11. Ibid., p. 167.
12. Ibid., pp. 164–5.
13. Ibid., p. 165.
14. Ibid., p. 176. Apparently still addressing Asad's critique, Barth asserted that, "the emphasis on peace, order and justice in no way represents a policy of defense of established class dominance…The Badshah, and later the Wali, continually encroached, contained, and progressively eliminated the power and prominence of Khans. In other words, the policy of the State in its exercise of law and order undermined the previous position of the dominant class." (Ibid., p. 165)
15. Ibid., p. 169.
16. Ibid., p. 174.
17. Reproduced from Curzon, 1923.
18. David Edwards, *Heroes of the Age: Moral Fault Lines on the Afghan Frontier*, Berkeley: University of California Press, 1996, Chapter 3.
19. Barth, *The Last Wali of Swat*, p. 154.
20. Ibid., p. 170.
21. Ibid., p. 171.
22. Ibid.
23. In *Taliban*, Ahmed Rashid discusses the way in which Taliban ministers kept their jobs as military commanders, meaning that they could be called to the front at any time,

thus keeping the civil administration effectively paralyzed, at the same time that the government itself retained the characteristics of a charismatic movement rather than that of a state. Ahmed Rashid, *Taliban: Militant Islam, Oil and Fundamentalism in Central Asia*, New Haven, CT: Yale University Press, 2000, pp. 100–1.

24. One well-placed Afghan official candidly commented that Karzai is "the product of three disorganized systems," the first of which is the tribal system of leadership within which he had inherited status, though "he never practiced it on the ground." As evidence of his lack of fitness for tribal leadership, my informant noted that "he was even known among his family as *diwana* [crazy], and his father would call him by this name. When he was in India, he [was known to] watch Indian movies and sell movie tickets in the black market in Simla, Himachel Pradesh." The second part of Karzai's background comes from his service with the "corrupt Jihadi parties, such as the Mujaddidi group, that got money without accountability. And third, he is a product of intelligence agencies whose accountability is always questionable."

25. It is worth pointing out that this was an area where the British proved especially successful in their efforts at state-building. The structures, routines, rituals, and general *esprit de corps* created by the British in the Indian army endure to this day and, particularly in the case of Pakistan, have provided the glue holding the state together when other institutions have failed.

26. See Antonio Giustozzi, *Decoding the New Taliban: Insights from the Afghan Field*, London: Hurst, 2009.

27. David Kilcullen, *The Accidental Guerrilla: Fighting Small Wars in the Midst of a Big One*, London: Hurst, 2009, pp. 70–109. Kilcullen also emphasizes in his study of counterinsurgency in Kunar the importance of road building, a point that, as previously noted, Barth also makes with regard to the Wali of Swat's success in solidifying state rule in his domain.

28. Ibid., p. 47.

BIBLIOGRAPHY

"Aama Itla" (a pamphlet, Pashto) Minjanib Tahrik Taliban Swat [April 2010].

Abid, Zain al-Abdin Khan, *Pashto Made Easy: Pushtu Rozmarra or "Everyday Pushtu"*, New Delhi, Madras: Asian Educational Services, 2001 [1917].

Abou Zahab, Mariam, "Sectarianism as a Substitute Identity: Sunnis and Shias in Central and South Punjab" in S. Mumtaz, J.L. Racine and I.A. Ali (eds), *Pakistan: The Contours of State and Society*, Oxford: Oxford University Press, 2002.

Abu-Lughod, Lila, "Romance of Resistance: Tracing Transformations of Power through Bedouin Women," *American Ethnologist*, 17, 1 (1990), pp. 41–55.

——— *Veiled Sentiments: Honor and Poetry in a Bedouin Society*, Berkeley: University of California Press, 1986.

Achcar, Gilbert, "Rethinking Imperialism: Past, Present and Future," *International Socialism*, 126 (2010), pp. 187–95.

Adamec, Ludwig W., *Historical and Political Who's Who of Afghanistan*, Graz: Akademische Druck und Verlagsanstalt, 1975.

AFP, "Army working towards development of S. Waziristan," 8 July 2010.

Ahmad, Sadaf, *Transforming Faith: The Story of Al-Huda and Isamic Revivalism among Urban Pakistani Women*, Syracuse, N.Y.: Syracuse University Press, 2009.

Ahmadi, Wali, "Kabul Literary Society," *Encyclopaedia Iranica* online edition http://www.iranica.com/articles/kabul-literary-society.

——— "Kabul Magazine," *Encyclopaedia Iranica* online edition http://www.iranica.com/articles/kabol-magazine.

Ahmed, Aijaz, *Iraq, Afghanistan and the Imperialism of Our Time*, New Delhi: Left Word, 2004.

Ahmed, Akbar, "Code of the Hills," *Foreign Policy*, http://www.foreignpolicy.com/articles/2011/05/06/the_code_of_the_hills.

——— *Journey into Islam: The Crisis of Globalization*, Washington: Brookings Press, 2007.

——— "Lose lawless tribal areas and you lose Pakistan itself," *The Independent*, 25/4/2009, http?://www.independent.co.uk/opinion/commentators/Akbar ahmed-lose-lawless tribal ....

——— *Millennium and Charisma among Pathans*, London: Routledge & Kegan Paul, 1976.

——— *Pakistan Society. Islam, Ethnicity and Leadership in South Asia*, Karachi: Oxford University Press, 1986.

——— *Pukhtun Economy and Society: Traditional Structures and Economic Development in a Tribal Society*, Boston: Routledge & Kegan Paul, 1980.

BIBLIOGRAPHY

―――― *Resistance and Control in Pakistan*, London; New York: Routledge, 1991.

Ahmed, Akbar and Gustaaf Houtman, "Swat in the Eye of the Storm," *Anthropology Today*, 25, 5 (2009), pp. 20–22.

Ahmed, Amineh, *Sorrow and Joy among Muslim Women*, Cambridge: Cambridge University Press, 2006.

Ahmed, Saghir, *Class and Power in a Punjabi Village*, London: Monthly Review Press, 1977.

Akbar, Said Hyder and Susan Barton, *Come Back to Afghanistan: My Journey from California to Kabul*, London: Bloomsbury, 2006.

Alam, Khurshid, "The Second big game & Pashtoons." Khushal Khan Khattack, *Poems From the Diwan of Khushal Khan Khattack*, D. MacKenzie (trans.), London: Allen and Unwin, 1965.

Alam, Muzaffar, "The Pursuit of Persian: Language in Mughal Politics," *Modern Asian Studies*, 32, 2 (1998), pp. 317–49.

Alavi, Hamza, "Kinship in West Punjab Villages," *Contributions to Indian Sociology*, 6, 1 (1972), pp. 1–27.

―――― "The Politics of Dependence: A Village in West Punjab," *South Asian Review*, 4, 2 (1971), pp. 111–28.

Albro, Robert, "Anthropology and the Military: AFRICOM, "Culture" and the Future of Human Terrain Analysis," *Anthropology Today*, 26, 1 (2010), pp. 22–4.

Ali, Kamran Asdar, "Pakistan's Troubled 'Paradise on Earth,'" *Middle East Report Online*, 29 April 2009, p. 6, http://www.merip.org/mero/mero04909.html

―――― "Strength of the State Meets Strength of the Street: The 1972 Labor Struggle in Karachi" in Naveeda Khan (ed.), *Beyond Crisis: Re-evaluating Pakistan*, London: Routledge, 2009.

'Alī, Khāksār Nādir, *Al-Habīb, jis-mēn A 'lā-Hazrat Hiz Majestī Amīr Habībullāh Khān kē Sayr ō Siyāhat-e Hindustān kē Vāqa'āt*, Agra: Sādiq Husayn, n.d. [c.1908].

Ali, Tariq, "The Perils of Islamophobia (Recorded talk)," *Marxism 2010: Ideas to Change the World*, 2 July 2010.

Allen, C., *God's Terrorists: The Wahabi Cult and the Hidden Roots of Modern Jihad*, London: Abacus, 2006.

Amir, Mahmud b. Khvand Amir, *Iran dar ruzgar-i Shah Isma'il-i avval va Shah Tahmasb-i safavi*, Tehran: Bunyad-i Mauqufat-i Duktur Mahmud Afshar Yazdi, 1991.

Anderson, David, *Histories of the Hanged: The Dirty War in Kenya and the End of Empire*, London: Weidenfeld & Nicolson and New York: W.W. Norton, 2005.

Anderson, Jon W., "There are no Khans Anymore," *Middle East Journal*, 32, 2 (1978).

―――― "Tribe and Community among the Ghilzai Pashtuns," *Anthropos*, 70 (1975).

Anis, Muhammad, "Militants nearing capital, Fazl tells NA," *The News International*, Islamabad/Rawalpindi edition, 23 April 2009.

Anonymous, "*Ta'mīr-e Pul-hā*," *Sālnāma-ye Kābul* 1313/1935, *qismat-e avval* [part 1].

―――― "*Wasā'il-e Hamal wa Naql: Tijārat: Rāh-hā*," *Sālnāma-ye Kābul* 1313/1935, *qismat-e avval* [part 1].

Ansari, Bayazid, *Khayr al-Bayan* (commentaries by Abd al-Hai Habibi, Abd al-Raouf Benawa and Abd al-Shakur Rashad), Kabul: Da Adabiyato aw Bashari Ulummo Pohanzai, 1974.

Arez, Ghulam Jailani and Andreas Dittmann (eds), *Kabul: Aspects of Urban Geography*, Peshawar: s.n., 2005.

BIBLIOGRAPHY

Arjomand, Said Amir "Defining Persianate Studies," *Journal of Persianate Studies*, 1, 1 (2008), pp. 1–4.

―――― "Evolution of the Persianate Polity and Its Transmission to India," *Journal of Persianate Studies*, 2, 2 (2009), pp. 115–36.

Arlinghaus, Joseph T., "The Transformation of Afghan Tribal Society: Tribal Expansion, Mughal Imperialism and the Roshaniyya Insurrection, 1450–1600," Ann Arbor: University Microfilms International, PhD thesis, Department of History, Duke University, 1988.

Armbruster, Heidi and Anna Laerke (eds), *Taking Sides: Ethnics, Politics and Fieldwork in Anthropology*, Oxford: Berghahn, 2008.

Asad, Amirzada and Robert Harris, *The Politics and Economics of Drug Production on the Pakistan Afghanistan Border: Implications for a Globalized World*, Aldershot: Ashgate, 2003.

Asad, Talal, "Market Model, Class Structure and Consent: a Reconsideration of Swat Political Organization," *Man* (New Series), 8, 1 (1972), pp. 74–94.

―――― *On Suicide Bombing*, New York: Columbia University Press, 2007.

Asian Development Bank, *Report and Recommendation of the President to the Board of Directors on a Proposed Loan to the Islamic Republic of Pakistan for the Malakand Rural Development Project*, Manila: ADB, 1999.

Atran, Scott, *Talking to the Enemy: Violent Extremism, Sacred Values and What it Means to be Human*, London: Allen Lane, 2010.

Awde, Nicholas and Asmatullah Sarwan, *Pashto: Dictionary and Phrasebook*, New York: Hippocrene Books, 2005 [2002].

Azadi Afghan Radio, "Afghans against Taliban Gestapo-like actions," Editorial Note, 22 May 2001. (http://www.afghanistannewscenter.com/news/2001/may/may22c2001.html, accessed May 2011).

Azar, Shaikh Muhammad Abdullah Khan, *My Heartrendingly Tragic Story*, Alberto M. Cacopardo and Ruth Laila Schmidt (eds), Oslo: Novus Press, 2006.

Aziz, Khalid, *Causes of Rebellion in Waziristan*, Peshawar: RIPORT, 22 February 2007.

―――― *The Reform of the Frontier Crimes Regulations (FCR) and Administration of the Tribal Areas of Pakistan*, www.khalidaziz.com, 22 November 2005.

Aziz, Muhammad and Ahmad Jamal-ud-din, *Afghanistan: a Brief Survey*, Kabul: Dar-Ut-Talif, 1934/1313AH.

Azoy, Whitney, *Buzkashi* (2nd edition), Long Grove: Waveland Press, 2003.

Baba, Rahman, *Selections from Rahman Baba*, J. Enevoldsen (trans.), Herning, Denmark: Poul Kristensen, 1977.

Babur, Zahiruddin Muhammad, *Baburnama: Part II*, W.M. Thackson Jr. (trans. and ed.), Cambridge, MA: Harvard University, Department of Near Eastern Languages and Civilizations, 1993 (Persian translation c. 1757–58 of Chaghatai Turkish text c. 1530).

―――― *Memories of Zehir-ed-Din Muhammad Babur*, (translated from Persian and Turkish manuscripts by John Leyden and William Erskine in 1826; annotated and revised by Sir Lucas White King in 1921), London: Oxford University Press, 1921.

Baha, Lal, *North-West Frontier Province Administration under British Rule 1901–1919*, Islamabad: National Commission on Historical and Cultural Research, 1978.

―――― "The Activities of the Mujahidin 1900–1936," *Islamic Studies*, 18 (1979), pp. 97–168.

BIBLIOGRAPHY

Bailey, Frederick, *Stratagems and Spoils: A Social Anthropology of Politics*, Oxford: Westview Press, 2001 [1969].

Baldauf, Ingeborg, "The Dāyi—Kārgil of Andkhoy: Language, History and Typical Professions. Discourse on Local Identity," *ASIEN* 1004 S (2007), pp. 135–52.

Banerjee, Mukulika, *The Pathan Unarmed: Opposition and Memory in the Khudai Khidmatgar Movement*, Oxford: James Currey, 2000.

Banks, Marcus, *Ethnicity: Anthropological Constructions*, London: Routledge, 1996.

Barakzai, Sultan Muhammad b. Musa Durrani, *Tarikh-i sultani*, Bombay: Karkhana-yi Muhammadi, 1881.

Barfield, Thomas, *Afghanistan: A Political History*, Princeton: Princeton University Press, 2010.

——— "Afghanistan is not the Balkans: Central Asian Ethnicity and Its Consequences" in Robert Canfield and Gabriele Rasuly-Paleczek (eds), *Ethnicity, Authority and Power in Central Asia: New Games, Great and Small*, London and New York: Routledge, 2011, pp. 95–109.

——— "Weak Links in a Rusty Chain: Structural Weaknesses in Afghanistan's Provincial Government Administration" in M. Nazif Shahrani and Robert L. Canfield (eds), *Revolutions and Rebellions in Afghanistan: Anthropological Perspectives*, Berkeley: University of California Press, 1984.

——— "Weapons of the not so Weak in Afghanistan: Pashtun Agrarian Structure and Tribal Organization for Times of War & Peace," Agrarian Studies Colloquium Series, *Hinterlands, Frontiers, Cities and States: Transactions and Identities*, Yale University, 23 February 2007, http://www.yale.edu/agrarianstudies/archive/colloq0607.html.

Barth, Fredrik, *Balinese Worlds*, Chicago: University of Chicago Press, 1993.

——— (ed.), *Ethnic Groups and Boundaries: The Social Organization of Cultural Difference*, Boston: Little Brown, 1969 and London: George Allen and Unwin, 1969.

——— *Features of Person and Society in Swat: Collected Essays on Pathans*, London: Routledge & Kegan Paul, 1981.

——— "Method in our Critique of Anthropology," *Man* (NS), 27 (1992), pp. 175–7.

——— *Models of Social Organization* (Occasional Papers 23), London: Royal Anthropological Institute, 1966.

——— *Nomads of South Persia: the Basseri Tribe of the Khamseh Confederacy*, London: Allen and Unwin, 1961.

——— "Nomadism in the Mountain and Plateau Areas of South West Asia," *Problems of the Arid Zone: Proceedings of the Paris Symposium* (Arid Zone Research 18), Paris: UNESCO, 1962, pp. 341–55.

——— "Overview: Sixty Years in Anthropology," *The Annual Review of Anthropology*, 36 (2007), pp. 1–16.

——— "Pathan Identity and its Maintenance" in Fredrik Barth (ed.), *Ethnic Groups and Boundaries The Social Organisation of Culture Difference*, London: Allen and Unwin, 1969, pp. 117–34.

——— *Political Leadership among Swat Pathans*, London: Athlone Press, 1959.

——— "Segmentary Opposition and the Theory of Games: a Study of Pathan Organization," *JRAI*, 89 (1959), pp. 5–21.

BIBLIOGRAPHY

——— "Swat Pathans Reconsidered" in *Features of Person and Society in Swat: Collected Essays on Pathans*, London: Routledge & Kegan Paul, 1981, pp. 121–81.

——— *The Last Wali of Swat: An Autobiography as told to Fredrik Barth*, New York: Columbia University Press, 1985.

Batchelder, C.C., *American Automotive Products in India*, Washington: Government Printing Office, 1923.

Baud, M. and Willem van Schendal, "Toward a Comparative History of Borderlands," *Journal of World History*, 8, 2 (1997), pp. 211–42.

Bausani, Alessandro, "Pashto Language and Literature" (translated from Italian by Bernard Blair), *Mahfil: A Quarterly of South Asian Literature*, 7, 1/2 (1971), pp. 55–69.

Bayly, C.A., *Empire and Information: Intelligence Gathering and Social Communication in India*, Cambridge: Cambridge University Press, 2000.

Bayly, Susan, *Asian Voices in a Postcolonial Age: India, Vietnam and Beyond*, Cambridge: Cambridge University Press, 2007.

Beattie, Hugh, *Imperial Frontier Tribe and State in Waziristan*, Richmond: Curzon, 2002.

Belasco, A., *The Cost of Iraq, Afghanistan, and other Global War on Terror Operations since 9/11*, Washington: Congressional Research Service, http://www.fas.org/sgp/crs/natsec/RL33110.pdf

Bellew, Henry Walter, *A General Report on the Yusufzai*, Lahore: Sang-e-Meel Publications 1977 [1864].

——— *Pushto Instructor: A Grammar of the Pukkhto or Pukshto Language, on a New and Improved System, Combining Brevity with Practical Utility, and Including Exercises and Dialogues, Intended to Facilitate the Acquisition of the Colloquial*, Peshawar: Saeed Book Bank & Subscription Agency, 1986 [1867].

al-Beruni, Abu Rayhan, *Alberuni's India*, Eduard Sachau (trans. and ed.), London: S. Chand, 1964 [c. 1020].

Bierschenk, Thomas, Jean-Pierre Chauveau and Jean-Pierre Olivier de Sardan, *Local Development Brokers in Africa. The Rise of a New Social Category*, Mainz, Germany: Working Paper No. 13. Institut für Ethnologie und Afrikastudien, Johannes Gutenberg-Universität, 2002.

Billaud, Julie, "Visible under the Veil: Dissimulation, Performance and Visibility in an Islamic Public Sphere," *Journal of International Women's Studies*, 11, 1 (2009), pp. 120–35.

Blumhardt, James Fuller, *Catalogues of the Hindi, Panjabi, Sindhi, and Pushtu Printed Books in the Library of the British Museum*, London: B. Quaritch, 1893.

——— *Catalogue of the Marathi, Gujarati, Bengali, Assamese, Oriya, Pushtu and Sindhi Manuscripts in the Library of the British Museum*, London: The British Museum, 1905.

Blumhart, James Fuller and D.N. Mackenzie, *A Catalogue of Pashto Manuscripts: in the Libraries of the British Isles*, London: The British Museum, 1965.

Boone, Jon and Ewan MacAskill, "Obama moves to bypass Karzai as drug abuses claim adds to dismay over his behaviour," *The Guardian*, 8 April 2010, p. 27.

Borger, Julian, "Assault deepens Afghan anxieties over what will happen when Nato troops leave," *The Guardian*, 14 September 2011, p. 14.

Bosworth, C.E., *The Ghaznavids: Their Empire in Afghanistan and Eastern Iran, 994–1040*, Edinburgh: Edinburgh University Press, 1963.

BIBLIOGRAPHY

Bowers, John and Kate Iwi, "The Discursive Construction of Society," *Discourse and Society*, 4, 3 (1993).

Bradburd, Daniel, *Ambiguous Relations: Kin, Class, and Conflict among Komachi Pastoralists*, Washington: Smithsonian, 1990.

Brahimi, Alia, *The Taliban's Evolving Ideology* (Global Governance Working Paper 02/2010), London: London School of Economics, 2010.

Brass, Paul, *Factional Politics in an Indian State: The Congress Party in Uttar Pradesh*, Berkeley: University of California Press, 1965.

Breman, Jan, *Patronage and Exploitation: Changing Agrarian Relations in South Gujarat, India*, Berkeley: University of California Press, 1974.

Brockes, Emma, "Why are Muslims so hypersensitive?" *The Guardian Weekend*, 8 May 2010, pp. 21–6.

Bruce, Richard, *The Forward Policy and its Results*, London: Longman Green, 1900.

Buchholz, Christine and Jan van Aken, *Afghanistan. Das wahre Gesicht des Krieges*, Berlin: Fraktion DIE LINKE im Bundestag, 2010.

Bukharin, Nikolai, *Imperialism and the World Economy*, London: Bookmarks, 2003.

Burke III, Edmund, "Islam and Social Movements: Methodological Reflections," in Edmund Burke III and Ira M. Lapidus (eds), *Islam, Politics, and Social Movements*, Berkeley: University of California Press, 1988, pp. 17–35.

Butt, Jan Mohammad, "Girls Education in Afghanistan," *Frontier Post*, 10–11 November 1998.

Byron, Robert, *The Road to Oxiana*, London: Macmillan, 1937.

Callinicos, Alex, *Imperialism and Global Political Economy*, Oxford: Polity, 2009.

Canfield, Robert (ed.), *Turko-Persia in Historical Perspective*, Cambridge: Cambridge University Press, 1989.

Canfield, Robert and Gabriele Rasuly-Paleczek (eds), *Ethnicity, Politics and Power in Central Asia: Games Great and Small*, London: Routledge, 2010.

Caroe, Sir Olaf, *The Pathans*, Karachi: Oxford University Press, 1958.

Caron, James, "Cultural Histories of Pashtun Nationalism: Public Participation, and Social Inequality in Monarchic Afghanistan, 1905–1960," PhD thesis, The University of Pennsylvania, 2009.

——— "Reading the Power of Printed Orality: Popular Pashto Literature as Historical Evidence and Public Intervention," *Journal of Social History*, 45 (2011).

Centlivres, Pierre "Le mouvement Taliban et la condition féminine," *Afghanistan Info* (Switzerland), 44 (1999), pp. 11–13.

——— *Les Bouddhas d'Afghanistan*, Lausanne: Favre, 2001.

——— "The Death of the Buddhas of Bamyan," *Viewpoints Special Edition, Afghanistan, 1979–2009: In the Grip of Conflict*, Washington: Middle East Institute, 2009, pp. 26–8.

Centlivres, Pierre and Micheline Centlivres-Demont, *Et si on parlait de l'Afghanistan?*, Neuchâtel: Editions de l'Institut d'Ethnologie, 1988.

Cheema, Pervaiz Iqbal and Maqsudul Hasan Nuri (eds), *Tribal Areas of Pakistan: Challenges and Responses*, Islamabad Policy Research Institute (IPRI)/Hanss Seidel Foundation, 2005.

Christensen, R., "Conflict and Change among the Khyber Afridis," PhD thesis, Leicester University, 1987.

BIBLIOGRAPHY

Clawson, Patrick, "Knitting Iran Together: The Land Transport Revolution, 1920–1940," *Iranian Studies*, 26 (1993), pp. 3–4.

Coghlan, Tom, "The Taliban in Helmand: An Oral History" in Antonio Giustozzi (ed.), *Decoding the New Taliban: Insights from the Afghan Field*, London: Hurst and New York: Columbia University Press, 2009, pp. 119–53.

Cohen, Abner, *Custom and Politics in Urban Africa: A Study of Hausa Migrants in Yoruba Towns*, London: Routledge & Kegan Paul, 1969.

——— "Introduction" in Abner Cohen (ed.), *Urban Ethnicity* (ASA Monographs 12), London: Tavistock Publications, 1974, pp. ix–xxiv.

Cohn, Bernard S., *Colonialism and Its Forms of Knowledge: The British in India*, Princeton: Princeton University Press, 1996.

Collier, Stephen and Aiwa Ong, "Oikos/anthropos: Rationality, Technology, Infrastructure," *Current Anthropology*, 44, 3 (2003), pp. 421–6.

Colville, Rupert C. "One massacre that didn't grab the world's attention," *International Herald Tribune*, 7 August 1999.

Corbridge, Stuart; Glyn Williams; Manoj Srivastava and René Véron, *Seeing the State: Governance and Governmentality in India*, Cambridge: Cambridge University Press, 2005.

Cowling, Geoff and John Newsinger, "Failing to learn the lessons of Afghan history," *The Guardian*, 29 July 2010.

Crews, Robert and Amin Tarzi, *The Taliban and the Crisis of Afghanistan*, Cambridge, MA.: Harvard University Press, 2009.

Curzon, George, *Tales of Travel*, New York: George H. Doran Co., 1923.

Darweza, Akhund, *Makhzan al-Islam* (introduction by Muhammad Taqwim al-Haqq Kaka Khel), Peshawar: de Pashto Academy, de Peshawar University, 1969.

Darwin, John, *The Empire Project: The Rise and Fall of the British World System, 1820–1970*, Cambridge: Cambridge University Press, 2009.

Das, Veena, *Life and Words: Violence and the Descent into the Ordinary*, Berkeley: University of California Press, 2007.

Dasti, Humaira, *Multan, A Province of the Mughal Empire*, Karachi: Royal Book Company, 1998.

Davies, Colin, *The Problem of the North-West Frontier 1890–1908*, 2nd edn., London: Curzon, 1975.

Dempsey, Judy, "Afghan leaks add to Europe's doubts," *International Herald Tribune*, 29 July 2010, p. 3.

Devji, Faisal, *Landscapes of jihad: Militancy, Morality, Modernity*, London: Hurst and New York: Columbia University Press, 2005.

——— *The Terrorist in Search of Humanity: Militant Islam and Global Politics*, London: Hurst and New York: Columbia University Press, 2008.

al-Dīn, Hājjī Mīr Shams, *Siyāhat-e Afghānistān, Mushtamil bar Kawā'if-e Ta'līmāt*, Lahore: Rafīq-e 'Ām Prēs, 1347/1929.

Djalili, M., A. Monsutti and A. Neubauer (eds), *Le Monde turco-iranien en question*, Geneva: Karthala, 2008.

Dorn, Bernhard, *History of the Afghans. Translated from the Persian of Neamet Ullah*, 2nd edn., London: Susil Gupta, 1965.

BIBLIOGRAPHY

Dorn, Bernhard (ed.), *A Chrestomathy of the Pushtu or Afghan Language, to which is Subjoined a Glossary in Afghan and English*, Saint Petersbourg: Imperial Academy of Sciences, 1847.

Dorronsoro, Gilles, *Revolution Unending: Afghanistan: 1979 to the Present*, London: Hurst and New York: Columbia University Press, 2005.

Dresch, Paul, "Mutual Deception: Totality, Exchange and Islam in the Middle East" in Wendy James and N. Allen (eds), *Marcel Mauss: A Centenary Tribute*, New York: Berghahn Books, 1998, pp. 111–33.

Duncan, Emma, *Breaking the Curfew: A Political Journey through Pakistan*, Reprint, London: Arrow Books Limited, 1990.

Durrani, 'Ashiq Muhammad Khan, *Tarikh-i Afghanistan*, Lahore: Sang-i-Meel, 1999.

The Economist, "Waziristan: The Last Frontier," 30 December 2009, http://www.economist.com/node/15173037

Edwards, David B., *Before Taliban: Genealogies of the Afghan Jihad*, Berkeley: University of California Press, 2002.

─── "Counterinsurgency as a cultural system," *Small Wars Journal*, December 2010, http://smallwarsjournal.com/jrnl/art/counterinsurgency-as-a-cultural-system.

───*Heroes of the Age: Moral Faultlines on the Afghan Frontier*, Berkeley: University of California Press, 1996.

─── "Learning from the Swat Pathans: Political Leadership in Afghanistan, 1978–1997," *American Ethnologist* 25, 4 (1998), pp. 712–28.

─── "Print Islam: Media and Religious Revolution in Afghanistan," in June Nash (ed.), *Social Movements: An Anthropological Reader*, Oxford: Blackwell, 2005.

Elkins, Caroline, *Imperial Reckoning: The Untold Story of Britain's Gulag in Kenya*, New York: Henry Holt, 2005.

Elphinstone, Mountstuart, *An Account of the Kingdom of Caubul, etc.*, 3rd edn. [1815], 2 vols., London, 1842.

Embree, Ainslee (ed.), *Pakistan's Western Borderlands: the Transformations of a Political Order*, New Delhi: Vikas Publishing, 1977.

Ewart, J.M., *Story of the North West Frontier Province*, Lahore: Sang-e-Meel, 2000 (reprint of the 1929 edition).

"Expats from Pakistan's Swat worry over relatives," Retrieved on 12 March 2008, http://khyberwatch.com/nandara/index2.php?option=com_content&task=view&id=475&po...

Fazal, Fazal Khaliq, *Barbarism in Disguise of Patriotism*, Mingora, Swat: Shoaib Sons Publishers & Booksellers, 2009.

Fenet, Annick, *Documents d'archéologie militante: La mission Foucher en Afghanistan (1922–1925)*, Paris: Académie des Inscriptions et Belles-Lettres, 2010.

Ferguson, James, *Kandahar Cockney: a Tale of Two Worlds*, London and New York: Harper Perennial, 2004.

Fleury, Antoine, *La Pénétration allemande au Moyen-Orient, 1919–1939: le cas de la Turquie, de l'Iran, et de l'Afghanistan*, Leiden: Brill, 1977.

Flood, Finbarr Barry, "Between Cult and Culture: Bamiyan, Islamic Iconoclasm, and the Museum," *Art Bulletin*, 84, 4 (December 2002), pp. 641–59.

Floor, Willem, "Chap (printing)," *Encyclopaedia Iranica* online edition http://www.iranica.

BIBLIOGRAPHY

com/articles/cap-print-printing-a-persian-word-probably-derived-from-hindi-chapna-to-print-see-turner-no.

Fofalzai, 'Aziz al-Dīn Vakili, *Tīmūr Shāh Durrānī*, repr. Kabul: Anjuman-i Tarikh, 1967.

Forster, George, *A Journey from Bengal to England through the Northern Parts of India, Kashmir, Afghanistan and Persia, and into Russia, by the Caspian Sea*, London: R. Fauldner, 1798.

Foust, Joshua, "The myth of Taliban tribalism," 2008, http://www.registan.net/index.php/2008/07/15/the-myth-of-taliban-tribalism/.

Frank, Andre Gunder and Barry K. Gills (eds), *The World System: Five Hundred Years or Five Thousand?*, Abingdon: Routledge, 1993.

Gazetteer of the Mooltan District, 1883–84, Lahore: Punjab Government, 1884.

Geiser, Urs, "Contested Forests in North-West Pakistan: The Bureaucracy between the 'Ecological', the 'National', and the Realities of a Nation's Frontier," in Gunnel Cederloef and K. Sivaramakrishnan (eds), *Ecological Nationalisms: Nature, Livelihoods and Identities in South Asia*, Seattle: University of Washington Press, 2005, pp. 90–111.

——— *Learning from the Kalam Integrated Development Project 1981–1998; Towards Sustainable Land Use and Livelihoods in North-West Pakistan*, Berne and Peshawar: Technical Report to Intercooperation, 2001.

——— "Reading Political Contestation in Pakistan's Swat Valley: From Deliberation to 'the Political' and beyond," *Geoforum*, 2012.

——— "The Urgency of (not Necessarily) Policy-Oriented Research—the Example of Power Devolution and Natural Resource Management in North-West Pakistan," in SDPI (eds), *Sustainable Development: Bridging the Research/Policy Gaps in Southern Contexts*, Karachi: Oxford University Press, 2005, pp. 67–76.

Geiser, Urs and Bernd Steimann, "State Actors' Livelihoods, Acts of Translation, and Forest Sector Reforms in Northwest Pakistan," *Contemporary South Asia*, 13, 4 (2004), pp. 437–48.

Gellner, Ernest, *Muslim Society*, Cambridge: Cambridge University Press, 1981.

——— *Saints of the Atlas*, London: Weidenfeld and Nicholson, 1969.

Ghani, Ashraf, "Impact of Foreign Aid on Relations Between State and Society," *Journal of Afghan Affairs*, 5/4 (1990), pp. 115–33.

———, "The Future of the Past," *Journal of Afghan Affairs*, 5/4 (1990), pp. 155–90.

Ghani, Asraf and Clare Lockhart, *Fixing Failed States: A Framework for Rebuilding a Fractured World*, Oxford: Oxford University Press, 2009.

Ghauri, Irfan, "Adult franchise system in FATA put clerics in Parliament: ISPR DG," *Daily Times*, 27 July 2006.

Ghosh, Anandita, *Power in Print: Popular Publishing and Politics of Language and Culture in a Colonial Society*, New Delhi: Oxford University Press, 2006.

Gilsenan, Michael, *Lords of the Lebanese Marches: Violence, Power and Narrative in an Arab Society*, London: I.B. Tauris, 1995.

——— *Saint and Sufi in Modern Egypt: An Essay in the Sociology of Religion*, Oxford: Clarendon Press, 1973.

Giustozzi, Antonio, (ed.), *Decoding the New Taliban: Insights from the Field*, London: Hurst and New York: Columbia University Press, 2009.

——— *Empires of Mud: Wars and Warlords in Afghanistan*, London: Hurst and New York: Columbia University Press, 2009.

BIBLIOGRAPHY

——— *Koran, Kalashnikov, and Laptop: The Neo-Taliban Insurgency in Afghanistan*, London: Hurst and New York: Columbia University Press, 2007.

——— *The Art of Coercion*, London: Hurst and New York: Columbia University Press, 2011.

——— *War, Politics and Society in Afghanistan*, London: Hurst and New York: Columbia University Press, 2000.

Glatzer, Bernt, "Centre and Periphery in Afghanistan: New Identities in a Broken State," *Sociologus*, Winter 2002.

——— "Political Organization of Pashtun Nomads and the State," in R. Tapper (ed.), *The Conflict of Tribe and State in Iran and Afghanistan*, London: Croom Helm, 1983, pp. 212–32.

Glover, William J., "Objects, Models, and Exemplary Works: Educating Sentiment in Colonial Punjab," *Journal of Asian Studies*, 64, 3 (2005).

Gluck, Sherna Berger and Daphne Patai (eds), *Women's Words: The Feminist Practice of Oral History*, New York: Routledge, 1991.

Gommans, Jos, *The Rise of the Indo-Afghan Empire c. 1710–1780*, Leiden: Brill, 1995.

Gonzalez, Robert J., *American Counterinsurgency: Human Science and the Human Terrain*, Chicago: Prickly Paradigm Press, 2009.

——— "Going 'Tribal': Notes on Pacification in the 21st Century," *Anthropology Today*, 25, 2 (2009), pp. 15–19.

——— "Human Terrain: Past, Present and Future Applications," *Anthropology Today*, 24, 1 (2008), pp. 21–6.

Goodhand, Jonathan, "Afghanistan in Central Asia," in M. Pugh, N. Cooper, and J. Goodhand (eds), *War Economies in a Regional Context: Challenges for Transformation*, Boulder, CO: Lynne Rienner Publishers, 2004, pp. 45–91.

——— *Bandits, Borderlands and Opium Wars: Afghan State Building Viewed from the Margins*, Copenhagen: DIIS Working Paper, 2009.

——— "From Holy War to Opium War?: A Case Study of the Opium Economy in North Eastern Afghanistan," in Christine Noelle-Karimi, Conrad Schetter, and R. Schlagintweit (eds), *Afghanistan: A Country without a State?* IKO-Verlag (Germany), 2002, pp. 139–60.

Gopal, Anand, "The Battle for Afghanistan. Militancy and Conflict in Kandahar," New America Foundation, Counterterrorism Strategy Initiative Policy Paper, 2010.

Gracia, J. Malcolm, "A Year Later, Life Resumes in the Swat Valley," 21 January 2010, http://www.allvoices.com/contributed news/5086650-a-year-later-life, etc.

Grant, B., "Shrines and Sovereigns: Life, Death and Religion in Rural Azerbaijan," *Comparative Studies in Society and History*, 53, 3 (2011), pp. 654–81.

Green, Nile, "Journeymen, Middlemen: Travel, Trans-Culture and Technology in the Origins of Muslim Printing," *International Journal of Middle East Studies*, 41, 2 (2009).

——— "The Afghan Afterlife of Phileas Fogg: Space and Time in the Literature of Afghan Travel," in Nile Green and Nushin Arbabzadah (eds), *Afghanistan in Ink: Literature between Diaspora and Nation*, London: Hurst, forthcoming.

——— "The Trans-Border Traffic of Afghan Modernism: Afghanistan and the Indian 'Urdusphere,'" *Comparative Studies in Society and History*, 53, 3 (2011).

——— "Tribe, Diaspora, and Sainthood in Afghan History," *The Journal of Asian Studies*, 67, 1 (2008), pp. 171–211.

BIBLIOGRAPHY

Gregorian, Vartan, "Mahmud Tarzi and Saraj-ol-Akhbar, Ideology of Nationalism and Modernization in Afghanistan," *Middle East Journal*, 21, 3 (1967), pp. 345–68.

——— *The Emergence of Modern Afghanistan: The Politics of Reform and Modernization, 1880–1946*, Palo Alto, CA: Stanford University Press, 1969.

Grierson, George Abraham, "Pashto," in George Abraham Grierson (ed.), *Linguistic Survey of India, Vol. X, Specimens of Languages of the Eranian Family*, Calcutta: Superintendent Government Printing, 1921.

Grima, Benedicte, *The Performance of Emotion among Paxtun Women*, Karachi: Oxford University Press, 1992.

Gutfreund, Owen D., *Twentieth-Century Sprawl: Highways and the Reshaping of the American Landscape*, New York: Oxford University Press, 2004.

Guyer, Jane, *Marginal Gains: Monetary Transactions in Atlantic Africa*, Chicago: University of Chicago Press, 2004.

Hackin, Joseph and Ria J. Hackin, *Bamian: Führer zu den buddhistischen Höhlenklöstern und Kolossalstatuen*, Paris: Les Éditions d'Art et d'Histoire, 1939.

——— *Le Site archéologique de Bāmiyān: Guide du visiteur*, Paris: Les Éditions d'Art et d'Histoire, 1933.

Haig, Wolseley (ed.), *The Cambridge History of India: Vol. 3, Turks and Afghans*, New York: Macmillan Co., 1928.

Hanifi, M. Jamil, "Editing the Past: Colonial Production of Hegemony Through the Loya Jerga in Afghanistan," *Iranian Studies*, 37, 2 (2004), pp. 299–322.

Hanifi, Shah Mahmoud, *Connecting Histories in Afghanistan: Market Relations and State Formation on a Colonial Frontier*, Palo Alto, CA: Stanford University Press, 2011.

——— "Henry George Raverty the Colonial Marketing of Pashto," in Cynthia Talbot (ed.), *Knowing India: Colonial and Modern Constructions of the Past*, New Delhi: Yoda Publishers, 2011.

——— "The Combined History of Pashto Printing and Resistance to Print," paper delivered at the 2010 SOAS "Rethinking the Swat Pathan" Conference http://www.soas.ac.uk/cccac/swat-pathan/file59663.pdf.

Hamilton, Angus, *Problems of the Middle East*, London: Eveleigh Nash, 1909.

Hannerz, Ulf, *Foreign News: Exploring the World of Foreign Correspondents*, Chicago: University of Chicago Press, 2004.

Hardy, Peter, *The Muslims of British India*, Cambridge: Cambridge University Press, 1972.

Harnisch, Chris, "Question Mark of South Waziristan: Biography and Analysis of Maulvi Nazir Ahmad," *Critical Threats*, 17 July 2009.

Haroon, Sana, *Frontier of Faith: Islam in the Indo-Afghan Borderland*, London: Hurst and New York: Columbia University Press, 2007.

Harpviken, K.B., *Social Networks and Migration in Wartime Afghanistan*, Basingstoke: Palgrave Macmillan, 2009.

Harrison, Selig, "Pakistan's ethnic fault line," *The Washington Post*, 11 May 2009, www.washingtonpost.com/wpdyn/content/article/2009/05/10/AR2009051001959.

Harvey, David, *The New Imperialism*, Oxford: Oxford University Press, 2003.

Hayat, Maira, "Still 'Taming the Turbulent Frontier?' The State in the Federally Administered Tribal Areas of Pakistan," *Journal of the Anthropological Society of Oxford*, (NS), 1, 2 (Winter 2009).

BIBLIOGRAPHY

Hedin, Sven, *Die Seidenstraße*, Leipzig: F.A. Brockhaus, 1936.

Hirschman, Albert, *The Passions and the Interests: Political Arguments for Capitalism before its Triumph*, Princeton: Princeton University Press, 1982.

Hodgson, Marshall, *The Venture of Islam: Conscience and History in a World Civilization: Vol. 2, The Expansion of Islam in the Middle Periods*, Chicago: University of Chicago Press, 1974.

Hopkins, B.D., *The Making of Modern Afghanistan*, Basingstoke: Palgrave Macmillan, 2008.

Hopkins, Benjamin D. and Magnus Marsden, *Fragments of the Afghan Frontier*, London: Hurst and New York: Columbia University Press, 2012.

Howell, Evelyn, *Mizh, A Monograph on Government's Relations with the Mahsud Tribe*, Karachi: Oxford University Press, 1979. First published Simla: Government of India Press, 1931.

Hugh-Buller, R., *Gazetteer of Balucistan*, v. 5, 1907.

Hughes, Thomas L., "The German Mission to Afghanistan, 1915–1916," *German Studies Review*, 25, 3 (2002).

Hughes, William J. and Joseph L. Thomas, *A History of Alley & MacLellan and the Sentinel Waggon Works: 1875–1930*, Newton Abbot: David & Charles, 1973.

Human Rights Watch, "Massacre in Mazar-i-Sharif," Afghanistan Report 10, No. 7 (C) (November 1998), http://www.hrw.org/legacy/reports98/afghan/.

Humphrey, Caroline, *The Unmaking of Soviet Life: Everyday Economies after Socialism*, Ithaca, NY: Cornell University Press, 2002.

Hussain, Khadim, *The Peace Deal with Swat Taliban, the Nizam-i-Adl Regulation and the Military Operation: The Discourse and the Narratives*, Islamabad: Aryana Institute for Regional Research and Advocacy, 2009.

al-Husaini, Imam al-Din, *Tarikh-i hhusainshahi or Tavarikh-i ahmadshahi* (1213/1798), National Archives Kabul.

Ibbetson, Denzil, *Outlines of Punjab Ethnography. Being Extracts from the Panjab Census Report of 1881, Treating of Religion, Language and Caste*, Calcutta, 1882.

Ibrahim, Muhammad b. Zain al-'Abidin Nasiri, *Dastur-i shahriyaran salaha-yi 1105 ta 1110 h.q.*, Tehran: Bunyad-i Mauqufat-i Duktur Mahmud Afshar Yazdi, 1994.

International Crisis Group, "Pakistan: Countering Militancy in FATA," *ICG Asia Reports*, Kabul/Brussels, 21 October 2009.

——— "Pakistan's Local Polls: Shoring up Military Rule," *ICG Asia Reports*, Kabul/Brussels, 2005.

——— "Report X," *ICG Asia Reports*, Kabul/Brussels, 2003.

International Herald Tribune, "The Afghan war logs," World News, 26 July 2010, pp. 1, 6–7.

Iqtidar, Humiera, "Jamaat-I Islami Pakistan: Learning from the Left" in Naveeda Khan (ed.), *Beyond Crisis: Re-evaluating Pakistan*, London: Routledge, 2009.

IRIN, "'NGOs should leave Swat'—insurgent leader," Humanitarian News and Analysis, UN Office for the Coordination of Humanitarian Affairs, 2009.

Islam, Riazul, *Indo-Persian Relations. A Study of the Political and Diplomatic Relations between the Mughal Empire and Iran*, Tehran: Iranian Culture Foundation, 1979.

Jalal, Ayesha, *Democracy and Authoritarianism in South Asia*, Cambridge: Cambridge University Press, 1995.

——— *Partisans of Allah: Jihad in South Asia*, New Delhi: Permanent Black, 2008.

BIBLIOGRAPHY

——— *State of Martial Rule: the Origins of Pakistan's Political Economy of Defense*, Cambridge: Cambridge University Press, 1990.

Jan, Delawar, "Time to act with a difference in Swat," *The News International*, Islamabad/Rawalpindi edition, 15 November 2008.

Jan, Mohammad Ayub, "Contested and Contextual Identities: Ethnicity, Religion and Identity among the Pakhtuns of Malakand, Pakistan," PhD thesis, University of York, 2010.

Jenkins, Simon, "A history of folly, from the Trojan Horse to Afghanistan," *The Guardian*, 28 July 2010, p. 31.

Jewett, A.C., *An American Engineer in Afghanistan: From the Letters and Notes of A.C. Jewett*, Marjorie Jewett Bell (ed.), Minneapolis: University of Minnesota Press, 1948.

Johnston, F., "Notes on Wana" (Recorded in 1903), reprinted in R. Nichols (ed.), *Colonial Reports on Pakistan's Frontier Tribal Areas*, Karachi: Oxford University Press, 2005.

Johnson, Thomas H. and M. Chris Mason, "Understanding the Taliban and Insurgency in Afghanistan," *Orbis: A Journal of World Affairs*, 51, 1 (2007), pp. 1–19.

Jones, Ann, *Kabul in Winter: Life without Peace in Afghanistan*, New York: Picador, 2006.

Jones, Phillip E., *The Pakistan People's Party: Rise to Power*, Karachi: Oxford University Press, 2003.

Kakar, Abdul Hai, "*Ghair mulki nahi hay, magar aa saktay hay*," 31 October 2007. http://www.bbc.co.uk/urdu/pakistan/story/2007/10/printable/071031_swat_commander_as.s…

——— "*Kharija policy mayn tabdili chahiyayn*," 30 November 2007. http://www.bbc.co.uk/urdu/pakistan/story/2007/11/printable/071130_taliban_uniform_sen.s…

——— "*Swat: mazeed pachas halakatu ka dawa*," 28 November 2007. http://www.bbc.co.uk/urdu/pakistan/story/2007/11/printable/071128_swat_deads_sen.shtml.

Kakar, Hasan, *Government and Society in Afghanistan*, Austin: University of Texas Press, 1979.

Kanwal, Brig. Gurmeet, (retd), "Losing Ground: Pak Army Strategy in FATA & NWFP," *IPCS Issue Brief, No. 84* (October 2008), New Delhi: Institute of Peace and Conflict Studies (IPCS).

Kasprowicz, M.D., "1857 and the Fear of Muslim Rebellion on India's North-West Frontier," *Small Wars and Insurgencies*, 8 (1997), pp. 1–15.

Kaye, John William, *History of the War in Afghanistan*, 3 vols, London: W. H. Allen, 1878.

Khan, Khan Abdul Wali, *Bacha Khan au Khudai Khidmatgari* (Pashto), Charsada: Wali Bagh, 3, 1998.

Khan, Muhammad Hayat, *Hayat-i afghani*, Lahore, 1867.

Khan, Ismail, "Army close to winding up first phase of operation," *Dawn*, 5 November 2009.

Khan, Mohammad Ilyas, "Nek Muhammad Wazir," *The Herald Monthly*, June 2004.

Khan, Navid Iqbal, "Functioning of Local Government in N.W.F.P.: A Case Study of Malakand Division (2001–2005)," MPhil thesis, National Institute of Pakistan Studies, Quaid-e-Azam University, Islamabad, 2009.

——— "Tehreek-i-Nifaz-i-Shariat-i-Muhammadi in Malakand Division (Khyber Pakhtunkhwa): A Case Study of the Process of 'State Inversion,'" *Pakistan Journal of History & Culture*, 31, 1 (2010), pp. 131–58.

BIBLIOGRAPHY

Khan, Sartaj, "Behind the crisis in Swat," *The News International*, 27 November 2008.

——— "Changing Pashtun society," *The News*, 14 January 2010.

——— "Imperialism, Religion and Class in Swat," *International Socialism*, 123 (2009), pp. 21–6.

Khan, Shoaib Sultan, *Rural Development in Pakistan*, Mumbai:Vikas Publishing House, 1981.

Khan, Sultan Mahomed (ed.), *Amir of Afghanistan*, 2 vols, Karachi; Oxford: Oxford University Press, 1980 [1900].

Khan, Umar Kamal, *Rise of the Saddozais and Emancipation of Afghans (1638–1747)*, Multan: Bazm-i Saqafat, 1999.

Khankhel, Essa and Daud Khattak, "NWFP govt, Taliban smell a rat," *The News International*, Islamabad/Rawalpindi edition, 4 April 2009.

Khattak, Ghaus Muhammad, *Issues in Forestry. Report to the Kalam Integrated Development Project*, Peshawar, 1987.

Khattak, Iqbal, "I did not surrender to the military, says Nek Mohammad," *The Friday Times*, 30 April-6 May 2004.

——— "Karzai restores monthly stipend to FATA elders," *Daily Times*, 26 September 2006.

——— "Maulvi Nazir decides to stay neutral," *Daily Times*, 19 October 2009.

——— "Mehsud unhappy over construction of Wana-Tank road," *Daily Times*, 2 March 2010.

——— "South Waziristan tense after cleric's killing," *Daily Times*, 25 August 2010.

——— "Wazir elder demands proportionate council seats," *Daily Times*, 5 December 2004.

——— "Wazir tribesmen want independent agency," *The Friday Times*, 17–23 October 2003.

Khazeni, Arash, *Tribes and Empire on the Margins of Nineteenth-Century Iran*, Seattle: University of Washington Press, 2010.

Kilcullen, David, "Taliban and Counter-Insurgency in Kunar," in Antonio Giustozzi (ed.), *Decoding the New Taliban: Insights from the Afghan Field*, London: Hurst and New York: Columbia University Press, 2009, pp. 231–45.

——— *The Accidental Guerrilla: Fighting Small Wars in the Midst of a Big One*, London: Hurst and NewYork: Columbia University Press, 2009.

Klaits, A. and G. Gulmamadova-Klaits, *Love and War in Afghanistan*, New York: Seven Stories, 2005.

Korpis, Craig, "Computing in Pashto: An Overview of a Major Language in Afghanistan and Pakistan," *Multilingual Computing and Technology*, 16, 2 (2005), pp. 27–30.

Krusinski, Judasz Tadeusz, *The History of the Revolutions of Persia Taken from the Memoirs of Father Krusinski*, New York: Arno Press, 1973.

Kuran, Timur, "The Islamic Commercial Crisis: Institutional Roots of Economic Underdevelopment in the Middle East," *Journal of Economic History*, 63 (2003), pp. 414–46.

Kūshān, Sūfī Pāyanda Muhammad, *Bā Kābul-e Qadīm Āshnā Shavīd*, Peshawar: Markaz-e Nashrāt-e Saʿīd, 1384/2006.

Kushev,V., "Areal Lexical Contacts of the Afghan (Pashto) Language (Based on the Texts of the XVI-XVIII Centuries)," *Iran and the Caucasus*, 1 (1997), pp. 159–66.

——— "The Dawn of Pashtun Linguistics: Early Grammatical and Lexicographical Works and Their Manuscripts," *Manuscripta Orientalia*, 7, 2 (2001), pp. 3–9.

BIBLIOGRAPHY

Kwon, H., *The Other Cold War*, New York: Columbia University Press, 2010.

Lamb, Christina, *Waiting for Allah: Pakistan's Struggle for Democracy*. New Delhi: Viking Penguin Books India (P) Ltd, 1991.

Lantz, François, "Mouvement et voies de communication en Asie centrale: L'avènement d'une colonie," *Cahiers d'Asie Centrale*, 17–18 (2009).

Leach, Edmund, *Political Systems of Highland Burma*, London: Athlone, 1954.

Lelyveld, David, 'Colonial Knowledge and the Fate of Hindustani,' *Comparative Studies in Society and History*, 35, 4 (1993), pp. 665–82.

Lenin, V.I., *Imperialism, the Highest Stage of Capitalism*, in *Collected Works*, XXII, Moscow, 1964.

Levi, Scott, *The Indian Diaspora in Central Asia and Its Trade, 1550–1900*, Leiden: Brill, 2002.

Lieven, Anatol "Insights from the Afghan Field," Open Democracy, October 2010, http://www.opendemocracy.net/anatol-lieven/insights-from-afghan-field.

Lindholm, Charles, "Contemporary Politics in a Tribal Society," *Asian Survey*, 19 (1979), pp. 485–505.

——— *Frontier Perspectives: Essays in Comparative Anthropology*, Karachi: Oxford University Press, 1996.

——— *Generosity and Jealousy: The Swat Pukhtun of Northern Pakistan*, New York: Columbia University Press, 1982.

——— "Models of Segmentary Political Action The Examples of Swat and Dir, NWFP, Pakistan" in S. Pastner and L. Flam (eds), *Anthropology in Pakistan: Recent Socio-Cultural and Archaeological Perspectives*, Ithaca, N.Y.: Cornell University Press, 1982, pp. 21–39.

——— *The Islamic Middle East: Tradition and Change*, Oxford: Wiley-Blackwell, 2002.

——— "The New Middle Eastern Ethnography," *JRAI*, 1, 4 (1995), pp. 805–820.

——— "The Segmentary Lineage System: Its Applicability to Pakistan's Political Structure" in Ainslee Embree (ed.), *Pakistan's Western Borderlands*, Durham, NC: Carolina Academic Press, 1977.

Lindholm Charles and Cherry Lindholm, "Marriage as Warfare," *Natural History* (October 1979), pp. 11–20.

Lindholm, Charles and M. Meeker, "History and the Heroic Pakhtun," *Man*, 16, 3 (1981), pp. 463–8.

Lindisfarne, Nancy, "Culture Wars," *Anthropology Today*, 24, 3 (2008), pp. 3–4.

——— *Dancing in Damascus: Stories*, Albany: State University of New York, 2000.

——— "Starting from Below: Fieldwork, Gender and Imperialism Now," *Critique of Anthropology*, 22, 4 (2002), pp. 403–423.

——— "Variant Masculinities, Variant Virginities: Rethinking "Honour and Shame," in Andrea Cornwall and Nancy Lindisfarne (eds), *Dislocating Masculinity: Comparative Ethnographies*, London: Routledge, 1994, pp. 82–96.

Lloyd, G.E.R., *Demystifying Mentalities*, Cambridge: Cambridge University Press, 1990.

Lodhi, A. Haroon Akram, "Attacking the Pakhtuns," *The Global Site*, October 2001.

Lomqani, Mulla Ghulam Jan, *Su'al wa Jawab-e Dawlati wa Band wa Bast Salatini*, Kabul: Dar al-Saltanah, 1886, http://afghanistandl.nyu.edu/books/adl0190/adl0190-fr01.html.

Luxemburg, Rosa and N. Bukharin, *Imperialism and the Accumulation of Capital*, Harmondsworth: Penguin, 1971.

Lydon, Ghislaine, *On Trans-Saharan Trails: Islamic Law, Trade Networks, and Cross-Cultural Exchange in Nineteenth Century Western Africa*, Cambridge: Cambridge University Press, 2009.

MacKenzie, D.N., "A Standard Pashto," *Bulletin of the School of Oriental and African Studies*, 22 (1959), pp. 231–5.

────── "The Development of the Pashto Script," in Shirin Akiner and Nicholas Sims-Williams (eds), *The Languages and Scripts of Central Asia*, London: School of Oriental and African Studies, 1997, pp. 137–43.

────── "The Xayr ul-bayan," in *Indo-Iranica: Mélanges présentés à Georg Mongenstierne à l'occasion de son soixante-dixième anniversaire*, Wiesbaden: Otto Harrassowitz, 1964, pp. 134–40.

Mahmood, Saba, *Politics of Piety: The Islamic Revival and the Feminist Subject*, Princeton: Princeton University Press, 2005.

Mahmood, Safdar, *Constitutional Foundations of Pakistan (Enlarged and Revised)*, Lahore: Jang Publishers, 1997.

Maillart, Ella, *The Cruel Way*, London: W. Heinemann, 1947.

Majlis-e Talif-e Pashtu, *Mu'allim-e Pashtu Kitab Duvvum*, 1935, Qandahar: Majlis-e Talif-e Pashtu, http://afghanistandl.nyu.edu/books/adl0180/.

Maku, Sulaiman, *Tazkerat ul-Awlia*, Abd al-Hai Habibi, Khushhal Habibi (ed. and trans.), 1942 [1216] http://www.alamahabibi.com/English%20Articles\Memoirs_of_Saints.htm.

Malekyar, Abdul Wahed, *Die Verkehrsentwicklung in Afghanistan*, Cologne: W. Kleikamp, 1966.

Malkki, Lissa, *Purity and Exile: Violence, Memory and National Cosmology among Hutu Refugees in Tanzania*, Chicago: University of Chicago Press, 1993.

Manor, James; Mark Robinson and Gordon White, *Civil Society and Governance, A Concept Paper*, Brighton: Institute for Development Studies, University of Sussex, 1999.

Mar'ashi, *Majma' al-tavarikh dar tarikh-i inqiraz-i ṣafaviya va vaqayi'-i ba'd ta sal-i 1207 hijri qamari* (1207/1792), 'Abbas Iqbal (ed.), 2nd ed., Tehran, 1362/1983.

Marchand, Trevor, "Preface and Introduction: Making Knowledge," *Journal of the Royal Anthropological Institute*, 16 (1993), pp. 1–21.

Markowski, Bruno, *Die materielle Kultur des Kabulgebietes*, Leipzig: Verlag Asia Major, 1932.

Marsden, Magnus, *Living Islam: Muslim Religious Experience in Pakistan's North-West Frontier*, Cambridge: Cambridge University Press, 2005.

────── "Talking the Talk: Debating Debate in Northern Afghanistan," *Anthropology Today*, 25, 2 (2009), pp. 20–24.

────── "Women, Politics and Islamism in Northern Pakistan," *Modern Asian Studies*, 42, 2/3 (2008), pp. 405–29.

Marshall, D.N., *The Afghans in India Under the Delhi Sultanate and the Mughal Empire: A Survey of Relevant Manuscripts*, C.J. Brunner (ed.), New York: Afghanistan Council of the Asia Society, 1976.

Martin, Frank A., *Under the Absolute Amir*, London: Harper & Brothers, 1907.

Martin, Nicolas, "The Political Economy of Bonded Labour in the Pakistani Punjab," *Contributions to Indian Sociology*, 43, 1 (2009), pp. 35–59.

Marwat, Fazal-ur-Rahim, "The Genesis of Change and Modernization in Federally Administered Tribal Areas of Pakistan," *IPRI Journal*, 7, 2 (Summer 2007).

Marwat, Fazal-ur-Rahim and Parvez Khan Toru, *Talibanization of Pakistan: (A Case Study of TNSM)*, Peshawar: Pakistan Study Centre, University of Peshawar, 2005.

BIBLIOGRAPHY

Matena, Rama Sundari, "Vernacular Futures: Colonial Philology and the Idea of History in Nineteenth-Century South India," *Indian Economic and Social History Review*, 42, 4 (2005), pp. 513–34.

McChesney, Robert D., *Kabul Under Siege: Fayz Muhammad's Account of the 1929 Uprising*, Princeton: Markus Wiener, 1999.

McFate M., and S. Fondacaro, "Cultural Knowledge and Common Sense. A Response to Gonzalez in this Issue," *Anthropology Today*, 24, 1 (2008), p. 27.

McMahon, Capt. A.H. and Lieut. A.D.G. Ramsey, *Report on the Tribes of Dir, Swat, and Bajour Together with the Utman-Khel and Sam Ranizai*, Lahore: Saeed Book Bank, 1981 [1901].

McNamara, Robert, "Address to the Board of Governors of the World Bank, Nairobi, Kenya, September 24, 1973" in World Bank (ed.), *The McNamara Years at the World Bank*, Baltimore, MD: Johns Hopkins University Press, 1981, pp. 233–61.

Meeker, Michael, "The Twilight of a South Asian Heroic Age: A Rereading of Barth's Study of Swat," *Man* (NS), 15 (1980), pp. 682–701.

Migdal, Joel, *Strong Societies and Weak States, State-Society Relations and State Capabilities in the Third World*, Princeton: Princeton University Press, 1988.

Migdal, Joel, Atul Kohli, and Vivienne Shue (eds), *State Power and Social Forces*, Cambridge: Cambridge University Press, 1994.

Miliband, David, "How to end the war in Afghanistan," *New York Review of Books*, 29 April 2010.

Mines, M., *The Warrior Merchants: Textiles, Trade and Territory in South India*, Cambridge: Cambridge University Press, 1984.

Mir, Farina, "Imperial Policy, Provincial Practices: Colonial Language Policy in Nineteenth-Century India," *Indian Economic and Social History Review*, 43, 4 (2006), pp. 395–427.

Mitchell, Timothy, *Rule of Experts: Egypt, Techno-politics, Modernity*, Berkeley: University of California Press, 2002.

de Modave, Comte, *Voyage en Inde du Comte de Modave, 1773–1776*, Paris: Ecole Française d'Extrême Orient, 1971.

Moghaddam, Sippi Azerbaijani, "Northern Exposure for the Taliban," in Antonio Giustozzi (ed.), *Decoding the New Taliban: Insights from the Afghan Field*, London: Hurst and New York: Columbia University Press, 2009, pp. 247–68.

Monsutti, Alessandro, "Afghan Migration Strategies and Three Solutions to the Refugee Problem," *Refugee Survey Quarterly*, 27, 1 (2008), pp. 58–73.

—— "Migration as a Rite of Passage: Young Afghans Building Masculinity and Adulthood in Iran," *Iranian Studies*, 40 (2007), pp. 167–85.

—— "The Impact of War on Social, Political and Economic Organisation in Southern Hazarajat" in R.D. Djalili, A. Monsutti and A. Neubauer (eds), *Le monde turco-iranien en question*, Geneva: Karthala, 2008, pp. 195–209.

—— *War and Migration: Social Networks and Economic Strategies of the Hazaras of Afghanistan*, P. Camiller (trans.), London: Routledge, 2005.

Morgenstierne, Georg, "Notes on an Old Pashto Manuscript Containing the Khair ul-Bayan of Bayazid Ansari," *New Indian Antiquary*, 2, 8 (1939), pp. 566–74.

—— *Report on a Linguistic Mission to North-western India*, Cambridge, MA: Harvard University Press, 1932.

Mousavi, Sayed Askar, *The Hazaras of Afghanistan*, Richmond: Curzon, 1998.

BIBLIOGRAPHY

Muhammad, Salih, *Lumra Kitab da Pashto I*, 1917, Kabul: Matba' Mashin Khana http://afghanistandl.nyu.edu/books/adl0146/index.html.

Munshi, Iskandar Beg, *Tarikh-i 'alamara-yi 'abbasi*, Tehran: Dunya-yi Kitab, 1998.

Mustafa, D. and K. Brown, "The Taliban, Public Space, and Terror in Pakistan," *Eurasian Geography and Economics*, 51, 4 (August 2010), pp. 496–512

Nadvī, Sayyid Sulaymān, *Sayr-e Afghānistān*, Lahore: Sang-e Mīl, repr. 2008.

Nawāz, Haq (ed.), *Siyāhat-e Iqbāl*, Lyallpur [Faisalabad]: Kitāb-e Markaz, 1976.

Neale, Jonathan, "Afghanistan: the Case Against the 'Good War,'" *International Socialism*, 120 (2008), pp. 31–60.

Newberg, Paula R., "Surviving State Failure: Internal War and Regional Conflict in Afghanistan's Neighborhood" in C. Arnson and I. W. Zartman (eds), *Rethinking the Economics of War: the Intersection of Need, Creed and Greed*, Washington DC: Woodrow Wilson Center Press and Baltimore, MD: Johns Hopkins University Press, 2005, pp. 206–233.

Niaz, Ilhan, *The Culture of Power and Governance of Pakistan, 1947–2008*, Karachi: Oxford University Press, 2010.

Nicholas, Ralph, "Factions: A Comparative Analysis," in K. Banton (ed.), *Political Systems and the Distribution of Power*, London: Routledge, 1965, pp. 21–9.

Nichols, Robert, *A History of Pashtun Migration, 1775–2006*, Karachi: Oxford University Press, 2008.

——— "Challenging the State: 1990s Religious Movements in the Northwest Frontier Province" in Craig Baxter and Charles Kennedy (eds), *Pakistan 1997*, Boulder: Westview Press, 1998.

——— "Introduction" in Robert Nichols (ed.), *Colonial Reports on Pakistan's Frontier Tribal Areas*, Karachi: Oxford University Press, 2005, pp. ix-xiv.

——— *Settling the Frontier: Land, Law and Society in the Peshawar Valley, 1500–1900*, Karachi: Oxford University Press, 2001.

Nizāmī, Khvāja Hasan, *Safarnāma-ye Afghānistān*, Lahore: Ātash Fishān, 2007 repr.

Noelle, Christine, *State and Tribe in Nineteenth-Century Afghanistan. The Reign of Amir Dost Muhammad Khan (1826–1863)*, Richmond: Curzon Press, p. 230.

Noelle-Karimi, Christine, "Historiography xi. Afghanistan," *Encyclopaedia Iranica*, 12 (2004), New York: Encyclopaedia Iranica Foundation, pp. 390–95.

Nojumi, Neamatollah, *The Rise of the Taliban in Afghanistan: Mass Mobilization, Civil War, and the Future of the Region*, New York: Palgrave, 2002.

Nojumi, Neamatollah, Dyan Nazurana and Elizabeth Stites, *Life and Security in Afghanistan*, Lanham, Maryland: Rowman & Littlefield, 2009.

Nordstrom, Carolyn, *Shadows of War: Violence, Power and International Profiteering in the Twenty First Century*, Berkeley: University of California Press, 2004.

Richard Norton-Taylor, "The wait for talks to start," *The Guardian*, 29 June 2010, p. 30.

Ogborn, Miles, *Indian Ink: Script and Print in the Making of the East India Company*, Chicago: University of Chicago Press, 2007.

Oppel, Jr., Richard A. and Taimoor Shah, "Attack killed 52, Afghans report," *International Herald Tribune*, World News Asia, 27 July 2010, p. 6.

Orakzai, Rifatullah, "*Swat: char muqamat par murchay khali*," 27 November 2007. http://www.bbc.co.uk/urdu/pakistan/story/2007/11/printable/071127_swat_areasfree_rzt.sht…

BIBLIOGRAPHY

——— "*Swat: lugu mayn adam tahafuz barqarar*," 8 December 2007. http://www.bbc.co.uk/urdu/pakistan/story/2007/12/printable/071208_swat_matta_capture_n...

——— "*Swat: Taliban kay murchay khali*," 27 November 2007, http://www.bbc.co.uk/urdu/pakistan/story/2007/11/printable/071127_swat_operation_updat...

——— "*Taliban hikmat amli tabdeel, Matta fauj kay pass*," 5 December 2007. http://www.bbc.co.uk/urdu/pakistan/story/2007/12/printable/071205_swat_update_zs.shtml.

Osella, Filippo and Caroline Osella, "Muslim Entrepreneurs in Public Life between India and the Gulf: Making Good and Doing Good," *Journal of the Royal Anthropological Institute*, 15 (2009), pp. 202–221.

Pain, Adam and S. Lister, "Markets in Afghanistan" in Adam Pain and J. Sutton (eds), *Reconstructing Agriculture in Afghanistan*, Rugby: Practical Action Publishing, 2007, pp. 235–50.

Parry, Jonathan and M. Bloch, *Money and the Morality of Exchange*, Cambridge: Cambridge University Press, 1989.

Pedersen, Morten, "From 'Public' to 'Private' Markets in Postsocialist Mongolia," *Anthropology of East Europe Review*, 25, 1 (2007), pp. 72–84.

Pehrson, Robert, *The Social Organization of the Marri Baluch*, compiled and analyzed from his notes by Fredrik Barth, Chicago: Aldine, 1966.

Pelsaert, Francisco, *Jahangir's India. The Remonstratie of Francisco Pelsaert*, Cambridge: W. Heffer & Sons, 1925.

Pelton, Robert Young, "The New War for Hearts and Minds," *Men's Journal*, 18, 3 (2009), pp. 78–83, 98.

Perlez, Jane and Pir Zubair Shah, "Lack of landowners could destabilize Swat valley," *International Herald Tribune*, News, 7 August 2009.

——— "The Taliban's latest tactic; Class warfare. Inroads are being made in Pakistan by playing poor against the wealthy," *International Herald Tribune*, 17 April 2009.

Physicians for Human Rights, *The Taliban's War on Women: A Health and Human Rights Crisis in Afghanistan*, 1998, http://physiciansforhumanrights.org/library/the-talibans-war-on-women.html.

——— *Women's Health and Human Rights in Afghanistan: A Population-Based Assessment*, 2001, http://physiciansforhumanrights.org/library/report-2001afgha-n-istan.html.

Picard, Elizabeth, "Managing Identities among Expatriate Businessmen across the Syrian-Lebanese Boundary" in I. Brandell (ed.), *State Frontiers: Borders and Boundaries in the Middle East*, London: I.B. Tauris, 2006, pp. 74–100.

——— "Trafficking, Rents and Diaspora in the Lebanese War" in C. Arnson and I.W. Zartman (eds), *Rethinking the Economics of War: the Intersection of Need, Creed and Greed*, Washington DC: Woodrow Wilson Center Press and Baltimore, MD: Johns Hopkins University Press, 2005, pp. 23–51.

Plowden, T.C., *Translation of the Kalíd-i-Afghání, the Text Book for the Pakkhto Examination, with Notes, Historical, Geographical, Grammatical, and Explanatory*, Lahore: Munshi Gulab Singh & Sons, 1893 [1874].

Powell, E. Alexander, "A Modern Magic Carpet," *The Century Magazine* 104, 2 (1922).

——— *By Camel and Car to the Peacock Throne: Syria, Palestine, Transjordania, Arabia, Iraq, Persia*, New York: Century Co., 1923.

Price, David, "Past Wars, Present Dangers, Future Anthropologies," *Anthropology Today*, 18, 1 (2002), pp. 3–5.

BIBLIOGRAPHY

Punjab Government, *Report on Waziristan and its Tribes*, Lahore: Sang-e Meel Publications, 2005 (reprint of the 1901 edition).

al-Qādirī, Mawlānā Zāhid, *A 'lā-Hazrat Shāh Amānullāh Khān Ghāzī Tājdār-e Afghānistān kā Safarnāma*, 2 vols, Delhi: Qurēshī Buk Depō, 1928.

Qandahari, Muhammad Abd al-Wasi, *Lumray Mashar da Marki da Pashto*, 1923, Kabul, http://afghanistandl.nyu.edu/books/adl0144/.

Qasmi, Sayyed Abdul Ghafoor, *Hidyah Wadudiah yani Sawanih Hayat Ala Hazat Badshah Abdul Wadud Khan Khudullahu Mulkahu Hukamran Riyasat-e-Yusufzai Swat wa Mutaliqat*, Braily: Matbua Saudagar Press, n.d.

Qazvini, Muhammad Tahir Vahid, *'Abbasnama*, Arak, 1951.

Qurashi, M.M. and Z.A. Khan, "Drift and Dissipation in Rural Development—an SOS for Survival" in M.A.K. Beg, H.M. Naqvi and H. Jonathan (eds), *International Conference on Challenge of Rural Development in the Eighties*, Peshawar: Pakistan Academy for Rural Development (PARD), 1986, pp. 400–431.

Qurēshī, Vahīd, *Urdū Adab main Safarnāma*, Lahore: Qawmī Prēs, n.d.

Rafi', Habībullāh, *Armaghān-e Tamaddun: Tārīkhcha-ye Vurūd-e Vasā'i-e 'Asrī beh Afghānistān*, Peshawar: Siyār Arīk, 1378/1999.

ur Rahim, Inam and Alain Viaro, *Swat: An Afghan Society in Pakistan. Urbanisation and Change in a Tribal Environment*, Karachi: City Press, 2002.

ur-Rahman, Iman and Alain Viaro, *Swat: An Afghan Society in Pakistan*, Karachi: City Press, 2002.

Rahman, Tariq, "The Learning of Pashto in North India and Pakistan: An Historical Account," *Journal of Asian History*, 35, 2 (2001), pp. 158–87.

——— "The Pashto Language Movement in Pakistan," *Contemporary South Asia*, 4, 2 (1995), pp. 151–70.

——— "The Teaching of Pashto: Identity versus Employment," http://www.tariqrahman.net/language/Teaching%20of%20Pashto.htm.

Rana, Muhammad Amir, "Swat De-Radicalization Model: Prospects for Rehabilitating Militants," *Conflict and Peace Studies*, 4, 2 (2011), pp. 5–12.

Rana, Muhammad Amir and Rohan Gunaratna, *Al-Qaeda Fights Back Inside Pakistani Tribal Areas*, Lahore: Pak Institute for Peace Studies (PIPS), 2007.

Rasanayagam, Johan, *Islam in Post-Soviet Uzbekistan: the Morality of Experience*, Cambridge: Cambridge University Press, 2010.

Rashid, Ahmed, *Taliban: Militant Islam, Oil and Fundamentalism in Central Asia*, New Haven, CT: Yale University Press, 2000.

Rasuly-Paleczek, Gabriele, "Alignment Politics and Factionalism among the Uzbeks of northeastern Afghanistan" in Robert Canfield and Gabriele Rasuly-Paleczek (eds.), *Ethnicity, Politics and Power in Central Asia: Games Great and Small*, London: Routledge, 2010.

Rathjens, Carl, "Karawanenwege und Pässe im Kulturlandschaftswandel Afghanistans seit dem 19. Jahrhundert" in Adolf Leidlmair and Hermann von Wissmann (eds), *Hermann von Wissmann-Festschrift*, Tübingen: Geographisches Institut der Universität Tübingen, 1962.

Rauf, A., "The British Empire and the Mujahidin Movement in the N.W.F.P., 1914–1934," *Islamic Studies*, 44 (2005), pp. 409–39.

BIBLIOGRAPHY

Raverty, Henry George, *A Dictionary of the Pukhto, Pushto, or, Language of the Afghans: With Remarks on the Originality of the Language and its Affinity to the Semitic and Other Oriental Tongues, Etc. Etc.*, Karachi: Indus Publishers, 1982 [1860].

——— *A Grammar of the Puk'hto, Pus'hto, or Language of the Afghans*, New Delhi: UBS Publishers, 1987 [1855].

——— *Gulshan-i Roh, Being Selections, Prose and Poetical, in the Pus'hto or Afghan Language*, London: Longman, 1860.

——— *Notes on Afghanistan and Baluchistan*, Vol. 1, 2nd edn., Quetta: Nisa Traders, 1982.

——— *Selections from the Poetry of the Afghans: From the Sixteenth to the Nineteenth Century, Literally Translated from the Original Pushto; with Notices of the Different Authors, and Remarks on the Mystic Doctrine and Poetry of the Sufis*, Peshawar: De Chapzai, 1981 [1867].

Reetz, Dietrich, *Hijrat: The Flight of the Faithful: A British File on the Exodus of Muslim Peasants from North India to Afghanistan in 1920*, Berlin: Das Arabische Buch, 1995.

Reeves, Madeleine, "Introduction: Contested Trajectories and a Dynamic Approach to Place," *Central Asian Survey*, 30, 304 (2011), pp. 307–330.

Reuter, Christopher and Borhan Younus, "The Return of the Taliban in Ander District, Ghazni," in Antonio Giustozzi (ed.), *Decoding the New Taliban: Insights from the Afghan Field*, London: Hurst and New York: Columbia University Press, 2009, pp. 101–118.

Rais, Rasool Baksh, "Elections in Pakistan: Is Democracy Winning?," *Asian Affairs*, 12, 47 (1985), pp. 81–102.

Richards, D., *The Savage Frontier: A History of the Anglo-Afghan Wars*, London: Macmillan, 1990.

Rico, J., *Blood Makes the Grass Grow Green: A Year in the Desert with Team America*, New York: Ballantine Books, 2007.

Risen, J., "US identifies vast mineral riches in Afghanistan," *The New York Times*, 13 June 2010, http://www.nytimes.com/2010/06/14/world/asia/14minerals.html?page-wanted=1.

Rittenberg, S., *Ethnicity, Nationalism and the Pukhtuns: The Independence Movement in India's NWFP*, Durham, NC: Carolina Academic, 1988.

Rishtiyyā, Sayyid Qāsim Khān, "*Mōtar dar Ahmiyyat-e ān dar Dunyā*," *Sālnāma-ye Kābul* 1314/1936, *qismat-e dovvum* [part 2], pp. 354–72.

Rittenberg, Stephen, "Continuities in Borderland Politics" in Ainslee Embree (ed.), *Pakistan's Western Borderlands: the Transformations of a Political Order*, New Delhi: Vikas Publishing, 1977, pp. 67–84.

Rodriguez, Deborah, *The Kabul Beauty School*, London: Hodder, 2008.

Roos-Keppel, George Olof and Qazi Abdul Ghani Khan, *A Manual of Pushtu*, Bombay: Oxford University Press, 1937 [1901].

Rosen, Nir "Western Media Fraud in the Middle East," 18 May 2011, http://english.aljazeera.net/indepth/opinion/2011/05/201151882929682601.html.

Rouse, Shahnaz, "Systematic Injustices and Inequalities: Maliki and Raiya in a Punjab Village" in H. Gardezi and J. Rashid (eds), *Pakistan, The Roots of Dictatorship: The Political Economy of a Praetorian State*, London: Zed Press, 1983, pp. 311–25.

Roy, Olivier, "Avec les talibans, la charia plus le gazoduc," *Le Monde Diplomatique*, November 1996, pp. 6–7.

BIBLIOGRAPHY

——— "Olivier Roy, politologue:'Les talibans incarnent la revanche des Pachtounes,'" *Le Monde*, 2 April 2001; http://www.radicalparty.org/it/node/5061122.

Rudnyckyj, Daromir, "Spiritual Economies: Islam and Neoliberalism in Contemporary Indonesia," *Cultural Anthropology* 24, 1 (2009), pp. 104–141.

Ruttig, Thomas, "How tribal are the Taleban? Afghanistan's largest insurgent movement between its tribal roots and Islamist ideology," Afghan Analysts Network Thematic Report 04/2010.

Sahlins, Marshall, *Tribesmen*, Englewood Cliffs: Prentice Hall, 1968.

Said, Edward, *Orientalism*, New York: Pantheon, 1978.

Salomon, Frank G., "A Preliminary Survey of Some Early Buddhist Manuscripts Recently Acquired by the British Library," *Journal of the American Oriental Society*, 117, 2 (1997), pp. 353–8.

Salzman, Philip, "Does Complementary Opposition Exist?" *American Anthropologist*, 80 (1978), pp. 53–70.

Sanson, Nicolas, *Estat présent du royaume de Perse*, Paris: Jacques Langlois, 1694.

Sarkar, Sir Jadunath, *History of Aurangzib*, Bombay: Orient Longman, 1973.

Scheper-Hughes, Nancy, "Making Anthropology Public," *Anthropology Today*, 25, 4 (2009), pp. 1–2.

Schetter, Conrad, *Ethnizität und ethnische Konflikte in Afghanistan*, Berlin: Dietrich Reimer Verlag, 2003.

——— "The 'Bazaar Economy' of Afghanistan" in Christine Noelle-Karimi, Conrad Schetter and Reinhard Schlagintweit (eds), *Afghanistan—A Country without a State?*, IKO-Verlag für Interkulturelle Kommunikation, 2000.

——— "Ungoverned Territories: Eine konzeptuelle Innovation im 'War on Terror,'" *Geographica Helvetica*, 65, 3 (2010), pp. 181–8.

Schinasi, May, *Afghanistan at the Beginning of the Twentieth Century: Nationalism and Journalism in Afghanistan: A Study of Seraj ul-Akhbar (1911–1918)*, Naples: Istituto Universitario Orientale, 1979.

Schwarzenbach, Annemarie, *Alle Wege sind offen: die Reise nach Afghanistan 1939/1940*, Basel: Lenos, 2000.

Scott, James C., *Domination and the Arts of Resistance: Hidden Transcripts*, New Haven, CT: Yale University Press, 1990.

——— *Seeing Like a State: How Certain Schemes to Improve the Human Condition have Failed*, New Haven, CT: Yale University Press, 1998.

Sen, Surendranath (ed.), *Indian Travels of Thevenot and Careri*, New Delhi: National Archives of India, 1949.

Sennet, Richard, *The Corrosion of Character: the Personal Consequences of Work in the New Capitalism*, New York: W.W. Norton, 1998.

Shafi, Muhammad, "Bayazid Ansari," *The Encyclopedia of Islam*, 2nd Edition, vol. 1, 1960, pp. 1121–4.

Shah, Sayyad Ali, *Da Shariat Karwan: Manzal ba Manzal* (Pashto), Lahore: Mukhtar Ahmad Khan Swati (Idara Nashr al-Maarif), 1995.

Shah, Sonia, "Unveiling the Taleban: Dress Codes are not the Issue, New Study Finds," *ZCom*, 10 July 2001, also circulated by UNDP Afghanistan, 7.8.01, http://www.zcom-

BIBLIOGRAPHY

munications.org/unveiling-the-taleban-dress-codes-are-not-the-issue-new-study-finds-by-sonia-shah.

Shah, Syed Bukhar, "PA warns India against 'adventurism,' Urges restoration of peace in Swat," *The News International*, Islamabad/Rawalpindi edition, 23 December 2008.

Shahbaz, Babar, *Dilemmas in Participatory Forest Management in Northwest Pakistan. A Livelihoods Perspective*, Zurich: Human Geography Series 25, University of Zurich, 2009.

Shaheed, Farida, "Gender, Justice and Civil Society in Unjust Societies," Lahore: Shirkat Gah, 2009.

Shahid, Tanvir Qaisar and Naim Mustafa, "Nek Mohammad kaun tha? [Who was Nek Muhammad?]," *Pakistan*, 19 June 2004.

Shaw, G.W., "Matb'a (printing) in Afghanistan," *Encyclopedia of Islam, 2nd Edition*, vol. 6, 1991, pp. 806–7.

Shirkat-Gah, "Shirkat Gah Female and Male Research Activities NWFP," in *Women's Empowerment in the Muslim Context (WEMC) Survey Reports*, Lahore: Shirkat Gah 2010.

Siddiqa, Ayesha, *Military, Inc.: Inside Pakistan's Military Economy*, London: Pluto, 2007.

Simpson, Edward and K. Kresse, "Introduction," in Edward Simpson and K. Kresse (eds), *Struggling with History: Islam and Cosmopolitanism in the Western Indian Ocean*, London: Hurst, 2007.

Singer, André, *Guardians of the North-West Frontier: The Pathans*, Amsterdam: Time-Life Books, 1982.

Singh, Chetan, *Region and Empire: Panjab in the Seventeenth Century*, Delhi: Oxford University Press, 1991.

Siu, Helen, "The Grounding of Cosmopolitans: Merchants and Local Cultures in South China" in Wen-Hsin Yeh (ed.), *Becoming Chinese: Passages to Modernity and Beyond*, Berkeley: University of California Press, 2000, pp. 191–227.

Smith, Graeme, "Talking to the Taliban," *The Globe and Mail*, 22 March 2008.

Sneath, David, *The Headless State: Aristocratic Orders, Kinship Society, and Misrepresentations of Nomadic Inner Asia*, New York: Columbia University Press, 2007.

Spencer, Jonathan, "The Perils of Engagement: A Space for Anthropology in the Age of Security?" *Current Anthropology* 52, 2 (2010), pp. 289–99.

Stafford, Charles, "Two Stories of Learning and Economic Agency in Yunnan," *Taiwan Journal of Anthropology*, 2, 1 (2004), pp. 171–94.

Steadman-Jones, Richard, *Colonialism and Grammatical Representation*, Oxford: Blackwell Publishing, 2007.

Steimann, Bernd, "Rural Livelihoods in a Highland-Lowland Context and the Role of Forest Resources (NWFP, Pakistan)" in SDPI (eds), *Troubled Times: Sustainable Development and Governance in the Age of Extremes*, Islamabad: City Press, 2006, pp. 44–65.

Steensgaard, Niels, "The Route through Qandahar: The Significance of the Overland Trade from India to the West in the Seventeenth Century" in S. Chaudhury and M. Morineau (eds), *Merchants, Companies and Trade: Europe and Asia in the Early Modern Era*, Cambridge: Cambridge University Press, 1999.

Stewart, Rory, *The Places in between*, London: Mariner Books, 2006.

Stinnes, Clärenore, *Im Auto durch zwei Welten*, Berlin: Reimar Hobbing, 1929.

Street, Brian, "Orientalist Discourse in the Anthropology of Iran, Afghanistan and Paki-

BIBLIOGRAPHY

stan" in Richard Fardon (ed.), *Localizing Strategies: Regional Traditions of Ethnographic Writing*, Edinburgh: Scottish Academic Press, 1990, pp. 240–59.

——— "Response to Barth," *Man* (NS), 27 (1992), pp. 177–9

Subrahmanyam, Sanjay, "Iranians Abroad: Intra-Asian Elite Migration and Early Modern State Formation," *The Journal of Asian Studies*, 51, 2 (1992), pp. 340–63.

——— "Of Imarat and Tijarat: Asian Merchants and State Power in the Western Indian Ocean, 1400 to 1750," *Comparative Studies in Society and History*, 37, 4 (2003), pp. 750–80.

Sultan-i-Rome, "Darakht, Taliban aur Fauj," *Roznama Azadi* (Urdu daily), Mingawara, Swat, 27 May 2010.

——— "Forestry in the Princely State of Swat and Kalam (North-West Pakistan). A Historical Perspective on Norms and Practices," Zurich: NCCR IP6 Working Paper No. 6, 2005.

——— "Judicial System, Judiciary and Justice in Swat: The Swat State Era and the Post-state Scenario," *Journal of the Pakistan Historical Society*, 49, 4 (2001) pp. 89–100.

——— "*Security kay naam par insaniat ki tazlil*," *Roznama Azadi* (Urdu daily), Mingawara, Swat, 3 June 2010.

——— "Swat: A Critical Analysis," *IPCS Research Paper 18*, New Delhi: Institute of Peace and Conflict Studies, January 2009.

——— The *Swat State, 1915–1969, From Genesis to Merger: An Analysis of Political, Administrative, Socio-Political, and Economic Development*, Karachi: Oxford University Press, 2008.

——— "Women's Right to Land Ownership in Swat State Areas—the Swat State Era and the Post-State Scenario," *Pakistan Journal of Gender Studies*, 1 (2008), pp. 105–20.

Tapper, Nancy, *Bartered Brides: Politics, Gender and Marriage in an Afghan Tribal Society*, Cambridge: Cambridge University Press, 1991.

——— "Direct Exchange and Brideprice: Alternative Forms in a Complex Marriage System," *Man* (NS), 16 (1981), pp. 387–407.

Tapper, Richard, "Afghan Articulations of Identity: Text and Context" in Jacques Hainard and Roland Kaehr (eds), *Dire les Autres: Réflexions et pratiques ethnologiques: Textes offerts à Pierre Centlivres*, Lausanne: Payot, 1997, pp. 89–103.

——— "Ethnicity and Class: Dimensions of Inter-group Conflict in North-Central Afghanistan" in M. Nazif Shahrani and Robert L. Canfield (eds), *Revolutions and Rebellions in Afghanistan: Anthropological Perspectives*, Berkeley: Institute of International Studies, 1984, pp. 230–46.

——— "Ethnicity, Order and Meaning in the Anthropology of Iran and Afghanistan" in Jean-Pierre Digard (ed.), *Le fait ethnique en Iran et en Afghanistan*, Paris: CNRS, 1987, pp. 21–34.

——— *Frontier Nomads of Iran: A Political and Social History of the Shahsevan*, Cambridge: Cambridge University Press, 1997.

——— "Historians, Anthropologists and Tribespeople on Tribe and State Formation in the Middle East" in Philip Khoury and Joseph Kostiner (eds), *Tribes and State Formation in the Middle East*, Berkeley: University of California Press, 1991, pp. 48–73.

——— "Holier than Thou: Islam in Three Tribal Societies" in Akbar S. Ahmed and David M. Hart (eds), *Islam in Tribal Societies: From the Atlas to the Indus*, London: Routledge & Kegan Paul, 1984, pp. 244–65.

BIBLIOGRAPHY

—— (ed.), *The Conflict of Tribe and State in Iran and Afghanistan*, Beckenham: Croom Helm, 1983, pp. 1–82.

—— (ed.), *Tribe and State in Iran and Afghanistan*, London: Routledge, 2011.

Tapper, Richard and Jon Thompson (eds), *The Nomadic Peoples of Iran*, London: Azimuth/ Thames & Hudson, 2002, pp. 10–39.

Teague-Jones, Reginald, *Adventures in Persia: To India by the Back Door*, London: Victor Gollancz, 1990.

Thompson, Edwina, *Trust is the Coin of the Realm: Lessons from the Money Men in Afghanistan*, Karachi: Oxford University Press, 2011.

Thornton, Thomas, *Colonel Sir Robert Sandeman: His Life and Works on Our Indian Frontier*, London: John Murray, 1895.

Tichy, Herbert, *Afghanistan: das Tor nach Indien*, Leipzig: W. Goldmann, 1940.

—— *Zum heiligsten Berg der Welt: auf Landstraßen und Pilgerpfaden in Afghanistan, Indien und Tibet*, Vienna: Seidel, 1937.

Titus, Paul, "Honour the Baluch, Buy the Pashtun: Stereotypes, Social Organisation and History in West Pakistan," *Modern Asian Studies*, 32, 3 (1998), pp. 689–716.

Toor, S., *The State of Islam: Culture and Cold War Politics in Pakistan*, London: Pluto Press, 2011.

Townsend, Mark, "Gita Sahgal's dispute with Amnesty International puts human rights group in the dock," *The Observer*, 25 April 2010. http://www.guardian.co.uk/world/ 2010/apr/25/ gita-sahgal amnesty international.

Trautmann, Thomas R. "Indian Time, European Time," in Diane Owen Hughes and Thomas R. Trautmann (eds), *Time: Histories and Ethnologies*, Ann Arbor: University of Michigan Press, 1995, pp. 167–97.

—— "The Lives of Sir William Jones" in Alexander Murray (ed.), *Sir William Jones 1746–1794: A Commemoration*, Oxford: Oxford University Press, 1998, pp. 93–121.

Trinkler, Emil, *Afghanistan: eine landeskundliche Studie auf Grund des vorhandenen Materials und eigener Beobachtung: mit 3 Textabbildungen, 4 Bilder- und 4 Kartentafeln*, Gotha: Perthes, 1928.

—— *Quer durch Afghanistan nach Indien*, Berlin: K. Vowinckel Verlag, 1925.

Trinkler, Emil and Paul Langhans, *Geologie Afghanistans und seiner Randgebiete: Orographie von Afghanistan*, Gotha: Perthes, 1928.

Tupper, Charles, *Customary Law of the Punjab*, Calcutta: Office of the Superintendent of Government Printing, 1881.

Udovitch, Anver, *Partnership and Profit in Medieval Islam*, Princeton, N.J.: Princeton University Press, 1960.

Vali Nasr, *Islamic Leviathan: Islam and the Making of State Power*, Oxford: Oxford University Press, 2001.

—— "The Rise of Sunni Militancy in Pakistan: The Changing Role of Islamism and the Ulama in Society and Politics," *Modern Asian Studies*, 34, 1 (2000), pp. 139–80.

van Schendel, W., "Geographies of Knowing, Geographies of Ignorance: Jumping Scale in Southeast Asia," *Environment and Planning. D, Society & Space*, 20 (2002), p. 647.

Vaughan, J. L., *A Grammar and Vocabulary of the Pooshtoo Language (as Spoken in the Trans-Indus Territories Under British Rule, &c. &c.)*, Calcutta: Thacker, Spink and Co. and R.C. Lepage and Co., 1864 [1854].

BIBLIOGRAPHY

von Hanstein, Otfrid *Im wilden Afghanistan: Reisen, Abenteuer und Forschungen*, Leipzig: Verlag Deutsche Buchwerkstätten, 1923.

Walsh, Declan, "Humanitarian crisis in Swat," *The Guardian*, 7 May 2009, http://www.Theage.com.au/world/humanitian crisis in Swat valley, 20090506 avaf.html.

——— "Pakistani troops continue assault on Taliban near Swat valley," *The Guardian*, 27 April 2009.

Warren, Alan, *Waziristan, The Faqir of Ipi and the Indian Army The North-West Frontier Revolt of 1936–37*, Karachi: Oxford University Press, 2000.

Waseem, Mohammed and Mariam Mufti, *Religion, Politics and Governance in Pakistan*, University of Birmingham: Working Paper 27, Religions and Development Research Programme, International Development Department, 2009.

Waterston, Alisse and Maria D. Verperi (eds), *Anthropology off the Shelf: Anthropologists on Writing*, Oxford: Wiley-Blackwell, 2009.

Wazir, Hafizullah, "Ex-MNA among 26 killed in Wana blast," *Daily Times*, 24 Aug. 2010.

Wazir, Maqbool, *Waziristan Chronology*, www.waziristanhills.com

Wedeen, Lisa, *Peripheral Visions: Publics, Power and Performance in Yemen*, Chicago: University of Chicago Press, 2007.

Weinbaum, M. and J. Harder, "Pakistan's Afghan Policies and their Consequences," *Contemporary South Asia*, 16, 1 (March 2008), pp. 25–38.

Weiss, Anita M., "A Provincial Islamist Victory in NWFP, Pakistan: The Social Reform Agenda of the Muttahida Majlis-i-Amal" in John L. Esposito and John Voll (eds), *Asian Islam in the 21st Century*, New York: Oxford University Press, 2008, pp. 145–73.

Werbner, Pnina, "Notes from a Small Place: Anthropological Blues in the Face of Global Terror," *Current Anthropology*, 51, 2 (2010), pp. 193–221.

West, Harry and T. Sanders (eds), *Transparency and Conspiracy: Ethnographies of Suspicion in the New World Order*, Durham, NC: Duke University Press, 2003.

Wilcox, Wayne Ayres *Pakistan: The Consolidation of a Nation*, New York: Columbia University Press, 1963.

Wild, Roland, *Amanullah: Ex-King of Afghanistan*, London: Hurst & Blackett, 1932.

World Bank, *Traditional Structures in Local Governance for Local Development. A Case Study of Pakhtuns residing in NWFP & FATA, Pakistan*, 2004.

Wright, Susan, "Constructing tribal identity in Iran; comment on Burkhard Ganzer," *Man* (NS), 29 (1994), pp. 182–6.

——— "Method in our Critique of Anthropology: a Further Comment," *Man* (NS), 27 (1992), pp. 642–4.

Writers Union of Free Afghanistan (WUFA), Association of Professors of Universities of Afghanistan, 1990, 155–90.

Yapp, Malcolm, "Tribes and States in the Khyber 1838–42" in R. Tapper (ed.), *The Conflict of Tribe and State in Iran and Afghanistan*, London: Croom Helm, 1983, pp. 150–91.

Younge, Gary, "Black presidents and women MPs do not alone mean equality and justice," *The Guardian*, 15 March 2010, p. 27.

Yousaf, Mohammad and Mark Adkin, *Afghanistan—The Bear Trap: The Defeat of a Superpower*, New Delhi: Bookwise (India) Pvt Ltd, 2007.

Yusufzai, Aqeel, *Talibanization: Afghanistan say FATA, Swat aur Pakistan tak*, Lahore: Nigarishat, 2009.

BIBLIOGRAPHY

Yusufzai, Rahimullah, "Military victory in Swat not in sight," *The News International*, Islamabad/Rawalpindi edition, 22 December 2008.

────── "Nizam-e-Adl and durable peace in Swat," *The News International*, Islamabad/Rawalpindi edition, 11 April 2009.

────── "This is not the first time," *The News International*, Islamabad/Rawalpindi edition, 4 April 2009.

Zaeef, Abdul Salam, *My Life with the Taliban*, Alex Strick van Linschoten and Felix Kuehn (eds), London: Hurst and New York: Columbia University Press, 2010.

Zaidi, Akbar S., *The Political Economy of Decentralisation in Pakistan*, Zurich: Working Paper No. 1, NCCR, 2005.

Zaloom, Caitlin, *Out of the Pits: Traders and Technology from Chicago to London*, Chicago: University of Chicago Press, 2006.

Zaman, Qasim, *The Ulama in Contemporary Islam: Custodians of Change*, Princeton: Princeton University Press, 2002.

Zebsar, Taj Muhammad Khan, *Uruj-e-Afghan* (Pashto verse), 1, Peshawar: Manzur-e-Aam Press, 1360 AH.

INDEX

Abbas I 32, 35
Abbas II 32, 36
Abdali 4, 5, chapter 2, 124
Abdul Ghuffar, Akhund 40
Abdul Jabbar Shah 150
Abdul Rahman, Maulana 21
Abdul Wadud, Miangul 137–8, 150, 217
Abdulla, Maulvi 43, 48
Abdur Rahman Khan, Amir 77, 81, 240–43, 254–6, 259, 262
Abid, Zain al-Abdin Khan 71
Abu-Lughod, Lila 194
Afghan jihad (against Soviet occupation) 51, 57, 109, 125, 127, 128, 130–1, 139, 152, 218, 227, 256
Afghan Motor Company 79
Afghanistan: history pre-1970s chapter 3, 46–7, 67, chapter 6, 243–7, 253–5; recent social and political situation 223–37, 255–63; trading and traders chapter 7; war since 2001, *see also* Taliban 15, 23, 56, 128, 131, 133, 141, 152, 191
Afridi 210, 214, 217
Afzal Khan 24
agriculture 18, 108–9, 14–15, 132, 160
Ahmad Shah Sadozai 31, 37, 242
Ahmad, Sayyid 40, 41, 48
Ahmed, Akbar 6, 127
Ahmedzai Wazir 54, 57–8, 210
aid 75–8, 146, 165–73, 177, 260
Ajaib al-Lughat 70
Ajar 137
Akbar 32
Akhunds 257, 258

AKRSP (Aga Khan Rural Support Programme) 170
al-Beruni 67
Alexander the Great 65–7, 180
'Ali Mardar Khan 35–6
Aligarh 89
al-Qaeda 52, 56, 218, 229
Amanullah Khan, Amir 78, 80, 81, 82, 83–4, 85, 86, 88, 91, 246
Amb 45
Ambela campaign 41–2, 45, 211
Anderson, Commissioner 214
ANP (Awami National Party) 128, 144, 155–7
Ansari, Bayazid 67–8
anthropology (general) 1–4, 119–33, 221–2, 224–5
Arif b. Tirin 33
Asad, Talal 108, 126, 138, 251
Ashoka 66
Asmas 44, 46–7
Aurangzeb 36
Ayub Khan, President 110, 181

Babur 32, 67
Bagram 56
Bahadur, Khan 21
Baitullah Mahsud 57, 60, 141, 153, 183, 219
Bajaur 47
Bakht Zeba 141
Bakht-i-Saywa 189
Balochistan 195, 213
Baluchi language 74
Bamiyan 84, 231

INDEX

Bannu 53, 209, 214
Baptist Missionary Press 70
Barikot 138
Barth, Fredrik 1–4, 6, 10, 15–16, 63–4, 75, 107–8, 126–7, 137, 145, 163, 171, 172, chapter 16, 249–53, 255–7
Bek Sagrana 110–15
Bellew, Henry Walter 71
Bengal 41
Bhittani 209
Bhutto, Benazir 113
Bhutto, Zulfikar Ali 53, 109, 110, 127, 139
Biha 20–21
bin Laden, Osama 229, 231
Birmal 209
Bonn 258
Britain 15, 26, 80, 81; British Raj in India 4, 5–6, 40–49, 69–72, 111, 181, chapter 15
Bruce, Richard 213–14, 219
Buddhas of Bamiyan 84, 231–2
Buner 138, 142, 143, 144, 158, 186
burqa 183–5, 201, 230
Byron, Robert 83, 84, 85

carpet making 98
Central Asia 7, 8, 9, 67, 81, 89, chapter 7
Chamarkand 45–7
Charikar 81
China 95
Chishti 33
Chitral 95–7, 167, 181, 186, 195
Chowdri Mazhar Ali 111
Christians 233
'civil society' 172–3
class and status 12–13, 52–60, 107–19, 126–33, 172, 175–8, chapter 10, 225–9
Cleveland, C.R. 45
Cold War, *see also* Soviet Union 122, 125, 127
Communist regime in Afghanistan 94, 256
community meeting houses 114
Community-Based Organisations (CBOs) 170, 172, 176
corruption 112, 113, 176, 229, 259, 263
crime and violence, *see also* military operations; Taliban impositions and punishments 18–19, 108–10, 113–17
Crump, L.M. 216

Dargai Khas 197–8, 199, 201, 202
Darweza, Akhund 67–8
Daud, President 247
Dawar 209
Deane, Sir Harold 216, 217
Defense Language Institute (USA) 73
Delhi Sultanate 67
Deobandi 23, 24, 149–50, 231
Dera Ismail Khan 54, 212
Derajat 211
development (general) 164–78
Dir 21, 139, 149, 152, 157, 158, 167, 181, 186, 217, 252
drug trafficking 102, 109–10, 116
dullah 19, 21–2, 23–4
Dura Shukuh 36
Durand Line 54, 214, 218
Durrani 10, chapter 2, 94, 123–4, 221–8, 234, 236
Durrani, Sultan Muhammad b. Musa Barakzai 34, 35
Dushanbe 96–7, 99, 100, 102

education 88, 97, 141, 143, 185–6, 203, 230
Edwards, David 94, 130, chapter 18
elections in Pakistan 21–2, 55–6, 108–9, 114, 116, 128
Elphinstone, Mountstuart 235, 240
Ethnic Groups and Boundaries 10, 64, 75, 223, 224
ethnicity 100–1, 123–7, 223–4, 234–6

Faqir of Ipi 47, 216
FATA (Federally Administered Tribal Areas) chapter 4, 143, 152, 193
Fazal, Fazal Khaliq 182
Fazlullah, Maulana/Mullah 25, 39, 128, 129, 136, 140, 141, 180, 143, 144, 153, 154–7, 175–7, 182–6, 193, 195, 200, 201
feudal society, *see also* land tenure 20–22, 108–18, 127–8, 130

INDEX

feuds in Swat 18–19
floods 129, 191
forest administration 167, 171–3
Fort William 70, 71
France 83, 125–6, 157
French travellers 32–3
Frontier Corps 56
Frontier Crimes Regulations 53, 140, 143
fruit cultivation 114, 115, 183

Gandhari 67
Gandhi, M.K. 26–7
German travelogues 80, 83
Germany 47, 82, 83, 168, 233, 258
Ghaffar Khan, Khan Abdul 26–7, 128
Ghaznavids 67
Ghilzai 35, 236
Gilani, Yusuf Raza 158, 161
Giustozzi, Antonio 130–32, chapter 17
Global War on Terror 4, 39, 63, 122, 163–4
Gondal, Abdullah 112–14
Gondal, Mazhar Ali 112–14
Gondals 110–16
Gregorian, Vartan 130
guesthouses in Afghanistan 87–8
Gujar 21–2, 24, 137, 139
Gulf 98, 99, 127, 135, 138
Gumal Pass 213

Habibullah Khan, Amir 77, 78, 80, 87, 247
Hackin, Joseph 84
Hadda, Mulla 46
Hamzullah, Mullah 214
Hanstein, Otfrid von 80, 88
Hashim Khan, Sardar Muhammad 89
Hayat Khan 36–7
Hazara 35, 95, 168, 226, 228, 231, 259
health services 111, 115, 150, 186, 187
Hedin, Sven 83
Helmand 15, 131
Herat 32, 33, 35, 36, 79, 80
Hindko 74
Hindus 232–3
Hindustani 70, 71, 72
'Hindustani Fanatics' 5–6, chapter 3
Hizb-i Islami 247

Human Terrain System 4, 12, 73, 121
Humayun 32
Hunter, W.W. 42
Husain Khan, Shah 36, 37
Husaini, Imam al-Din 33
Hussain, Mian Iftikhar 156

Ibbetson, Sir Denzil 211
imperialism 121–7, 132–3
India (modern) 120, 232–3
India (pre-1947) 31, 32, 33, 65–72, 79
Indian nationalists and terrorists (fighting British rule) 44, 46, 47, 48
Ipi 47
Iqbal, Muhammad 83, 91
Iran 32–7, 81, 125, 126, 221–2, 230, 233
Iraq 122, 125
Iskandar Beg 32
Islam 3, 5, 10, 17, 22, 23, 25, chapter 3, 58–9, 88, 97–9, 125–6, 128, 132–3, 139–42, 194–5, 205, 225–7, 233, 260
Islamabad 57, 158, 175
Islamophobia 125–6, 132–3
Israel 125
Italy 82

Jahan, Shah 32, 36
Jahanzeb, Miangul 137, 150
Jalalabad 79, 86–7, 232, 243
Jan Muhammad 87
Jan, Delawar 156
Javaid, Muhammad 158
Javed, Syed Muhammad 144
Jhang 117
Jhangvi, Haq-Nawaz 117
JI (Jamaat-i Islami) 139, 200
jirga 19, 55, 58, 166, 215, 218–19, 242–5
Johnston, F.W. 213, 215–16
Joint Forest Management Committees 173
Jones, Sir William 65, 70
JUI (Jamiat-i-Ulema-i-Islam) 21, 23, 24, 55, 139
JUI-F (Jamiat-i-Ulema-i-Islam-Fazlur Rahman) 55, 59, 158
justice 23–4, 74, 139–40, 152–4, 174, 201, 261

361

INDEX

Kabal 146, 154
Kabul 74, 77, 79, 80, 81, 83, 84, 86, 89, 95, 96, 98, 228, 230, 231
Kabul Literary Society 78, 81, 84
Kakar, Hasan 241, 243
Kalabagh 217
Kalam 150
Kaniguram 54, 60
Karachi 54, 127, 218
Karzai, Hamid 11, 122, 129, 131, 132, 255, 258–60, 261–3
*kashar*s chapter 4
Kashmir 141
Khair al-Bayan 67–9
Khaksar Nadir Ali 79
khans, *see also* class and status 17, 20–22, 24, 137–9, 171, 225, 245–7, 258
Kharki 201–4
Khudad Khan 36
Khudakka, 'Ali Muhammad Khan 34, 35
Khurasan 33, 34
Khushal Khan Khattak 18, 26, 27, 68–9
Khyber Pakhtunwa 11, 149, 180, chapter 14
Khyber Pass 78, 79, 87
Kohat 211
Kohistan 64, 182, 186
Kunar 131
Kunduz 93, 96

Laddah 60
Lahore 33, 44, 111
Lahori Gate 196, 202
Lal Masjid 57, 152, 166, 175
Lala Pir 214
land tenure, landlords, land reform 20–22, 108–18, 126–30, 137–40, 171–4
*lashkar*s 39, 60, 159, 200
Last Wali of Swat, The 64–5, 251–3
Lindholm, Charles 6, chapter 1, 119, 127, 163, 171, 172
Lodi dynasty 34
Lucknow 33
Lyallpur 45

*madrasa*s 55, 58–9, 146, 153, 182, 234, 257
Mahmakhtel 21, 24

Mahmood, Saba 194–5
Mahmud of Ghazna 89
Mahsud (Mehsud) 54–5, 57, 209–19
Maillart, Ella 84
Makhdooms 110–12
Makhzan al-Islam 67–9
Malakand 21, 139, 140, 142–6, 157, 167, 180, 183, 186, 200, 201
Malaysia 138
*malik*s 22, 52–3, 55, 58–9, 213–19
Mamdherai/Imamdherai 153, 182
Mangal Thana 41
Manglawar 179, 185, 189
Maqami Taliban 57
Mar'ashi, Muhammad Khalil 33–7
Marobi 214
Mas'ud, Sir Ross 89
*mashar*s 52
Mashhad 33
Massoud, Ahmed Shah 231
Matta 183, 185
Maudud Khan Sadozai 35–6
Maulvi Nazir 57
Mazar-e Sharif 80, 89, 93, 96, 231
media 228–30
Merk, William 214–17
Miangul state 137–9
Migdal, Joel 143–4
migration 20, 23, 51, 53, 54, 127, 135, 136, 138, 173, 218
military operations (Pakistani) 39, 55, 56–7, 59, 60, 129, 141–6, 154–61, 163, 181, 186, 187, 190, 193, 218
Mingora 129, 141, 143, 144, 170, 187–8, 191
Miraj Khalid, Malik 53
Miran Shah 214
MMA (Muttahida Majlis-e-Amal) 23, 25, 56, 153, 175, 182
Moghaddam, Azerbaijani 130
Mohmand 214, 217
Monsutti, Alessandro 94–5
mosques 17–18, 58
motor vehicles 77–91
Mughals 32, 33, 34, 35, 69
Muhiy-ud-Din (Mullah Powindah) 214–15

362

INDEX

Mujahidin (Afghanistan, 1980s) 13, 227, 228–9, 262
mullahs 58, 60, 225–6
Multan 32, 37
Murshidabad 33
Musa Qala 133
Musharraf, President 10, 53, 112–13, 141, 154, 155
Muslim Khan 136, 142–3, 176
Muslim League 47

Nadir Shah 31, 33, 78, 80, 81, 82, 86
Nadwi, Sulayman 83, 85–90
Najibullah, President 9, 229
Nangarhar 243, 247
National Accountability Bureau (Pakistan) 112, 113
NATO 5, 15, 99, 129
Nawaz Sharif 112–13
Nazir, Mullah 59
Nek Mohammad 56, 57, 59
neo-Taliban, *see also* Taliban; TNSM; TTP 130–32, chapter 14, 235, 260
NGOs 165–6, 191, 195, 201–3, 233
Ni'matullah 33
Niamatullah, Amir 44–6
Nifaz-e-Nizam-e-Sharia Regulation, 1994 153
Nizam-e-Adl 2009 pact 141, 186
Nizami, Hasan 85, 86–90
Noor Mohammad, Maulana 55
Northern Alliance (United Front) 229, 233, 235
Nul 183
NWFP (North-West Frontier Province) 11, 23, 127, 128, 140, 155, 165, 166–74, 175, 180, 216

Obama, President 129
Omar, Mullah 131, 229, 235

Pakistan: administration of Frontier regions 24, 53–4, 135, 150–53, 166–78, 181–2; elections 21–2, 55–6, 108–9, 114, 116, 128; international relations 39, 56, 129, 152, 233; military operations 25, 39, 55, 56–7, 59, 60, 129, 141–6, 154–61, 163, 181, 186, 187, 190, 193, 218
Panjshiris 93, 97, 100, 123–4
Pashto language chapter 5, 154, 226
Pashto Tolena 72
PATA (Provincially Administered Tribal Areas) 140, 149, 151, 152–3, 180–82
Pathan/Pashtun/Pukhtun/Pushtun people *passim*; *see* Pashto language
PDPA (People's Democratic Party of Afghanistan) 94, 227, 228, 229
peasant resistance 127
Persia 32–7
Persian language 64, 68, 69, 70, 71, 72, 74, 99, 226
Persianate culture 6, 69, 99–100
Peshawar 25, 33, 40, 43, 74, 80–81, 86, 89, 95, 135, 138, 167, 168, 187, 262
Picard, Elizabeth 95
Plowden, Trevor 71, 211
PNA (People's National Alliance) 21, 23
Political Leadership among Swat Pathans 1–4, 250–51
Political Parties Order (2002) 54
population of Swat 138
PPP (Pakistan People's Party) 21, 109–10, 128, 139, 161
printing 70–72
prostitution 197–8
Pukhtun/Pushtun/Pashtun/Pathan people *passim*; *see* Pashto language
Pukhtunwali/Pashtunwali 17–18, 23, 56, 164, 194, 197
Punjab 13, 43, 60, 107–18, 129, 195, 210, 213, 219

Qamaluddin, Mullah 200–1
Qandahar 31–7, 65, 71, 74, 79, 80, 132, 234, 258, 259
Qazi Kabir 242
Qazvini, Muhammad Tahir Vahid 32
Quetta 74, 79

Rahman Baba 26, 27
Rahman, Tariq 72
Rai Bareilly 40, 41
railways 79, 81, 217

INDEX

Ranjit Singh 34
Rashid, Ahmed 200
Raverty, Henry George 70–71, 160
Razmak 216, 218
Red Shirts (Khodoi Kidmatgar) 26–7, 128, 132
refugees and internally displaced people 23, 59, 60, 129, 139, 141, 159, 163, 188–9, 218, 234; refugee-traders 95–7
Reza Shah 81
Rishtiyya, Sayyid Qasim Khan 84, 91
rivaj chapter 12
Riyaz al-Mahabbat 69–70
roads 57, 79–91, 217
Roos-Keppel, George 44–5
Russia 96, 102, 103, 213

Sado 35
Sadozai dynasty 33–7
Sadozai, Ahmad Khan 31, 33, 34
Safavids 32–5, 69
Saidu Sharif 170, 174, 177, 185, 191
Salafi doctrine 98, 231
Samar Minallah 157
Samiullah, Pir 141
Sandeman, Sir Robert 213
Sanson 32–3
Sararogha 57, 60
Sargodha 210–15
Saudi Arabia 23, 40, 230
Schwarzenbach, Annemarie 84, 85
Sebujni 137, 139, 141
Sentinel Waggon Works 82
September 11 attacks 9, 140, 152–3, 163–4
Shabana 141
Shahbaz-e-Jang, Nawwab Mahabbatallah 69–70
Shahr-i Safa 35
Shakai 59
Shams al-Din, Hajji 82, 85, 88
Shamser Ali Khan 144
Shangla 157, 186
sharia 24, 59, 139–41, 143, 157, 166, 176–7, 182, 183, 200, 201
Shari-Nizam-e-Adl Regulation, 1999 153, 157

Shasevan 221–2
Shelter Now International 233
Shia Islam 117, 226, 231, 234
'Shin Bagh' (pseudonym for community studied) 17–27
Shinwari 12, 137, 243–6
Shirkat Gah 193–205
Shirkat-e Badaran-e Afghan 81
Shirkat-e Pitrul 82
Sikhs 41, 46, 48, 232
Sindh 195
Sipah-e Sahaba 108, 117
Sitana 41–3
Soviet Union 46–7, 48, 81, 99, 125, 152, 228–9, 256
Sufi Muhammad 129, 135, 136, 139–41, 143–4, 153, 157–8, 175, 182, 186, 199–201
Sufism 17, 48
suicide attacks 25, 55, 144
Sultan Husain, Shah 32
Sultanat Khan 24
Sunni Islam 125, 226, 231, 234
Swat uprisings 24–7, 127–9, 142–6, 180–92
Swat valley scenery, vegetation 18–20

Tablighi-Jama'at 98
Tajikistan 96–7, 99–100
Tajiks 226, 228
Taliban, *see also* neo-Taliban; TNSM; TTP 1, 5, 10–13, 39, 52, 55–60, 91, 108, 120, 122, 123, 129–33, 139–46, 152–61, 163–4, 183–92, 193–6, 199–205, 224, 227–37, 257–61; Taliban impositions and punishments 141–2, 183–7, 200–4, 229–34, 258
Tank 54, 209, 213, 214, 217, 218
Taraki, Nur Muhammad 94
Tarbela 158
Tarkanri 137
Taylor, Rennell 42, 211
Thompson, Edwina 95
Tichy, Herbert 83
TNSM (Tehrik-i-Nifaz-i-Shariat-i-Muhammadi) 23, 39, 117, 128–9, 135, 139, 140, 144, 152–3, 157, 159, 166, 171, 174–5, 177–8, 182–3, 200

INDEX

Tor Mulla 142
Torkham 86, 243
tourism 18, 173
trading networks 13–14, 37, chapter 7
traditional economy of Swat 17–18
transport chapter 6
Trinkler, Emil 83
TTP (Tehrik-i-Taliban Pakistan) 23, 25, 55, 57, 141, 143, 153, 180, 183, 191, 200, 218, 219
Tupper, Sir Charles 211
Turangzai 43
Turkmens 96–7

United Nations 161, 233
Urdu 64, 70, 72, 85; Urdu travelogues 5, 78, 80, 84–90
Uruzgai 131
USA 8, 13, 23, 39, 56, 72–3, 74, 84, 109, 122, 123, 124–6, 128–9, 136, 141, 142, 143, 146, 152, 153, 233
Uthmani/Utmanzai Wazir 57, 210, 216
Uzbeks 52, 56, 96–7, 226, 228, 242

Vajpayee, A.B. 233

Village Organisations (VOs) 170

Wahhabi doctrine 23, 40, 42, 231
Wali, Asfandyar 128
Walis of Swat 11, 23–4, 64, 150, 167, 181, chapter 18, 263
Wana 55, 56, 59, 213, 216
Wazir 52, 54–8, 209, 212, 214, 218
Waziristan 5, 52, 53–60, 129, 201, chapter 15; North 53, 54–5, 57, 214; South 53, 54–5, 56, 59, 60, 131, 214, 217, 218
Wild, Ronald 80, 83–4, 91
'Women Groups' 173
women's situation 10–11, 132–3, chapter 13, chapter 14, 230
World Food Programme 129, 233
World War I 43–5
World War II 47

Yargurkhel 56
Yusufzai 126, 127, 137, 149, 222

Zahir Shah 80
Zardari, President 54, 156, 157
Zia ul-Haq 22, 109, 112, 117, 139

365